The travel guide

Footprint

Ecuador & Galápagos Handbook

Robert and Daisy Kunstaetter
Alan Murphy

I have too deeply enjoyed the voyage, not to recommend any naturalist..., to take all chances, and to start on travels by land... He may feel assured, he will meet with no difficulties or dangers (excepting in rare cases) nearly so bad as beforehand anticipated. ... Travelling ought also to teach him distrust; but at the same time he will discover, how many truly goodnatured people there are, with whom he never before had, or ever again will have any further communication, who yet are ready to offer him the most disinterested assistance.

Charles Darwin, *Voyage of the Beagle* (1839)

Ecuador & Galápagos Handbook
Third edition
© Footprint Handbooks Ltd 2001

Published by Footprint Handbooks
6 Riverside Court
Lower Bristol Road
Bath BA2 3DZ. England
T +44 (0)1225 469141
F +44 (0)1225 469461
Email discover@footprintbooks.com
Web www.footprintbooks.com

ISBN 1 900949 82 2
CIP DATA: A catalogue record for this
book is available from the British Library
Library of Congress Catalog Card
Number on file

Distributed in the USA by
Publishers Group West

Neither the black and white nor
coloured maps are intended to have
any political significance.

Credits

Series editors
Patrick Dawson and Rachel Fielding

Editorial
Editor: Jo Williams
Maps: Sarah Sorensen

Production
Typesetting: Richard Ponsford, Leona
Bailey and Angus Dawson
Maps: Robert Lunn and Claire Benison
Colour maps: Kevin Feeney

Cover: Camilla Ford

Design
Mytton Williams

Photography
Front cover: Robert Harding
Picture Library
Back cover: Art Directors & Trip
Inside colour section: Jamie Marshall,
Patti Zway, Robert Kunstaetter, Impact,
Robert Harding Picture Library, Trip
Photographic Library, South American
Pictures, Alois Speck, David Horwell,
Edward Paine

Print
Manufactured in Italy by LEGOPRINT

Every effort has been made to ensure
that the facts in this Handbook are
accurate. However, travellers should still
obtain advice from consulates, airlines
etc about current travel and visa
requirements before travelling. The
authors and publishers cannot accept
responsibility for any loss, injury or
inconvenience however caused.

Ecuador

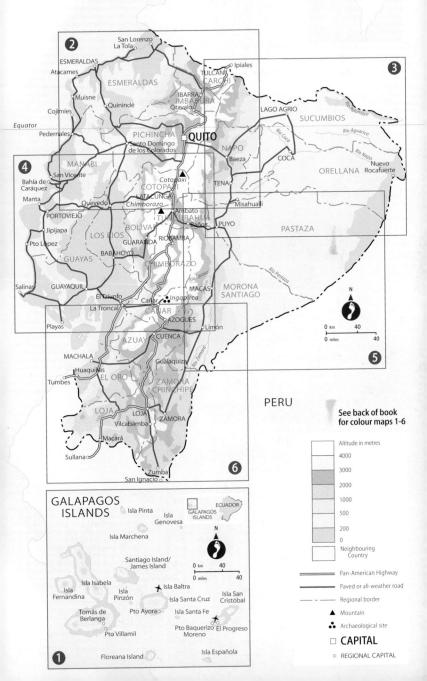

Pacific Ocean

COLOMBIA

❷

San Lorenzo
La Tola

ESMERALDAS
Atacames

Ipiales **❸**

TULCÁN
CARCHI

ESMERALDAS

IBARRA
IMBABURA
Otavalo

LAGO AGRIO

SUCUMBÍOS

Río Putumayo

Muisne

Quinindé

PICHINCHA

Equator

Pedernales

Santo Domingo
de los Colorados

□ QUITO

NAPO

Baeza

COCA

Río Coca

Río Aguarico

Río Napo

ORELLANA

Nuevo
Rocafuerte

❹

MANABÍ

San Vicente

Bahía de
Caráquez

Manta

Quevedo

Cotopaxi ▲
LATACUNGA
COTOPAXI
Chimborazo ▲

TENA

Misahualí

Ambato
TUNGURAHUA
Baños

PORTOVIEJO

BOLÍVAR

PUYO

PASTAZA

Jipijapa

Pto López

LOS RIOS

GUARANDA

RIOBAMBA

BABAHOYO

Río Pastaza

GUAYAS

Salinas

CHIMBORAZO

Río Upano

MACAS

MORONA
SANTIAGO

GUAYAQUIL

El Triunfo

Cañar ⁂ Ingapirca

N

La Troncal

CAÑAR

Playas

AZOGUES

Limón

0 km   40

0 miles   40

AZUAY

CUENCA

MACHALA

Guálaquiza

❺

Huaquillas

EL ORO

Río Zamora

Tumbes

ZAMORA
CHINCHIPE

PERU

LOJA

LOJA
Vilcabamba

ZAMORA

See back of book
for colour maps 1-6

Macará

Sullana

❻

Zumba
San Ignacio

Altitude in metres
4000
3000
2000
1000
500
200
0
Neighbouring
Country

═══ Pan-American Highway
━━━ Paved or all-weather road
- - - Regional border
▲ Mountain
⁂ Archaeological site
□ CAPITAL
○ REGIONAL CAPITAL

GALAPAGOS ISLANDS

Isla Pinta

Isla
Genovesa

ECUADOR

GALAPAGOS
ISLANDS

Isla Marchena

N

Santiago Island/
James Island

0 km   40

0 miles   40

Isla Isabela

Isla Baltra

Isla
Fernandina

Isla
Pinzón

Isla Santa Cruz

Isla San
Cristóbal

Tomás de
Berlanga

Pto Ayora

Isla Santa Fe

Pto Villamil

Pto Baquerizo
Moreno

El Progreso

Floreana Island

Isla Española

❶

Contents

Left: why did the chicken cross the road? At Otavalo market they're just going along for the ride.

4

Right: Feeling active today? Guagua Pichincha volcano lets off some steam.

A foot in the door

6

Right: riding piggyback in Alausí, a town in the Southern Highlands.
Below: few cities have a setting to match that of Quito.

Above: it's peak time along the so-called 'Valley of the Volcanoes', where giants such as Cotopaxi and Chimborazo line the main highway south of Quito.
Right: the colonial city of Cuenca has many fine churches such as this one, El Carmen de la Asunción.
Next page: no visit to Ecuador would be complete without at least one full-blown Andean market experience. A truly exotic assault on the senses.

Highlights

The phrase 'small is beautiful' could have been coined specifically with Ecuador in mind. By South American standards it is tiny (only half the size of France) and dwarfed by its neighbours Colombia and Peru. But it is this relative compactness which is one of its main attractions. If you've only got a few weeks in which to explore a place, you really don't want to spend half your time in an aircraft or on a bus. Here, you can watch dawn break over the jungle canopy, have lunch high in the Andean mountains, then watch the sun slip into the Pacific Ocean; all in the same day.

Ecuador also boasts great biological diversity; a fact that did not escape the attention **Equatorial** of 18th and 19th century scientists and explorers, who came, saw and compiled large **explorers** volumes extolling its many virtues. The first to put Ecuador on the map was French aristocrat, Charles-Marie de la Condamine, who determined the precise location of the equatorial line here, hence the country's name. Today, tourists can still write home about impenetrable jungles, snow-capped volcanoes, weird and wonderful creatures and exotic peoples. Two centuries of 'progress' have not diminished the keen sense of adventure which this country inspires.

The capital city, Quito, is the perfect base from which to explore the delights of the **Capital gains** country. Although it stands a mere 23 kilometres south of the Equator, Quito's mountain setting means it enjoys a pleasant, spring-like climate all year round. The city has enough to satisfy the culture vulture and hedonistic night-owl, and you don't have to be an architecture buff to appreciate its elegant and beautifully preserved colonial heart. In sharp contrast is its modern alter ego, boasting sleek contemporary buildings with shiny glass and concrete towers, making Quito one of the most attractive cities in the whole of Latin America.

South of the capital runs the country's main traffic artery, bordered on both sides by so **Under the** many snow-covered volcanoes they look like giant traffic cones deployed to section **volcanoes** off a lane of motorway. The early 19th-century explorer Alexander Von Humboldt dubbed this the 'Avenue of the Volcanoes', a most appropriate tag which has stuck to this day. Living in the shadow of these volcanoes - many of which are still active - are the indigenous peoples of the highlands, going about their business in much the same way as they did before the Spanish arrived, still wearing traditional dress and conversing in the ancient language of the Incas.

Not content with admiring the volcanoes from a distance, adventure-hungry visitors are climbing them in search of the biggest natural high this little country has to offer.

On the western side of the Andes lies Ecuador's coast, so different in atmosphere from **Coastal votes** the highlands that you could be in another country. If your idea of a good time is to lie on a beach all day soaking up rays and partying into the small hours of the morning, then Ecuador's more popular beach resorts are for you. Those who prefer their activity during daylight hours can swim, surf, scuba dive, or watch humpback whales getting it together in the warm waters off the shores of Manabí province.

Right and below: when you've shopped until you drop in Otavalo's famous market, buying anything from dressed-up dolls to dough figurines, there's loads of stunning countryside to explore just outside town.

Above: where do Panama hats come from? Ecuador, of course! The superior straw hat was once a powerful status symbol and remains the country's most famous export.
Right: hedging your bets...topiary at Tulcán cemetery is one of the more unusual sights in this northern town on the Colombian border.
Next page: if you only climb one of Ecuador's many volcanoes, then Cotopaxi, in the heart of a beautiful national park, should probably be the one.

Artesanía

Ecuador is a shopper's paradise. Everywhere you turn there's some particularly seductive piece of *artesanía* on offer. This word loosely translates as 'handicrafts', but that doesn't really do them justice. The indigenous peoples make no distinction between fine arts and crafts, so *artesanía* are valued as much for their practical use as for their beauty.

During Inca times, textiles held pride of place, and things are no different today. **Weaving** Throughout the northern highlands beautiful woven textiles are still produced, often **& dealing** using techniques unchanged for centuries. A few hours north of Quito is one of Ecuador's main weaving centres and most popular attractions, the market town of Otavalo, where local indigenous women dress in very beautiful traditional fashion. Here it seems the world and his wife are busily engaged in producing beautiful wall hangings, handbags, pillow covers, ponchos, belts and, of course, those ubiquitous sweaters. You can shop to your heart's content in the town and in the surrounding hills and valleys, where each tiny community specialises in its own particular type of *artesanía*, be it hats, baskets or leather wallets, purses and bags. When you run out of money you could explore the beautiful hinterland of volcanoes, lakes and valleys.

Most people don't know that the Panama hat, Ecuador's most famous export, comes **Hats off** from Ecuador, but this natty piece of headwear with an identity crisis has been woven in the southern sierra and on the coast for more than a century. The confusion over the origin dates back to when the isthmus of Panama was the major trading post for South American goods and the quickest and safest seafaring route to Europe and North America. In the mid-19th century gold seekers from the east coast of the US heading for the California gold rush picked up the straw hats on their way out west. Fifty years later, workers on the Panama Canal found them ideal protection against the tropical sun and, like the forty-niners before them, named them after the point of purchase rather than their place of origin. The name stuck. In the colonial city of Cuenca you can see the *superfinos* being made. These are Panama hats of the highest quality. The genuine article should hold water as surely as a glass and, when rolled up, should be slim enough to pass through a wedding ring.

Though proud of these ancient techniques passed on through the centuries, there are **Carrying on** times when the indigenous peoples of Ecuador have preferred the sheer convenience **the tradition** of mass production. In Cotopaxi province, in the Central Highlands, *shigras*, which are bags made from sisal, were originally used to store foodstuffs and even to carry water from the wells. These bags almost died out with the arrival of plastic containers, until Western demands ensured that the art survived. *Shigras* can be found at the market in Salcedo, south of Latacunga.

The indigenous communities throughout the Andes produce many other examples **Market forces** of fine work; from the intricate woodcarvings of San Antonio de Ibarra, north of Otavalo, to the people of Calderón, near Quito, who earn an honest crust from figures made of bread dough. You could easily spend a few weeks wandering around these sleepy little Andean towns and villages, all of which burst into life in a riot of colours, sounds and smells on their respective market days.

A wildlife paradise

The greatest natural show on earth The reason many people come to Ecuador is to visit a group of 19 islands lying almost a thousand kilometres due west. The Galápagos Islands came to the world's attention following a visit by a young Charles Darwin, whose short stay in the archipelago proved to be not insignificant for science and the study of evolution. The islands, which get their name from the giant tortoises that live there, are home to numerous endemic species of birds and reptiles. Now, this wildlife paradise has become a national park dedicated to the conservation of its many unique species. Everyone returns from this 'showcase of evolution' with a sense of wonder and a feeling of being privileged. This is enhanced by the fact that visitor numbers are strictly regulated. The movement of tourists is also carefully co-ordinated and everyone pays a park fee on arrival, which is earmarked for conservation. It's a small price to pay for the greatest natural show on Earth. See also the colour wildlife section in the Galápagos chapter.

Fearless fauna But it is not just the scientific importance of this place that makes it so special. The animals here are so tame you could walk up and shake their hand (or flipper, wing or claw). This is nature in all its naked glory and in startling close-up. Each island also has its own particular main event; from the bizarre love dance of the blue-footed booby to the magnificent 'red balloon' courtship display of male frigate birds.

Underwater magic If the animals on land seem indifferent to the prying camera lenses of tourists, those beneath the waves are positively gregarious. Impossibly cute sea lion pups are always on the lookout for a new playmate, and the cheeky little Galápagos penguins dart around checking out the latest visitors. Slightly more reserved are marine turtles and graceful manta rays, while hammerhead sharks thankfully prefer to remain aloof.

Jungle adventure No visit to Ecuador would be complete without venturing into its steamy jungles. Only a few hours away from Quito by bus, the eastern slopes of the Andes give way to a vast green carpet stretching into the horizon. This is home to all manner of strange and exotic mammals, birds, fish, amphibians and reptiles. Parrots and macaws on the wing, and troops of screeching monkeys provide the noisy score for capybara (sheep-sized rodents), caiman, armadillos, tapirs, peccaries and, if you are really lucky, jaguars. There are also a million and one butterflies, some the size of your hand, and spiders as big as next door's cat. It's all part of the authentic jungle experience.

Wet & wild Any trip to the rainforest is an adventure in itself, but those who crave even more excitement can ride the rapids on some of Ecuador's wildest and most spectacular rivers. White water rafting here is described as some of the best in the world, with the added advantage of warm, tropical water.

Eco-ethno-tourism The tropical forests are also home to the country's few remaining lowland ethnic groups. National parks and wildlife reserves have been set up to protect the region's precious natural assets and, of course, its indigenous people. Tourist dollars are invested into local community development by the more enlightened eco-tourism projects in an attempt to preserve one of the most biologically diverse places on earth as well as the traditional way of life of its inhabitants.

Creature comforts There are various ways of experiencing the jungle, depending on how much you value your creature comforts. It's not everyone's idea of fun to bathe in a jungle river with piranhas and electric eels and then sleep on the floor of a native hut at the end of a hot, sweaty hike. For those who prefer to embark on their rainforest adventure from a comfortable room with private shower, there are many jungle lodges to choose from.

Left: lazing on a sunny afternoon. The Amazon can be explored at your leisure by organising a trip through the jungle on a boat.
Below: staying in a jungle lodge is one way of experiencing the jungle firsthand in relative comfort.
Bottom left: toucan play that game!

Above: the beautiful San Rafael Falls are the highest in the country and along the gateway to the Oriente, Ecuador's vast tropical lowlands.
Next page: balsa wood parrots. Light as a feather and brightly painted in eye-catching colours, an example of Ecuador's many handicrafts.

Essentials

2

Essentials

Planning your trip

Where to go

One of Ecuador's great attractions is its relative compactness. Travelling around is easy and unlike its larger neighbours, much of what you want to see is only a few hours by road from the capital, Quito. The exceptions are the Galápagos Islands, which are usually reached by air, and the jungle, which is accessible by air and road. The latter overland journey can take up to 14 hours on poor roads, especially in the rainy season; but that is still a fraction of the time required to reach the jungle overland in other countries.

Ecuador is small enough to allow you to cross it in less than 24 hours, from north to south (or vice versa). Obviously, this won't give you much of a flavour of the place, but it does emphasize the fact that you can pack a lot into even the tightest of schedules. In fact, the biggest problem in trying to suggest various itineraries for the tourist is that there are just too many alternatives. So, instead, we'll point out some of the highlights in each region. Mix and match the options according to the time available and your own particular interests. Take a look at the section on Special interest travel (page 65) for information about climbing, trekking, rafting, kayaking and other adventure sports as well as birdwatching, hot springs and fishing. We also provide information about volunteer programmes.

Quito The point of arrival for most visitors is the capital, Quito. It is actually two distinct cities: the old city, which contains all the beautiful colonial churches and historic buildings, and the new city, with a million-and-one hotels, restaurants, bars and cafés. Quito boasts a wide range of excellent museums and it is the language course capital of South America. Just about any type of holiday or activity can be arranged here. There are many opportunities for day trips, to cultural as well as natural attractions. You could easily spend a few weeks in and around Quito without exhausting all possibilities.

North of Quito Almost everyone will make the two-hour bus journey to Otavalo, home to one of the finest craft markets in all of Latin America. It can be visited in less than a day, but many choose to extend their stay, so that they can also explore the numerous little craft villages nearby, or visit natural wonders such as Lake Cuicocha or any of the several nature reserves in the area. There are also several hiking possibilities. Alternatively, you can stay in Ibarra, a bit further north, which is the starting point for the trip to San Lorenzo on the coast, or a good stop on the way north to the Colombian border. North of Ibarra is El Angel Ecological Reserve, with interesting trekking amid the area's unique *frailejón* plants.

South of Quito South of the capital is the spectacular 'Avenue of the Volcanoes' and Cotopaxi National Park, which can be visited in a day; longer if you want to climb or trek. Two hours south of Quito is Latacunga, the starting point for the beautiful Quilotoa circuit, which has become very popular with visitors. It can be done in one day with a car, but needs longer without. Nearby is Saquisilí, with its colourful Thursday market – 2½ hours from Quito. Baños is a very popular spa town situated at the foot of Tungurahua, an imposing snow-capped volcano which became active again in 1999. There is good day hiking and cycling nearby and it is one of the gateways to the jungle - only 3½ hours from Quito. Riobamba, four hours from Quito, is the main city of the central highlands. It is a good base for trekking and climbing and a convenient stop on the journey south. Towering over the city is Chimborazo, the highest mountain in the country. Ingapirca, Ecuador's most important Inca archaeological site, lies 3½ hours further south, between Riobamba and Cuenca. Allow a day to visit Ingaprica by bus from Cuenca, or you can find accommodation nearby. Cuenca is a lovely colonial city, the heart of the southern highlands and also a great place to buy Panama hats (yes, they're made in Ecuador). It is 10-12 hours from Quito by bus and 45 minutes by air. Allow yourself a couple of days to fully appreciate its fine churches and museums and to take a trip out to the nearby Cajas National Park. Four to five hours south of Cuenca is the provincial capital of Loja, another convenient stop and the jumping-off point for a trip into the wilds of Podocarpus National Park. Only 1½ hours from Loja is lovely Vilcabamba, once a fabled fountain of youth, today the southern terminus of Ecuador's 'gringo trail'. New crossings to Peru are opening up and the country's entire southern border is expected to undergo a good deal of tourist development in coming years, facilitating outstanding travel circuits through the two nations.

Guayaquil   Guayaquil is 45 minutes by air from Quito and eight hours by bus, 5½ hours from Cuenca, and five hours from Riobamba. It can also be reached from many foreign destinations and has the country's only international airport outside Quito. Guayaquil is Ecuador's largest city and main port, bustling with commerce and industry. It is mostly visited by business people but has undergone something of a cultural revival in recent years, and boasts a lovely new *malecón* (riverfront promenade) as well as a few other tourist attractions. Guayaquil is especially well supplied with luxury hotels, restaurants and shops. Trips to the Galápagos can also be arranged from here.

The Pacific   From Guayaquil it is 2½ hours west to the seaside resort of Salinas, Ecuador's answer to
Coast   Miami Beach, on the Santa Elena peninsula. Northwards the coast has much more to offer. The little town of Puerto López (about 4½ hours from Guayaquil) is a good base from which to explore Machalilla National Park. Here, you can go hiking through dry tropical forest, horse riding, scuba diving, whale watching or just lie on the dazzling white sands of Los Frailes beach - one of the finest in all of Ecuador. Further north is Bahía de Caráquez, a resort city on the estuary of the Río Chone, with some interesting natural attractions such as the Isla de Fragatas (island of frigate birds). On the north side of the estuary are more excellent beaches, stretching for 20 km from San Vicente to the little village of Canoa. In the far north are the palm-fringed beaches of Same, Súa and Atacames, well known for their party atmosphere. Atacames is 40 minutes by road south of the city of Esmeraldas, which is only five to six hours from Quito or 30 minutes by air. From Esmeraldas you can also travel further north to San Lorenzo, a little corner of Africa in Ecuador, from which you can head up to Ibarra by road, thus completing a circuit from Quito. It is difficult to suggest the length of time you should spend on the coast since it depends how long you want to spend lazing on the beach, but a week would be enough to give a taste.

Oriente Jungle   A worthwhile and enjoyable jungle trip requires a little more preparation. You can either arrange a tour in Quito (or from abroad) to one of the many jungle lodges, which should be of at least three or four nights because of the time required to travel to and from the lodge. The alternative is to travel under your own steam to one of the main jungle towns and arrange a tour from there with a local agency or freelance guide. Tours can be arranged from Puyo, Tena, Misahuallí, Coca, Lago Agrio and Baños, which is on the road from the highlands to the Oriente. The southern Oriente is less developed for tourism, but interest in the region is growing, and tours here can be arranged from Macas and Zamora. Independent travel in the Oriente takes time, especially during the rainy season, so you should allow for five to seven days if you want to go far enough to see good wildlife. Late 2000 saw the first Amazon sailings for tourists from the Ecuadorean Oriente to Brazil via Peru.

Galápagos   Most people arrange their tours from Quito, Guayaquil or abroad, but those with more
Islands   time and less money can try flying directly from Quito or Guayaquil to Puerto Ayora on

Santa Cruz island, main town of the Galápagos. If you are lucky, you can get a good last-minute deal on a sailing tour there, but you can also be stuck waiting for weeks, especially in high season. Galápagos tours range from four days up to 14 days, but seven days would be optimal if you can afford it, to fully appreciate this once-in-a-lifetime experience.

When to go

Ecuador's climate is so varied and variable that any time of the year is good for a visit. In the highlands, every valley seems to have its own micro-climate but, generally, in the northern and central Andes, the driest months are June to September. In the southern highlands the driest months are August to January. Rainfall drops almost linearly from north to south along the Pacific coast, so that it can rain throughout the year in northern Esmeraldas and seldom at all near the Peruvian border. The coast can be enjoyed year-round, although it may be cool from June to September, when mornings are often grey and misty. In the Oriente, as in the rest of the Amazon basin, heavy rain can fall at any time, but it is usually wettest from April to September. The Galápagos are hot from January to April, when heavy showers are likely. From May to September is the cooler misty season.

Climate

Please remember that these are only broad generalizations and, simply stated, the weather in most of Ecuador is highly unpredictable

Ecuador's high international tourist season is from June to early September, which is the best time for trekking or climbing. There is also a shorter tourist season between December and January, when Galápagos tours may be booked well in advance. Most Ecuadoreans take long weekends around Carnival, Holy Week, and over New Year; vacations in the highlands are from July to September, on the coast January to March. While a few resort areas may become busy at these times, and prices rise accordingly, Ecuador is not overcrowded at any time of the year.

High/low seasons

Essentials

Finding out more

Tourist Information
Tourist information and promotion is handled at the national level by the **Ministerio de Turismo**, Eloy Alfaro 1214 y Carlos Tobar, Quito, T500719, 507555/560, F507564/565, mtur1@ec-gov.net Details of tourism offices throughout Ecuador are given under the respective towns and cities.

The **Cámara Provincial de Turismo de Pichincha (CAPTUR)** operates information booths at Quito airport and in the old city and new city (see the chapter on Quito). Their administrative offices are located at 6 de Diciembre 1424 y Carrión, T224074, F507682.

Outside Ecuador, tourist information can sometimes be obtained from Ecuadorean embassies and consulates (see box on page 25). **South American Explorers** in Quito (see below) provides a great deal of useful information for its club members and the **Latin American Travel Advisor** (see page 22) operates a reliable on-line information service; both are recommended. See their websites along with the others listed below.

South American Explorers (SAE)
This is a US based non-profit organization staffed by volunteers, which provides a wide range of travel information about South America. It offers a resource centre, an extensive file on volunteer work programmes, a library and a quarterly journal as well as selling guidebooks, maps and equipment (both new and used) and providing email and fax facilities. They can hold postal mail and email for members: write to PO Box 17-21-431, Quito, or send email to member@saec.org.ec and put the member's full name in subject field. The Quito facilities are at Jorge Washington 311 y Leonidas Plaza, T/F225228, explorer@saec.org.ec, www.samexplo.org Open Mon-Fri 0930-1700. It is located in a lovely spacious house and services are only available for members. Annual membership US$50 single, US$80 for a couple. Membership is highly recommended, visit first and have a look around. There are also SAE clubhouses in Lima and Cusco, Peru. US head office: 126 Indian Creek Rd, Ithaca, NY 14850, T1-607-2770488, F1-607-2776122, explorer@samexplo.org It offers books, maps, trip-planning service and can ship books and maps worldwide. Official representatives in UK: Bradt Publications, 41 Nortoft Rd, Chalfont St Peter, Bucks, SL9 0LA, T/F01494-873478.

Websites
Thanks to the many quality websites devoted to reporting the ins and outs of Ecuador, it is now possible to find up-to-date on-line information for just about anything you are interested in. Some sites may be commercial and include advertising or their directories may only list paying customers, but they nonetheless contain a good deal of useful information. Here are some of the best:

EcuadorExplorer (www.ecuadorexplorer.com): travel guide to Ecuador and the Galápagos Islands. The site includes up-to-the-minute information about the best places to stay, what to do, tips on staying healthy plus good background information about different regions, business, economy, government and more. English.

Latin American Travel Advisor (www.amerispan.com/lata/): this travel information service maintains an up-to-date detailed and reliable site about Ecuador and 16 other Latin American countries. English.

South American Explorers (www.samexplo.org): this has information on membership and the club's services as well as updates on travel conditions in Ecuador and other South American countries. English.

The Naturalist Net (www.naturalist.net): a site dedicated to the Galápagos with emphasis on the Islands' unique ecosystems with lots of up-to-date information and news. English.

GalápagosIslands (www.galapagosislands.com): a booking service for Galápagos tours that also has natural history information, geography, history, a wildlife photo gallery, and an extensive travel planning section. English.

The Charles Darwin Foundation (www.darwinfoundation.org): the foundation dedicated to conservation of the Galápagos has tons of educational information and resources for those planning a visit. English.

British Embassy in Quito (www.britembquito.org.ec): has necessary contact information, advice, on-line consular registration, and business information. English.

United States Embassy in Quito (www.usis.org.ec): contains useful contact information, a good link list, and US Embassy reports on Ecuador, including a Human Rights Report, an Economic Trend Report, an Investment Climate Report and an International Narcotics Control Strategy Report. English and Spanish.

Ecuadorean Embassy in Washington (www.ecuador.org): updated almost daily, it is the most up-to-date Ecuadorean government site. The site contains loads of general information about Ecuador's economy, government, and history, as well as a directory of authorities and Ecuadorean State owned and private institutions. The site also contains a useful current issues and news section. English and Spanish.

List of Embassies in Quito and Visa regulations (www.ecuadorexplorer.com/html/visas_embassies.html): has a complete list of embassies located in Quito with contact information and the most up-to-date source of Ecuadorean visa regulations and requirements for immigrants, students and travellers. English.

Explored (www.explored.com.ec): a developing Ecuadorean portal with a substantial amount of information about the nation and a digital archive of *Hoy* (one of Ecuador's major daily newspapers); includes articles dating back to 1990. Their travel section, called Ecuador Online, includes maps and a great guide to Ecuador's national parks. Spanish.

Hoy Digital (www.hoy.com.ec): an excellent on-line version of one Ecuador's major daily newspapers. *Hoy Digital* offers extras that are not included in its print version, a big selling point for Web junkies. Spanish.

El Comercio (www.elcomercio.com): the on-line version of Quito's largest circulation newspaper. Spanish.

El Universo (www.eluniverso.com): the on-line version of Guayaquil's largest circulation newspaper. Spanish.

Miami Herald (www.herald.com): arguably the best coverage of Latin America of any English language newspaper. Contains daily country updates including Ecuador. English.

Yupi Ecuador (www.ec.yupi.com): the Latin American portal and search engine's Ecuadorean site. Spanish.

Conciudadanos (www.conciudadanos.com): a portal that unites Ecuadoreans living abroad and other 'Ecuaphiles' to create a fully functional virtual community. English and Spanish.

Ecuatorianos (www.ecuatorianos.com): the largest virtual Ecuadorean community on the Web. It hosts numerous chats, works as a search engine and provides loads of news and other information about Ecuador. Spanish.

Bacan (www.bacan.com): a popular Ecuadorean search engine. Spanish.

Mande (www.mande.com.ec): an Ecuadorean search engine. Spanish.

Essentials

Before you travel

Getting in

Passports & visas

Visiting Ecuador as a tourist for a period of less than 3 months is very simple, with only a passport required for most travellers

All visitors to Ecuador must have a passport valid for at least six months and, in principle, an onward or return ticket. The latter is seldom asked for, but can be grounds for refusal of entry in some cases. Only citizens of the following countries require a consular visa to visit Ecuador as tourists: Algeria, Bangladesh, China, Costa Rica, Cuba, Honduras, India, Iran, Iraq, Jordan, North and South Korea, Lebanon, Libya, Nigeria, Pakistan, Palestinian Authority, Sri Lanka, Sudan, Syria, Tunisia, Vietnam and Yemen. Upon entry all visitors are required to complete a brief **international embarkation/disembarkation card**, which is then stamped along with your passport. **Keep this card in your passport**, losing it can cause all manner of grief when leaving the country or at a spot check.

Spot checks

Warning: you are required by Ecuadorean law to carry your passport at all times. Failure to do so can result in imprisonment and/or deportation. An ordinary photocopy of your passport is not an acceptable substitute and you will generally not be permitted to return to your hotel to fetch the original document. A photocopy certified by your embassy or the immigration police may be acceptable, but you should also have your original passport close at hand. For the best way to protect your passport see the section Protecting money and valuables, page 45. Spot checks for passports are most often carried out near border areas and at police checkpoints on highways throughout the country, as well as in bars, discos and resorts popular with foreigners. Be cautious however when approached by someone

Ecuadorean embassies and consulates

Australia, 11 London Circuit, 1st Floor, Canberra ACT 2601, T(6)62811009, F(6)62625285, embecu@canberra.hotkey.net.au

Austria, Goldschmiedgasse 10/2/24, A-1010 Vienna, T(1)5353208, F(1)5350897, mecuaustria@council.net

Belgium, Av Louise 363, 9th Floor, 1050 Brussels, T(2)6443050, F(2)6442813, ecuador@skypro.be

Canada, 50 O'Connor St No 316, Ottawa, ON K1P 6L2, T(613)5638206, F(613)2355776, embecuca@sprint.ca; 151 Bloor St West, Suite 470 Toronto, ON M5S 1S4, T(416)9682077, F(416)9683348, ctoronto@ican.net; 1010 Sainte Catherine W No 502, Montreal, QC H3B 1G4, T(514)8744071, F(514)8749078, consecuador-montreal@iq.ca

France, 34 Ave de Messine, 75008 Paris, T(1)45611021, F(1)42560664, ambecuad@infonie.fr

Germany, Kaiser-Friedrich Strasse 90, 1 OG, 10585 Berlin, T(30)2386217, mecuadoral@aol.com

Israel, 4 Rehov Weizmann (Asia House), 4th floor, Tel Aviv 64239, T(3)6958764, F(3)6913604, mecuaisr@infolink.net.il

Italy, Via Guido d'Arezzo 14, 00198 Roma, T(6)8541784, F(6)5354434, mecuroma@flashnet.it

Japan, No 38 Kowa Building, Room 806, 12-24 Nishi-Azabu 4 Chome, Minato-Ku, Tokyo 1060031, T(3)34992800, F(3)34994400, ecujapon@twics.com

Netherlands, Koning innengracht 84, 2585 GG The Hague, T(70)3463753, F(70)8658910, embecua@bart.nl

New Zealand, Ferry Bldg, 2nd Floor, Quay St, Auckland, T(09)3090229, F(09)3032931.

Spain, Príncipe de Vergara No 73, 7th Floor, 28006 Madrid, T(1)5627215, F(1)7450244, embajada@mecuador.es

Sweden, Engelbrektsgatan 13, S-100 41 Stockholm, T(8)6796043, F(8)6115593, suecia@embajada-ecuador.se

Switzerland, Ensingerstrasse 48, 3006 Berne, T(031)3511755, F(031)3512771, edesuiza@bluewin.ch

UK, Flat 3B, 3 Hans Crescent, Knightsbridge, London SW1X 0LS, T020-7584 1367, F7823 9701, 101543.2243@compuserve.com

USA, 2535 15th Street NW, Washington, DC 20009, T(202)2347200, F(202)6673482, mecuawaa@pop.erols.com

Essentials

claiming to be an immigration officer on the street. If they are in uniform, they will have a tag with their name, which you should first write down. If they are plain clothed (which is unusual) then politely ask for their ID, seek assistance from several bystanders, and insist on walking to the nearest police station before you hand over any documents. Do not get in a taxi or other vehicle with such an individual. **A legitimate immigration officer should not ask to see your money at a spot check**, if this is asked for then you are probably being set up to be robbed.

   As long as your documents are in order, serious hassles with the immigration authorities in Ecuador are fortunately very rare. Remember however, that tourists are not permitted to work under any circumstances. If you should encounter serious difficulties with the immigration police, then these may be reported to your embassy or consulate. Some embassies also recommend that you register with them details of your passport and accommodation in case of emergency.

In principle, tourists are entitled to visit Ecuador for up to 90 days during any 12 month period. This may (or may not) be extended to a maximum of 180 days at the discretion of the Policía Nacional de Migración (national immigration police). In practice, those travelling by land from Peru or Colombia are seldom granted more than 30 days on arrival, but this can usually be extended to at least 90 days, and sometimes to 180 days (see below). When arriving at Quito or Guayaquil airport you will generally be asked how long you plan to stay in the country. Whether or not you are asked, it is best to

Length of visit

Essentials

request at least two weeks more than you think you will need, just to be on the safe side. If you have no idea how long you will stay, ask for 90 days.

Extensions At present only a nominal fee/fine of US$0.40 is charged for extensions, but this will most likely increase substantially. **Extensions up to 90 days, total stay may only be requested at the following locations: 1) in Quito** at the Jefatura Provincial de Migración de Pichincha, Isla Seymour 44-174 y Río Coca, T247510 (note that this is not the same as the Dirección Nacional de Migración listed below); **2) in Guayaquil** at the Jefatura Provincial de Migración del Guayas, Av. Río Daule, near the *terminal terrestre*, T297004; **3) in Cuenca** at the Jefatura Provincial de Migración del Azuay, Luis Cordeo 662 entre Presidente Córdova y Juan Jaramillo, T831020; **4) in Puerto Baquerizo Moreno** at the Jefatura Provincial de Migración de Galápagos, on San Cristóbal Island, F520129. To request **extensions beyond 90 days**, you must first be authorized for a 90 day stay (either on arrival or through an initial extension as above), and then you must go to **immigration police headquarters in Quito**: Dirección Nacional de Migración, Amazonas 171 y República, T454122. All of the above offices are normally open Monday-Friday 0800-1200 and 1500-1800. Immigration offices in cities other than the above cannot grant tourist visa extensions. If you are lucky, obtaining an extension can take less than an hour, but always leave yourself a few days' slack as there may be delays. Also note that the above regulations are frequently subject to change, if you are unsure about current requirements then enquire well before your time expires. Polite conduct and a neat appearance are important when dealing with the immigration authorities.

Longer stays There are many options for foreigners who wish to stay in Ecuador longer than six months a year, but if you enter as a tourist then you cannot change your status while inside the country. Types of consular visas for longer stays include: student, retiree, investor, business person, foreign employee, volunteer, cultural exchange, spouse of an Ecuadorean citizen and parent of an Ecuadorean child. Each visa has its own particular requirements and corresponding fees, which vary from US$50 to US$500, plus an initial application fee of US$30 for all visas. Information is available from Ecuador's diplomatic representatives (see box on page 25) where applications must be filed. Allow several months for the application process.

After arriving in Ecuador, all foreigners **except tourists** must register first with the Dirección Nacional de Extranjería in Quito, Edificio de la Corporación Financiera Nacional, Juan León Mera N19-36 y Patria, sixth floor, open Monday-Friday 0800-1300, and then with the immigration police office in the province where they will live, in order to obtain their *censo* (foreign resident census card), which must be renewed annually. Those with immigrant visas must additionally get a *cedula* (national identity card) from the *registro civil*, and foreign men must also obtain two separate permits from the military. Subsequent visa renewals and modifications are handled either by Extranjería (as above), for immigrant visas; or, for non-immigrant visas, by the Cancillería in Quito, Departamento de Asuntos Migratorios, Carrión corner Paez, second floor, open Monday-Friday 0930-1230. These are complex time-consuming procedures whose regulations frequently change. Many expatriates therefore choose to retain the services of a specialized immigration lawyer, although this is not strictly indispensable. Be sure to get a personal recommendation however, before hiring such an attorney, as some are unscrupulous and will overcharge as well as creating more problems than they resolve.

Tourists may leave the Ecuador at any time with only their passport and the international embarkation/disembarkation card which they were issued on arrival. Other foreigners face varying requirements, including a *salida* (exit permit) issued by the immigration police and valid for one year; as well as the *censo, cedula,* and military documents mentioned above.

Leaving Ecuador
Remember to reconfirm international flights 72 hours in advance

In addition to your passport, the following documents are important for a visit to Ecuador.

Important documents

International vaccination certificate: a vaccination certificate is seldom asked for in Ecuador but must nonetheless be carried by all international travellers. For details see Vaccination and immunization, page 65.

Driver's license: a valid local driver's license from any country in the world is generally sufficient to rent a car and drive in Ecuador. An international driver's license is therefore not indispensable. For details see under Car, page 52.

ISIC card: the International Student Identity Card (ISIC) may help you obtain discounts when travelling in Ecuador. For details see Student travellers, page 39.

Leave the following documents at home with a friend or relative whom you can easily contact in case of emergency: your birth certificate or citizenship certificate, a photocopy of your passport, copies of your airline tickets and copies (not originals) of purchase receipts for any travellers' cheques you bring with you. Do not bring any unnecessary personal documents which you cannot use in Ecuador, but which would be inconvenient to replace should they be lost or stolen. Examples include a work ID or social security card, purge your purse or wallet of these before you travel.

Documents to leave at home

Travel insurance is extremely important for all visitors to Ecuador. An adequate insurance policy should include coverage for the damage, loss, or theft of your belongings as well as health care in the event of accident or illness. You may also wish to consider coverage for repatriation by air ambulance in the event of a serious mishap. There are so many different types of policies offered worldwide that it is difficult to make specific recommendations. In all cases however, you should read the

Insurance

Essentials

fine print before leaving home and be sure to bring all the necessary contact information with you. Notify your insurer as soon as possible in the event of a claim. You will almost certainly have to pay all expenses out-of-pocket in Ecuador (be sure to keep detailed receipts) and request reimbursement after you return home. For this reason having some extra cash on hand is also part of your travel insurance.

Customs **On arrival** Customs inspection is carried out at airports after you clear immigration. When travelling by land, customs authorities may also set up checkpoints along the country's highways. Tourists seldom encounter any difficulties but if you are planning to bring any particularly voluminous, unusual, or valuable items to Ecuador (for example professional video equipment, a boat or desktop computer) then you should enquire beforehand with an Ecuadorean diplomatic representative (see box on page 25) and obtain any necessary permits, or be prepared to pay the prevailing customs duties. Reasonable amounts of climbing gear and one used laptop computer per family are generally not a problem. For details on bringing a vehicle into Ecuador see under Documents, page 54. Never bring any firearms.

Shipping goods to Ecuador Except for documents, customs duties must be paid on all goods shipped to Ecuador. Enforcement is strict, duties are high and procedures are slow and complicated. You are therefore advised to bring anything you think you will need with you when you travel, rather than having it sent after you once you are in the country.

On departure Your baggage may be inspected by security personnel and will always be sniffed by dogs searching for drugs. **Never transport anything you have not packed yourself**, you will be held responsible for the contents. No export duties are charged on souvenirs you take home from Ecuador, but there are various items for which you require special permits. These include specimens of wild plants and animals, original archaeological artifacts, certain works of art and any objects considered part of the country's national heritage. When in doubt, enquire well in advance.

What to take Everybody has their own list. Obviously what you take depends on your individual

A good general principle is to take half the clothes and twice the money you think you will need travel style, your budget and what you plan to do. Listed below are a few things which are particularly useful for travelling in Ecuador. There are a million-and-one other travel accessories and gadgets on the market, all of which may well prove useful under the appropriate circumstances. At the same time however, you should try to think light and compact. The less weight you have to carry around and the fewer your belongings which might be lost or stolen, the more carefree and enjoyable will be your travels. All but the most specialized products are available in Quito and Guayaquil, while many basic commodities are readily purchased throughout the country.

A **moneybelt or pouch** is absolutely indispensable for everyone, see Protecting money and valuables, page 45. Be sure to bring an adequate supply of any **medications** you take on a regular basis, plus two weeks spare, as these may not be available in Ecuador. **Sturdy comfortable footwear** is a must for travels anywhere, and Ecuador's uneven sidewalks, dirt roads and muddy country trails are no exception. **Sun protection** is very important in all regions of the country and for visitors of all complexions. This should include a **sun hat, high quality sun glasses and sun screen for both skin and lips**. Take **insect repellent** if you plan to visit the coast or jungle. Also recommended are **rubber sandals or thongs** for use on the beach, at hot springs and in hotel showers, where they protect against both athlete's foot and electric shock when instant-heating shower heads are used. If you use contact lenses, be sure to also bring a pair of **eye glasses**. A **small lightweight towel** is an asset, as is a short length of **travel clothesline**, which can be purchased or made of braided elastic, eliminating the need for pegs. A **compact torch (flashlight)**, **alarm watch** and **pocket knife** may all be useful. Always carry some **toilet paper**, as this is seldom found in public washrooms unless it is sold at the entrance.

For full details of recommended vaccinations, see page 83. Check malaria prophylaxis for lowland rural areas to be visited, including the Oriente and Pacific coast, but not Galápagos.

Vaccinations & malaria

Money

There are a variety of different ways for visitors to bring their funds to Ecuador. You are strongly advised to use two or more of these, so as not to be stuck if there are problems with any one alternative. US cash in small denominations is by far the simplest and the only universally accepted option, but clearly a serious risk for loss or theft. Travellers' cheques are safe, but can only be exchanged for cash in the larger cities and up to 5% commission may be charged (although it is usually less). Credit cards can be used to obtain a cash advance at some branches of some banks, and to pay at most upmarket establishments, but a surcharge may be applied. Internationally linked banking machines or ATMs are common in Ecuador, although their use involves certain risks (see below) and they cannot always be relied on. Funds may be rapidly wired to Ecuador by Western Union, but high fees and taxes apply. It is best not to bring any currencies other than US dollars to Ecuador, neither as cash nor travellers' cheques; they are difficult to exchange and generally fetch a poor rate.

There is simply no substitute for cash-in-hand when travelling in Ecuador. Always bring some (but not all) of your funds as small US dollar bills

Since September 2000, the US dollar is the only official currency of Ecuador. Only US dollar bills circulate, in the following denominations: $1, $2 (rare), $5, $10, $20, $50 and $100. US coins are used alongside the equivalent size and value Ecuadorean coins for $0.01, $0.05, $0.10, $0.25 and $0.50. These Ecuadorean coins have no value outside the country. Many merchants are reluctant to accept bills larger than $20, both because counterfeit notes are a problem and because change may be scarce. Even legitimate banknotes which look old or rumpled or have a small tear are often refused. Travellers should therefore carefully check any bills they receive as change.

Currency

At the close of this edition (January 2001), Ecuador was reluctantly coming to terms with its new currency. Many people, especially in small towns, still think in terms of the country's previous monetary unit, the sucre, which was used for over a century. The last exchange rate for the sucre was 25,000 to US$1 and you might find some prices still quoted in sucres, although this should gradually disappear. Sucre notes and coins have no value except as souvenirs.

US dollar travellers' cheques can be exchanged for cash in Ecuador, but usually only in Quito, Guayaquil, Cuenca and occasionally in some of the larger provincial capitals. American Express travellers' cheques are the most widely accepted brand. Produbanco and Banco del Pacifico exchange travellers' cheques at some but not all of their branches, and there may be restrictions on the amount, paperwork and long queues involved. A few *casas de cambio* (exchange houses) are still operating following dollarization of the economy and some exchange travellers' cheques, usually quite efficiently. Commissions typically range between 1.5% and 5%. Your passport is always required to cash travellers' cheques and you may also have to show the original purchase receipt. The more expensive hotels, restaurants and tour agencies generally accept payment in travellers' cheques, but smaller establishments may not, especially outside major centres. A good strategy therefore is to gradually convert your travellers' cheques to cash, whenever you visit a larger city. American Express has offices in Quito and Guayaquil and they offer a very efficient service. They sell travellers' cheques against an Amex card (or a cardholder's personal cheque) and

Travellers' cheques

replace lost or stolen travellers' cheques, but they do not give cash for travellers' cheques nor travellers' cheques for cash. A police report is required if travellers' cheques are stolen.

Credit cards The most commonly accepted credit cards in Ecuador include Visa, MasterCard, Diners, and to a lesser extent American Express. Many smaller hotels, restaurants, tour agencies and shops may display credit card signs but not honour the cards 'just at the moment', or they may apply a surcharge (typically 10%) for credit card customers. Luxury or first class establishments will usually have no difficulty in honouring most credit cards. MasterCard holders can obtain cash advances at the company's offices in Quito, Guayaquil, Cuenca and Ambato as well as at branches of ABN-AMRO Bank, Banco del Pacifico and Mutualista Pichincha in larger centres throughout the country. Those with Visa cards can obtain cash advances at the main branches of Banco de Guayaquil in Quito and Guayaquil and some branches of Banco Amazonas, Banco del Austro, Banco Bolivariano, Banco Pichincha and Filanbanco, but most reliably in larger centres. Remember that you will be charged interest on cash advances, check with your home bank or credit card company before travelling to see what interest rates and regulations apply.

ATMs ATMs or banking machines are very common throughout Ecuador, and many are linked to international systems such as Plus or Cirrus. Visitors with the appropriately encoded credit cards or bank cards can therefore obtain cash from these machines. Always check with your home bank before travelling regarding which networks they work with and their Ecuadorean affiliates, as well as the charges and conditions which apply to such transactions. Also bear in mind that these electronic systems are not always reliable in Ecuador. They may be out of order or run out of cash, they may refuse to accept a valid card or even confiscate it, and the card is then very difficult to retrieve. ATMs linked to Cirrus are found in most banks affiliated with MasterCard, whereas those linked to Plus are found in most (but not all) banks affiliated with Visa.

Money transfers In addition to the above means of payment, you may need to have funds sent from your home, either on a routine basis or in an emergency. Bank transfers, wires, telexes or cables to Ecuador are not recommended for this purpose, because of potentially long delays, high taxes and service charges. Western Union has offices throughout Ecuador and can reliably transfer funds into or out of the country in a matter of minutes, but high taxes and charges also apply. The most efficient and economical alternative is to purchase travellers' cheques on an Amex card or with a personal cheque, as described above. Note that money orders are not accepted anywhere in Ecuador. If all else fails, you might have someone send you a small amount of US cash by regular airmail, with each bill carefully concealed in a separate envelope. This is prone to theft of course, and contravenes international postal regulations.

Cost of living

For hotel prices, see Where to stay, page 47; for restaurant prices, see Food and drink (page 61)

With the implementation of dollarization in 2000 the economy finally stabilized and, at the same time, real prices slowly began to rise. Ecuador nonetheless remains a cheap country for the budget traveller and even among the cheapest in South America. It is impossible to predict the future, but a reasonable assumption is that the cost of living will continue to slowly increase for some time. **The prices listed in this book are current at the time of publication, and the traveller should expect them to gradually rise thereafter.** Despite the US dollar economy however, it seems most unlikely that prices in Ecuador will reach or even approach international levels, and the country should remain a good travel bargain for the foreseeable future.

Overall, tourists in Ecuador can live quite comfortably on a daily budget of US$15-20 per person, including transport, or as little as US$10-15 per person without sacrificing too much in the way of comfort or quality. Small cities and towns in the

highlands offer the lowest prices. Quito is only slightly more expensive, and cheap accommodation and places to eat are still plentiful in the capital. Visitors will also find local handicrafts excellent value. Guayaquil is also more expensive, as are seaside resort towns and tourist facilities deep in the Oriente, but cheap accommodation and meals can be found almost anywhere if you take the time to shop around.

Getting there

Air

International flights into Ecuador arrive either at Quito or Guayaquil. Unless going immediately to the Galápagos from Guayaquil, it may be a good idea to start your visit in Quito. This is where you will find most sources of tourist information, travel agencies, language schools and the widest selection of hotels and restaurants in the intermediate price range. If your flight only goes to Guayaquil, there are frequent shuttle flights up to the capital if you do not want to go overland. International airfares from North America and Europe to Ecuador vary substantially with low and high season. The latter is generally July to September and December. International flights to Ecuador from other South or Central American countries however, usually have one price year-round. The monthly guide *Transport*, available at most travel agencies, gives details of international and national flights and phone numbers of airlines in Quito and Guayaquil. Flight frequency changes regularly. You should always check current timetables.

From Europe KLM offers departures from many European cities, including 16 UK airports, to Quito via Amsterdam. Iberia flies to Quito from Madrid via Santo Domingo, Dominican Republic.

Discount flight agents in the UK and Ireland

Council Travel, 28a Poland St, London, W1V 3DB, T020-7437 7767, www.destinations- group.com

STA Travel, Priory House, 6 Wrights Lane, London, W8 6TA, T0870-160 6070, www.statravel.co.uk
They have other branches in London, as well as in Brighton, Bristol, Cambridge, Leeds, Manchester, Newcastle-Upon-Tyne and Oxford and on many University campuses. Specialists in low-cost student/youth flights and tours, also good for student IDs and insurance.

Trailfinders, 194 Kensington High Street, London, W8 7RG, T020-7938 3939, www.trailfinders.com

Usit Campus, 52 Grosvenor Gardens, London, SW1 0AG, T0870-2401010, www.usitcampus.co.uk Student/youth travel specialists with branches also in Belfast, Brighton, Bristol, Cambridge, Manchester and Oxford. The main Ireland branch is at 19 Aston Quay, Dublin 2, T01-6021777.

Lufthansa and Air France fly from Frankfurt and Paris, respectively, to Bogotá, where passengers are transferred to local carriers for the flight to Quito. Continental Airlines flies to Quito and Guayaquil from London Gatwick, Dublin, Shannon, Paris, Frankfurt, Dusseldorf, Rome, Milan, Lisbon and Madrid; all flights are via Newark or Houston. American Airlines flies to Quito and Guayaquil from various European cities via Miami.

Miami's heavily congested international airport is by far the most important air transport hub linking Ecuador with all of North America. American Airlines has at least one flight daily from Miami to each of Quito and Guayaquil; on some days there are two flights. Cheaper fares from Miami to Quito or Guayaquil may be offered by Copa Airlines, which flies via Panama City, and TACA, which flies via San José, Costa Rica. Several South American airlines may also offer competitive fares from Miami to Quito or Guayaquil via their respective capital cities. These include Avianca and Aces of Colombia and Avensa/Servivensa of Venezuela. Continental Airlines flies to Quito and Guayaquil from less congested Houston and Newark, with some flights routed through Panama City. Ecuatoriana flies from New York City's JFK to Quito and Guayaquil. **From North America**

There are three options: 1) To Los Angeles (USA) with Quantas or Air New Zealand, continuing to Quito via Houston with Continental. 2) To Papetete (Tahiti) with Quantas or Air New Zealand, continuing to Quito via Easter Island and Santiago (Chile) with Lan Chile. 3) To Buenos Aires (Argentina) with Quantas or Aerolineas Argentinas, continuing to Quito with Lan Chile or another South American carrier. **From Australia & New Zealand** *See also box on page 37*

Essentials

www.journeylatinamerica.co.uk GO

JOURNEY LATIN AMERICA

BRITAIN'S FOREMOST LATIN AMERICAN SPECIALIST
20 YEARS
SINCE 1980

🕊 Flights only

🕊 Escorted Groups

🕊 Active Adventures

🕊 Cruises

🕊 Insurance

🕊 Brochures

🕊 **Tailor-made Tours**

Search | Favourites ▶ | ▲

- Amazon
- Banos
- Cotopaxi
- Cuenca
- **Galapagos**
- Otavalo
- Quito
- Saquisili
- Train Journeys
- Volcanoes ▼

Jungle
Markets
Cities
History
Wildlife

Search | Regions ▶ | ▲

- Argentina
- Bolivia
- Brazil
- Caribbean ▶
- Central America ▶
- Chile
- Colombia
- **Ecuador**
- Mexico
- Peru
- Uruguay
- Venezuela ▼

Fully Bonded

AITO
ABTA
IATA

JOURNEY LATIN AMERICA

12-13 Heathfield Terrace, Chiswick
LONDON
W4 4JE
020 8747 8315
Fax 020 8742 1312

28-30 Barton Arcade Deansgate
MANCHESTER
M3 2BH
0161 832 1441
Fax 0161 832 1551

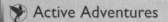

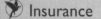

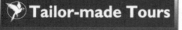
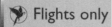
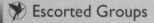

Discount flight agents in North America

Air Brokers International, 323 Geary St, Suite 411, San Francisco, CA 94102, T 01-800-883 3273, www.airbrokers.com Consolidator and specialist on RTW and Circle Pacific tickets.
Council Travel, 205 E 42nd St, New York, NY 10017, T1-888-COUNCIL, www.counciltravel.com Student/budget agency with branches in many other US cities.
Discount Airfares Worldwide On-Line, www.etn.nl/discount.htm A hub of consolidator and discount agent links.
International Travel Network/Airlines of the Web, www.itn.net/airlines Online air travel information and reservations.
STA Travel, 5900 Wilshire Blvd, Suite 2110, Los Angeles, CA 90036, T1-800-777 0112, www.sta-travel.com Also branches in New York, San Francisco, Boston, Miami, Chicago, Seattle and Washington DC.
Travel CUTS, 187 College St, Toronto, ON, M5T 1P7, T1-800-667 2887, www.travelcuts.com Specialist in student discount fares, Ids and other travel services. Branches in other Canadian cities.
Travelocity, www.travelocity.com Online consolidator.

Essentials

There are regular flights to Quito and/or Guayaquil from Buenos Aires, Santiago, La Paz and Santa Cruz (Bolivia), Lima, Bogotá, Caracas, Panama City, San José (Costa Rica) and Havana. From Brazil Ecuatoriana/VASP flies to Quito from São Paulo and Manaus. The latter can be a particularly useful route for those travelling through South America from the Andes to the Atlantic or vice versa. Copa Airlines has a hub in Panama City which offers convenient connections between Ecuador and various destinations in Central America, Mexico and the Caribbean. (See also Getting around, page 50.) **From Latin American cities**

Airlines will only allow a certain weight of luggage without a surcharge; this is normally 30 kg for first class and 20 kg for business and economy classes, but these limits are often not strictly enforced when it is known that the plane is not going to be full. On some flights from the UK via Paris special outbound concessions are offered of a two-piece allowance up to 32 kg, but you may need to request this. Passengers seeking a larger baggage allowance can route via USA, but with certain exceptions, the fares are slightly higher using this route. On the other hand, weight limits for internal flights within Ecuador are often lower. It's best to enquire beforehand. **Baggage allowance**

Most airlines offer discounted fares on scheduled flights through agencies who specialize in this type of fare. For a list of these agencies see Tour operators (page). The very busy seasons are 7 December - 15 January and 10 July – 10 September. If you intend travelling during those times, book as far ahead as possible. Between February-May and September-November special offers may be available. **Prices & discounts**
It is generally cheaper to fly from London rather than a point in Europe to Latin America

Other fares fall into three groups, and are all on scheduled services: **a) Excursion (return) fares** with restricted validity, eg five to 90 days. Carriers are introducing flexibility into these tickets, permitting a change of dates on payment of a fee. **b) Yearly fares** These may be bought on a one-way or return basis. Some airlines require a specified return date, changeable upon payment of a fee. To leave the return completely open is possible for an extra fee. You must fix the route (some of the cheapest flexible fares now have six months' validity). **c) Student (or under 26) fares** Do not assume that student tickets are the cheapest; though they are often very flexible, they are usually more expensive than a) or b) above. Some airlines are flexible on the age limit, others strict. One way and returns available, or 'Open Jaws' (see below). **NB** If you foresee returning home at a busy time (eg Christmas, August), a booking is advisable on any type of open-return ticket.

For people intending to travel a linear route and return from a different point from that at which they entered, there are 'Open Jaws' fares, which are available on student, yearly, or excursion fares.

Essentials

If you buy discounted air tickets *always* check the reservation with the airline concerned to make sure the flight still exists. Also remember the IATA airlines' schedules change in March and October each year, so if you're going to be away a long time it's best to leave return flight coupons open. In addition, check whether you are entitled to any refund or re-issued ticket if you lose, or have stolen, a discounted air ticket. Some airlines require the repurchase of a ticket before you can apply for a refund, which will not be given until after the validity of the original ticket has expired. The Iberia group and Air France, for example, operate this costly system. Travel insurance in some cases covers lost tickets.

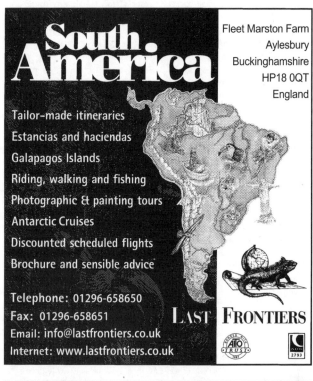

Discount flight agents in Australia and New Zealand

Flight Centres, 82 Elizabeth St, Sydney, T13-1600; 205 Queen St, Auckland, T09-309 6171. Also branches in other towns and cities.
STA Travel, T1300-360960,

www.statravelaus.com.au; 702 Harris St, Ultimo, Sydney, and 256 Flinders St, Melbourne. In NZ: 10 High St, Auckland, T09-366 6673. Also in major towns and university campuses.

Road

There are regular connections by bus to Quito and Guayaquil from Peru and Colombia, as well as South American countries farther afield, but no vehicle road connecting Central and South America. The most commonly-used overland routes are via the Tulcán-Ipiales border crossing in the north, and the Huaquillas-Aguas Verdes border in the south, although Macará-La Tina-Sullana is an increasingly attractive border crossing with Peru. A new crossing with Peru opened in late 2000 between Zumba (Ecuador) and San Ignacio (Peru), allowing for a more direct route from Loja and Vilcabamba to Jaen and Chachpoyas (Peru), but you can only cross on foot here. Other new border posts with Peru might be opened in coming years. For details on immigration procedures at these borders, see under the relevant sections of respective towns. Note that it is usually much cheaper to buy bus tickets as far as the nearest border town, cross on foot or by taxi, and then purchase tickets locally in the country you have just entered. There are some exceptions however, or times when the convenience of a direct service outweighs additional cost. For example, there is now a particularly convenient service from Loja direct to Piura, Peru.

If entering Ecuador by car, details of customs procedures are given on page 52.

Boat

Enquiries regarding passages should be made through agencies in your own country, or through the Strand Cruise and Travel Centre, Charing Cross Shopping Concourse, The Strand, London WC2N 4HZ, T020-7836 6363, F7497 0078. In Switzerland, contact Wagner Frachtschiffreisen, Stadlerstrasse 48, CH-8404 Winterthur, T052-2421442, F2421487. In the USA, contact Freighter World Cruises, 180 South Lake Ave, Pasadena, CA 91101, T818-4493106, or Traveltips Cruise and Freighter Travel Association, 163-07 Depot Rd, PO Box 188, Flushing, NY 11358, T(800)8728584.

The Strand Cruise and Travel Centre can book passages on the following two routes. A 74-day round trip, with space for about five passengers, costs £3,730 per person in a double cabin, from Felixstowe to Guayaquil via the Panama Canal and then down to various ports in Chile, before returning to Felixstowe via the Panama Canal and Cartagena, Colombia. Another shipping company carries a maximum of 12 passengers on a 70-day round trip, costing £4,100, from the mediterranean port of Leghorn, calling at ports on the east coast of Spain, Miami, Cartagena, Panama Canal, various ports in Peru and Chile, Guayaquil, Panama Canal, Cartagena, various Spanish ports and up to Leghorn.

Touching down

Airport information

For most visitors, the point of arrival will be Mariscal Sucre airport in Quito. For details of Guayaquil's Simón Bolívar airport see page 286.

Public transport to & from airport

Taxi The safest and easiest way to and from town from the airport is to take a taxi. You can catch one from the rank right outside arrivals. The fare from the airport to the new town is about US$2; to the old town or to a first-class hotel US$3 (more at night). Alternatively, you can use the Trans-Rabbit van service, they have a booth at international arrivals, T568755, US$6 to the new town in a van with room for up to 10 passengers. This is good value if there are a few people sharing. To order a taxi by phone, see Taxis, on page 51.

Bus This is **not recommended** unless you have virtually no luggage or are desperately low on funds. Buses and trolley alike are usually too crowded for you to enter with even a small backpack and the chances of having something vanish *en route* are very high. If you really have no other choice, the bus stop is one block from the terminal to the west (towards Pichincha), in front of *Centro Comercial Aeropuerto*. For the new city take a southbound red bus marked 'Carcelén-Congreso' or 'Pinar Alto-Hotel Quito' these run along Av Amazonas and later C Juan León Mera, fare US$0.15. For the old city and parts of the new city, take a green *alimentador* (feeder bus line) at the same bus stop, it goes to the northern terminus of the trolley, where you transfer to the trolley line; combined fare US$0.15. There is no bus or trolley service late at night when most flights from North America arrive. Do not even think of walking into town at such times, take a cab. See also under Quito, Ins and outs (page 100).

Airport facilities
See Sleeping in Quito, page 111, for details of hotels near the airport

Quito airport is a bit cramped but functional. There are often long queues for international departures and most airlines recommend you arrive three hours before your flight. Always reconfirm international flights 72 hours in advance.

The airport is divided into four contiguous sections which are only a minute's walk from each other. From north to south are: international arrivals, international departures, national arrivals and national departures. Left luggage facilities are just outside international arrivals. There is a telephone office upstairs in international departures, plus a few debit card-operated public phones downstairs; buy the debit cards at one of the airport shops. There is a post office outside, between international departures and national arrivals. Also upstairs in international departures is a bar-restaurant which serves meals and snacks, and a fast food place in national departures; both are expensive. There are expensive souvenir shops in international departures and luxury duty-free in the international departure lounge, after you clear immigration. All the main car rental companies are located just outside international arrivals. For details of their offices in Quito, see page 139.

NB Beware of self-styled porters: men or boys who will grab your luggage and offer to find you a cab in the hope of receiving a tip or stealing your bags. Legitimate porters wear ID tags and there is no shortage of taxis right at hand. Watch your gear at all times.

Airport departure tax

A 12% tax is charged on international air tickets for flights originating in Ecuador, regardless of where bought, as well as on domestic tickets, and a departure tax of US$25 is payable by all passengers leaving on international flights (except those who stay less than 24 hours in the country). Pay the departure tax when checking in with your airline, or at a booth in the international departures area. You will not be allowed to board without proof of payment.

Touching down

Official time _5 hours behind GMT. The Galápagos is 6 hours behind._

Voltage _110 volts, 60 cycles, AC throughout Ecuador. Very low wattage bulbs are the rule in many cheaper hotel rooms, keen readers might want to carry a bright bulb._

Weights and measures _The metric system is generally used in foreign trade and must be used in legal documents. English measures are understood in the hardware and textile trades. Spanish measures are often used in the retail trade and in Indian markets._

Tourist information

For full details of the Ecuadorean Ministry of Tourism, and for on-line information, see under Finding out more (page 22). The addresses of local tourist offices are given in the main travelling text. See Tours and tour operators (page) for a list of specialist tour operators operating from outside of Ecuador.

This non-profit, educational organization functions primarily as a comprehensive travel information network for its club members. For full details, see page 22. **South American Explorers**

This travel information service maintains an up-to-date detailed and reliable website about Ecuador and 16 other Latin American countries, www.amerispan.com/lata/ They also carry out research and can help organize logistic support for special projects and expeditions, such as scientists, authors, documentary film-makers, etc. For details see their website or contact LATA@pi.pro.ec **The Latin American Travel Advisor**

The Instituto Geográfico Militar in Quito (see page 144) produces a series of topographic maps covering most of the country at the following scales: 1:250,000, 1:100,000, 1:50,000 and 1:25,000. The latter two scales are most useful for trekking. Maps of the seacoast and border areas are classified, and cannot be purchased without a military permit. ITMB's 1:1,000,000 map of Ecuador, by Kevin Healey, 1994-96 edition, is available from ITMB Publishing Ltd, 345 West Broadway, Vancouver, BC, Canada. A recommended series of maps and city guides by Nelson Gómez, published by _Ediguias_ in Quito, includes handy pocket maps/guides of Quito, Guayaquil, Cuenca, Otavalo and Galápagos (the latter two in English). These are available in bookshops throughout the country, but most reliably in the capital. Stanfords, 12-14 Long Acre, Covent Garden, London, WC2, T020-78361321, F020-78360189, www.stanfords.co.uk stocks good road maps. **Maps & guidebooks**

This is available from Trade Partners UK, a government network for British businesses overseas. Contact Pippa Lodge, T020-72154715, F78288141, pippa.lodge@ tradepartners.gov.uk The _Ecuadorean News Digest_ is published by the Ecuadorean American Association, 150 Nassau St, New York, NY 10038. **Information for business travellers**

Special groups

Foreign students visiting Ecuador may be eligible for some discounts, while other concessions are restricted to those who are Ecuadorean citizens. This is in a way unfair, but you should keep in mind that - no matter how tight your budget - you probably have far more resources at your disposal than the average Ecuadorean student. By all means, shop around and bargain for the best student deal you can find, but also remember to be fair, especially when dealing with individuals or small family-run operations. **Student travellers**

Those tourist establishments in Ecuador which offer discounts to foreign students generally honour the International Student Identity Card (ISIC), but only if the card was issued in your home country. If you need to find the location of your nearest ISIC office contact: The International Student Travel Confederation, Herengracht 479, 1017 BS Amsterdam, The Netherlands, T31-20-421 2800, F31-20-421 2810, www.istc.org Student cards must carry a photograph if they are to be any use in Latin America for discounts.

Senior travellers Mainland Ecuador has long been a popular destination for the young and adventurous, while older travellers have traditionally focused their visits on Galápagos, Quito and perhaps Otavalo. There is however no good reason for more mature travellers to shun the less beaten path. Those in good health should face no special difficulties travelling independently, but it is very important to know and respect your own limits and to give yourself sufficient time to acclimatize to altitude in the highlands. If you require a special diet or medications, these must be brought from home, as they may not be available locally. Seniors' discounts in Ecuador, even more so than those for students (see above), tend to be restricted to Ecuadorean citizens, but bear in mind that a local retiree may have to make do with a pension under US$30 a month. You are more likely to benefit from the strong traditional respect for the elderly in Ecuadorean society. At the same time, you will be sure to notice that the country's demographic profile is the inverse of that in most parts of the developed world. People under 25 years of age are the majority here, so it should be no surprise that older *gringo* travellers tend to stand out. For general information about active, adventurous travel for those 50 or better, see *Travel Unlimited: Uncommon Adventures for the Mature Traveler* by Alison Gardner, Avalon Travel Publishing, 2000; and www.travelwithachallenge.com

Disabled travellers As with most Latin American countries, facilities for the disabled traveller are sadly lacking in Ecuador. Wheelchair ramps are a rare luxury in most of the country, but they are present in the resort town of Baños, see page 212. Getting a wheelchair into a bathroom or toilet is well nigh impossible, except for some of the more upmarket hotels. Pavements are often in a poor state of repair. Disabled Ecuadoreans obviously have to cope with these problems and mainly rely on the help of others to move around; fortunately most bystanders are very helpful. Quito's trolley system has wheelchair access in principle, but it is often too crowded to make this practical.

But of course only a minority of disabled people are wheelchair-bound and it is now widely acknowledged that disabilities do not stop you from enjoying a great holiday. The website www.geocities.com/Paris/1502 is dedicated to providing travel information for 'disabled adventurers' and includes reviews and travel tips. *Nothing Ventured*, edited by Alison Walsh, gives personal accounts of worldwide journeys by disabled travellers plus advice and listings.

Gay & lesbian travellers The 1998 constitution prohibits discrimination on the basis of sexual orientation and attitudes have gradually become more liberal in Quito and Guayaquil. Outside these two largest cities however, values are still intensely conservative and there remains a general bias, even hostility, against gay people. As in most Latin countries, effeminate behaviour in men is condemned, and the derogatory term *maricón* is commonly used to describe such a person, irrespective of their sexual orientation. Same-sex couples travelling in Ecuador should avoid public displays of affection. A place to meet or obtain information is the Matrioshka bar in La Mariscal neighbourhood of Quito, Pinto 376 y Juan León Mera, T552668, matrioshka@ecuabox.com

Bus travel People contemplating overland travel in Ecuador with children should remember that a lot of time can be spent waiting for and riding buses. You should take reading material with you, as it is difficult, and expensive to find. Also look for the locally available comic strip *Condorito*, which is quite popular and a good way for older children to learn a bit of Spanish. Many children become nauseous however on the winding roads of the highlands, and reading while the bus is moving can make this even worse. Always keep some plastic bags at hand.

Fares On all long-distance buses you pay for each seat, and there are no half-fares if the children occupy a seat each. For shorter trips it is cheaper, if less comfortable, to seat small children on your knee. Sometimes there are spare seats which children can occupy after tickets have been collected. In city buses, small children generally do not pay a fare, but are not entitled to a seat when paying customers are standing. All foreign children over 1 year 11 months of age must pay full fare on domestic flights in Ecuador. For children under this age, only taxes are charged. Make sure that any children accompanying you are fully covered by your travel insurance policy.

Food can be a problem if the children are not adaptable. It is easier to take food with you on longer trips than to rely on meal stops where the food may not be to taste. Avocados are safe, readily available, easy to eat and nutritious; they can be fed to babies as young as six months and most older children like them. Bananas, papayas and tangerines are also good choices, for all the same reasons. A small immersion heater and jug for making hot drinks is invaluable, but remember that electric current is 110v in Ecuador. In restaurants, you can normally buy a *media porción* (half portion), or divide one full-size helping between two children.

Hotels Try to negotiate family rates; if charges are per person, insist that two children will occupy one bed only, therefore counting as one tariff. You can almost always get a reduced rate at cheaper hotels. Occasionally when travelling with a child you will be refused a room in a hotel that is 'unsuitable', ie intended for short stay couples. Travel with children can bring you into closer contact with local families and, generally, presents no special problems – in fact the path may even be smoother for family groups. Officials are sometimes more amenable where children are concerned and they are pleased if your child knows a little Spanish. For more detailed advice, see *Travel with Children* by Lonely Planet (3rd ed, 1995).

Travelling with children
Make sure you pack that favourite toy. Nothing beats a GameBoy, unless it's two Gameboys and a link cable

Essentials

Rules, customs and etiquette

Most Ecuadoreans, if they can afford it, devote great care to their clothes and appearance. It is appreciated if visitors do likewise. How you dress is mostly how people will judge you. This is particularly important when dealing with officials. Buying clothing locally can help you to look less like a tourist. In general, clothing is less formal in the lowlands, both on the coast and in Oriente, where men and women do wear shorts. In the highlands, people are far more conservative, though wearing shorts is considered acceptable for sports and on hiking trails, but not at a church or cemetery. Men should not be seen bare-chested in populated areas in the highlands. You should pack spring clothing for Quito (mornings and evenings are cold), but in Guayaquil tropical or light-weight clothes are needed. Women should pack one medium to long length skirt and men might want to consider bringing a smart sweater or jacket. Suits and dresses are compulsory for business people. Good quality sweaters and wool shawls can be easily purchased in Ecuador and make good additions to your wardrobe.

Clothing

Remember that politeness – even a little ceremoniousness – is expected and appreciated in Ecuador. In this connection professional or business cards are very useful. Men should always remove any headgear and say "con permiso" when entering offices, and be prepared to shake hands often; always say "Buenos días" (until midday)

Conduct

or "Buenas tardes" and wait for a reply before proceeding further. Remember that the traveller from abroad has enjoyed greater advantages in life than most Ecuadorean minor officials, and should be friendly and courteous in consequence. Never be impatient and do not criticize situations in public: the officials may know more English than you think and they can certainly interpret gestures and facial expressions. Politeness can be a liability, however, in some situations; most Ecuadoreans are disorderly queuers, except - interestingly enough - when lining up for the Quito trolley! In commercial transactions (buying a meal, taxis, goods in a shop etc) politeness should be accompanied by firmness; always ask the price first.

Politeness should also be extended to street vendors; saying "No, gracias" with a smile is far better than an arrogant dismissal. Whether you give money to beggars is a personal matter, but your decision should be influenced by whether a person is begging out of need or trying to cash in on the *gringo* trail. In the former case, local people giving may provide an indication. Giving money or candies to children is a separate issue, upon which most agree: don't do it. There are occasions where giving food in a restaurant may be appropriate, but first inform yourself of local practice.

Time-keeping   Ecuadoreans, like most Latin Americans, have a fairly relaxed attitude towards time. They will think nothing of arriving an hour or so late on social occasions. If you expect to meet someone at an exact time, you can tell them that you want to meet at such and such an hour "en punto".

Tipping   In most of the better restaurants a 10% service charge is included in the bill, but you can give an extra 5% as a tip if the service is good. The most basic restaurants do not include a tip in the bill, and tips are not expected. US$1 is a generous tip for airport porters, US$0.50 for car 'watch' boys. Taxi drivers are usually not tipped, but you can pay a little extra for particularly good service if you get it. Tipping for all other services is entirely discretionary, how much depends on the quality of service given.

Prohibitions   **Almost all the foreigners serving long sentences in Ecuador's squalid jails are there for possession of illegal drugs.** To paraphrase the slogan: just don't do it! For further details see Drugs, page 46. Never carry firearms, their possession could also land you in serious trouble.

Responsible Tourism

Travel to the furthest corners of the globe is now commonplace and the mass movement of people for leisure and business is a major source of foreign income and economic development in many parts of South America. In some areas of Ecuador such as the Galápagos Islands it is by far the most significant economic activity.

The benefits of international travel are self-evident for both hosts and travellers: employment, increased understanding of different cultures, business and leisure opportunities. At the same time there is clearly a downside to the industry. Where visitor pressure is high and/or poorly regulated, adverse impacts to society and the natural environment may be apparent. Paradoxically perhaps, this is as true in undeveloped and pristine areas (where culture and the natural environment are less prepared for even small numbers of visitors), as in major resort destinations.

The travel trade is growing rapidly and impacts of this supposedly 'smokeless' industry are becoming increasingly apparent worldwide. Ecuador is no exception, and may be especially vulnerable to adverse effects because of the country's small size and the high volume of tourism concentrated in certain areas. Sometimes these impacts may seem remote and unrelated to an individual trip or holiday (eg air travel is clearly implicated in global warming and damage to the ozone layer), but individual choice and awareness can make a difference in many instances (see box opposite),

Travelling responsibly

Where possible choose a destination, tour operator or hotel with a proven ethical and environmental commitment - if in doubt ask.

Spend money on locally produced (rather than imported) goods and services and use common sense when bargaining - your few dollars saved may be a week's salary to others.

Use water and electricity carefully - travellers may receive preferential supply while the needs of local communities are overlooked.

Learn about local etiquette and culture - consider local norms and behaviour and dress appropriately for local cultures and situations.

Protect wildlife and other natural resources - don't buy souvenirs or goods made from wildlife unless they are clearly sustainably produced and are not protected under CITES (the Convention on International Trade in Endangered Species).

Don't give money or sweets to children - it encourages begging - instead give to a recognized project, charity or school.

***Always ask before taking photographs or videos of people**, this is by far the most common indiscretion committed by most tourists in Ecuador.*

Consider staying in local accommodation rather than foreign-owned hotels - the economic benefits for host communities are far greater - and there are far greater opportunities to learn about local culture.

Mark Eckstein, Washington, DC, USA.

Essentials

and collectively, travellers are having a significant effect in shaping a more responsible and sustainable industry.

In an attempt to promote awareness of and credibility for responsible tourism, organizations such as Green Globe, T0207-9308333, www.greenglobe21.com and the Centre for Environmentally Sustainable Tourism (CERT) (T01268-795772, F01268-795772, www.c-e-r-t.org) now offer advice on destinations and sites that have achieved certain commitments to conservation and sustainable development. Generally these are larger mainstream destinations and resorts but they are still a useful guide and increasingly aim to provide information on smaller operations.

Of course travel can also have beneficial impacts and this is something to which every traveller can contribute - many national parks are in part funded by receipts from visitors. Similarly, travellers can promote patronage and protection of important archaeological sites and heritage through their interest and contributions via entrance fees. They can also support small-scale enterprises by staying in locally run hotels and hostels, eating in local restaurants and by purchasing local goods, supplies and crafts.

In fact, during the past decade there has been a phenomenal growth in tourism that promotes and supports the conservation of natural environments and is also fair and equitable to local communities. This 'eco-tourism' segment is probably the fastest growing sector of the travel industry in all of South America and especially in Ecuador. Perhaps the best known Ecuadorean example of such development on a large scale is the Kapawi lodge in southern Oriente (see under Macas, page 384). The more grassroots projects include: *Ricancie* on the upper Río Napo near Tena (see page 375), Sani Isla lodge and Añangu on the lower Río Napo below Coca (see page 370) and Yachana lodge which is accessed from Misahuallí (see page 378). There are also many others.

While the authenticity of some eco-tourism operators' claims needs to be interpreted with care, there is clearly both a huge demand for this type of activity in Ecuador and also significant opportunities to support worthwhile conservation and social development initiatives.

Organisations such as Conservation International (T1-202-4295660, www.ecotour. org), the Eco-Tourism society (T1-802-4472121, www.ecotourism.org), Planeta (www2.planeta.com/mader) and Tourism Concern (T020-7753 3330, www.tourismconcern.org.uk) have begun to develop and/or promote eco-tourism projects and destinations and their websites are an excellent source of information and details for sites and initiatives throughout South America. Additionally, organizations such as Earthwatch (US/Canada T1800-7760188, UK T01865-311601, www.earthwatch.org) and Discovery International (T020-7229 9881, www.discoveryinitiatives.com) offer opportunities to participate directly in scientific research and development projects throughout the region.

Ecuador offers unique and unforgettable experiences often based on the natural environment, cultural heritage and local society. These are the reasons many of us choose to travel here and why many more will want to do so in the future. Shouldn't we provide an opportunity for future travellers and hosts to enjoy the quality of experience and interaction that we take for granted?

The gringo trail   There exists in Ecuador a well defined route for many travellers. It runs roughly from north to south through Otavalo, Quito (from which a climbing excursion is usually taken), Baños (from which a jungle excursion is usually taken) and Vilcabamba. This 'gringo trail' offers the best opportunities for socializing with other travellers, finding facilities and services geared specifically to foreign tastes and of course seeing a few of the tourist highlights of the country. There is however more - so much more - to be experienced in Ecuador. You are heartily encouraged to venture further afield and do some real exploring on your own, to get to know Ecuadoreans as well as fellow tourists and to take home a more sincere impression of the country - always keeping in mind the principles of responsible travel described above.

Living in Ecuador

Since the early 1990s, Ecuador has attracted increasing numbers of foreign residents. They have swelled the ranks of the country's traditional expatriates (diplomats, NGO volunteers and multinational employees), with retirees of all ages, as well as those seeking a new and interesting start. Many of the latter have opened businesses in the tourist trade and their growing numbers, as well as the presence of illegal migrants, has prompted the authorities to tighten controls. For information about visas for living in Ecuador, see Longer stays, page 26.

Ecuadoreans have traditionally welcomed outsiders warmly, although a certain cultural barrier was always noticeable, especially in the highlands and even more so among indigenous inhabitants. Growing numbers of successful foreign-owned businesses however, particularly when heavily concentrated in small towns like Otavalo, Baños or Vilcabamba, have generated their share of envy and anti-gringo sentiment among some segments of the local population.

Ecuador as a whole remains, in many ways, a pleasant and thoroughly interesting place for a foreigner to make his or her home. It is not, however, without its important risks and challenges, for which the outsider must be well prepared. Come and enjoy an extended visit and get to know the country before making major life choices.

Safety

More specific safety warnings are given under each town, city or region. See also the website of The Latin American Travel Advisor (see page 39)   Ecuador lost its innocence during the 1990s, prior to which it had been a remarkable island of peace and tranquillity. The incongruously peaceful reputation still lingers however, leading some visitors to mistakenly let down their guard. The truth is that Ecuador today is probably neither more nor less safe than most other Andean nations, except for notoriously violent Colombia. **Safe and hassle-free travels remain the rule in Ecuador but you should always be vigilant and take routine precautions.** An ounce of prevention here is worth ten pounds of cure.

Keep all documents (including your passport, airline tickets and credit cards) secure and hide your main cash supply in several different places. If one stash is lost or stolen, you will still have the others to fall back on. The following means of concealing cash and documents have all been recommended: extra pockets sewn inside shirts and trousers; pockets closed with a zip or safety pin; moneybelts (best worn below the waist and never within sight); neck or leg pouches; a thin chain for attaching a purse or wallet to your belt; and elastic support bandages for keeping money and travellers' cheques above the elbow or below the knee.

Protecting money & valuables

Make photocopies of important documents and give them to your family, embassy and travelling companion, this will speed up replacement if documents are lost or stolen and will still allow you to have some ID while getting replacements.

You should keep cameras in bags or briefcases and generally out of sight. Do not wear expensive wrist watches or any jewellery. Even prescription eyeglasses can be a target if they have expensive looking frames; take a spare set or your prescription just in case. If you wear a shoulder-bag in a market, carry it in front of you. Backpacks should be lockable but are nonetheless vulnerable to slashers: in crowded places wear your day-pack on your chest with both straps looped over your shoulders. Whenever visiting an area which is particularly unsafe (see below) take the bare minimum of belongings with you.

The cheapest hotels are usually found near markets and bus stations but these are also the least safe areas of most Ecuadorean towns. Look for something a little better if you can afford it, and if you must stay in a suspect area, always return to your hotel before dark. It is best, if you can trust your hotel, to leave any valuables you don't need in their safe-deposit box. But always keep an inventory of what you have deposited. If you don't trust the hotel, change hotels to one you feel safe in. If there is only one choice for places to stay, lock everything in your pack and secure that in your room; a light bicycle chain or cable and a small padlock will provide at least a psychological deterrent for would-be thieves. Even in an apparently safe hotel, do not leave valuable objects strewn about your room. Would *you* be tempted to pocket a camera worth two years of your salary?

Hotel security

Pickpockets, bag snatchers and slashers are always a hazard for tourists, especially in crowed areas such as markets or the downtown cores of major cities. Keep alert and avoid swarms of people. Crowded city buses are another magnet for thieves. Criminal gangs, at times well armed, also operate in the larger cities of Ecuador, especially in poor neighbourhoods and at night. You should likewise avoid deserted areas, such as parks or plazas after hours. If you are the victim of an armed assault, never resist or hold back your valuables; they can always be replaced but your health or life cannot.

Urban street crime

Banditry on the roads of Ecuador is currently an important problem, especially at night. This includes car-jackings and intercity bus hold-ups. **Travel by daylight whenever possible.** See Bus travel tips (page 52) for important safety suggestions.

Highway robbery

Be especially careful arriving at or leaving from bus stations. They are obvious places to catch people (tourists or not) with a lot of important belongings. Do not set your bag down without putting your foot on it, even to just double check your tickets or look at your watch; it will grow legs and walk away. Day-packs are easy to grab and run with, and are generally filled with your most important belongings. Take taxis to bus stations in major cities, when carrying luggage, before 0800 and after dark (look on it as an insurance policy).

Ignore mustard smearers and paint or shampoo sprayers, and strangers' remarks like "what's that on your shoulder?" or "have you seen that dirt on your shoe?" Furthermore, don't bend over to pick up money or other items in the street. These are all ruses intended to distract your attention and make you easy for an accomplice to steal from. If

Avoiding con tricks

someone follows you when you're in the street, slip into a nearby shop, or - if there are enough people around - let him catch up with you and "give him the eye".

Be wary of 'plainclothes policemen', politely insist on seeing identification and know that you have the right to write it all down. Do not get in a cab with any police officer, real or not. Tell them you will walk to the nearest police station. The real police only have the right to see your passport (not your money, tickets or hotel room) but before handing anything over, ask why they need to see it and make sure you understand the reason. Do not hand over your identification freely and insist on going to the station first. On no account take them directly back to your lodgings. Be even more suspicious if they seek confirmation of status from a passer-by.

Dangerous areas The countryside and small towns are generally the safest parts of Ecuador. The big cities - Guayaquil, Quito, and to a lesser extent Cuenca - call for the greatest care. The coast is somewhat more prone to violence than the highlands, but hard drinking at *fiestas* can bring out the worst in people anywhere. The northern border with Colombia, including the provinces of Esmeraldas, Carchi, and especially Sucumbíos, call for additional precautions. There was concern at the close of this edition that implementation of the US-sponsored 'Plan Colombia' might cause an influx of Colombian refugees, insurgents or drug runners into these border areas. This had not yet happened to any significant extent but the situation (particularly in Sucumbíos) was evolving rapidly. Be sure to carefully inform yourself before visiting these areas.

Drugs Some *gringos* come to Ecuador specifically to do or buy drugs and many live to regret it. Although certain illegal drugs are readily available, anyone found carrying even the smallest amount is automatically assumed to be a trafficker. If arrested on any charge the wait for trial in prison can take several years and is particularly unpleasant. Your foreign passport will not shield you in this situation, indeed you may be dealt with more harshly because of it. If you are unconvinced then visit an Ecuadorean prison to see for yourself (your embassy or consulate might be able to give you the names of citizens of your country serving sentences who would appreciate a visitor). **Drugs' use or purchase is punishable by up to 15 years' imprisonment.**

Unfortunately, we have received occasional reports of drug-planting, or mere accusation of drug-trafficking by the police on foreigners in Quito, with US$1,000 demanded for release. If you are asked by the narcotics police to go to the toilets to have your bags searched, insist on taking a witness. Better yet, avoid those hotels, bars and other establishments where drugs are common. Tricks employed to get foreigners into trouble over drugs include being invited to a party or somewhere involving a taxi ride, or simply being asked on the street if you want to buy cocaine. In all cases, a plain clothes 'policeman' will discover the planted cocaine – at your feet in the taxi – and will ask to see your passport and money. He will then return them, minus a large part of your cash. Do not get into a taxi, do not show your money, and try not to be intimidated. Single women may be particularly vulnerable, but being in pairs is no guarantee of security.

Women travellers Generally women travellers should find visiting Ecuador an enjoyable experience. However, machismo is alive and well here and you should be prepared for this and try not to overreact. When you set out, err on the side of caution until your instincts have adjusted to the customs of a new culture.

It is easier for men to take the friendliness of locals at face value; women may be subject to much unwanted attention. Minimize this by not wearing suggestive clothing and do not flirt. By wearing a wedding ring, carrying a photograph of your 'husband' and 'children', and saying that your 'husband' is close at hand, you may dissuade an aspiring suitor. If politeness fails, do not feel bad about showing offence and departing. When accepting a social invitation, make sure that someone knows the address and the time you left. Ask if you can bring a friend (even if you do not intend to do so).

If, as a single woman, you can befriend an Ecuadorean woman, you will learn much more about the country as well as finding out how best to deal with the barrage of suggestive comments, whistles and hisses that might come your way. Travelling with another *gringa* may not exempt you from this attention, but at least should give you moral support.

Police

Emergency police phone number: 911 in Quito, 101 elsewhere

In recent years the authorities have taken measures to improve public safety for visitors and Ecuadoreans alike, albeit with limited success. A special tourist police (uniformed and identified by arm-bands) operates in old town Quito, Otavalo, Cotopaxi National Park and the Chimborazo Fauna Reserve as well as a few other locations; they may be approached for advice and assistance. Police on bicycles now patrol some of Quito's parks, and mounted police sometimes do likewise in La Mariscal nightlife district. Indeed almost all police officers are helpful and friendly to tourists.

Unfortunately institutional corruption, including police corruption, is an important problem in Ecuador. Tourists are seldom affected but should be sensitive to the situation. If you are asked for a bribe (the polite euphemism is *'algo para la colita'*, a little something for a soft drink), then it is best to play innocent; be patient and the official will usually relent. This will also discourage harassment of other *gringos*. Never offer to bribe a police officer, since you don't know the rules you should not try to play the game.

Social unrest

Ecuadorean society has a remarkably long fuse. Despite several episodes of political and social unrest in recent years, these have not led to bloodshed. While it seems that a process of stabilization is now underway, visitors should know how to react (and not overreact) in the event of social unrest. Strikes and protests are usually announced days or weeks in advance, keep abreast of the local news and make your travel plans accordingly. The most significant impact of strikes on tourists is the restriction of overland travel; activities in towns and especially the countryside often go on as usual. Stay put at such times and make the most of visiting nearby attractions, rather than trying stick to your original itinerary or return to Quito at all costs; the situation will soon blow over. Ecuador is an open democratic society, where freedom of speech is highly respected. Nonetheless, as an outsider, you should avoid involvement in local politics.

The last word on safety

Above and beyond all of the foregoing, a relaxed and confident attitude is by far your best defence. A friendly smile, even when you've just thwarted a thief's attempt, can help you out of trouble. You should take even more comfort from the fact that the overwhelming majority of people in Ecuador are exceptionally well meaning. They are far more likely to go out of their way to help you than to hurt you.

Where to stay

Hotels

At Christmas, Easter and Carnival accommodation can sometimes be hard to find and prices are likely to rise. It is advisable to book in advance at these times and during school holidays and local festivals (see Holidays and festivals, page 81)

There are hotels to suit every budget and in many places there are establishments which offer excellent value while catering to international travellers' tastes, particularly where foreign tourists go and foreigners have opened facilities (eg Otavalo, Baños, Vilcabamba) and in larger towns and cities. In less visited places the choice of better class hotels may be limited but this does not mean that only basic conditions are to be expected. The best value accommodation can be found in the busiest tourist centres, especially Quito, which is full of excellent value hotels to suit all budgets. Accommodation tends to be a bit more expensive on the coast and in the Oriente. In the Oriente, there are some first-class lodges and nature reserves to stay in, built in a rustic style, but offering good standards of service, food and guiding. Most places are friendly and helpful, irrespective of the price, particularly smaller *pensiones* and *hospedajes*, which are often family-run.

Essentials

Essentials

 Hotel prices and facilities

Prices are for two people sharing a double room, including taxes and service charges **LL** *(US$150 and over) and* **L** *(US$100-149)   Hotels in these categories are usually only found in Quito, Guayaquil and the main tourist centres. They should offer pool, sauna, gym, jacuzzi, all business facilities (including email and internet access), meeting rooms, banquet halls, several elegant restaurants, bars and often a casino. Most will provide a safe deposit box in each room. Another set of options in this price range - although sometimes cheaper - are* haciendas *(country estates), a number of which have opened their doors to tourists. They generally provide a gracious and very traditional atmosphere, excellent food, activities such as horseback riding and the opportunity to experience life as it was lived by the country's élite in centuries gone by.*
AL *(US$66-99),* **A** *(US$46-65) and* **B** *(US$31-45)   The better value hotels in these categories provide a good deal more than standard facilities and comfort. Most will include breakfast and many offer 'extras' such as international cable TV, minibar, and tea and coffee making facilities. They may also provide tourist information and their own transport. Service is generally good and most accept credit cards. Some may have a swimming pool, sauna and jacuzzi.*
C *(US$21-30) and* **D** *(US$16-20)   Hotels in these categories range from very comfortable to functional, but there are some real bargains to be had. At these prices you should expect your own large bathroom, unlimited hot water, a towel,*

soap and toilet paper, TV, a restaurant, communal sitting area and a reasonably sized, comfortable room with air conditioning (in tropical regions).
E *(US$11-15) and* **F** *(US$7-10)   In the hotels in this range you can expect cleanliness and a reasonable degree of comfort, a private bathroom with hot water, maybe a small TV and a fan (in tropical areas) but no other frills. The best value hotels in this price range will be recommended in the travelling text. Many of those catering for foreign tourists in the more popular regions offer excellent value for money and many have their own restaurant and services such as laundry, safe deposit box, and luggage store.*
G *(US$4-6) and* **H** *(US$3 and under)   A room in this price range usually consists of little more than a bed and four walls, with barely enough room to swing the proverbial cat. If you're lucky you may have a window, a table and chair but seldom your own bathroom. Anywhere that provides these facilities, as well as being clean, will normally be recommended in our hotel listings. You may have a shared electric shower for hot water in this category in the highlands, cheap places in tropical areas only have cold water. Soap, towels, toilet paper or a toilet seat are seldom supplied. In colder (higher) regions they may not have enough blankets, so take your own or a sleeping bag. In the lowlands insects are common in cheap hotels, use the mosquito net if one is provided (or bring your own) and ignore the cockroaches - they are harmless.*

If you want a room with air conditioning expect to pay around 30% extra. Most mid-range or better hotels have their own restaurants serving all meals. Few budget places have this facility, though some may serve a simple breakfast. Better hotels will often have their own secure parking but even more modest ones can usually recommend a nearby safe public parking lot. Most places have sufficient room to safely park a motorcycle.

Hotel owners may try to let their less attractive rooms first, but they are not insulted if you ask for a bigger room, better beds or a quieter area. The difference is often marked. Likewise, if you feel a place is overpriced then do not hesitate to bargain politely. Always take a look at the rooms and facilities before you check in, there are usually several nearby hotels to choose from and a few minutes spent selecting among them can make the difference between a pleasant stay and miserable one. In cheaper places, do not merely ask about hot water (or any water for that matter); open the tap and see for yourself. The electric showers frequently used in cheaper hotels should be treated with respect. If you do not know how to use them, then ask someone to show you, and always wear rubber sandals or thongs. Tall travellers (above 180 cm) should note that many cheaper hotels, especially in the highlands, are built with the modest stature of local residents in mind. Make sure you fit in the bed and remember to duck for doorways.

Some hotels charge per person or per bed, while others have a set rate per room regardless of the number of occupants. If travelling alone, it is usually cheaper to share with others in a room with three or four beds.

Due to increasingly strict tax enforcement even some cheaper hotels now charge 12% *IVA* (VAT or sales tax), but enquire beforehand if this is already included in their price. At the higher end of the scale 22% (12% tax + 10% service) is usually added to the bill.

The hotel prices given in the text were correct at the time of publication. Due to the effects of dollarization of the economy they might be expected to *gradually* increase thereafter. As you travel, identify hotel categories that satisfy both your tastes and budget, then look for hotels in this category whenever you arrive in a new location.

Advice & suggestions

The cheapest (and often the nastiest) hotels can be found around bus and train stations. If you're just passing through and need a bed for the night, then they may be okay. The better value accommodation is generally found on and around the main plaza.

When booking a hotel from an airport or bus station by phone, always talk to the hotel yourself; do not let anyone do it for you (except an accredited hotel booking service). You may be told the hotel of your choice is full and be directed to one which pays a higher commission.

Many cheap hotels (as well as simple restaurants and bars) have inadequate water supplies. **Almost without exception used toilet paper should not be flushed, but placed in the receptacle provided**. This is also the case in most Ecuadorean homes and may apply even in quite expensive hotels, when in doubt ask. Tampons and sanitary napkins should likewise be disposed of in the rubbish bin. Failing to observe this custom will block the drain, a considerable health risk.

Camping

Camping in protected natural areas can be one of the most satisfying experiences during a visit to Ecuador. For details see Trekking, page 68. Organised campsites, car or trailer camping on the other hand are virtually unheard of. Because of the abundance of

cheap hotels you should never *have to* camp in Ecuador, except for cyclists who may be stuck between towns. In this case the best strategy is to ask permission to camp on someone's private land, preferably within sight of their home for safety. It is not safe to pitch your tent at random near villages and even less so on beaches. Those travelling with their own trailer or camper van can also ask permission to park overnight on private property, in a guarded parking lot or at a 24-hour gas station (although this may be noisy). It is unsafe to sleep in your vehicle on the street or roadside.

Homestays Homestays are a good idea and growing in popularity, especially with travellers attending Spanish schools in Quito. The schools can make these arrangements as part of your programme. You can live with a local family for weeks or months, which is a good way to practise your Spanish and learn about the local culture. Do not be shy to change families however, if you feel uncomfortable with the one you have been assigned. Look for people who are genuinely interested in sharing (as you should also be), rather than merely providing room and board.

Getting around

Air TAME is the main internal airline. It offers return flights from Quito to Cuenca, Esmeraldas, Galápagos (Baltra and San Cristóbal, for details see page 405), Guayaquil, Lago Agrio, Loja, Macas, Manta, Portoviejo and Tulcán (continuing to Cali, Colombia); also from Guayaquil to Cuenca, Loja, Machala and Galápagos. Routes and frequencies change frequently and up-to-date information may not be available outside Ecuador, so always enquire locally. TAME offices are given under each relevant town or city, or contact them via email or the web: tamecom@impsat.net.ec, www.tame.com.ec

The only other significant internal carrier, SAN/SAETA, suspended operations in 2000. At the close of this edition it was not known whether their flights would be resumed. Smaller airlines include Aerogal which flies Quito-Coca, and Austro Aereo which flies Guayaquil-Cuenca. A few military fights serve isolated communities in Oriente, but these are generally not open to foreigners. Air taxis and charters can be organized to any airstrip in the country; to the jungle best from Quito or Shell, to the coast best from Guayaquil.

Ecuador is a small country and internal airfares are generally less than US$50 one way for all destinations, although they may be expected to gradually rise alongside fuel prices in the dollarized economy. Flying times are typically under one hour. Foreigners must pay more than Ecuadoreans for flights to Galápagos and the Oriente.

Seats are not assigned on internal flights, including to the Galápagos. Passengers may have to disembark at intermediate stops and check in again, even though they have booked all the way to the final destination of the plane. Flights between Quito and Guayaquil are operated as a *puente aereo* (shuttle service) and no reservations are permitted. You go directly to the airport, purchase your ticket and board the next available aircraft on a first come first served basis. For all other routes make sure you confirm and reconfirm flight reservations frequently in order to avoid being bumped off your flight.

Train Sadly, the spectacular Ecuadorean railway system has all but ceased operations. In 2000 tourist rides were still being offered over the Devil's Nose from Riobamba to Sibambe and back and there was talk of possibly reopening the line as far as Bucay. From Quito, the only service was a weekend excursion to the El Boliche station in Cotopaxi National Park. Trains were running just a few kilometres out of Ibarra and the line to San Lorenzo was closed. Foreigners pay a much higher fare than Ecuadoreans on these few remaining routes.

The road network is extensive and because the country is not large and travelling times in many parts are not excessive, getting around by public transport is easy. The Panamericana runs down the length of the Andes connecting all the major towns and cities. A curiosity is that almost any large paved road may be referred to by locals as 'La Pana'.

Road network
Throughout Ecuador, intercity travel by car or bus is safest during the daytime

The state of Ecuador's roads is constantly changing due to the cyclical forces of nature and the lack of ongoing maintenance. Rainy seasons in general, and the *El Niño* climatic phenomenon in particular, can cause heavy damage in both the highlands and coast. When the roads reach an intolerable state, a reconstruction campaign is focused on the most heavily affected areas, but usually only the surface is repaired. These roads are then excellent for a while, until the cycle of deterioration begins all over again. At the close of this edition (January 2001) coastal roads were recently repaired and in very good shape, while many of those in the highlands were sorely in need of work.

Several important roads, mostly paved, link the highlands and the Pacific coast. These include from north to south: Quito to Esmeraldas via San Miguel de los Bancos and Quinindé, Quito to Guayaquil via Alóag and Santo Domingo de los Colorados (the busiest highway in Ecuador), Latacunga to Quevedo via La Maná (unpaved but beautiful), Ambato to Babahoyo via Guaranda, Riobamba to Guayaquil via Pallatanga and Bucay, Cuenca to Guayaquil via Zhud and La Troncal, Cuenca to Machala via Girón and Pasaje, and Loja to Machala or Huaquillas.

Santo Domingo de los Colorados is the hub of most roads on the coast of Ecuador. From Guayaquil, the coastal route south to Peru is a major artery. From Guayaquil north, there are now roads all the way to San Lorenzo near the Colombian border. A road from San Lorenzo to Ibarra, although subject to landslides, has replaced the railway journey on the same route. More details are given in the relevant sections.

On the eastern side of the Andes, the roads in Oriente are mostly unpaved and may be impassable during the rainy season. The *Carretera Perimetral de la Selva* (jungle perimeter road, a seldom-used term) runs from Lago Agrio in the north to Zamora in the south, via Baeza, Tena, Puyo and Macas. Roads connect Coca to both Lago Agrio and Baeza, the latter is especially beautiful. There are road links from the highlands to the jungle by the following routes, also from north to south: Quito to Baeza via Papallacta (upper half is paved), Ambato to Puyo via Baños (upper half is paved), Cuenca to Macas via Gualaceo (unpaved and rough but beautiful), and Loja to Zamora (fully paved and in good condition in 2000). Those driving in the Oriente should be reasonably self sufficient and pay special attention to safety, especially in the province of Sucumbíos.

Bus travel is generally more convenient, and cheaper, than in other Andean countries. Some companies have comfortable air conditioned units for use on their longer routes. Fares for these are higher and some companies have set up their own stations, away from the main bus terminals, exclusively for these better buses.

Bus

Most buses, though, leave from the central bus terminal (*terminal terrestre*) in each town. They are small and fill up quickly, so leave at frequent intervals. These buses are sometimes crowded and tall people may find the lack of leg room uncomfortable. For more information see box, page 52.

Taxis are a particularly convenient, safe and cheap transport option for tourists in the cities and towns of Ecuador. In Quito, all taxis must have meters by law; for details of taxi service in the capital see page 51. Meters are not used in other cities, where a flat rate is charged within the central part of town, generally under US$1 at the present time. Ask around to ascertain the going rate. All legally registered taxis have the number of their co-operative and the individual operator's number prominently painted on the side of the vehicle. Note these and the licence plate number if you feel you have been seriously overcharged or mistreated. You may then complain to the

Taxis

Essentials

☞ *Bus travel tips*

Avoid night time travel if at all possible. *The risks are highest after dark, both for traffic accidents and for hold-ups. While the incidence of the latter is relatively low when you consider the number of buses on the road, highway banditry is increasing and its consequences can be particularly severe. Buses are usually held up by heavily armed gangs, never resist or hold back your valuables. Shootings and rapes have occurred during hold-ups and foreign women may be at higher risk. Under the circumstances, travelling overnight in order to save on hotel accommodations is a particularly poor strategy, besides you miss the views and arrive too tired to enjoy the next day's touring. Bus hold-ups can take place anywhere, but are most common on the coast, along isolated stretches of road (eg in Oriente) and especially after dark. So travel by daylight in order to enjoy the spectacular scenery and arrive safely at your destination.*

Politely refuse any food, drink, sweets or cigarettes offered by strangers on a bus. These may be drugged as a way of robbing you. Such tricks are fortunately uncommon in Ecuador, but they do happen occasionally.

Always carry money and valuable documents in your money belt with you on the bus, but also pack a little spare cash and travellers' cheques in with your luggage. If you want to hold your seat at a stop, leave a newspaper or other insignificant item on it, never your bag.

Luggage can be checked-in with the larger bus companies and will be stowed in a locked compartment. On smaller busses it usually rides on the roof, in which case you should make sure it is covered with a tarpaulin to protect against dust and rain. In all cases it is your own responsibility to keep an eye on your gear, never leave it unattended at bus stations. Many travellers place their luggage in a costal (potato or flour sack) for bus rides, this helps keep it clean and makes it a bit less conspicuous.

Only the most modern buses have toilets on board; neither these nor the sanitary facilities at reststops are likely to be spotlessly clean. Avoid the very back of the bus if you can, as you will be right next to the toilet and the ride can be particularly dusty and bumpy. Take warm clothing when travelling in the highlands.

It is always possible to buy food and drinks on the roadside, as buses stop frequently, but keep an eye out for hygiene and make sure you have small change on hand. Bus drivers usually know the best places for meal stops and some roadside comedores can be quite good. On a longer journey however, take snacks and a small bottle of mineral water just in case.

Despite all these caveats, bus travel in Ecuador can be safe, pleasant and lots of fun; an excellent way to get to know the country and its people. Bon voyage!

transit police or tourist office, but be reasonable as the amounts involved are usually small and the vast majority of taxi drivers are honest and helpful.

Car   Driving in Ecuador has been described as 'an experience', partly because of unexpected potholes and other obstructions and the lack of road signs, partly because of local drivers' tendency to use the middle of the road. Some roads in Oriente that appear paved are in fact crude oil sprayed onto compacted earth. Beware the bus drivers, who often drive very fast and rather recklessly (passengers also please note).

There are only two grades of gasoline sold in Ecuador, 'Extra' (82 octane, currently US$0.80 per US gallon) and 'Super' (92 Octane, currently US$1.20 per US gallon). Both are unleaded. Extra is available everywhere, while super may not be available in more remote areas. Diesel fuel (currently US$0.60 per US gallon) is notoriously dirty and available everywhere. These prices are expected to gradually increase in 2001.

The road maps published by *Ediguías* (Nelson Gómez) are probably the most useful (see under Maps and Guidebooks, page 38).

To rent, buy or bring? The big choice for would-be foreign motorists, is whether to rent a vehicle, buy one in Ecuador, or bring their own from home. Each option has its own advantages and drawbacks. Rentals are of course the most convenient for short term visitors, but they are quite expensive and the insurance deductibles are sky-high. If you will stay for a few months or longer, it can make sense to purchase a local car and sell it before you leave. Vehicles are relatively expensive in Ecuador but there are many used ones on the market and they tend to maintain their value. There will be paperwork involved with transfer of ownership, registration, insurance, etc, but this is not an insurmountable obstacle. Bringing your own vehicle from home makes sense if you are travelling through Ecuador (for up to 30 days, see documents below) as part of a longer journey, and offers the advantage of driving something you know and trust. It is not a good idea however to bring a car from abroad if you wish to stay only in Ecuador for an extended period, as the import procedures are prohibitively complex, time consuming and expensive.

Preparation Preparing your own car for the journey is largely a matter of common sense: obviously any part that is not in first class condition should be replaced. It's well worth installing extra heavy-duty shock-absorbers (such as Spax or Koni) before starting out, because a long trip on rough roads in a heavily laden car will give heavy wear. Fit tubes on 'tubeless' tyres, since air plugs for tubeless tyres are hard to find, and if you bend the rim on a pothole, the tyre will not hold air.

Take spare tubes, and an extra spare tyre. Also take spare plugs, fan-belts, radiator hoses and headlamp bulbs. Even though local equivalents for some models can easily be found in the larger cities, it is wise to take spares for those occasions when you might need them. You can also change the fanbelt after a stretch of long, hot driving to prevent wear (eg after 15,000 km/10,000 miles). If your vehicle has more than one fanbelt, always replace them all at the same time (make sure you have the necessary tools if doing it yourself).

If your car has sophisticated electrics, spare 'black boxes' for the ignition and fuel injection are advisable, plus a spare voltage regulator or the appropriate diodes for the alternator, and elements for the fuel, air and oil filters if these are not a common type. (Some drivers take a spare alternator of the correct amperage, especially if the regulator is incorporated into the alternator.)

Dirty fuel is a problem in Ecuador, so be prepared to change filters more often than you would at home: in a diesel car you will need to check the sediment bowl often, too. An extra in-line fuel filter is a good idea if feasible (although harder to find, metal canister type is preferable to plastic), and for travel on dusty roads an oil bath air filter is best for a diesel car. It is wise to carry a spade, jumper cables, tow rope and an air pump. Fit tow hooks to both sides of the vehicle frame. A 12 volt neon light for repairs will be invaluable. Spare fuel containers should be steel and not plastic, and a siphon pipe is essential for those few places where fuel is sold out of the drum. Take a 10 litre water container for yourself and your vehicle.

Security Apart from the mechanical aspects, spare no ingenuity in making your car secure. Use heavy chain and padlocks to chain doors shut, fit security catches on windows, remove interior window winders (so that a hand reaching in from a forced vent cannot open the window). All these will help, but none is foolproof. Anything on the outside – wing mirrors, spot lamps, motifs etc – is likely to be stolen too. So are wheels if not secured by locking nuts.

Try never to leave the car unattended except in a locked garage or guarded parking space. Remove all belongings and leave the empty glove compartment open when the car is unattended. Also lock the clutch or accelerator to the steering wheel with a heavy, obvious chain or lock. Street children will generally protect your car in exchange for a tip. Be sure to note down key numbers and carry spares of the most important ones (but don't keep all spares inside the vehicle).

Essentials

Documents   There are police checks on many roads in Ecuador and you will be detained if you are unable to present your documents. Always carry your passport and driving licence. An international drivers license is not, strictly speaking, required in Ecuador but it may nonetheless be helpful. You also need the registration document (title) in the name of the driver, or, in the case of a car registered in someone else's name, a notarized letter of authorization. The original invoice from when the car was purchased may also be required in order to ascertain its value. All documents must be originals accompanied by a Spanish translation, preferably certified by an Ecuadorean embassy or consulate.

The rules for bringing a foreign car into Ecuador are complex, change frequently and are inconsistently applied. At the present time there appear to be three options. **1) To cross Ecuador with your car from north to south or vice versa in a maximum of three days**, you do not need any papers other than the above. You must however be accompanied throughout this period by a customs official and will be required to pay for their meals and accommodation. **2) To travel with your car in Ecuador for up to 30 days**, you must have a *carnet de passage en douane* (sometimes locally called a *tríptico*), which is an international customs document - a sort of passport for your car - issued by the automobile club of your home country (AAA, CAA, RAC, AA, etc) or the country where the vehicle is registered. The requirements for obtaining a *carnet* vary from country to country but usually involve leaving a deposit ranging from 100% to 400% of the value of the vehicle, enquire well before you travel. To obtain an entry permit (stamp) you must present your *carnet* at the Ecuadorean consulate nearest the border point where you will enter the country. There are Ecuadorean consulates in Ipiales, Colombia, and Tumbes, Peru. You must show this entry permit (stamp) when crossing the border, on entry and departure, and always have it on hand for police checkpoints. The 30 day period cannot normally be extended. **3) To travel with your car in Ecuador for up to 180 days**, you must obtain a *permiso de internación temporal* (temporary import permit) from Ecuadorean customs. This involves endless paperwork and leaving a deposit for 120% of the value of the vehicle. This option is not recommended in most cases.

Insurance for a foreign-registered vehicle against accident, damage or theft can only be arranged in the country of origin, not in Ecuador, but it is getting increasingly difficult to find agencies who offer this service. It is very expensive to insure against accident and theft, especially as you should take into account the value of the car increased by duties. If the car is stolen or written off you may be required to pay very high import duty on its value.

Shipping   Shipping in a vehicle through Guayaquil is hazardous due to theft; you will be charged by customs for every day the car is left there and will need assistance from an agent. Spare cash may be needed. Manta is a smaller, more relaxed and efficient alternative port. If bringing in a motorcycle by air it can take over a week to get it out of customs. You need a customs agent, who can be found around the main customs building near Quito airport; try to fix the price in advance. Best to accompany the agent all the time and a letter from the Ecuadorean Automobile Club (ANETA) may be helpful. For details of required documents, see above.

Car hire   Various international and local car hire companies are clustered around the airports of Quito, Guayaquil and Cuenca. It may be difficult to rent a vehicle in smaller cities however, where there are usually only a few rental cars available and these are often in use. Even in Quito, rental cars may be scarce during high season (June to September, and December to January), it is best to reserve in advance for these times. The names and addresses of agencies are given in the main text.

In order to rent a car you must be 25 and have an international credit card. You may pay cash, which is cheaper and may allow you to bargain, but they want a credit card for security. You may be asked to sign two blank credit card vouchers, one for the rental fee itself and the other as a security deposit, and authorization for a charge of as much as US$2,500 may be requested against your credit card account. These arrangements are all above board and the uncashed vouchers will be returned to you when you return the vehicle, but the credit authorization may persist on your account (reducing your credit limit) for up to 30 days. Always make certain that you fully understand the rental agreement before signing the contract, and be especially careful when dealing with some of the smaller agencies. Also, check the car's condition, not forgetting things like wheel nuts, and make sure it has good ground clearance. Always garage the car securely at night.

Rates vary depending on the rental company and vehicle, but a small car suitable for city driving currently costs about US$250 per week including all taxes and insurance. A sturdier four-wheel-drive can be twice as much.

Car hire insurance   Some car hire firms do not have adequate insurance policies and you will have to pay heavily in the event of an accident. Check exactly what the hirer's insurance policy covers. All policies include a deductible, which you will have to cover out-of-pocket. This deductible is typically US$500 in the event of a minor accident and US$1,200 or more in the event of theft or complete destruction of the vehicle. Beware of being billed for scratches which were on the vehicle before you hired it.

Drive carefully

It is best to try and settle minor fender-benders amicably without notifying the police. In case of a serious accident it is common for both the drivers and vehicles to be detained. The ensuing judicial process can be long and complicated and, as a foreigner, you will be at a considerable disadvantage. For this reason, and because you are on unfamiliar turf, you should **drive defensively at all times.** Always be on the lookout for pedestrians, especially near elevated crosswalks which are seldom used. The recklessness of the locals should make you more, not less, careful.

Motorcycling

People are generally very amicable to motorcyclists and you can make many friends by returning friendship to those who show an interest in you. Simple motorcycles are a common means of transport, often carrying an entire family, while fancy dirt bikes have become popular in recent years with some wealthy young Ecuadoreans.

The machine   It should be off-road capable: a good choice would be the BMW R80/100/GS for its rugged and simple design and reliable shaft drive, but a Kawasaki KLR 650s, Honda Transalp/Dominator, or the ubiquitous Yamaha XT600 Tenere would also be suitable. A road bike can go most places an off road bike can go at the cost of greater effort.

Preparations   Fit heavy duty front fork springs and the best quality rebuildable shock absorber you can afford (Ohlins, White Power). Fit lockable luggage containers such as Krausers (reinforce luggage frames) or make some detachable aluminium panniers. Fit a tank bag and tank panniers for better weight distribution. A large capacity fuel tank (Acerbis), +300 mile/480 km range is helpful if going off the beaten track. A washable air filter is a good idea (K&N), also fuel filters, fueltap rubber seals and smaller jets for high altitude Andean motoring. A good set of trails-type tyres as well as a high mudguard are useful. Get to know the bike before you go, ask the dealers in your country what goes wrong with it and arrange a link whereby you can get parts flown out to you (but beware of high customs duties). If riding a chain driven bike, a fully enclosed chaincase is useful. A hefty bash plate/sump guard is invaluable.

Spares   Reduce service intervals by half if driving in severe conditions. Take oil filters, fork and shock seals, tubes, a good manual, spare cables (taped into position), a plug cap and spare plug lead. A spare electronic ignition is a good idea, try and buy a second hand one and make arrangements to have parts sent out to you. A first class tool kit is a must and if riding a bike with a chain then a spare set of sprockets and an 'o' ring chain should be carried. Spare brake and clutch levers should also be taken as these break easily in a fall. Parts may be few and far between, but mechanics are skilled at making do and can usually repair things. Castrol oil can be bought everywhere and relied upon. Take a puncture repair kit and tyre levers. Find out about any weak spots on the bike and improve them. Get the book for international dealer coverage from your manufacturer, but don't rely on it. They frequently have few or no parts for modern, large machinery.

Clothes and equipment A tough waterproof jacket, comfortable strong boots, gloves and a helmet with which you can use glass goggles (Halcyon) which will not scratch and wear out like a plastic visor. The best quality tent and camping gear that you can afford and a petrol stove which runs on bike fuel is helpful. Also see Camping, page 49.

Security Never leave a fully laden bike on its own. An Abus D or chain will keep the bike secure. A cheap alarm gives you some peace of mind if you leave the bike outside a hotel at night, but this is not recommended. Most hotels will allow you to bring the bike inside. Look for hotels that have a courtyard or more secure parking and never leave luggage on the bike overnight or whilst unattended.

Documents Passport, driving licence and registration (title) documents are all necessary. The rules for bringing a motorcycle into Ecuador are, in principle, the same as those for a car (see above) but may sometimes be applied more leniently.

Cycling   At first glance a bicycle may not appear to be the most obvious vehicle for a major journey, but given ample time and reasonable energy it most certainly is the best. It can be ridden, carried by almost every form of transport from an aeroplane to a jungle canoe, and can even be lifted across one's shoulders over short distances. Cyclists can be the envy of travellers using more orthodox transport, since they can travel at their own pace, explore more remote regions and meet people who are not normally in contact with tourists.

Choosing a bicycle The choice of bicycle depends on the type and length of expedition being undertaken and on the terrain and road surfaces likely to be encountered. Unless you are planning a journey almost exclusively on paved roads – when a high quality touring bike such as a Dawes Super Galaxy would probably suffice – a mountain bike is strongly recommended. The good quality ones (and the cast iron rule is **never** to skimp on quality) are incredibly tough and rugged, with low gear ratios for difficult terrain, wide tyres with plenty of tread for good road-holding, cantilever brakes, and a low centre of gravity for improved stability. Although bikes and spares are available in the larger cities, high quality equipment is expensive and the cheap stuff does not last. Within reason, buy everything you possibly can before you leave home.

Bicycle equipment A small but comprehensive tool kit (to include chain rivet and crank removers, a spoke key and possibly a block remover), a spare tyre and inner tubes, a puncture repair kit with plenty of extra patches and glue, a set of brake blocks, brake and gear cables and all types of nuts and bolts, at least 12 spokes (best taped to the chain stay), a light oil for the chain (eg Finish-Line Teflon Dry-Lube), tube of waterproof grease, a pump secured by a pump lock, a Blackburn parking block (a most invaluable accessory, cheap and virtually weightless), a cyclometer, a loud bell, and a secure lock and chain. *Richard's Bicycle Book* makes useful reading for even the most mechanically minded.

Luggage and equipment Strong and waterproof front and back panniers are a must. When packed these are likely to be heavy and should be carried on the strongest racks available. Poor quality racks have ruined many a journey for they take incredible strain on unpaved roads. A top bag cum rucksack (eg Carradice) makes a good addition for use on and off the bike. A Cannondale front bag is good for maps, camera, compass, altimeter, notebook and small tape-recorder. (Other recommended panniers are Ortlieb – front and back – which is waterproof and almost 'sandproof', Mac-Pac, Madden and Karimoor.) 'Gaffa' tape (duct tape) is excellent for protecting vulnerable parts of panniers and for carrying out all manner of repairs.

All equipment and clothes should be packed in plastic bags to give extra protection against dust and rain. (Also protect all documents etc, carried close to the body from sweat.) Always take the minimum clothing. It's better to buy extra items en route when you find you need them. Generally it is best to carry several layers of thin light clothes than fewer heavy, bulky ones. Always keep one set of dry clothes, including long trousers, to put on at the end of the day. The incredibly light, strong, waterproof and wind resistant Gore-Tex jacket and overtrousers are invaluable. Training shoes can be used for both cycling and walking.

Useful tips Wind, not hills, is the enemy of the cyclist. Try to make the best use of the times of day when there is little; mornings tend to be best but there is no steadfast rule. Take care to avoid dehydration, by drinking regularly. In hot, dry areas with limited supplies of water, be sure to carry an ample supply. For food, carry the staples (sugar, salt, dried milk, tea, coffee, porridge oats, raisins, dried soups etc) and supplement these with whatever local foods can be found in the markets. Give your bicycle a thorough daily check for loose nuts or bolts or bearings. See that all parts run smoothly. A good chain should last 2,000 miles, 3,200 km or more but be sure to keep it as clean as possible – an old toothbrush is good for this – and to oil it lightly from time to time.

Remember that thieves are attracted to towns and cities, so when sight-seeing, try to leave your bicycle with someone such as a café owner or shopkeeper. Country people tend to be more honest and are usually friendly and very inquisitive. However, don't take unnecessary risks; always see that your bicycle is secure (most hotels will allow bikes to be kept in rooms). In more remote regions dogs can be vicious; carry a stick or some small stones to frighten them off. Traffic on main roads can be a nightmare; it is usually far more rewarding to keep to the smaller roads or to paths if they exist. Most towns have a bicycle shop of some description, but it is best to do your own repairs and adjustments whenever possible. If you need boxes/cartons to send bicycles home, the German-run Global Transportes, Veintimilla 878 y Av Amazonas, 3rd floor, Quito, might be able to help you.

The Expedition Advisory Centre, administered by the Royal Geographical Society, 1 Kensington Gore, London SW7 2AR, T020-7591 3030, www.rgs.org/eac has a useful monograph entitled *Bicycle Expeditions*, by Paul Vickers, which can be downloaded free from their website. In the UK there is also the Cyclist's Touring Club, CTC, Cotterell House, 69 Meadrow, Godalming, Surrey GU7 3HS, T01483-417217, www.ctc.org.uk for touring and technical information. In addition to the *Ediguía*s road maps mentioned for cars (above), a series of very practical *hojas de ruta* are available from the IGM in Quito. They include detailed road maps and elevation profiles for routes between the major towns.

Most cyclists agree that the main danger comes from other traffic. A rearview mirror has been frequently recommended to forewarn you of vehicles which are too close behind. You also need to watch out for oncoming, overtaking vehicles, unstable loads on trucks, protruding loads etc. Make yourself conspicuous by wearing bright clothing and a helmet.

Essentials

Hitchhiking Public transport in Ecuador is so cheap and abundant that there is seldom any need to hitchhike along the major highways. On small out-of-the-way country roads however, the situation can be quite the opposite, and giving passers-by a ride is common practice and safe for drivers and passengers alike, especially in the back of a pickup or larger truck. A small fee is usually charged, best ask in advance. In truly remote areas there may not be enough traffic to make hitching worthwhile.

For obvious reasons, a lone female should not hitch by herself. Besides, you are more likely to get a lift if you are with a partner, be they male or female. The best combination is a male and female together. Three or more and you'll be in for a long wait. Your appearance is also important. Someone with matted hair and a large tattoo on their forehead will not have much success. Remember that you are asking considerable trust of someone. Would you stop for someone who looked unsavoury?

Keeping in touch

Points of contact Details of organizations which can help sort out problems or give advice, such as the South American Explorers, British Council and Alliance Française, or addresses of embassies and consulates, can be found in the Quito directory (page 139).

Language
See also page 466 for basic Spanish words & phrases

The official languages of Ecuador are Spanish and Quichua. English and a few other European languages may be spoken in some establishments catering to tourists in Quito and the most popular tourist destinations. Away from these places, knowledge of Spanish is essential. Indeed, learning some Spanish is the single most important way to prepare for your visit, or you can begin with a period of language study. With even a modest knowledge of Spanish you will be able to befriend Ecuadoreans, to interchange ideas and insights with them. Without any language skills, you will feel like someone trying to peep through the keyhole at Ecuador.

There are now very few people, even in remote highland villages, who speak only Quichua. Spanish however, may be relegated to the role of a second language in some native communities. Those who are planning to work or have extensive contact with highland Indian groups, would do well to learn some Quichua beforehand. There are opportunities to do so in Quito.

Internet services
The internet is exceptionally accessible in Ecuador and has replaced postal and telephone services for most travellers

Almost every place that offers Internet will also have Net2Phone. There are so many cyber cafés in the larger cities and towns that you will be tripping over them. They are frequented not only by tourists, but also by many locals, and are sometimes crowded and noisy.

Some form of Internet access may be found almost everywhere in Ecuador, except for remote locations in the Oriente. Both the cost and speed of access vary greatly however, with the best service available in Quito, Guayaquil and Cuenca. In smaller towns a cyber café may have to call their Internet Service Provider (ISP) in one of the main cities over a noisy long distance phone line, hence service will be slower and more expensive. Hourly Internet rates currently range from about US$1 (in Quito) to US$7 (in Coca), Net2Phone rates are typically around US$0.20 per minute to North America and Europe. These prices might rise however, if state telephone companies are able to carry through their plans to regulate public internet access.

Since public internet access is so easy in Ecuador, there is really no need to bring your own laptop just to keep in touch. If you have your own computer and modem however, you can connect to CompuServe and America Online via the SCITOR network, the Quito dialup is 505000. This is usually expensive though, check prices with your ISP beforehand. For those planning an extended stay, there are also many local ISPs offering service throughout Ecuador.

During 1999-2000 the Ecuadorean post office was unreliable for both sending and receiving mail, a shame in view of its previously reasonable track record. We have received numerous reports of parcels, letters and especially postcards which never arrived, and *correo certificado* (registered mail) seemed even more prone to problems than ordinary airmail. Those items which did arrive, were at times delayed for several months. It is hoped that this situation will once again improve, but visitors are advised to seek advice from local residents before sending all but the most trivial items through the mail. **Urgent or valuable documents should never be entrusted to the post office.** National and international courier service is available as an alternative, for details see below.

    Opening hours for post offices are generally Monday-Friday 0730-1900 and Saturday 0730-1400, although there may be some variation from town to town. Postal branches in small towns may not be familiar with all rates and procedures. Your chances are better at the main branches in provincial capitals or, better yet, in Quito: at Colón corner Almagro in La Mariscal district, or at the main sorting centre on Japón near Naciones Unidas (behind the CCI shopping centre).

    Letters and postcards Ordinary airmail rates for up to 20 g are currently US$0.68 to the Americas, US$0.84 to the rest of the world. Registered mail costs an additional US$0.48 per item.

    Parcels Up to 30 kg, maximum dimensions permitted are 70 by 30 by 30 cm. Current rates by air parcel post: to the Americas approximately US$13.50 for the first kg, US$3.50 for each additional kg; to the rest of the world approximately US$22 for the first kg, US$12.50 for each additional kg. Current rates by SAL/APR (surface air lifted) reduced priority service: to the Americas approximately US$13 for the first kg, US$3 for each additional kg; to the rest of the world approximately US$20 for the first kg, US$10 for each additional kg. There is no surface (sea) mail service from Ecuador.

Postal services

Essentials

Essentials

Letters and parcels for Europe bearing the correct Ecuadorean postage can be dropped off at the Lufthansa office, 18 de Septiembre E7-05 y Reina Victoria, Quito, to be sent in the next international bag (be there by 1200 on the day before the flight).

Receiving mail Letters can be sent to Poste Restante/General Delivery (*lista de correos*, but you must specify the postal branch in larger cities), some embassies (enquire beforehand), or, for card or travellers' cheque holders, American Express offices. Foreign names can cause considerable confusion, for the smallest risk of misunderstanding, use the initial and surname only (eg J Smith). Items sent to you by courier must have a specific street address (eg your hotel or embassy) and will be subject to customs inspection and possibly high duties. See Shipping goods to Ecuador, page 28. Never send anything to Ecuador by surface (sea) mail, it is most unlikely to arrive.

Courier service Courier companies are the only safe alternative for sending or receiving valuable time-sensitive mail in Ecuador. For rapid and reliable international service, **DHL** has offices throughout the country; the most convenient locations in Quito include Colón 1333 y Foch and República 433 y Almagro, T485100. It is friendly and efficient. For courier service within Ecuador, **Servientrega** has offices throughout the country, reliable one to two day service is available to all areas, US$2.50 for up to 2 kg. There are many other courier companies operating in Ecuador, but quality of service and reliability vary greatly.

Telephone services Ecuador's telephone system has been restructured several times in recent years and is tentatively slated for privatization in 2001 or 2002. It is currently operated by three regional state companies, whose names you should look for on telephone offices: **Andinatel** in the northern highlands and Oriente; **Pacifictel** on the coast, in the southern highlands and Oriente; and **ETAPA** in Cuenca. There are also two private companies, **Bell South** and **Porta**, which provide cellular phone service, including convenient but expensive debit card operated public cell phones. Since this system is wireless, public phones have been installed in previously inaccessible locations, such as the mountain shelter on Chimborazo. Short term cell phone rentals are also available. The service provided by all of the above is generally fair, best in the larger cities, worst in small towns and villages. Most public cellular phones have their numbers posted and allow you to receive calls. So you can make a brief contact with home and have someone call you back.

Debit cards for public cell phones may be purchased at kiosks and many small shops; they are specific to one company (ie you cannot use Porta cards in Bell South phones nor vice versa). There are also a few coin operated private phones in shops and restaurants but almost no public phones *per se*. The best places to make local, national or international calls are telephone company offices, with at least one such office in each city or town. You are assigned a cabin, dial your own calls, and pay on the way out. For international calls however, you may be asked to specify how many minutes you would like to speak and pay in advance.

Rates fluctuate. For international calls, compare the current price charged at the phone company office with those charged by the card operated cell phones (**NB** the amount shown on the cell phone LCD display may be per 15 second increments rather than one minute, best check with the operator). Examples of current state phone company rates are: US$1.32/minute to the USA, US$2.11/minute to the UK, US$2.61/minute to Australia. Hefty surcharges may be applied to calls made from hotels, ask for their rates in advance.

Country-direct access is available free of charge from private phones and telephone company offices throughout Ecuador (except Galápagos), although not every office knows about this nor are they familiar with the access numbers (see box, page opposite).

Country-direct access numbers

To reach an operator from one of the countries shown below, dial the following numbers free of charge from private phones or a telephone company office. You can then make a collect call or credit card call. Ask about rates beforehand as these may be expensive.

Argentina: 999161, 999186.
Bolivia: 999169.
Brazil: 999177.
Canada: 999175.

Chile: Entel 999179, ChileSat 999183, Telefónica 999188.
Dominican Republic: 999165.
France: 999180.
Italy: 999164.
Mexico: 999184.
Peru: 999167.
Spain: 999176.
UK: 999178, 999181.
USA: ATT 999119, WorldPhone 999170/2, Sprint 999171.
Venezuela: 999173.

Faxes may be sent and received at phone company offices, some post offices, hotels and many private locations. Shop around for the best rates.

Newspapers The main newspapers in Quito are El Comercio and Hoy, in Guayaquil El Universo. All three are available nationwide as well as on-line (see websites, page 22). El Mercurio of Cuenca is also highly regarded. There are several smaller regional or local papers published in the provincial capitals. Foreign newspapers are only available in some luxury hotels and a few speciality shops in Quito and Guayaquil.

Media

World Band Radio South America has more local and community radio stations than practically anywhere else in the world, and Ecuador is well known in this field for the presence of pioneer evangelical broadcaster HCJB. A shortwave (world band) radio offers a practical means to brush up on the language, sample popular culture and absorb some of the richly varied regional music. International broadcasters such as the BBC World Service (www.bbc.co.uk/worldservice/index.shtml for schedules and frequencies), the Voice of America (www.voa.gov), Boston (Mass)-based Monitor Radio International (operated by Christian Science Monitor, www.csmonitor.com) and the Quito-based HCJB (89.3 FM in Quito, 102.5 FM in Guayaquil), keep the traveller abreast of news and events, in both English and Spanish.

Compact or miniature portables are recommended, with digital tuning and a full range of shortwave bands, as well as FM, long and medium wave. Detailed advice on radio models (£150 for a decent one) and wavelengths can be found in the annual publication, Passport to World Band Radio (Box 300, Penn's Park, PA 18943, USA). Details of local stations is listed in World TV and Radio Handbook (WTRH), PO Box 9027, 1006 AA Amsterdam, The Netherlands, US$19.95. Both of these, free wavelength guides and selected radio sets are available from the BBC World Service Bookshop, Bush House Arcade, Bush House, Strand, London WC2B 4PH, UK, T020-7257 2576, www.bbc.co.uk/worldservice

Food and drink

One of the most important considerations for the traveller is food. You can economize on accommodation without risking your health, but unless you really want to spend most of your time sitting on the toilet, you need to eat well. Fortunately, this presents no real problems in Ecuador, for you can eat reasonably well for very little.

Essentials

Eating out
See box opposite for our price categories, which are also on the inside front cover

In Quito you can find restaurants to suit every possible taste or budget – everything from a slice of pizza to sushi. The most economical way to eat is to ask for the set meal in restaurants. This is called *almuerzo* at lunch time, and *merienda* in the evening. It is very cheap and wholesome, and costs around US$1-2 for three courses. You can go a little upmarket and spend around US$2-4 for a set lunch in a pretty swanky place. A la carte dining doesn't cost the earth, however. You can eat very well indeed for under US$10 a head, and if you really want to push the boat out, it won't set you back more than US$10-15. Many hotels have their own restaurant or cafeteria which serves *desayuno* (breakfast, sometimes included in the hotel price), *almuerzo* and *merienda*.

Service of 10% and tax of 12% are added to first and second class restaurant bills. Cheaper restaurants usually don't charge any service.

Markets
An even cheaper option is to eat in the *comedores* of markets, but you may be putting yourself at considerable risk for the sake of a few cents. Remember that the commonest affliction of visitors to Ecuador is traveller's diarrhoea. If you're preparing food yourself, however, markets are the best places to find fresh ingredients, and shopping can be an experience in itself.

Vegetarians
Vegetarians are now pretty well catered for; they should find no problems in the main towns and tourist centres. Even the tiniest village restaurant will rustle up some kind of edible vegetarian option. You're safer being able to list all the foods you can't eat – saying "Soy vegetariano/a" (I'm a vegetarian) or "no como carne" (I don't eat meat) is often not enough.

NB Shellfish is always a risk and so is *ceviche* (see below), but they should be safe in well run hygienic establishments. Fruit is plentiful and excellent, but ensure it is washed or peel it yourself. Avoid lettuce, raw strawberries, undercooked food (including eggs) and reheated food. Food that is cooked in front of you and offered hot all through is generally safe. **Tap water anywhere in Ecuador is not safe to drink**. The better hotels have their own water purification systems and in many restaurants you can get boiled water, water that has been filtered or, more popular these days, commercially bottled water.

Different cuisines
The cuisine varies extensively with each region. Seafood is very good, especially on the coast, while Andean dishes tend to be based around maize and meat and are 'warming' to suit the altitude. The following are some typical dishes worth trying.

In the highlands *Locro de papas* is a potato and cheese soup. *Mote* (corn burst with alkali) is a staple in the region around Cuenca, but used in a variety of dishes in the Sierra. *Caldo de patas* is cow heel soup with *mote*, but more appealing are *llapingachos* (fried potato and cheese patties) and *empanadas de morocho* (a ground corn shell filled with meat). *Morocho* is a thick drink or porridge made from the same white corn, milk, sugar and cinnamon. *Sancocho de yuca* is a meat and vegetable soup with manioc root. The more adventurous may want to try the delicious roast *cuy* (guinea pig). Also good is *fritada* (fried pork) and *hornado* (roast pork). *Humitas* are tender ground corn steamed in corn leaves, and similar are *quimbolitos*, which are prepared with coarse wheat flour and steamed in *achira* leaves. *Humitas* and *quimbolitos* come in both sweet and savoury varieties.

On the coast As mentioned above, seafood is excellent and popular everywhere. *Ceviche* is marinated fish or seafood which is usually served with popcorn and *tostado* (roasted maize). Only *ceviche de pescado* (fish) and *ceviche de concha* (clams), which are marinated raw, potentially pose a health hazard. The other varieties of *ceviche* such as *camarón* (shrimp/prawn), and *langostino* (jumbo shrimp/king prawn) all of which

Essentials

Restaurant price categories

All of the following prices are based on a complete meal for one person including a non-alcoholic beverage, tax and service:
Very expensive: above US$25

Expensive: US$12.50 to US$24.99
Mid range: US$5 to US$12.49
Cheap: US$1 to US$4.99
Seriously cheap: less than US$1

are cooked before being marinated, are generally safe delicacies, though you should check the cleanliness of the establishment. *Langosta* (lobster) is an increasingly endangered species but continues to be illegally fished; so please be conscientious. Other coastal dishes include *empanadas de verde* which are fried snacks: a ground plantain shell filled with cheese, meat or shrimp. *Sopa de bola de verde* is plantain dumpling soup. *Encocadas* are dishes prepared with coconut milk and fish or seafood, which are very popular in the province of Esmeraldas. *Cocadas* are sweets made with coconut. *Viche* is fish or seafood soup made with ground peanuts, and the ubiquitous *patacones* are thick fried plantain chips served as a side dish.

In the Oriente most dishes are prepared with yucca (manioc or cassava root) and a wide variety of river fish.

Special foods are prepared for certain holidays. *Fanesca* is a fish soup with beans, many grains, ground peanuts and more, sold during Easter Week throughout the country. *Colada morada* (a thick dark purple fruit drink) and *guaguas de pan* (bread dolls) are made around the time of *Finados*, the day of the dead at the beginning of November. Special *tamales* and sweet and sticky *pristiños* are Christmas specialities.

Ecuadorean food is not particularly spicy. However, in most homes and restaurants, the meal is accompanied by a small bowl of *ají* (hot pepper sauce) which may vary greatly in potency. Those unfamiliar with this condiment are advised to exercise caution at first. *Colada* is a generic name which can refer to cream soups or sweet beverages. In addition to the prepared foods mentioned above, Ecuador offers a large variety of delicious temperate and tropical fruits, some of which are unique to South America.

Drink The variety of tropical fruits on offer in Ecuador is bewildering. Not surprisingly, then, fruit juices are wonderful here. Among the most popular are *naranjilla*, *maracuya* (passion fruit), *tomate de arbol*, *piña* (pineapple), *taxo* (another variety of passion fruit) and *mora* (blackberry). But anything can be made into a mouth-watering *jugo* (juice prepared with water) or *batido* (prepared with milk). A note of caution, however. Make sure the place is clean and the juice is made with boiled water, and ask for your drink *sin hielo* (without ice, which may be made from tap water). The usual soft drinks, known as *colas*, are widely available. On the downside, this is not coffee paradise. Instant coffee or liquid concentrate is common, so ask for *café pasado* if you want real filtered coffee. Places where you can get a decent cup of coffee are few and far between outside Quito and the more popular tourist spots.

As for alcohol, the main beers are Pilsener, Biela and Club, all of which are reasonable (and after a few bottles, who cares anyway?). A wide selection of foreign beers are also available in many of Quito's bars. Good quality Argentine and Chilean wines are available in the larger cities and cheaper than European or US ones. *Aguardiente* (literally 'fire-water') is potent unmatured rum, also known as *paico* and *trago de caña*, or just *trago*.

Shopping

For more details of handicrafts & where to find them, see Arts & crafts (page 453). For local markets & shops see under the relevant town, city or village

Almost everyone who visits Ecuador will end up buying a souvenir of some sort from the vast array of arts and crafts (*artesanía*) on offer. The best, and cheapest, places to shop for souvenirs, and pretty much anything else in Ecuador, are the street markets which can be found absolutely everywhere. The country also has its share of shiny, modern shopping centres, especially in Guayaquil and the capital, but remember that the high overheads are reflected in the prices.

Otavalo's massive market is the best-known place for buying wall hangings and sweaters. Another market, at Saquisilí, south of Quito, is renowned for shawls, blankets and embroidered garments. Fewer handicrafts can be found on the coast, but this is where you can buy an authentic Panama hat at a fraction of the cost in Europe. The best, called *superfinos*, are reputed to be made in the little town of Montecristi, but the villages around Cuenca claim to produce superior models. Cuenca is a good place to buy Panama hats, and other types of hat can be bought throughout the Andes. Ecuador also produces fine silver jewellery, ceramics and brightly painted carvings, usually made from balsa wood. Other good buys are the many beautiful items fashioned from *tagua*, or vegetable ivory.

All manner of *artesanía* can be bought in Quito, either on the street or in any of the shops. There's not actually much difference in the price. The advantage of buying your souvenirs in a shop is that they'll usually package your gifts well enough to prevent damage on the flight home. Craft cooperatives are also a good place to shop, since there is a better chance that a fair share of the price will go to the artisan.

Bargaining

Stall holders in markets expect you to bargain, so don't disappoint them. Many tourists enjoy the satisfaction of beating down the seller's original price and finding a real 'bargain', but don't take it too far. Always remain good natured, even if things are not going your way (remember that you're on vacation and they're working). And don't make a fool of yourself by arguing for hours over a few cents. The item you're bargaining for may have taken weeks to make and you're probably carrying more cash in your wallet than the market seller earns in a month.

Photography

Kodachrome cannot be purchased or processed anywhere in Ecuador. Kodak Ektachrome is available but Fuji Sensia and Konica are the most common brands of slide film. A variety of colour print film is sold in Ecuador, but always be sure to check the expiry date. If you are a serious photographer, then it is best to bring all your supplies from home.

Machine processing for colour prints is available in most towns but the results are usually no better than fair. Colour slide and black and white processing is harder to find, and may be of even lower quality. A highly recommended professional lab for all types of work is run by Ronald Jones in Quito and among the commercial labs, Difoto is recommended, see page 129.

Modern airport X-ray machines are supposed to be safe for any speed of film, but it is worth trying to avoid X-rays as the doses are cumulative. Many airport officials will allow film to be passed outside X-ray arches; they may also hand-check a suitcase with a large quantity of film if asked politely. Or use a commercially available lead-lined pouch. Avoid sending film home by mail, both because of X-rays and because the post office is unreliable.

Cameras, lenses and film should be protected in humid areas such as Oriente by putting them in a plastic bag.

Special interest travel

Climbing

Ecuador's mountains are one of its greatest attractions and there are 10 mountains over 5,000 m high, of which nine have glaciers, with routes ranging from easy snow-plods to hard and technical routes. Michael Koerner, in his *The Fool's Climbing Guide to Ecuador and Peru*, wrote: "The mountains are beautiful but above all exotic. On the same climb one can fight tropical vegetation, stroll up a glacier, and look down the crater of a live volcano." From Quito, using public transport, you can arrive at the base of seven of the country's big 10 mountains the same day and summit the next day – after you have acclimatized.

Outrageously easy access makes Ecuador a fantastic place to get some high altitude climbing experience

Acclimatization means letting your body adapt to the high altitude. No one should attempt to climb over 5,000 until they have spent at least a week at the height of Quito (2,800 m) or equivalent. Many of the sub-5,000 mountains are enjoyable walk-ups and a number of the big 10 are suitable for beginners, while others are technically challenging and only suitable for experienced mountaineers.

Cotopaxi If you've never climbed and want to suck some air at high altitude, Cotopaxi (5,897 m) is your best bet. While not, as often stated, the highest active volcano in the world, Cotopaxi is undoubtedly one of the most beautiful mountains in the world and the view down into the crater from the rim is unforgettable. Access is easy: you drive to 4,600 m in three hours from Quito, and the normal route is suitable for complete beginners climbing with a competent guide. Starting in Quito, you spend one night at the hut, climb the next morning and are back in town that afternoon. On the down side, Cotopaxi is the most climbed mountain in the Andes, the hut is often crowded and so is the normal route. (See also page 195.)

The big ten

Tungurahua The lowest of the big 10, Tungurahua, at 5,016 m, is not a good first climb because you start in the resort town of Baños at 1,800 m, leaving a massive 3,200 m of ascent to the summit. If you do climb Tungurahua you must have crampons and ice axe and be roped up to cross the summit glacier. **NB** At the close of this edition Tungurahua was dangerous and off limits to climbers and trekkers due to volcanic activity. For details see Baños, page 222.

Chimborazo Ecuador's highest peak, the giant Chimborazo, at 6,310 m, was long considered the highest mountain on Earth. It is, if you measure its height from the centre of the planet. Stand on the summit and thanks to the equatorial bulge you are closer to the sun than at any other point on the Earth's surface. However, the climb is long – 1,300 m of ascent from the hut – and cold. (See also page 236.) Opposite Chimborazo is **Carihuairazo** (5,020 m), which is technically more interesting than its neighbour.

Other mountains regularly climbed include **Cayambe** (5,789 m), the only place on the planet where the latitude is 0° and so is the temperature. It's a technically easy climb but dangerous, because of the large number of crevasses and the fact that its eastern location means that cloud rolls in most days from the jungle, reducing visibility to another zero. (See page 162.)

Access to **Antisana** (5,705 m) has improved dramatically with the opening of a new road. You can now drive to base camp in three hours from Quito. The normal route is technically easy but, as with Cayambe, it is dangerous due to the large number of crevasses. (See also page 358.)

Iliniza Norte (5,116 m) is the only one of the big 10 that does not have a glacier. It is a rock scramble but parts of the route are exposed, unstable and dangerous. You need a rope and the experience to use it or hire a guide. Opposite Iliniza Norte is **Iliniza Sur** (5,263 m), which is beautiful but technically challenging and only for experienced climbers. (See page 192.)

Essentials

The least climbed of the big 10 are **El Altar** (5,319 m) and **Sangay** (5,323 m). El Altar is a spectacularly beautiful blown out volcano with an emerald-green crater lake and nine separate peaks, all of them technically difficult (see page 238). Sangay is the world's most continuously active volcano. The route is long – five to seven days – and technically easy, but extremely dangerous due to the likelihood of being hit by lumps of rock being ejected from the volcano. (See page 384.)

The normal routes (and huts) on Cotopaxi, Chimborazo, Tungurahua, and Iliniza Norte can be crowded. Outside these four you are likely to have the mountains to yourself, and if you climb any route other than the normal route on these four you will also keep away from the crowds.

Other mountains Apart from the big 10 there are many other mountains worth climbing in Ecuador, whether you are acclimatizing for the bigger peaks, don't like the ice and snow or just want to try something different. Around Otavalo are three mountains: Ecuador's 11th highest peak **Cotacachi** (4,939 m) which is made of loose and dangerous rock, **Imbabura** (4,630 m), a walk-up best started from the La Esperanza to the north, and **Fuya Fuya** (4,263 m), the highest point of the massive Mojanda volcano. (See page 171.)

Above Quito are the **Pichinchas**: Guagua (4,794 m) and Rucu (4,790 m). Guagua is a good acclimatization climb, but enquire beforehand about the current level of volcanic activity. Unfortunately, Rucu should not be climbed due to continuous problems with muggers, sometimes armed. (See page 155.)

In the Cotopaxi national park are the triple peaked **Rumiñahui** (4,722 m) and **Sincholagua** (4,901 m). For Rumiñahui Norte and Sincholagua, a rope and helmet are essential to reach the summits. Rumiñahui Central is the easiest scramble, starting from Limpiopungo, while Rumiñahui Sur is climbed from the northwest via Machachi and Pansaleo (see page 195). Opposite, on the other side of the central valley, is **Corazón** (4,791 m), which is a long but easy walk-up and gives fantastic views of Cotopaxi and the Ilinizas.

Two of the most esoteric peaks in Ecuador are **Sara Urcu** (4,676 m) and **Cerro Hermoso** (4,571 m). Sara Urcu is south of Cayambe. Whymper climbed it in 1880 but the climb was not repeated until 1955. It has Ecuador's lowest and easternmost glacier. You thrash about in the wet and vegetation for several days while your ice axe and crampons rust, before getting to the glacier and putting them on. It is very easy to get extremely lost in this area. A map and compass and the ability to use them are essential. Map reading is also a requirement for Cerro Hermoso, the highest point of the mysterious **Llanganates** range, where dense vegetation and complicated topography allegedly help conceal 750 tons of Inca gold collected for Atahualpa's ransom and stashed after his murder (see box, page 432). The peak is a walk-up, once you've found it. Access is easier from the north but it is still a five-day plus expedition and only for the fit, acclimatized and experienced.

To the east, in the jungle, are two active volcanoes **Reventador** (3,562 m) and **Sumaco** (3,900 m), whose position was not determined until 1921. These two can be climbed if you like hot and sweaty conditions and have your machete-user's licence to hack your way through the vegetation to get to base of the volcanoes. (See also page 360.)

When to climb There are two climbing seasons in Ecuador: June to August and December to February. Allegedly, the eastern cordillera is drier December-February and the western cordillera June-August (though it is often windy in August) and Cotopaxi has more clear days than any other peak. It is best to avoid the wetter seasons March-May and September-November. However, the weather can be good or bad on any day of the year and it is worth remembering that Cotopaxi has been climbed on every day of the year and that Whymper's grand tour in 1880, when he made seven first ascents, was December to July. Bad weather is just predominant for the mountains on the eastern side of the eastern cordillera (eg El Altar, Sangay, Llanganates, Sara Urcu). Being on the equator, days and nights are 12 hours long. As a result, climbs are attempted all year round all over the country.

More important than the time of year is the time of day. You should aim to reach the summit of any of the snowcapped peaks at 0700 so that descent is completed well before midday. As the equatorial sun warms the snow it attains the consistency of sugar which makes it hard going and also dangerous, and avalanches are far more likely. On top of this, any rock held in place by ice will start its gravity-induced downward journey once the sun has melted the cementing ice.

Nights and early mornings are generally clear. However, cloud normally comes in by midday if not earlier, often reducing visibility to zero. This is another reason to climb at night but if the route is not tracked out by previous parties it is worth marking the way with flags; white footsteps in white snow in a white-out are difficult to follow. The weather tends to be better at full moon and the equatorial moon is so strong that you do not need to use your headtorch if climbing by moonlight, from full moon down to half moon.

Essentials

Sunburn & altitude

In good weather the heat is incredible: you want to strip off but if you do so you will get the worst sunburn of your life

Ultra violet light at high altitude on or near the equator is very, very strong. Without proper eye protection it is possible to get snowblindness after as little as 15 minutes above 5,000 m. It does not matter if it is sunny or cloudy, in fact more UV light is reflected on cloudy days. Snowblindness is not normally apparent until the night after the damage has been done. The pain has been described as what it must be like to have acid or boiling water poured into your eyes. The next day, the victim often cannot see and will have to be led down the mountain. Snowblindness counts as a permanent eye injury – part of the retina is burnt out – which means victims are more susceptible in the future. Wear sunglasses that give 100 protection against UV light. Ski goggles with 100 UV protection lenses are useful for cloudy days, bad weather, and as spares in case you break or lose your glacier glasses. Sunburn is a serious business at high altitude and will happen on completely overcast days. The power of the equatorial sun reflecting off snow will burn the skin under the chin, up the nostrils and behind the ears, so remember to apply protection to all these areas. Use weatherproof sun block with a rating of factor 25 or higher.

Guides & rescue

ASEGUIM (Asociación Ecuatoriana de Guias de Montaña), the Ecuadorean mountain guides association, was formed in 1993 and has very high standards for its members who have a rigorous training programme monitored by mountain guides from the French national mountain training school ENSA. Another advantage of climbing with ASEGUIM guides is that should you need rescuing they have the best and fastest rescue organization in the country (see also Trekking below). The usual cost is around US$1,500 per rescue. All ASEGUIM guides carry a two-way radio. There is no helicopter rescue and, as yet, little cooperation from the army, police or government. If you will be climbing extensively in Ecuador, it is a good idea to register with your embassy or consulate and advise them of any insurance you may have to cover the costs of rescue or repatriation by air ambulance. The first place the authorities usually contact in the event of an emergency involving a foreign climber is the embassy of their home country.

Equipment

Everything you might lose, break or forget is usually available from one of the Quito climbing and outdoor shops, but sometimes none of them will have what you want. Duracell MN1203 headtorch batteries, when available, cost about US$8. Gear from the US tends to be cheaper in Ecuador than in Europe but European gear tends to be very expensive. A number of shops hire gear as do agencies for their clients, but always check the condition of rented equipment very carefully before you take it out.

Mountain refuges	These are mainly of international standard with many improvements in recent years. Most provide the basic services: electric light; running water; and cooking facilities. They usually have a warden throughout the main climbing season. Nightly tariffs are usually US$10.
Rock & ice climbing courses	Courses are offered on Cayambe, Cotopaxi and Chimborazo. There is usually only one per year, but ASEGUIM might organize others if there is sufficient interest; ie if a reasonable number of tourists organize themselves into a group. *Safari* run an ice glacier school, the only one in the country (see Tour operators in Quito, page 133).
Further reading	*Ecuador: A Climbing Guide*, by Yossi Brain (The Mountaineers, Seattle, 2000) is the most up-to-date reference and covers routes on all the 'big 10' plus 10 additional mountains. *Climbing and Hiking in Ecuador* (see below under Trekking) covers a number of treks and sub-5,000 m peaks suitable for acclimatizing as well as general descriptions of routes on the 'big 10'. *The Fool's Climbing Guide to Ecuador and Peru*, by Michael Koerner (Buzzard Mountaineering, 1976), is concise and funny more than practical due to its age, but a very enjoyable read. *Montañas del Ecuador* by Marco Cruz (Dinediciones, Quito 1993, Spanish) is a beautiful coffee-table book packed full of colour photographs, taken by Ecuador's leading guide of the last 20 years.

Montañas del Sol, by Freddy Landazuri, Ivan Rojas, and Marcos Serrano (Campo Abierto, Quito, 1994, Spanish), is a good climbing guidebook but it lacks top diagrams and public transport information. *Cotopaxi: Mountain of Light*, by Freddy Landazuri (Campo Abierto, 1994; in English and Spanish), is a thorough history of the mountain. *Die Schneeberge Ecuador*, by Marco Cruz, is a German translation from Spanish and is excellent. *Travels Amongst the Great Andes of the Equator*, by Edward Whymper (published by Gibbs M Smith, Salt Lake City), is an absolute classic; one of the best books written about climbing anything anywhere (especially if you ignore any paragraph discussing the differences between the mercurial and aneroid barometers).

Mountaineering journals include: *Campo Abierto* (not produced by the Travel Agency of the same name), an annual magazine on expeditions, access to mountains etc, US$1; *Montaña* is the annual magazine of the *Colegio San Gabriel* mountaineering club, US$1.50. Jorge Anhalzer publishes a series of five concise mountain guides, for each of Ecuador's most frequently climbed peaks, with updated information on routes to the summits. Available from book and camping shops.

Trekking

Ecuador's varied landscape, diverse ecological environments, and friendly villagers within a compact area, make travelling by foot a refreshing break from crowded buses. Although the most commonly travelled routes are in the Sierra, there are also excellent trekking opportunities on the Coast and in the Oriente. Likewise you can descend from the windswept páramo through Andean Slope cloud forest to tropical rain forest and hence observe most of the ecosystems of Ecuador during a single excursion.

Most hikes pass through protected areas which are managed by the Ministerio del Ambiente. Currently about 17% of the country lies within national parks, ecological reserves and recreation areas, but most of these are threatened by development pressures. The only areas that are well-staffed and have reasonably good infrastructure are **Cotopaxi, Galápagos, Cajas, Podocarpus** and **Machalilla** National Parks. Thanks to foreign technical and financial assistance other areas such as the **Cayambe-Coca** and **Antisana** Ecological Reserves and **Sangay, Sumaco Napo-Galleras** and **Yasuní** National Parks are becoming more than 'paper parks', with increased staff and real environmental policing.

A detailed map of Ecuador's protected areas can be purchased at the Ministerio del Ambiente's offices in the MAG (Ministerio de Agricultura Y Ganadería) building on Av

Eloy Alfaro and Av Amazonas, Quito, T548924/563816/541921, F564037. The official entrance fees for parks and conservation units are typically US$10 to US$20 for foreigners (much less for Ecuadoreans).They vary from park to park and also with the time of year, see National Parks, page 447, for a complete list. In any event, the less-visited parks will have no one around to collect the fee.

It is still the ruggedness and lack of access, however, that protects most of these areas from environmental impacts and makes them so appealing to wilderness travellers.There are not many well-marked trails as you would find in national parks in developed countries. In some places ancient routes have been used for thousands of years by campesinos and are relatively easy to follow. In other areas you may be bush-whacking through the forest with a machete. A basic knowledge of how to ask for directions in Spanish and map and compass skills are perhaps the most important elements to a successful trek. It is also possible to hire experienced guides (US$50-100 per day) from the major cities or less expensive local *campesino* guides (US$10 per day) if you are unsure about the route.

Topographic maps should be purchased at the IGM (Instituto Geográfico Militar) in Quito, see page 39. The 1:50,000 scale maps are most useful, of which there is coverage of most of the country. For more remote locations bring a handheld GPS, but remember that this is no substitute for comprehensive navigation and map-reading skills.

It is best to carry trekking equipment from home, but if you are travelling light most gear can be purchased or hired at outfitters in Quito. Always check rented gear very carefully.

Quito companies which offer guiding services include: *Safari*, *Sierra Nevada*, *Pamir* and *Surtrek*. Complete contact information is found under Quito Tour operators, page 133. For a complete list of Quito shops which sell or rent gear, see Camping, climbing and trekking equipment, page 129, some of these shops also offer guiding. Guides and gear can also be hired at agencies in Baños and Riobamba. Otavalo agencies offer trekking tours. In Cuenca there are several operators offering trekking and many private guides, one company in Cuenca also rents tents. *Biotours* in Loja has a few items for rent and guides for southern Ecuador, see the corresponding sections.

Guiding & equipment rental

The standard hiking shoe for Ecuador is the rubber boot, which is worn by most *campesinos* while working in the countryside. Travellers may balk at using footwear that only costs US$5 and can be purchased in any town, but they keep feet warm and dry through muddy terrain, unlike conventional leather or goretex hiking boots. As long the trail is not rocky they are also very comfortable. **All drinking water must be boiled or treated.** Iodine tablets are easy and reliable but may be difficult to locate in Quito. Common stove fuels which may be found in Ecuador include white gas (this may be difficult, try Ace Hardware or Kywi in Quito), kerosene (most hardware stores), and gas canisters (outfitters listed above).

Equipment

High altitude sickness (locally called *soroche*) can be a problem for recent arrivals. It is important to drink lots of water and not push yourself too hard when you have just arrived. If an accident occurs self-evacuation may be quickest, but rescues can be arranged with ASEGUIM, see Guides and rescue, page 67. You will be charged for the expenses of the rescue.

Sunburn, altitude & safety

For information on sunburn and altitude, see page 67 and 86. **NB** Some of the more popular hikes in the country such as Laguna Cuicocha, Lagunas de Mojanda and especially Rucu Pichincha (best avoided) have experienced armed robberies. The basic rule of thumb is that the farther off the beaten gringo track, the safer you are. It is important to enquire locally about the safety of a particular trek.

Different terrains Hiking in the Sierra is mostly across high elevation *páramo*, through agricultural lands, and past indigenous communities living in traditional ways. There are outstanding views of glaciated peaks in the north and precolumbian ruins in the south. On the coast there are only a few areas developed for hiking ranging from dry forest to coastal rain forest. The Oriente is mostly virgin tropical rain forest and offers excellent hiking even outside the protected areas. The forest canopy shades out the brushy vegetation, making cross-country travel relatively easy. Since there are no vantage points to get a bearing it is also easy to get lost, and a GPS does not work in a dense forest. Local guides are often required because of this difficulty in navigation and because you will be walking on land owned by indigenous tribes. The Andean Slopes are steep and often covered by virtually impenetrable cloud forests and it rains a lot. Many ancient trading routes head down the river valleys. Some of these trails are still used. Others may be overgrown and difficult to follow but offer the reward of intact ecosystems. You may be travelling across land that is either owned outright by indigenous people or jointly managed with the Miniterio de Ambiente. It is important to be respectful of the people and request permission to pass through or camp. Sometimes a fee may be charged by locals but it is usually minimal.

When to go Although each region has its own wet and dry seasons, climate can be unreliable especially during an El Niño year. The Oriente is wet all year but somewhat dryer December to February. Since the eastern Sierra is most influenced by weather patterns from the Oriente these are the best months for hiking. The western Sierra is dry June to September with a short dry spell in December and January. The southern coast experiences a very dry season May to December, while the northern coast is generally much wetter during this dry period. Since air temperatures vary with altitude it is important to dress appropriately. The coast and the Oriente are hot and humid, so wear light clothes and leave your Gore-Tex coat at home. In the valleys of the Sierra temperatures are moderate but snow is possible in the páramo.

Trek descriptions There are five treks described in detail in the main travelling text. These are: **Trek of the Condor** (page 153); **Cajas National Park** (page 264); **Saraguro to Yacuambi** (page 267); **Volcan Reventador** (page 360); and **Ingapirca** (page 246).

Further reading A comprehensive hiking guide is *Climbing and Hiking in Ecuador*, 4th Edition, by Rachoweicki, Thurber and Wagenhauser (Bradt, 1997). A new book due out in late 2001 is *Trekking in Ecuador*, by Robert and Daisy Kunstaetter (The Mountaineers, Seattle), with in-depth coverage of 30 different treks.

Rafting and kayaking

Ecuador is a whitewater paradise. Warm waters, tropical rainforest and dozens of accessible rivers concentrated in such a small area have made the country a 'hotspot' for rafters and kayakers the world over. Regional rainy seasons occur at different times throughout the year so the action never stops – there's always a river to run.

Rafting is an activity open to almost anyone with a sense of adventure. Worldwide the sport continues to grow, as is the case in Ecuador, with the majority of participants first-timers. No previous rafting experience is needed to join a trip as each boat has an experienced guide at the helm. Trips can run from one to eight days.

Rafting trips are offered by operators in Quito, Tena and Baños with guides, equipment, transport and food provided. Although not new, the rafting industry has until recently remained relatively undeveloped. Standards vary so it is really important to ask a few questions before booking a trip. The most important things to look for are experienced guides and top notch equipment. Without exception, the reputable companies are run by foreign or foreign-trained Ecuadorean guides. Ask about the guides' rafting, river rescue and first aid training, about the rafting and personal safety equipment, if they carry first aid, raft repair and river rescue kits, if they utilize safety kayakers and have on-river emergency communications. Although there are some inherent dangers in river running, these are the factors that make a rafting trip relatively safe.

Kayakers find the biggest problem is choosing which of the dozens of enticing rivers to run in the time they have available. The following river descriptions include the most popular runs. However as new rivers are being 'opened' every year the list is by no means exhaustive. For information on river conditions, the ins and outs of travelling with kayaks, rental of kayaking equipment and guiding services, contact Steve Nomchong at Yacu Amu Rafting in Quito or Gynner Coronel at Ríos Ecuador in Tena (see below). Both these companies also offer 'learn to' courses that give newcomers the chance to find out what they've been missing out on. After all, there's no better place to learn this exciting sport than on Ecuador's warm tropical rivers.

Grades The majority of Ecuador's whitewater rivers share a number of characteristics. Plunging off the Andes the upper sections are very steep creeks offering, if they're runnable at all, serious technical grade V, suitable for expert kayakers only. As the creeks join on the lower slopes they form rivers navigable by both raft and kayak (ie less steep, more volume). Some of these rivers offer up to 100 km of continuous grade III-IV whitewater, before flattening out to rush towards the Pacific Ocean on one side of the ranges or deep into the Amazon Basin on the other.

Water quality Unfortunately, some of Ecuador's rivers are not very clean. Water quality may vary significantly depending on such factors as proximity of towns, local agricultural practices, last rainfall, river volume, and the relative proportions of surface and ground water. It's a complex equation but as a general rule the rivers running straight off the eastern and western slopes of the Andes are less subject to pollution than the highland rivers which drain some of the most densely populated regions of the country before their descent into the jungle or to the Pacific. Ask about water quality before signing up for a trip.

Pacific Coast rivers Owing to their proximity to Quito, the Blanco river and its tributaries are the most frequently run in Ecuador. There is almost 200 km of raftable whitewater in the Blanco valley, with the Toachi/Blanco combination and the Upper Blanco being the most popular day trips. The former starts as a technical grade III-IV run, including the infamous rapids of the El Sapo canyon, before joining the Blanco where big waves abound (year round). The latter is most probably the world's longest day trip – 47 km of non-stop grade III-IV rapids in a little over four hours on the river (February-June only). Trips are also offered on the Caoni (grade II-III) and Mulate (grade III) rivers.

In addition to those already mentioned, kayakers have a number of other possibilities to choose from depending on the time of year and their skills and experience. The Mindo (grade III-IV), Saloya (grade IV-V), Pilaton (grade IV-V) and Upper Toachi (grade IV-V) are options.

Quijos river The waters of the Quijos river and its tributaries are a whitewater playground. Within a 30 km radius of the town of El Chaco you'll find everything from steep, technical grade V creek runs to big volume, roller coaster grade III and IV. Popular runs include sections on the main Quijos (grade III-V) for rafting and kayaking and the Papallacta (grade V), Cosanga (grade III-IV) and Oyacachi (grade IV) tributaries for kayaking. Day tripping is the norm on the upper runs although further downstream a two day trip is possible starting near the town of El Reventador. At the end of the upper section the collected waters of the Quijos catchment plunge dramatically over San Rafael Falls, which at 145 m is the highest waterfall in Ecuador. Access to the Quijos valley is generally easy as it forms the main corridor from Quito down into the jungle. The most popular put ins and take outs are accessible by road although putting in for the run from El Reventador requires a 40 minute scramble down muddy slopes from the main road.

The best time to dip your paddle depends on how hard you want to push yourself. The rainy season generally runs from March to September so at this time you can expect high flows and truly continuous whitewater (for expert kayakers only). The rest of the year, the dry season, is when the commercial rafting and kayaking operators run trips. During these months there's still plenty of action and water and air temperatures are more comfortable.

Oriente About 1½ hours from Lago Agrio the Upper Aguarico river, from Puerto Libre (on the new Lumbaquí-Tulcán road) to Lumbaquí, offers big volume grade II-III rapids. A short distance to the south the clear waters of the Dué river (grade III-IV), a major tributary of the Aguarico, run refreshingly cool off the flanks of Volcán El Reventador. Both rivers are best run between February and July. Regular rafting departures are not offered on either river but special trips can be arranged through one of the Quito-based operators.

In the jungle surrounding Tena, the **Napo river** and its tributaries offer a tremendous amount of whitewater in a small area. It's very easy to spend a week based here and paddle a different river every day. The grade III Upper Napo is the most popular rafting trip. However, the gem of this region, the **Misahuallí** (grade IV), is rafted less frequently as it is subject to sudden and dramatic variations in water level. This river passes through pristine jungle in a remote canyon, the highlight being the heart-stopping portage around Casanova Falls.

Additional kayaking options include various sections of the Misahualli, Jondachi, Anzu and Hollín rivers. Difficulty is very much water level dependent but most are grade IV or V when they have sufficient water to paddle.

Pastaza This is generally not run on the lower reaches although a canyon between Shell and the Puyo-Macas road bridge contains some good grade IV rapids at high levels. It should be noted that the Patate river, a highland tributary, has been rafted regularly out of Baños. Another tributary, the Topo (grade V), has been reported by some expert kayakers to be the best steep creek run in the country.

Upano Best known for the Namangosa Gorge in which dozens of waterfalls plummet up to *The vertical walls of the* 100 m into the river, to date this spectacle has been witnessed by few river runners. *Namangosa Gorge are* While the gorge is undoubtedly the highlight, what makes a journey down the Upano *covered by a thick layer* special is witnessing the changing character of an Amazonian river. Trickling from a *of primary rainforest* string of mountain lakes the Upano quickly gathers force, carving a path southward *broken only by the* through the province of Morona Santiago. As it rushes past Macas it is shallow and *waters spilling* braided. Picking a route from the myriad channels is a real challenge; make the wrong *spectacularly off the* choice and an unscheduled portage will result. *lip of the gorge*

The pace steadily increases until the river plunges into the magnificent Namangosa Gorge. Some falls cascade down staggered cliffs while others freefall into the jungle below. This 'Lost World' atmosphere is made even more daunting by the seething rapids below. The rapids are big class IV with lots of funny water including raft-flipping boils and kayak(er)-swallowing eddylines.

Once out of the gorge, the river broadens and deepens to become a calm but powerful giant on its way to meet the mighty Amazon.

Five to eight day rafting trips start near Macas. A few kayakers have attempted the upper reaches of the river and returned with stories to be filed under E for epic. The run from Macas to the end of the gorge is about 120 km and takes four to five days. Some choose to continue another day or so further downstream to the village of Santiago Mayatico which is the final possible take-out. From here it's only a few miles as the toucan flies to the border with Peru.

Recommended months are October to February and this is when commercial trips are offered. During the rest of the year the river can flood unexpectedly. In fact during April and May, when the river peaks, the gorge fills so much that a local Shuar indian once travelled upstream to Macas in a motorized canoe.

Quito All agencies in Quito offer one and two day trips on the Toachi and Blanco rivers. Some of them offer additional trips which are mentioned below. *Yacu Amu Rafting*, Baquedano E5-27 y Juan León Mera, T236844, F226038, rafting@yacuamu.com, www.yacuamu.com Also one and two day trips on the Quijos and five and eight day trips on the Upano October-February, customized itineraries, kayaking information, equipment rental, courses with qualified instructors, guiding service and all inclusive packages for those who want to leave the organizing to someone else. Highly recommended as professional and with highest quality equipment. *ROW Expediciones*, Robles 653 y Amazonas, 3rd floor, T239224, F522977, row@uio.satnet.net Also seven day trips on the Upano November-February, guides from Idaho, USA. *Sierra Nevada*, Joaquin Pinto 637 y Cordero, T553658, F554936, snevada@accessinter.net French-trained guides and good equipment. *Eco-Adventur*, Calama 339 entre J L Mera y Reina Victoria, T520647, F223720, info@adventour.com *Explorandes*, Presidente Wilson 537 y Diego de Almagro, T222699, F556938, explora@hoy.net

Tena *Ríos Ecuador*, 15 de Noviembre y 9 de Octubre, T06-887438, info@riosecuador.com Year-round rafting trips on the Upper Napo, and on the Misahualli October-March. Also kayaking trips, instruction, rental and information. Good guides and high safety standards. Run by Gynner Coronel, who is highly respected and recommended.

Baños *Río Loco* Maldonado y Martínez, T/F03-740929, rioloco@ecuadorexplorer.com Year-round trips on the Patate and Pastaza rivers.

Agencies

Other adventure sports

The coast of Ecuador is a paradise for divers, combining both cool and warm water dive destinations in one of the most biologically diverse marine environments on earth. The Galápagos Islands are undoubtedly the most popular destination, but diving in lesser known waters such as those off the central coast of Ecuador has been gaining popularity in recent years. The secluded coves of Isla de la Plata, 45 km off the coast of Machalilla National Park, contain an abundance of multicoloured tropical fish which make diving and snorkelling a great experience. Colonies of sea lions can be seen, as well as migrating humpback whales, from late June to October, and many species of marine birds.

The Galápagos Islands are well known for their distinctive marine environments and offer more than 20 dive sites including opportunities for night diving. Each island contains its own unique environment and many are home to underwater life forms endemic to this part of the world. For a detailed description of dive sites and marine life, see page 403.

Diving is becoming more popular with tourists since the cost of doing a PADI course in Ecuador is relatively low. There are several agencies in Quito which feature diving and full instruction on their programmes. Equipment can be hired easily from most of the adventure tour operators, but it is advisable to check everything thoroughly. The larger bookshops also stock diving books and identification guides for fish and other marine life.

Among the agencies specializing in diving are *Nixe Cruises*, *Quasar Nautica* and *Tropic Ecological Adventures* (see page 133 for their addresses). See also the Galápagos chapter (page 416) for diving agencies in Puerto Ayora.

Diving

Essentials

Mountain biking   Increasingly more and more people come to Ecuador to ride through the spectacular mountain scenery or along the coastal roads. The upper Amazon basin also offers a relatively traffic-free route from north to south.

What many people don't take into account is the frequently extreme conditions in which they find themselves biking. Dehydration can be a very real issue when cycling at high altitudes or in the hot tropical lowlands. Bottled water is available at many small stores in villages, but along some of the more spectacular routes they are few and far between. A water pump or other sterilizing systems should always be carried. Sunscreen is essential at high altitudes even on cloudy days. Wrap around sunglasses help to restrict the amount of dust which gets into the eyes.

When planning routes it is best to use 1:50,000 topographical maps as they give a more accurate measurement of the distances. The IGM in Quito also produces a series of very practical *hojas de ruta* which include elevation profiles. You should in addition seek a little local knowledge, since maps are not updated frequently and new roads are often not indicated, nor are landslides which may make certain routes impassable. Maps do not always distinguish between cobbled and good *lastre* (gravel) graded surfaces. The latter are normally far superior for biking and should be taken where possible.

Routes   Departing from Quito in northerly and southerly directions it is difficult to avoid the busy paved Panamericana for about the first 30 km. For those going south the **Machachi** area makes a good destination for a first day. To the north a lot of traffic can be avoided by biking to **Mitad del Mundo**, an easy first day, and then taking the old road with its dramatic scenery via **San Jose de Minas** to travel to the **Otavalo** area. Those who wish to stay on the paved road should consider **Guayllabamba** (easy) or **Cayambe** (harder) a first day destination.

The road **east from Baños** toward the jungle is very popular and beautiful, and there are ample opportunities to rent bikes here. Unfortunately holdups of bikers have (rarely) taken place on this route, so enquire about public safety before heading out. In general, for biking just like for hiking, the farther from the main gringo trail, the safer you are.

Trying to cover too great a distance, especially at the beginning of a trip, is a common mistake; 40-50 km a day is a respectable distance to cover at altitudes above 2,500 m. Beyond 50 km from Quito the traffic decreases and more alternative roads become available. In many areas the Panamericana is paralleled by older dirt roads, with very little traffic.

General advice   A good bike lock should be considered essential equipment, the best will be long enough to pass through both wheels and the frame. Most bus lines will carry bicycles on the roof racks for little or no extra charge. It is advisable to supervise the loading and assure that the derailer is not jammed up against luggage which might damage it. If you take a long journey with major altitude changes let a little air out of the tyres especially when going from lower to higher altitudes. Bikes may be taken on commercial flights in place of a suitcase, always double check that there will be space. Routes to the Jungle have more luggage restrictions, as do those to the Galápagos. For agencies offering mountain bike tours and bike shops, see Quito Sports (page 132). Also see cycling, page 56.

Paragliding   This is a pretty special activity amid the high mountains, and its devotees can sometimes be seen in the rays of the afternoon sun drifting off Pichincha toward Quito. *Escuela Pichincha* have an office at Carlos Endara 160, between Av Amazonas and La Prensa, near the airport, T/F256592, home T455076, cellular T09-478349, parapent@uio.satnet.net They offer seven day intensive courses for US$450, or every second day for 15 days for US$350, which includes 30 to 40 flights near Quito (though no tandem flights as it is too dangerous for landing), minimum of two people; or every Saturday over eight weeks for US$250. They also sell equipment, which is cheaper than in Europe.

Birdwatching

The lowlands are rich in Cotingas, Manakins, Toucans, Antbirds and spectacular birds of prey, while the cloud forests are noted for their abundance of Hummingbirds, Tanagers, Mountain Toucans and Cock of the Rock. As a result of this wonderful avian diversity, a network of birding lodges has sprung up and ecotourism has never been easier.

Ecuador is one of the richest places in the world for birds, and some of the planet's most beautiful species can be found here

Here we list the best lodges and roads for birding according to their biological region; both the sites and the regions are more fully described in the main text. For further information about Ecuador's wonderful biodiversity, see Flora and fauna, page 445. Within each region described below, the sites are listed from north to south.

Bilsa (400-700 m), a virgin site in Esmeraldas province, contains even the rarest foothill birds (such as Banded Ground-cuckoo and Long-Wattled Umbrellabird), though access can be an ordeal in the wet season. This site has 305 known species.

Western lowlands & lower foothills

 Aldea Salamandra (200 m) on the Calacalí-Esmeraldas road offers cabins with access to several forest reserves nearby.

 Tinalandia (700-900 m) near Alluriquín on the Alóag-Santo Domingo road is a great introduction to the world of tropical birds. There are lots of colourful species (more than 360 have been seen here) and they are easier to observe here than at most other places, but some of the larger species have been lost from this area. The lodge itself is very accessible and comfortable.

 Río Palenque (200 m) between Santo Domingo and Quevedo is one of the last islands of western lowland forest. It is a very rich birding area, with 370 species. It has begun to lose some species because of its isolation from other forests.

 Parque Nacional Machalilla (0-850 m) on the coast near Puerto López has lightly disturbed dry forest and cloud forest, with many dry-forest specialties. The higher areas are slightly difficult to access. There are 115 known species here.

 Ecuasal ponds (0 m), on the Santa Elena peninsula, which hold a variety of seabirds and shorebirds; famous for their Chilean Flamingos.

 Cerro Blanco (250-300 m) just outside Guayaquil is one of the best remaining examples of dry forest. There have been breeding Great Green Macaws on occasion, and even Jaguars have been spotted. It has 190 known species of birds.

 Manta Real (300-1200 m) is a rainforest-to-cloud forest transition area on the Guayaquil-Cuenca road, with some very rare birds endemic to southwestern Ecuador and adjacent Peru. There are 120 species known from the area.

 Manglares-Churute (50-650 m) just southeast of Guayaquil contains a dry-to moist forest and a mangrove forest. The bird list includes only 65 species but the area is poorly studied.

 The petrified forest of **Puyango** (300-400 m) has live trees as well, and typical dry forest birds. It has 130 known species.

Páramo del Angel (2500-4500 m) south of Tulcán is a spectacular grassland dotted with tall tree-like herbs called *frailejones*; 160 bird species are known from here.

Western Andes

 Cerro Golondrinas (2000-4000 m) is near the Páramo del Angel, and there are highly recommended guided treks available through both.

 Intag Cloud Forest Reserve (1800-2800 m), **Junín Community Reserve** (1500-2200 m), and **Siempre Verde** are all cloud forests near the Reserva Ecológica Cotacachi-Cayapas , with a full set of cloud forest birds. Access is via Otavalo.

 Los Cedros Reserve (1000-2700 m) near the Cotacachi-Cayapas Ecological Reserve has excellent forest over an interesting range of elevations. Populations of many bird species are higher here than in more accessible places.

 Yanacocha (3300-4000 m) is a surprisingly well preserved high elevation forest on the west side of the Pichincha volcano. Access is from Quito.

Essentials

The Nono-Mindo road (1500-3400 m) is a famous birding route starting from Quito and passes through a wide variety of forest types. It is somewhat disturbed in its higher sections but quite good in its lower half, where there are now several excellent lodges.

Tandayapa Lodge (1700 m) on the Nono-Mindo road is well done, easily accessible and comfortable. Serious birders seeking rarities will benefit from the knowledgeable guides who can show practically any species they are asked to find. There are 318 species that have been seen here.

Bellavista (1800-2300 m) on the Nono-Mindo road is a perfectly situated lodge with colourful easy-to-see birds, and plenty of rarities for hardcore birders.

El Pahuma (1600-2600 m) is an easy day trip from Quito (about an hour) on the Calacalí-Esmeraldas road, with lots of birds and even an occasional Spectacled Bear. A visitor centre with lodging is under construction, along with a botanical garden. A preliminary survey found about 130 species of birds here.

Maquipucuna (1200-2800 m) just off the Calacalí-Esmeraldas road has extensive forest, and cabins for guests. There are about 300 species here.

Mindo (1300-2400), the most ecotourism-conscious town in Ecuador (see page 149) has many good lodges. Even the road into town (easily reached from Quito in two hours) is excellent for good views of beautiful birds like quetzals and tanagers. More than 400 species occur in the whole area.

The Chiriboga road (900-3200 m) from the south of Quito to near Santo Domingo is good for birds in its middle and lower sections, but it can be very muddy; a four-wheel-drive vehicle is recommended. **Guajalito** (1900-2400 m) is situated halfway down the Chiriboga Road and could be used as a base and as a place to do forest-interior birding.

La Hesperia (1000-2000 m) off the Aloag-Santo Domingo road has good mid-elevation forest (which is otherwise hard to reach in the west) and good facilities.

Otonga (800-2300 m) is a private reserve rising into the mountains south of the Aloag-Santo Domingo road. The bird life here is known for not being shy, especially the Dark-backed Wood-Quails.

Chilla, Guanazán, Manú, and Selva Alegre (2800-3000 m), on the road from Saraguro to the coast, have remnant forests and good birds.

Piñas Forest / Buenaventura (800-1000 m) 24 km north of the road from Loja to the coast is an important area for bird conservation, since there are few remaining tracts in the area. Many rare birds are present. Piñas has over 310 bird species.

Guachanamá Ridge (2000-2800 m) between Celica and Alamor in extreme southwest Ecuador contains many rare southwestern endemic birds.

Sozoranga-Nueva Fátima road (1300-2600 m) near the Peruvian border in Loja has remnants of a wide variety of mid-elevation forests, and has many southwest endemics. There are 190 known species in the area.

Inter-Andean forests & páramos

Guandera (3100-3800 m), near the Colombian border, has beautiful temperate forest with Espeletia *páramo* and many rare birds.

Pasochoa (2700-4200 m) provides a very easy cloud forest to visit just south of Quito. Not virgin, but lots of birds (about 120 species).

Parque Nacional Cotopaxi (3700-6000 m), 1½ hours south of Quito, is a spectacular setting in which to find birds of the high arid *páramo*. There is also a birdy lake and marsh, Limpiopungo. About 90 species are known from the park.

Parque Nacional Cajas (3000-4500 m) has extensive *páramo* and high elevation forest, accessible from Cuenca. It has 125 known species, including Condor and the Violet-tailed Metaltail, a hummingbird endemic to this area.

The Oña-Saraguro-Santiago road (2000-2600 m) between Cuenca and Loja has great roadside birding in high-elevation forest remnants. About 145 species have been seen here.

Papallacta (3000-4400 m), 1½ hours east of Quito, has a dramatic cold wet landscape of grassland and high elevation forest. Condors are regular here, along with many other highland birds. **Eastern Andes**

Guango (2700 m) is a new lodge with good birding in temperate forest below Papallacta. 95 high-elevation species have been found here so far.

Baeza (1900-2400 m), about two hours east of Quito, has forest remnants near town which can be surprisingly birdy. The road to the antennas above town is especially rich.

San Isidro (2000 m), half an hour from Baeza just off the Baeza-Tena road, is a comfortable lodge with bird-rich forests all around, and wonderful hospitality. The bird list exceeds 260 species.

SierrAzul (2200-2400 m), 12 km beyond San Isidro, protects a slightly higher elevation; good birds and some endangered mammals. About 140 bird species seen here so far.

Guacamayos Ridge (1700-2300 m) on the Baeza-Tena road has excellent roadside forest rich in bird life.

San Rafael Falls (1400 m) on the Baeza-Lago Agrio road is a very good place to see Cocks-of-the-Rock and other subtropical birds. Access is an easy walk once you reach the site. Over 200 bird species have been found there, and the true total is certainly higher.

The Loreto road (300-1400 m) connecting the Baeza-Tena road to Coca makes a fabulous subtropical transect with many very rare birds. More than 300 species have been found there.

The Baños area (1500-5000 m) has good forests at a wide range of elevations, though much of it can only be reached after serious hiking.

The Gualaceo-Limon road (1400-3350 m) northeast of Cuenca has perhaps the best roadside birding on the east slope, in a spectacular natural setting. It is not well studied, but already the bird list exceeds 200 species. A complete list will probably exceed 300 species.

Parque Nacional Podocarpus (950-3700 m) near Loja is one of the most diverse protected areas in the world. There are several easy access points at different elevations. The park is very rich in birds, including many rarities and some newly discovered species; there could be up to 800 species in the park!

The Loja-Zamora road (1000-2850 m): some segments of the old road (parallel to the current one) are very good for birds. A total of 375 species have been found along the new and old roads.

Cuyabeno lodges (200-300 m) in the northern Oriente are located in seasonally flooded forests not found elsewhere, and lots of wildlife. These lodges have well over 400 species of birds. **Oriente jungle**

Rio Napo area lodges (200-300 m) in the north and central Oriente provide a wide spectrum of facilities and prices, in forest ranging from moderately disturbed to absolutely pristine. Some of these lodges are among the most bird-rich single-elevation sites in the world, with lists exceeding 550 species.

Archidona / Tena / Misahuallí area lodges (300-600 m) in west-central Oriente are much easier and cheaper to reach than other sites, and the lodges are especially comfortable. The forest in this area is somewhat disturbed however, so larger birds and mammals are scarce or absent.

Pastaza area lodges (200-300 m) in the southern Oriente have a slightly different set of birds than the other areas, and a different cultural environment.

Only the inhabited islands may be visited without taking an organized and guided tour. To visit the uninhabited ones independently, you have to obtain scientific permission, which is difficult. **The Galápagos**
See also the Galápagos chapter, page 389

Essentials

Guided tours There is great pleasure in coming to grips with tropical birds on your own, but a good professional bird guide can show you many more species than you will find by yourself. The quality of guides varies greatly; if you choose to take a guided tour, make sure you get a guide who knows bird calls well, since this is the way most tropical birds are found. There are excellent professional bird tour companies in Europe and the US; in addition, there are some Ecuadorean companies which specialize in bird tours. Price is usually a good indicator of quality.

Quito birding companies include: **BirdEcuador**, contact Irene Bustamante, Carrion N21-01 entre Juan Leon Mera y Reina Victoria, T547403, F228902, birdcua@hoy.net; **Neblina Forest**, contact Mercedes Rivadeneira, Centro Comercial La Galeria, local #65, Los Shyris y Gaspar de Villaroel, T460189, cellT09-723169, USA toll-free T1-800-5382149, mrivaden@pi.pro.ec, www.neblinaforest.com; **Avestravel**, contact Robert Jonsson, Jorge Washington E7-23 entre 6 de Diciembre y Reina Victoria, T224469, cellT09-206628, avestrav@impsat.net.ec, www.angelfire.com/biz/Avestravel

Conservation issues Natural habitat is quickly being destroyed in Ecuador, and many birds are threatened with extinction. Responsible ecotourism is one way to fight this trend; by visiting the lodges listed above you are making it economically feasible for the owners to protect their land instead of farming or logging it. Another way you can help protect important Ecuadorean forest tracts is by donating to foundations that buy land for nature reserves. The **Jocotoco Foundation** specializes in buying up critical bird habitat in Ecuador; it is a small, lean foundation directed by the world's top experts on South American birds (eg Robert Ridgely, author of *Birds of South America*, and Neils Krabbe, co-author of *Birds of the High Andes*). Their work deserves support. For more information see www.jocotoco.org

Further reading For the moment, *A Guide to the Birds of Colombia,* by S Hilty and W Brown (Princeton University Press, USA, 1986) is the best field guide. Virtually all northern Ecuadorean birds are treated there. In the south, however, this guide is less useful. There *Birds of the High Andes,* by J Fjeldsa and N Krabbe (Apollo Books, Svendborg, Denmark, 1990) covers some additional species, but for full coverage we must wait for R Ridgely and P Greenfield's *Birds of Ecuador,* to be published in 2001. Much detailed site information is contained in the excellent *A Guide to Birdwatching in Ecuador and the Galápagos,* by R Williams, B Best and T Heijnen (Biosphere Publications, UK) and some information presented here comes from that book. *An Annotated List of the Birds of Mainland Ecuador,* by R Ridgley, P Greenfield and M Guerrero (CECIA, Quito, 1998) is an unillustrated but useful distributional checklist, with English and Spanish common names. An excellent book on the natural history of tropical birds is S Hilty's *Birds of Tropical America: A Watcher's Guide to Behavior, Breeding and Diversity* (Chapters Publishing, Shelburne, VT, USA). *Common birds of Amazonian Ecuador: a guide for the wide-eyed ecotourist,* by C Canaday and L Jost (Ediciones Libri-Mundi, Quito, 1997) is a nice beginner's guide with excellent illustrations. Finally John V Moore's tapes and CDs of Ecuadorean birds are highly recommended and are available in Quito at Libri Mundi (Juan Leon Mera y Pinto) or directly from John V Moore Nature Recordings, 333 West Santa Clara Street #1212, San Jose, CA 95125 USA.

Hot springs

Ecuador is located on the 'Ring of Fire' and has many volcanoes: active, dormant and non-active (dead). Hot springs are associated with all three, although they are mostly found with the older volcanoes where sufficient time has elapsed since the last eruptions for water systems to become established. There are several areas where you can look for hot springs:

1 On the coastal lowlands, pressure from the collision of the continental and oceanic plates causes friction and heat is dissipated into the water system. Many of these springs have a high mineral content and these sulphurous waters are frequently praised for their curative properties. Very few are large enough to warrant development. Temperatures range from 20°C to 30°C.

2 At the foot of the Andes, water temperatures are elevated by pressure caused by plate tectonics. South of Guayaquil there are several springs with minimal or no development, all-in temperature ranges from 40°C to 55°C. To the north of Guayaquil there are fewer springs and the temperatures are much lower.

3 In the Andes above 1,500 m most of the springs are directly associated with older volcanic action. The vast majority of Ecuadorean hot springs are found in the Andes north of Riobamba and up to Colombia. To the south of Riobamba the only major hot springs are a few kilometres south of Cuenca.

4 The few springs at the foot of the Andes in the upper Amazon are mostly associated with secondary ridges of mountains, and the heat source seems to be pressure caused by uplifting and folding. None of these has been developed and access to all is difficult.

5 In the craters of Alcedo Volcano, in the Galápagos Islands, and Guagua Pichincha, direct contact with heat sources causes rainwater to boil. In the Galápagos this produces an intermittent geyser. On Pichincha, prior to the 1999 eruptions, a small hot stream with minimal mineral content flowed down from the active crater. **NB** At the close of this edition the crater of Guagua Pichincha was dangerous and off limits to visitors due to volcanic activity.

Here is a selection of Ecuador's best springs, from north to south.

Aguas Hediondas are about 1½ hours west of Tulcán, see page 187.

Chachimbiro   is accessed from Ibarra, see page 84.

Nangulví can be reached from Otavalo, see page 175.

Oyacachi These springs have recently undergone development. There is public transport from Cayambe to Canguahua hourly; beyond there, only infrequently, but rental trucks are available. Alternatively, hire a horse or walk about 25 km. Several families in the village will provide floors to sleep on, or you can ask to sleep in one of the churches or in the school.

The hot springs at **Papallacta**, the best developed site in the country, can be visited in a day trip from Quito, as can the more modest ones at **El Tingo** and **La Merced**. For details about Papallacta, see page 152.

The hot springs of **Baños** (Tungurahua) are the best known in Ecuador. There are four separate bathing complexes here, and the town of Baños is overflowing with *residencias, pensiones,* guest houses, restaurants and activities, all of which can be full during national holidays, especially Carnival. See page 213.

Palitagua About one hour south of Baños on the flanks of Tungurahua, these springs are a couple of hours' walk up from the village of Puela. Tucked into a narrow mountain valley, surrounded by forest and below a cold waterfall, are three water sources, the two hotter ones contained in small cement tanks. **NB** At the close of this edition the Palitagua area was dangerous and off limits to visitors due to the volcanic activity of Tungurahua.

El Placer   Access to this spring takes a couple of days' trekking, but it's well worth the effort. It is located in Sangay National Park by the headwaters of the Río Palora. Access is from the village of Alao, which is in turn reached from Riobamba. The trail is clear and easy to follow. The pool has been enlarged and deepened and a new refuge built to shelter about 15 people. Take food, adequate clothing, sleeping bags, mats, etc.

There is another **Baños**, near Cuenca, which has the hottest commercial springs in the country. It is only 10 minutes by city bus from the city, see page 262.

Baños San Vicente These springs are close to Salinas and Libertad on the coast. They are famed for the curative properties of the warm mud lake which people slide into before baking themselves dry. There are also several indoor pools of different temperatures, some steam rooms and massage facilities. Take a bus running between Guayaquil and Libertad and get off about 15 km east of Santa Elena. Small trucks and cars pick up passengers at this junction. There are a couple of small hotels in the village.

Yanayacu Two hours east of Guayaquil on the road to Cuenca is the village of Cochancay. About 1 km up the hill from the village there is a small turning on the left; this is the old unpaved road to the mountains. One kilometre along the road there is another turning to the left which leads down to the Baños of Yanayacu. There are numerous small and medium-sized hot pools on a rock outcrop beside the Río Bulu Bulu. The small *residencia* here has a few rooms and food on the weekend.

Fishing

Fishing is possible in the lakes of the central Sierra, north and south of Quito, and in the rivers of the Oriente. This is more popular with locals than with tourists, but excursions can, nevertheless, be organized. The lakes near Papallacta offer trout fishing. There is also big-game fishing for bonito and marlin off Playas, Salinas and Manta.

Recommended lakes and rivers north of Quito are Lagunas del Voladero, near El Angel, and Lagunas San Marcos, Mojanda and Cojos, all in the province of Imbabura. South of Quito are Lagunas de Secas and Lagunala Mica or Micacocha, both near Pintag, and Río Chalupas, near Cotopaxi. In the Oriente is the Río Quijos (between Baeza and Lago Agrio), Río Cosanga (south of Baeza) and Laguna Pañacocha, east of Coca.

Volunteer programmes

'Voluntourism' has been growing in popularity in Ecuador, attracting many visitors - from students to retirees. It is a good way to become more intimately acquainted with the country (blemishes and all) and, at the same time, to try and lend a hand to its people. If you are seriously interested in volunteering, you should research organizations before you leave home. Try to choose a position which matches your individual skills. Think carefully about the kind of work that you would find most satisfying, and also be realistic about how much you might be able to achieve. The shorter your stay, the more limited should be your expectations in all regards.

You must speak at least basic Spanish, and preferably a good deal more, in order to work effectively in a local community setting. Also remember that you are volunteering in order to get to know and help the 'real Ecuador' and that conditions can sometimes be pretty harsh. In almost all cases you will have to pay your own airfare, and also possibly contribute toward your room and board. For information about visas see Longer stays, page 26.

There are a number of different areas where voluntary work is possible. We list a few here but South American Explorers in Quito has details of many other opportunities. **Environmental opportunities Cerro Golondrinas Cloud Forest Conservation Project** aims to conserve as much as possible of the highland cloud forest situated on the western slopes of the Andes and to introduce new agro-forestry techniques. Volunteers are required to work in the tree nursery and to assist with seed collection, planting, cutting weeds and clearing trails. Contact: Casa de Eliza, Isabel La Católica 1559 y Cristóbal Gangotena, Quito, T/F502640, funordex@pi.pro.ec, www.ordex-ec.com

Fundación Jatun Sacha has three different sites at which volunteers can work. Either at the Jatun Sacha biological reserve in the Napo area of the Ecuadorean Amazon, the Bilsa Reserve which is lowland cloud forest in the Mache hills near Quinindé or at Guandera in high altitude inter-Andean cloud forest near San Gabriel in

Carchi province. Volunteers may participate in research, education, station maintenance and agro-forestry activities. At the Amazon reserve, volunteers can assist at the new Amazon plant conservation centre. Contact: Fundación Jatun Sacha, Pasaje Eugenio de Santillán N34-248 y Maurian (PO Box 17-12-867), Quito, T432246, F453583, volunteer@jatunsacha.org, www.jatunsacha.org

Fundación Maquipicuna supports the conservation of biodiversity and sustainable use of natural resources. They need help with reforestation, trail building, environmental education and organic gardening at their reserve northwest of Quito. Contact: Bert Witteveen, Baquerizo Moreno E9-153 y Tamayo (PO Box 17-12-167), Quito, T507200, F507201, arodas@uio.satnet.net, www.maqui.org

Fundación Natura is a large Ecuadorean NGO which promotes environmental awareness and education. They require volunteers to assist at their reserve south of Quito. Pasochoa is humid Andean forest where volunteers may help with the with the reforestation programme. Contact: Fundación Natura, Av República 481 y Almagro, (PO Box 17-01-253), Quito, T503367, natura@fnatura.org.ec

The best way to learn about the rainforest is to become a guide at one of the lodges. Qualified field biologists with good interpersonal skills are always in demand, especially if they know birds well. The job can be difficult but will leave a lasting imprint on your life. Check with any of the lodges listed in the Oriente chapter, page 351. You should carefully enquire about the terms in advance.

Teaching opportunities Intercambio Selvatico (Jungle Exchange) seeks to help indigenous communities by teaching them the basics of the English language to maximize their effectiveness in the tourist industry. Volunteers do not need to be qualified teachers but must have an excellent command of the language, an outgoing spirit and a concern for the survival of Amazon cultures and ecosystems. Minimum of one month's commitment. Contact: Chris Canaday, T447463.

Working with children Centro de Hospederia La Tola/Los Ninos Migrantes provides overnight shelter for homeless children and is also an educational centre for older children, teaching them skills such as carpentry. Volunteers should be able to make a commitment of at least one month. Contact: Padre Pio Baschirotto, Valparaiso 887 y Don Bosco (PO Box 17-11-117), Quito, T581312, F223426; or South American Explorers, Quito, T/F225228.

Holidays and festivals

Festivals are an intrinsic part of Ecuador's social fabric and for many the highlight of the year. For a description of the most important festivals, see under Festivals, page 456. The dates of local festivals are given under each town. The main holidays are given below.

1 January, *New Year's Day*; **6 January**, *Reyes Magos y Día de los Inocentes*; **27 February**, *Día del Civismo*; **Lent**, *Carnival* (Monday and Tuesday before Lent); **Easter**, *Holy Thursday; Good Friday; Holy Saturday*; **1 May**: *Labour Day*; **24 May**, *Battle of Pichincha, Independence Day*; **June**, *Corpus Christi* (40 days after Easter); **10 August**, *first attempt at independence*; **9 October**, *Independence of Guayaquil*; **12 October**, *Columbus' arrival in America*; **1 November**, *All Saints' Day*; **2 November**, Finados, *All Souls' Day*; **3 November**, *Independence of Cuenca*; **6 December**: *Foundation of Quito*; **25 December**: *Christmas Day*.

Health

For anyone travelling overseas health is a key consideration. With the following advice and routine sensible precautions the visitor to Ecuador should remain as healthy as at home. Most visitors return home having experienced no problems at all apart from some travellers' diarrhoea.

The health risks, especially in the lowland tropical areas, are different from those encountered in Europe or North America. It also depends on where and how you travel. There are clear differences in risks for the business traveller, who stays in international class hotels in large cities and the backpacker trekking in remote areas, and there is huge variation in climate, vegetation and wildlife. There are no hard and fast rules to follow; you will often have to make your own judgement on the healthiness or otherwise of your surroundings.

There are English (or other foreign language) speaking doctors in Quito and Guayaquil who have particular experience in dealing with locally-occurring diseases, but don't expect facilities to international standards away from the major centres. Your embassy representative will often be able to give you the name of local reputable doctors and most of the better hotels have a doctor on standby. If you do fall ill and cannot find a recommended doctor, try the Outpatient Department of a hospital – private hospitals or *clínicas* are usually less crowded and may offer a more acceptable standard of care to foreigners.

Before travelling

Take out medical insurance. Make sure it covers all eventualities, especially evacuation to your home country by a medically equipped plane if necessary. You should have a dental check up, obtain a spare glasses prescription, a spare oral contraceptive prescription (or enough pills to last) and, if you suffer from a chronic illness (such as diabetes, high blood pressure, ear or sinus troubles, cardio-pulmonary disease or nervous disorder), arrange for a check up with your doctor, who can at the same time provide you with a letter explaining the details of your disability in English and if possible Spanish. Check the current recommendations for malaria prophylaxis (prevention). If you are on regular medication, make sure you have enough to cover the period of your travel plus two weeks spare.

Children   More preparation is probably necessary for babies and children than for an adult and perhaps a little more care should be taken when travelling to remote areas where health services are primitive. This is because children can become more rapidly ill than adults (on the other hand they often recover more quickly). Diarrhoea and vomiting are the most common problems, so take the usual precautions, but more intensively.

Breastfeeding is best and most convenient for babies, but powdered milk and formulas are widely available in Ecuador and so are baby foods in the larger cities. Papaya, bananas and avocados are all nutritious and can be cleanly prepared. The treatment of diarrhoea is the same as for adults, except that it should start earlier and be continued with more persistence. Children get dehydrated very quickly in hot countries and can become drowsy and uncooperative unless cajoled to drink water or juice plus salts.

Upper respiratory infections, such as colds, catarrh and middle ear infections, are also common and if your child suffers from these normally take some antibiotics against the possibility. Outer ear infections after swimming are also common and antibiotic eardrops will help. Wet wipes are always useful and sometimes difficult to find in Ecuador. Disposable nappies (diapers) on the other hand, can be found throughout the country, all too often improperly disposed of; please be conscientious in this regard.

Medicines   There is very little control on the sale of drugs and medicines in Ecuador. You can buy anything except drugs of addiction without a prescription. Be wary of this because pharmacists can be poorly trained and might sell you drugs that are unsuitable, dangerous or old. Many drugs and medicines are manufactured under licence from American or European companies, so the trade names may be familiar to you. This means you do not have to carry a whole chest of medicines with you, but remember that the shelf life of some items, especially vaccines and antibiotics, is markedly reduced in hot conditions.

Buy your supplies at the better outlets where there are refrigerators, even though they are more expensive, and always carefully check the expiry date of all preparations you buy. Immigration officials occasionally confiscate scheduled drugs (Lomotil is an example) if they are not accompanied by a doctor's prescription.

What to take

Self-medication may be forced on you by circumstances so the following text contains the names of drugs and medicines which you may find useful in an emergency or in out-of-the-way places. You may like to take some of the following items with you from home: **sunglasses**, ones designed for intense sunlight; **earplugs**, for sleeping on aeroplanes and in noisy hotels; **suntan cream**, a high protection factor for skin and lips; **insect repellent** preferably containing DET; **mosquito net**, if you will be travelling extensively in the costal lowlands or the Oriente jungle; lightweight, permethrin-impregnated ones are best; **motion sickness tablets**, if you suffer from this condition; for winding mountain bus rides or boat travel in Galápagos; **tampons** can be hard to find outside major cities; **condoms**; **contraceptives**; **water sterilizing tablets**; **antimalarial tablets**; **anti-infective ointment** eg Cetrimide; **dusting powder** for feet etc containing fungicide; **antacid tablets** for indigestion; **sachets of rehydration salts** if you are travelling with young children; **mild painkillers** such as Paracetamol or Aspirin; **antibiotics** for diarrhoea etc.

Vaccination & immunization

Have a check-up with your doctor if necessary and arrange your immunizations well in advance. Try a specialist travel clinic if your doctor is unfamiliar with health in Latin America

Smallpox vaccination is no longer required anywhere in the world. Neither is cholera vaccination recognized as necessary for international travel by the World Health Organization – it is not very effective either. Nevertheless, some immigration officials may rarely request proof of vaccination against cholera.

Vaccination against the following diseases are recommended:

Yellow Fever This is a live vaccination not to be given to children under nine months of age, pregnant women or persons allergic to eggs. Immunity lasts for 10 years, an International Certificate of Yellow Fever Vaccination will be given and should be kept because it is sometimes asked for. Yellow fever is not very common in Ecuador, but the vaccination is practically without side effects and almost totally protective. Yellow fever is a fatal disease and you should not visit the Oriente jungle without being vaccinated.

Typhoid A disease spread by the insanitary preparation of food. A number of new vaccines against this condition are now available; the older TAB and monovalent typhoid vaccines are being phased out. The newer, eg Typhim Vi, causes less side effects, but are more expensive. For those who do not like injections, there are now oral vaccines.

Poliomyelitis Despite its decline in the world this remains a serious disease if caught and is easy to protect against. There are live oral vaccines and in some countries injected vaccines. Whichever one you choose it is a good idea to a have booster every three to five years if visiting developing countries regularly.

Tetanus One dose should be given with a booster at six weeks and another at six months, and 10 yearly boosters thereafter are recommended. Children should already be properly protected against diphtheria, poliomyelitis and pertussis (whooping cough), measles and HIB, all of which can be more serious infections in Ecuador than at home. Measles, mumps and rubella vaccine is also given to children throughout the world, but those teenage girls who have not had rubella (german measles) should be tested and vaccinated. Hepatitis B vaccination for babies is now routine in some countries. Consult your doctor for advice on tuberculosis inoculation: the disease is still widespread in Ecuador.

Infectious Hepatitis is less of a problem for travellers than it used to be because of the development of two extremely effective vaccines against the A and B form of the disease. It remains common, however, in Ecuador. A combined hepatitis A & B vaccine is now available – one jab covers both diseases.

Other vaccinations These might be considered in the case of epidemics, eg meningitis. There is an effective vaccination against rabies which should be considered by all travellers, especially those going through remote areas or if there is a particular occupational risk, eg for zoologists or veterinarians.

Further information

Further information on health risks abroad, vaccinations etc may be available from a local travel clinic. If you wish to take specific drugs with you such as antibiotics these are best prescribed by your own doctor. Beware, however, that not all doctors can be experts on the health problems of remote countries. More detailed or more up-to-date information than local doctors can provide are available from various sources, including the following.

In the UK there are hospital departments specializing in tropical diseases in London, Liverpool, Birmingham and Glasgow, and the Malaria Reference Laboratory at the London School of Hygiene and Tropical Medicine provides free advice about malaria, T0891-600350; calls cost 60p a minute. In the USA the local Public Health Services can give such information and information is available centrally from the Centre for Disease Control (CDC) in Atlanta, T404-3324559, www.cdc.gov In Canada information is available from the McGill University Centre for Tropical Diseases, T514-9348049, www.medcor.mcgill.ca/~tropmed/td/txt

There are additional computerized databases which can be assessed for destination-specific up-to-the-minute information. In the UK there is MASTA (Medical Advisory Service to Travellers Abroad), T0906-8224100, calls cost 60p a minute. The Scottish Centre for Infection and Environmental Health has an excellent website providing information for travellers at www.fitfortravel.scot.nhs.uk Other information on medical problems overseas can be obtained from *Travellers' Health - How to stay healthy abroad*, edited by Dr Richard Dawood (OUP 1992, £7.99). General advice is also available in the UK in *Health Information for Overseas Travel* published by the Department of Health and available from HMSO and post offices and *International Travel and Health* published by WHO, Geneva. Handbooks on first aid are published by the British and American Red Cross and by St John's Ambulance in the UK.

Staying healthy

Intestinal upsets

The commonest affliction of visitors to Ecuador is probably travellers' diarrhoea. Diarrhoea and vomiting is due, most of the time, to food poisoning, usually passed on by the insanitary habits of food handlers. As a general rule the cleaner your surroundings and restaurant, the less likely you are to suffer.

Foods to avoid: uncooked, undercooked, partially cooked or reheated meat, fish, eggs, raw vegetables and salads, especially when they have been left out exposed to flies. Stick to fresh food that has been cooked from raw just before eating and make sure you peel fruit yourself. Avoid raw food, undercooked food (including eggs) and reheated food. Food that is cooked in front of you and offered hot all through is generally safe. Always wash and dry your hands before eating.

Shellfish are always a risk eaten raw (as in *ceviche*) and at certain times of the year some fish and shellfish concentrate toxins from their environment and cause various kinds of food poisoning. The local authorities notify the public not to eat these foods. Do not ignore the warning.

Heat treated milk (UHT), pasteurized or sterilized in Tetra-Brik or similar containers, is safe and available in all but the smallest villages of Ecuador as is pasteurized cheese. Standards vary for ordinary pasteurization however and the milk sold refrigerated in plastic bags cannot always be trusted. If you can, boil it before drinking. On the whole matured or processed cheeses are safer than the fresh varieties and fresh unpasteurized milk from whatever animal can be a source of food poisoning germs, tuberculosis and brucellosis. This applies equally to ice cream, yoghurt and cheese made from unpasteurized milk, so avoid these homemade products – the factory made ones are probably safer.

Tap water anywhere in Ecuador is unsafe to drink. Filtered or bottled water (with or without gas) is universally available and safe. Ice for drinks should be made from boiled water, but rarely is, so stand your glass on the ice cubes, rather than putting them in the drink. The better hotels have water purifying systems. Stream and well water, if you are in the countryside, is often contaminated by communities or livestock living surprisingly high in the mountains.

Travellers' diarrhoea

This is usually caused by eating food which has been contaminated by food poisoning germs. Drinking water is rarely the culprit. Sea water or river water is more likely to be contaminated by sewage and so swimming in such dilute effluent can also be a cause.

Infection with various organisms can give rise to travellers' diarrhoea. They may be viruses, bacteria, eg Escherichia coli (probably the most common cause worldwide), protozoal (such as amoebas and giardia), salmonella and cholera. The diarrhoea may come on suddenly or rather slowly. It may or may not be accompanied by vomiting or by severe abdominal pain and the passage of blood or mucus, when it is called dysentery.

How do you know which type you have caught and how to treat it? If you can time the onset of the diarrhoea to the minute ('acute') then it is probably due to a virus or a bacterium and/or the onset of dysentery. The treatment in addition to rehydration is Ciprofloxacin 500 mg every 12 hours; the drug is now widely available and there are many similar ones.

If the diarrhoea comes on slowly or intermittently ('sub-acute') then it is more likely to be protozoal, ie caused by an amoeba or giardia. Antibiotics such as Ciprofloxacin will have little effect. These cases are best treated by a doctor as is any outbreak of diarrhoea continuing for more than three days. Sometimes blood is passed in amoebic dysentery and for this you should certainly seek medical help. If this is not available then the best treatment is probably Tinidazole (Fasigyn), one tablet four times a day for three days. If there are severe stomach cramps, the following drugs may help but are not very useful in the management of acute diarrhoea: Loperamide (Imodium) and Diphenoxylate with Atropine (Lomotil). They should not be given to children.

Any kind of diarrhoea, whether or not accompanied by vomiting, responds well to the replacement of water and salts, taken as frequent small sips of some kind of rehydration solution. There are proprietary preparations consisting of sachets of powder which you dissolve in boiled water or you can make your own by adding half a teaspoonful of salt (3.5 g) and four tablespoonsfuls of sugar (40 g) to a litre of boiled water.

Thus the lynchpins of treatment for diarrhoea are rest, fluid and salt replacement, antibiotics such as Ciprofloxacin for the bacterial types and special diagnostic tests and medical treatment for the amoeba and giardia infections. Salmonella infections and cholera, although rare, can be devastating diseases and it would be wise to get to a hospital as soon as possible if these were suspected.

Fasting, peculiar diets and the consumption of large quantities of yoghurt have not been found useful in calming travellers' diarrhoea or in rehabilitating inflamed bowels. Oral rehydration has on the other hand, especially in children, been a life saving technique and should always be practised, whatever other treatment you use. As there is some evidence that alcohol and milk might prolong diarrhoea they should be avoided during and immediately after an attack.

Diarrhoea occurring day after day for long periods of time (chronic diarrhoea) is notoriously resistant to amateur attempts at treatment and again warrants proper diagnostic tests (most Ecuadorean towns have laboratories for stool samples). There are ways of preventing travellers' diarrhoea for short periods of time by taking antibiotics, but this is not a foolproof technique and should not be used other than in exceptional circumstances. Doxycycline is possibly the best drug. Some preventatives such as Enterovioform can have serious side effects if taken for long periods.

Paradoxically **constipation** is also common, probably induced by dietary change, inadequate fluid intake in hot places and long bus journeys. Simple laxatives are useful in the short-term and bulky foods such as maize, beans and plenty of fruit are also useful.

High altitude Spending time at high altitude in Ecuador, is usually a pleasure – it is not so hot, there are fewer insects and the air is clear and spring like. Travelling to high altitudes, however, can cause medical problems, all of which can be prevented if care is taken.

On reaching heights above about 3,000 m, heart pounding and shortness of breath, especially on exertion, are a normal response to the lack of oxygen in the air. A condition called acute mountain sickness (*soroche*) can also affect visitors. It is more likely to affect those who ascend rapidly, eg by plane and those who over-exert themselves (teenagers for example). *Soroche* takes a few hours or days to come on and presents with a bad headache, extreme tiredness, sometimes dizziness, loss of appetite and frequently nausea and vomiting. Generally, most travellers adjust to the altitude in Quito (2,800 m) quickly but often experience mild cases of altitude sickness above 4,000 m.

Insomnia is common and is often associated with a suffocating feeling when lying in bed. Keen observers may note their breathing tends to wax and wane at night and their face tends to be puffy in the mornings – this is all part of the syndrome. Anyone can get this condition and past experience is not always a good guide: the author, having spent years travelling constantly between sea level and very high altitude, never suffered symptoms, then was severely affected whilst climbing Kilimanjaro in Tanzania.

The treatment of acute mountain sickness is simple – rest, painkillers (preferably not aspirin based) for the headache and anti sickness pills for vomiting. Oxygen is actually not much help, except at very high altitude. Unlike Bolivia and Peru, coca leaves are illegal in Ecuador but *mate de coca* in tea bags can be found in a few Quito shops and will alleviate some of the symptoms.

To **prevent** the condition: on arrival at places over 3,000 m have a few hours rest in a chair and avoid alcohol, cigarettes and heavy food. If the symptoms are severe and prolonged, it is best to descend to a lower altitude and to reascend slowly or in stages. If this is impossible because of shortage of time or if you are going so high that acute mountain sickness is very likely, then the drug Acetazolamide (Diamox) can be used as a preventative and continued during the ascent. There is good evidence of the value of this drug in the prevention of *soroche*, but some people do experience peculiar side effects. The usual dose is 500 mg of the slow release preparation each night, starting the night before ascending above 3,000 m.

A more unusual condition can affect mountaineers who ascend rapidly to high altitude – **acute pulmonary oedema**. Residents at altitude sometimes experience this when returning to the mountains from time spent at the coast. This condition is often preceded by acute mountain sickness and comes on quite rapidly with severe breathlessness, noisy breathing, coughing, blueness of the lips and frothing at the mouth. Anybody who develops this must be brought down as soon as possible, given oxygen and taken to hospital.

A rapid descent from high places will make sinus problems and middle ear infections worse and might make your teeth ache. Lastly, don't fly to altitude within 24 hours of Scuba diving. You might suffer from 'the bends'.

Watch out for **sunburn** at high altitude. The ultraviolet rays are extremely powerful. The air is also excessively dry at high altitude and you might find that your skin and lips dry out and the inside of your nose becomes crusted. Use a moisturiser for the skin and lips and some vaseline wiped into the nostrils. Some people find contact lenses irritate because of the dry air.

It is unwise to ascend to high altitude if you are pregnant, especially in the first three months, or if you have a history of heart, lung or blood disease, including sickle cell.

Heat & cold

Full acclimatization to high temperatures takes about two weeks. During this period it is normal to feel a bit apathetic, especially if the relative humidity is high. Drink plenty of water (up to 15 litres a day are required when working physically hard in the tropics), use salt on your food and avoid extreme exertion. Tepid showers are more cooling than hot or cold ones. Large hats do not cool you down, but do prevent sunburn. Remember that, especially in the highlands, there can be a large and sudden drop in temperature between sun and shade and between night and day, so dress accordingly. Warm jackets or woollens are essential after dark at high altitude. Loose cotton is still the best material when the weather is hot.

Insects

These are mostly more of a nuisance than a serious hazard and if you try, you can prevent yourself entirely from being bitten. Some, such as mosquitoes, are, of course, carriers of potentially serious diseases, so it is sensible to avoid being bitten as much as possible.

Sleep off the ground and use a mosquito net or some kind of insecticide. Preparations containing Pyrethrum or synthetic pyrethroids are safe. They are available as aerosols or pumps and the best way to use these is to spray the room thoroughly in all areas (follow the instructions rather than the insects) and then shut the door for a while, re-entering when the smell has dispersed. Mosquito coils release insecticide as they burn slowly. They are widely available and useful out of doors. Tablets of insecticide which are placed on a heated mat plugged into a wall socket are probably the most effective. They fill the room with insecticidal fumes in the same way as aerosols or coils.

You can also use insect repellents, most of which are effective against a wide range of pests. The most common and effective is diethyl metatoluamide (DET). DET liquid is best for arms and face (care around eyes and with spectacles – DET dissolves plastic). Aerosol spray is good for clothes and ankles and liquid DET can be dissolved in water and used to impregnate cotton clothes and mosquito nets. Some repellents now contain DET and Permethrin, insecticide. Impregnated wrist and ankle bands can also be useful.

If you are bitten or stung, itching may be relieved by cool baths, antihistamine tablets (care with alcohol or driving) or mild corticosteroid creams, eg hydrocortisone (but take care: never use if there's any hint of infection). Careful scratching of all your bites once a day can be surprisingly effective. Calamine lotion and cream have limited effectiveness and antihistamine creams are not recommended – they can cause allergies themselves. Bites which become infected should be treated with a local antiseptic or antibiotic cream such as Cetrimide, as should any infected sores or scratches.

When living rough, skin infestations with body lice (*piojos*, crabs) and scabies (*rasca bonita*) are easy to pick up. They may be treated with topical Benzyl Benzoate (Benzoato de Bencilo) or Gamma-benzene Hexachloride (Davesol or Lindano), available in most pharmacies. Fleas (*pulgas*) are generally harmless but annoying and usually acquired in crowded buses or markets. Bedbugs (*chinches*) are occasionally a plague in very cheap hotels, and leave you incredibly itchy.

Crotamiton cream (Eurax) alleviates itching and also kills a number of skin parasites. Malathion lotion 5 (Prioderm) kills lice effectively, but avoid the use of the toxic agricultural preparation of Malathion, more often used to commit suicide.

Ticks

They attach themselves usually to the lower parts of the body often after walking in areas where cattle have grazed. They take a while to attach themselves strongly, but swell up as they start to suck blood. The important thing is to remove them gently, so that they do not leave their head parts in your skin because this can cause a nasty allergic reaction some days later. Do not use petrol, vaseline, lighted cigarettes etc to remove the tick, but with a pair of tweezers remove the beast gently by gripping it at the attached (head) end and rock it out in very much the same way that a tooth is extracted.

Certain tropical flies (generically called *el tupe* in the Oriente) which lay their eggs under the skin of sheep and cattle also occasionally do the same thing to humans, with the unpleasant result that a maggot grows under the skin and pops up as a boil or pimple. The best way to remove these is to cover the boil with oil, vaseline or nail varnish so as to stop the maggot breathing, then to squeeze it out gently the next day.

Sunburn The burning power of the tropical sun, especially at high altitude, is phenomenal. Always wear a wide brimmed hat and use some form of suncream lotion on untanned skin. Normal temperate zone suntan lotions (protection factor up to seven) are not much good; you need to use the types designed specifically for the tropics or for mountaineers or skiers with protection factors up to 15 or above. Glare from the sun can cause conjunctivitis, so wear sunglasses especially on tropical beaches, where high protection factor sunscreen should also be used.

Prickly heat This very common intensely itchy rash is avoided by frequent washing and by wearing loose clothing. It's cured by allowing skin to dry off through use of powder and spending two nights in an air-conditioned hotel!

Athletes foot This and other fungal skin infections are best treated with Tolnaftate or Clotrimazole.

Other risks and more serious diseases

Meningitis epidemics occur from time to time.

Rabies Remember that rabies is endemic in Ecuador, so avoid dogs that are behaving strangely and in Oriente and parts of the coast cover your toes at night from the vampire bats, which also carry the disease. If you are bitten by a domestic or wild animal, do not leave things to chance: scrub the wound with soap and water and/or disinfectant, try to have the animal captured (within limits) or at least determine its ownership, where possible, and seek medical assistance at once.

The course of treatment depends on whether you have already been satisfactorily vaccinated against rabies. If you have (this is worthwhile if you are spending lengths of time in developing countries) then some further doses of vaccine are all that is required. Human diploid vaccine is the best and is now available in many parts of Ecuador; other, older kinds of vaccine, such as that derived from duck embryos, may be the only types available in some small towns. These are effective, much cheaper and interchangeable generally with the human derived types. If not already vaccinated then anti rabies serum (immunoglobulin) may be required in addition. It is important to finish the course of treatment whether the animal survives or not.

AIDS AIDS (*SIDA*) in Ecuador is increasing and is not confined to the well known high risk sections of the population, ie homosexual men, intravenous drug abusers and children of infected mothers. Heterosexual transmission is now the dominant mode and so the main risk to travellers is from casual sex. The same precautions should be taken as with any sexually transmitted disease.

The Aids virus (HIV) can be passed by unsterilized needles which have been previously used to inject an HIV positive patient, but the risk of this is negligible. Sterile disposable syringes are routinely available throughout Ecuador. The risk of receiving a blood transfusion with blood infected with the HIV virus is greater than from dirty needles because of the amount of fluid exchanged. Supplies of blood for transfusion should now be screened for HIV in all reputable hospitals, so again the risk is very small indeed.

Catching the AIDS virus does not always produce an illness in itself (although it may do). The only way to be sure if you feel you have been put at risk is to have a blood test for HIV antibodies on your return to a place where there are reliable laboratory facilities. The test does not become positive for some weeks.

In Ecuador malaria exists in both the Oriente jungle and the coastal lowlands, with **Malaria** important seasonal variations in the latter region. Mosquitos do not thrive above 2,500 m, so you are safe at altitude. There are different varieties of malaria, some resistant to the normal drugs. Make local enquiries if you intend to visit possibly infected zones and use a prophylactic régime.

Start taking the tablets a few days before exposure and continue to take them for six weeks after leaving the malarial zone. Remember to give the drugs to babies and children also. Opinion varies on the precise drugs and dosage to be used for protection. All the drugs may have some side effects and it is important to balance the risk of catching the disease against the albeit rare side effects. Until recently, only the older, less efficacious drugs such as Chloroquine (Aralen) and Fansidar could be routinely purchased in Ecuador. This is currently changing and a variety of anti-malarial preparations including Mefloquine (Larium) and Proguanil (Paludrine) should soon be available, either at pharmacies or directly through physicians.

The increasing complexity of the subject is such that as the malarial parasite becomes immune to the new generation of drugs it has made concentration on the physical prevention from being bitten by mosquitos more important. This involves the use of long sleeved shirts or blouses and long trousers, repellants and nets. Clothes are now available impregnated with the insecticide Permethrin or Deltamethrin, or it is possible to impregnate the clothes yourself. Wide meshed nets impregnated with Permethrin are also available, are lighter to carry and less claustrophobic to sleep in.

Prophylaxis and treatment If your itinerary takes you into a malarial area, seek expert advice before you go on a suitable prophylactic régime. This is especially true for pregnant women who are particularly prone to catch malaria. You can still catch the disease even when sticking to a proper régime, although it is unlikely. If you do develop symptoms (high fever, shivering, headache, sometimes diarrhoea), seek medical advice immediately. If this is not possible and there is a great likelihood of malaria, the treatment is: Chloroquine, a single dose of four tablets (600 mg) followed by two tablets (300 mg) in six hours and 300 mg each day following. Falciparum type of malaria or type in doubt: take local advice. Various combinations of drugs are being used such as Quinine, Tetracycline or Halofantrine. If falciparum type of malaria is definitely diagnosed, it is wise to get to a good hospital as treatment can be complex and the illness very serious.

The main symptoms are pains in the stomach, lack of appetite, lassitude and yellowness **Infectious** of the eyes and skin. Medically speaking there are two main types. The less serious, but **hepatitis** more common is Hepatitis A for which the best protection is the careful preparation of **(jaundice)** food, the avoidance of contaminated drinking water and scrupulous attention to toilet hygiene. The other, more serious, version is Hepatitis B which is acquired usually as a sexually transmitted disease or by blood transfusions. It can less commonly be transmitted by injections with unclean needles and possibly by insect bites. The symptoms are the same as for Hepatitis A. The incubation period is much longer (up to six months compared with six weeks) and there are more likely to be complications.

A vaccination against Hepatitis A (Havrix) gives immunity lasting up to 10 years. After that boosters are required. Havrix monodose is now widely available as is Junior

Havrix. The vaccination has negligible side effects and is extremely effective; it is available in Ecuador.

Hepatitis B can be effectively prevented by a specific vaccine (Engerix) – three shots over six months before travelling. If you have had jaundice in the past it would be worthwhile having a blood test to see if you are immune to either of these two types, because this might avoid the necessity and costs of vaccination or gamma globulin. There are other kinds of viral hepatitis (C, E etc) which are fairly similar to A and B, but vaccines are not available as yet.

Typhus This can still occur and is carried by ticks. There is usually a reaction at the site of the bite and a fever. Seek medical advice.

Intestinal worms These are common and the more serious ones such as hookworm can be contracted from walking barefoot on infested earth or beaches; try to wear sandals or thongs.

Various other tropical diseases can be caught in jungle areas, usually transmitted by biting insects. They are often related to African diseases and were probably introduced by the slave labour trade. Leishmaniasis (Espundia) is carried by sandflies and causes a sore that will not heal or a severe nasal infection. Wearing long trousers and a long sleeved shirt in infected areas protects against these flies. DET is also effective. In addition to jungle areas, Leishmaniasis is present in remote areas of the coastal provinces of Manabí and Esmeraldas, away from the sea shore. Be careful about swimming in piranha or caribe infested rivers. It is a good idea not to swim naked: the Candiru fish can follow urine currents and become lodged in body orifices. Swimwear offers some protection.

Leptospirosis Leptospirosis occurs in Ecuador, transmitted by a bacterium which is excreted in rodent urine. Fresh water and moist soil harbour the organisms which enter the body through cuts and scratches. If you suffer from any form of prolonged fever consult a doctor.

Snake bites This is a very rare event indeed for travellers. If you are unlucky (or careless) enough to be bitten by a venomous snake, spider, scorpion or sea creature, try to identify the creature, but do not put yourself in further danger. Snake bites in particular are very frightening, but in fact rarely poisonous – even venomous snakes bite without injecting venom.

What you might expect if bitten are: fright, swelling, pain and bruising around the bite and soreness of the regional lymph glands, perhaps nausea, vomiting and a fever. Signs of serious poisoning would be the following symptoms: numbness and tingling of the face, muscular spasms, convulsions, shortness of breath and bleeding. Victims should be got to a hospital or a doctor without delay.

Commercial snake bite and scorpion kits are available, but usually only useful for the specific type of snake or scorpion for which they are designed. Most serum has to be given intravenously so it is not much good equipping yourself with it unless you are used to making injections into veins. It is best to rely on local practice in these cases, because the particular creatures will be known about locally and appropriate treatment can be given.

Treatment of snake bite Reassure and comfort the victim frequently. Immobilize the limb by a bandage or a splint or by getting the person to lie still. Do not slash the bite area and try to suck out the poison because this sort of heroism does more harm than good. If you know how to use a tourniquet in these circumstances, you will not need this advice. If you are not experienced do not apply a tourniquet.

Precautions Avoid walking in snake territory in bare feet or sandals – wear proper shoes or boots, preferably the knee-high rubber boots used by most Ecuadorean *campesinos*. If you encounter a snake stay put until it slithers away, and do not investigate a wounded snake. Spiders and scorpions may be found in the more basic hotels. If stung, rest and take plenty of fluids and call a doctor. The best precaution is to keep beds away from the walls and look inside your shoes and under the toilet seat every morning.

Certain tropical sea fish when trodden upon inject venom into bathers' feet. This can be exceptionally painful. Wear plastic shoes when you go bathing if such creatures are reported. The pain can be relieved by immersing the foot in extremely hot water for as long as the pain persists.

This is increasing worldwide, including Ecuador. It can be completely prevented by avoiding mosquito bites in the same way as malaria. No vaccine is available. Dengue is an unpleasant and painful disease. Symptoms are a high temperature and body pains, but at least visitors are spared the more serious forms (haemorrhagic types) which are more of a problem for local people who have been exposed to the disease more than once. There is no specific treatment for dengue – just pain killers and rest.

Dengue fever

This is a chronic disease, present in the province of Manabí and a few other parts of Ecuador. It is very rarely caught by travellers and difficult to treat. It is transmitted by the simultaneous biting and excreting of the Reduvid bug, locally known as the *chinchorro*. Somewhat resembling a small cockroach, this nocturnal bug lives in poor adobe houses with dirt floors often frequented by opossums. If you cannot avoid such accommodation, sleep off the floor with a candle lit, use a mosquito net, keep as much of your skin covered as possible, use DET repellent or a spray insecticide. If you are bitten overnight (the bites are painless) do not scratch them, but wash thoroughly with soap and water.

Chagas' disease (South American Trypanosomiasis)

When you get home

Remember to take your antimalarial tablets for six weeks after leaving the malarial area. If you have had attacks of diarrhoea it is worth having a stool specimen tested in case you have picked up amoebas. If you have been living rough, blood tests may be worthwhile to detect worms and other parasites. Report any untoward symptoms to your doctor and tell the doctor exactly where you have been and, if you know, what the likelihood of disease is to which you were exposed.

Further reading

The Cambridge Encyclopedia of Latin America and the Caribbean, Simon Collier, Thomas E Skidmore and Harold Blakemore (editors), 2nd edition 1992; *The Penguin History of Latin America*, Edwin Williamson (1992); and *The Discovery of South America*, J H Parry (1979). Anyone interested in the Spanish conquest should read the excellent *The Conquest of the Incas* (1983), by John Hemming. Other historical accounts are given in: *The Discovery of the Amazon*, edited by José Toribio Medina, translated by Bertram T Lee, edited by HC Heaton (New York: Dover, 1988); *Return of the Indian: Conquest and Revival in the Americas*, by Phillip Wearne (London: Cassell/LAB, 1996); *El poder político en el Ecuador*, by Osvaldo Hurtado (Barcelona: Ariel, 1981); and *5000 años de ocupación: Parque Nacional Machalilla*, edited by Presley Norton and Marco Vinicio García (Quito: Centro cultural Artes and Ediciones Abya-Yala, 1992), especially 'Las culturas cerámicas prehispánicas del Sur de Manabí', by Presley Norton, pages 9–40. An excellent overall guide to politics, society and culture is *Ecuador In Focus* (Latin American Bureau, 1997). Also good are *Ecuador* (Ediciones Libri Mundi); *Ecuador: Island of the Andes* by Kevin Kling and Nadia Christianson (London: Thames & Hudson, 1988); and *The Ecotourist's Guide to the Ecuadorean Amazon*, by Rolf Wesche, 1995.

General

Essentials

Other reading   More personal accounts are given in the travelogues of early gringo visitors to Ecuador. These include **Charles Darwin**'s excellent *Voyage of the Beagle* [1839] (London, 1989); *Travels Amongst the Great Andes of the Equator* [1891], by **Edward Whymper** (Gibbs M Smith, Salt Lake City, 1987); *Diario del viaje al Ecuador* [1745], by **Charles-Marie de la Condamine**, N Gómez ed (Ediguias, Quito, 1994); and two books by **Darío Lara**: *Viajeros Franceses al Ecuador en el Siglo XIX* (Casa de la Cultura Ecuatoriana, Quito, 1972) and *Gabriel Lafond de Lurcy: Viajero y testigo de la historia ecuatoriana* (Banco Central del Ecuador, Quito, 1988). Other recommended personal accounts are: *Living Poor*, by **Moritz Thomsen** (London: Eland) (also by Thomsen is *The Saddest Pleasure* and *Farm on the River of Emeralds*); *Huasipungo*, by Jorge Izaca (London 1962); *Ecuador* [1929], by **Henri Michaux** (OUP, 1952); and *The Panama Hat Trail*, by **Tom Miller** (Abacus, 1986). Recommended works of fiction based in Ecuador are *Galápagos*, by **Kurt Vonnegut** (New York/London, 1986), and *Queer*, by **William Burroughs** (1985).

The country is presented through the eyes of an orphaned Ecuadorean child in *El País de Manuelito*, by **Alfonso Barrera Valverde** (Editorial El Conejo, Quito, 1991). Its title at least has become a contemporary classic.

The Climbing, Trekking, Birdwatching, Literature and Galápagos Islands sections all contain suggestions for further reading. Also interesting is South American Explorer, published quarterly by South American Explorers (see page 22).

A very useful book, highly recommended, aimed specifically at the budget traveller, is *The Tropical Traveller*, by **John Hatt** (Penguin Books, 3rd edition, 1993). Along similar lines is *The Practical Nomad*, by **Edward Hasbrouck** (Moon Publications, Chico CA, USA, 1998).

Useful addresses

UK   *Adventure Travel Centre*, 131-135 Earls Court Rd, London SW5 9RH, T020-7244 6411, www.topdecktravel.co.uk Organizes short tours as well as longer expeditions.
Condor Journeys and Adventures, 1 Valley Rise, Mill Bank, Sowerby Bridge HX6 3EG, T01422-822068, www.condorjourneys-adventures.com
Cox & Kings Travel, Gordon House, 10 Greencoat Place, London SW1P 1PH, T020-7873 5001, F7630 6038, www.coxandkings.co.uk
Destination South America, T01285-885333, www.destinationsouthamerica.co.uk
Discover Adventure, 5 Netherhampton Cottages, Netherhampton, Salisbury, SP2 8PXUK, T01722-741123, www.discoveradventure.co.uk
Dragoman Camping/Hotel Adventures, Camp Green, Debenham, Stowmarket, Suffolk IP14 6LA, T01728-861133, F861127, www.dragoman.co.uk Overland camping and/or hotel journeys throughout South and Central America.

Encounter Overland, 267 Old Brompton Rd, London SW5 9JA, T020-7370 6845, www.encounter.co.uk

Exodus Travels, 9 Weir Rd, London SW12 0LT, T020-8772 3822, www.exodustravels. co.uk Experienced in adventure travel, including cultural tours and trekking and biking holidays.

Explore Worldwide, 1 Frederick St, Aldershot, Hants GU11 1LQ, T01252-319448, F343170, www.explore.co.uk Highly respected operator with offices in Eire, Australia,New Zealand, USA and Canada, who run two to five week tours in more than 90 countries worldwide, including Ecuador.

Galápagos Adventure Tours, 37-39 Great Guildford St, London SE1 0ES, T020-7261 9890, F7922 1138. Run by David Horwell who has an abundant knowledge of the Galápagos. Escorted tours to the islands as well as the Andes and rainforest.

Galápagos Classic Cruises, 6 Keyes Rd, London NW2 3XA, T020-8933 0613, F8452 5248. Specializes in tailor-made cruises and diving holidays. Will also organize land tours to mainland Ecuador.

Guerba Expeditions, Wessex House, 40 Station Rd, Westbury, Wilts BA13 3JN, T01373-826611, F858351, info@guerba.demon.co.uk Specializes in adventure holidays, from canoeing safaris to wilderness camping.

Hayes & Jarvis, 152 King St, London W6, T020-8748 0088. Long established operator offering tailor-made itineraries as well as packages.

High Places, Globe Works, Penistone Rd, Sheffield S6 3AE, T0114-2757500, F2753870, www.highpl.globalnet.co.uk

International Wildlife Adventures, T800-5938881, info@wildlifeadventures.com, www.wildlifeadventures,com

Journey Latin America, 12-13 Heathfield Terrace, Chiswick, London W4 4JE, T020-8747 8315, www.journeylatinamerica.co.uk The world's leading tailor-made specialist for Latin America, running escorted tours throughout the region, they also offer a wide range of flight options.

Latin American Language Services, 96 Cotteril Road, Surbiton, Surrey, KT6 7UK, F020-8241 3483, info@lals.co.uk

Last Frontiers, Fleet Marston Farm, Aylesbury, Buckinghamshire HP18 0QT, T01296-658650, F658651, www.lastfrontiers.co.uk South American specialists offering tailor-made itineraries to Ecuador including the Galápagos, as well as discounted air fares and air passes.

Naturetrek, Chautara, Bighton, Alresford, Hants SO24 9RB, T01962-733051, F736426/733368, www.naturetrek.co.uk Birdwatching tours throughout the continent; also botany, natural history tours, treks and cruises.

Nomadic Thoughts, 81 Brondesbury Rd, London NW6 6BB, T020-7604 4408, F7604 4407, www.nomadicthoughts.com. Specializes in tailor-made itineraries.

Quasar Nautica, Steeple Cottage, Easton, Winchester, Hants SO21 1EH, England, T01962-779317, F779458, pkellie@yachtors.u-net.com. Specializes in Galápagos cruises and diving holidays. Also offer standard country tours, as well as customized nature, cultural and adventure group tours.

Reef & Rainforest Tours, Prospect House, 1 The Plains, Totnes, TQ9 5DR, T01803-866965, F865916, www.reefrainforest.co.uk

South American Experience, 47 Causton St, Pimlico, London SW1P 4AT, T020-7976 5511, F7976 6908, www.southamericanexperience.com Flights, accommodation and tailor-made trips.

STA Travel, Priory House, 6 Wrights Lane, London W8 6TA, T020-7361 6100, F7938 9570, www.statravel.co.uk.

Trailfinders, 42-50 Earl's Court Rd, London W8 6FT, T020-7938 3366, www.trailfinders.com

Tucan Travel, T020-8896 1600, www. tucantravel.com Offers adventure tours and overland expeditions.

For further information on specialist travel firms, contact the **Latin American Travel Association** at PO Box 1338, Long Ashton, Bristol BS41 9YA, T01275-394484.

Elsewhere in Europe Travellers starting their journey in continental Europe may try: Uniclam-Voyages, 63 rue Monsieur-le Prince, 75006 Paris, www.uniclam.com for charters. The Swiss company, Balair (owned by Swissair) has regular charter flights to South America, www.swissair.com For cheap flights in Switzerland, Globetrotter Travel Service, Renweg, 8001 Zürich, has been recommended. Also try Nouvelles Frontières, Paris, T1-41415858, or Hajo Siewer Jet Tours, Martinstr 39, 57462 Olpe, Germany, T02761-924120. The German magazine Reisefieber is useful.

USA & Canada *eXito Latin American Travel Specialists*, 5699 Miles Avenue, Oakland, CA 94618, USA, T1800-6554053 toll free, F510-6554566, exito@wonderlink.com.

ExpeditionTrips.com, 4509 Interlake Avenue North, 179 Seattle, Washington WA

98103, T1-877-412-8527, www.ExpeditionTrips.com info@expeditiontrips.com

Galápagos Holidays, 14 Prince Arthur Av, Suite 109, Toronto ON M5R, Canada, T1800-6612512 toll free, www3.sympatico.ca/galapagos.holidays. Long established company running customized itineraries to Ecuador. Daily departures to the Galápagos Islands.

Ladatco Tours, T305-8548422, F305-2850504, www.ladatco.com. Based in Miami, run 'themed' explorer tours.

Quasar Nautica, 7855 NW 12th St, Suite 221, Miami, Florida 33126, T1305-5999008/2472925, F5927060, tumbaco@gate.net See entry under UK, above, for further details.

Wildland Adventures, 3516 NE 155 Street, Seattle, WA 98155, USA, T800-3454453, F800-3650686, www.wildland.com Specializes in cultural and natural history tours to the Galápagos, Andes and Amazon.

Southtrip, Sarmiento 347, 4th floor, of 19, Buenos Aires, Argentina, T11-43287075, **South America** www.southtrip.com

Essentials

Quito

3

Quito

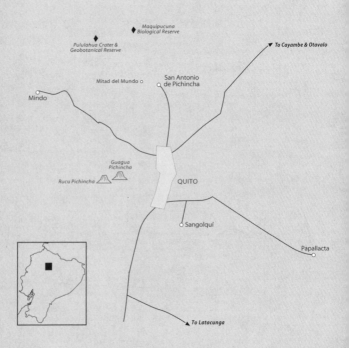

Few cities have a setting to match that of Quito, the second highest capital in Latin America after La Paz. It lies in a long narrow valley running north to south, wedged between the slopes of the volcano Pichincha (4,794 metres) to the west and a steep canyon to the east, formed by the Machángara River.

Quito is very much a city of two halves. The old city, a UNESCO World Heritage Trust site, is the colonial centre, where pastel-coloured houses and ornate churches line a warren of steep and narrow streets. The new city extends north of the colonial city and is an altogether different place. Its broad avenues are lined with fine private residences, parks, embassies and villas. Here you'll find Quito's main tourist and business area: banks, tour agencies, airlines, language schools, smart shops and restaurants, bars and cafés, and a huge variety of hotels and cheap residenciales, *in the district known as La Mariscal, and further north as far as Avenida Naciones Unidas.*

Ins and outs

Getting there

Phone code: 02
Colour map M2, grid C4
Population: 1,487,513
Altitude: 2,850m

Air Quito's airport, Mariscal Sucre, lies only about 5 km to the north of the main hotel district. The easiest way to get to your hotel is by taxi, which is recommended as safe, relatively cheap and reliable (see below). Taxis can be caught outside international arrivals. For full details of transport to and from the airport and other airport facilities, see Touching down, on page 38. For car hire companies, see page 139. For full details of flights into and out of Quito, see Getting there by air, page 32. For ground transportation see Getting around, below.

Bus The main bus station (*Terminal Terrestre*) is at Maldonado and Cumandá, south of Plaza Santo Domingo, in the Old City. Most long distance bus services start and end here, and this is really the only place to get information on bus schedules. Several companies with long-distance luxury coach services have offices and terminals in the New City. (See also under Transport on page 137). From the Terminal Terrestre to anywhere in the city, take a taxi, or the trolley bus (see Getting around below). Note that the area around the Terminal Terrestre is unsafe and you need to pay close attention to your belongings at all times, as robberies are common.

Train There is no regular passenger service. For details on tourist rides from Quito, see under Transport, page 137.

Getting around

See also Transport, page 137

Bus There are two levels of city buses, *selectivos* are red, take only sitting passengers (not always respected) and charge US$0.15. *Populares* are light blue, cost under US$0.10, can get very crowded. *Interparroquial* buses are pink, these run to the outer suburbs, including the valleys of Tumbaco and Los Chillos.

Trolley bus 'El Trole', is an integrated transport system of trolley buses, running on exclusive lanes across the city from north to south, and feeder bus lines (*alimentadores*, painted green), serving suburbs from the northern and southern terminals and from El Recreo station. The Trole has 2 routes running mainly along Av 10 de Agosto (see map on page 102); one running north to south and the other south to north. The northern station is north of 'La Y', the junction of 10 de Agosto, Av América and Av de la Prensa; at El Recreo, on Av Maldonado is an important transfer station and the southern terminus is in Ciudadela Quitumbe in the far south of the city. The main bus terminal is served on both the northern and southern routes by the Cumandá stop, at Maldonado y 24 de Mayo. In the north, a feeder line marked 'Aeropuerto' goes near the airport. Some trolleys run the full length of the line, while others run only a section, the destination is marked in front of the vehicle. There is a special entrance for wheelchairs. The trolley bus is not designed for heavy luggage and can be very crowded at peak hours. **NB** Beware of pickpockets. ■ *0530-2400 Mon-Fri and 0530-2200 at weekends. The fare is US$0.15.*

Taxi Taxis are a safe, cheap and efficient way to get around the city. From the airport to the New Town costs US$2, to the old city US$3; from the Terminal Terrestre to the new town is US$2; and journeys around the new city cost from US$1. Expect to pay around 50-100% more at night. There is no increase for extra passengers. At night it is safer to use a radio taxi, there are several companies including: Taxi Amigo, T222222/333333, City Taxi, T633333 and Central de Radio Taxis, T500600. To hire a taxi by the hour costs from US$5.

Orientation & safety

Quito is a long, narrow city, stretching from north to south for over 35 km, and east to west only between 3 and 5 km. The best way to get oriented is to look for Pichincha, the mountain which lies to the west of the city.

Flying into Quito at night

Quito airport is normally open from 0400 to 0000 and most flights from North America arrive between 2100 and midnight. If a flight to Quito is delayed much after midnight, then it is usually diverted to land in Guayaquil. Most Quito airport services are closed at night and it is difficult to make a phone call. There is nowhere to wait until dawn and it can get quite cold outside.

There is only one hotel right by Quito airport, across the street from domestic arrivals. It is mediocre and overpriced however, and you are much better off selecting a couple of hotels near one another in the new town, and taking a taxi to check them out. There is no bus service after about 2000 and walking is out of the question.

Try to team up with at least one other traveller and ask one of the many taxis to take you to your hotel of first choice. One person can remain with the luggage in the cab while the other checks out the hotel; if it is unsuitable or there is no vacancy, have the cab take you to the next place on your list. If you are in a group of six or more the Trans-Rabbit van service from the airport can be a good deal.

In the words of an old saying, 'All dogs look black at night'. Remember that it is always intimidating to arrive in an unfamiliar place after dark. Spend a bit more for safe and comfortable accommodation for your first night in Quito. After a good sleep, you will quickly get your bearings the next morning.

The areas of most interest to visitors are the colonial city, with its many churches, historical monuments, museums and some hotels, best accessed by trolley; la Mariscal or Mariscal Sucre district, which extends east from Av 10 de Agosto to Av 12 de Octubre, and north from Av Patria to Av Orellana, where you find many more hotels, restaurants, bars, discos, travel agencies and some banks; and the environs of Parque La Carolina, north of La Mariscal as far as Av Naciones Unidas and between Av 10 de Agosto and Av Eloy Alfaro to the east, where the newer hotels, restaurants, main banking district, airline offices and a number of shopping malls are located. Efforts are being made to revitalize the old city.

Street numbers In 1998, the city introduced a new street numbering system. The north-south axis is C Rocafuerte. All streets north of this street are lettered N and numbered in sequence, and likewise streets running south, which are lettered S. The east-west axis is Av 10 de Agosto, C Guayaquil and C Maldonado; streets running east are lettered E and numbered in sequence, and those running west are lettered Oe (*oeste*). Street numbers are followed by a dash, then the individual building number, indicating the distance in metres from the corner – eg E5-127, or N12-43. This system was partly implemented in the north, but ran into major difficulties in the old city as streets are not perpendicular. Renumbering then stopped. At the time of writing, both numbering systems are in operation, creating some confusion. The addresses listed below use both systems.

Public safety Theft and violent crime are serious problems, despite some innovative efforts by the police and neighbourhood associations. It is hoped that mounted and bicycle police patrols, the tourist police and new police stations will all have a positive effect. For the time being however, both the new and old cities are dangerous at night and pickpockets are active at all hours. Take the necessary precautions, watch your belongings at all times, avoid crowds and use taxis at night. Be careful on crowded buses and on the *Trole*. Even more caution is required around the Terminal Terrestre and La Marín. Do not walk through city parks in the evening or even in daylight at quiet times. This includes Parque La Carolina, where joggers are advised to stay on the periphery. The parks are quite safe and pleasant however when frequented by locals,

Quito orientation

Quito

To Mitad del Mundo

National & International Terminals

Av Gato Plaza Lasso

Av Amazonas

Av De La Prensa

Av Occidental

Av El Inca

Av De Las Palmeras

Av Eloy Alfaro

Plaza de Toros

Terminal Norte

Av 10 de Agosto

Av Amazonas

Av De Los Shyris

Av Gaspar de Villarroel

Av América

La Y

Quincentro Shopping Centre

Estadio Atahualpa

Av 6 De Diciembre

Av Rep del Salvador

Av Eloy Alfaro

Av De Los Granados

Plaza de las Américas

CCI Shopping Centre

Av Naciones Unidas

Estadio

Parque La Carolina

La Carolina

El Florón

Av De La República

Av Eloy Alfaro

Fundación Guayasamín

Av Mariana de Jesús

Hospital Metropolitano

Mariana de Jesús

El Jardín Shopping Centre

Av Occidental

Cuero y Caicedo

Av América

Av 10 de Agosto

Colón

Av Colón

D

Av 6 de Diciembre

Av Coruña

Av Federico González Suárez

GUAPULO

Santa Clara

E

Av 12 de Octubre

Av 10 de Agosto

Av Amazonas

Mariscal

C

Parque El Ejido

El Ejido

La Alameda

Parque Alameda

B

Banco Central (North-South)

San Blas (South-North)

Teatro Sucre (North-South)

Av Pichincha

Av Libertador Simón Bolívar

To San Rafael & Sangolquí

Marín (South-North)

Plaza San Francisco

Plaza de la Independencia

Plaza Grande (North-South)

Santo Domingo

Terminal Terrestre

Cumandá

Av Cumandá

Terminal Terrestre

A

Related maps
A *Old Town, page 106*
B *South from El Ejido,
page 113*
C *El Ejido north to Colón,
page 114*
D *North from Colón,
page 116*
E *Northeast from
Mariscal Sucre, page 117*

Av Bahía de Caráquez

Panecillo

To Pan-American Highway South

N

0 km 1
0 miles

24 hours in Quito

If you only do one thing in Quito then make sure it's a tour of the Old Town. Here you can wander up and down a maze of steep cobbled streets jam-packed with indigenous street vendors as you admire the stunning colonial architecture.

Start in Plaza de la Independencia, the heart of the old colonial part of the city, and from there proceed to Plaza de San Francisco, dominated by its impressive church and monastery. Then head down to Plaza de Santo Domingo, where there's another fine colonial church to see.

For a wonderful view of the city and encircling volcanoes and mountains, take a taxi up to the top of Cerro Panecillo, which is instantly recognizable by the statue of the Virgen de Quito.

By now you'll no doubt be feeling peckish so catch the 'Trole' from near the bus station to the New Town for lunch. The ever-popular Super Papa, or Grain de Café are both good choices and great value.

After lunch, you might want to indulge in a little culture, so get yourself down to the Casa de la Cultura in Parque El Ejido , where you can bone up on Modern Art, indigenous costumes, musical instruments and archaeology, as well as many temporary exhibits.

Continuing with the culture theme, take a break for coffee and postcard writing in the ever-so-tasteful Café Cultura, before catching up on your emails in one of the city's myriad cybercafés.

Following dinner in the excellent Magic Bean, it's time to sample Quito's nightlife. Turtle's Head Bar and Ghoz are perennial gringo faves, but if you want to experience a night of hot and sweaty salsa, get on down to Seseribó, where you can wiggle your hips with the best of them.

Quito

such as on weekends. The Mariscal tourist hotel and nighlife district has also had its share of problems, be particularly careful between Reina Victoria and 6 de Diciembre, Foch and Pinto; this applies to male as well as female travellers, attacks by transvestites have been reported. Also beware of young children selling flowers, groups of them occasionally swarm tourists and find a way to their belongings. The Policía de Turismo has its headquarters at Reina Victoria y Roca, T543983.

Visiting the **Panecillo** has long been considered a risky business, but neighbourhood brigades are patrolling the area and improving public safety; they charge visitors US$0.20 per person, to finance their safety operation. However, taking a taxi up is a lot safer than walking. Do not carry valuables and seek local advice before going.

Pichincha volcano Guagua Pichincha is an active volcano, its crater is located 14 km west of Quito. Eruptions during 1999 made for some spectacular viewing but caused only minor inconvenience to the city, in the form of light ash fall. At the close of this edition there had been little or no activity for many months and most Quiteños had become totally blasé about their volcanic neighbour. More than Quito itself, the zones of significant risk are situated on the western and northwestern flanks of Pichincha, and include the area around the popular tourist destination of Mindo. If volcanic activity should resume, then visitors are advised to enquire locally before visiting these areas.

Quito is within 25 km of the equator, but it stands high enough to make its climate **Climate** much like that of spring in England; the days pleasantly warm and the nights cool. Because of the height, visitors may initially feel some discomfort and should slow their pace for the first day or so. The mean temperature is 13°C; rainfall, 1,473 mm. The rainy season is from October to May with the heaviest rainfall in April, though heavy storms in July are not unknown. Rain usually falls in the afternoon. The day length (sunrise to sunset) is almost constant throughout the year. Quito suffers from air and noise pollution, principally due to traffic congestion. These are worst at rush hours and especially severe during the Christmas shopping season.

Tourist information The Cámara Provincial de Turismo de Pichincha (CAPTUR) has information offices at the airport, in the new city in Parque Gabriela Mistral at Cordero y Reina Victoria, T551566, and in the old city at Venezuela y Chile, T954044. It is helpful and friendly, some staff speak English. Their administrative offices are located at 6 de Diciembre 1424 y Carrión, T224074, F507682. The **Ministerio de Turismo** is located at Eloy Alfaro 1214 y Carlos Tobar (between República and Shyris), T500719/507555, F507564, mtur1@ec-gov.net Information counter downstairs.

History

Quito gets its name from the **Quitus**, a tribe which inhabited this region in pre-Inca times. By the beginning of the 16th century, the northern highlands of Ecuador were conquered by the Incas and Quito became the capital of the northern half of the empire under the rule of Huayna Capac and later his son Atahualpa. As the Spanish conquest approached this region, **Rumiñahui**, Atahualpa's general, razed the city, to prevent it from falling into the invaders' hands.

The colonial city of Quito was founded by Sebastián de Benalcázar, Pizarro's lieutenant, on December 6, 1534. It was built at the foot of Panecillo on the ruins of the ancient city, using the rubble as construction material and today you can still find examples of Inca stonework in the façades and floors of some colonial buildings such as the Cathedral and the church of San Francisco. Following the conquest, Quito became the seat of government of the **Real Audencia de Quito**, the crown colony, which governed current day Ecuador as well as parts of southern Colombia and northern Peru.

The city changed gradually over time. The Government Palace, for example, was built in the 17th century as the seat of government of the Real Audiencia, yet changes were introduced at the end of the colonial period and the begining of the republican period in the 19th century.

The 20th century saw the expansion of the city both to the north and south, first with the development of residential neighbourhoods and later with a transfer of the commercial and banking heart of the city north of the colonial centre. In the 1980s and 1990s the number of high-rise buildings increased, the suburban valleys of **Los Chillos** and **Tumbaco** to the east of town were incorporated into a new **Distrito Metropolitano**, and a number of new poor neighbourhoods sprawled in the far north and south. The city continues to grow, and at the start of the millennium Quito stretched over 35 km from north to south.

Sights

Old Town

The **Red Centro Histórico** offers guided tours along five different circuits in the colonial city. These include visits with English speaking guides, who are part of the Metropolitan Police Force, to museums, plazas, churches, convents and historical buildings. A good way to see some of the less known sights.
■ *Mon-Fri 0900-1800, Sat-Sun 0800-1600. US$4-6, depending on route, includes museum entrance fees. At Plaza de la Independencia, Chile y García Moreno, ground floor of the Palacio Arzobispal.*

Plaza de la Independencia The heart of the colonial city is Plaza de la Independencia or Plaza Grande, dominated by the **Cathedral**, built 1550-1562, with grey stone porticos and green tile cupolas. The portal and tower were only completed in the 20th century. On its outer walls are plaques listing the names of the founding fathers of

Quito. Inside is the tomb of the independence hero, General Antonio José de Sucre, in a small chapel tucked away in a corner, and a famous Descent from the Cross by the Indian painter Caspicara. There are many other 17th and 18th century paintings and some fine examples of the works of the Quito School of Art (see Painting and sculpture, page 461). The interior decoration, especially the roof, shows Moorish influence. ■ *Mon-Sat 0600-1000.*

Beside the Cathedral, around the corner, is **El Sagrario**, originally built in the 17th century as the Cathedral's main chapel and is very beautiful. It has some impressive baroque columns, its inner doors are gold plated and built in the Churrigueresque style. ■ *Mon-Sat 1900-2000, Sun 0800-1300.*

Facing the Cathedral is the **Palacio Arzobispal**, the Archbishop's palace. The Red Centro Histórico offers guided tours of the Old Town from here; for details see above. Part of the building now houses shops. Next to it, in the northwest corner, is the former **Hotel Majestic**, with an eclectic façade, including baroque columns. Built in 1930, it was the first building in the old city with more than two stories; today it houses municipal administrative offices. On the east side of the Plaza is the new concrete **Municipio** which fits in surprisingly well.

The low colonial **Palacio de Gobierno**, silhouetted against the flank of Pichincha, is on the west side of the Plaza. It was built in the 17th century and remodelled in neoclassical style by Carondelet, president of the Crown Colony and later by Flores, first president of the Republic. On the first floor is a gigantic mosaic mural of Orellana navigating the Amazon. The ironwork of the balconies looking over the Plaza are from the Tuilleries in Paris and were sold by the French government shortly after the French Revolution. ■ *Visits with special permit only, Tue and Thu, 0930-1230. A written request must be presented several days in advance at the gate.*

Calle Morales, the main street of La Ronda district, is one of the oldest streets in the city, worth seeing for its narrow cobbled way and wrought iron balconies. It is better known as **Calle La Ronda** and is now part of a red light district, beware of pickpockets. The area should be avoided after dark.

From Plaza de la Independencia two main streets, Calle Venezuela and García Moreno, lead south towards the Panecillo (see below) to the wide Avenida 24 de Mayo, at the top of which is a new concrete building where street vendors are supposed to do their trading since the street markets were officially abolished in 1981. Street trading still takes place, however, and there are daily street markets from Sucre down to 24 de Mayo and from San Francisco church west up past Cuenca.

Plaza de San Francisco (or Bolívar) is west of Plaza de la Independencia. On the northwest side of this plaza is the great church and monastery of the patron saint of Quito, **San Francisco** (see below).

Plaza de Santo Domingo (or Sucre), to the southeast of Plaza San Francisco, has the church and monastery of **Santo Domingo**, with its rich wood carvings and a remarkable Chapel of the Rosary to the right of the main altar. In the centre of the plaza is a statue to Sucre, pointing to the slopes of Pichincha where he won his battle against the Royalists. On the south side of the plaza is the **Arco de la Capilla del Rosario**, one of the city's colonial arches. Going through it you enter **La Mama Cuchara** (the 'great big spoon'), a dead-end street which conserves its colonial flavour.

Quito

Cerro Panecillo Cerro Panecillo (little breadloaf) lies to the south of the Plaza de San Francisco. From its top, 183 metres above the city level, there is a fine view of the city below and the encircling cones of volcanoes and other mountains. Gazing benignly over the Old City from the top of the Cerro Panecillo is the impressive statue of the Virgen de Quito, a replica of the painting by Legarda found in the San Francisco Church. Mass is held in the base on Sunday. There is a good view from the observation platform up the statue. ■ *Daily 1030-1730. Access US$0.20. Entry to the interior of the monument is US$1.*

Quito Old Town

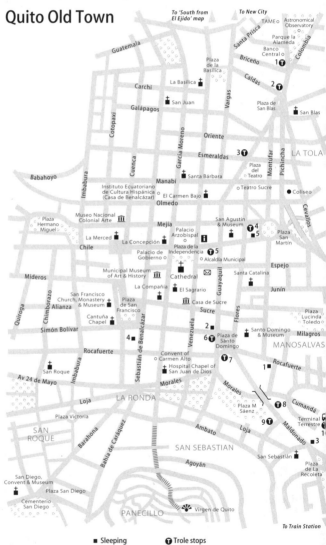

Related maps
Quito Orientation,
page 102
South from El Ejido,
page 113

0 metres 100
0 yards 100

■ Sleeping
1 Grand Hotel
2 Real Audencia
3 Reino de Quito
4 Residencial Sucre
5 Viena International

🚊 Trole stops
1 Banco Central
2 San Blas
3 Teatro Sucre
4 Marín
5 Plaza Grande
6 Santo Domingo (south-north)
7 Santo Domingo (north-south)
8 Cumandá (south-north)
9 Cumandá (north-south)
10 Terminal Terrestre

NB It is not safe to walk up the Panecillo by the series of steps and paths which begin on García Moreno (where it meets Ambato). See Public safety above. You should take a taxi up and down, which costs US$3, including time at the top to admire the spectacular view.

Outside of the old town

Between the old and new towns is Parque la Alameda at the northern end of the old city, which has the oldest astronomical observatory in South America. ■ *Sat 0900-1200*. There is also an impressive monument to Simón Bolívar, various lakes, and in the northwest corner is *el churo*, a spiral lookout tower with a good view.

In El Ejido, on the south side of Av Patria in the new city, there are exhibitions of paintings on the weekend,when the park fills with local families, as does **La Carolina** park, north of Eloy Alfaro and between Amazonas and Los Shyris. You can also enjoy aerobics, boating and horseriding in Carolina on Sunday (but see Orientation and safety on page 100). The **Parque Metropolitano**, behind Estadio Atahualpa, is reputed to be the largest urban park in South America and is good for walking, running or biking through the forest. There are some picnic areas with grills. On Sunday at 0800 there are birdwatching tours, call CECIA (T464-359) for further information. Take a bus along 6 de Diciembre to the stadium and walk 30 minutes uphill or a bus along Eloy Alfaro to Plaza Costa Rica from where it is a 20 minute walk to the park.

The beautiful district of Guápulo is perched on the edge of a ravine on the eastern fringe of the city, overlooking the Río Machángara. It is popular with Quito's bohemian community and a worthwhile place to visit. To get there, take bus 21 (Guápulo-Dos Puentes) from Mejía y Venezuela, or walk down the steep stairway which leads off Av González Suárez, near the *Hotel Quito*. One of the main points of interest is the **Iglesia de Guápulo**, It is well worth seeing for its many paintings, gilded altars, stone carvings of indigenous animals and, above all, the marvellously carved pulpit, one of the loveliest in the whole continent. This 17th-century church, built by Indian slaves and dedicated to Our Lady of Guápulo, was the founding spot for the famous Quito School of Art.

Parque la Alameda

El Ejido, La Carolina & Parque Metropolitano

Guápulo

Quito

Churches

NB Beware of unofficial guides who offer to show you the churches in order to practise their English and later ask for money.

The fine Jesuit church of **La Compañía**, on Calle García Moreno, one block south of Plaza de la Independencia, has the most ornate and richly sculptured façade and interior. Several of its most precious treasures, including a painting of the Virgen Dolorosa framed in emeralds and gold, are kept in the vaults of the Banco Central del Ecuador and appear only at special festivals. In January 1996, during restoration work, the interior was badly damaged by fire. It was closed to the public in late 2000 due to restoration work.

La Merced, not far away to the north, was built at the beginning of the 17th century, in baroque and moorish style, to commemorate Pichincha's eruptions which threatened to destroy the city. General Sucre and his troops prayed here for the wellbeing of the nation, following the decisive battle which gave Ecuador its independence in 1822. In the adjacent monastery of La Merced is Quito's oldest clock, built in 1817 in London. Fine cloisters are entered through a door to the left of the altar. La Merced church contains many

There are 86 churches in Quito; if you don't have much time, make sure you visit San Francisco and Santo Domingo

splendidly elaborate styles, the main altar has wood carvings by Legarda; note the statue of Neptune on the main patio fountain. ■ *Mon-Sat 0600-1200 and 1230-1800.*

The **Basílica**, on Plaza de la Basílica (Calle Venezuela), is very large, has many gargoyles, stained glass windows and fine, bas-relief bronze doors. Its construction started in 1926 and took 72 years; some final details still remain unfinished due to lack of funding. It is possible to go up to the tower, where there is also a cafeteria. The views of the city are magnificent. Recommended. ■ *Daily 0930-1730, US$1.40.*

San Francisco, Quito's largest church, is said to be the first religious building constructed in South America by the Spanish, in 1553. The two towers were felled by an earthquake in 1868 and rebuilt. A modest statue of the founder, Fray Jodoco Ricke, the Flemish Franciscan who sowed the first wheat in Ecuador, stands at the foot of the stairs to the church portal. Worth seeing are the fine wood carvings in the choir, a magnificent high altar of gold and an exquisite carved ceiling. The church is rich in art treasures, the best known of which is *La Virgen de Quito* by Legarda, which depicts the Virgin Mary with silver wings. The statue atop the Cerro Panecillo is based on this painting. There are also some paintings in the aisles by Miguel de Santiago, the colonial *mestizo* painter. His paintings of the life of Saint Francis decorate the monastery of San Francisco close by, where the collection of painting and sculpture by artists of the Quito School of Art was renovated in 1994. (See museums below) ■ *Mon-Sat 0900-1200 and 1500-1700, Sun 0900-1200.* Adjoining San Francisco is the **Cantuña Chapel** which has impressive sculptures. ■ *0800-1200.*

Many of the heroes of Ecuador's struggle for independence are buried in the monastery of **San Agustín** on Flores y Mejía. The church has beautiful cloisters on three sides where the first act of independence from Spain was signed on 10 August 1809, it is now a national shrine. The church was extensively renovated due to earthquake damage, the wood carved columns and gilded altars are among the few remains of the original 16th-century construction. The monastery was once the home of the Universidad de San Fulgencio, Quito's first university, founded in the 16th century, it has a large collection of paintings by Miguel de Santiago and an attractive fountain made from a single block of stone. ■ *Mon-Sat 0900-1200 and 1300-1800.*

In the restored monastery of **San Diego** (by the cemetery of the same name, just west of the Panecillo) are some unique paintings with figures dressed in fabrics sewn to the canvas – a curious instance of present-day collage. ■ *Tue-Sun 0930-1230, 1430-1730; US$0.75. Ring the bell to the right of the church door to get in; all visitors are shown around by a guide.*

Other churches of note are: **La Concepción**, at Mejía y García Moreno and **San Blas**, at Guayaquil y 10 de Agosto.

Museums

Quito prides itself on its art and the city's galleries, churches and museums boast many fine examples. Check museum opening times in advance.

Casa de la Cultura
The place to go if you only have time for one museum

Opposite **Parque El Ejido**, at the junction of 6 de Diciembre and Avenida Patria, there is a large cultural and museum complex housing the **Casa de la Cultura** and the museum of the Banco Central del Ecuador (entrance on Patria).

In addition to the many temporary exhibits, the following permanent collections are presented in museums belonging to the Casa de la Cultura: **Museo**

de Arte Moderno, paintings and sculpture since 1830; **Museo de Traje Indígena**, a collection of traditional dress and adornments of indigenous groups; **Museo de Instrumentos Musicales**, an impressive collection of musical instruments, said to be the second in importance in the world. ■ *All three open Tue-Fri 1000-1700, Sat 1000-1400, US$1, T223392.*

If you have time to visit only one museum in Quito, it should be the **Museo Nacional del Banco Central del Ecuador**, also housed in the Casa de la Cultura. It has three floors, with five different sections. The **Sala de Arqueología** is particularly impressive. It consists of a series of halls with exhibits and illustrated panels with explanations in English as well as Spanish. It covers successive cultures from 4000 BC to 1534 AD with excellent diagrams and extensive collections of beautiful precolumbian ceramics. The **Sala de Oro** has a good collection of pre-hispanic gold objects. The remaining three sections house art collections. The **Sala de Arte Colonial** is rich in paintings and sculptures especially of religious themes. The **Sala de Arte Republicano** houses works of the early years of the Republic. The **Sala de Arte Contemporáneo** presents contemporary art. There are also temporary exhibits, videos on Ecuadorean culture, the various indigenous groups and other topics, a bookshop and cafeteria, which serves good coffee. For guided tours in English, French or German call ahead and make an appointment. Highly recommended. ■ *Tue-Fri 0900-1700, Sat-Sun 0900-1500, US$2, US$1 for students with ISIC or national student card, T223259.*

Museo Nacional de Arte Colonial features a small collection of Ecuadorean sculpture and painting, housed in the 17th-century mansion of Marqués de Villacís, which also has an attractive patio and fountain. ■ *Tue-Fri 1000-1800, Sat 1000-1500 and Sun 1000-1400, US$0.50, Cuenca y Mejía, T282297.*

In the colonial city

Housed in the restored 16th-century Hospital San Juan de Dios is the **Museo de la Ciudad**. It takes you through Quito's history from pre-hispanic times to the 19th century. ■ *Tue-Sun 0930-1730, US$4, students US$2, guide service extra, Rocafuerte 572 y García Moreno, T283882.*

Museo del Convento de San Francisco has a fine collection of religious art which was restored between 1991 and 2000; there are pieces by many reknowned local and European artists. The architecture of the convent is also of interest. ■ *Mon-Sat 0900-1800, Sun 0900-1200, US$1, Plaza de San Francisco, T281124.*

Museo de San Agustín has an interesting exhibition of religious restoration work. ■ *Mon-Sat 0830-1200 and Mon-Fri 1500-1800, US$0.25, Chile y Guayaquil.* There is a similar collection in the **Museo Dominicano Fray Pedro Bedón** on Plaza Santo Domingo.

An impressive colonial building which belonged to the Jesuits, later housing the royal Cuartel Real de Lima and most recently the municipal library, was restored and reopened in September 2000 as the **Centro Cultural Metropolitano**. By 2001 it is due to house several museums and temporary exhibits. The first operating is the restored **Museo de Cera** depicting the execution of the revolutionaries of 1809. The museum, housed in the original cell, is well worth a visit, but is not for the claustrophobic. ■ *Tue-Sat 0900-1700, Sun 0900-1300, free, Espejo y García Moreno near Plaza de la Independencia.*

Museo Histórico Casa de Sucre is the beautiful, restored house of Sucre, with a museum. ■ *Tue-Fri 0830-1600, Sat-Sun 0830-1300, US$1, Venezuela 573 y Sucre, T952860.*

The house of Benalcázar is a colonial house with a courtyard and some religious statues on public view. ■ *0900-1300, 1400-1600, Olmedo y Benalcázar.*

The house of Camilo Egas, a contemporary Ecuadorean artist, is on Venezuela and has been restored by the Banco Central. It has different exhibitions during the year. ■ *Mon-Fri 1000-1300, US$0.75.*

In the new city The **Museo Jijón y Caamaño**, housed in the library building of the Universidad Católica at 12 de Octubre y Patria, has a private collection of archaeological objects, historical documents, portraits, uniforms and so on, which are very well displayed. ■ *Mon-Fri 0900-1600. US$0.40.* There is also a museum of jungle archaeology at the university. ■ *0830-1200.*

There is a fine museum in Bellavista in the northeast of Quito, **Museo Guayasamín**. As well as the eponymous artist's works there is a precolumbian and colonial collection, which is highly recommended. You can buy works of art and jewellery. Ask to see the whole collection as only a small portion is displayed in the shop. ■ *Mon-Fri 0900-1230 and 1500-1830, Sat 0900-1230, US$1.50, Bosmediano 543, Bellavista, near the Channel 8 TV station, T446455, F446277; easiest to take a taxi here, or try the Batán-Colmena bus, marked Bellavista.*

The **Museum of Ethnology**, is at Departamento de Letras, Ciudad Universitaria. ■ *Tue-Fri 0900-1230, Wed and Fri 1500-1700, Tue and Thu 1500-1830, at Universidad Central.*

The **Abya-Yala** cultural centre runs a small interesting museum of Amazon cultures. ■ *12 de Octubre 1430 y Wilson, T562633.*

Museo de Artesanía has a good collection of Indian costumes and crafts, with helpful guides and a shop. ■ *Mon-Fri 0800-1600, 12 de Octubre 1738 y Madrid.*

Museo-Biblioteca Aureliano Pólit is in the former Jesuit seminary beyond the airport. It has a unique collection of antique maps of Ecuador. ■ *Mon-Fri 0900-1200, 1500-1700, José Nogales y F Arcos, Cotocollao, take a Condado bus from Plaza San Martín in Avenida Pichincha.*

Museo de Ciencias Naturales is at Rumipamba 341 y Los Shyris, at the east end of Parque La Carolina. ■ *Mon-Fri 0830-1630, Sat 0900-1300. US$2, students, US$1.*

Museo del Colegio Mejía has natural science and ethnographic exhibits. ■ *Mon-Fri 0700-1300, 1530-2000, Ante y Venezuela.*

Vivarium, run by Fundación Herpetológica Gustavo Orces, is an organization whose aims are to protect endangered species through a programme of education. They have an impressive number of South American and other snakes, reptiles and amphibians, and run a successful breeding programme. You can take good photos of the boa constrictors. Staff are very friendly and there are good explanations (in Spanish, though information is available on request in English, French and German). ■ *Mon-Sat 0900-1300 and 1430-1600, Sun 1100-1800, US$1 (children half price), Reina Victoria 1576 y Santa María, T230988, F448425, touzet@orstom.ecx.ec*

In a similar vein is **Museo Amazónico**, which has interesting displays of Amazonian flora and fauna and tribal culture, and shows the effects of oil exploration and drilling. There is also an extensive bookstore, with books mostly in Spanish. ■ *Mon-Fri 0830-1230, 1430-1830, Sat 0900-1200, US$0.40, Centro Cultural Abya Yala, 12 de Octubre 1430 y Wilson, T506247/562633.*

Out of town **Cima de la Libertad** is a museum at the site of the 1822 Battle of Pichincha, with a great view. ■ *0900-1200 and 1500-1800, US$1.25.* The Tourist Office recommends taking a taxi there as the suburbs are dangerous. A good idea is to take the trole south to El Recreo and a taxi from there.

For museums at Mitad del Mundo, see Excursions from Quito below

Art galleries

Fundación Guayasamín, in Bellavista, see Museums above. **Posada de las Artes Kingman**, Almagro 1550 y Pradera, T526335. **Galería Pomaire**, Amazonas 863 y Veintimilla, T540074. **La Galería**, Juan Rodríguez 168 y Almagro, T225807. **Viteri**, Orellana 473 y Whimper, T561548.

Essentials

Sleeping

Finding good value accommodation is not a problem in Quito. There is a wide selection from which to choose in all price ranges. The vast majority of top-class hotels and also the more popular budget places are all in the new city. Note that in some hotels there is a different price structure for Ecuadoreans and sometimes even for citizens of other Latin American countries. Note that there can be water shortages in August in the cheaper hotels in the old town. Those travelling by car may have difficulty parking in the centre of Quito and are therefore advised to choose the less central hotels. Likewise, those who are sensitive to air and noise pollution should choose their lodgings accordingly, away from the city's main traffic arteries.

Sleeping
■ *on maps, pages 106, 113, 114, 116 & 117*
Price codes: see inside front cover

LL *Hilton Colón*, Amazonas y Patria, T560666, F563903, reserv@hiltoncolon.com Excellent Italian restaurant (1200-1530 and 1700-2230) and cafeteria (24 hrs), international newspapers, business centre, arcade with quality shops, casino. **LL** *Marriott*, Av Orellana 1172 y Amazonas, T972000, marriott@andinanet.net www.marriotthotels. com Breakfast included for executive rooms and suites, buffet restaurant with international and Ecuadorean food, Mediterranean restaurant, spa, pool, business centre. The most modern and grandiose of the luxury hotels. **LL** *Swissôtel*, 12 de Octubre 1820 y Cordero, T566497, F569189, ecswq@uio. satnet.net. Superb 5-star accommodation, 185 rooms, 53 suites and 2 presidential suites, has 3 non-smoking floors and handicapped facilities, state-of-the-art fitness centre, VIP limousine service, full range of shops, including *Olga Fisch* which is recommended for handicrafts, business centre, Japanese, French and Italian restaurants, also bar, deli and café.

In the new city

    L *Alameda Real*, Roca 653 y Amazonas, T562345, F565759, apartec@uio.satnet.net Mostly suites, good buffet breakfast, 24-hr cafeteria, business centre, use of internet included. **L** *Dann Carlton*, República de El Salvador 513 e Irlanda, T249008, F448007, dannres@punto.net.ec www.carltonquito.com Restaurant with international food, special menu with Colombian dishes on Sun, business centre, spa. **L** *Holiday Inn Crowne Plaza*, Shyris 1757 y Naciones Unidas, T445305, F251985, admihote@ accessinter.net Luxury suites, non-smoking suites, includes breakfast, restaurants, free transport to the airport. **L** *Mansión del Angel*, Wilson E5-29 y JL Mera, T557721, F237819. Refurbished old building, very elegant, lovely atmosphere, includes breakfast. **L** *Radisson Royal*, Cordero 444 y 12 de Octubre, at World Trade Centre building, T233333, F235777, quito@radisson.com.ec www.radisson. com/quitoec Luxury rooms, **LL** in suites, sushi bar, grill and international restaurants, business centre, spa. **L** *Sheraton Four Points*, Av Naciones Unidas y República de El Salvador, T970002, F433906, sheraton@uio.satnet.net International restaurant, bar, travel agency, business centre, gym, craft shop.

    AL *Akros*, 6 de Diciembre N34-120, T430610, F431727, akroshtl@hoy.net www.hotelakros.com Spacious rooms, includes welcome cocktail and buffet breakfast, excellent restaurant, bar. Small and friendly. **AL** *Hostal Mi Casa*, Andalucía N24-151 y Francisco Galavis, La Floresta, T/F225383, micasa@ecuanex.net.ec 6 exclusive rooms, good beds, includes large breakfast, **L** in suites, sauna, gardens. Small,

Quito

family run and atmosphere, multilingual owner, quiet, 2 blocks east of *Swissôtel*. **AL** *Howard Johnsons La Carolina*, Alemania E5-103 y Av República, T267239 F264264, reservas@ecuabox.com Restaurant (24 hrs), bar, gym. **AL** *Reina Isabel*, Amazonas 842 y Veintimilla, T544454, F221337, hrisabel@accessinter.net Includes breakfast, very nice. **AL** *Sebastián*, Almagro 822 y Cordero, T222400, F222500, hsebast1@hsebastian.com.ec www.ecua.net/sebastian Heating, a/c, cafeteria, restaurant, cable TV, free email. Comfortable. Recommended. **AL** *Villa Nancy*, Muros 146 y 12 de Octubre, behind the British Embassy, T550839, F562483, nancita@pi.pro.ec Rooms with view of the city, includes buffet breakfast, airport transfers, email, cable TV, multilingual staff, spotlessly clean. Good area for walking. Recommended.

A *Café Cultura*, Robles 513 y Reina Victoria, T504078, T/F224271, cafecult@ ecuacadorexplorer.com, www.cafecultura.com. Beautifully decorated rooms, honeymoon and family suites are **AL**, garden, luggage store, good restaurant serves excellent breakfasts, shop with local crafts and foods, fax and email service. *Cultura Reservation Centre* next door where you can book a variety of tours (see Tour operators below). Excellent service, great atmosphere. English, French and German spoken. Highly recommended. **A** *Chalet Suisse*, Reina Victoria N24-191 y Calama, T562700, F563966, hosuisse@impsat.net.ec Nice rooms, excellent restaurant, 12 safes. Rooms on the street are very noisy Fri and Sat nights. Price negotiable in low season. **A** *Hostal de la Rábida*, La Rábida 227 y Santa María, T222169, F221720, larabida@uio.satnet.net. Bright rooms with big baths, good restaurant, laundry service. Clean, comfortable, excellent service very friendly and helpful, Italian owner. Highly recommended. **A** *Hostal Los Alpes*, Tamayo 233 y Washington, behind US Embassy, T561110, F561128, alpes@ accessinter.net Alpine-style interior, excellent restaurant with reasonable prices, breakfast included, many handicrafts and artworks. Friendly and comfortable, free papers, English paperbacks, popular with Americans. Warmly recommended. **A** *Hostal La Pradera*, San Salvador 222 y Pasaje Martín Carrión, T/F227309, hpradera@uio. satnet.net, www.hostalpradera.com Fourteen comfortable rooms with private bath, cable TV, restaurant, includes breakfast. Located in a quiet and selective zone behind the Ministerio de Agricultura. **A** *Hostal Satori*, Pedro Ponce Carrasco 262, entre 6 de Diciembre y Almagro, T/F239575, satori@ecuabox.com Price includes breakfast, restaurant serves set meals and à la carte, international and Ecuadorean and vegetarian food, open 0700-1000, 1300-1500 and 1800-2200, mid-range prices. New in 2000. **A** *Hostal Villantigua*, Jorge Washington 237 y Tamayo, T528564 F545663, alariv@uio.satnet.net, www.angelfire.com/vt/villantigua Older house furnished with antiques, suites with fireplace more expensive. Quiet. Multilingual staff. **A** *Madison*, Roca 518 y Reina Victoria, T508617, F509547, hmadison@waccom.net.ec Nicely furnished rooms and suites, 1 suite with jacuzzi, lovely restaurant, internet service. Multilingual staff. **A** *Quito*, González Suárez N27-142 y 12 de Octubre, T544600, F567284, hotelquito@orotels. com Includes buffet breakfast, good restaurant. Nice pool, good views, A good place for afternoon coffee, open to non-residents. Part of Orotel chain. **A** *Río Amazonas Internacional*, Cordero 1342 y Amazonas, T556666 F556670, amazonas@hoy.net Safety deposit box in each room, restaurant, room service.

A *Santa Bárbara*, 12 de Octubre N26-15 y Coruña, T225121, F275121, santabarbara@porta.net Beautiful refurbished colonial-style house, laundry service, parking, English, French and Italian spoken. **A** *Sierra Madre*, Veintimilla 464 y Luis Tamayo, T505687/505688, F505715, htsierra@hoy.net Comfortable rooms, nice restaurant, sun roof, cable TV, laundry service. Colonial style, well furnished. **A** *Sierra Nevada*, Pinto 637 y Amazonas, T553658, F554936, snevada@accessinter.net, www.hotel.snevada.tours.com Price includes breakfast, cafeteria (open 0700-1100), laundry service, multilingual staff, gardens and terrace, climbing wall, part of *Sierra Nevada Expeditions* (see Tour operators below). **A** *Sol de Quito*, Alemania N30-170 y Vancouver, T541773, solquito@interactive.net.ec www.solquito.com Includes breakfast. Friendly, helpful, has received very good reports.

B *Embassy*, Wilson 441 y 6 de Diciembre, T563192, hembassy@interactive.net.ec Clean, well furnished, parking, restaurant, noisy disco next door at weekends. **B** *Floresta*, Isabel La Católica 1015 y Salazar, behind Swissôtel, T500422, floresta@impsat.net.ec With bath, TV, phone, parking, restaurant, laundry service. Safe and very quiet. Recommended. **B** *Hostal Charles Darwin*, La Colina 304 y Orellana, T234323, F529384, chdarwin@ecuanex.net.ec Includes full breakfast, cable TV. Very quiet, safe, friendly. Recommended. **B** *Hostal El Portón*, San Javier 203 y Av Orellana, T231712, F232662, elporton@rdyec.net Rooms in rustic style cabins and suites, breakfast included, carpeted, cable TV, cafeteria (0700-2100), room service, safety deposit. Small, clean, quiet, friendly. **B** *Hostal Plaza Internacional*, Plaza 150 y 18 de Septiembre, T522735, F505075, hplaza@uio.satnet.net. Clean, comfortable, multilingual staff, very helpful, good location. **B** *Hostal La Villa*, Toledo 1455 y Coruña, T222755, F226082, nevadatu@uio.satnet.net Carpeted rooms and suites with minibar, cable TV, includes full breakfast, laundry service, restaurant 0700-2200, mid-range prices. European style building. **B** *Hothello*, Amazonas N20-20 y 18 de Septiembre, T/F565835, hothello@cometoecuador.com www.cometoecuador.com/hothello Modern rooms with heating, cable TV, safety deposit, French cafeteria, room service, discounts during low season. Multilingual staff. New in 1999. **B** *Palm Garten*, 9 de Octubre 923 y Cordero, T526263, F568944. Very clean, good breakfasts, beautiful house, luggage store. **B** *Residencial Sunshine*, Pinto 241 y Reina Victoria, T223183. Large rooms with bath, hot water, includes full breakfast. German-run, also English spoken, clean, cosy. Recommended. **B** *Tambo Real*, 12 de Octubre y Patria opposite US Embassy, T563822, F554964, reservac@hoy.net Good rooms, ideal for business visitors, very good restaurant. Recommended.

C *Alston Inn*, JL Mera 741 y Baquedano, T/F229955, alston@uio.satnet.net With bath, hot water, TV, laundry service, many restaurants nearby, no charge for credit card payment. English spoken. **C** *Casa Sol*, Calama 127 y 6 de Diciembre, T230798, F223383, www.lacasasol.com Includes breakfast, cheaper with shared bath, small with courtyard, 24-hr cafeteria, cable TV, living room with fireplace, laundry service, luggage stored, safe deposit boxes, very helpful, English and French spoken. Highly

South from El Ejido

Related maps
Quito Orientation,
page 102
Quito Old Town,
page 106
El Ejido north to Colón,
page 114

■ Sleeping
1 Hostal L'Auberge Inn   3 Tambo Real
2 Kinara Hostel

recommended. **C** *El Centro del Mundo*, Lizardo García 569 y Reina Victoria, T229050. With bath, hot water, rooms with shared bath slightly cheaper,cable TV in lounge Clean, safe, modern, good meeting place.

C *Hostal Alcalá*, Cordero E5-48 y Reina Victoria, T227396, hostalalcala@hotmail. com With bath, includes breakfast, **F** in dormitory. Same management and services as Posada del Maple. **C** *Hostal La Carolina*, Italia 324 y Vancouver, T542471, F222744, hoscarol@uio.satnet.net Rooms and suites, hot water, safe deposit, cable TV, internet, credit cards accepted. Friendly, helpful, very clean, ask for quiet rooms at the back. **C** *Hostal Jardín del Sol*, Calama 166 y Almagro, T/F230950, h.j.sol@uio.satnet.net includes breakfast, TV, restaurant. Modern, nice. **C** *Magic Bean*, Foch E5-08 y JL Mera, T566181, www.ecuadorexplorer.com/magic/home.html Two rooms with bath, 2 dormitories with 3 and 4 beds (**F**), good beds, hot water, restaurant, includes breakfast. American owned, secure. Highly recommended. **C** *Orange Guest House*, Foch 726 y Amazonas, T569960. With bath, hot water. Clean, good location for bars and clubs. **C** *Posada del Maple*, Rodríguez E8-49 y Almagro, T544507, admin@ posadadelmaple.com www.posadadelmaple.com With bath, **D** without, **G** in dormitory, includes full breakfast, cable TV, laundry and cooking facilities, free tea and coffee, internet, meals and drinks in their *Café La Molienda de Jose*, travel information and reservations service, bus ticket purchase. Friendly, warm atmosphere. **C** *Rincón de*

El Ejido north to Colón

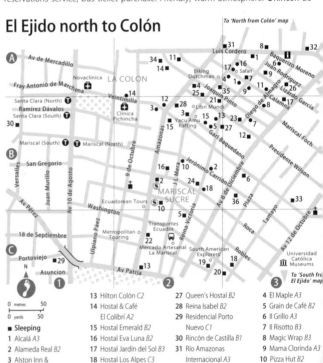

To 'North from Colón' map

To 'South from
El Ejido' map

Related maps
Quito Orientation,
page 102
South from El Ejido,
page 113
North from Colón,
page 116

0 metres 50
0 yards 50

■ Sleeping
1 Alcalá *A3*
2 Alameda Real *B2*
3 Alston Inn &
　Super Papa *B2*
4 Amazonas Inn *A2*
5 Café Cultura *C2*
6 Casa Helbling *B3*
7 Chalet Suisse *A3*
8 El Cafecito *A3*
9 El Centro del Mundo *A3*
10 El Kapulí *B2*
11 El Taxo *A2*
12 Embassy *B3*

13 Hilton Colón *C2*
14 Hostal & Café
　El Colibrí *A2*
15 Hostal Emerald *B2*
16 Hostal Eva Luna *B2*
17 Hostal Jardín del Sol *B3*
18 Hostal Los Alpes *C3*
19 Hostal Plaza
　Internacional *C2*
20 Hostal Villantigua *C3*
21 Hostelling
　International *B2*
22 Hothelo *C2*
23 La Estancia Inn *B3*
24 Madison *B2*
25 Pickett *A2*
26 Posada del Maple *A3*

27 Queen's Hostal *B2*
28 Reina Isabel *B2*
29 Residencial Porto
　Nuevo *C1*
30 Rincón de Castilla *B1*
31 Río Amazonas
　Internacional *A3*
32 Sebastián *A3*
33 Sierra Madre *B3*
34 Sierra Nevada *A2*
35 The Magic Bean *A2*
36 Villa Nancy *B3*

● Eating
1 Adam's Rib *A3*
2 El Holandés *B2*
3 El Hornero *B2*

4 El Maple *A3*
5 Grain de Café *B2*
6 Il Grillo *A3*
7 Il Risotto *B3*
8 Magic Wrap *B3*
9 Mama Clorinda *A3*
10 Pizza Hut *B2*
11 Shorton Grill *A3*
12 Terraza del Tártaro *B2*
13 Tex Mex *B2*
14 Viejo José *A2*

● Bars & nightclubs
15 Alkerke *B2*
16 Arribar *A3*
17 No Bar *A3*
18 Reina Victoria *B2*

Bavaria, Páez 232 y 18 de Septiembre, T509401, bavariainn@punto.net.ec Large rooms with bath, colour TV, restaurant with good German food. Clean. **C** *Rincón Escandinavo*, Leonidas Plaza 1110 y Baquerizo Moreno, T540794, hotelres@porta.net www.escandinavohotel.com Well furnished rooms, with bath, TV, cafeteria, restaurant. Small, modern, friendly, English spoken. Recommended. **C** *Villa Nancy*, Carrión 335 y 6 de Diciembre, T563084, F549657, villa_nancy@yahoo.com Includes breakfast, offers free airport transfer, washing/drying machines, travel book library and travel information.

D *Ambassador*, 9 de Octubre 1046 y Colón, T503712. With bath, cafeteria. Clean. Recommended. **D** *Casa Helbling*, Veintimilla 531 y 6 de Diciembre, T226013, casahelbling@accessinter.net Good breakfast US$3.50, hot water, use of kitchen , luggage store, use of washing machine US$3. Very friendly and helpful, German spoken, family atmosphere, good information on tours. Highly recommended. **D** *Crossroads*, Foch N5-23 y J L Mera, T234735. Excellent rooms, good hot showers, **F** in dormitory, very clean and friendly, opposite good internet café. Recommended. **D** *Hostal El Ciprés*, Lérida 381 y Pontevedra, T/F549558, elcipres@hotmail.com With bath, **E** without, **G** in dorm, includes breakfast, use of kitchen, safety deposit, transport to airport/terminal if staying at least 3 days, parking. Very helpful owner. **D** *Hostal Vizcaya*, Rumipamba 1726 y Manuela Sáenz, opposite Colegio San Gabriel's coliseum, T452252. Comfortable beds, bath, colour TV, good breakfast and evening meal on request, laundry service, Owned by Sra Elsa de Racines, reservations essential, English spoken, kind and friendly family. Recommended. **D** *Majestic*, Mercadillo 366 y Versalles, T543182, F504207, hmajestic@accessinter.net Well furnished rooms, with bath, hot water, bar, cafetería, restaurant. Clean, quiet and friendly. **D** *Posada del Arupo 2*, Juan Rodríguez y Reina Victoria, T557543, F242189, pitaemi@uio.satnet.net With bath, **E** without, includes breakfast and hot drinks all day, sitting room with cable TV, laundry service, use of kitchen.

E *Amazonas Inn*, Pinto 471 y Amazonas, T225723. Carpeted rooms with bath, TV, some sunny rooms, those on first floor are best. Very clean, friendly. **E** *El Cafecito*, Luis Cordero 1124 y Reina Victoria, T234862. Shared bath, hot water but you have to ask for it, the room called 'tomato' has a nice balcony. Canadian-owned, relaxed atmosphere, café serves superb pancakes and pastries and an excellent vegetarian dish of the day, good information. **E** *La Casa de Eliza*, Isabel La Católica 1559 y Coruña, T226602, F502640, manteca@uio.satnet.net Hot water, kitchen and laundry facilities, safe for valuables.Very popular and homely, no smoking in the house. Eliza organizes treks through the Cerro Golondrinas Cloudforest Reserve with research and volunteer opportunities, see page 80. Recommended. **E** *La Casona de Mario*, Andalucía 213 y Galicia, near Universidad Católica, T230129, F230129, lacasona@punto.net.ec Shared bath, kitchen, laundry and storage facilities, sittingroom, big garden, cable TV, book exchange.

Argentine-run, very comfortable. Highly recommended. **E** *Dan Internacional*, Av 10 de Agosto 2482 y Colón, T221727, F225083. A/c, with bath, hot water, good food and laundry. In a busy street, clean. Recommended. **E** *Emerald*, Veintimilla 1069 y Amazonas, T525991, F564746. Carpeted rooms with bath, hot water, rooms with TV are more expensive, laundry service. Modern, clean, friendly. **E** *Hostal Húngaro*, Tamayo 21-209 y Roca, T559450, with bath, hot water. In a quiet street, simple, clean. **E** *Hostal La Quinta*, Cordero 1951 y Páez, T230723, came@uio.satnet.net Large rooms with bath and TV, breakfast available, parking. An old renovated mansion, Italian owner speaks English, excellent service, safe, quieter rooms at rear. Recommended. **E** *Hostal Tierra Alta*, Wilson E7-79 y Almagro, T235993. With bath, electric shower, some rooms with cable TV. Secure, clean, helpful. **E** *Loro Verde*, Rodríguez 241 y Almagro, T226173. With bath, includes breakfast, kitchen. Clean, secure, friendly, good location. **E** *Nuestra Casa*, Bartolome de las Casas 435 y Versalles, T225470, mlo@uio.satnet.net Converted family house, shared bath, hot water, cooking facilities, dinner available for US$3-4 (including vegetarian), camping possible in the garden for US$1.50, laundry facilities and service. Highly recommended. **E** *Queen's Hostal* Reina Victoria 836 y Wilson, T551844, F406690. With bath, cafeteria, cooking facilities, sitting room with fireplace, safety deposit. Nice. **E** *Residencial Carrión*, Carrión 1259 y Versalles, T548256. With bath, **F** without**,** TV, restaurant, bar, garden, luggage stored. Friendly staff, good value, accepts Visa, fills early. Recommended. **E** *El Taxo*, Foch 909 y Cordero, T225593, fzalamea@yahoo.com www.ecuadorexplorer.com/taxo Large family house, open fire, constant hot water, kitchen facilities. Friendly, helpful, good meeting place.

F *Casa Paxee*, Romualdo Navarro 326 y La Gasca, T500441. Price includes fruit for breakfast, use of kitchen area, laundry facilities, clean bath, 3 rooms only. Discounts for longer stays. Highly recommended. **F** *Casapaxi*, Navarro 364 y La Gasca, at the end of the lane, T542663. Hot water, TV, kitchen, stores luggage, Clean, friendly, owner Luigiana Fossati speaks perfect English and is very helpful. Repeatedly recommended as providing excellent value. **F** *Hostal Basc*, Lizardo García 537 y Reina Victoria, T503456. hostalbask@latinmail.com With bath, cheaper without, hot water, sitting room with cable TV, kitchen facilities, free coffee, cafeteria serves breakfast and

North from Colón

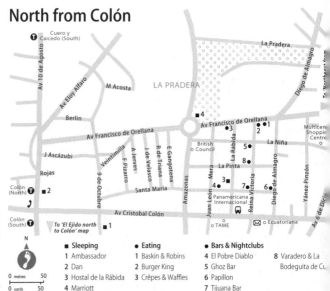

Related maps
Quito Orientation,
page 102
El Ejido north to Colón,
page 114
Northeast from
Mariscal Sucre,
page 117

■ **Sleeping**
1 Ambassador
2 Dan
3 Hostal de la Rábida
4 Marriott

● **Eating**
1 Baskin & Robins
2 Burger King
3 Crêpes & Waffles

● **Bars & Nightclubs**
4 El Pobre Diablo
5 Ghoz Bar
6 Papillon
7 Tijuana Bar
8 Varadero & La
  Bodeguita de Cu

snacks. Friendly atmosphere. **F** *Hostal La Galería*, Calama 233 y Almagro, T500307. Twelve carpeted rooms with bath, pool bar, cafeteria. English spoken, discounts for longer stay. **F** *Hostal Jardín Quiteño*, Versalles 1449 y Mercadillo, T/F526011. Carpeted rooms with bath, TV, restaurant, parking. **F** *Hostal El Yuco*, Cordero 1145 y Amazonas, T225381. With bath, hot water, cable TV, cafeteria. Small, homey, on quiet street yet central, discounts for long stays. **F** *El Kapulí*, Robles 625 y Amazonas, T/F221872, sunlight87@hotmail.com With bath, 2 larger rooms with several beds and shared bath, hot water, sheets changed daily, laundry service, luggage stored, English spoken. Very clean, very friendly and helpful. Recommended.

 F *Lafayette*, Baquedano 358 y J L Mera, T224529. Hot water, carpeted, TV. Very clean. Recommended. **F** *Nueve de Octubre*, 9 de Octubre 1047 y Colón, T552424. With bath, TV, luggage storage, laundry service. Clean, very comfortable, friendly, secure, night watchman. Recommended. **F** *Pickett*, Wilson 712 y JL Mera, T551205, Carpeted rooms with bath, cable TV, hot water, all rooms have outside window, free coffee, laundry. Friendly, popular. **F** *Tortuga Verde*, JL Mera N24-41 y Pinto, T556829. Shared bath, hot water, **H** in dorm, airport transport, tours. Good location but noisy, very popular with young backpackers. New Swiss management in 2000, English, German and French spoken. Recommended. Breakfast in *El Bacalao* downstairs. **F** *Versalles*, Versalles 1442 y Mercadillo, T526145. Restaurant serves breakfast daily and lunch on weekdays. Nice, clean.

 G per person *Gan Eden*, Pinto 163 y 6 de Diciembre, T223480. Eighteen beds in double rooms or dormitory, shared bath, hot water, soap, towel and toilet paper provided, restaurant serves cheap breakfast and Israeli food, cable TV, luggage store, laundry and fax service (for anyone who needs to fax home their dirty clothes). Very clean, very helpful owner. Highly recommended. **G** per person *Hostal Eva Luna*, Pasaje de Roca 630, between Amazonas y JL Mera, T234799, admin@safari.com.ec. Women-only hostel, kitchen facilities.Secure, comfortable, family atmosphere. Highly recommended. **G** per person *Hostal del'Hoja*, Gerónimo Leyton N23-89 y Av La Gasca, T560832, delhoja@mixmail.com Shared bath, hot water, includes breakfast, kitchen facilities, free coffee and tea, airport transport. **G** *Pensión Lotys*, Marchena 592 y América, T522531, F226438. With bath, electric shower, garden, all rooms are on the ground floor and are a bit gloomy and cold, good value laundry. Friendly, secure, peaceful. Recommended. **G** *Posada del Arupo 1*,

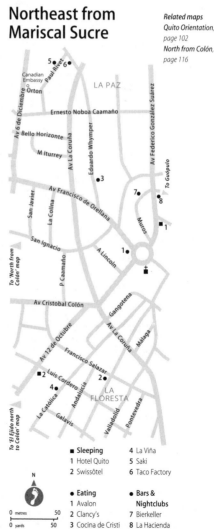

Northeast from Mariscal Sucre

Related maps
Quito Orientation,
page 102
North from Colón,
page 116

■ **Sleeping**
1 Hotel Quito
2 Swissôtel

● **Eating**
1 Avalon
2 Clancy's
3 Cocina de Cristi

4 La Viña
5 Saki
6 Taco Factory

● **Bars &**
Nightclubs
7 Bierkeller
8 La Hacienda

Berlin 147 y 9 de Octubre, T525041. Ten rooms with bath, laundry service. Same owners as *Posada del Maple*, English and French spoken. **G** per person *Rincón de Castilla*, Versalles 1127 y Carrión, T224312, F548097. Shared bath, hot water, 1 room with bath, luggage stored, laundry facilities, parking, travel agency. Clean, friendly, safe, owner speaks German, French and English. Recommended.

Youth hostel *Hostelling International*, Pinto 325 y Reina Victoria, T543995, F508221, hostellingquito@hotmail.com Large hostel with capacity for 75. **F** per person in private room with bath. Cheaper in dormitory with lockers and shared bath. Discounts for IYHF members and International Student Card holders. Restaurant, cafetería, laundry sevice, coin operated washing machines, hot water, TV on request, safe deposit, luggage store, fax service, closed circuit TV security system. Rather characterless modern building, refurbished in 2000.

Near the airport **B** *Aeropuerto*, opposite the terminal, T435899. With bath, hot water, restaurant serves lunch only. Overpriced. **F** *Hostal El Pinar*, Av La Prensa 4937 y N López, 2 blocks south of the airport, T241697. One room with bath, cheaper without. Not too clean but friendly and helpful, safe.

Between the **E** *L'Auberge Inn*, Av Colombia 1138 y Yaguachi, T552912, auberge@uio.satnet.net
new & old cities www.ioda.net/auberge-inn With bath, **F** without, duvets on beds, fax service, garden, lovely terrace and communal area, sauna. Clean, helpful, good atmosphere. **F** *Dorado*, 18 de Septiembre 805 y Larrea, T525072. Big rooms with bath, electric shower, cable TV, restaurant (0730-2200). Rooms by second floor TV lounge can be noisy. **F** *Hostal El Ejido*, Juan Larrea 1519 y Riofrío, T526066. With bath, **G** without, hot water. Clean, friendly, good value. **F** per person *Kinara Hostel for Foreigners*, Bogotá 534 y Av América, T224086, F525179, kinara@impsat.net.ec. Includes American breakfast, use of kitchen, safe deposit boxes, laundry service, library, cable TV, luggage storage, free tea and coffee, English and French spoken, immaculately clean. Highly recommended. **F** *Old Port*, Asunción 750 y Venezuela, T225211. With bath, **G** without, hot water, cable TV, videos, laundry service, kitchen facilities, Spanish lessons, tours. Multilingual staff. **F** *Residencial Marsella*, Los Ríos 2035 y Julio Castro, T/F515884, marcella@andinanet.net With bath, **G** without, hot water good rooftop terrace with views over Parque La Alameda, top floor rooms best but noisy, luggage stored for US$1 per bag per 15 days, often full by 1700, expensive laundry, safe deposit, notice board, security guard. Clean, good value.

G *Coral*, Manuel Larrea 1266 y Ante, T572337. With bath, hot water. Spacious, popular with families, clean, cafetería open 0730-2200. **G** *Residencial Margarita 1*, Elizalde 410 y Colombia (near Los Ríos), T952599. With bath, hot water,luggage stored. Helpful. Recommended. **G** *Residencial Margarita 2*, Los Ríos 1995 y Espinoza, T950441. With bath, hot water, good beds, sheets changed daily,luggage stored, safety deposit. Very clean, friendly, great value. Highly recommended. **H** *Hostal San Blas*, Caldas 121 y Pedro Fermín Cevallos, Plaza San Blas, T281434. With bath, cheaper without, hot shower, kitchen and laundry facilities, terrace, cable TV, great value. Recommended.

In the old city **B** *Real Audiencia*, Bolívar 220, T950590, F580213, realaudi@hoy.net,
On map, page 106 www.realaudiencia.com Spacious, well furnished, carpeted rooms, includes breakfast, TV, laundry service, baggage stored, restaurant/bar on top floor, safety deposit box. Great views, at Plaza de Santo Domingo Trole stop. Highly recommended.

D *Viena Internacional*, Flores 600 y Chile, T954860, vienaint@uio.satnet.net Large rooms, hot water, phone, laundry, good meals. English spoken, clean, good value, safe. **E** *San Francisco de Quito*, Sucre 217 y Guayaquil, T287758, hsfquito@andinanet.net With bath, hot water, luggage storage. In stylishly renovated colonial building with nice patio, clean, friendly.

F *Cumandá*, Morales 449, next to the terminal terrestre, T956984 With bath, hot showers, TV, phone, laundry, restaurant, garage. Comfortable, excellent service, clean, safe, rooms at the front are noisy but quieter at the back. Recommended. **F** *Grand Hotel*, Rocafuerte 1001 y Pontón, T959411. With bath, hot water, **G** without bath, kitchen facilities, laundry service, good breakfast in cafeteria (0700-1200), safety deposit, luggage storage. Some rooms dingy, rundown, secure, friendly Spanish school attached. **F** *Hostal La Casona*, Manabí 255 entre Flores y Montúfar, T957923. Carpeted rooms, with bath, hot water, TV, restaurant, bar, disco, discount for longer stays. **F** *Huasi Continental*, Flores 332 y Sucre, T957327. With bath, **F** without, hot water, TV, phone, luggage stored, good restaurant.Clean, safe, helpful. **F** *Internacional Plaza del Teatro*, Guayaquil, 1373 y Esmeraldas, T959462. Carpeted rooms with bath, TV, restaurant, parking. Stylish, clean, good service. Recommended. **F** *Piedra Dorada*, Maldonado 3210, near bus terminal, T957460. Renovated, with bath, hot shower, phone, TV, restaurant. Clean, helpful.

G *Catedral Internacional*, Mejía 638 y Cuenca, T955438. Good rooms with bath, hot shower, restaurant. In colonial building, very clean, pleasant. **G** *La Posada Colonial*, Paredes 188 y Rocafuerte, T282859. With bath, **H** without, hot water, parking. Beautiful old building, clean. Recommended. **G** *Reina de Quito*, Maldonado 2648 y Portilla, 2 blocks from the bus terminal, T/F950347. With bath, hot water, some rooms dark, restaurant (midday only), luggage store. Great views from the terrace, run by the army, secure. **G** *Rumiñahui*, Montúfar 449 y Junín, T289325. With bath, hot water, clean, safe deposit box, laundry facilities. **G** *San Agustín*, Flores 626 y Chile, T282847. With bath, hot water, restaurant variable (0700-1600). Clean. **G** *Santo Domingo*, Rocafuerte 1345 y Maldonado, Plaza Santo Domingo, T952810. With bath, **H** without, hot water, noisy, best rooms 8a or 9a, luggage store, not a safe area at night or early morning.

H *Colonial*, Maldonado 3035 y Quijano (at the end of an alley), T950338. With bath, hot water 0600-0900, laundry. Quiet, safe although not a safe area at night, close to the bus terminal. **H** *Flores*, Flores 355 y Sucre, T280435. With bath, hot water, ask for a room on the first floor, laundry facilities. Safe, friendly, convenient for the bus station.

H *Guayaquil*, Maldonado 3248 y Paredes, near bus terminal, T959937. With bath, cheaper without, hot water, will store luggage for small fee. Basic, safe. **H** *Hostal Félix*, Guayaquil 431 y Rocafuerte, T954645. Shared bath, hot shower in basement, friendly, reliable. **H** *Montúfar*, Sucre 160 y Montúfar, T281419. With bath, hot water. Clean, safe, good value. **H** *Residencial San Marcos*, Junín 452 y Almeida. Hot shower, cooking and washing facilities, safe, clean, friendly. Recommended. **H** *Residencial Sucre*, Bolívar 615 y Cuenca, Plaza San Francisco, T954025. Some rooms with bath, cold showers, has terrace with great views over the old city, laundry facilities. A bit noisy, not for the hygienically minded but phenomenally cheap.

Sra Anita Gomezjurado, Julio Zaldumbide N24-741 entre Miravalle y Coruña, near *Hotel Quito* (take Colón-Camal bus), T237778. **E** per person half board in rooms with private bath, hot water, laundry. In quiet, residential neighbourhood, convenient for Universidad Católica, German and some English spoken, friendly, clean, safe. *Sra Rosa Jácome* has an apartment in the new city, T503180 (evenings), 1 double room with bath and 2 singles, **E** per person, use of kitchen and phone, she will arrange outings and is friendly and helpful, she meets most incoming flights at the airport in her taxi. *Sra Leonor de Maldonado*, Hungría N31-192 y Mariana de Jesús, 1 block west of Av Amazonas, T256489/434046, maldonado_maria_@hotmail.com One double room with private bath, **E** per person full board, includes laundry service, airport transport. Daughters speak English and French, they can accompany visitors to local sights. *Cecilia Rivera*, a doctor, offers half board, **E** per person, at Salazar 327 y Coruña, T548006. Good view across the valley, quiet, safe, hot water, laundry, luggage store.

Accommodation in private homes

Quito

Apartments for rent

Apartments for rent are also advertised in El Comercio, especially in 'Suites (Sector Norte)' section; prices from US$125-300 per month, usually unfurnished

For longer stays with room, kitchen, TV, laundry service etc, the following have been recommended: *Apart-Hotel Amaranta*, Leonidas Plaza N20-32 y Washington, T560585, amaranta@impsat.net.ec Comfortable, well-equipped suites, from US$900 a month, daily rate **A** includes breakfast, good restaurant. *Apartamentos Modernos*, Amazonas 2467 y Mariana de Jesús (near El Jardín Mall), T234321, F233766, modernos@uio.satnet.net Fully furnished 2 and 3 bedroom appartments with kitchen, US$450-US$500/month. Daily rate **B-C**. Daily towel and cleaning service, very clean, friendly, English spoken, convenient location. Recommended. *Apart-Hotel Antinea*, Rodríguez 175 y Diego de Almagro, T506839, hotelant@accessinter.net.ec Suites and apartments, lovely rooms. Daily rate **A** includes breakfast. *Apartotel Mariscal*, Robles 958 y Páez, T528833. Rooms and suites, daily rate **E**. *Mireya Vergara*, Av París y Río Coca, T441492, has some large apartments, fully furnished, from US$250-400 per month. *Marcia de Sandoval*, Galavis 130 y Toledo, La Floresta, T543254. Rents small studio apartments, well equipped, US$120-180 per month.

Eating

For restaurant price classification, see inside front cover

The vast majority of restaurants are in the new city, where almost any type of cuisine can be found, to suit any budget. Those in the old city tend to offer only local and fast food. It is also difficult to find places to eat in the old city in the evenings, especially after 2200. Note that hygiene at hamburger and *salchipapa* stalls is sometimes poor. Many restaurants throughout the city close on Sunday evening. **NB** Prices listed in less salubrious places are often inaccurate, so check first. Also note that restaurants with stickers indicating acceptance of credit cards do not necessarily do so. In many of the more expensive restaurants 22 percent tax and service is added to the bill. There are a number of restaurants in the food courts of shopping malls, for their addresses see Shopping below. The following list is by type and all restaurants are in the new city unless otherwise stated. In all cases, assume good food, service and value.

Ecuadorean

Los Adobes, La Terraza Quicentro Shopping, T254917. Traditional meals, specially 'fritada'. Mid-range prices. *La Choza*, Av 12 de Octubre N24-551 y Cordero, T507901. Good music and special decoration. Expensive. Mon-Fri 1200-1600 and 1900-2230, Sat and Sun 1200-1630. *Mama Clorinda*, Reina Victoria 1144 y Calama, T544362. A la carte and set meals. Filling, good value. Cheap. *El Pajonal*, Homero Salas S/N y El Altar, near the airport, T449816. Very good Ecuadorean food, also live music on Fri night. Mid-range prices. *La Querencia*, Eloy Alfaro N34-194 y Catalina Aldaz. Good views and atmosphere. Mid-range prices. *Rincón La Ronda*, Belo Horizonte 406 y Almagro, T540459. Very good food and atmosphere, Sun buffet. Expensive. Daily 1200-2300.

Fast food

For pizza restaurants also see below

There has been something of a fast food explosion in the new city and you can find most of the better-known US outlets here. All the shopping centres have food courts with a variety of fast food outlets including traditional Ecuadorean, Chinese and Italian food in addition to the ubiquitous hamburger, pizza, etc.

In the Food Garden at Mall El Jardín are *Taco Bell*, *Burger King* and *KFC*, among others. *Taco Bell* is also on JL Mera y Carrión. There is also a branch of *Burger King* at Centro Comercial Iñaquito, Quicentro Shopping and at Orellana y Reina Victoria, with *Baskin & Robbins* vast ice cream emporium next door on Orellana and at Quicentro. *McDonalds*, Av Amazonas corner Naciones Unidas and several other locations, but no breakfast menu or milkshakes. *TropiBurger* at Av de los Shyris y Naciones Unidas and several other locations is a local fast food chain.

French & Swiss

Chalet Suisse, Reina Victoria N24-191 y Calama, T562700. Good steaks, also some Swiss dishes, good quality. Mid-range prices. *Chantilly*, Roca 736 y Amazonas. Good restaurant and bakery, they have a second branch at Whymper 394. Mid-range prices.

Quito

Ile de France, Reina Victoria N26-143 y la Niña, T553292. French-Swiss cuisine and fondue bar, very good. Expensive. Open daily 1230-1500 and 1830-0000. *Lafite*, La Niña 559 y JL Mera, T222266. Excellent food and atmosphere, live music on weekends. Expensive. *Raclette*, Eloy Alfaro 1348 y Andrade Marín, T237753. Swiss specialties including raclette, fondue, some international dishes. Alpine décor. Expensive. Open Mon-Sat 1230-2300, Sun 1200-1600. *Rincón de Francia*, Roca 779 y 9 de Octubre, T554668. Excellent, reservation essential, slow service. Very expensive.

Biergarten, San Juan de Cumbayá, T895797. Beer garden and restaurant. In the sub- **German** urbs to the east of the city. *Café Colibrí*, Pinto 619 y Cordero, T564011. German food, also cafeteria, breakfast, coffee and snacks, good atmosphere, German and English newspapers, open 0700-2100. *Hansa Krug*, Salazar N11-131 y 12 de Octubre, T237334. Typical German fare, Raclette on Fri night.

La Casa de Mi Abuela, JL Mera 1649 y la Niña, T521922. Very good food and great vari- **Grill** ety. Mid-range prices. *Columbia*, Colón 1262 y Amazonas and Tarqui 851 y 10 de Agosto, T551857. Popular. Mid-range prices. Open Sun. *Columbus*, Amazonas 1539 y Santa María, T540780 and Amazonas 3463 y Atahualpa, T444859. More upmarket. *Roasters*, República N6-238 y Eloy Alfaro, behind El Jardín Mall. Good roast chicken, also nice corn bread. *Shorton Grill*, Calama E7-73 y Almagro, T523645. Large portions. Mid-range prices. *Los Troncos*, Los Shyris 1280 y Portugal, T437377. Good Argentine grill, serves beef, chicken, pork, fish, salads. Small and friendly. Expensive. Mon-Sat 1200-2300, Sun 1200-1700.

Chandani Tandoori, Reina Victoria y Wilson, T558991. Simple little place, with good **Indian** authentic cuisine. Mid-range prices.

All of the luxury class hotels have very good international restaurants (see Sleeping **International** above). The *Swissôtel*, has several superb restaurants. The *Hilton Colón*, has an excel- lent Sunday buffet, all you can eat for US$13, from 1200 to 1500. Also an excellent Ital- ian restaurant. In the *Hotel Quito*, the buffet breakfast is excellent value.

Amadeus Restaurant and Pub, Coruña 1398 y Orellana, T230831. Very good interna- tional cuisine and concerts, usually 2300 on Fri, rather formal. *Cocina de Kristy*, Whymper y Orellana. Upmarket, great view from the terrace and equally great food. Expensive. Recommended. *Cafetería Sutra*, at Calama 380 y JL Mera, above *Safari* Tours. Very good food, drinks, friendly, reasonable prices, nice vibe, popular meeting place.

Cafetería Stop, Amazonas N24-15 y Moreno Bellido, T567960. International and Chilean dishes. Very good atmosphere. Overpriced. *Cantagallo* Los Laureles E14-138 y Av. Eloy Alfaro, T434672. Excellent food, a number of seafood and highbrow dishes,

Quito

live music, great atmosphere. Very expensive. Mon-Sat 1200-1530 and 1900-2300, Sun 1200-1600. *Clancy's*, F Salazar y Toledo, T554278, good food and service. Mid-range prices. Open daily 1200-2400. *Crêpes & Waffles*, La Rábida 461 y Orellana. Succulent savoury crêpes and salads and delicious desserts. Mid-range prices. Highly recommended. *La Escondida Bar & Grill*, General Roca N33-29 y José Bosmediano, T242380. Seafood, salads, pastas, tapas. Young crowd, informal atmosphere. Expensive. Closed Mon. Recommended. *Grain de Café*, Baquedano 332 y Reina Victoria. Excellent set lunch, also vegetarian meals, good cakes and coffee, good service, book exchange, films in English on Tue afternoon, informative French Canadian owner (Daniel). Mid-range prices. Mon-Sat 1200-2230. Highly recommended. *Terraza del Tártaro*, Veintimilla 1106 y Amazonas (no sign), at the top of the building, T527987. Excellent views, pleasant atmosphere. Recommended. *La Viña*, Isabel la Católica y Cordero, T566033. Extensive and unusual menu, Peruvian chef, beautifully presented and excellent food. Expensive. Highly recommended. *El Zócalo*, JL Mera y Calama. Varied menu. Lively atmosphere, live music on Fri night, terrace, a meeting place for young people.

Italian *La Briciola*, Toledo1255 y Cordero, T547138. Extensive menu, excellent food, homey atmosphere. Expensive. 1230-1500 and 1930-2300, closed Sun. *Capuletto*, Eloy Alfaro N32-544 y Los Shyris, T550611. Excellent fresh pasta and desserts, Italian deli, lovely outdoor patio with fountain. Mid-range prices. Mon-Sat 0900-0000, Sun 0900-2200. Recommended. *Il Grillo*, Baquerizo Moreno 533 y Almagro, T225531. Great pizzas, upmarket style. Mid-range prices. Closed Mon. *Pavarotti*, Av 12 de Octubre 1955 Cordero, above Restaurant La Choza, T566668. *Il Risotto*, Pinto 209 y Almagro, T220400. Very popular and very good. Expensive. Closed Mon. *La Scala*, Salazar y 12 de Octubre. Good atmosphere, quite expensive. *Siboney*, Atahualpa y 10 de Agosto. Homemade pasta, great huge pizzas. Cheap. *Spaghetti*, Plaza de las Américas, at Av América y República, near Naciones Unidas, T260340 and Portugal y Eloy Alfaro, T446288. Very good food at reasonable prices. *La Trattoria de Renato*, San Javier y Orellana. Nice atmosphere. Expensive.

Latin American *La Bodeguita de Cuba*, Reina Victoria y la Pinta. Good Cuban food. Good music at the *Varadero* bar next door (see Bars below). Expensive. *Café Tequila*, Portugal y Eloy Alfaro, T453466. Mexican food and drinks. Open daily 1200-1600 and 1830-0000, closed Sun evening. *Churrascaría Tropeiro*, Veintimilla 564 y 6 de Diciembre, T548012. Brazilian-style, salad bar and *espeto* grill, *feijoada completa* on weekends. *La Guarida del Coyote*, Av Eloy Alfaro E25-94 y Portugal, T467882. Excellent Mexican Food, live music. Mid-range prices. *Rincón Ecuatoriano Chileno*, 6 de Diciembre y Orellana. Delicious, very good value, small. Recommended.

Middle Eastern *Aladdin*, Almagro y Baquerizo Moreno, T229435. Varied menu. Cheap. Open daily 1030-2330, Fri and Sat until 0200. *Amizlala*, Reina Victoria y Pinta. Varied middle eastern dishes. Cheap. 0900-2200 daily. *El Arabe*, Reina Victoria y Carrión. Good food. Mon-Sat 1130-0000, Sun 1200-1800. *Cactus*, Calama y JL Mera. Israeli food. Nice terrace. Cheap. *Gan Eden*, Pinto y 6 de Diciembre, T223480. Israeli snacks, falafel. Cheap.

Oriental *Casa de Asia*, Eloy Alfaro 3027 y Germán Alemán, T464517.Excellent, Korean and Japanese. Expensive. *Chifa Asiático*, Robles y Páez. Authentic Chinese cuisine. Mid-range prices. *Chifa China*, Carrión Oe 2-82 y Versalles, T229954. Good. *Fuji*, Robles 538 y JL Mera, T529634. Japanese food. *Happy Panda*, Cordero E9-348 e Isabel la Católica, T547322. Excellent. Mid-range prices. *Hong Kong*, Wilson 246 y Tamayo, T225515. Good. *Hong Tai*, La Niña 234 y Yanez Pinzón. Good. Cheap. *Hou Wah*, Av Orellana sin número y 6 de Diciembre, T505363. Very good. Mid range prices.*Pekín*, Whimper 300 y Orellana, T235273. Excellent food, very nice atmosphere. Expensive. *Sake*, Paul Rivet

N30-166 y Whymper, T524818. Sushi bar and other Japanese dishes. Very trendy, great food, nicely decorated. Mon-Sat 1200-1530 and 1900-2300. Sun 1230-1600. Recommended. *Siam*, Calama E5-104 y JL Mera. Good Thai food, slow service, nice balcony. Mid-range prices. 1200-2300. *Thai-an*,Eloy Alfaro N34-230 y Portugal, T446639. Excellent Thai food and ambience. Expensive. Mon-Sat 1200-1530 and 1830-2230, Sun 1200-1600.

Pizza

There are many good pizzerías, most with several outlets and home delivery service (phone numbers listed below), those most central are listed. Prices are generally mid-range. *Le Arcate*, Baquedano 358 y JL Mera, T237659. Wood oven pizza, good, same management as *Il Risotto*. 1100-1500 and 1800-2300, closed Mon. *Domino's*, Coruña 1239 y San Ignacio, T508506. More expensive than average. *Ch Farina*, Carrión, entre JL Mera y Amazonas, T558139 and Naciones Unidas y Amazonas (open 24 hrs), T444400. Fast service, good, popular. *El Hornero*, Veintimilla y Amazonas, T542518, Naciones Unidas y Shyris and on Gonzalez Suárez, T230378. Very good wood oven pizzas, try one with *choclo* (fresh corn). Recommended. 1200-2300. *Pizza Hut*, JL Mera 566 y Carrión, T500143, Naciones Unidas y Amazonas, T454288 and at several shopping centres. *Pizza Net*, Calama E5-37 y JL Mera. Large screen TV, internet. *Pizza Pizza*, Santa María y Almagro. Good and relatively cheap.

Seafood

Be selective when choosing a seafood restaurant, visitors have become ill after eating at some of the cheaper establishments

Avalón, Av Orellana 155 y 12 de Octubre, T509879. Excellent food, upmarket. Very expensive. *Barlovento*, 12 de Octubre 251 y Orellana. Seafood, also cheap steak, outside seating. *Bambu Bar*, Diego de Almagro 213 y Andrade Marín, T509442. Excellent seafood and ceviches. Very expensive. *Bar y Grill Buon Gustaio*, Isla San Cristóbal 881. Seafood and local food. Recommended. *La Canoa Manabita*, Calama y Reina Victoria. Great seafood and very clean. Opening hours vary depending on the owner's mood. *El Cebiche*, JL Mera 1236 y Calama, T526380 and on Amazonas 2428 y Moreno Bellido, T504593. Delicious *ceviche*. *Cebiches y Banderas de la Foch*, Av 12 de Octubre 1533 y Foch, T526963. Reasonably priced. *Cebiches de la Rumiñahui*, 7 branches: *Real Audiencia* entre Av del Maestro y Tufiño (the original branch and less clean); *La Casa del Ajedrez*, Amazonas 3008 y Rumipanba, at Parque La Carolina; *Quicentro Shopping Centre*: all are popular for *ceviche*, seafood and fish. Mid-range prices. *Delmónicos* Mariano Aguilera 331 y Pradera, T544200. Very good seafood. Expensive. Daily 1230-1500 and 1930-2300, closed Sun evening. *La Jaiba*, Reina Victoria N25-20 y Colón, T543887. An old favourite, varied menu, good service. Expensive. *Mare Nostrum*, Foch 172 y Tamayo, T528686. Very upmarket, fine ambiance. Very expensive. Daily 1200-2300. *Las Palmeras*, Japón y Naciones Unidas, opposite Parque la Carolina. Very good *comida Esmeraldeña*, try their *ceviche*, outdoor tables, good value. Mid-range prices. Open lunchtime only. *Puerto Camarón*, Av 6 de Diciembre y Granaderos, Centro Comercial Olímpico, T265761. Good quality, varied menu. Mid-range prices. Recommended. *Las Redes*, Amazonas 845 y Veintimilla, T525691. Lovely atmosphere. Expensive. Closed Sunday. Highly recommended. *El Viejo José*, Veintimilla y Páez, opposite Clínica Pichincha. Good, try their *cazuelas*. Cheap and good value. Recommended.

Spanish

El Mesón de Triana, Isabel La Católica 1015 y Salazar, T502844. Varied Spanish menu, tapas, nice décor with Talavera ceramics. Mon-Fri 1230-1600 and 1900-2300, Sat 1900-2300. *La Paella Valenciana*, República y Almagro. Huge portions, superb fish, seafood and paella. Expensive. *La Puerta de Alcalá*, Lizardo García 664 y JL Mera. Delicious *tapas*. *La Vieja Castilla* La Pinta 435 y Amazonas. Typical Spanish food. Expensive.

US

Adam's Rib, Calama E6-15 y Reina Victoria, T563196. American ribs, wonderful steaks, great pecan pie, a popular meeting place for American expats. Mid-range prices. Happy hour 1730-2100. Mon-Fri 1200-2230, Sat closed, Sun 1200-2100. *American*

Deli, República de El Salvador 1058 y Naciones Unidas, T451252, also at Mall El Jardín and Centro Comercial Iñaquito. Sandwiches, hamburgers, desserts. *TGI Friday's*, at Quicentro Shopping, food and drinks. *Hunters*, 12 de Octubre 2517 y Muros, T234994. BBQ wings, ribs, beer, drinks. *The Magic Bean*, Foch 681 y JL Mera, T566181. Excellent food, huge portions, outdoor eating, specializes in fine coffees and natural foods, more than 20 varieties of pancakes, good salads, gets very busy. Mid-range prices. Recommended. *The Magic Wrap*, Foch E8-15 y Almagro, T527190. Make your own tortilla wraps with salad bar style offerings, desserts. Cheap. 1100-0300 daily. *Red Hot Chilli Peppers*, Foch 713 y JL Mera. Amazing fajitas, the best daiquiris in town, friendly. Cheap. Mon-Sat 1200-2200. *Sports Planet*, at Plaza de las Américas, Av América y Naciones Unidas, T267790. Bar and restaurant. The complex also houses cinemas and other restaurants. *The Taco Factory*, at Whymper y Paul Rivet. Relatively cheap, generous portions, US TV. *Texas Ranch*, JL Mera y Calama. For steak, also good burgers, seafood, soups, salads. Cheap. Daily 1200-0000. *Tex Mex*, Reina Victoria 847 y Wilson. The Tex Mex Mixta is especially recommended. Lively atmosphere, draught beer. Mid-range prices. Open daily.

Vegetarian *Le Champignon*, Robles 543 y JL Mera, T224373. Nice atmosphere. Mid-range prices. *Casa Naturista*, Lizardo García 630. Also a health food store. *Las Ensaladas/Mi Frutería*, Quicentro Shopping. Gorgeous fresh fruit salads and coastal Ecuadorean food. *El Holandés*, Reina Victoria 600 y Carrión, T522167. Delicious Dutch Indian, Indonesian, Greek and Italian dishes. Cheap, wine expensive. Mon-Fri 1200-2300. Recommended. *Manantial*, 9 de Octubre 591 y Carrión and Luis Cordero 1838 y 9 de Octubre. Good and cheap set lunch. *El Maple*, JL Mera y Calama. Good, varied, good fruit juices, Stylish décor. Cheap set lunch, otherwise mid-range prices. Open daily except Sun for dinner. Recommended. *Maranatha*, Riofrío y Larrea, between old and new cities. Very good vegan food, set lunch, good value, very clean, open 1200-1500. *El Marquez*, Calama 433, between JL Mera and Amazonas. Good set lunch served Mon-Fri. Seriously cheap. *La Vid*, JL Mera N24-277, between Cordero and Colón, T221063, good and cheap. *Windmill*, Versalles y Colón 2245. Reasonable prices.

In the Old City *La Chimenea*, Rodrigo de Chávez 455 y P de Alfaro. Excellent meat and steaks, reasonable prices. *El Criollo*, Flores 731 y Olmedo. Tasty chicken specialities. Clean, cheap. *La Cueva del Oso*, Edificio Pérez Pallares, Chile 1046 y Venezuela, across from the Plaza de la Independencia, T586823. In elegant covered courtyard, art deco interior, great atmosphere. Expensive. Mon-Sat 1200-0100. *Las Cuevas de Luis Candelas*, Benalcázar 713 y Chile, T287710. Open since 1963, Spanish and Ecuadorean dishes served in a nice atmosphere with flamenco music. Mid-range prices, closed on Sun. *Chifa El Chino*, Bolívar y Venezuela. Chinese, cheap, good lunch. *Girasol*, Oriente 581 y Vargas. Vegetarian. Cheap, closes at 1700. *Viena*, Chile y Flores. For breakfasts. *Tianguez*, Plaza de San Francisco. Ecuadorean food, cafetería, crafts. Run by Fundación Sinchi Sacha. *Cafetería Dimpy*, Venezuela y Mejía. Cheap lunches, snacks, juices, breakfast and coffee.

Cafés *Bangalô*, Foch y Almagro. Excellent cakes, quiches, coffees. Great atmosphere, good jazz at weekends. Mon-Sat lunchtime and 1600-2000. *Books & Coffee*, JL Mera 12-27 y Calama, T528769. Capuccino, espresso, book exchange, English and German newspapers, a good place to sit and write a letter. *El Cafecito*, Luis Cordero 1124 y Reina Victoria, at the hotel. Pancakes, set meal of the day and the best chocolate brownies. Daily 0900 until late. *Café Cultura*, Robles 513 y Reina Victoria, at the hotel. Relaxed atmosphere, tasteful décor, excellent cakes and homemade bread, good service. Daily 0800-1130 and 1500-1700. Recommended. *Café Galletti*, Amazonas 1494 y Santa María. Great coffee bar, New York owner. Recommended. *Café Libro*, Almagro 24-15 y Moreno Bellido, T567960. Coffee, snacks, excellent magazines and great atmosphere. *Fried Bananas*, JL

Mera y Roca. Funky little café, great menu. Cheap. Open Mon-Sat 0730-2230. *Super Papa*, JL Mera 761 y Baquedano. Stuffed baked potatoes, some vegetarian, sandwiches and salads, excellent cakes, takeaway service, great breakfasts, popular for notices and advertisements. Cheap. Mon-Fri 0700-2130, Sat-Sun 0700-2000. *Tianguez*, Reina Victoria 1780 y la Niña, at Plaza San Francisco and on Rafael León Larrea (behind Hotel Quito). Good café and shop, Run by Fundación Sinchi Sacha. *Hothello*, Amazonas N20-20 y 18 de Septiembre, at the hotel. Parisian style café, serves sandwiches. 0700-2200. *Lennon*, Calama 434 y Amazonas. Coffee bar, nice atmosphere. Recommended. *Sun Café*, Reina Victoria 1343 y Rodríguez, T236085. Generous portions. English spoken, occasional films shown and live entertainment. *Swiss Corner*, Los Shyris y El Telégrafo. Very good sandwiches, snacks, cakes, pastries. Expensive. 0700-2200. *Yogurt Persia*, Reina Victoria y Luis Cordero and Mariana de Jesús y Amazonas. Delicious home-made yoghurt with fresh fruit, small menu.

In the Old City *Cafetería Imperio*, Pasaje Amador B-9, T583370. Very good coffee and snacks, reasonable prices. *Café Modelo*, Sucre y García Moreno. Cheap breakfast. *Café Royal*, Portoviejo 161, T521320. Very good breakfasts, seriously cheap.*Las Cerezas*, García Moreno 1355 y Olmedo. Nice patio, friendly, good juices and fruit salads. *Café Condal*, Sucre 350 y García Moreno, T565244. Cappuccino, snacks, also Internet. *Heladería Zanzibar*, on Guayaquil, near Plaza Santo Domingo and on Benalcázar 860. Excellent ice cream. *Jugos Naturales*, Oriente 449 y Guayaquil. Safe juices and extracts.

Bakeries Quito seems to have a good bakery on every street corner. A few of the most outstanding include: *La Cosecha*, Los Shyris y El Comercio, try their garlic breads. *Cyrano*, Portugal y Los Shyris, excellent pumpernickel and whole wheat breads, outstanding pastries. *Sal y Pimienta* at the Hilton Colón and other locations. *Swissôtel* has its own bakery with excellent speciality breads.

Ice cream parlours *Corfú*, Portugal y los Shyris, next to Cyrano, excellent. *Helados de Paila*, Los Shyris, opposite and just north of the grandstands. Good sherbet from local fruits, just like in Ibarra. *Gelateria 1*, Av 6 de Diciembre, Centro Comercial Olímpico, north of the stadium. Very good Italian ice cream. At the south end of the same shopping centre is *Venezia*, Italian ice cream, also coffee, snacks and pizza.

Bars and nightclubs

Bars **NB** Bars and nightclubs are subject to frequent drug raids by police (see Drugs, page 46). You can also be arrested for not having your passport. *Alkerke*, Baquedano 340 y Reina Victoria. Good bar-café. Mon-Fri 1230-1600, Thu-Sat 1900-0200. *Arribar*, JL Mera 1238 y Lizardo García (upstairs). Good music (rap, hip hop, techno, etc), happy hour 1600-1800, very popular with gringos, pool table and table football. Good local ale and stout, but a pretty rough place. *Bierkeller*, Muros y González Suárez, T232435. Steaks, German sausages and *parrilladas*, good salads, imported German beer, pool and darts, good atmosphere, live music on Fridays. Variable schedule, call for reservations, Austrian owner, *Taberna Austriaca* bar upstairs. *La Boca del Lobo*, Calama 284 y Reina Victoria, T234083. Café-bar, snacks, nice atmosphere. Mon-Sat 1700-0100. *Bogarín*, Reina Victoria N24-217 y Lizardo García, T555057. Café-bar, snacks, live music. Tue-Sat 1800-0200. *Café Toledo 1*, Toledo 720 y Lérida and number 2, Francisco Salazar y Tamayo. Café-bar, live music every night. *La Casa de la Peña*, C Galápagos, towards the top of the hill, in the old city. Café-bar, snacks and drinks, in the house of the well-known painter Miguel de Santiago, views down to the Cathedral. *La Cascada Mágica*, Foch 476 y Almagro next to the Magic Wrap restaurant, T527190. Pool (billiards), air-hockey and other games, live music Tue, Thu and Sat.

Quito's nightlife is largely concentrated in a square, bordered by Colón & Orellana, & 6 de Diciembre & Amazonas

1700-0200. *Catz*, Calama y Reina Victoria. Small, warm atmosphere, pool table. *La Estación*, Lizardo García y JL Mera. Swiss-owned, pool and billiards, live music on Saturday (US$4 cover charge), popular with locals and tourists alike. Recommended. *Ghoz Bar*, La Niña 425 y Reina Victoria, T239826. Swiss owned, excellent Swiss food, pool, darts, videos, games, music, German book exchange. The *Hotel Hilton Colón* is good for cocktails with canapés and a resident jazz band. *Kings Cross Bar*, Reina Victoria 1781 y La Niña. Recommended for old hippies. *Kizomba*, Almagro y L García. Brazilian music, good atmosphere, friendly staff, dancing at weekends, good *caipirinhas*. Highly recommended. *Matices Piano Bar*, Av Isabel La Católica y Cordero, T555020. Excellent food, live piano music, owner is a well known local pianist and composer, Dr Nelson Maldonado. Mid-range prices. Open 1630- 0200. *Matrioshka*, Pinto 376 y JL Mera, T552668. Gay and lesbian bar. *No Bar*, Calama y JL Mera. Good mix of latin and Euro dance music on weekdays, always packed on weekends, entry US$2 at weekends, happy hour 1800-2000. Open till 0200, closed on Sun. *Papillon* and *Tijuana Bar* are at Santa María and Reina Victoria, they are popular with local yuppies. *El Pub*, San Ignacio y González Suárez. English menu, including fish and chips. popular with expats. *El Pobre Diablo*, Isabel La Católica y Galavis, 1 block north of Madrid, T235194. Good atmosphere, relaxed and friendly, jazz music, sandwiches and Ecuadorean snacks for US$3-5, a good place to hang out and chill. Mon 1800-0200, Tue-Sat 1100-0200. *Reina Victoria Pub*, on Reina Victoria 530 y Roca. Mon-Sat from 1700, darts, English style beer, moderately priced bar meals, ask about Thu dinner specials, can be a bit quiet at times, popular meeting points for British and US expats. *San Antonio de Cabeza*, Whimper 358 y Av Orellana, T235559, excellent atmosphere, live music, drinks and international food. *Snappy Bar*, J L Mera 22-83 y Veintimilla, T501040. Karaoke, net café, good American food, you can sing and have a good time with excellent prices. Open 2000-0200. *The Turtle´s Head Bar*, La Niña 626 y JL Mera, great fish, chips and amazing microbrews. Open daily 1700 to 0200. *Varadero*, Reina Victoria 1721 y La Pinta, T542575. Bar-restaurant, live Cuban music most nights, meals and snacks (US$7-9), good cocktails for around US$3, older crowd and couples.

Nightclubs   *Carpenix*, Almagro y La Niña. Cover charge, popular with young crowd. *Cerebro*, Av 6
Many of the bars turn   de Diciembre y Los Shyris, Sector El Inca. Large disco, they have contests and occa-
into informal nightclubs   sionally well known artists performing. *La Hacienda*, Camino de Orellana near Hotel
after 2200. Most of   Quito. Varied music, young crowd, beautiful views down to Guápulo. Open
the places listed are   2200-0200. *Macks*, Maldonado y Pujilí, in the south near El Recreo Trole stop. Fine mix
open until 0300   of music and people, huge, 5 dance halls. Wed-Sat 2000-0200. *Mayo 68*, Lizardo
García 662 y JL Mera. Salsoteca, small, an absolute must for all you authentic salseros. Highly recommended. *Le Pierrot*, Carrión N22-54 y Amazonas. *P.P. Botella*, Ponce Carrasco 282 y Almagro, T239627. Restaurant and later lively disco, ladies night on Thu. Mon-Wed 1230-0100, Thu-Sat 1230-0300, Sun 1230-1700. *Seseribó*, Veintimilla y 12 de Octubre, T563598. Caribbean music and salsa. Thu-Sun 2100-0200, US$6. Recommended. *Seven*, Los Shyris y Naciones Unidas, opposite Parque la Carolina. Tecno disco, liveliest 0300-0600. Open Thu-Sat. *Tabujas*, Almagro y La Niña. *Vauzá*, Tamayo y F Salazar. Varied music. Large bar in the middle of the dance floor, mature crowd. Wed-Sat 2200-0300.

Entertainment

There are always many cultural events taking place in Quito, usually free of charge. See the listings section of *El Comercio* and other papers for details. August is a particularly active month, see festivals below.

Cinemark 7, at Plaza de las Américas, Av América y República, www.cinemark.com.ec **Cinema**
Multiplex, many salons, restaurants in the same complex, US$2.35, or US$1.25 on
Wed. *Multicines*, CCI, Amazonas y Naciones Unidas (in the basement), T259677.
Excellent selection of movies, 8 salons, T259677. *Multicines*, El Recreo, at El Recreo
Trole stop in the south of the city. Same movies as in CCI, 10 salons, convenient if stay-
ing in the old city, US$1.85 or US$1.05 on Wed. *Colón*, 10 de Agosto y Colón. Often has
documentaries with Latin American themes. *Universitario*, América y Av Pérez
Guerrero, Plaza Indoamérica, Universidad Central, US$0.70. *Benalcázar*, 6 de
Diciembre y Portugal, US$1. *24 de Mayo*, Granaderos y 6 de Diciembre, US$1. The
Casa de la Cultura (see Museums) often has film festivals, as well as showing foreign
films. There are many others, especially in the old city, mostly showing violent and sex
films. Usually there is a standard entry charge (US$0.80) and you can stay as long as
you like. Section C or D of *El Comercio* lists the films every day.

Ritmo Tropical, Av 10 de Agosto 1792 y San Gregorio, Edif Santa Rosa, oficina 108, **Dance classes**
T227051. Teaches Salsa, Merengue, Cumbia, Vallenato and Folkloric dance in groups
or one-to-one, US$5 per hr.

The *Orquesta Sinfónica Nacional* presents weekly concerts on Fri evenings. Since the **Music & dance**
Teatro Sucre is being restored (see below), concerts are held at *Teatro Politécnico*,
Queseras del Medio, opposite Coliseo Rumiñahui, or in one of the colonial churches.
Call for information, T565733, US$1.50. There are concerts on Tue evenings, 3 times
per month, Oct-Dec and Feb-Aug, at the *Auditorio de las Cámaras* (Chamber of Com-
merce) Av Amazonas y República. Call for information, T260265/6 Ext 231.
   Local folk music is popular and the entertainment, as well as where it takes place,
are known as a *peña*. Most *peñas* do not come alive until 2230. *Dayumac*, JL Mera y
Carrión. This meeting place for local music groups is dark and bohemian, and warms
up after 0000. Fri-Sat 2100-0200. *Cuerdas Andinas Disco Bar*, Carrión y JL Mera.
Entrance only for couples. Thu-Sat 2200-0200. *Ñucanchi*, Av Universitaria 496 y
Armero. Thu-Sat 2230-0300.
   Popular concerts are held at the *Plaza de Toros*, Amazonas y Juan de Azcaray, in
the north or at the *Coliseo Rumiñahui*, Toledo y Queseras del Medio, La Floresta.
Tickets are sold in advance and go fast for the better known groups.

Teatro Sucre, at Plaza del Teatro, Manabí between Flores and Guayaquil, T281644, **Theatre**
was built in the 1880s. Its interior is small and distinguished. Restorations were under-
way in 2000. *Teatro Bolívar*, Flores 421 y Junín, T582486. Another classic theatre in the
old city. It was damaged by fire in 1999, but despite restoration work, there are still
theatrical presentations, the proceeds are used for the renovations. Call to enquire if a
performance is on. *Teatro Aeropuerto*, Juan J Pazmiño y Av de la Prensa, T506651, Ext
121. The Ecuadorean folk ballet 'Jacchigua' is presented here on Wed and Fri at 1930,
and is entertaining and colourful. Reserve ahead. *Teatro Humanizarte*, Leonidas Plaza
N24-226 y Baquerizo Moreno. Presents the 'Ballet Andino', a folk presentation every
Wed at 1930. *Teatro Charles Chaplin*, Cordero 1200 y JL Mera, has regular theatrical
presentations on weekends, check the paper for events. *Teatro Prometeo* adjoining
the Casa de la Cultura Ecuatoriana, 6 de Diciembre y Tarqui. *Agora*, the open-air theatre of the Casa de la Cultura, at 12 de Octubre y Patria, stages many concerts. There are
also plays at the *Patio de Comedias*, 18 de Septiembre, between Amazonas and 9 de
Octubre. *Centro Cultural Afro-Ecuatoriano* (CCA), Tamayo 985 y Lizardo García,
T522318. Sometimes has cultural events and published material, and is a useful contact for those interested in the black community.

Quito

Festivals

For details of national festivals see page 81

In Quito *años viejos* are on display throughout the city before New Year's; a good spot to see them is on Amazonas, between Patria and Colón. Water throwing is common at Carnival. The solemn *Good Friday* procession in the old city is most impressive, with thousands of devout citizens taking part. **August** is *Mes de las Artes*, organized by the municipality, with cultural events, dancing and music in different places throughout the city.

The city's main festival, *Día de Quito*, is celebrated throughout the week ending **6 December**. It commemorates the founding of the city with elaborate parades, bull-fights, performances and music in the streets. It is very lively and there is a great deal of drinking. The main events culminate on the evening of December 5, and the sixth is the day to sleep it all off; everything (except a few restaurants) closes.

Shopping

In the old city, streets are lined with shops of every imaginable kind

Trading hours are generally 0900 to 1900 on weekdays, although some shops close at midday, as they do in smaller cities. Saturday afternoon and Sunday most shops are closed. The old city remains a very important commercial area. Outside the colonial centre, especially to the north, much of the shopping is now done in shopping centres (malls), which are as insipid as anywhere else in the world. These are usually open Monday to Saturday 1000-2000, and Sunday 1000-1400. They include: *Mall El Jardín*, Amazonas between Mariana de Jesús and República; *Centro Comercial Iñaquito*, known as CCI, Amazonas and Naciones Unidas; *Quicentro Shopping*, Naciones Unidas between Los Shyris and 6 de Diciembre; *El Bosque*, Av Occidental and Carvajal, to the northwest; *El Recreo*, Av Maldonado at the Trole stop, in the south of the city.

Bookshops *Libri Mundi*, JL Mera N23-83 y Veintimilla, T234791. Excellent selection of Spanish, English, French and also some Italian books. Sells the Ecuador Handbook, South American Handbook and Central America and Mexico Handbook. Knowledgeable and helpful staff. It has a noticeboard of what's on in Quito. Very highly recommended. Open Mon-Sat, 0800-1800. There is also a branch at Quicentro Shopping, open daily. *Mr. Books*, Mall El Jardín, 3rd floor, T980281. Excellent bookshop, good selection, many in English including travel guides. Open daily. Recommended. *The Travel Company*, JL Mera 517 y Roca and JL Mera 1233 y Lizardo García. For books (secondhand at No 1233), postcards, T-shirts and videos. Recommended. *Imágenes*, 9 de Octubre y Roca. For books on Ecuador and art, also postcards. *Libro Express*, Amazonas 816 y Veintimilla, T548113, also at Quicentro Shopping and El Bosque. Has a good stock of maps, guides and international magazines. *Librería Selecciones*, Veintimilla E5-27 y Amazonas. Nice stock of magazines. *Confederate Books*, Calama 410 y JL Mera, T527890. Has an excellent selection of second-hand books, including travel guides, mainly in English but German and French are also available. Open 1000-1900. *Libros para El Alma*, DAlmagro 129 y Pinto, T226931. Also has café and library and will even organize jungle trips. *Abya-Yala*, 12 de Octubre 14-30 y Wilson, T506247. Good for books about indigenous cultures and anthropology. Also has an excellent library and museum (see Museums above). *South American Explorers* (see page 22) sell guidebooks in English and maps of other South American countries. *Biblioteca Luz*, Oriente 618 y Vargas. Runs a book exchange (mainly Spanish), for which they charge US$2. There is a bookshop at *Centro Comercial Popular*, Flores 739 y Olmedo, T212550. Sells half price books and magazines, some French and English books, also book exchange. Foreign newspapers are for sale at the news stand in *Hotel Colón* (approximately US$3 each) and in some shops along Amazonas. Lufthansa will supply German newspapers if they have spare copies.

Difoto, Amazonas 893 y Wilson, T224676. Good quality processing, English and German spoken. Recommended. *Foto Imágen*, Mariana de Jesús E5-11 e Italia, T469762. Camera sales and repairs. *Kis Color*, Amazonas 1238 y Calama. Develops and prints 36 exposure film for US$12, better quality for 24-hr printing than 1 hr service, passport photos in 3 mins. *Ecuacolor/Kodak*, Amazonas 888 y Wilson, Orellana 476 y 6 de Diciembre, and 10 de Agosto 4150 y Atahualpa and at several shopping centres. A highly recommended professional lab is that of *Ron Jones*, Lizardo García E9-104 y Andrés Xaura, 1 block east of 6 de Diciembre, T507622. He develops slides and prints, black and white or colour. He is helpful and informative. *Color Power*, Vancuver 505 y Alemania, T568287. Good lab. *Fotomania*, 6 de Diciembre N19-23 y Patria, T547512. For new and second-hand cameras, also for black and white developing. The average price for processing prints is US$10 for 24, US$12 for 36. Lots of shops on Amazonas sell film at good prices, but always check the expiry date. In the old city: *Suba Foto*, Maldonado 1371 y Rocafuerte. Sells second-hand cameras. *Foto Estudio Grau*, Bolívar 140 y Plaza Santo Domingo. For repairs and parts.

Camera repairs & equipment

Los Alpes, Reina Victoria N23-45 y Baquedano, T/F232362. Equipment sale and hire, guides for climbing and trekking. *Altamontaña*, Jorge Washington 425 y 6 de Diciembre, T524422, F558380. Imported climbing equipment for sale, equipment rental, good advice, experienced climbing and trekking guides. *The Altar*, JL Mera 615 y Carrión, T523671. Equipment rental at good prices. Imported and local gear for sale. *Andísimo*, 9 de Octubre 479 y Roca, T223030, F508347. Equipment rental and some for sale, guiding service for climbing and trekking. *Antisana*, Centro Comercial El Bosque, ground floor, T451605. Local and imported equipment, no rentals. *Aventura Sport*, Quicentro Shopping, top floor, T924373. Tents, good selection of glacier sunglasses, upmarket. *Camping Sports*, Colón 942 y Reina Victoria, T521626. Local and imported equipment, no rentals. *Cotopaxi*, Av Colón 942 y Reina Victoria. Good value equipment. *Equipos Cotopaxi*, 6 de Diciembre 927 y Patria, T500038. Ecuadorean and imported gear for sale, no rentals. Lockable pack covers, made to measure can be ordered here. *The Explorer*, Reina Victoria E6-32 y Pinto, T550911. Reasonable prices for renting or buying, very helpful, will buy US or European equipment. Offers guiding service for climbing, trekking and jungle. Recommended.

Camping, climbing & trekking equipment

Bluet Camping Gas is generally available in the above shops. For primus stoves and parts try *Almacenes Jácome*, Chile 955 (near C Guayaquil, in the old city). White gas is sometimes available at *Kywi* hardware shops, at Centro Comercial Olímpico, 6 de Diciembre, 2 blocks north of the stadium or 10 de Agosto south of Colón, ask for *'combustible para lámparas Coleman'*. It is better to have a multifuel stove, but some white gas stoves (eg the SVEA Optimus) will also burn unleaded gasoline, which is available at service stations everywhere.For hiking boots try *Calzado Beltrán*, Cuenca 562, and other shops on the same street, also see the Shopping section for Ambato.

Camping fuel

Supermaxi supermarkets at CCI, El Bosque, Centro Comercial Plaza Aeropuerto (Av de la Prensa y Homero Salas), at the Multicentro shopping complex on 6 de Diciembre y La Niña, about 2 blocks north of Colón, Mall El Jardín and El Recreo. This is a very well stocked supermarket and department store with a wide range of local and imported goods, not cheap. All branches are open Mon-Sat 1000-2000, Sun 1000-1300. *Mi Comisariato* is another supermarket and department store at Quicentro Shopping and García Moreno y Mejía in the old city. *La Feria* supermarket, Bolívar 334, between Venezuela and García Moreno. Sells good wines and spirits, and Swiss, German and Dutch cheeses. Supermercado Santa María with good prices, Av Iñaquito y Pereira and Versalles y Carrión. Macrobiotic food is available at *Vitalcentro Microbiótico*, Carrión 376 y 6 de Diciembre. *Sangre de Drago*, the Indian cure-all, is sold in markets and at homeopathic pharmacies.

Foodstuffs

Handicrafts A large selection of typical Ecuadorean *artesanías* can be found at the *Mercado Artesanal La Mariscal*, on Jorge Washington, between Reina Victoria and JL Mera. This interesting and worthwhile market, which occupies most of a city block, was built by the municipality to house street vendors. ■ *Daily 1000-1800*. There are carved figures, plates and other items of local woods, balsa wood boxes and birds, silver of all types, Indian textiles, buttons, toys and other things fashioned from tagua nuts, hand-painted tiles, naïve paintings, hand-woven rugs and a variety of antiques dating back to colonial days. Panama hats are a good buy. There are also souvenir shops on García Moreno in front of the Palacio Presidencial and some street vendors sell along Av Amazonas in the new city and C Guayaquil in the colonial city. Indigenous garments (for natives rather than tourists) can be seen and bought on the north end of the Plaza de Santo Domingo and along the nearest stretch of C Flores.

The following craft shops have been recommended, but this list is far from comprehensive. *Hilana*, 6 de Diciembre 1921 y Baquerizo Moreno. Beautiful and unique 100% wool blankets in Ecuadorean motifs, excellent quality, purchase by metre possible, inexpensive. *Casa Indo Andina*, Roca y JL Mera. Alpaca, wool fashions, good quality. Near *Hotel Quito* at Colón E10-53 y Caamaño, T541315, is *Folklore*, the store of the late Olga Fisch. It stocks a most attractive array of handicrafts and rugs, and is distinctly expensive, as accords with the designer's international reputation. Her stores can also be found at *Hotel Hilton Colón*, where *El Bazaar* has a good selection of crafts, and at the *Swissôtel*. *Productos Andinos*, Urbina 111 y Cordero, T224565. An artisans' co-operative selling a great variety of good quality, reasonably priced items. Recommended. *Camari*, Marchena 260 y Versalles. Direct sale shop run by an artisan organization. *La Bodega Exportadora*, JL Mera 614 y Carrión. Recommended for antiques and handicrafts, as is *Renacimiento*, Carrión y JL Mera. *Fundación Sinchi Sacha*, Reina Victoria 1780 y La Niña, and Plaza San Francisco, co-operative selling select ceramics and other arts and crafts from the Oriente. Recommended. *Marcel Creations*, Roca 766, entre Amazonas y 9 de Octubre. Good panama hat selection. *Artesanías Cuencanas*, Av Roca 626 entre Amazonas y JL Mera. Friendly, knowledgeable, wide selection. *Galería Latina*, next to Libri Mundi at JL Mera 823 y Veintimilla, T221098. This has a fine selection of alpaca and other handicrafts from Ecuador, Peru and Bolivia. Occasionally visiting artists demostrate their crafts. *Centro Artesanal*, JL Mera 804, *El Aborigen*, Washington 536 y JL Mera, and *Ecuafolklore*, Robles 609 entre Amazonas y JL Mera (also stocks guide books) have all been recommended. *Coosas*, JL Mera 838 and Quicentro Shopping. The factory outlet for Peter Mussfeldt's attractive animal designs (bags, clothes etc). *The Ethnic Collection*, Amazonas 1029 y Pinto. T522887. Wide variety of clothing, leather, bags, jewellery, balsa wood and ceramic items from across Ecuador. *Antigüedades el Chordeleg*, at Hilton Colón. For goldwork. *Handicrafts Otavalo*, Sucre 255 and García Moreno. Good selection, but expensive. *Nomada*, Pinzón 199 y Colón. Excellent quality T-shirts at factory prices *Amor y Café*, Foch 721 y JL Mera. Quality ethnic clothing. *Los Colores de la Tierra*, JL Mera 838 y Wilson. Hand-painted wood items and unique handicrafts.

Leather goods can be found at *Chimborazo*, Amazonas y Naciones Unidas (next to El Espiral shopping centre) and *Aramis*, Amazonas 1234. *Su Kartera*, Sucre 351 y García Moreno, T512160, also at Veintimilla 1185, between 9 de Octubre y Amazonas. Manufacturers of bags, briefcases, shoes, belts etc.

Jewellery *H Stern's*, has stores at the airport, *Hotel Hilton Colón* and *Hotel Quito*. *Alquimia*, Juan Rodríguez 139. High quality silversmith. *Jewelry & Design*, Mall El Jardín, local 166. *Taller Guayasamín*, in Bellavista (see Museums above). *Edda*, Tamayo 1256 y Cordero. Custom-made jewellery. Recommended. *Argentum*, JL Mera 614. Reasonably priced. *La Guaragua*, Washington 614 y Amazonas. Also sells *artesanías* and antiques, excellent selection, reasonable prices. *Tinta*, JL Mera 1020 y Foch, good selection of silver jewellery, reasonable prices, good service. *Jeritsa*, Veintimilla E4-162 y Amazonas, good selection of gold and silver items, good prices and service.

There is an exhibition and sale of paintings at *Parque El Ejido*, opposite *Hotel Hilton Colón*, on Saturday and Sunday mornings. On Amazonas, northeast of *Hotel Colón*, are a number of street stalls run by Otavalo Indians, who are tough but friendly bargainers. Bargaining is customary in small shops and at street stalls.

For fruits and vegetables and to get the overall *mercado* experience, the main markets are: *Mercado Central*, Av Pichincha y Olmedo, in the old city, Teatro Sucre Trole stop southbound or San Blas northbound; *Mercado Santa Clara*, Versalles y Ramírez Dávalos, Santa Clara Trole stop, *Mercado Iñaquito*, Iñaquito y Villalengua, west of Amazonas, La Y Trole stop.

Mercado Ipiales, on Chile from Imbabura uphill, or *Mercado Plaza Arenas* on Vargas, next to Colegio La Salle, are where you are most likely to find your stolen camera for sale (also try *Grau*, a camera shop on Plaza Santo Domingo, on your left as you face the church). The other market is on 24 de Mayo and Loja from Benalcázar onwards. Not surprisingly, these are unsafe parts of town.

Markets & street sellers
Watch your belongings & pockets at all markets

Sports

A local game, *pelota de guante* (glove ball), is played on Saturday afternoons and Sundays at Estadio Mejía and in Parque El Ejido. **Basketball** is played in the Coliseo Julio César Hidalgo on Av Pichincha and Coliseo Rumiñahui on Toledo y Queseras del Medio. **Football** (soccer) is played at Estadio Atahualpa, 6 de Diciembre y Naciones Unidas and at Estadio Casa Blanca, in Carcelén to the north, the schedules vary for each tournament, check the newspapers. **Rugby** is played at Colegio Militar on Sunday 1000, ask for details at *El Pub* (see Bars above). Another group plays friendly rugby, women and children are welcome to join, enquire at the *Turtle's Head Bar* (see above).

Ball games

The agencies and guides listed here have all been recommended to us, their contact information is listed under Tour operators below. *Safari Tours* Chief guide Javier Herrera speaks English and uses only ASEGUIM guides. Maximum 2 climbers per guide, large and small groups, several languages spoken, very knowledgeable, well organized and planned. *Safari* also runs a high altitude glacier school, with courses of 3-5 days with bilingual guides. *Surtrek* Arranges guided climbs of most peaks, also rents and sells equipment. Chief guide is Camilo Andrade, 8 languages spoken (including English and German), only uses ASEGUIM guides, 1 guide per 2 climbers, large and small groups. *Compañía de Guías*, Jorge Washington y 6 de Dicembre, T533779, guiasmontania@accessinter.net English, German, French and Italian spoken. All ASEGUIM guides: Julio Mesías, Cesar Román, Edison Salgado, Diego Zurita. *Sierra Nevada* Chief guide Freddy Ramírez uses mostly ASEGUIM guides and is fluent in French, English and German, he has his own equipment, and takes mostly large groups. *Pamir Travel and Adventures* Chief guide Hugo Torres is very experienced and speaks English. Independent guides do not normally provide transport or a full service (ie food, equipment, insurance). The following are all ASEGUIM: *Cosme León*, T603140. *Oswaldo Friere*, T265597. *Benno Schlauri*, T340709. *Gabriel Llano*, T450628.

Climbing clubs The Quito climbing clubs welcome new members, but they do not provide guiding services. It is not really worth joining if you are in Ecuador for only a few weeks. However, the clubs are a good source for locating professional guides. Padre José Ribas at *Colegio San Gabriel Climbing Club* is helpful, and their club meets on Wednesday at 1930. *Club de Andinismo* of the Universidad Católica meets every Tuesday and Thursday at 1930 and welcomes visitors. It is probably the most active club at this time. *Nuevos Horizontes Club* at Colón 2038 y 10 de Agosto, T552154, welcomes non-members onto their increasingly infrequent trips and will provide climbing information. *Sadday* is at Alonso de Angulo y Galo Molina.

Equipment Stores which sell climbing and camping equipment (see Shopping above) also rent some items and are a good source of general information. They are

Climbing
Complete information on climbing is found under Special interest travel, see page 65

Quito

often looking for used European/North American equipment, contact them if you wish to sell before leaving.

Mountain biking *The Biking Dutchman*, Foch 714 y JL Mera, T542806/568323, after hours 09730267, F567008, dutchman@uio.satnet.net, www.ecuadorexplorer.com/dutchman The pioneers of mountain biking in Ecuador, one and two day tours, great fun, good food, very well organized, English, German and Dutch (of course) spoken. *Safari* (see Tour operators below) rents bikes and has free route planning. *Páramo Mountain Bike Shop*, 6 de Diciembre 3925 y Checoslovaquia, T255403. Stocks high quality bikes. *Bicisport*, in *Quicentro* Shopping, top floor, and 6 de Diciembre 6327 y Tomás de Berlanga, T460894.. Stocks imported bikes and parts. *Biciteca y Renta Bike*, Av Brasil 1612 y Edmundo Carvajal (subida al Bosque), T/F241687. For sales, spares, repairs, tours, rentals and information, rents high quality bikes for US$20 per day. *Bike House*, Av Gaspar de Villaroel E11-14 y 6 de Diciembre. Stocks Cannondale, Bell, Blackburn, etc. *Bike Tech*, Andagoya 498 y Ruiz de Castilla south of Mariana de Jesús. Owners Santiago and Regis have informal 'meets' every Sunday, anyone is welcome, no charge, they ride 20 or more routes around Quito, they also have a good repair shop and cheap parts, they are friendly and glad to advise on routes. *Sobre Ruedas*, Av 10 de Agosto N52-162, Ciudadela Kennedy, T416781. Repairs, tours, rentals and sales. For more information on mountain biking, see under Special interest travel, page 74.

Other activities **Bowling** At El Molinón, Amazonas y Eloy Alfaro. **Bullfighting** At Plaza de Toros Iñaquito, Amazonas y Tomás de Berlanga, the first week of December is the main season. Tickets are on sale at 1500 the day before the bullfight. An above-average ticket costs US$10 but you may have to buy from touts. The Unión de Toreros, Edif Casa Paz, Av Amazonas, has information on all bullfights around the country; these take place all year. They do not have details of the parochial *toros de pueblo*, these take place during each village's *fiestas patronales*. **Bungee jumping** Every Sunday at 1000 with *Andes Bungee*, T524796, US$50 for 2 jumps. Be mindful of safety however, as accidents have occurred. **Cockfighting** Takes place in the Pollodrome, C Pedro Calixto y Chile, on Saturday, 1400-1900. Entry is US$0.25 plus bet. **Jogging** The Hash House Harriers is a club for runners and walkers. Enquire at *Reina Victoria Pub*, T229369. **Paragliding** *Escuela Pichincha de Vuelo Libre*, Carlos Endara Oe3-60 y Amazonas, T256592 Offers a complete course for US$400. (See also Special interest travel, page 74). **Snorkelling** *El Globo* shops, 10 de Agosto y Roca, and Amazonas y Gaaspar de Villaroel,stock cheap snorkelling gear, as do *Importaciones Kao*, Colón y Almagro, at Quicentro Shopping and at El Bosque. **Swimming** There is a cold spring-water pool on Maldonado beyond the Ministry of Defence building (US$1), hot shower (US$1). A public heated, chlorinated pool is in Miraflores, at the upper end of C Universitaria, a 10-minute walk from Amazonas. You must take swimming cap,

towel and soap to be admitted. It's open Tue-Sun, 0900-1600; entry US$1.50. There is another public pool at Batán Alto, on Cochapata, near 6 de Diciembre and Gaspar de Villaroel, very good but expensive at US$3. **Whitewater rafting** For complete information on rafting and kayaking, see under Special interest travel, page 70.

Tour operators

The following companies have all been recommended. Most are clustered in the Mariscal district, especially along Av Amazonas between Colón and Patria, where you are encouraged to have a stroll and shop around. They are divided into those which specialize in Galápagos tours or jungle tours; those which offer a variety of tours are listed under General tours, below. For companies specializing in climbing/trekking, river rafting or mountain biking, also see above under Sports, starting on page 131. Choosing a responsible tour operator is very important, not only as a way of getting the best experience for your money, but also to limit impact on areas you will visit and ensure benefits for local communities. See Responsible tourism, page 42. **NB** When booking tours, note that national park fees are rarely included (for park fees, see page 449).

General tours *Alta Montaña*, JL Mera 12-27 y L García, T528769. For climbing and trekking. *Andes Adventures*, Av Amazonas N23-04 y Wilson, T/F222651, andes@adventures.com.ec. Climbing, trekking, rafting, jungle tours, Galápagos cruises. *Andisimo Travel & Outdoors*, Av 9 de Octubre 479, T508347, tours@andisimo.com, www.andisimo.com Trekking, climbing and other tours. *Angermeyers Expediciones y Turismo Cía Ltda*, Foch 726 y Amazonas, T569960, F569956, angermeyer@accessinter.net, www.angermeyer.com Galápagos cruises, jungle and mountain tours. *Canodros*, Av Portugal 448 e Isabel de Aldaz, T256759, eco-tourism1@ecu.net.ec, www.galapagosexplorer.com, run Galápagos cruises and jungle tours in the Kapawi Ecological Reserve, also have an office in Guayaquil. *Cultura Reservation Center (CRC)*, at *Café Cultura*, Robles 513 y Reina Victoria, T/F558889, info@ecuadortravel.com, www.ecuadortravel.com Booking and information centre for a collection of small, privately owned hotels and lodges throughout Ecuador and the Galápagos. *Ecoventura*, Av Colón 535 y 6 de Diciembre, T507408, F507409, info@galapagosnetwork.com, www.ecoventura.com Miami office: Galapagos Network, USA and Canada toll-free T1-800-633-7972 Tours throughout Ecuador and to the Galápagos. *Ecuadorian Tours* (American Express agent), Av Amazonas 329 y J Washington, T560488, F501067, www.ecuadoriantours.com They also sell local student cards for US$20 to those with proof of home student status, useful for discounts. They also have an office at *Hotel Colón*. *Ecuaviajes*, Av Eloy Alfaro 1500 y Juan Severino, T238544, F563510. Cristina Latorre de Suárez speaks excellent English and is very helpful. *Elinatour*, J. Bejarano 150 y Suárez, T529053. Seven blocks

Quito

from *Hotel Quito*. Very helpful. *Etnotur*, Luis Cordero 13-13 y JL Mera, T564565, F502682, etnocru@uio.satnet.net. English and German spoken, jungle, mountain, rafting and Galápagos tours. *Explorandes*, Wilson 537 y Diego de Almagro, T556936, F556938, explora@hoy.net Trekking, rafting, climbing, jungle tours. *Free Biker Tours*, Guipuzcoa 339 y La Floresta, T560469, or in Switzerland, Grenzweg 48, 3645 Gwatt, T03-3365-128. Run by Patrick Lombriser, spectacular tours on 600cc Enduro motorcycles. *Inti Travel*, in Ecuador T599297, www.wonderlink.com, US agent *Exito*, 1212 Broadway Ave, Suite #910, Oakland, CA 94612, T1-800-6554053. Small group hiking and climbing adventures in the Andes and Amazon. *Klein Tours*, Av Los Shyris 1000 y Holanda, T430345, F442389, ecuador@kleintours.com.ec, www.kleintours.com Galápagos and mainland tours, tailor-made, specialist and adventure, English, French and German spoken. *KBtours*, Marco Aguirre N48-142, T241209, kbtours@hotmail.com, Quito city tours, Indian markets and Cotopaxi. *Metropolitan Touring*, Av República de El Salvador 36-84, T464780, F464702, www.ecuadorable.com, also has office at Amazonas 239 y 18 de Septiembre. A very large organization. Run Galápagos cruises, also arranges climbing, trekking expeditions led by world-known climber, as well as city tours of Quito, Machalilla National Park, private rail journeys, jungle camps. *Transturi S.A.*, Isla Pinzón 701 near Río Coca,

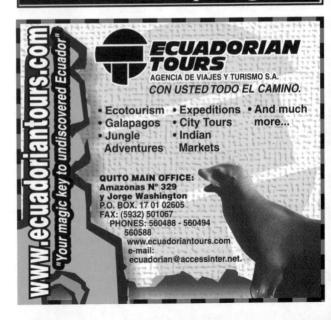

T245055. This is part of Metropolitan Touring, and operate a cruise ship, the *Flotel Orellana*, in 4-5 day trips along the jungle rivers. **Naturgal**, Foch 635 y Reina Victoria, T522681, T/F224913. English spoken, specializes in trips to the Llanganates. Also recommended as good value for Galápagos. **Nomadtrek**, Av América 5677, T254368/369, nomadtre@uio.satnet.net Offers trips to the Galápagos, white river rafting and tours to the jungle. Good for adventure travel. **Pablo Prado**, Rumipamba 730 y República, T446954. Tours in 4WD vehicle, nature adventures, ecological excursions, Galápagos, rainforest. **Pamir Travel and Adventures**, JL Mera, 721 y Ventimilla, T542605/220892, F547576, pamir@travels.com.ec. Galápagos cruises, climbing tours and jungle tours (see also under Climbing above). **Positiv Turismo**, Voz Andes N41-81, T440604, F257883, www.positurs.com Swiss-Austrian-run company offers trips to Galápagos, cultural round trips, trekking and special interest tours. **Quasar Nautica**, Av Los Shyris 2447 y Gaspar de Villaroel, T257822/448786, qnautic1@ecnet.ec, wwwquasarnautica.com Tailor-made tours to historic sites, haciendas, national parks and jungle lodges with highly qualified guides. They have a fleet of 6 luxurious sail and power yachts for their highly recommended Galápagos cruises. UK agent: Penelope Kellie, T01962 779317, F01962 779458, pkellie@yachtors. u-net.com; US agent: T1-800-2472925, F1-305-5927060, tumbaco@gate.net **Rain Forestour**, Av Amazonas 420, between Robles and Roca, T239822, rainfor@interactive.net.ec, also have an office in Baños. Offers highland and jungle trips. **Ranft Turismo**, Shyris y Río Coca, Edif Eurocentro, T255954, F432622, ecuador@ranfturismo.com Trips to Galápagos, Andes and Amazon. **Safari**, Calama 380 y JL Mera (also at Pasaje Roca 630 y Amazonas, the small dead-end street opposite *Hotel Alameda Real*), T552505, F223381, admin@safari.com.ec, www.safari.com.ec Run by Jean Brown, Pattie Serrano and mountaineer Javier Herrera. Excellent adventure travel, customized trips, mountain

climbing, rafting, trekking and Oriente jungle including Huaorani territory. They also book Galápagos tours, run a high altitude glacier school and are an excellent source of travel information. Highly recommended. Calama office open 7 days a week 0900-1900 (see also under Climbing, above). *Sherpa Tours*, Versalles 1127 y Carrión, T/F224312, sherpatours@ accessinter.net. Agent for *Guacamayo Bahía Tours* in Bahía de Caráquez (see page 334), also contact for *Enduro Adventure* motorcycle tours. *Sierra Nevada*, Pinto 637 y Amazonas, T553658/224717, F554936, snevada@ accessinter.net. Specialized adventure tours and jungle expeditions (see also Climbing and Whitewater rafting above). *Sudamericana de Turismo*, Av Amazonas 11-15 y Pinto, T233233 Ricardo speaks German. *Surtrek*, Amazonas 897 y Wilson, T561129, F561132, info@surtrek.de, www.surtrek. com Climbing and trekking expeditions, jungle and Galápagos tours, also flights (see also Climbing above). *Terracenter*, Reina Victoria 1343 y J Rodríguez, T/F507858. Wide variety of tours, including to the Galápagos (special arrangement with Simón Bolívar language school). *Tierra del Sol*, Amazonas 338 y Jorge Washington, T/F228655. Galápagos tours, rafting, climbing and adventure tours. *Vasco Tours*, L García 537 y Reina Victoria, T/F235348, vascotours@andinanet.net Mounatains and Oriente jungle.

For more details of tours to the Galápagos, see page 407 **Galápagos tours** *Andes Discovery Tours*, Av Amazonas 645 y Ramírez Dávalos, T550952, F437470. Helpful. *Ecoventura/Galápagos Network* see contact information above. Operate three 20-passenger motor yachts and a 48-passenger ship. *Ecuagal*, Amazonas 1113 y Pinto, T229579, F550988. Own 2 boats in the Galápagos. *Galasam Cía Ltda*, Pinto 523 y Av Amazonas, and Amazonas 1354 y Cordero, T507080, F567662, galasam@accessinter.net Operates economic Galápagos Tours as well as Condor Tours, Uniclán, Yanasacha, Sol Mar Tours. Their tours can be booked in Europe: Switzerland,

Monorama, T01-2615121, F01-2622306; Holland, Cross Country Travel, T025-2077677, F025-2023670. Also in Australia through Latin American Travel, T61-33295211, F61-33296314. And in the USA: Galápagos Worldwide, T1-800-3279854, F1-305-6611457; Latin American Specialized Tours, T1-410-9223116, F1-410-9225538; Galapagos Yacht Cruises, T1-800-4252778; Forum Travel, T1-510-6712993, F510-9461500. The above are exclusive representatives and prices are the same as in Ecuador. **Neptunotour**, 290 Gangotena Enrique y Orellana,PO Box 17-04-10502. Galápagos cargo boat tour. **Nixe Cruises**, Cordero 1313 y JL Mera, T230552 (ask for Consuelo). Catamaran cruises of Galápagos, maximum 10 passengers, 4 crew, 1 guide, diving available, also tours of the coast, Machalilla National Park and the Oriente. **Palmar Voyages**, Alemania 575 (N31-77) y Mariana de Jesús, T569809, F506915, palmarro@impsat.net.ec Small specialist company, good rates. **Rolf Wittmer**, Foch E7-81 y Almagro, T526938, F228520, rwittmer@tiptop.com.ec, www.rolfwittmertiptoptours.com Two yachts available, *Tip Top 11* and *111*, for tours of the Galápagos. **Taurus Viajes**, Amazonas 678 y Ramirez Davalos, 2nd Flr, T223639. **The Galápagos Boat Company**, Pasaje Roca 630, T220426. Broker for up to 80 boats in the islands, will find you the best deals around.

Jungle tours *Explorer Tours*, Reina Victoria 1235 y Lizardo García, T508871, F222531. Owns *Sacha Lodge* and *La Casa del Suizo* on the Río Napo, first rate educational jungle tours. **Green Planet**, JL Mera N23-48, T520570, greenpla@interactive.net.ec Friendly staff and guides, good food. **Kempery Tours**, Pinto 539 y Amazonas, T226715, kempery@ecuadorexporer.com, www.ecuadorexplorer.com/kempery/home Good value tours. **Native Life**, Foch E4-167 y Amazonas, Quito, T505158, F229077, natlife1@natlife.com.ec Run tours to their Nativo Lodge in the Cuyabeno Reserve. **Napo Tour**, JL Mera 1312 y Cordero, T547283. Has been recommended as efficient and cheap, it is better value to book Napo's *Anaconda Hotel* (near Misahuallí) in Quito than to book in Misahuallí (it is also cheaper to make your own way there than to go with Napo Tour). **Tropic Ecological Adventures**, Av República E7-320 y Almagro, Edif Taurus, Apto 1-A, T225907, F560756, tropic@ uio.satnet.net, www.tropiceco. com Run by Welshman Andy Drumm, a naturalist guide and divemaster on the Galápagos. He also works closely with conservation groups. Winners of an award for responsible tourism in 1997, this small company runs ecologically responsible and educational jungle tours and is recommended for anyone seriously interested in the environment. A sizeable percentage of each fee is given to indigenous communities and ecological projects.

Also see Jungle lodges, page 354

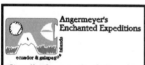
Transport

Bus All tickets are bought on the buses; the exact fare is sometimes expected. Buses are very slow in the Old City owing to traffic jams. To reduce worsening air pollution in the city, the municipal authorities attempt to control motor

Local
See also Ins & outs, page 100

vehicle emissions. The situation was helped slightly by the introduction of the electrified trolley bus service and further improvement might come with the implementation in 2001, of the *Ecovía*, an exclusive lane for 'ecologically sound' buses, along Av 6 de Diciembre. Many bus lines go through *La Marín* (officially called Plaza San Martín) at the north end of the old city. Extra caution is advised here, as it is a rough area, pickpockets abound and it should be avoided at night.

Suburban service: buses for destinations near Quito, leave from 'La Marín', which extends the length of Av Pichincha; a few others leave from Cotocollao (Trans Minas) in the north, Villaflora in the south, or near the Patria/10 de Agosto intersection.

Taxis All taxis must have working meters by law, but make sure the meter is running (drivers may sometimes say their meters are out of order). Do not ask the price if the meter is running as this will offend bona fide drivers. If the meter is not running, you should always fix the fare before getting in. Also insist that the taxi drops you precisely where you want to go.

All legally registered taxis have the number of their co-operative and the individual operator's number prominently painted on the side of the vehicle and on a decal on the windshield. They are safer and cheaper than unauthorized taxis. Note the registration and the license plate numbers if you feel you have been seriously overcharged or mistreated. You may then complain to the transit police or tourist office. But be reasonable and remember that the majority of taxi drivers are honest and helpful.

For trips outside Quito taxi tariffs should be agreed beforehand. Expect to pay US$50-70 a day. Outside the main hotels cooperative taxi drivers have a list of agreed excursion prices and most drivers are knowledgeable. Arrangements can also be made through the radio taxi numbers listed above. For taxi tours with a guide, try Hugo R Herrera, T267891/236492. He speaks good English and is recommended.

Long distance
Watch your belongings at the Terminal Terrestre at all times

Bus The main *Terminal Terrestre* for all national services is in the old city, on Maldonado (see page 100). There is a 24-hr luggage store which is safe, US$1.75 per day. There are company booking offices in the terminal but staff shout destinations of buses leaving and you can pay them when you get on board. For the less frequent routes, or at busy times of the year (long weekends or holidays) it may be a good idea to purchase your ticket a day in advance, but this is usually not necessary. See under the relevant destinations for fares and schedules.

Quito's *Terminal Terrestre* is neither particularly safe nor pleasant, so try to spend as little time here as possible. If going to the *Terminal Terrestre* by taxi, you can pay the driver a little extra to take you inside directly to the departure ramps, so as to avoid walking through the station. This is an especially good idea at night or very early in the morning. When arriving in Quito by bus, you and your luggage will be unloaded next to a large taxi rank. Cab drivers wait for the buses; choose one, either agree to use the meter or agree on a price, and get going. If you have almost no luggage and know Quito well, then there is a trolley stop right outside the bus station which is convenient, but riding the trolley with a backpack is not recommended because of crowding and theft.

Several companies now run better quality coaches on their longer routes. Those which have stations in the new city are: Flota Imbabura, Manuel Larrea 1211 y Portoviejo, T236940, for Cuenca and Guayaquil; Transportes Ecuador, JL Mera 330 y Jorge Washington, to Guayaquil; Panamericana Internacional, Colón 852 y Reina Victoria, T501585, for Huaquillas, Machala, Cuenca, Loja, Guayaquil, Manta and Esmeraldas. They also run international service: daily to **Bogotá**, changing buses in Tulcán and Ipiales, US$74, 29 hrs; to Lima, changing buses in Aguas Verdes and Túmbes, US$60, 38 hrs. For these and other South American destinations it is cheaper to take a bus to the border and change there. The route for crossing the Peruvian border via Loja and Macará takes longer than the Huaquillas route, but Macará is a more relaxed place to cross. Ormeño Internacional, from Perú, has an office on Shyris N34-432 y Portugal, opposite Parque la Carolina, T460027. They go twice per week to Lima (US$40, 36 hrs), **Santiago** (US$130, 4 days) and **Buenos Aires** (US$170, 1 week).

The main car hire companies are at the airport: Avis, Budget, Ecuacars, Expo and Localiza. City offices: **Budget**, Colón y Amazonas, T221814 and *Hotel Hilton Colón* (closed Sat-Sun), T525328. **Avis**, at the airport, T440270. **Ecuacars**, Colón 1280 y Amazonas, T529781. **Expo**, Av América N21-66 y Bolívia, T228688. **Localiza**, 6 de Diciembre E8-124 y Veintimilla, T505986. **Santitours**, Maldonado 2441, T212267/251063, also rent minibuses, buses and four-wheel drive vehicles, chauffeur driven rental only. **Trans-Rabbit**, in the international arrivals section of the Airport rent vans for up to 10 passengers with driver for trips in Quito and out of town, T568755. Budget and Ecuacar have been particularly recommended as being helpful. For rental prices and procedures see Car hire, page 54. Drivers should note that there is a ring road around Quito, and a bypass to the south via the Autopista del Valle de Los Chillos and the Carretera de Amaguaña. ·

Car hire

AMIPA, *Auxilio Mecánico Inmediato para Automóviles*, T464931, cellular 734222. Reliable roadside mechanical assistance in the Quito metropolitan area (including Los Chillos and Tumbaco valleys), service for members and non-members. **Land rover** Specialists at Inglaterra 533, *Talleres Atlas*. Also *Luis Alfredo Palacios*, Iturralde y Av de la Prensa, T234341. **Motorcycle repairs** *Sr Lother Ranft*, Euro Servicio, Av Los Shyris y Río Coca, T454261. His main business is BMW, Mercedes and Porsche cars (very busy) but he is a bike enthusiast and can get BMW motorcycle parts from Germany in 2 weeks. *Paco Olmedo*, Domingo Espinar 540 y La Gasca, T550589, has a well-equipped mechanical shop. *Talleres Kosche*, Eiffel 138 y Los Shyris, T442204. Recommended. *Juan Molestina*, Av 6 de Diciembre y Bélgica, T564335, fuel and travel equipment shop, helpful for motorbike spare parts.

Car & motorcycle repairs

Train The railway station is 2 km south of the centre, along the continuation of C Maldonado, reached by trolley, Chimbacalle stop if northbound, Machángara if southbound and walk uphill along Maldonado. The ticket office (T656142) at this beautiful but decrepit old station is supposedly open Mon-Fri 0800-1630, Sat 0800-1200, but is frequently closed and employees are not well-informed. You can also get information from railway head office, T582921 (Mon-Fri 0800-1600).

Regular passenger service has been discontinued throughout the country. See Getting around, page 50. A tourist train runs from Quito to the Cotopaxi station in Area Nacional de Recreación El Boliche , Saturday and Sunday at 0800, returning at 1430. It costs US$10 each way, purchase tickets in advance as it is a popular ride. If you wish to return by bus, it is a 2 km walk from the Cotopaxi ststion to the Panamerican highway. Metropolitan Touring (T464780) offers various tours involving train travel; see Tour operators on page 133.

Directory

Domestic *Aerogal*, Av Amazonas 7997, T257202. *TAME*, Av Amazonas 13-54 y Colón, T509382. **International** *ACES*, Edif Banco La Previsora, Torre B, #411, Av Naciones Unidas y Amazonas, T466461. *AeroPerú*, Jorge Washington 718, 3rd Flr, T561699. *Air France*, World Trade Center, Torre A, #710, Av 12 de Octubre N24-562 y Cordero, T524201. *American Airlines*, Av Amazonas 4545 y Pereira, T260900. *Avensa/Servivensa*, Av Portugal 794 y República de El Salvador, T253972. *Avianca*, Edif Twin Towers, Av República de El Salvador 780 y Portugal, T262736. *Continental Airlines*, World Trade Center, Av 12 de Octubre 1830 y Cordero, T557170. *Copa Airlines*, Veintimilla 910 y JL Mera, T563358. *Ecuatoriana*, Torres de Almagro, Reina Victoria y Colón, T563923. *Iberia*, Av. Amazonas 239 y Jorge Washington, T560546. *KLM*, Edif Torre 1492, #1103-1104, Av 12 de Octubre y A Lincoln, T986828. *LanChile*, 18 de Septiembre E7-05 y Reina Victoria, T508396.

Airline offices

Quito

Lufthansa, 18 de Septiembre E7-05 y Reina Victoria, T541300. *TACA*, Av República de El Salvador 3567 y Portugal, T923169. *Varig*, Edif Porto Lisboa, Av Portugal 794 y Rep de El Salvador, T250126.

Banks   For the best way to bring your funds, see Money, page 29. Banks are open 0900-1800 Mon-Fri, cash advance usually till 1600, and Sat 0900-1400. Expect queues and paperwork at all banks. The procedures and commissions indicated below are subject to frequent change. *Banco del Pacífico* deals with Mastercard through ATMS, and TCs in US$ only, maximum US$200/day, US$3 charge per transaction. Main branch at Naciones Unidas between Shyris and Amazonas, also Amazonas y Roca, Mall El Jardín and Swissôtel. For cash advances on *Mastercard* without using an ATM, you must go to the Mastercard office, Naciones Unidas 825, next door to Banco del Pacífico, good service. *Banco Guayaquil*, Colón y Reina Victoria, 3rd Flr. Visa ATM with maximum withdrawal of US$100, cash advances on Visa without limit, fast and efficient. *Filanbanco*, Amazonas y Robles. Visa ATM and cash advance, helpful if cards are lost, does not change TCs. Also at 10 de Agosto, opposite Central Bank, and at the airport. *Lloyds Bank*, Av Amazonas 580 y Carrión. Quick service, closes 1530. Recommended. *Banco de Pichincha*, Amazonas y Colón, VISA cash advace. Also on Venezuela in the old town, half a block from Plaza de la Independencia. *Produbanco*, Amazonas N35-211 y Japón (near CCI), and Amazonas y Robles. Cash and TCs in various currencies, 1% to 2% commission, good service, no credit cards. Closed on Sat. The *American Express* representative is *Ecuadorean Tours*, Amazonas 329 y Jorge Washington, T560488. Sells and replaces Amex TCs, but not does not deal with any cash.

Casas de Cambio   There are not too many exchange houses left following dollarization, and some of those listed below might soon close due to shrinking business. They may be more efficient than banks but charge a higher commission. Shop around. *Multicambios*, Venezuela 689, T511364, Roca 720, T567344, and Colón 919 y Reina Victoria, T561747, also at the airport. Open Mon-Fri, 0830-1330, 1430-1730 and Sat morning. *Vazcambios*, Amazonas y Roca, *Hotel Alameda Real*, T225442. Charges 1.5% commission for US$ TCs, 2% for TCs in other currencies.

Communications   **Post Office**   There are 22 postal branches throughout Quito, all are open Mon-Fri 0730-1900, Sat
See Postal services, page   0730-1400. In principle all branches provide all services, but your best chances are at Colón y
59, for rates, procedures   Almagro in the Mariscal district, and at the main sorting centre on Japón near Naciones Unidas,
& precautions   behind the CCI shopping centre. The branch on Eloy Alfaro 354 y 9 de Octubre is especially chaotic and unhelpful, best avoided. There is also a branch in the old city, on Espejo, between Guayaquil y Venezuela, and between the old and new towns at Ulloa and Ramírez Dávalos, behind the Mercado Santa Clara. This used to be the centre for parcel post, and you may still be directed there to send large pckages. *Poste Restante* is available at the post offices at Espejo and at Eloy Alfaro. All *poste restante* letters are sent to Espejo unless marked 'Correo Central, Eloy Alfaro', but you are advised to check both *postes restantes*, whichever situation you use. For those with an Amex card or TCs, letters can be sent care of American Express, Apdo 2605, Quito. *South American Explorers*, see page 22, holds mail for members.

Telecommunications   National and international calls can be made from the **Andinatel** offices: at Av 10 de Agosto y Colón; in the Old City at Benalcázar between Chile and Mejía; the Terminal Terrestre and the airport (above international departures); all open 0800-2200. For information about making long distance calls from Bell South and Porta public phones, see Telephone services, page 60.

Internet   Quito has very many cyber cafés. In the Mariscal tourist district it is difficult to walk two steps without bumping into one. Rates start at about US$1/hour, net2phone around US$0.25 per minute. Only a very few are listed below, you will have no difficulty finding others. Since there are so many to choose from, you can select a cyber café to suit your particular mood; do you prefer to surf to the sounds of classical music or heavy metal? Since they are so popular some places get crowded, smoky, and very noisy - especially distracting for net2phone. Also remember that internet access is cheapest and fastest in Quito, Guayaquil and Cuenca, more expensive and slower in small towns and more remote areas.

A few of the recommended favourites include: *British Council*, Amazonas 1646 y La Niña, open 0900-1800 daily; *Café Net*, Edificio Torres de Almagro, local 14 (downstairs), Reina Victoria y Cordero, open 0730-0200 Mon-Fri and 0900-0000 Sat-Sun, private booths, music not too loud, highly recommeded; *Papaya Net*, Calama 413 y JL Mera, open 0900-0000 daily, very popular with *gringos*; *Pizza Net*, Calama 354 y JL Mera, open 0800-0000 daily, spacious, pizzas and pastas, large screen TV; *Pool Net*, Calama 233 y Diego de Almagro, open 0900-0000 daily, popular with locals.

British Council, Amazonas N26-146 y La Niña, T540225/508282, F223396, british4@uio.satnet.net. Open Mon-Fri, 0900-1900. Language school, library, *La Galería* café serves a full English breakfast for US$3 and has back copies of British newspapers, also book exchange, vegetarian restaurant, tea and cakes, free films every Wed, internet facilities. Books are loaned if you join the library and pay a returnable deposit. *Alliance Française* at Eloy Alfaro 1900. French courses, films and cultural events. *Casa Humboldt*, Vancouver y Polonia, T548480. German centre, films, talks, exhibitions.

Cultural centres

Argentina, Amazonas 477, 8th flr, T562292. *Austria*, Veintimilla 878 y Amazonas, 4th flr, T524811. *Belgium*, JL Mera N23-103 y Wilson, T545340. *Bolivia*, Bosmediano 526 y José Carbo, T446450. *Brazil*, Edif España, Av Amazonas y Colón, T563086. *Bulgaria*, De Los Cabildos 115, T444873. *Canada*, Edif Josueth González, 4th flr, Av 6 de Diciembre 2816 y Paul Rivet, T223114. *Chile*, Edif Xerox, 4th flr, Juan Pablo Sanz 3617 y Av Amazonas, T466780. *China*, Av Atahualpa 349 y Amazonas, T458337. *Colombia*, Av Colón 1133 y Amazonas, T222486. *Costa Rica*, Rumipamba 692 y República, 2nd floor, T254945. *Cuba*, Av 6 de Diciembre 5113, T260981. *Czech Republic/Slovakia*, Grecia 210, T460220. *Dominican Republic*, Edif Albatros, 2nd flr, Av de Los Shyris 1240 y Portugal, T434232. *El Salvador*, Diego de Almagro 1118, T565346. *Egypt*, Baquedano 922 y Reina Victoria, T225240. *France (embassy)*, General Plaza 107 y Patria, T560789. *France (consulate)*, Edif Kingman, 2nd flr, Diego de Almagro 1550 y La Pradera, T569883. *Germany*, Edif City Plaza, Av Naciones Unidas y República de El Salvador, T970822. *Guatemala*, Edif Gabriela 3, 3rd flr, República de El Salvador 733 y Portugal, T459700. *Honduras*, Av 12 de Octubre 1942, T504047. *Israel*, Edif Plaza 2000, 9th flr, Av 12 de Octubre y Gen Francisco Salazar, T562152 *Italy*, La Isla 111 y H Albornoz, T561077. *Japan*, Edif Corp. Financiero Nacional, JL Mera N19-36, T561899. *Korea*, Reina Victoria 1539, T223619. *Mexico*, Av 6 de Diciembre N36-165 y Naciones Unidas, T285788. *Netherlands*, World Trade Center, 1st flr, 12 de Octubre 1942 y Cordero, T229229. *Nicaragua*, Edif World Trade Center, Torre A, #405, Av 12 de Octubre 1942 y Cordero, T230810. *Panama*, Edif Kingman, Diego de Almagro 1550, T557838. *Paraguay*, Obispo Andrade 330, T448060. *Peru*, Edif Irlanda, Av República de El Salvador 495 e Irlanda, T468410. *Poland*, Eloy Alfaro 2897, T453466. *Russia*, Reina Victoria 462 y Roca, T526375. *Spain*, La Pinta 455 y Amazonas, T564377. *Sweden*, Pasaje Alonso Jerves 134 y Orellana, T509423. *Switzerland*, Edif Xerox, 2nd flr, Juan Pablo Sanz 120 y Amazonas, T434948. *UK*, Edif City Plaza, 14th flr, Av Naciones Unidas y República de El Salvador, T970800. *Uruguay*, Edif Josueth González, 9th flr, Av 6 de Diciembre 2816 y Paul Rivet, T544228. *Venezuela*, Los Cabildos 115 e Hidalgo de Pinto, T268635. *USA*, Av 12 de Octubre y Patria, T562890.

Embassies & consulates

Quito

Quito has become one of the most important centres for Spanish language study in all of Latin America, with over 100 schools operating in the city. Students range from executives pursuing an intensive period of technical training, to travellers beginning an extended journey with a few informal classes. Many people combine language study with touring and opportunities for cross-cultural exposure, and some schools are well set up to organize this. Homestays with an Ecuadorean family are often part of the experience. There are schools and programs to suit every taste and budget, far too many to list here. Instead we will try to focus on how to choose a language school, and list just a few of those who have received consistently favourable recommendations.

Language courses

If you are short on time then it can be a good idea to make your arrangements from home, either directly with one of the schools or through an agency such as *AmeriSpan Unlimited*, USA and Canada toll-free T1-800-879-6640, info@amerispan.com,

Quito

www.amerispan.com who can offer you a wide variety of options. If you have more time and less money, then it may be cheaper to organize your own studies after you arrive. *South American Explorers* provides a free list of recommended schools and these may give club members discounts.

Identify your budget and goals for the course: rigorous grammatical and technical training, fluent conversation skills, getting to know Ecuadoreans or just enough basic Spanish to get you through your trip. Visit a few places to get a feel for what they charge and offer. Prices vary greatly, from US$3 to US$10 per hour, but you do not always get what you pay for. There is also tremendous variation in teacher qualifications, infrastructure and resource materials. A great deal of emphasis has traditionally been placed on one-to-one teaching, but remember that a well structured small classroom setting such as that provided by the *Universidad Católica* (see below) can also be very good.

The quality of homestays likewise varies, the cost including meals runs from US$10 to US$15 per day. Try to book just one week at first to see how a place suits you, don't be pressed into signing a long term contract right at the start. For language courses as well as homestays, deal directly with the people who will provide services to you, and avoid local intermediaries. Always get a detailed receipt when you make a payment.

Finally, remember that Quito is not the only place in Ecuador where you can study Spanish. Although some of the best schools are located in the capital there are also good options in Otavalo, Baños, Cuenca and elsewhere (listed in the corresponding sections of the text). Do you prefer the

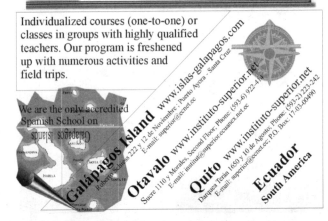

cosmopolitan bustle and nightlife of Quito, or the clean air and tranquillity of a smaller town?

The following are some of the recommended Spanish schools in Quito: **In the New City:** *Academia de Español Equinoccial*, Roca 533 y JL Mera, T/F564488, www.equadorspanish.com *Academia de Español Quito*, Marchena 130 y Av 10 de Agosto, T553647, F506474, edalvare@pi.pro.ec, www.academquito.com.ec *Academia Latinoamericana*, José Queri 2 y Eloy Alfaro, T528770, F465500, delco@spanish.com.ec, www.ecu.net.ec/academia *Amazonas One to One Spanish School*, Washington 718 and Amazonas, Edif Rocafuerte, 3rd Flr, T/F504654, amazonas@pi.pro.ec, www.ecu.net.ec/amazonas *American Spanish School*, 9 de Octubre 564 y Carrión, T229166, F229165, as.school@accessinter,net *Bipo & Toni's Academia de Español*, Carrión E8-183 y L Plaza, T/F500732/556614, info@bipo.net, www.bipo.net *Centro de Español Siglo 21*, Carrión 768 y 9 de Octubre, T568501, F237359, info@centro21.com.ec, www.centro21.com *Columbus Travel* in the same building, also offer salsa lessons on Fri. *Cristóbal Colón*, Av Colón 2088 y Versalles, T506508, F222964, ccolon@southtravel.com, www.southtravel. com *Escuela de Español Ecuador*, Lazarazo 2328 y C Zorilla, T557529, cellular T09-478801, provide classes at students' homes. *Estudio de Español Pichincha*, Andrés Xaura 182, entre Lizardo García y Foch, T528051, F601689, lvite@uio.satnet.net *Galápagos Spanish School*, Amazonas 258 y Washington, 2nd floor, T565213, info@ galapagos.edu.ec, www.galapagos.edu.ec *Instituto Superior de Español*, Darquea Terán 1650 y 10 de Agosto, T223242, F221628, superior@ecnet.ec, www. instituto-superior.net They also have a school in Otavalo (Sucre 1110 y Morales, 2nd flr, T922414, F922415, institut@ superior.ecuanex. ec) and can arrange voluntary work with La Cruz Roja Ecuatoriana, at Mindo, Fundación Jatun Sacha and others. *La Lengua*, Colón 1001 y JL Mera, 8th Flr, T/F501271, lalengua@hoy.net, www.la-lengua.com (Switzerland T/F8510533 E peter-baldauf@ bluewin.ch). *Mitad del Mundo*, Gustavo Darquea Terán Oe2-58 y Versalles, 2nd Flr, T/F567875, mitmund1@mitadmundo.com, wwwpub.ecua.net.ec/mitadmundo Repeatedly recommendeded. *San Francisco*, Sucre 518 y Benalcázar (Plaza San Francisco), 3rd flr, T282849, sanfranciscoss_@latinmail.com *Simón Bolívar*, Leonidas Plaza 353 y Roca, T/F236688, info@simon-bolivar.com, www. simon-bolivar.com Have their own travel agency *South American Spanish Institute*, Av Amazonas 1549 y Santa María, T544715 T/F226348 (UK 0181-9836724). *Universidad Católica*, 12 de Octubre y Roca, contact Carmen Sarzosa, T228781, csarzosa@puceuio. puce.edu.ec

In the Old City: *Beraca School*, García Moreno 858 between Sucre and Espejo, Pasaje Amador, 3rd flr, T288092, beraca@interactive.net.ec It has a second location in the new town. *Quito's Information Center*, Guayaquil 1242 y Olmedo, 2nd Flr, F229165.

Recommended course books: *Español, Curso de Perfeccionamento*, by Juan Felipe García Santos (Universidad de Salamanca, Sep, 1990). *Learn Spanish One to One*, by José Aguirre and *1001 Ejercicios* by Marcia García, T449014.

Laundry

Laundromats *Lavandería*, 552 Olmedo, T213992. Will collect clothes. *Lavahotel*, Almagro 818 y Colón. Good value, US$2.15 per load, including soap powder, US$2.15 per dryer. *Lavamatic*, Pinto 539 y Amazonas. US$0.70 per kilo. Mon-Sat 0800-1900, Sun 0800-1300. Also 3 others on Pinto between Reina Victoria y JL Mera. The laundry next to *Hotel Pickett Inn* does a good deal, US$0.70 per kilo. *Rainbow*, JL Mera y Cordero. JL Mera y Cordero. Will deliver prepaid laundry to hotels in La Mariscal. *Almagro*, Wilson 470 y Almagro, T225208. US$2.30 per load. **Dry cleaning** *Martinizing*, 1 hr service, 12 de Octubre 1486, Diego de Almagro La Pradera, and in 6 shopping centres, plus other locations, expensive. *La Química*, Mallorca 335 y Madrid and Olmedo y Cotopaxi in the old city. *Norte*, Amazonas 7339, 6 de Diciembre 1840 y Eloy Alfaro, and Pinzón y La Niña.

Maps

For more information on maps and guide books, see page 39

The *Instituto Geográfico Militar* is on top of the hill to the east of El Ejido park. From Av 12 de Octubre, opposite the Casa de la Cultura, take Jiménez (a small street) up the hill. After crossing Av Colombia continue uphill on Paz y Miño behind the Military Hospital and then turn right to the guarded main entrance. You have to deposit your passport or identification card. There is a beautiful view from the grounds. Map and aerial photo indexes are all laid out for inspection. The map sales room (helpful staff) is open 0800-1600, Mon-Fri. Map and geographic reference libraries are located next to the sales room. Some maps are also available at the *Centro de Difusión Geográfica* in the Casa de Sucre, Venezuela 573; they are also helpful.

Medical services

For all emergencies in Quito call 911.
For information on health in Ecuador see page 81

Dentists Drs *Sixto y Silvia Altamirano*, Av Amazonas 2689 y Av República, T452414. Excellent. Dra *Rosa Oleas*, Amazonas 252 y Washington, T507164. *Dr Fausto Vallejo*, Madrid 744 (1 block from the end of the Colón-Camal bus line), T554781. Recommended, very reasonable. *Dr Roberto Mena*, Coruña E24-865 e Isabel la Católica, T559923. Speaks English and German. *Dr Víctor Peñaherrera*, Coruña 1898, T234284. Speaks English. Recommended.

Doctors Most embassies have the telephone numbers of doctors who speak non-Spanish languages. The following are recommended. **General surgeons**: Dr Francisco Gándara, Centro Médico Metropolitano, Mariana de Jesús y Calle 'B', office 314, T249477, cellular T09-556573, paging service T555000. Friendly and helpful, speaks French.

General practice and internal medicine: *Dr Wilson Pancho*, Av República de El Salvador 112, T463139/469546. Speaks German. *Dr John Rosenberg*, Med Center Travel Clinic, Foch 476 y Almagro, T521104, cellular T09-739734, paging service 227777 beeper 310, internal and travel medicine with a full range of vaccines, speaks English and German, very helpful. *Dr Rodrigo Sosa Cevallos*, Jerónimo Leyton 1248, T226803. English-speaking. *Dr Wilson Vargas Uvidia*, Colombia 2548, T953152. Speaks English and French.

Gynaecology: *Dr Stephen Contag*, Centro Médico Meditrópoli, Mariana de Jesús opposite Hospital Metropolitano, T267972/3. Speaks English. *Dr Juan Molina*, also at Meditrópoli, T432171/260581, speaks German and English.

Paediatrics: Dr Ernesto Quiñones, at Centro Materno Infantil, Manuel Barreto 167 y Coruña, at north end of Coruña, T232965/564538. Speaks English and Italian. Dr Guillermo Luna, Av. América 4343 y Hernández de Girón, T245317. Speaks English. **Dermatology**: Dr Rodrigo Armijos, at the pathology laboratory in the Medical Faculty of the Universidad Central, entrance below Iquique y Sodiro. For treatment of leishmaniasis and other tropical cutaneous horrors, he is a researcher developing a vaccine for leishmaniasis. *Dra Mónica Santamaría*, Edificio Diagnóstico 2000 on Mariana de Jesús, 1 block below Hospital Metropolitano, T460404. For all skin problems. Speaks English and some French.

Hospitals Among the recommended health centres are: *Hospital Voz Andes*, Villalengua Oe 2-37 y Av 10 de Agosto, T262142 (reached by Trole, la Y stop). Emergency room, quick and efficient. American, British and Ecuadorean doctors and nurses on staff, fee based on ability to pay, run by Christian HCJB organization, has out-patient department, T439343. *Hospital Metropolitano*, Av Mariana de Jesús y Av Occidental, just east of the western city bypass, T261520, ambulance T265020. Catch a Quito Sur-San Gabriel bus along Av América, or the Trole (Mariana de Jesús stop) and walk up or take a cab from there. Very professional and recommended, but prices are almost the same as in the USA. *Clínica Pichincha*, Veintimilla E3-30 y Páez, T562296, ambulance T501565. Another very good, expensive hospital. *Clínica Pasteur*, Av Eloy Alfaro 552 y 9 de Octubre, T234004. Also good and cheaper than the above. *Novaclínica Santa Cecilia*, Veintimilla 1394 y 10 de Agosto, T545390/545505, emergency T545000. Reasonable prices, good.

Medical laboratories All the hospitals listed above have reliable laboratories for all tests. Other reliable labs include *Dra Johanna Grimm*, República de El Salvador 112 y Shyris, Edificio Onyx, 3rd floor, T462182. English and German spoken. *Dr Jaime Silva*, at Medcenter, Foch 476 y Almagro, T521104.

Opticians *Optica Los Andes*, several locations including 10 de Agosto 520 y Arenas, T545159 and Quicentro Shopping. Professional. *Optica Gill*, Amazonas 1068, opposite the British Council, English spoken, glasses, contact lenses, helpful.

Pharmacies *Fybeca* is a reliable chain of 33 farmacies throughout the city. Their 24 hr branches are at Av Amazonas y Tomás de Berlanga near the Plaza de Toros, and at Centro Comercial El Recreo in the south. *Farmacia Colón*, Av 10 de Agosto 2292 y Cordero, T226534, also 24 hr. Check the listing of *farmacias de turno* in *El Comercio* on Sat for 24-hr chemists during the following week. Always check expiry dates on any medications and avoid purchasing anything that requires refrigeration in the smaller drug stores.

Places of worship Joint Anglican/Lutheran service is held (in English) at the *Advent Lutheran Church*, Isabel la Católica 1419, Sun at 0900. A Synagogue is located in the far north of the city, for information contact T483800.

South American Explorers Jorge Washington 311 y Leonidas Plaza, T/F225228, explorer@saec.org.ec, www.samexplo.org Open Mon-Fri 0930-1700. For full details on this organization, see page 22.

Useful addresses **Immigration Offices** See Getting in, Extensions, page 26. **Police** Criminal Investigations are at Cuenca y Mideros, in the old city. To report a robbery, make a *denuncia* within 48 hrs on official paper; if one officer is unhelpful, try another. Thefts can also be reported at the Policía Judicial, Roca y JL Mera. If you wait more than 48 hrs, you will need a lawyer. Policía de Turismo is at Reina Victoria y Roca, T543983.

Excursions from Quito

Mitad del Mundo and surroundings

Equator monument Twenty three kilometres north of Quito is the Mitad del Mundo Equatorial Line Monument at an altitude of 2,483 m near San Antonio de Pichincha. The location of the equatorial line here was determined by Charles-Marie de la Condamine and his French expedition in 1736, and agrees to within 150 metres with modern GPS measurements. A paved road runs from Quito to the Monument, which you can reach by a 'Mitad del Mundo' bus (US$0.50, one hour) from Avenida América or the Parque Hermano Miguel (see Old Town map, page 106). The bus fills instantly, but outside rush hour you can board anywhere along Avenida América (beware of pickpockets on the bus). An excursion to Mitad del Mundo by taxi with a one hour wait is about US$25 per taxi.

The monument forms the focal point of a park and leisure area built as a typical colonial town, with restaurants, gift shops, a Post Office with philatelic sales, tourist office (open 0900-1600), international pavilions (mostly not open) and so on. There are free live music and dance demonstrations on weekends. The monument itself has a very interesting ethnographic museum inside. It is run by the Consejo Provincial. A lift takes you to the top, then you walk down with the museum laid out all around with exhibits of different indigenous cultures every few steps. ■ *Mon-Fri 0900-1800, Sat and Sun 0900-1900 (very crowded on Sun). Admission to the monument and the museum is US$2 (includes guided tour of museum in Spanish or English), parking US$0.40.*

There is a Planetarium with hourly 30 minute shows and an interesting model of old Quito, about 10 m², with artificial day and night, which took seven years to build, and is very impressive; entry US$0.65. Two minutes' walk before the Monument is the restaurant *Equinoccio*, which charges about US$10 a meal, live music, open from 1200 daily, T394091, F545663. Nearby is another museum called *Inti-Ñan*, eclectic and interesting, entry US$1, T395122. Available at the restaurant, or at the stalls outside, are 'certificates' recording the traveller's visit to the Equator. These are free if you have a meal.

Sleeping **D** *Hostería Alemana*, on the approach road from Quito, 8 blocks south, T394243. Very good restaurant. **E** *Residencial Mitad del Mundo*, in San Antonio de Pichincha. Simple. **F** *Sol y Luna*, 2 blocks from monument, T394979. Private bath.

Pululahua A few kilometres beyond the Monument, off the paved road to Calacalí, is the Pululahua crater, which is well worth visiting. It is a geobotanical reserve; the park entry fee is US$5 (if you go in by the road). Try to go in the morning, as there is often cloud later. Trucks will take you from the Mitad del Mundo bus stop; the round trip costs US$5. *Calimatours*, Manzana de los Correos, Oficina 11, Mitad del Mundo, T394796 in Quito, PO Box 17-03-638, organizes tours to all the sites in the vicinity for US$5 per person. Recommended.

Continue on the road past the Monument towards Calacalí. After nearly 5 km (one hour's walk) the road bears left and begins to climb steeply. The paved road to the right leads to the rim of the volcano and a view of the farms on the crater floor. There are infrequent buses to Calacalí which will drop you at the fork, from where it is a 30 minute walk. There is plenty of traffic at weekends for hitching a lift. There is a rough track down from the *mirador* into the crater, to experience the rich vegetation and warm micro-climate inside. It's a half hour walk down, and one hour back up. Or continue past the village in the crater, turn left and follow an unimproved road up to the rim and back to the main road; a 15-20 km round trip. There is a restaurant, *El Crater*, at the rim of the crater, with fantastic views, open only on weekends.

It is also possible to drive to the reserve. Eight kilometres from the Mitad del Mundo monument on the way to Calacalí, take the turn off to the right past the gas station; it is 2.4 km to the Moraspungo Park gate where a very scenic drive into the crater begins. In 8 km you reach the valley floor. From there you can turn right towards the village of Pululahua, or left and continue downhill to the sugar-cane growing area of Nieblí. There are two cabins near the Moraspungo entrance, US$1 per person, take sleeping bag, warm clothing and food.

Other excursions near Mitad del Mundo Also in the vicinity of the Mitad del Mundo Monument, 3 km from San Antonio beyond the Solar Museum, are the Inca ruins of **Rumicucho**. Restoration of the ruins is poor, but the location is magnificent.

Eight kilometres from Quito on the road to San Antonio de Pichincha, is the village of **Pomasqui**, near where was a tree in which Jesus Christ appeared to perform various miracles, El Señor del Arbol, now enshrined in its own building. In the church nearby is a series of paintings depicting the miracles (mostly involving horrendous road accidents), which is well worth a visit. You may have to find the caretaker to unlock the church.

From San Antonio a dirt road heads north towards **Perucho**. South of Perucho another road turns sharply southeast to **Guayllabamba** via **Puéllaro** (eat at the house on the plaza which is also a radio/TV workshop). A left turn (northeast) off this road, just before Guayllabamba, goes to **Malchinguí**, **Tocachi** and **Cayambe** (see page 161).

The Equator line also crosses the Panamericana 8 km south of Cayambe, where there is a concrete globe beside the road. Take a Cayambe bus (two hours, US$0.80) and ask for Mitad del Mundo by Guachala. For nearby accommodation, see *Hostería Guachala*, under Cayambe (page 161).

North of Quito

The Quito municipal zoo is situated in the small town of Guayllabamba, 45 minutes north of the capital, see page 160. Take a Flota Pichincha bus from América y Colón. The zoo is spacious and well designed, a worthwhile family outing. ■ *US$1.20, children $0.60*. It gets quite warm in Guayllabamba, so take something to drink.

Guayllabamba Zoo

Northwest of Quito

Despite their proximity to the capital, the western slopes of Pichincha and its surroundings are surprisingly wild, with fine opportunities for walking and especially birdwatching. There are four roads that drop into the western lowlands from Quito. Each has a unique character, and each has interesting ecotourism reserves. The northernmost, the **Calacalí-Esmeraldas road**, starts near the Mitad del Mundo monument, goes through Calacalí and San Miguel de los Bancos, and ends up in the province of Esmeraldas. This is the simplest of the four roads to drive, since it is paved and traffic is light. Parallel to this road is the much rougher **Nono-Mindo road**, famous for its excellent birdwatching. This road begins off Av Occidental, Quito's western ring road; you must ask for directions to find it. At the beginning of this road is **B** *Hostería San Jorge*, T494002, just above Quito. Here there is horseriding, birdwatching, sauna, pool, peace, quiet and fresh air within 20 minutes of the airport. There are several connections between the paved Calacalí road and the rough Nono-Mindo road, so it is possible to drive on the paved road most of the way even if your destination is one of the lodges on the Nono-Mindo road.

The major reserves on the paved road are **Maquipucuna** and **El Pahuma**; the major lodges on the Nono-Mindo road are **Tandayapa** and **Bellavista**. Both roads meet just before the turnoff to **Mindo**, a town with many more lodges. **Aldea Salamandra** is on the paved road beyond the Mindo turnoff.

The **El Pahuma Reserve** has 600 hectares. It is an interesting collaboration between a local landowner and the Ceiba Foundation for Tropical Conservation. Less than one hour from Quito on the Calacalí-Esmeraldas road, El Pahuma features an orchid garden and an orchid propagation program. Trails start at 1,600 m and go to 2,600 m. Birds such as mountain toucans and tanagers are present, and Spectacled Bear have been seen. ■ *US$5, guide US$2.50/day*. Very rustic **G** accommodation in a cabin, two hours' climb from the entrance, no facilities. A visitor centre with more comfortable accommodation was being built in 2000. Contact Alejandro Trillo T252053, cellT09-392040, or see www.ceiba.org

The **Tandayapa Lodge** is on the Nono–Mindo road and can be reached in 1½ hours from Quito via the Calacali-Esmeraldas road; take the signed turnoff to Tandayapa at Km 32, just past Café Tiepolo. It is longer but more scenic to

Reserves & lodges

take the Nono road all the way from Quito. This is a very comfortable lodge at about 1,700 m, with trails going higher. The lodge is owned by dedicated birders who strive to keep track of all rarities on the property; they can reliably show you practically any of 318 species, even such rare birds as the White-faced Nunbird or the Lyre-tailed Nightjar. Recommended for serious bird watchers. Contact T543045, cellT09-735536, tandayapa@tandayapa.com, www.tandayapa.com Accommodation in our **L** range, including three meals.

The **Maquipucuna Reserve** contains 4,500 ha, surrounded by an additional 14,000 ha of protected forest. It can be reached in two hours from Quito with a private vehicle. The cloud forest at 1,200-2,800 m contains a tremendous diversity of flora and fauna, including over 325 species of birds. Especially noteworthy are the colourful tanager flocks, mountain-toucans, parrots and quetzals. The reserve has trails ranging in length from 15 minutes to all day. There is also a research station and an experimental organic garden. Entry US$6, guide US$10/day. Accommodation in our **L** range, including three meals. Contact Fundacion Maquipucuna, Baquerizo Moreno E9-153 y Tamayo, Quito, T507200, F507201, arodas@uio.satnet.net, www.maqui.org The British charity, Rainforest Concern, can also be contacted for information (and fundraising), c/o Peter Bennett, 27 Lansdowne Crescent, London W11 2NS, T020-72292093, F020-72214094.

Getting there Take the Calacalí-Esmeraldas road, at Nanegalito turn right on a dirt road to Nanegal; keep going until a sign on the right for the reserve (before Nanegal). Pass through the village of Marianitas and it's another 20 minutes to the reserve. The road is poor, especially in the January-May wet season, four-wheel drive vehicles recommended. For Maquipucuna and Bellavista - see below - take a bus to Nanegalito (two basic hotels, better is **H** *Don Fabra* on main plaza) and hire a truck, or arrange everything with the lodges or in Quito.

Near Maquipucuna are a couple of community conservation and eco-tourism projects. By the upper elevation border of Maquipucuna, to the southeast, is Yunguilla, reached by pickup truck from Calacalí, with a cabin for visitors (**E** per person full board) and guiding service for treks in the forest and down to Maquipucuna (US$10 per person). Further information from Germán Collaguazo, cellular T09-580694, yunguilla@yahoo.com To the east of Maquipucuna in a beautiful tract of cloudforest is Santa Lucía, with a cabin for visitors. Information in Quito from Paulina Tapia T573904 or Fiona Woodward T457143.

Bellavista is located at Km 68 on the Nono-Mindo road. This dramatic dome-shaped lodge is perched in beautiful cloud forest. Faster access is possible along the Calacalí-Esmeraldas road, via a turnoff at Km 42 (past Nanegalito), or via a slightly better road at Km 58; both have Bellavista signs. The reserve is part of a mosaic of private protected areas dedicated to conservation of one of the richest accessible areas of west slope cloud forest. Bellavista at 2,200 m is the highest of these, and the easiest place to see the incredible Plate-billed Mountain-Toucan. About 300 species of birds have been seen here, including large numbers of hummingbirds drawn to the many feeders at the lodge. The area is also rich in orchids and other cloud forest plants. Recommended. Accommodation in our **L** range, with private bath, hot shower, and full board (good vegetarian food); dormitory-style room with shared bath is **AL**. Camping is also possible, US$5. A biological station on the property is available for researchers. Package tours can be arranged including transport from Quito; to get there on your own take a bus to Nanegalito and hire a pickup truck, or get off at Km 42 and walk 12 km on the side road to the left. For reservations, contact T232313 in Quito, Cellular T09-490891 at the reserve, bellavista@ecuadorexplorer.com

Mindo is a small town surrounded by dairy farms and lush cloud forest climbing the western slopes of Pichincha. Some 19,200 ha, ranging in altitude from 1,400 to 4,780 m (the rim of the crater of Guagua Pichincha) have been set aside as a nature reserve, **Bosque Protector Mindo-Nambillo**. The reserve features spectacular flora and fauna, beautiful cloud forest and many waterfalls. A total of 350 species of birds have been identified and this is one of the best places in the country to see Cock-of-the-rock, Golden-headed Quetzal and Toucan-Barbet. The steep access road into town is particularly good for birdwatching, as is the private 'Yellow House Trail' (owned by the Garzón family). Unfotunately, there has been some conflict in the area over the future of the reserve which includes both state and private land.

Mindo
Population: about 1,700

Amigos de la Naturaleza de Mindo runs the Centro de Educación Ambiental (CEA), 4 km from town, within the 17 ha buffer zone at the edge of the reserve, with capacity for 25-30 people. Guide service, lodging and food are available. There is also a reasearch station for the exclusive use of scientists. There are well maintained trails near the shelters.

Admission to the reserve is US$2, lodging US$6 per person; package with accommodation, full board and excursion US$25 per person. Take food if you wish to prepare your own, there are good kitchen facilities. Volunteer programmes can be arranged for US$200/month. All arrangements have to be made in advance, contact in Mindo: Amigos de la Naturaleza de Mindo, one block from the *parque central*. If closed, look for Viviana Murcia. In Quito: Ing Humberto Ochoa, Quito, T490958 (best on weekends), amigosmindo@hotmail.com During the rainy season, access can be rough. In addition to the reserve, Mindo also has an orchid garden across from the sports stadium and a butterfly farm 3 km from town. Activities include rappelling in the La Isla waterfalls and 'inner-tubing' regattas in the rivers. Vinicio Pérez is an excellent resident birding guide; he speaks a little English.

Sleeping and eating **A** *Mindo Gardens*, next to the CEA. Luxurious, beautiful setting, good birdwatching. **B** per person *Hostería El Carmelo de Mindo*, in 32 hectares, 700 m from town centre, T224713, T/F546013, hcarmelo@uio.satnet.net, www.mindo.com.ec Cabins or room with or without bath, **E** per person dormitory, **F** per person camping, meals available, horse rental, excursions, 50% discount for IYHA card holders. **C** *El Monte*, www.ecuadorexplorer.com/elmonte Lovely cabins set in the forest overlooking the river, good food available. Check at the café one block from the plaza in town, or book through the *Cultura Reservation Center* (see Quito Tour operators, page 133). Recommended. **E** per person *Hacienda San Vicente*, 'Yellow House', 500 m south of the plaza. Includes all meals, family-run, very friendly, clean, nice rooms, TV, excellent food, good walking trails nearby, great value. Recommended. **E** *El Bijao*, on the left approaching the village. Good. Recommended. **E-F** *Gypsy*. 2 attractive cabins, clean, friendly, family-run, ask at *Restaurant Omarcito*. Good value, recommended. **F** per person *Alexandras*, T (Quito) 240317 and ask for Alexandra (speaks Spanish only). Family-owned *finca* with accommodation for 8, hot water, kitchen, fridge, quiet, cosy, clean. Recommended. **F** *Hostal Arco Iris*. Basic, clean, some rooms with private bath. There are several others. Places to eat include *Salón Arco Iris, San Francisco, La Choza. Omarcito*, also has rooms for 10.

Transport From Quito, Cooperativa Flor del Valle, M Larrea y Asunción, T527495. leaves daily at 1530 and at 0800 Fri-Sun, US$1.50, 2½ hrs. Also Cooperativa Kennedy from Santo Domingo; 4 hrs. The most direct access from Quito is along the Calcalí-Esmeraldas road; at Km 59 to the left is the turnoff for Mindo. It is about 5 km down a side road to the town.

Mindo can also be reached on a 3-day walk from the town of Lloa (10 km west of the the southern end of Quito). There are 3 buses a day to Lloa, no fixed schedule, which leave from Calle Angamarca, in the area of Quito called Mena 2. **NB** You must check about the current level of volcanic activity of Guagua Pichincha before undertaking this trek. Also be careful fording the Río Cristal.

West of Mindo Beyond the turnoff for Mindo the main road continues to descend westward to **San Miguel de los Bancos, Pedro Vicente Maldonadao** and **Puerto Quito** before joining the main road from Santo Domingo to Esmeraldas. The climate here is subtropical and these small towns have a couple of basic hotels and places to eat. There are also a growing number of tourist developments in the area.

Resorts & farms Accessed from Pedro Vicente Maldonado is **C** *Reserva Río Guaycuyacu*, an exotic fruit farm with 400 varieties of fruit and birdwatching. Includes 3 hearty vegetarian meals a day, maximum 8 guests. One month agricultural apprenticeships can be arranged. From Pedro Vicente Maldonado take a truck to Mashpi, from where it is a 2-4 hour hike. Booking essential, write to: Galápagos 565, Quito, guaycuyacu@hotmail.com

Four kilometres west of Pedro Vicente Maldonado is **LL** *Arasha*, elegant and very upmarket, new in 2000, pools, waterfalls (artificial and natural), jaccuzzi, spa center and hiking trails. World class chef and kitchen (meals not included in price of accommodation). Quito office Los Shyris N39-41 y Río Coca, 8th floor, T253967, F260902, arasharv@interactive.net.ec, www.arasha1spa.com

Two kilometres east of Puerto Quito, 140 km northwest of Quito, is **Aldea Salamandra**. This beautiful nature reserve is set in tropical rainforest. Accommodation is in bamboo and thatch cabins, some of which are built in the trees on the riverbank. This is a great place to take a birdwatching excursion, swim in the river, trek through the forest to isolated waterfalls, take a kayak trip or simply relax and enjoy nature. Note that weekends tend to be busy when it is used as the local beach. Aldea Salamandra work with Fundación Natura to preserve the environment and raise awareness of environmental issues.

A price range including all meals and excursions; or accommodation only, in our **D** range. Vegetarian food is available, as well as typical dishes. Discounts are available for groups of 15 or more and IYHA members. For reservations contact Quito T228151, aldeasalamandra@yahoo.com, www.aldeasalamandra.com It is three hours by bus from Quito. Take any Esmeraldas bus and ask the driver to stop 2 km before Puerto Quito. It is a 10-minute walk from the main road; well signposted. You can also go from Esmeraldas with Trans Esmeraldas, two hours; tell the driver to stop 2 km after Puerto Quito.

Southwest of Quito

Just south of Quito are two other roads to the western lowlands, the **Chiriboga Road** and the main **Alóag-Santo Domingo road**. The Chiriboga road is complicated to find; go to Quito's southern neighbourhood of Chillogallo and then on to San Juan de Chillogallo. There is irregular bus service on the first half of the Chiriboga road, but it is often muddy and difficult, especially November to April when a four-wheel drive is needed. For a description of the Santo Domingo road see Quito to Santo Domingo, page 310.

Nature reserves

Guajalito is a rustic lodge on the the Chiriboga road. The lodge is surrounded by a very large forest reserve, with a wide variety of birds. This would be a good base for birdwatching along the road and for getting inside the forest, which is normally impossible elsewhere because of steepness or deforestation. Accessible by bus from Chillogallo. Price is in our **B** range, meals included. Reservations are required, contact T600531, vlastimilz@mail.usfq.edu.ec

Otonga is an extensive private reserve near **Las Pampas**, south of the Alóag-Santo Domingo road. There is a basic shelter about two hours' walk from the end of the side road which branches off the Santo Domingo road at **Union de Toachi**. Much of the forest is virgin and rich in unusual orchids, gesneriads, and birds. Bring a sleeping bag and flashlight. Prices in our **D** range, includes basic food. Contact the Tapias or Dr Onore in Quito, T567550.

La Hesperia is an old hacienda with new facilities for ecotourism. Some of the hacienda is still used for farming and raising cattle, but most of it has been kept in forest. There are many birds (such as Cock-of-the-rock) and even some monkeys. Most of the forest is at around 1,500-2,000 m elevation, with a mild pleasant climate. Access is from the Aloag-Santo Domingo road 8 km past **Tandapi**. Prices in our **L** range. Reservations required, Contact Juan Pablo Játiva, Quito, T241877, 464800, pjativa@la-hesperia.com, www.la-hesperia.com

Tinalandia, near Santo Domingo, is one of the best places to see many species of birds with minimal effort. Complete details are given under Santo Domingo de los Colorados, page 310.

Southeast of Quito

Sangolquí
Population: 18,000

Sangolquí is about 20 minutes from Quito by bus. There is a busy Sunday market (and a smaller one on Thursday) and few tourists. There are thermal baths nearby (see below). Stay at **C** per person *Hostería Sommergarten*, Urb Santa Rosa, Chimborazo 248 y Río Frío, 30 minutes by bus from Quito in the valley of Los Chillos, T/F330315/332761, rsommer@uio.satnet.net, www.ecuador-sommer.com This is a bungalow resort surrounded by a subtropical park, price includes breakfast, lots of activities are available, sauna, pool. Also **A** *La Carriona*, km 2½ via Sangolqui-Amaguaña, T331974. This is a beautiful colonial *hacienda* with pool and spa, includes breakfast.

El Tingo & La Merced hot springs

In the valley of Los Chillos, to the southeast, are the thermal pools of **La Merced** and **El Tingo**. These thermal pools are among the easiest to get to, and are both within 30-40 minutes of Quito. There are numerous complexes all with comfortably warm water for swimming. Both are extremely crowded at the weekend. At El Tingo, there is excellent food and a good atmosphere at the German-owned *Mucki's Garden* restaurant, T320789. Four kilometres from

La Merced is **Ilaló**, privately owned pools, admission US$2. These are cleaner, with fewer mosquitoes and people, but also best on weekdays. Take a 'La Merced' bus from La Marín (lower end of Avenida Pichincha). They leave about every 30 minutes throughout the day. If driving, take Autopista de Los Chillos to San Rafael and, where the divided highway ends, turn left at the traffic lights. It is 4 km to El Tingo, and a further 7 km to La Merced.

From **Alangasí**, along the road to La Merced, a good paved road branches 10 km southeast to **Píntag**. The road then turns to rough gravel and divides, the right fork goes to the base of Sincholagua (4,899 m), the left fork goes to Laguna La Mica at the base of the snow-covered volcano Antisana (5,704 m). This is a magnificent area for hiking and camping where condors may be seen. There are no services, so visitors must be self sufficient. An access permit from the landowner is required; enquire beforehand in Píntag, Sr José Delgado, T435828. See also Trek of the Condor below.

Pasochoa The Refugio de Vida Silvestre Pasochoa (formerly known as Bosque Protector Pasochoa), 45 minutes southeast by car from Quito, is a private park set in mountain forest, run by Fundación Natura. Entrance for foreigners US$7 and it is very touristy at weekends. The reserve is classified as humid Andean forest, but much of the fauna has been frightened away by the noise of visitors. This is nonetheless a good place for a family picnic or an acclimatization hike close to Quito. There are walks of 30 minutes, one hour, two, four and eight hours. Camping is permitted in the park (US$3 per person), but take food and water as there are no shops and take your rubbish away with you. There is also a refuge (US$5 per person per night, with shower, has cooking facilities), but you will need a sleeping bag.

Getting there / From Quito buses run from La Marín to Amaguaña (ask the driver to let you off at the 'Ejido de Amaguaña'); from there follow the signs for Pasochoa. It's a walk of about 8 km, with not much traffic for hitching, except at weekends. By car, take the highway to Los Chillos; at San Rafael (traffic light) continue straight on towards Sangolquí and on to Amaguaña. About 1½ km past Amaguaña turn left onto a cobblestone road and follow the signs to Pasochoa. Tours from Quito cost US$40 per person. A price negotiated with a taxi driver from a good hotel is about US$15 per person. A pick-up truck from Amaguaña is about US$5.

East of Quito

Underground An unusual place on the road heading east from Quito toward the Oriente is
Lodge A *Cuevas de Alvaro*, near Pifo. The price includes three meals and it is in a fascinating location built right into the rock. It is a good spot to see condors at certain times of the year. Quito office: Carrión N21-01 entre JL Mera y Reina Victoria, T547403, F228902, birdecua@hoy.net, www.cuevasdealvaro.com.ec

Termas de These baths, 65 km east from Quito, 1 km from the road to Baeza, are the most
Papallacta attractively developed set of hot springs in Ecuador. The hot water is channelled into three pools large enough for swimming, three smaller shallow pools and two tiny family-size pools. There is also a steam room, hot showers and two cold plunge pools as well as access to the river. The area offers good walking, with a few well maintained trails nearby, and many more rugged ones up the valley; guided walks available. The baths are crowded at weekends but usually quiet through the week. The view, on a clear day, of Antisana from the Papallacta road or while enjoying the thermal waters is superb. ■ *0700-2300, US$2.* Next door are the **Jambiyacu** baths, with five large pools, very crowded

on weekends. ■ *US$1*. More springs in this area provide the village of Papallacta with abundant hot water and fill three simple but clean pools at the **Balneario Municipal** of the village. ■ *US$0.50*.

The Fundación Ecológica Rumicocha has a small office on the main street in the village, run by Sra Mariana Liguia, who is friendly. There are leaflets on the Cayambe-Coca reserve. ■ *0800-1200, 1400-1600*.

Within the Termas de Papallacta complex there are 6 cabins for up to 6 people each and 2 good restaurants serving trout and other dishes (US$4-5). One of the cabins has a private thermal bath, the other has kitchen facilities, US$75 per cabin. Across the road is **B** *Hostal La Posada*, comfortable double rooms with private bath, **C** in small rooms with bunk beds and shared bath. It has its own indoor and outdoor pools. Reservations are recommended for weekends and holidays. Quito office at Foch E6-12 y Reina Victoria, #4, T557850, F557851, papallacta@ecnet.ec, www.papallacta.com.ec

Sleeping & eating

Along the access road to the Termas **F** *Hostal Antisana*, shared bath, clean, simple. **G** *Pampas de Papallacta*, private bath, basic. Also several simple places to eat, trout is the local speciality.

In Papallacta village **G** *Residencial El Viajero*. Very basic, shared bath, restaurant with reasonable meals, avoid the rooms in the old building. **G** *Hotel Quito*, with private bath, cheaper without. Clean and friendly, popular restaurant. There are also a couple of shops with basic supplies.

Many buses a day pass the village on their way to and from Lago Agrio or Baeza (drivers sometimes charge full fare). From Quito, 2 hours, US$1: Ask to be let off at the road to the springs; it is then a short half hour walk up the hill to the complex.

Transport

East of Papallacta is **L** *Guango Lodge*, including three good meals. Situated in temperate forest, Grey-breasted Mountain-toucans are regularly seen here along with many other birds. Reservations needed, Quito T 547403, F228902, birdecua@hoy.net, www.ecuadorexplorer.com/sanisidro

Birding at Guango

Trekking near Quito

The **Trek of the Condor** is a classic three to four day páramo hike with excellent views of snow-capped volcanoes and a chance to see the endangered Andean Condor. You will be travelling through Antisana Ecological Reserve and Cotopaxi National Park, two of the most spectacular highland parks. This trek is physically demanding and requires route-finding skills across untrailed alpine grasslands and bogs. It can snow so it is important to bring warm clothing. The IGM 1:100,000 Píntag map covers the whole area but for more detail obtain IGM 1:50,000 Píntag, Papallacta, Laguna Micacocha, Sincholagua and Cotopaxi.

The start of the trek is located at **El Tambo** (a grouping of kiosks just before a bridge) about 1½ hours by bus from Quito on the road to Baeza. To get an early start it is possible to spend the night at the hostel next to the thermal springs in Papallacta (see above). An entrance fee of US$1 may be collected in El Tambo which compensates the community for crossing their land. You can also arrange a local guide and mules at El Tambo. Begin by following a muddy livestock path on the right side of the Río Tambo. Cross to the left side of the river after 20 minutes and contour up one of the livestock paths to the top of the ridge on the left. Cross the ridge and head southeast on a way-trail until you are within sight of **Laguna Tumiguina** (also called Laguna Vulcán).

The trail descends to the upstream end of the lake. The lake is three to four hours from the road. This lake was created by a parasitic lava eruption of Antisana in the 18th-century which dammed the stream. If camping here the blocky lava flow with abundant orchids makes an interesting afternoon excursion. From the river gauging station at the lake, head upstream (south) about 300 m to the point where three rivers form a confluence. Find the well-defined trail located between **Quebrada Sunfohuaycu** and the stream directly to the east. Switch back up grassy slopes to a muddy path through cloud forest.

Above the cloud forest the trail climbs around to the east side of **Antisanilla** (shown as Loma Chosalongo Grande on IGM map). Higher up the trail is easy to lose but you can head cross-country more or less in the direction of Antisana. As the terrain flattens a faint car track heads to a shallow lake called **Laguna Santa Lucía** which is home to herds of semi-wild horses, lapwings, and Andean gulls. Camping next to the lake is outstanding but the weather can be cold and foggy. Laguna Santa Lucía is about four to five hours from Laguna Tumiguina.

An obvious track begins on the west side of Laguna Santa Lucía and heads over páramo to a gravel road which connects to **Hacienda Antisana** and the road to Píntag. The hacienda is a stone house below a large eroded hillside. The owner, José Delgado (T435828, Quito), may require a fee (US$10) to cross his land but usually no one is around to collect it.

From here the route is cross-country without the benefit of an established trail so there are other possibilities than what is described below. Head out across the golf course-like plain skirting the north side of Loma Mangourcu and drop down to **Quebrada Jatunhuaycu**. Cross this stream and head up to the pass directly to the east. You will be walking across cushion plants which are tussock-like mounds of spongy vegetation that make walking awkward. Cross over a pass and descend a marshy draw to a broad valley. Cross another section of cushion plants, a new gravel road not shown on the map, and then cross **Quebrada Pullurima Viejo**.

Follow the trail leading to the right up a hill and then drop down to Quebrada de los Ladrillos. Ascend the next hill and drop down to **Quebrada Huallanta**. Quebrada Huallanta is a U-shaped valley which currently supports at least three

Trek of the Condor

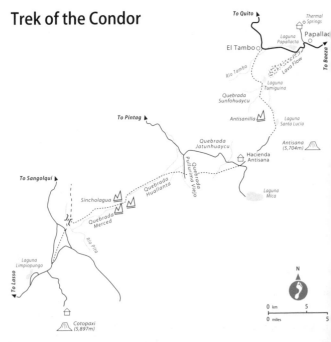

condors often seen soaring above the valley on sunny days. This is a good camping site (about six to seven hours from Laguna Santa Lucía) with views up the valley of the red cliffs of **Sincholagua**.

Head up the valley to the base of Sincholagua and then up the steep trail to the right of the waterfall. Keep climbing to a pass between Sincholagua and the small peak to the left. Contour around to another pass between Sincholagua and a second small peak. Descend scree and cushion plant-covered slope to the basin and find a trail that contours the right side of the **Quebrada Merced valley**. Once on the ridge connect with the car track that heads down to the bridge that crosses the Río Pita. It takes five to seven hours from Quebrada Huallanta to the **Río Pita bridge**.

Once across the bridge you are walking over gravel outwash plains. Either follow the road towards the peak of Cotopaxi or short-cut across the plain to reach the turn off to the climbers' refuge. A pleasant camping site is on the back side of **Laguna Limpiopungo**. There is usually traffic to hitch a ride to the Panamericana from the climbers' refuge turn off or you can walk the road in four to five hours from the Río Pita. Frequent buses head north and south on the Panamericana.

Climbing near Quito

Cruz Loma is the low, southern one of the two antenna-topped peaks overlooking Quito from the west (to the north is a peak with loads of antennas, known as Las Antenas). On a clear day you can see about 50 km down the central valley and to the east.

Warning Both Cruz Loma and especially Rucu Pichincha are notorious for armed robbery, and rapes have also occured. A large group does not necessarily confer protection. Never walk in these areas without carefully checking safety first, ask at South American Explorers, see page 22, or Tourist Police.

Rucu Pichincha
Beware of muggings on Cruz Loma & Rucu Pichincha

Rucu Pichincha (4,627 m) can be seen from some parts of Quito, and can be climbed either via Cruz Loma or via its neighbouring hill to the north. The path to its foot runs due west over and around hummocks on the rolling, grass-covered *páramo*. The climb up to the peak is not technical, but it is rocky and requires a bit of endurance. From Cruz Loma to Rucu Pichincha peak takes about four hours up and two down. Take rainproof and cold weather gear just in case. You can continue from Rucu to Guagua Pichincha, the higher of the two peaks. Be careful at Paso de la Muerte, a narrow ledge, about 30 minutes beyond Rucu Pichincha.

To save time and energy take a taxi or bus, for example No 14, to Toctiuco, to the upper reaches of the city and start climbing to Cruz Loma from there (allow at least five hours to reach the summit). There are poor roads up to both peaks, but traffic is sparse. Try hitching early in the morning, but remember that it is difficult to hitch back after about 1730 and you will have to walk in the dark. The road to the radio station on the northern hill is better for hitching.

NB No water is available so be sure to carry adequate supplies, especially if going to Rucu Pichincha. Please pick up your flotsam; the area is rubbish-strewn enough as it is.

After almost 350 years of dormancy, Guagua Pichincha renewed its volcanic activity in 1999. The level of activity subsequently diminished but could increase again at any time. **Descent into the crater is extremely dangerous and strictly prohibited.** Climbing to the refuge and crater rim may be

Guagua Pichincha
Enquire about volcanic activity before climbing

reasonably safe but always enquire beforehand. The Geophysics Institute of the *Escuela Politecnica Nacional* posts daily reports on the web at www.epn.edu.ec/~igeo and the *El Comercio* newspaper has a small daily summary on its front page.

A recommended route for climbing Guagua Pichincha volcano (4,794 m) is to take a bus to Mena 2 at Calle Angamarca (dump trucks go to a mine near Lloa on weekdays), or to Chillogallo (US$1), from where the road goes to the town of **Lloa**, then a four by four track goes to the rim of the crater. There are three buses a day to Lloa but no fixed schedule. It is possible to catch a lift on a truck or *camioneta*, or take a taxi, which costs around US$12. Set off early as you will need all day to walk up to the *refugio*, just below the summit at 4,800 m.

Lloa is a small, friendly village set in beautiful surroundings. The road to the summit is signposted from the right-hand corner of the main plaza as you face the volcano, and is easy to follow. There are a couple of forks, but head straight for the peak each time. It can take up to eight hours to reach the *refugio*, allowing for a long lunch break and plenty of rests. The *refugio*, which is maintained by the Defensa Civil, is manned and will provide a bed and water for US$2 per person. The warden has his own cooking facilities which he may share with you. It gets very cold at night and there is no heating or blankets. Be sure to keep an eye on your things.

The walk from the *refugio* to the summit is very short. You can scramble a bit further to the 'real' summit (above the *refugio*) which is tricky but worth it for the views; many other volcanoes can be seen on a clear morning.

The descent back to Lloa takes only three hours, but is hard on the legs. There is a restaurant in Lloa, on the main road to Quito, which sells good but expensive soup. To get back to Quito, walk a few hundred metres down the main road until you reach a fork. Wait here for a truck, which will take you to the outskirts of the city for around US$1. A taxi from the southern outskirts to the New City costs around US$4.

Northern Highlands

4

Northern Highlands

North from Quito to the border with Colombia is an area of considerable ecological importance and natural beauty, where several organizations are working to protect its assets. The landscape is mountainous, with views of the Cotacachi, Imbabura, Chiles and glacier-covered Cayambe, interspersed with lakes. This is also a region renowned for its artesanía. Countless villages specialize in their own particular craft, be it hats, woodcarvings, bread figures or leather goods. And, of course, there is Otavalo, with its outstanding Saturday market, a must on everyone's itinerary.

The Panamericana, fully paved, runs northeast from Quito to Otavalo (94 km), Ibarra (114 km), and Tulcán (240 km), from where it continues to Ipiales in Colombia. Secondary roads go west from all these cities, and descend to subtropical lowlands. From Ibarra a road runs northwest all the way to the Pacific port of San Lorenzo. To the east is the impressive snow capped cone of Cayambe (5790 m), part of the Reserva Ecológica Cayambe-Coca.

Quito to Cayambe

Calderón   Thirty two kilometres north of Quito's centre, and 5 km from the periphery, Calderón is the place where figurines are made of bread dough and glue. You can see them being made, though not on Sunday, and prices are lower than in Quito. Especially attractive is the Nativity collection. Prices range from about US$0.10 to US$4, which is excellent value. The figures can be seen in the cemetery on 1-2 November, when the graves are decorated with flowers, drinks and food for the dead. (See also Arts and Crafts, on page 454.) The Corpus Christi processions are very colourful. Many buses leave from Santa Prisca and along Avenida América in Quito, but drivers are often unwilling to take backpackers at rush hour.

Guayllabamba   After Calderón the road for the north descends into the spectacular arid Guayllabamba gorge and climbs out again to the fertile oasis of **Guayllabamba** village, noted for its avocados and delicious *chirimoyas* or custard apples (D *Hostería Guayllabamba*, cabins on eastern outskirts of town). The Quito municipal zoo is located in Guayllabamba (worthwhile, see page 147). The area is also a popular destination for Quiteños, who flock here on weekends to eat *comida típica* in a number of good *paradores*. Along the road to Cayambe, 2 km north of town is the **Bosque de Bromelias**, a small protected area.

At Guayllabamba, the highway splits into two branches. To the right, the Panamericana runs northeast to Cayambe. The left branch goes towards the town of **Tabacundo**, from where you can rejoin the Pamamericana travelling east to Cayambe or northeast to Cajas. Many buses take the latter route, which is faster. There is an access road from Tabacundo to the **Lagunas de Mojanda**, see page 173. Four kilometres north of Tabacundo by the village of Tupigachi is **B** *Hostería San Luís*, T360464, F360103, hosteriasanluis@accessinter.net It has 36 rooms with large fireplaces, a good restaurant, horses, mountain bikes, fishing, pool, spa, games room. There are great views of Cayambe.

Tolas de   Ten kilometres past Guayllabamba on the road to Tabacundo (8 km before
Cochasquí   Tabacundo), a cobbled road to the left (signed Pirámides de Cochasqui) leads to **Tocachi** and further on to the Tolas de Cochasqui archaeological site, administered by the Consejo Provincial de Pichincha. The protected area contains 15 truncated clay pyramids, nine with long ramps, built between 900 and 1500 AD by Indians of the Cara or Cayambi-Caranqui tribe. The pyramids are covered by earth and grass but a few have been excavated, giving a good idea of their construction. Festivals take place with dancing at the equinoxes and solstices. There is a site museum with interesting historical explanations in Spanish. The views from the site, south to Quito, are marvellous. ■ *0930-1630. Visits to the pyramids are guided and a small entry fee is charged. Take a bus that goes on the Tabacundo road and ask to be let off at the turnoff. From there it's a pleasant 8 km walk through an agricultural landscape. If you arrive at the sign around 0900, you could get a lift from the site workers. A taxi from Cayambe costs US$8 for the round trip.*

El Quinche   Six kilometres southeast of Guayllabamba is the small village of El Quinche, where there is a huge sanctuary to Nuestra Señora del Quinche in the plaza. The image was the work of the sculptor Diego Robles around 1600 in Oyacachi. It was brought to El Quinche because the local Indians did not wish to worship the image. There are processions on 21 November in El Quinche. There are many paintings illustrating miracles, ask the caretaker for the details. There is a bus service from Guayllabamba and direct buses from Quito via Cumbayá and Pifo (*Pensión Central*, basic, clean).

Northern Highlands

Cayambe

Cayambe, on the righthand branch of the Panamericana, 25 km northeast of Guayllabamba, is dominated by the snow capped volcano of the same name. The town itself is fairly unremarkable, but quiet and pleasant.

The surrounding countryside consists of rich dairy farms and flower plantations. The area is noted for its *bizcochos*, which are small shortbread-type biscuits served with *queso de hoja*, tasty string cheese. There is a fiesta in March for the equinox with plenty of local music. Inti Raymi during the summer solstice blends into the San Pedro celebrations around June 29.

On the edge of town are the pyramids of the Sun and Moon at Puntiachil. Worth a visit is the private museum of Marco Sandoval Ortíz. He'll give a detailed explanation of the Puntiachil culture in exchange for a small donation.

Phone code: 02
Colour map M2, grid B5
Population: 16,849

B *Hacienda Guachala*, south of Cayambe on the road to Cangahua, T363042. A beautifully restored hacienda built in 1580, owned by Diego Bonifaz, Mayor of Cayambe (2000-2004), spring-fed swimming pool, basic but comfortable rooms with fireplaces, delicious food, good walking, Anglo-Arabian horses for rent, excursions to nearby pre-Inca ruins. Highly recommended. **F** *Cabañas de Nápoles*, Panamericana Norte Km 1½, T360366. With bath, TV, good restaurant. **F** *Shungu Huasi*, 1 km northwest of town.

Sleeping
Hotels may be full on Fridays during June-September

Northern Highlands

Cayambe

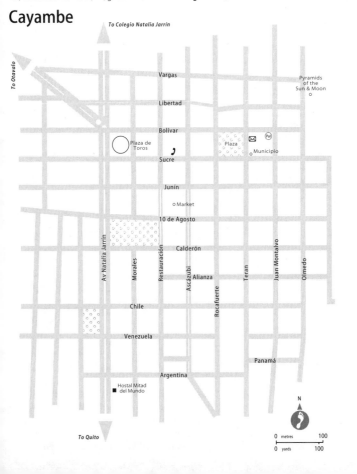

To Colegio Natalia Jarrín

To Otavalo

Vargas
Libertad
Bolívar
Plaza de Toros
Sucre
Junín
○ Market
10 de Agosto
Av Natalia Jarrín
Morales
Restauración
Ascázubi
Alianza
Rocafuerte
Calderón
Teran
Juan Montalvo
Olmedo
Chile
Venezuela
Panamá
Argentina
■ Hostal Mitad del Mundo

Pyramids of the Sun & Moon ○

Plaza
✉
Pol
○ Municipio

To Quito

N

0 metres 100
0 yards 100

Accommodation for only 6 people, meals available, excellent horse riding programmes for US$45 per person per day (minimum 2 people). **F** *La Gran Colombia*, on the Panamericana, north of town, T361238. Double rooms, restaurant. Clean, noisy. **G** *Hostal Mitad del Mundo*, on the Panamericana south of town, T360226. With bath, TV, cheaper with shared bath. Clean, pool, sauna, restaurant. **G** *Hostal Cayambe*, Bolívar 23 y Ascázubi, T361007. Youth hostel, clean, friendly, stores luggage.

Eating *Casa de Fernando*, Panamericana Norte Km 1½. Good. *El Molino*, Panamericana norte, Km 3. Excellent breakfasts, French cuisine, cosy atmosphere. Open for lunch and early dinner. There are several cheap restaurants on Bolívar.

Transport Direct bus with Flor del Valle, leaves from M Larrea y Asunción in Quito, every 10 minutes, 0500-1900, US$0.80, 1½ hrs. Some Quito-Otavalo buses stop in Cayambe. They depart every few minutes from the Terminal Terrestre in Quito. Cayambe-Otavalo, US$0.30, 40 mins. Cayambe-Olmedo buses leave every 30 mins till 1600 Mon-Fri, and 1800 Fri-Sun (1 hr, US$0.35). To Ibarra at 0700 only, 1½ hrs, US$0.50, returns 1230.

Reserva Ecológica Cayambe-Coca

Cayambe is a good place to access the western side of the Reserva Ecológica Cayambe-Coca which spans the Cordillera Central and extends down to the eastern lowlands.

Cayambe
Volcano
The highest point in the world which lies directly on the Equator

At 5,790 m, Cayambe is Ecuador's third highest peak. About 1 km south of Cayambe is an unmarked cobbled road heading east via Juan Montalvo, leading in 26 km to the Ruales-Oleas-Berge refuge at about 4,800 m. The *refugio* costs US$10 per person per night; it can sleep 37 people in bunks, but bring a sleeping bag, as it is very cold. There is a kitchen, fireplace, and eating area with tables and benches, running water, electric light and a radio for rescue. It is named after three Ecuadorean climbers killed by an avalanche in 1974 while pioneering a new route up from the west.

This is now the standard route, using the refuge as a base. The route heads off to the left of a rocky outcrop immediately above the *refugio*. To the right of the outcrop is an excellent area of crevasses, seracs and low rock and ice walls for practising technical skills. The climb is heavily crevassed, especially near the summit, there is an avalanche risk near the summit and south-easterly winds are a problem. It is more difficult and dangerous than either Chimborazo or Cotopaxi. An alternative route is to the northeast summit (5,570 m), which is the most difficult, with the possible need to bivouac.

Getting there You can take a camioneta from Cayambe to *Hacienda Piemonte El Hato* (at about 3,500 m) or a taxi for US$15. From the *hacienda* to the *refugio* it is a 3-4 hr walk, sometimes longer if heavily laden, and the wind can be very strong, but it is a beautiful walk. It is difficult to get transport back to Cayambe. A milk truck runs from Cayambe hospital to the *hacienda* at 0600, returning between 1700-1900. Four-wheel drive jeeps go to the refugio (see *Safari Tours* in Quito, page 133), 1½-2 hrs. An alternative route is via Olmedo (see below), through *Hacienda La Chimba* to Laguna de San Marcos, which is the end of the vehicle track. This gives access to the northeast summit.

Oyacachi to El
Chaco trek
An adventurous trek takes you from the highlands to the Oriente lowlands in three to four days. Starting in the village of Oyacachi at 3,100 m, it follows the Oyacachi river first along the north bank and later on the southern bank, crossing several tributaries along the way (a pulley may be necessary for these crossings). The walk ends at El Chaco, at 1,550 m, on the western shore of the

Quijos river and along the Baeza-Lago Agrio road. The season for this walk is November to February, it is impassable during the rainy season.

Getting there Take a truck from Cayambe to Oyacachi via Cangahua, the route is very scenic. From El Chaco there is bus service to Quito via Baeza or to Lago Agrio in the northern Oriente.

Cayambe to Otavalo

The road forks north of Cayambe. **To the right** is a cobbled road in good condition, the very scenic *carretera vieja* or old road, which runs to **Olmedo**. There are no hotels or restaurants in Olmedo, but there are a couple of shops and lodging may be available with the local nuns. There is also an Andinatel office, in the old Tenencia Política, on the plaza. The surrounding countryside is pleasant for strolling. A road runs east from Olmedo to the **Laguna de San Marcos**, 40 minutes by car, three hours on foot.

After Olmedo the road is not so good (four-wheel drive vehicles are recommended). It is 9 km from Olmedo to **Zuleta**, where beautiful embroidery is done on napkins and tablecloths. There is a *feria* on Sunday. You can see the beautiful Hacienda Zuleta of the former president Galo Plaza, which offers accommodation. Fifteen kilometres beyond Zuleta is La Esperanza (see Excursions from Ibarra, page 179), 8½ km before Ibarra.

To the left the main paved road crosses the *páramo* at the Nudo de Cajas and suddenly descends to the basin of Lago San Pablo and beyond to Otavalo.

An alternative route from Quito to Otavalo is via San Antonio de Pichincha, past the Inca ruins of Rumicucho (see page 146) and San José de Minas. The road curves through the dry but impressive landscape down to the Río Guayllabamba, then climbs again, passing some picturesque oasis villages. After Minas the road is in very bad condition and a jeep is necessary for the next climb and then descent to join the Otavalo-Selva Alegre road about 15 km west from Otavalo. The journey takes about three hours altogether and is rough, hot and dusty, but the scenery is magnificent. This is a great biking route since there is little traffic. In **San José de Minas** is **F** *La Carreta*, on the plaza, with hot shower, restaurant, clean. In the valley below, at Cubi there are warm springs. Buses to San José de Minas leave from Asunción y Larrea and from Anteparra y San Blas in Quito.

Otavalo

Otavalo is set in beautiful countryside which is worth exploring for three or four days. The town itself is nothing to write home about, consisting as it does of rather functional concrete buildings. But then visitors don't come here for the architecture. Otavalo is one of South America's most important centres of ethno-tourism and its enormous Saturday market, featuring a dazzling array of textiles and crafts, is second to none and not to be missed. It's best to travel on Friday, in order to avoid overcrowded buses on Saturday and to enjoy the nightlife.

Phone code: 06
Colour map M2, grid B5
Population: 28,000
Altitude: 2,530m

Getting there The bus terminal is at Atahualpa and Ordoñez in the northeast of the city and just off the Panamericana (see map). Through buses going further north drop you at the highway which is not recommended. See under transport, page 170, for further details. Near the terminal is a lifelike monument, showing Otavaleños performing a traditional dance. There are few hotels around the bus terminal; take a taxi or city bus into the centre. There is no longer a train service to Otavalo.

Ins & outs

Getting around The centre is bounded by the Río El Tejar to the west and the disused rail tracks in the east. It is quite small and you can walk between the *artesanías* market at Plaza de Ponchos and the produce market at plaza 24 de Mayo. The livestock market is more of a hike.

Tourist office and information *Cámara Provincial de Turismo de Imbabura*, Bolívar 8-14 y Montalvo, Mon-Sat 0900-1200, Mon-Fri 1500-1700, general information about attractions, hotels in Otavalo and region. Otavalo tourist information is available at www.otavalo-web.com **Maps:** the IGM produces a detailed tourist map of the province of Imbabura. There is also a handy pocket map of this region from *Ediguias*, with good maps of the province and city maps of Otavalo and Ibarra.

Safety Otavalo is a prime tourist destination. The presence of large numbers of foreign visitors attracts pickpockets and thieves. Be careful with your belongings especially in crowded markets. Don't leave anything unattended, even in locked cars.

Sights

While most visitors come to Otavalo to meet its native people and buy their crafts, you cannot escape the influence of the modern world here, a product of the city's very success in trade and tourism. The streets are lined not only with small kiosks selling homespun wares, but also with wholesale warehouses and international freight forwarders, as well as numerous hotels, cafés and restaurants catering to decidedly foreign tastes.

In the Plaza Bolívar is a statue of Rumiñahui, Atahualpa's general. There was outrage among indigenous residents over suggestions that the monument be replaced with a statue of Bolívar himself, symptomatic of the ongoing rivalry between native Otavaleños and their *mestizo* neighbours.

Markets

The artesanías industry is so big that the Plaza de Ponchos is now filled with vendors every day of the week

The Saturday market actually comprises three different markets in various parts of the town and the central streets are filled with vendors. The *artesanías* (crafts) market starts at 0700 and goes on till 1800, and is based around the Plaza de Ponchos (officially called Plaza Centenario). The livestock section begins at 0500 and lasts until 1000. It takes place outside town in the Viejo Colegio Agrícola. To get there, go west on Calle Colón from the town centre. The produce market lasts from 0700 till 1400, in Plaza 24 de Mayo.

Bargaining is appropriate in the market and in the shops. The Otavaleños sell goods they weave and sew themselves, as well as *artesanías* from throughout Ecuador, Peru and Bolivia. *Mestizo* and indigenous vendors from Otavalo, and from elsewhere in Ecuador and South America, sell paintings, jewellery, shigras, baskets, leather goods, woodcarvings from San Antonio de Ibarra and the Oriente, ceramics, antiques and almost anything else you care to mention.

The *artesanía* market has more selection on Saturday but prices are a little higher than other days when the atmosphere is more relaxed. There is a good book market also at Plaza de Ponchos. Indigenous people in the market respond better to photography if you buy something first, then ask politely. Reciprocity and courtesy are important Andean norms.

Museums **Instituto Otavaleño de Antropología** has a library, an archaeological museum with artefacts from the northern highlands, a collection of musical instruments, as well as a good ethnographic display of regional costumes and traditional activities. ■ *Mon-Fri 0800-1200, 1430-1830, free, Av de los Sarances west of the Panamericana Norte, T920321.*

The Otavaleños

In a country where the term indio *can still be intended as an insult and a few highland Indians continue to address whites as* patroncito *(little master), the Otavaleños stand out in stark contrast. They are a proud and prosperous people, who have made their name not only as successful weavers and international businessmen, but also as unsurpassed symbols of cultural fortitude.*

There is some considerable debate over the origin of the Otavaleños. In present-day Imbabura, pre-Inca people were Caranquis, or Imbaya, and, in Otavalo, the Cayambi. They were subjugated by the Caras who expanded into the highlands from the Manabí coast. The Caras resisted the Incas for 17 years, but the conquering Incas eventually moved the local population away to replace them with vassals from Peru and Bolivia. One recent theory is that the Otavaleños are descended from these forced migrants and also Chibcha salt traders from Colombia, while some current-day Otavaleños prefer to stress their local pre-Inca roots.

Otavalo men wear their hair long and plaited under a black trophy hat. They wear white, calf-length trousers and blue ponchos. The women's colourful costumes consist of embroidered blouses, shoulder wraps and a plethora of gold coloured necklace beads. Their ankle-length skirts, known as anacos, *are fastened with an intricately woven cloth belt or* faja. *Traditional footwear for both genders is the* alpargata, *a sandal whose sole was originally made of coiled hemp rope, but today has been replaced by rubber.*

Impeccable cleanliness is another striking aspect of many Otavaleños' attire. Perhaps the most outstanding feature of the Otavaleños, however, is their profound sense of pride and self-assurance. This is aided not only by the group's economic success, but also by achievements in academic and cultural realms. All families speak Quichua as their first tongue and Spanish as their second. It is ironic perhaps that these fascinating people, whom many tourists come to regard as typical representatives of Ecuador's highland Indians, are in fact so atypical.

The **Museo Arqueológico César Vásquez Fuller** has an excellent collection from all over Ecuador and is recommended. ■ *Mon-Sat 1400-1800, US$1, the owner gives free tours, Roca y Montalvo.* **Museo Jaramillo** has a small collection of regional ceramic and stone pieces. It was renovated in 1998. Recommended. ■ *Thu-Sat 1000-1300, 1500-1700, Bolívar, off Parque Central.* **Centro Histórico** is just outside town, in the direction of Cotacachi. There is also a museum in Peguche, see Sleeping, Out of town below.

Essentials

B *Ali Shungu*, Quito y Miguel Egas, T920750, alishngu@uio.telconet.net Nice rooms with firm mattresses, safety deposit boxes, good restaurant with vegetarian dishes on request, folk music at weekends, lovely garden, apartment suites, **AL**. Accepts cash only. US run. Recommended. **B** *El Indio Inn*, Bolívar 904, T922922, F920325. Very attractive rooms, also has suites with sitting room. Clean and pleasant. **C** *El Coraza*, Calderón y Sucre, T921225, F920459. Nice rooms. Very clean, friendly, quiet. **C** *Doña Esther*, J Montalvo 4-44, T/F920739. Stylish rooms in beautifully renovated colonial house, with courtyard, excellent restaurant with wood-burning pizza oven, French-Otavaleño-run, very friendly. Recommended.

E *Cabañas El Rocío*, Barrio San Juan y Panamericana, T922136. Attractive rooms with bath, hot water, cafeteria serves full breakfast for US$1, parking. Views of the garden. **E** *Inca Real*, Salinas across from Plaza de Ponchos, T/F922895. With good mattresses, **F** without bath. Modern, clean, nice. **E** *El Indio*, Sucre 1214 y Salinas, T920060.

Sleeping
■ *on map, page 167*
Hotels may be full on Friday nights, before market, when prices go up. Make sure to keep your room locked and your valuables stowed, there have been some reports of theft

Northern Highlands

Carpeted rooms, with bath, TV, restaurant. **E** *Otavalo*, Roca 504 y J Montalvo, T920416. **F** without bath, good popular restaurant, refurbished colonial house with attractive patio, parking. New management in 2000, good service, friendly. **E** *Riviera Sucre*, García Moreno 380 y Roca, T920241. **F** with shared bath, laundry facilities, cafeteria, good breakfasts, book exchange, attractive garden. Popular, a good place to meet other travellers, staff not always helpful, good place to stay. Mostly recommended. **E** *Samay Inn 1*, Abdon Calderon 10-05 y Sucre, T/F922871. With bath, hot water. Friendly. **E** *Samay Inn 2*, Colon y Roca, T/F922995. Sixteen rooms, with private or shared bath, good beds. In modern building, very friendly and helpful, good value. Recommended. **E** *Valle del Amanecer*, Roca y Quiroga, T920990, F920286. With bath, hot water, cheap laundry, good restaurant. Attractive colonial building with courtyard, relaxed atmosphere, very clean, popular, mountain bike hire, friendly, medical service available (owner is a physician), help arranging tours. Recommended. **E** *Yamor Continental*, at the north end of Bolívar near the bus terminal, T920451. Pool, parking, pleasant gardens, restaurant. Ageing but comfortable, quiet.

F *Kikinpaq*, Sucre 1414 y Quiroga, T922408. With bath, hot water, TV, parking, **G** with shared bath. **F** *Los Ponchos Inn*, Sucre y Quiroga by Plaza de Ponchos, T/F923575. With bath, hot water, TV. Modern, with views of the plaza. **F** *Residencial Irina*, Jaramillo 5-09 y Morales, T920684. With bath, **G** without, tepid showers, laundry facilities, restaurant, excellent breakfast. Clean, friendly, discount for longer stay, top rooms best, mountain bike hire. Recommended. **F** *Residencial Rocío*, Morales between Ricaurte y Egas, T520584. Hot showers, breakfast available. Popular, friendly, good value. **F** *Rincón de Belén*, Roca 8-20 y J Montalvo, T921860. With bath, electric shower, TV, parking, restaurant. Nice, modern. **F** *Rincón del Viajero*, Roca 407 y Quiroga, T921741. A couple of rooms with bath, most with shared bath (cheaper), hot water, sitting room with fireplace, terrace with hammocks, ping pong table, breakfast available, parking. English spoken. **F** *Runa Pacha*, Roca y Quiroga, T921730. With bath (outside the room, but private), hot water, **G** with shared bath, restaurant bike and motorbike rentals. **F** *Samay Inn 3*, 31 de Octubre 901 y Quito, T922438. With bath, hot water, TV, cafeteria.

G *El Cacique* 31 de Octubre, entre Quito y Panamericana Norte, T921740, F920930. With bath, TV, parking, nice terrace. Clean, spacious, friendly. **G** *La Herradura*, Bolívar 10-05 y Colón, T923418. Shared bath, hot water, restaurant. Clean. Recommended. **G** *Hostal El Geranio*, Ricaurte between Colón y Morales, T920185. With bath, electric shower, cheaper with shared bath, laundry facilities, also 1 apartment for 9, with kitchen, nice backyard, internet service. Popular, very friendly, family run, quiet, clean, helpful with local excursions. **G** *Inti Ñan*, J Montalvo 602 y Sucre, by the main park, T921373. Shared bath, hot water, nice clean rooms, laundry facilities. Small, friendly, noisy during the day. **G** *María*, Jaramillo y Colón, T/F920672. Modern, with bath, hot water, parking. Good location. **G** *Residencial San Luís*, Abdón Calderón 6-02 y 31 de Octubre, T920614. Shared bath, family run, safe, café, friendly. **G** *Pensión Los Angeles*, Colón 4-10 y Bolívar, T920058. Clean, friendly, hot shower US$0.50 extra, nice patio, quiet. **G** *Samac Tarina*, Abdón Calderón 7-13 y Av 31 de Octubre, T920182. Eleven rooms with shared bath, 2 rooms with bath and TV, good beds, safety deposit, rooms at the front with balcony are better, rooms with bath are dark. Clean, friendly, family run, good location for market. **G** *Samaj Huasy*, Jaramillo 6-11 y Salinas. Half a block from the Plaza de Ponchos, T921126. Dark rooms, shared bath, hot water.Clean, friendly. **H** *Residencial Colón*, Colón 7-13, T920022. Hot water, good.

Youth hostel *Jatun Pacha*, 31 de Octubre 19 y Panamericana, T922223, F922871. IYHF hostel, nice, modern, breakfast and 1 hr cycling included, **F** per person in dormitory, cheaper for members and students with valid ID, private room with bath **D**, bicycle rentals.

Out of town   Towards Mojanda: **A** *Casa de Mojanda*, Vía Mojanda Km 3, F922969, mojanda@uio.telconet.net Beautiful setting on a mountainside near the main road on 25 acres of farmland and forested gorge, organic garden, 7 cottages and 1 dormitory for 12, price includes all meals, healthy cooking, cosy, comfortable, quiet, library, horse riding, mountain bikes. Highly recommended. At Km 4.5 is **E** per person *La Luna de Mojanda*, T/F09-737415/816145. Run by young Argentine couple, includes breakfast, with bath, cheaper without, **G** per person in dormitory with kitchen and dining room, they organize cheap four-wheel drive tours, games room, library, taxi service to Otavalo, good restaurant, cable TV, English and German spoken. Highly recommended. **C** *Hospedaje Camino Real*, via a Mojanda Km 2, T920421. Cabins with hot water, equipped kitchen, laundry, good meals, full breakfast for US$2, library. Owner is an anthropologist, English spoken. Bus to the village of Punyaro takes you very close. Recommended.

North of town L *Vista del Mindo*, 5 km north of Otavalo, T946112, F946109, smarmon@spavistadelmundo.com Hotel spa, rooms and suites. Personalized health programs. New in 2000. **AL** *Hacienda Pinsaqui*, 3½ km north of Otavalo along the

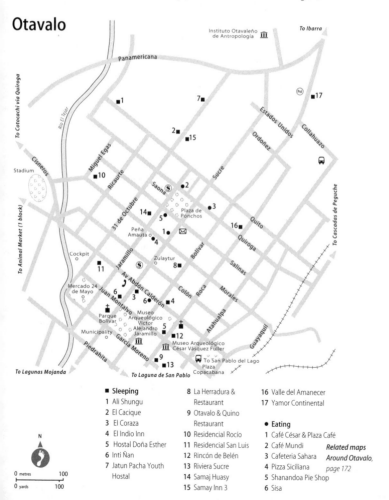

Otavalo

■ Sleeping	8 La Herradura &	16 Valle del Amanecer
1 Ali Shungu	Restaurant	17 Yamor Continental
2 El Cacique	9 Otavalo & Quino	
3 El Coraza	Restaurant	● Eating
4 El Indio Inn	10 Residencial Rocío	1 Café César & Plaza Café
5 Hostal Doña Esther	11 Residencial San Luis	2 Café Mundi
6 Inti Ñan	12 Rincón de Belén	3 Cafeteria Sahara
7 Jatun Pacha Youth	13 Riviera Sucre	4 Pizza Siciliana
Hostal	14 Samaj Huasy	5 Shanandoa Pie Shop
	15 Samay Inn 3	6 Sisa

Related maps
Around Otavalo,
page 172

Panamericana, 300 m north of the turn off to Cotacachi, just west of the highway, T/F946116/7, info@pinsaqui.com Immaculate rooms, one with a private sunken jacuzzi, some with fireplace, includes breakfast, beautiful original antiques, lovely dining room, lounge with fireplace, stylish colonial ambience, beautiful gardens, horse riding. **B** *Hosteria la Casa de Hacienda*, entrance at Panamericana Norte Km 3, then 300 m east along the old road, between Peguche and Ilumán, T946336, F923105, casadhda@imbanet.net Tasteful cabins with fireplace, restaurant, price includes breakfast. At the foot of Imbabura volcano, horse riding.**C** *Troje Cotama*, 4 km north of Otavalo along the Panamericana and 1½ Km west, by Carabuela, T/F946119. Converted grain house, very attractive, fireplace in rooms, good cheap food, home made bread. Quiet country setting, 1 hr and 15 mins walk from Otavalo on a country road. Dutch run, Dutch, English and German spoken.

In Peguche 2 km north of Otavalo, (see Around Otavalo below). **B** *Peguche Tío*, near centre, T922619. Rooms with bath, hot water, fireplace, restaurant, includes breakfast. Andean construction with round communal area, decorated with works of art, small interesting museum with archaeological and antiques collections. From the Panamericana walk 50 m east and then 50 m north. **D** *Aya Huma Hotel*, on the railway, T922663, F922664, ayahuma@imbanet.net Excellent restaurant with vegetarian food and delicious pancakes, lovely place, hot water, clean, quiet, **E** with shared bath, run by a Dutch lady, great place to make contact with local indigenous culture, live folk music on Saturday, 15 mins from the falls. Highly recommended.

Eating
● *on map, page 167*

Ecuadorean *El Indio*, Sucre y Salinas. Good fried chicken (weekends especially) and steaks, local speciality *fritada* (fried pork). *Mi Otavalito*, Sucre y Morales. Good for lunch also international food à la carte. *La Herradura*, Bolivar 10-05. Good set meal and à la carte, outdoor tables. *Cafetería Camba Huasi*, Bolívar y J Montalvo. Self service, varied food, good coffee. *Royal*, on the main plaza. Clean (even the toilets), home cooking. *Ali Micuy*, Jaramillo y Quiroga, on the Plaza de Ponchos. Set meals, vegetarian dishes available.

International The restaurant of *Hotel Ali Shungu* (see above) serves all meals. Open 0700-2100, wide variety. Recommended. *SISA*, Abdón Calderón 409 entre Bolívar y Sucre, T920154. Coffee shop, cappuccino, excellent food in clean restaurant upstairs, reports of slow service, also bookstore, cultural centre shows weekly international films, live music Fri-Sun. Open 0700-2200. *Geminis*, on Salinas between Sucre and Bolívar. Excellent food, good atmosphere and music. Highly recommended. *Café Mundi*, Quiroga 608 y Jaramillo, Plaza de Ponchos. Nice atmosphere, varied menu, vegetarian available. *Tabasco's*, Sucre y Salinas, Plaza de Ponchos, Mexican, attractive, good food.

Italian *Café César*, Sucre 12-05 entre Salinas y Morales, 2nd Floor, good views from top balcony. *Pizza Siciliana*, Sucre 10-03 y Calderón, Morales 5-10 y Sucre and Jaramillo y Salinas. Good large pizzas, vegetarian dishes, good juices, friendly. *Il de Roma*, J Montalvo 4-44. Good food, warm atmosphere.

Middle Eastern *Cafetería Sahara*, Quiroga, between Sucre y Bolívar. Good for falafel and humus, fruit and vegetable juices, water pipes, Arabic coffee and sweets. Small portions, cushions on the floor for sitting.

Seafood *Fuente del Mar*, Bolívar 815. Half a block from the main plaza. Also has some rooms with hot showers. Recommended. *Quino Pequeño*, Roca 740 y Juan Montalvo. Good typical coastal cooking, good value. *Marisquería Delfín Azul*, Salinas y Sucre. Good value.

Cafés and bars *Cafetería Shanandoa Pie Shop*, Salinas y Jaramillo. Good pies, milk shakes and ice cream, expensive, good meeting place, popular and friendly, recommended for breakfast, book exchange, daily movies at 1700 and 1900. *Empanadas Argentinas*, Morales y Sucre. Good savoury and sweet *empanadas*. *Terraza Café Sol*, Jaramillo at Plaza de Ponchos. Good views of the plaza and mountains. *Oraibi Bar*, Colón y Sucre. Open Thu-Sat, Jul-Aug, Swiss owner, pleasant courtyard, snacks, live music Fri and Sat evenings, good service, book exchange. *Agua Fresca*, Salinas at Plaza de Ponchos, some vegetarian, mainly snacks, open Mon, Wed, Fri, Sat only, good music and atmosphere. *Huaqui Inti*, Salinas at Plaza de Ponchos. Popular with foreigners, live music on weekends.

Peña Amauta, Jaramillo y Morales. Good local bands, friendly and welcoming, mainly foreigners, Italian food upstairs. *Peña la Jampa*, Jaramillo 5-69 y Morales, T922988. Popular. *Peña Tuparina*, Morales y 31 de Octubre. Recommended. *Peñas* are normally only on Fri and Sat from 2200, entrance US$1. *Habana Club*, Quito y 31 de Octubre. Lively disco, cover US$1. On Fri and Sat nights there are nightlife tours on a chiva (open sided bus with a musical group on board), it stops at the Plaza de Ponchos and ends its route at the *Habana Club*.

Entertainment
Otavalo is generally safe until 2200. Avoid deserted streets & plazas

Indigenous celebrations overlap with *mestizo* Catholic holidays, prolonging festivities for a week or more. At the **end of June** the *Inti Raymi* celebrations of the summer solstice (**June 21**), are combined with the *Fiesta de San Juan* (**June 24**) and the *Fiesta de San Pedro y San Pablo* (**June 29**). There are bullfights in the plaza and regattas on the beautiful Lago de San Pablo, 4 km away (see Around Otavalo below for transport). These combined festivities are known as *Los San Juanes* and participants are mostly indigenous. The celebration begins with a ritual bath in the Peguche waterfall (a personal spiritual activity, best carried out without visitors and certainly without cameras). Most of the action takes place in the smaller communities surrounding Otavalo. Groups of musicians and dancers compete with each other as they make their way from one village to another over the course of the week; there is much drinking along the way. In Otavalo, indigenous families have costume parties, that at times spill over onto the streets. In the San Juan neighbourhood, near the Yanayacu baths, there is a week-long celebration with food, drink and music. If you wish to visit fiestas in the local villages, ask the musicians in the tourist restaurants, they may invite you, but be aware that outsiders are not always welcome. The music is good and there is a lot of drinking, but transport back to Otavalo is hard to find.

Festivals

The *Fiesta del Yamor* and *Colla Raimi* (fall equinox or festival of the moon) are held during the **first 2 weeks of September**. This is the largest festivity in the province of Imbabura, it takes place in several cities and is mainly a mestizo celebration. Special *yamor chicha* is prepared from seven varieties of corn and served to the participants. Local dishes including *llapingachos* and *fritada* are cooked, also amusement parks are set up, bands play in the plaza and there is much dancing. Other events include bullfighting (corner 31 de Octubre y Quito), fireworks and sporting events, including swimming and reed boat races across Lago San Pablo.

Mojandas Arriba is an annual 2-day hike from Quito over Mojanda to reach Otavalo for the **31 October** foundation celebrations commemorating the day Simon Bolívar elevated Otavalo to the status of a city. It is walked by hundreds each year and follows the old trails with an overnight stop at Malchingue.

Shopping

Otavalo can seem like a giant souvenir shop at times. As well as the market, there are countless shops selling sweaters, tapestries and other souvenirs

The Ethnic Collection, on Jaramillo at Plaza de Ponchos, has selected, upmarket crafts. *Tagua Muyu*, Sucre 10-11 y Colon, is good for *tagua* (vegetable ivory) carvings. *Galeria de Arte Quipus*, Sucre y Morales, and *Galeria Inti Ñan*, Salinas 509 y Sucre, Plaza de Ponchos, are both good for paintings with native motifs. *Le Petit Cadeau*, Roca 9-03, sells religious art. *Palos de Lluvia*, Morales 506 y Sucre, is good for rain sticks and other crafts. *Hilana*, Sucre esquina Morales, sells wool blankets.

The Book Market, at Jaramillo 6-28 y Salinas, is highly recommended for buying, selling or exchanging books in English, French, German and other languages at cheap prices. They also stock guidebooks, maps, postcards, CDs and cassettes. *Fruti Hortalizas*, Colon 310 y Bolivar, is good for for organic fruits and vegetables.

Sports

Mountain bikes For hire at *Ecoturismo*, Jatun Pacha Youth Hostel (see above), US$3 per hour, US$10 for 5 hours or US$12 per day, includes helmet. *Taller Ciclo Primaxi*, García Moreno y Atahualpa 2-49, has good bikes for rent, US$5 per day. Recommended. *Hostal Valle del Amanecer* (see above). US$4 per day.

On the Panamericana, *Yanayacu* has 3 swimming pools, volleyball courts and is full of locals on Sun. *Neptuno*, at Morales and Guayaquil, also has a popular pool. Near the market, on Quiroga y Sucre, a ball game is played in the afternoons called *pelota de mano*. It is similar to the game in Ibarra (described on page 178) except that the ball is about the size of a table-tennis ball, made of leather, and hit with the hands, not a bat. There is a cockpit (*gallera*) at 31 de Octubre y Montalvo, fights are on Sat and Sun 1500-1900, US$0.50.

Tour operators

All agencies offer similar tours and prices. One-day tours with English-speaking guides to artisans' homes and villages, which usually provide opportunities to buy handicrafts cheaper than in the market, cost US$15-17 pp. Day trips to Cuicocha or Mojanda, US$15-20 pp. Horse riding tours around Otavalo: 5 hrs to Tangali thermal springs US$15 pp; full day to Cuicocha crater lake US$30 pp. Trips to the Intag subtropical region and Nangulví thermal baths. *Zulaytur*, Sucre y Colón, 2nd flr, T921176, F922969. Run by Rodrigo Mora. English spoken, information, map of town, slide show, horse-riding, tours, interesting day tour of local artisan communities, US$10 pp. Their tours, especially the latter, have been repeatedly recommended. *Intiexpress*, Sucre 11-06, T921436, F920737, also on Bolívar y Salinas esquina, T921588. Recommended for horse-riding tours, US$15 pp, ask them to prepare the horses before you arrive or time is wasted, good for those with or without experience, beautiful ride. *Diceny Viajes*, Sucre 10-11 y Colón, T921217. Run by Zulay Sarabino, an indigenous Otavaleña, English and French spoken, native guides knowledgeable about the area and culture, climbing trips to Cotacachi volcano, favourable reports. Recommended. *Suni Tours*, Morales y Sucre, T923383. Interesting itineraries, trekking and horse riding tours, trips to Intag US$20 pp per day. Guides carry radios for communications with the office. *Ecuapanorama*, Calderón y Roca, T920889/563. Ecological tours of Intag, horseriding, hikes. *Chachimbiro Tours*, Roca 904 y Morales, T923633 (cellT(09)727100). Trips to the *Complejo de Ecoturismo Chachimbiro* (thermal baths, see Excursions from Ibarra, page 179), US$18 pp for a day trip, US$25 pp for 2 days, including meals. *Intipungo*, Garcia Moreno 4-59 y Bolívar, T921171. For airline reservations, DHL/Western Union representative, international collect calls through AT&T, also tours. *Yuraturs*, Morales 505 y Sucre, T/F921861. For reservations and tours. *Leyton's Tours*, Quito y Jaramillo, T922388, horseback and bicycle tours.

Transport

Bus From **Quito** by bus from the Terminal Terrestre. It's best to take a Cooperativa Otavalo or Cooperativa Los Lagos bus, as they are the only ones which go into Otavalo; other companies, such us those going north to Ibarra or Tulcán, will drop you off on the highway but this is not safe, muggings have been reported, especially after dark. From the Terminal, buses go along the Av Occidental and later Av de la Prensa in

Cotocallao, where you can also get on. Frequent service, US$1.25, 2 hrs. **Taxi** A fast and efficient alternative is by taxi with Supertaxis Los Lagos (in Quito at Asunción 3-81, T565992; in Otavalo at Roca 8-04, T923203) who will pick you up at your hotel (in the new city only); hourly from 0830 to 1900, 2 hrs, US$4 per person, buy ticket at their office the day before travelling. A regular taxi costs US$20 one way. *Hotel Ali Shungu* (see above) runs a shuttle bus from any hotel in the new city, Quito, to Otavalo, US$15 per person. It's not restricted to *Ali Shungu* guests and is a dependable service.

Other buses To Ibarra, every 15 mins, US$0.35, 30 minutes. To **Tulcán**, via Ibarra, frequent departures. To **Cayambe**, every 15 mins, US$0.50. To **Cotacachi**, from the terminal, on Sat also from Morales y Miguel Egas, every 15 mins (some via Quiroga), US$0.25. To the communities around Lago San Pablo there's frequent service, US$0.15. To **Peguche**, take a city bus (blue), they leave every 15 mins, US$0.15. Buses and trucks to **Apuela, Peñaherrera, García Moreno** and points west leave from Colón y 31 de Octubre.

Banks *Filanbanco*, on Sucre y Colón. Visa ATM and cash advances. *Banco del Pacífico*, Mastercard ATM. *Vaz Cambios*, Jaramillo y Saona, Plaza de Ponchos.   **Directory**
   Communications Post Office: corner of Plaza de Ponchos, entrance on Sucre, 1st flr. **Andinatel:** Calderón between Jaramillo and Sucre. Open 0800-1245, 1300-1845, 1900-2145. **Internet:** Prices run about US$1.60 per hour. *Café Net*, Sucre y Morales. *Native Café Net*, Sucre y Colón, T923540. Also food service and drinks, open 0800-2200. *Micro Control*, Bolívar 14-22 y Ordóñez. Open Mon-Sat 0800-1300, 1500-2000. *Amor y Café* (sweater shop), Bolívar y Quito.
   Language schools *Instituto Superior de Español*, have a school at Sucre 11-10 y Morales, 2nd Flr, T992414, F922415, institut@superior.ecuanex.net.ec (see also Language course, Quito, page 141). *Academia de Español Mundo Andino*, Salinas 404 y Bolívar, T/F921801, espanol@interactive.net.ec Classes also with Helena Paredes Dávila, at C Colón 6-12, T920178. Recommended. *Fundación Jacinto Jijón y Caamaño*, Bolívar 8-04 y Montalvo, p 2, T920725, Spanish and Quichua lessons.
   Laundry *Tecno Clean*, C Olmedo 32. Dry cleaning. *New Laundry*, Roca 942 y Calderon. US$1.20 per kilo.

Around Otavalo

The Otavalo weavers come from dozens of communities, but it is easiest to **Weaving** visit the nearby towns of Peguche, Ilumán, Carabuela and Agato which are **villages** only 15-30 minutes away and all have a good bus service. Buses leave from the terminal and stop at Plaza Copacabana (Atahualpa y Montalvo). You can also negotiate a price with a taxi driver.

In **Ilumán**, the Conterón-de la Torre family of *Artesanías Inti Chumbi*, on the northeast corner of the plaza, gives backstrap loom weaving demonstrations and sells crafts. There are also many felt hatmakers in town who will make hats to order. In **Agato**, the Andrango-Chiza family of *Tahuantinsuyo Weaving Workshop* gives weaving demonstrations and sells textiles. In **Carabuela** many homes sell crafts including wool sweaters. Carlos de la Torre, a backstrap weaver, can be found above the Evangelist Church. In **Peguche**, the Cotacachi-Pichamba family, off the main plaza behind the church, sells beautiful tapestries, finished with tassels and loops, ready to hang.

To get to this waterfall, situated near the village of Peguche, follow the old rail- **Cascada de** way track through the woods in the direction of Ibarra until the track drops **Peguche** away to the left and a dirt path continues up the hill towards the waterfall. The patch of eucalyptus forest near the base of the falls is a popular spot for weekend outings and picnics. Allow 1-1½ hours each way. A wooden bridge at the foot of the falls leads to a steep path on the other side of the river which leads to Ibarra. From the top of the falls (left side) you can continue the walk to Lago de

San Pablo (see below). **NB** The tracks go through an unsafe neighbourhood. Avoid it by taking a bus to the trailhead near Peguche.

Four kilometres north of Otavalo are cold ferrous baths at the **Fuente de Salud**, said to be very curative, but opening hours are very irregular.

Lago de San Pablo

Robberies of lone walkers have been reported, best go in a group

There is a network of old roads and trails between Otavalo and the Lago de San Pablo area, none of which takes more than an hour or two to explore. It is worth walking either to or back from Lago de San Pablo for the views. The walk there via *El Lechero* (a large tree, considered sacred among indigenous people) is recommended, though you will be pestered by children begging. The trail starts at the south end of Calle Morales in Otavalo. The walk back via the outlet stream from the lake, staying on the right hand side of the gorge, takes two to three hours, and is also recommended, or you can flag down a passing bus. Alternatively, take a bus to San Pablo, then walk back towards the lake. The views of Imbabura are wonderful. To explore the lake itself, canoes can be hired at the *Club de Tiro, Caza y Pesca, Cabañas del Lago* or *Puerto Lago* (see Sleeping below).

Sleeping Around the lake: **L** *Hostería Cusín*, in a converted 17th-century *hacienda* on the east side of the lake, San Pablo del Lago, T918013, F918003, hacienda@cusin.com.ec, www.haciendacusin.com Twenty five rooms with fireplaces, includes breakfast, fine expensive restaurant, sports facilities (horses, mountain bikes, squash court, pool, games room), library, large screen TV, lovely courtyard and garden, book in advance, run by an Englishman, Nick Millhouse, French and German also spoken, credit cards not accepted. **AL** *Hostería Jatun Cocha*, Panamericana Km 5½, on the west side of the lake, T/F918191. Tasteful rooms with fireplaces, restaurant. On the lakeshore, kayaks, windsurfing, bicycles. **A** *Hostería Puerto Lago Country Inn*, Panamericana Sur, Km 5½ y Lago San Pablo on the west side of the lake, T920920,

Around Otavalo

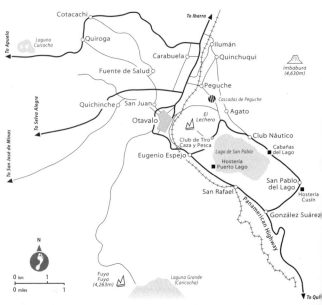

Related map
Otavalo, page 167

F920900, efernand@uio.satnet.net. Includes breakfast and dinner. Beautiful setting, a good place to watch the sunset, very hospitable, good expensive restaurant (try trout in walnut sauce), motor boat trips on the lake. **B** *Cabañas del Lago*, on northeast side of the lake, T/F918001 (in Quito, T435936), cablago@access.net.ec Nice cabins with bunk beds, on the lakeside.Clean, restaurant, nice garden, boats and pedalos for hire.

From **San Pablo del Lago** it is possible to climb the **Imbabura** volcano, at 4,630 m and almost always under cloud – allow at least six hours to reach the summit and four hours for the descent. An alternative access, preferred by many, is from La Esperanza, south of Ibarra (see page 179). Easier, and no less impressive, is the nearby **Cerro Huarmi Imbabura**, 3,845 m. Buses from Otavalo to San Pablo del Lago leave every 30 minutes (US$0.15), from the bus terminal. A taxi costs US$1.70.

It is possible to take a tour or hike southwest to an impressive crater lake 18 km from Otavalo. **Caricocha** (or Laguna Grande de Mojanda) is 1,200 m higher than Otavalo. Twenty-five minutes' walk above Caricocha is **Laguna Huarmicocha** and a further 25 minutes is **Laguna Yanacocha**. Take a warm jacket, food and drinks; there is no entrance fee. The views on the descent are excellent.

    From Caricocha the route continues south about 5 km before dividing: the left-hand path leads to **Tocachi**, the right-hand to **Cochasqui** (see page 160). Both are about 20 km from Laguna Grande and offer beautiful views of Quito and Cotopaxi (cloud permitting). You can climb **Fuya Fuya** (4,263 m) and **Yanaurco** (4,259 m), but the mountain huts on the shore of Laguna Grande and on the path to Fuya Fuya are derelict. (See Out of town, page 167, for hotels on the way to Mojanda.) Get there by car on a cobbled road. Take a tent, warm sleeping bag, and food; there is no accommodation. Or take a Quito bus as far as Tabacundo, hitch to Lagunas (difficult at weekends), then walk back to Otavalo by the old Inca trail, on the right after 2-3 km. A taxi or camioneta from Otavalo is US$18 return, arrange in advance but don't pay the full fare; one way is US$7.

    Safety There have been several reports of armed holdups of campers by Mojanda and those travelling the nearby roads. At the Otavalo Police station you can request an escort to visit Mojanda.

West of the road between Otavalo and Ibarra is Cotacachi, where leather goods are made and sold, although quality varies a lot. The collapsible leather duffle bags are recommended. Credit cards are widely accepted but you have to pay a 10% surcharge. There is also access along a cobbled road directly from Otavalo.

Sleeping LL *La Mirage*, ex-hacienda 500 metres west of town, T915237, F915065, mirage1@mirage.com.ec, www4.hosteria_la_mirage.com.ec Beautiful garden, pool and gymnasium, very good suites with fireplace and antiques, lovely restaurant, excellent chocolate cake, arrive early for lunch as tour parties stop here, expensive, good excursions, price including breakfast and dinner. Recommended. **A** *Hostería La Banda*, 10 de Agosto, T915176, F915873. Bungalows and suites, country estate-style restaurant, cafeteria. **C** *El Mesón de las Flores*, García Moreno 1376 y Sucre, T916009, F915828. Converted ex-hacienda off main plaza, meals in a beautiful patio, live music at lunch Sat-Sun, parking. Highly recommended. **D** *Cotacachi Inn*, 10 de Agosto 12-38 y Bolívar, above leather shop, T915490, F915286. Includes breakfast. Restaurant, internet, no outside views. **D** *Sumac Huasi*, Montalvo 11-09 y Moncayo, T915873. Large modern rooms, includes breakfast, nice. **F** *Plaza Bolívar*, Bolívar 12-35 y 10 de Agosto, Edificio de la Sociedad de Artesanos, 3rd floor, T915755. With bath, hot water, parking. **G** *Bachita*, Sucre y Peñaherrera, T914490. Modern, bath, clean, quiet. Recommended.

Lagunas de Mojanda

Be sure to enquire about safety before visiting this area

Cotacachi

Northern Highlands

Eating A local speciality is *carne colorada*. **Fortunatos**, Sucre 913 y Montalvo, Local and international food. **Asadero La Tola**, Rocafuerte 018 y 9 de Octubre, in an old courtyard. *El Leñador*, Sucre 1012 y Montalvo. Varied menu, good value. *Inty Huasi*, Bolívar 12-48 y 10 de Agosto. Good value.

Transport Frequent buses run from Otavalo terminal (US$0.20) and on Saturday also also from Morales y Egas (US$0.25). There are 4 buses direct to Quito, leaving in the early morning; US$2.

Laguna Cuicocha The lake lies about 15 km beyond Cotacachi, past the town of Quiroga, at an altitude of 3,070 m. The area has been developed for tourism and is part of the **Reserva Ecológica Cotacachi-Cayapas**, which extends from Cotacachi volcano to the tropical lowlands on the Río Cayapas in Esmeraldas. The US$5 park fee need not be paid if only visiting the lake. This is a crater lake with two islands, although these are closed to the public for biological studies.

There is a well-marked, 8 km path around the lake, which takes four to five hours and provides spectacular views of the Cotacachi, Imbabura and, occasionally, glacier-covered Cayambe peaks. The best views are to be had in the early morning, when condors can sometimes be seen. There is a lookout at 3 km, two hours from the start. It's best to do the route in an anticlockwise direction and take water and a waterproof jacket. A community group is managing the lake area, they offer guides for the walk around the lake and run interesting tours (Spanish only) on motor boats, US$2 per person, for minimum six people. **Cerro Cotacachi** (4,944 m), north from the lake, is also part of the reserve. To climb it, it's best to approach from the ridge, not from the side with the antenna which is usually shrouded in cloud. Detailed maps of the Otavalo-Ibarra region are available from the IGM in Quito.

Enquire about safety before walking around the lake **Warning** Public safety has been a problem in the past. A local community group is now in charge of safety in the area, always enquire locally before going around the lake, especially on your own. *Do not eat the blueberries, they are poisonous.* Also, many people have been badly poisoned by eating the blueberries which grow near the lake. They are tasty but are *not* blueberries; they render the eater helpless within two hours, requiring at least a stomach pump. **NB** On the road between Cotacachi and Cuicocha, children stretch string across the road to beg, especially at weekends, Christmas and New Year.

Sleeping and eating G per person *El Mirador*, above the restaurant and pier (follow trail, T09-559053). With food, rooms with hot water and fireplace, friendly service, camping possible, hikes arranged with knowledgeable guide up Cotacachi, but you must be fit, excellent view, return transport to Otavalo provided for US$7. **G** per person *Refugio Cuicochamanta*, 1 km beyond the park entrance, on the road to Intag, T916313. In native family's home, breakfast and dinner included, trekking, climbing and horseback tours offered, English and French spoken. The restaurant at the lakeshore, El Muelle, has a dining room overlooking the lake, clean, moderate prices.

Transport Buses from Otavalo to **Quiroga** (US$0.20) leave from the terminal. Bus Cotacachi-Quiroga US$0.10; *camioneta* Quiroga-Cuicocha US$2.50, Cotacachi-Cuicocha US$3.50. Alternatively, hire a taxi (US$12.50) or a *camioneta* (US$7) in Otavalo for Laguna Cuicocha. A taxi costs US$4 one way from Cotacachi. The 3-hr walk back to Cotacachi is beautiful. After 1 km on the road from the park entrance, turn left (at the first bend) on to the old road. You can also walk from Otavalo.

Just west of the Panamericana, 11 km north of the turoff for Cotacachi, is **Atuntaqui**, a quiet, pretty town with many sweater factories. Its *fiesta* is around March 2. It can also be reached from Cotacachi via a secondary road, good for cycling or walking. Here is *El Manantial*, a swimming pool and sauna, and **H** *Hostal Colombia*, T911490, with restaurant, clean, quiet.

To the northwest of Otavalo lies the lush subtropical region of Intag. Access to this area is along the road that follows the southern edge of Cuicocha, then continues northwest to the town of **Apuela** from where it goes southwest to **García Moreno**, five to six hours from Otavalo.

Before Apuela is the **Intag Cloud Forest Reserve**, a two hour drive from Otavalo followed by an hour's hike to a friendly lodge with good vegetarian food. The reserve contains primary cloud forest at elevations from 1,800 m to 2,800 m, and there is a trail to Los Cedros (see below). The owners are very involved in community environmental work, see www.decoin.org The lodge only accepts groups of 6 or more and specializes in university groups. Prices depend on group size US$25-50 per person per day. Reservations by mail only: Casilla 18, Otavalo.

South of Apuela are the thermal baths of **Nangulví**. As with most developed springs in the country they tend to be busy and full at weekends. There are four hot pools here and one large cold one for plunging. From Otavalo three buses a day and several trucks pass right by these springs, a fourth bus passes within 20 minutes' walk. All depart from one of the corners where Calle Colón and 31 de Octubre intersect.

Sleeping and eating In Apuela: **G** *Residencial Don Luís*. Basic, cold showers, fairly clean, friendly. There are also some cabins (new in 2000), without name or sign, ask in town. **Southwest of Apuela**: **D** *Gualiman*, up the road to Peñaherrera, T953048. Cabins overlooking the Nangulví area, pre-Inca *tolas* and archaeological finds in the area. **In Nangulví**: **D** *Cabañas Río Grande* (T(06) 920442, Otavalo). Also **G** *Cabañas*, basic.

Beyond García Moreno is the **Junín Cloud Forest Reserve**, a 800 ha forest which spans elevations of about 1,500-2,000 m. The local community is trying ecotourism as an alternative to forest destruction and has built accommodations, prices in our **A** range. From García Moreno, the lodge can be reached by a 1½ hour truck ride or four hour hike depending on road conditions (worst January-April). When hiking, mules carry your luggage. There are good walking possibilities, including a trail to Los Cedros (see below). Further information from decoin@hoy.net, www.decoin.org

On the southwest boundary of Reserva Cotacachi-Cayapas is **Los Cedros Research Station**, 6,400 ha of pristine cloud forest famous for the number of new orchid species discovered there. Bird life is abundant, and large species are more common and less shy than in many other places. Nice facilities, with prices in our **L** range including meals. Access involves a six to eight hour walk from **Saguangal**, north of **Pacto** and west of **García Moreno**, which can be reached by bus (from the plaza at Cotocollao in Quito, 6 hours). A four-wheel drive vehicle can shorten the walk by 1½ hours, *Safari Tours* can provide transport. There is a hotel at the road-head so the trip does not have to be done all in one day. In Quito contact: T540346, cibt@ecuanex.net.ec, www.ecole-adventures.com

Ibarra

Phone code: 06
Colour map M2, grid B3
Population: 119,243
Altitude: 2,225

This pleasant colonial town, founded in 1606, has many good hotels and restaurants. Prices are lower than Otavalo and there are fewer tourists. The city has an interesting ethnic mix, with blacks from the Chota valley and Esmeraldas alongside Otavaleños and other highland Indians.

Ins & outs

Getting there There is no central bus terminal; buses leave from their own terminals all in the west of the city: Trans Andina on Chica Narváez; Expreso Turismo and others at Moncayo between Flores y Vacas; Trans Otavalo, Av F E Vacas cuadra 3 (beside the railway track). Other bus companies leave from alongside the railway tracks near the obelisk, on the corner of Velasco, at the entrance to the city. Beware of bagslashers here.

Getting around No problem here as the city is compact although the Santo Domingo church is a few blocks from the centre. There is a *Ministerio de Turismo* office at Olmedo 956 y P Moncayo, T958547, F958759. It is very helpful; free city map and various tourist leaflets available, English spoken, open Mon-Fri.

Sights

Take care in the downtown area, especially at night

The city has two plazas with flowering trees. On **Parque Pedro Moncayo** stand the Cathedral and Casa Cultural, the Municipio and Gobernación. One block away is the smaller **Parque Dr Victor Manuel Peñaherrera**, at Flores y Olmedo, more commonly called Parque de la Merced after its church.

Some interesting paintings are to be seen in the church of **Santo Domingo** and its museum of religious art. ■ *Mon-Sat 0900-1200, 1500-1800, US$0.15, at the end of Simón Bolívar.* At García Moreno y Rocafuerte is the back of **San Agustín** church, whose façade is on the small Parque Abdón Calderón. On Sucre, at the end of Avenida A Pérez Guerrero, is the **Basílica de La Dolorosa**, damaged by an earthquake in May 1987, but reopened in December 1992. A walk down Pérez Guerrero leads to the large covered **market** on Cifuentes, by the railway station, open daily.

Essentials

Sleeping
■ *on map*
Price codes:
see inside front cover

The better class hotels tend to be fully booked during Holy Week, *Fiesta de los Lagos* and at weekends. Along the Panamericana Sur, at **San Antonio de Ibarra**, are several country inns, some in converted haciendas. **From south to north B-C** *Hostería Natabuela*, Km 8, T932032, F640230. Comfortable rooms, covered pool, sauna, restaurant. **C** *Hostería Chorlaví*, set in a converted hacienda, Km 4, T955777, F956311. US$2.50 for extra bed, also cabins, excellent *parrillada* and folk music and crafts on Sun, disco at weekends, sauna, good restaurant, very traditional, pool open to non-residents US$0.30. Recommended. Next door to *Hostería Chorlaví*, up the same drive is **C** *Rancho Carolina*, T953215, F955215. Nice cabins, restaurant. **C-B** per person *Hostería San Agustín*, Km 2, T955888. Clean, friendly, good service, hot water, good food. **F** *Hostal Los Nogales*, Sucre y Plaza (in San Antonio de Ibarra), T932000. Cheaper without bath, restaurant, good value.

In Ibarra B *Ajaví*, Av Mariano Acosta 18-38 y Circunvalación, T955221, F952485. Along the main road into town from the south, with pool and good restaurant. **D** *Hostería El Prado*, off the Panamericana at Km 1, barrio El Olivo, T/F959570. Includes breakfast, luxurious, set amongst fruit orchards, restaurant, pool and sauna. **E** *Royal Ruiz*, Olmedo 940 y P Moncayo, T/F641999. With bath, cable TV, parking, restaurant, sauna. **F** *Montecarlo*, Av Jaime Rivadeneira 5-63 y Oviedo, T958266, F958182. Restaurant, heated pool, Turkish bath, jacuzzi, same management as *Hostería El Prado*.

F *Fenix*, Pedro Moncayo 7-44, T643903. With bath, nice, modern, good value, smaller rooms cheaper. **F** *Royal Ruiz*, Olmedo 940 y Moncayo, T641999. Clean, quiet, private bath, cable TV, good.

G *El Dorado*, Oviedo 5-47 y Sucre, T950699, F958700. Clean, hot water on request, good restaurant, parking. Undergoing renovations in 2000. **G** *Hostal Madrid*, Moncayo 741 y Sánchez, T956177. Clean, comfortable, with bath, TV, parking, doors locked at 2300. Recommended. **G** *Hostal El Retorno*, Pasaje Pedro Moncayo 4-32, between Sucre and Rocafuerte, T957722. With bath, **H** without, hot water, clean, nice view from terrace, restaurant, friendly. Recommended. **G** *Imbabura*, Oviedo 9-33 y Narváez, T950155. Nice colonial building, shared bath, great showers, cheap, clean, will store luggage, big rooms, breakfast and snacks in the patio, basic, take your own padlock, the owner has considerable local knowledge, very friendly, recently refurbished. Highly recommended. **G** *Nuevo Colonial*, Olmedo 5-19 y Grijalva, T952918. Old colonial building, quiet, clean, restaurant, parking. **G** *Residencial Madrid*, Oviedo 857 y Moncayo, T951760. With bath, hot water, TV, friendly, parking, good views from upper rooms. **H** *Residencial Colón*, Narváez 862, T958695. With bath, hot water, pleasant, clean, friendly, laundry facilities, stores luggage, will change money. Recommended. **H** *Residencial Imperio*, Olmedo 8-62 y Oviedo, T952929. With bath, hot water, TV in lobby, reasonable value, disco at weekends till 0400. There are several other cheap hotels along Bolívar, Moncayo and Olmedo.

The restaurant at *Hostería Chorlaví* is recommended, but is crowded with tour buses on Saturday lunchtime, likewise *Hotel Ajaví*. *El Chagra*, Olmedo 7-48. *Platos típicos*,

Eating
● *on map*

Northern Highlands

Ibarra

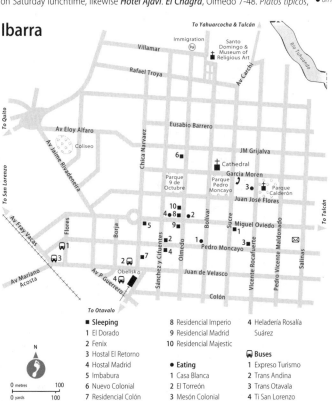

good river trout, reasonable prices. Recommended. *Marisquería Las Redes*, Moreno 3-80. Seafood. *Marisquería Rosita*, Olmedo 7-42. Cheap fish and seafood. Breakfast with good bread at *Café Pushkin*, Olmedo 7-75. Opens 0730. A classic. *Rith's*, Olmedo 7-61. Good set meals and à la carte.

There are many other restaurants on Olmedo: *Miravalle*, No 7-52. Good value *almuerzo* and *merienda*. *El Cedrón*, No 7-37. Vegetarian food, poor coffee and breakfast. *Chifa Muy Bueno*, No 7-23. Chinese, does a good *Chaulafan*. *Chifa Gran Kam*, at No 7-62. Exceptionally good food, not expensive.

Mr Peter's, Oviedo 7-30 y Bolívar. Good pizza, wide ranging à la carte, modern surroundings, good service, nice atmosphere, not cheap, open 1100-2200. *Casa Blanca*, Bolívar 7-83. Excellent, family-run, located in colonial house with seating around a central patio with fountain, open for breakfast and on Sun, delicious food, 'amazingly cheap'. Warmly recommended. *Mesón Colonial*, Rocafuerte 5-53, at Parque Abdón Calderón. Also in a colonial house, extensive à la carte menu, good food and service, most main dishes around US$3-4. Recommended. *El Torreón*, Oviedo 7-62 y Olmedo. Smart, expensive, extensive à la carte, good service, good wine list. *Café Floralp*, Bolívar y Gómez de la Torre. Open 0700-2100, Swiss-owned, good breakfast, bread, has its own cheese factory behind the restaurant, yoghurt, excellent coffee, good selection of Chilean wines, the 'in place' to meet and eat. Warmly recommended. *La Casa de Chef*, Oviedo y Sánchez. Popular and good. *Pizza El Horno*, Rocafuerte y Sucre. Good pizzas. *La Trattoría Rusticana*, Sucre 5-08 y García Moreno, good pizza, cheap and friendly.

There are several excellent *heladerías*, including: *La Bermejita*, at Olmedo 7-15. Directly opposite is *Hielo y Dulce*, at Olmedo 7-08. Also *Heladería Rosalía Suárez*, Oviedo y Olmedo (100 years old in 1996). Excellent home made fruit sherbets called *helados de paila*, try the *mora* (raspberry) or *guanábana* (soursop) flavours. An Ibarra tradition, highly recommended.

Local specialities Local sweet specialities including walnut nougat (*nogadas*) and bottled blackberry syrup concentrate (*arrope de mora*). These are both made locally and sold in the small shops along Olmedo 700 block. The best selection of these, plus others such as guava jam, are to be found in the line of kiosks opposite the Basílica de la Merced, in Parque Peñaherrera. *Helados de paila* made in large copper basins (*pailas*, see above), are available in many heladerías throughout the town.

Bars & nightclubs *El Encuentro*, Olmedo 9-59. Piano bar, interesting drinks, very popular, pleasant atmosphere, unusual décor. *Blue Sky*, G Moreno y Sánchez. Open Tue-Fri, popular bar with live music. *El Zarape*, on Circunvalacíon. *Peña* and Mexican restaurant. Discos include *Tequila Rock* and *Sambuca* both at Oviedo y Bolívar, also *Studio 54* at Laguna Yaguarcocha.

Festivals *Fiesta de los Lagos* is held over the last weekend of **September**, Thu-Sun, it begins with *El Pregón*, a parade of floats through the city. On **16 July** is *Virgen del Carmen*.

Shopping There are a number of good supermarkets in the centre of town: *Supermaxi*, south of the centre on Eugenio Espejo. *Supermercado El Rosado*, at Olmedo 9-46. *Supermercado Universal*, Cifuentes y Velasco. *Mi Supermercado*, Bolívar 7-83.

Sports **Paddle ball** A unique form of paddle ball is played on Sat and Sun near the railway station and other parts of town; ask around for details. The players have huge spiked paddles for striking the 1 kg ball. On weekdays they play a similar game with a lighter ball. *Balneario Primavera*, Sánchez y Cifuentes 3-33. **Turkish bath** Heated pool, Turkish bath, also offers aerobics classes and remedial massage, for membership T957425. Also *Baños Calientes*, at Sucre 10-68. **Tennis** *Ibarra Tennis Club*, at Ciudad Jardín, T950914. **Paragliding** is possible from Ibarra; ask for information at *Hotel Imbabura*.

Bus To/from **Quito** buses leave frequently, 2-3 hrs, US$2. Shared taxis with **Supertaxis Los Lagos** (in Quito at Asunción 3-81, T565992; in Ibarra at Flores 924 y Sánchez Cifuentes, Parque La Merced) who will pick you up at your hotel (in the new city only); hourly from 0830 to 1900, 2½ hrs, US$4 per person, buy ticket at their office the day before travelling. To **Tulcán**, US$2, 2 hrs. To **Otavalo**, 30 mins, US$0.35. to **Cotacachi** (US$0.25, 1 hr) some continue to **Quiroga**. **Train** See under Ibarra to the Coast (page 180). | **Transport**

Banks The following banks all have ATMs and are open Mon-Fri 0845-2000. *Banco Continental*, Olmedo 11-67. *Filanbanco*, Olmedo 11-49, for Visa. *Banco del Pacífico*, Moncayo y Olmedo, MC and TCs. *Banco del Austro*, Colón 7-51, VISA. Casa de Cambio: *Imbacomer*, Oviedo 770 y Bolívar, poor rates. **Communications** Post Office: Salinas 6-64, between Oviedo y Moncayo. **Andinatel:** at Sucre 4-56, just past Parque Pedro Moncayo. Opens 0900. **Internet**: prices around US$1/hr. Two places, one on Pérez Guerrero y Bolívar, the other on Theodoro Gómez y Bolívar. **Hospitals and medical services** *Clínica Médica del Norte*, at Oviedo 8-24. Open 24 hrs. **Language courses** *Centro Ecuatoriano Canadiense de Idomas (CECI)*, Pérez Guerrero y Bolívar, US$3/hr. *CIMA*, Obelisco Casa No 2, 2nd floor, US$1/hr. **Tour operators** *Nevitur Cia Ltda*, Bolívar 7-35 y Oviedo, T958701, F640040. Excellent travel guides, new vans for trips throughout the country, as well as the Pasto region of Colombia. *Turismo Intipungo*, Rocafuerte 4-47 y García Moreno, T955270. *Delgado Travel*, Moncayo y Oviedo, T/F640900. Excellent service. *Imbaviajes*, Oviedo 8-36. A recommended **taxi driver** for excursions is Luis Cabrera Medrano, Cooperativa de Taxis, Pascual Monge, 'El Obelisco'. **Useful addresses** Immigration: Olmedo y LF Villamar (T951712). | **Directory**

Excursions from Ibarra

Ten minutes from Ibarra, just off the main road between Otavalo and Ibarra, is this village, which is well known for its wood carvings. The trade is so successful that the main street is lined with galleries and boutiques. Bargaining is difficult, but it is worth seeing the range of styles and techniques and shopping around. Visit the workshop of Moreo Santacruz, and the exhibition of Osvaldo Garrido in the Palacio de Arte. Luís Potosí's gallery on the main plaza has some beautiful carvings. | **San Antonio de Ibarra**

A pretty village to visit close to Ibarra, 10 km directly south on the road to Olmedo, is La Esperanza, set in beautiful surroundings on the pre-Inca road which goes to Cayambe. Eugenio makes good quality leather bags and clothes cheaply to measure, for example US$60 for trousers. One particular lady does extremely fine embroidery; ask in the village for her house. | **La Esperanza**

You can climb **Cubilche** volcano in three hours from La Esperanza for beautiful views. From the top you can walk down to Lago de San Pablo, another three hours.

You can also climb Imbabura volcano more easily than from San Pablo del Lago. Allow 10-12 hours for the round trip, take a good map, food and warm clothing. The easiest route is to head right from *Hotel Casa Aída*, take the first road to the right and walk all the way up, following the tracks up past a water tank. It's a difficult but enjoyable walk with superb views; watch out for some loose scree at the top. You can go back to La Esperanza from the summit or go on to Otavalo, which is about another three to four hours.

Sleeping G per person *Casa Aída*. With bath, clean, hot water, friendly, Aída speaks some English and cooks good vegetarian food, Sr Orlando Guzmán is recommended for Spanish classes, US$2.40 per hour. Next door is **G** per person *Café María*. Basic rooms, will heat water, friendly, helpful, use of kitchen, laundry facilities. The bus from Parque Germán Grijalva in Ibarra passes the hotels, US$0.17, 1 hour. A taxi from Ibarra is US$5.

Urcuquí Urcuquí is a pretty little town with a basic hotel and a park. On Sunday the locals play unusual ball games. To get there, a bus from Ibarra leaves from the open space opposite the old bus station (now a car showroom). Urcuquí is the starting point for walking to the Piñán lakes.

Chachimbiro About two hours' drive on a bumpy track northwest from Ibarra, in the parish of Tumbabiro, are the clean, hot mineral swimming pools of Chachimbiro. These are part of the *Complejo de Turismo Ecológico Chachimbiro*, run by *Fundación Cordillera*. The complex is part of a project to encourage sustainable development and environmental education in the region. *Proyecto Chachimbiro* has made many improvements including trails, organic gardens and a medical centre for treatment in the thermal waters. Weekends can be quite crowded. There is one exceedingly hot pool for therapy and several of mixed water for soaking and playing. There are new cabins in the complex with private bath and showers with thermal water, and others by the entrance, both in our **F** price range. There are also two restaurants. There is a bus daily direct to the complex from the Expreso Turismo terminal on Calle Flores in Ibarra; be there by 0700 as it leaves when full. Tours are available from *Chachimbiro Tours* in Otavalo (see page 170).

Lago Yahuarcocha It is possible to walk the 4 km to Lago Yahuarcocha in about 1½ hours. Follow Calle 27 to the end of town, cross the river and walk to the right at the first junction. At the end of this road, behind two low buildings on the left, there is a small path going steeply uphill. There are beautiful views of Ibarra and then, from the top of the hill, over the lake surrounded by mountains and the village of the same name. The beauty of the lake has been disfigured by the building of a motor-racing circuit round its shores. The lake is gradually drying up with *totora* reeds encroaching on its margins. They are woven into *esteras* (mats) and sold in huge rolls at the roadside. Reed boats can sometimes be seen.

Sleeping D *Parador El Conquistador*, 8 rooms, large restaurant. Recommended. *Hotel del Lago*, no accommodation, only refreshments. *Rancho Totoral*, T/F955544. Excellent cooking, many local dishes, US$3-4 for a meal, beautiful, tranquil setting, accommodation planned. Camping on the lakeside is possible, but mind your gear. There are frequent buses between Ibarra (market area) and the village (30 mins, US$0.10).

Ibarra to the Coast

The spectacular train ride from Ibarra to the Pacific coast, once very popular with tourists, no longer operates (see Transport below). Instead, a road, prone to landslides, drops northwest following the valley of the Río Mira to the subtropical lowlands and passes through the village of **Guallupe**, from where you can visit the Cerro Golondrinas cloud forest (see page 183). The road then reaches **Lita** (*Altitude*: 512 m), 93 km before San Lorenzo on the Pacific coast, three hours from Ibarra. The road continues to the coast through lush tropical vegetation.

Sleeping & eating In Guallupe D *Bospas Farm*, 800 m from the village. Private bath, bed and breakfast. Also offer volunteer opportunities on experimental organic farm. Contact Piet Sabbe, bospas22@hotmail.com **F** *Martyzu*, has pool and restaurant. Better is **F** *El Limonal*, T648688. **In Lita** One kilometre uphill from the station is a **G** *residencia*, adequate, clean, frequent water cuts. There are now several restaurants owing to the increase in road traffic. Lights go out at 2200.

Bus The road to San Lorenzo is paved as far as Guallupe, 20 km before Lita. To **San** **Transport**
Lorenzo, there are 6 buses daily between 0530 and 1600 (always crowded), it's a
beautiful scenic route; 6 hours, US$3.75, returning from 0700. *Coop Valle de Chota*
(Ibarra stop near the train station) and *Coop Espejo* (Av Pérez Guerrero by the Mobil
gas station) serve this route. There are also buses which go as far as **Lita**, at 0600, 0900
and 1300, 3 hrs, US$2.30. They return to Ibarra at 0600, 1000 and 1300. The last San
Lorenzo-Ibarra bus passes Lita at 1800. For buses from San Lorenzo, see page 348.

Train These now only run for 1½ hrs to Tulquizán, US$7 one way. Always enquire in
advance to see if and when trains are operating, T955050.

North to Colombia

The Panamericana goes past Laguna Yahuarcocha and then descends to the
hot dry Chota valley. Twenty-four kilometres north of Ibarra is the turnoff
west for Salinas and Lita along the road to San Lorenzo. Six kilometres further
north, at Mascarilla, is a police checkpoint (have your documents at hand),
after which the highway divides.

One branch follows an older route northeast through Mira and El Angel to
Tulcán on the Colombian border (see below). This road is paved and in excellent condition as far as El Angel, but deteriorates rapidly thereafter. The El
Angel-Tulcán section is unpaved and in very poor condition but the scenery is
beautiful. It is now seldom used and there are no facilities along its 49 km.

The second branch (the modern Panamericana), in good repair but with
many heavy lorries, runs east through the Chota valley to Juncal, before turning north to reach Tulcán via Bolívar and San Gabriel. An excellent paved road
runs between Bolívar and El Angel, connecting the two branches. A second lat-
eral road, between San Gabriel and El Angel, is in poor shape and is often
impassable during the rainy season.

The old route to the border

Along the old route, which climbs steeply from Mascarilla, is the town of Mira, **Mira**
15 km past the fork. Some of the finest quality woollens come from this part of *Population: 5,500*
the country. There are two women in Mira who produce them for export and a
cooperative up the hill opposite the bus station which sells them in the town at
export prices. There are two carnivals held each year, on 2 February and 18
August, with fireworks and free flowing Tardón, the local *aguardiente*.
H *Residencial Mira*, behind church. Basic but clean, good beds. There are very
few restaurants. Bus from Ibarra, US$0.55, one hour. From Tulcán, 1600, 1½
hours, US$1.

Twenty kilometres northeast along the old Panamericana is **El Angel**, a sleepy **El Angel**
highland town that comes to life during its Monday market. It is the birthplace of *Population: 5,700*
José Franco, designer of the famous topiary in the Tulcán cemetery, and the *Altitude: 3,000 m*
main plaza retains a few trees that were originally sculpted by him. *Photo Estudio*
Narváez, José Grijalva by plaza, sells good photos of the surrounding area.

Sleeping and eating **E** *Hostería El Angel*, at the village entrance, T/F06-977584,
www.ecuador-sommer.com. Includes breakfast, hot showers, trips into the reserve
(see below), US$20 per person (minimum 4 people), reservations in Quito T/F221480.
H *Residencial Viña del Mar*, José Grijalva 05-48 on the main plaza. Shared bath, basic,
restaurant next door. **H** *Residencial Alvarez*, run by Sra Ofelia López Peñaherrera, José

Northern Highlands

Grijalva 02-59, no sign. Basic, shared bath, cold water, no shower, but very friendly. Recommended. Eating places include *Asadero Los Faroles*, José Grijalva 5-96. Roast chicken and trout, expensive. Several other chicken places in town. *Pastelería Mi Pan*, José Grijalva corner Bolívar. Very good bread and pastries. The shops are well stocked with provisions.

Transport   *Trans Espejo*, hourly to **Quito** via Ibarra, US$2.50, 4 hrs. To **Tulcán** at 0530 and 0700 daily, US$0.95. *Trans Mira*, hourly to **Mira** and **Tulcán**.

La Calera   Three kilometres south of town, along the road to Mira, is the turnoff for the thermal baths of **La Calera**. From here a steep but good cobbled road descends for 6½ km into a lovely valley to the baths themselves, with good views along the way. There are two pools with warm water in pleasant surroundings, admission US$0.50. The baths are deserted during the week, when only the smaller pool is filled. There is no public transport; hire a jeep from El Angel, US$15 round trip, or take a *camioneta*; contact Fernando Calderón, T977274. The baths are crowded with locals on weekends and holidays, when the same jeeps charge US$0.50 per person. With a sleeping bag it is possible to stay the night in the main building, but take food.

Reserva   El Angel is the main access point for this reserve, created in 1992 to protect
Ecológica   15,715 ha of *páramo* ranging in altitude from 3,400 to 4,150 m. The reserve
El Angel   contains the southernmost large stands of the velvet-leaved *frailejón* plant, also found in the Andes of Colombia and Venezuela. Also of interest are the spiny *achupallas* with giant compound flowers, related to the *Puya Raymondi* of Peru and Bolivia. The fauna includes *curiquingue* hawks, deer, foxes, and a few condors. There are several small lakes scattered throughout the reserve. It can be very muddy during the rainy season; The best time to visit is May to August.

The reserve is administered by the Ministerio del Ambiente. Their El Angel office is at José Grijalva 04-26, in an old school, upstairs to the left. The staff are friendly and helpful. The Reserve entry fee is US$10 for foreigners. The *Fundación El Angel* can also provide information about visiting the reserve. Their offices are in the municipal building. Gerardo Miguel Quelal knows the area well and can be hired as a guide. Contact him through either of the above offices.

Excursions into the reserve: from El Angel follow the poor road north towards Tulcán for 16 km to **El Voladero** (parking area but no sign) where a trail climbs over a low ridge (30 minutes' walk) to two crystal clear lakes. Camping is possible here, but you must be self-sufficient and take great care not to damage the fragile surroundings. Jeeps can be hired in the main plaza of El Angel for a day trip to El Voladero; US$40 return, but bargain.

Another, longer, excursion follows an equally poor road to **Cerro Socabones**, beginning in the town of **La Libertad**, 3½ km north of El Angel. This route climbs gradually through haciendas, where fighting bulls are bred, to reach the high *páramo* at the centre of the reserve. After Socabones, in the village of **Morán**, the local guide Hugo Quintanchala can take you further through the valley. There are many paths criss-crossing the *páramo* and it is easy to get lost. Jeeps from El Angel to Cerro Socabones, US$50 return. A helpful driver is Sr Calderón, T977274.

A third access to the reserve is from the north along the Tufiño-Maldonado road (see below) from which the Lagunas Verdes (green lakes) can be seen. Like many of the lakes in the *páramo* these are gradually drying. According to local legend, they are enchanted. There are sulphur gas vents here, so take care.

Cerro Golondrinas Cloudforest

Beyond the Morán valley, in the forested hills towards the Mira valley, is the Cerro Golondrinas Cloudforest.

A four day trek begins in the Andean highlands, west of El Angel, at 4,000 m, crosses three eco-systems, and finishes in Guallupe, at 1,000 m in the subtropical lowlands. Horses carry your luggage and meals are prepared by local farmers along the way. The trek leaves every Saturday morning and costs US$210 per person (all inclusive, slightly less per person for large groups) for groups of six to eight. Guides and horses can be arranged in Guallupe to take you to the foundation's *Corazón Lodge* in the middle of the reserve. You need to bring a sleeping bag, rubber boots and raingear.

There are opportunities for volunteers on the conservation project on a short-term (minimum one month) or full-time basis (minimum one year). Many different skills are needed and help is always welcome in the tree nursery and permaculture farm in Guallupe. Volunteers pay US$210 per month for food and accommodation. Those interested in working, or merely visiting the reserve, should contact: *La Casa de Eliza*, Quito, T/F502640, funorex@pi.pro.ec, www.orex-ec.com There are also volunteer opportunities at **Bospas Farm** outside Guallupe, see page 180. *Hostería El Angel* have the *Cotinga Lodge* here (T/F06-977584, www.ecuador-sommer.com). Situated at 2,500 m there is accommodation for 14 in simple, comfortable rooms.

The new route to the border

El Chota

Following the new route of the Panamericana east past Mascarilla for 2 km is the turnoff for the town of El Chota with the **Honka Monka** museum of Afro-Ecuadorean culture. A further 8 km leads to a series of tourist complexes for Colombians and Ecuadoreans who come down from the highlands for the *sabor tropical*.

Sleeping B *Aruba Hostería*, T06-937005. Modern, small pool, very smart restaurant, expensive. **C** *Hostería Oasis*, Casilla 208, Ibarra, T/F06-941200. Cabins for up to 6 and mini-cabins for 2, best facilities including 3 large pools (one is a wave pool), waterslide, playground, several snack bars, disco, good restaurant with live music on weekends, good value, day use US$3 per person. Tours throughout the region. **E** *Hostería El Jordán*, T06-937002. Similar but not as elaborate. There are several others.

Just beyond is **El Juncal**, the turnoff east to Pimampiro, after which the highway turns north to cross the Río Chota into the province of Carchi and begins its steep climb out of the valley.

Pimampiro The quiet town of Pimampiro lies 8 km off the Panamericana along a paved road. The surrounding countryside offers excellent walking. There is a Sunday market. **H** *Residencial* is run by the Hurtado family on Calle Flores. It has no sign so ask around; it is basic and friendly, but has a poor water supply. *El Forastero*, on the corner of Flores and Olmedo, serves good food. Buses from Ibarra, Cooperativa Oriental, leave every 20 minutes, US$0.60, 45 minutes; also Expreso Turismo from P Moncayo y Flores.

Sigsigpamba From Pimampiro follow a steep dirt road along the beautiful canyon of the Río Pisquer 20 km to the village of Sigsigpamba. There are many forks in the road, so you'll need to ask directions frequently if you're walking. The views are magnificent. Four-wheel drive vehicles are recommended if driving. There are no hotels or restaurants in Sigsigpamba, only a few basic shops. A bus (crowded) leaves from Pimampiro at 1100, Thursday to Sunday.

Sigsigpamba is the best access to the **Laguna de Puruanta**, a four to five hour strenuous hike. The lake is set amid the high *páramo* and you can camp and fish for trout. The area is very muddy during the rainy season (November to May). From the lake you can walk to the village of Mariano Acosta, from which buses run back to Ibarra through Pimampiro. The direct road from Mariano Acosta to Ibarra is in very poor shape and no longer has a bus service. Allow three or more days for the excursion and take a tent, sleeping bag, warm waterproof clothing, food, stove and fuel.

Bolívar A further 17 km north is Bolívar, a neat little town with houses and the interior of
Population: 15,175 its church painted in lively pastel colours, a well kept plaza and a Friday market. There is the basic **H** *Hospedaje* run by Sra Lucila Torres, on Carrera Julio Andrade s/n, one block north of the plaza. There is no sign; shared bath. *Restaurant Los Sauces*, by the highway, serves good food, good value. Recommended. There's a good bakery on the main plaza at García Moreno esq Julio Andrade.

La Paz Five kilometres north of Bolívar is the turnoff east for the town of La Paz, from which a steep but good cobbled road descends for 5 km to the **Gruta de La Paz**. Views along the road are breathtaking, including two spectacular waterfalls. The place is also called *Rumichaca* (Quichua for stone bridge) after the massive natural bridge which forms the *gruta* (grotto). Not to be confused with the Rumichaca on the Colombian border.

The entire area is a religious shrine, receiving large numbers of pilgrims during Holy Week, Christmas, and especially around 8 July, feast day of the Virgin of La Paz. In addition to the chapel in the grotto itself, there is a large basilica, a Franciscan convent, a guest house for pilgrims **G**, a restaurant and shops selling religious articles. These are open on weekends and pilgrimage days only and there are very few visitors at other times. It is possible to camp for free opposite the convent. The river which emerges from the grotto is rather polluted, and the sewer smell detracts from its otherwise great natural beauty.

There are clean thermal baths (showers and one pool) just below the grotto, open Wednesday to Sunday (crowded at weekends), admission US$0.50, showers US$0.25. Look for the caretaker if the gate to the pool is locked. Several scenic trails through the valley start from behind the hotel.

Transport There is public transport to La Paz from Tulcán on Sat and Sun. Also jeeps from San Gabriel, US$0.60 per person (20 min) on weekends. It costs US$10 to hire a vehicle during the week. A second, signposted access road has been built from the Panamericana, 3 km south of San Gabriel.

Ten kilometres north of La Paz is San Gabriel, an important commercial centre. The spectacular 60 metre high **Paluz** waterfall is 4 km north of town. Follow Calle Bolívar out of the main plaza and turn right after the bridge. It's well worth the walk. There is a rather chilly 'thermal' bath along the way. Jeeps for Tulcán leave from the main plaza in San Gabriel when full. There are also buses to Quito, every 45 minutes, US$2.50, four hours.

San Gabriel
Population: 19,500

Sleeping and eating H *Residencial Ideal*, Montúfar 08-26. Basic, hot water US$0.25 extra, a bit smelly, lousy beds. H *Residencial Montúfar*, Colón 03-44. Some rooms with private bath, hot water, clean, safe, motorcycle parking, basic, 'has seen better days'. For eating, try *Su Casita*, Bolívar 12-07. Good set meal. *Asadero Pío Riko*, Bolívar 10-15. Chicken and others. *Heladería Zanzibar*, Colón 3-16. For ice cream.

Twenty kilometres east of San Gabriel is the tiny community of Mariscal Sucre, also known as Colonia Huaquenia, which has no tourist facilities but is very hospitable. It can be reached by taxi from San Gabriel in one hour; sometimes shared four wheel drive vehicles also go there, which are a cheaper option. This is the gateway to the **Guandera Reserve and Biological Station**, part of the Jatun Sacha Foundation's system of reserves. It includes over 1,000 ha of Frailejon *páramo* and twisted mossy temperate forest. There are rare birds like the Chestnut-bellied Cotinga and Crescent-faced Antpitta and many orchids. There is a guest house (**C**), 30 minutes' walk from Mariscal Sucre. It is very cold at night so bring warm clothes. Reservations and further information about visits and volunteer programmes from Jatun Sacha Foundation in Quito, Pasaje Eugenio de Santillán N34-248 y Maurián, T432246, F453583, volunteer@jatunsacha.org, www.jatunsacha.org

Mariscal Sucre

This small town before Tulcán (**H** *Residencial Bolivia*, very basic) is the access for **El Carmelo** and **La Bonita**. The former is a back way for contraband into Colombia, the latter is on a new road into Sucumbíos province, which should eventually connect with the Baeza-Lago Agrio road at Lumbaquí; very scenic. **Warning** Do not enter this area straddling Carchi and Sucumbíos, near the Colombian border, without first inquiring about public safety (see Dangerous areas, page 46).

Julio Andrade

Tulcán

The old and new branches of the Panamericana join at Las Juntas, 2 km south of Tulcán, a commercial centre and capital of the province of Carchi. It is always chilly. For decades the economic life of the town has revolved around smuggling between Ecuador and Colombia and Tulcán remains an important shopping destination for Colombians, who arrive by the busload from as far

Phone code: 06
Colour map M2, grid A6
Population: 37,069
Altitude: 2,960

Northern Highlands

away as Bogotá and Medellín. There is a frantic textile and dry goods fair on Thursday and Sunday. Prices are generally lower than Colombia, but higher than other parts of Ecuador.

Tulcán and the traditionally tranquil border province of Carchi have seen an increase in tension due to drug trafficking and the *guerrilla* conflict in neighbouring Colombia (see Dangerous areas, page 46). It is prudent not to wander about late at night.

Sights   The centre is very compact but it is a little way out to the **cemetery**, which is two blocks from Parque Ayora. In the cemetery the art of topiary is taken to incredible, beautiful extremes. Cypress bushes are trimmed into archways and fantastic figures of animals, angels, geometric shapes and so on, in *haut* and *bas* relief. Note the figures based on the stone carvings at San Agustín in Colombia, to the left just past the main entrance. To see the various stages of this art form, go to the back of the cemetery where young bushes are being pruned. The artistry, started in 1936, is that of the late Sr José Franco, now buried among the splendour he created. His epitaph reads: 'In Tulcán, a cemetery so beautiful that it invites one to die!' The tradition is carried on by his sons. There is also an amazing cantilevered statue of Abdón Calderón and his horse leaping into mid-air in the Parque Ayora.

Sleeping
■ *on map*
On Fri nights & at weekends it can be difficult to find a room as the town is usually busy with Colombian shoppers

D *Machado*, Ayacucho 403 y Bolívar, T984221, F980099. Private bath, hot water. Includes breakfast. Comfortable. **D** *Sara Espíndola*, Sucre y Ayacucho, T985925. With private bath, hot water. Comfortable. **E** *Azteca*, Bolívar y Atahualpa, T981447, F980481. TV, restaurant, good, clean rooms, but noisy from the disco downstairs. **E** *Frailejón*, Sucre y Rocafuerte, T981129/980149. With bath, hot water, TV, good but expensive restaurant. **E** *Parador Rumichaca*, on the old road to the frontier, a short walk from the old bridge, T980276. Swimming and thermal pools, popular, reservations required. Recommended. **E** *Sáenz Internacional*, Sucre y Rocafuerte, T981916, F983925. Very nice, modern, friendly, good value. **F** *España*, Sucre entre 10 de Agosto y Pichincha, T983860. Modern, some rooms with bath. **F** *Florida*, Sucre y 10 de Agosto, T983849. With bath, cheaper without, modern section at back, good value. **F** *Hostal Alejandra*, Sucre y Quito, T981784. Bath, clean, hot water, TV, safe indoor parking, restaurant, good value. Recommended. **F** *Los Alpes*, opposite the bus station. With hot shower, TV, clean. Recommended. **F** *Torres de Oro*, Esquina Sucre y Rocafuerte, T980226. With bath and TV. **G** *Carchi*, Sucre 50-044. Shared bath, cold water, basic. **H** *Pensión Minerva*, Olmedo 40-50. Hot water, a bit smelly but otherwise clean, beds not too comfortable, friendly, quiet. **H** *Residencial Colombia*, Colón 52-017 y Ayacucho, T982761. Shared bath, basic. **H** *Residencial Oasis*, 10 de Agosto 6-39, T980342. Large rooms. **H** *Quito*, Ayacucho 450, T980541. OK.

Eating
● *on map*

Terminal, in the bus station, reasonable. You can find Colombian specialities at *Los Arrieros*, Bolívar 51-053 and *El Patio*, on Bolívar, more expensive. **Seafood at:** *Cevichería el Viceño*, Bolívar 48-049. *Marisquería Anzuelo Manabita*, Sucre y Boyacá. There are various Chinese restaurants on Sucre: *Café México*, Bolívar 49-045. Excellent vegetarian dishes, good value, friendly. Recommended. *Parrilladas*, Sierra y Bolívar, near the cemetery. Good typical food. There are many other places to eat in town.

Transport   **Air** TAME flies to **Quito** (check schedules in advance) and to **Cali** in Colombia. The airport is on the new road to Rumichaca, the Colombian border.

Bus The bus terminal is a long uphill walk 1½ km from the centre. It's best to take a taxi, US$1 from Parque Ayora, or a little blue bus from Parque Ayora. Keep a sharp look out on the right for the terminal, or the bus will not stop. Bus to **Quito**, 5 hrs,

ulcán

US$4.10, every 15 mins. To **Ibarra**, 2 hrs, US$2. To **Otavalo**, US$1.95, 3 hrs (make sure the bus is going to Otavalo; best not to get out on the Highway at the turnoff, because of the risk of robberies), or take a bus to Ibarra and then a colectivo. To **Guayaquil**, 20 a day, 11 hrs, US$7. To **Huaquillas**, with Panamericana Internacional, 1 luxury coach a day. There are also plenty of colectivos.

Directory

Banks *Filanbanco*, Sucre y Junín, for Visa. *Banco del Austro*, Bolívar y Ayacucho, for Visa. Few places accept credit cards. There is an association of informal money changers in Tulcán. Look for photo ID and note down the name in case of any disagreement. A good place to change *pesos colombianos* for US$ cash or vice versa is in the main plaza, where the rates are better than at the border.

Excursions from Tulcán

To the west of Tulcán lies a scenic area of páramos with geothermal activity at the foot of Volcán Chiles.

Aguas Hediondas

A complex of pools fed by a stream of boiling sulphurous mineral water in a wild, impressive, lonely valley

By far the best hot springs of the region are Aguas Hediondas (stinking waters). These waters are said to cure everything from spots to rheumatism. The baths are deserted on weekdays. Condors can sometimes be seen hovering above the high cliffs surrounding the valley. The area has been developed with indoor and outdoor pools, and camping is possible but bring all gear and food. **Warning** The area around the source is walled off because of extremely dangerous sulphur fumes (deaths have occured in the past), never attempt to enter.

Several buses a day leave Tulcán for Tufiño, but only the midday one goes up the hill to the turning for the walk into Aguas Hediondas. On Sundays there are two direct buses. One leaves from the Cathedral and the other from Calle Sierra, both at 0700-0730. Follow the winding road 3 km west of Tufiño, to where a rusting white sign marks the turnoff to the right. From here it is 8 km through strange scenery to the magnificent natural hot river.

Northern Highlands

Past the turnoff for Aguas Hediondas the road climbs to the *páramo* on the southern slopes of **Volcán Chiles**, whose summit is the border with Colombia. The volcano can be climbed in about six hours, but you must be self-sufficient. Enquire about the route in Tufiño, where guides can sometimes be hired.

To the south lies the Reserva Ecológica El Angel and the Lagunas Verdes (see above). The road then begins its long descent to **Maldonado** and Chical in the subtropical lowlands. One bus leaves from opposite Colegio Nacional Tulcán, Calle Sierra, daily at noon, US$2, five hours, returning early the next morning. **Warning** Do not enter this remote area along the Colombian border without first inquiring about public safety (see Dangerous areas, page 46).

Frontier with Colombia

Leaving Ecuador Colectivos from Tulcán to the border (blue and white minivans) leave when full from Parque Ayora (near the cemetery), US$0.60. From the bus terminal to the border, US$1. A city bus from the terminal to Parque Ayora is often too crowded for luggage. A taxi to the border from Parque Ayora is US$2.50, from the bus terminal to the border it is US$3.50. It's a 3 min walk across the bridge from the Ecuadorean side to the Colombian side. Taxi drivers may take you for free.

At the border The border is open 24 hrs. There is an Andinatel office for phone calls. Try to ask for 90 days on entering Ecuador if you need them, although you will most likely only be given 30.

NB You are not allowed to cross to Ipiales for the day without having your passport stamped. Both Ecuadorean exit stamp and Colombian entry stamp are required. Although no one will stop you at the frontier, you risk serious consequences in Ipiales if you are caught with your documents 'out of order'.

Exchange The many money changers on both sides of the border will exchange cash. Always do your own arithmetic and beware of tricks.

Into Colombia Two kilometres from the border bridge is the Colombian town of **Ipiales**, 'the city of the three volcanoes'. It has an Indian market every Friday morning. There is a good selection of hotels and transport links by air and road into Colombia are frequent. Seven kilometres east of Ipiales is the famous Sanctuary and pilgrimage centre of **Las Lajas**, on a bridge over the Río Guáitara, which is definitely worth a visit for its architecture and setting. For more details see the *Colombia Handbook* or *South American Handbook*.

Central Highlands

5

Central Highlands

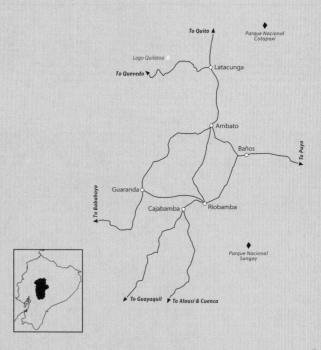

To Quito

Parque Nacional Cotopaxi

Lago Quilotoa

To Quevedo

Latacunga

Ambato

Baños

To Puyo

To Babahoyo

Guaranda

Cajabamba

Riobamba

Parque Nacional Sangay

To Guayaquil

To Alausí & Cuenca

South from Quito is some of the loveliest mountain scenery in Ecuador. This part of the country was named the 'Avenue of the Volcanoes', by the German explorer, Alexander Von Humboldt, and it is easy to see why. An impressive roll call of towering peaks lines the route south: Cotopaxi, the Ilinizas, Carihuairazo and Chimborazo, to name but a few. This area obviously attracts its fair share of trekkers and climbers, while the less active tourist can browse through the many colourful Indian markets and colonial towns that nestle among the high volcanic cones.

Baños, named and famed for its thermal baths, is a spa popular with tourists and Ecuadoreans alike on the main road from the Central Highlands to the Oriente jungle. It is the base for activities ranging from mountain biking to café lounging, and Ecuador's latest attraction: volcano watching.

The Panamericana climbs gradually out of the Quito basin towards Cotopaxi. At Alóag, a road heads west to Santo Domingo de los Colorados and the northern Pacific Lowlands; this is the main link between coast and mountains.

Machachi
Phone code: 02
Altitude: 2,900 m

In a valley nestled between the summits of Pasochoa, Rumiñahui and Corazón, lies this town, with good views from its pleasant *parque central*. The area is famous for its mineral water springs and icy cold, crystal clear swimming pool. ■ *0800-1530 daily, entry US$0.25*. The water, 'Agua Güitig', is bottled in a plant 4 km from the town and sold throughout the country. Free, self-guided tours of the plant can be made 0800-1200 (take identification). Machachi is in the middle of an important dairy area. An annual highland 'rodeo', El Chagra, is held during the third week of July.

Sleeping In town: F-G *Castillo del Valle*, at gasoline station on the Panamericana, south of the northern entrance to town, T314807. With bath, hot water, restaurant. **F** *La Estancia Real*, Luis Cordero y Panzaleo, 3 blocks east of park, T315760. With bath, hot water, parking, **G** in old section with shared bath. **H** *Miravalle*, Luis Luis Cordero y Barriga, east of the centre, T315222. Shared bath, parking. Basic.

Out of town: **D** *La Estación de Machachi*, 1½ km west of the Panamericana, in the village of Aloasí, T309246. With bath, fireplaces. Beautiful, family-run, access to Corazón (a mountain which can be climbed). **E** *Hostal Casa Nieves*, 500 m west of the Panamericana, turnoff 4 km south of Machachi, T315092. With bath, electric shower, heater, cheaper with shared bath, sitting room with fireplace and many interesting old books, also offer meals and horse trips. In farmhouse of Hacienda Bolívia, owned by descendants of Simón Bolívar. Very friendly. A bit overpriced. **E** *Tambo Chisinche*, 200 m east of the Panamericana, entrance 5½ km south of Machachi, T315041. Shared bath, hot water, breakfast included, meals on request or can use kitchen, small sign, horse riding on Rumiñahui. Clean and spartan. See below for accommodation in El Chaupi.

Eating Café de la Vaca, 4 km south of Machachi on the Panamericana. Very good lunches and dinners using fresh produce from the farm. Pricey. Open Wed-Sun. *El Pedregal*. Colón 4-66, 1 block from the park. Roast chicken. Good, mid-range prices log-cabin style. *El Chagra*. Take the road that passes in front of the church, on the right-hand side and it's about 5 km further on. Good Ecuadorean food. *Kibi's Burguer*, Colón y Mejía, 1 block from the park. Snacks, fruit salads. Popular with locals. Cheap.

Transport Bus to Quito from Av Amazonas 1 block south of the park,(Ejecutivos go to the Terminal Terrestre, Populares to El Recreo, 2-3 blocks north of the Trole station of the same name), 1 hr, US$0.45. To **Latacunga** from obelisk at the Panamericana, 1 hr, US$0.45. To **El Chaupi**, from Av Amazonas opposite the market, every ½ hr, US$0.20. Taxi to **Cotopaxi**, about US$30 per car.

Directory Internet: prices around US$1/hr. *Compusystems*, Mejía y Colón, opposite the park. *Internet Zone*, Colón 4-77, US$1/hr.

Reserva Ecológica Los Ilinizas

Machachi is a good starting point for a visit to the northern section of the **Reserva Ecológica Los Ilinizas**, a 150,000 ha nature reserve created in 1996 to preserve remnants of western slope forest and *páramo*. It includes El Corazón, Los Ilinizas and Quilotoa. The area is suitable for trekking and the twin peaks of Iliniza are popular among climbers. ■ *US$5*.

Access is through a turnoff west of the Panamericana 6 km south of Machachi, from where it is 7 km to the village of El Chaupi. A very badly rutted

Bus travel in the Andes

Stepping onto a bus at the beginning of a journey in the Ecuadorean Andes can be an unnerving experience. Maybe it's the sight of those shiny, bald tyres which look as if they haven't seen tread since the driver was last in short trousers. Or maybe it's the comprehensive collection of religious imagery decorating the driver's cab, leaving one to contemplate prayer as the best means of ensuring a safe trip. On the other hand, it could simply be the fact that the bus is packed to suffocation point. For you can bet your last banana pancake that on board there will be enough passengers, luggage and livestock to fill your average super-tanker. Overcrowded, it seems, is a word not included in the Andean vocabulary.

As the bus heads off and you settle down into your 10 sq cm of available space, thoughts may turn to the road. In the Andean backwoods roads tend to range from badly potholed dirt tracks, barely wide enough for two buses to pass, to badly potholed dirt tracks, barely wide enough for two anorexic llamas to stand shoulder-to-shoulder without one of them falling off the side.

Such a prevalence of pot holes does have its compensations, though. It makes for some amusing near head-on collisions as your driver veers back and forth across the carriageway in an attempt to avoid them. In places, the potholes join up, so that the road becomes one giant pothole with the driver veering wildly from one side to the other in a desperate attempt to avoid hitting the few remaining bits of original road that stick up like stalagmites, turning the road into a kind of obstacle course.

But potholes are only a minor distraction. Rather more worrying are the crosses that all too frequently appear by the side of the road. These are placed by the relatives of those who have perished in road accidents at the precise spot where the vehicle plunged over the side. This means that they can serve as some macabre point-scoring system to indicate the degree of difficulty of any particular bend. On the most dangerous bends, there may be so many that they form a makeshift crash barrier, preventing others from suffering the same fate.

Guiding you along these thin strips of mountain roads which coil their way through the Andes are people you will come to fear and respect – the drivers. At times you may be convinced that many of these drivers are members of a strange religious cult whose sole aim is to wipe out the entire travelling public. What other explanation could there be for hurtling at breakneck speed along roads that would make a tortoise slow down?

Some drivers manage to combine their formula one racing skills with a nice line in sadistic humour. There you'll be, crawling along behind an excruciatingly slow-moving farm vehicle on a road as straight as a pool cue. Then, as you approach the first bend for miles, the driver will suddenly pull out to overtake. Just as suddenly, he pulls back in, comfortably missing the onrushing 10-ton truck by, oh, at least 2 mm. You have to laugh.

Though you will often curse the driver's apparent disregard for your wellbeing, you'll also have occasion to sing his praises. For when the bus breaks down (as it invariably does), he can display his breathtaking mechanical genius. More often than not, this will happen in the middle of the night, far from the nearest dwelling, with the temperature outside well below zero. The engine has blown up, the wheels fallen off and the driver disappears into a cloud of black smoke wielding nothing more than a metal pipe, an old cigarette packet and a length of string. Miraculously, an hour later, you're on your way once more. Uncanny.

But it's not all discomfort and near-death experiences. The intimacy of bus travel makes for some interesting encounters and, if your Spanish is up to it, can prove the beginning of many a beautiful friendship. Buses can also be a unique insight into Andean life. And at dinner parties in years to come, it'll be these experiences that have your guests glancing anxiously at their wristwatches and reaching for their jackets.

Central Highlands

dirt road continues from here to 'La Vírgen' (statue) about 9 km beyond. Nearby are some woods where you can camp. It takes three hours to walk with a full pack from 'La Vírgen' to the *refugio*, a shelter below the saddle between the two peaks, at 4,750 m.

Climbing the Ilinizas **Iliniza Norte** (5,105 m) can be climbed without technical equipment in the dry season but a few exposed, rocky sections require utmost caution. Allow two to four hours for the ascent from the refuge, and take a compass as it's easy to mistake the descent. **Iliniza Sur** (5,245 m) is a four hour ice climb. There are some steep, technical sections on this route, especially a 50-65° 400 m ice slope, and full climbing gear and experience are absolutely necessary.

The southern section of Reserva Ecológica Los Ilinizas is accessed from Latacunga, see Quilotoa Circuit (page 201).

Sleeping *Refugio*, the shelter is fully equipped with beds for 12 and cooking facilities, take a mat and sleeping bag because it fills quickly, US$10 per person per night (the caretaker locks the shelter when he is out). **D** *Hacienda San José del Chaupi*, 3 km southwest of El Chaupi, T09-713986, or T02-891547 (ask for Rodrigo). Includes breakfast, shared bath, hot water, meals available if requested in advance, kitchen facilities, horse riding US$5 per hr, US$20 per day. Converted farm house and cabins. **G** per person *Hacienda Nieves*, T315092,2½ km from El Chaupi, along the road to los Ilinizas. Cabin for 6, electric shower, kitchenette, fireplace. Horse riding US$5 per hr, US$25 up to 6 hrs. Rodeo BBQ, US$30 per person. **G** per person *Cabañas Los Ilinizas*, near main plaza in El Chaupi (ask at the store on the plaza, where you'll also find the key). One room with 4 beds, hot shower, kitchen facilities, no electricity but candles available.

Transport There is a frequent bus service from Machachi to El Chaupi (see above), from where you can walk to the shelter in 7 to 8 hours. Horses can be hired at *Hacienda San José* or *Hacienda Nieves*. A pickup from Machachi to 'La Virgen' is about US$20. From there it is 3 hours' walk to the refuge.

Parque Nacional Cotopaxi

Cotopaxi volcano (5,897 m) is at the heart of this beautiful national park and is one of the prime tourist destinations in the country. If you only climb one of Ecuador's many volcanoes, then this should probably be the one. Many agencies run tours here.

Getting there
Colour map 4, grid A5

There are three entrances to Parque Nacional Cotopaxi. The first, 16 km south of Machachi, starts at a sign for the Clirsen satellite tracking station, which cannot be visited. This route goes past Clirsen and the old Cotopaxi railway station, then via **Area Nacional de Recreación El Boliche**. There is a shared entry fee for El Boliche and Cotopaxi; you only pay once. Follow the route for over 30 km along a signposted dirt road to reach the museum and Limpio Pungo plateau described below.

The second entrance, most frequently used, lies about 9 km further south along the Panamericana and is marked by a small Parque Nacional Cotopaxi sign; it is 6 km north of Lasso. Turn east off the Panamerican highway at the sign; nearly 1 km beyond, turn left at a T-junction and a few hundred metres later turn a sharp right. Beyond this road is either signed or you take the main fork. This is the main entrance and it is quicker and easier to follow than the first route described above. It leads first to a gate where you pay your fee (see below), then climbs to a small museum and on to the plateau and lake of Limpio Pungo (3,850 m). Past Limpio Pungo the road deteriorates and a branch right climbs steeply to a parking lot

(4,600 m). From here it is 30 mins to 1 hr on foot to the José Ribas refuge, at 4,800 m (beware of altitude sickness). Walking from the Panamerican highway to the refuge takes an entire day or more, and may exhaust you for the climb to the summit.

The third entrance is from the north. **Cyclists** should consider this approach, rather than from the west because the latter route is too soft to climb on a bike. From Machachi it is 13 km on a cobbled road, then 2 km of sand to Santa Ana del Pedregal. A further 5 km of sand leads to the park entrance, then it is 15 km to the car park. The last 7 km are steep and soft. The descent takes 1½ hrs, as opposed to 7 hrs going up. Ask Jan But, *The Biking Dutchman* (see page 133, and Mountain Biking, page 74); he has all the equipment.

If you don't have a car it is best to take a **Quito-Latacunga** bus (or vice-versa) and get off at **Lasso** (see below). Do not take an express bus as you cannot get off before Latacunga. A truck from Lasso to the parking lot costs US$25 for 4 people, one-way. If you do not arrange a truck for the return you can sometimes get a cheaper ride down in a truck which has just dropped off another party. Alternatively, get off the bus at the southern entrance and hitchhike into the park from there. This is usually possible on weekends. Frequently, but not always, there are pickups which wait for passengers at this entrance, US$20 for up to 4 people, US$40 return including wait; make sure you agree on the price beforehand. Trucks and a jeep are available from Latacunga for about US$30 round trip (ask at the *Hotel Estambul* in Latacunga), the jeep leaves at 0700.

Check out snow conditions with the guardian of the refuge before climbing. In April 1996, a freak avalanche buried about 30 people on the patio behind the refuge. The ascent from the refuge takes five to eight hours. It's best to start climbing at 0100 as the snow deteriorates in the sun. A full moon is both a practical and magical experience. Equipment and experience are required. Take a guide if you're inexperienced on ice and snow. For a list of climbing guides, see page 131. Climb the sandy slope above the hut and head up leftwards on to the glacier. The route then goes roughly to the right of Yanasacha (a bare black rock cliff) and on to the summit. Allow two to four hours for the descent.

The best season is December to April. There are strong winds and clouds August to December but the ascent is still possible for experienced mountaineers. The route is more difficult to find on Cotopaxi than on Chimborazo (see page 236) and the snow and ice section is more heavily crevassed and is also steeper, but the climbing time is less.

From the left branch at the fork for the José Ribas refuge, a narrow dirt road continues along the *páramo*, making an incomplete circuit around the Cotopaxi volcano. Beautiful views and undeveloped archaeological sites can be found in this area, but a four-wheel drive vehicle is advised as parts are washed out. Just north of Cotopaxi are the peaks of **Sincholagua** (4,893 m), **Rumiñahui** (4,712 m and **Pasochoa** (4,225 m). To the southeast is **Qulindaña** (4,878 m).

Climbing Cotopaxi
It is advisable to seek information from Quito tour operators or climbing clubs. Also see Climbing, page 65

Rumiñahui can be climbed from the park road, starting at Laguna Limpio Pungo. The area around the base of the mountain is excellent for birdwatching and it is possible to see several species peculiar to the *páramo*. However, you should also watch out for wild horses, mountain lions and, most of all, wild bulls. From Laguna Limpio Pungo to the mountain base takes about 1-1½ hours.

The climb itself is straightforward and not technical. There is no difficulty, though it is quite a scramble on the rockier parts and it can be very slippy and muddy in places after rain. There are three summits: *Cima Máxima* is the highest, at 4,722 m; *Cima Sur* and *Cima Central* are the others. The quickest route to *Cima Máxima* is via the central summit, as the climb is easier and not as steep. There are excellent views of Cotopaxi and the Ilinizas. From the base to

Climbing Rumiñahui

the summits takes about three to four hours. Allow around 3-3½ hours for the descent to Limpio Pungo.

This is a good acclimatization trek. Take cold/wet weather gear. Even outside the winter months there can be showers of sleet and hailstones.

Park essentials

Park fees & facilities Visitors to the Parque Nacional Cotopaxi must register at the main entrance and pay the entrance fee of US$10 during high season (usually Jul-Dec), US$7 the rest of the year, but these dates vary. The park gates are open 0700-1500, although you can stay until 1800. The park administration and a small museum are located 10 km from the park gates, just before the plateau of Laguna Limpio Pungo, where wild horses may be seen. The museum has a 3D model of the park and stuffed animals. It is open 0800-1200 and 1400-1600. On the pine-forested lower slopes you may see the llamas which were bred by the park authorities and released in the park. Their numbers are diminishing as they are prey to an increasing number of mountain lions.

Sleeping There are 2 very run down *cabañas* and some campsites (US$2 per tent, no facilities), at La Rinconada and Cóndor Huayco, both between the museum and Laguna Limpio Pungo, camping is not permitted around the lake itself. It is very cold, water needs to be purified, and food should be protected from foxes. The José Ribas refuge has a kitchen, water, and 30 bunks with mattresses. It costs US$12 per person per night, bring a sleeping bag and mat, as well as a padlock for your excess luggage when you climb; or use the lockable luggage deposit, US$2.50.

Outside the park To the east of the Panamericana and south of the park is a rounded hill known as Cerro Callo or Cerro San Agustín, a volcanic bubble, once thought to be a prehistoric burial site. At its base are some Inca structures now part of an *hacienda*-hotel: **LL** *Hacienda San Agustín de Callo*, entrance from the Panamericana just north of the southern park entrance, marked by a painted stone, it is 10 min ride from the highway, T03-719160, www.incahacienda.com Suites with fireplaces in room and bath, bathtub, breakfast and dinner included. Horse rides and bicycles US$10 per hr. To the southeast of the park lies an area of rugged *páramos* and mountains dropping down to the jungle. The area has several large *haciendas* which form the Fundación Páramo, a private reserve with restricted access. Here is **L** *Hacienda Yanahurco*, Quito T241593, F445016, yanahurco@impsat.net.ec, www.yanahurco.com Ranch style rooms with bath, hot water, fireplace or heater, meals. Two to four day programs, all-inclusive. Yearly rodeo in Nov. **AL** per person *Volcanoland*, Between El Pedregal and the northern access to the park, www.volcanoland.com Dormitory accommodation. Package includes transport from Quito, breakfast, dinner and horse riding or mountain-bike tour. They can arrange access to the base of Quilidaná. **B** *Cuello de Luna*, 1 km west of the Panamericana, access directly opposite the southern entrance to the park, cellular T09-700330. Includes breakfast, hot shower. Lovely converted *hacienda* with nice views, cosy atmosphere, good food, French, English and German spoken, transport and tours, a good place to acclimatize at 3,125 m. **G** per person *Tambopaxi*, just outside the park by the northernmost entrance from Machachi, Quito T546256 Compañía de Guías.

Lasso
Phone code: 03
Altitude: 3,000 m

The railway tracks and the Panamericana cross one another at Lasso, a small town, 33 km south of Alóag, with a milk bottling plant. It has some simple *comedores*, including *Express*, by the railway station, which serves Ecuadorean food, simple hardy meals. In the surrounding countryside are several *hosterías*, converted country estates offering accommodations and meals. Along the Panamericana are *paradores* or roadside restaurants.

Sleeping B *Hostería La Ciénega*, 2 km south of Lasso, west of the Panamericana, T719052, hcienega@uio.satnet.net Nice rooms with heater or fireplace, good expensive restaurant, horse riding (US$2 per hr). Reservations necessary Thu-Sun. In a historical *hacienda* reached via an avenue of massive, old eucalyptus trees. There are nice gardens and a private chapel. It belongs to the Lasso family (whose land once spread from Quito to Ambato), but is administered by others. A camioneta from here to the refuge parking area on Cotopaxi costs US$35. **C** *Posada del Rey*, facing La Ciénega, T719319. Carpeted rooms, mid-range priced restaurant with choice of 3 set meals, covered pool. Clean but a bit characterless and overpriced. **C** *Hostería San Mateo*, 4 km south of Lasso on the west side of the Panamericana, T/F719471, san_mateo@yahoo.com Bright rooms with bath, pricey restaurant with set meals and *à la carte*, horse riding included. Small but nice, with friendly service, adjoining working *hacienda* can be visited.

Eating places include *Parador La Avelina*, on the Panamericana, 5 km south of Lasso. Cafeteria known for its cheese and ice cream. A traditional stop for Ecuadoreans travelling this route. *Parador Chalupas*, opposite La Avelina. Similar cafeteria.

Latacunga

The capital of Cotopaxi Province, Latacunga, was built largely from the local light grey pumice and the colonial character of the town has been well preserved. Cotopaxi is all of 29 km away and can still be seen clearly. In fact, as many as nine volcanic cones can be seen from the city – provided they are not hidden in the clouds, which unfortunately is all too often. Your best chance of seeing them is early in the morning.

Phone code: 03
Colour map 2, grid C4
Population: 39,882
Altitude: 2,800 m

Central Highlands

Getting there The road from Quito enters from the north. A few simple hotels and restaurants are dotted around the highway, with better quality and more selection in the centre. **Getting around** The centre is compact and it is quite pleasant to walk around it.

Ins & outs

Sights

The central plaza, **Parque Vicente León**, is a colourful and beautifully maintained garden. It is locked at night. There are several other gardens in the town including **Parque San Francisco** and **Lago Flores**, also known as La Laguna. On Avenida Amazonas, by the Palacio de Justicia, is an interesting statue of a market vendor.

Casa de los Marqueses de Miraflores, at Sánchez de Orellana y Abel Echeverría, is housed in a restored colonial mansion with a lovely inner courtyard and gardens. Some of the rooms have been converted into a modest museum and it includes exhibits about the Mama Negra celebrations (see below), colonial art, archaeology, numismatics and a library. The house itself is worth a visit. ■ *Mon-Fri 0800-1200 and 1400-1800, free, T801410.*

Casa de la Cultura was built in 1993 around the remains of a Jesuit Monastery and incorporates the old Monserrat watermill. The finely designed modern building contains an excellent museum with precolumbian ceramics, weavings, costumes and models of festival masks. There is also an art gallery, library and theatre. The Casa de la Cultura has week-long festivals with exhibits, concerts and so on, around April 1 (Fiesta de la Provincia), August 9 (Día de la Cultura) and November 11 (Fiesta de Latacunga). ■ *Tue-Fri 0800-1200 and 1400-1800 Sat 0800-1500, US$0.20, Antonia Vela 3-49 y Padre Salcedo, T813247.*

Escuela Isidro Ayora, Sánchez de Orellana y Tarqui, and the **Cathedral** both have museums.

The Latacunga spaceport

Let's face it, Ecuador does not cut the highest profile on the world scene. This is no news to those who have returned home from travels here only to face their politely ignorant friends and relatives. Perhaps the Galápagos islands might ring a bell with some, or Quito with your exceptionally well read uncle and of course Baños with that dyed-in-the-wool mochilero classmate.

But Latacunga? Surely only those who have climbed Cotopaxi, or spent the night on route to or from Quilotoa or Saquisilí, will have ever heard of the place. That might change drastically however, and Latacunga could be thrust into the international limelight by becoming home to the first ever launching site for recreational space travel.

The highlands of Ecuador are in a uniquely privileged position for sending spacecraft into orbit. Their location close to the equator, where the planet bulges and the velocity of its rotation is greatest, combined with altitudes between 2,000 and 3,000 m above sea level, mean important technical advantages and cost savings for such a venture. An aerospace consulting firm called Mach 25 Technologies apparently carried out a year long pre-feasibility study comparing Ecuador with other potential equatorial launch sites such as Kenya and Sumatra. Its conclusions, as published in El Comercio in September 2000 read: "Ecuador is the best place on earth to build a new spaceport." and Latacunga could be a likely venue.

The idea has already captured the imagination of local authorities ranging from the Civil Aviation Board and Quito Chamber of Commerce to the Ecuadorean Astronomy Association. But will it fly? NASA, the US space agency, suggests that extraplanetary tourism might be a reality as soon as 2017 and a survey carried out in Japan indicated that folks would be willing to pay US$10,000 per person for a brief flight. That makes the cost of a Galápagos cruise seem like a cheap almuerzo at the Latacunga market.

Intriguing as all this may be, an Ecuadorean spaceport is likely still some time off in the future, and there remain a great many unanswered questions about just how it might work. For those who are familiar with the country's current transportation systems one of those questions might be, "Will the Latacunga space shuttle carry luggage strapped to its roof?"

Essentials

Sleeping
■ *on map*
Price codes:
see inside front cover

D *Rodelú*, Quito 16-31, T800956, F812341, rodelu@uio.telconet.net With bath, TV, excellent restaurant, parking. Clean. Recommended. **D** *Rosim*, Quito 16-49, T/F800853, carpeted rooms, with bath. Quiet, comfortable, friendly. **E** *El Marquez*, Roosevelt y Marquez de Maenza, in La Laguna neighbourhood, southeast of the centre, T811150, F912334. Bright rooms, cafeteria serving breakfast. Quiet, modern, good value, but out of the way.

F *El Alamo*, 2 de Mayo 8-01 y Echeverría, T812043. With bath. Area gets busy on market days, helpful. Recommended. **F** *Central*, Sánchez de Orellana y Padre Salcedo, T802912. With bath. A bit faded, friendly owner. **F** *Cotopaxi*, Padre Salcedo 5-61 at Parque Vicente León, T801310. With bath, cafeteria, parking nearby, hot water after 0700. Rooms with view over plaza are noisy at weekends. **F** *Estambul*, Belisario Quevedo 6-46 y Padre Salcedo, T800354. Shared bath, clean, quiet, luggage store, tours. Highly recommended. **F** *Santiago*, 2 de Mayo y Guayaquil, T802164. With bath, **G** without bath. Comfortable, good value. **F** *Tilipulo*, Guayaquil y Belisario Quevedo, T810611. Spacious well-furnished rooms, with bath, TV, cafeteria, parking. Comfortable, friendly and helpful, tours and transport in good four wheel drive vehicle. Recommended.

Convenient for the bus station, along the Panamericana, known as Avenida Eloy Alfaro, are: **F** *Hostal Quilotoa*, No 78A-17, T801866, F802090. With bath, *Pollo a la Brasa* restaurant downstairs. **F** *Llacta Cunga*, No 79-213, T/F811461. With bath, TV, hot water, restaurant, parking, request rooms away from the road, group discounts. In the same building is **F** *Los Ilinizas*, T/F801895. With bath, TV, hot water, good restaurant, parking. Comfortable, helpful.

By the central market, Mercado El Salto are: **G** *Amazonas*, Valencia 4-67, T812673. Simple rooms, with bath, electric shower, **H** without bath, good chicken restaurant. Basic, best place to eat in vicinity of the market. **G** *Jaqueline*, Antonia Vela 9-34, T801033. Shared bath, electric shower. Clean, basic, friendly. **H** *El Salto*, Valencia 4-49, T803578. Small rooms, with bath, cheaper without bath, warm showers, restaurant. Very basic, noisy.

Also by the Panamericana: **G** *Costa Azul*, Av 5 de Junio. Shared bath, good restaurant. Very basic. **G** *Los Nevados*, Av 5 de Junio 53-19 y Eloy Alfaro, T800407. With bath, hot water, cheaper without bath, restaurant. **H** *El Turismo*, 5 de Junio 53-09 y Alfaro, T800362. electric shower. Friendly, basic.

Finca Parador Don Diego, south of the train station and the Rumipamba bridge on the Panamericana. Trout, steak, chicken. Clean and classy with great service. Expensive. *Parrilladas El Coyote*, in *Hotel El Marquez*, T812246. Grill. Mid-range. Open 1100-1500 and 1800-2200. *Los Copihues*, Quito 14-25 y Tarqui. International menu, 4 course set lunch, good, generous portions, popular with business people. Mid-range. Open Mon-Sat 1000-2200. Recommended. *Rodelú* (see hotel above). Good breakfasts, steaks and pizzas, popular with travellers. Mid-range. *Chifa China*, Antonia Vela 6-85 y 5 de Junio, Chinese food, large portions. Mid-range. Open daily to 2130. *Chifa*

Eating
● *on map*
Price categories:
see inside front cover

Central Highlands

Latacunga

■ Sleeping
1 Amazonas & El Salto
2 Central
3 Costa Azul
4 Cotopaxi
5 El Alamo
6 El Turismo & Los Nevados
7 Estambul
8 Hostal Quilotoa
9 Ilinizas & Llacta Cunga
10 Jaqueline
11 Rodelú
12 Rosim
13 Santiago
14 Tilipulo

● Eating
1 Buon Giorno
2 Chifa China & Chifa Fortuna
3 El Mashca & La Borgoña
4 La Gaviota
5 Los Copihues
6 Pingüino
7 Sabores de Italia

Fortuna, Antonia Vela 6-91, Chinese food. Mid-range. Open daily 1000-2230. *Pizzería Buon Giorno*, Sánchez de Orellana y General Maldonado, opposite the main park. Great pizzas and lasagne, huge selection. Mid-range. Open late. *Pizzería Los Sabores de Italia*, Padre Salcedo, opposite the main park. Good pizza and Italian dishes. Mid-range. Open daily 1300-2300. *La Borgoña*, Valencia 41-40. Ecuadorean food. Good value, friendly. *La Gaviota*, Pastaza 2-56 y Av Amazonas. Seafood. Mid-range. Open daily 0800-1800. *El Porteño*, Sánchez de Orellana y General Maldonado, near main park. Seafood. Mid-range. *El Mashca*, Valencia 41-54. Chicken. Cheap and good value. Open until 2200. Recommended. *Pingüino*, Quito 73-106, 1 block from Parque Vicente León. Good milk shakes and coffee. *Cafetería El Pasaje*, Padre Salcedo 4-50, on pedestrian mall. Snacks, burgers, coffee. Closed Sun. Local dishes include *chugchucaras*, pork skins served with corn, bananas, potatoes, popcorn and small pieces of roast pork (the ultimate high-cholesterol snack), best at *Rosita* on the Panamericana. Also try *allullas con queso de hoja*, biscuits with string cheese.

Bars & nightclubs *Beer Center*, Sánchez de Orellana 74-20. Bar and disco. Good atmosphere, young crowd. *Galaxy*, Barrio El Calvario, on a hill to the east of the centre. Disco, varied music, nice atmosphere. *Kahlúa*, Padre Salcedo 4-50, on pedestrian mall. Bar. Open Wed-Sat 1900-0100.

Festivals The *Fiesta de la Mama Negra* is held on **24 Sep**, in homage to the Vírgen de las Mercedes. It celebrates the black slaves brought by the Spanish to work on the plantations and is similar to the *morenada* at Oruro in Bolivia. There is dancing in the streets with colourful costumes, head-dresses and masks. Market vendors are among the most enthusiastic participants in this event. The *civic festival of Mama Negra* is on the **first Sun in Nov**, when all the elected officials of the Municipio participate.

Shopping **Crafts** Souvenir shops sell regional items including *shigras* (finely stitched colourful straw bags) and 'primitivist' paintings as well as items from other parts of Ecuador. *Azul*, Padre Salcedo 4-14, on pedestrian mall, ceramics, bronze and wooden items. *La Mama Negra*, Padre Salcedo 4-43, on pedestrian mall. *Las Orquídeas*, Belisario Quevedo 6-08 y Padre Salcedo, large selection. **Markets** There is a Sat market on the Plaza de San Sebastián at Juan Abel Echeverría. Goods for sale include *shigras*, reed mats, and homespun wool and cotton yarn. On C Guayaquil, between Sánchez de Orellana and Quito, is the Plaza de Santo Domingo, where a Tue market is held. The quality of *artesanía* is rated by some as better than Saquisilí. The main fruit and vegetable market, the *mercado central* or Plaza El Salto, is between Félix Valencia and 5 de Junio. Market days are Tue and Sat, but there is also daily trading. **Supermarkets** *Aki*, Av Rumiñahui y Unidad Nacional, southeast of centre, largest. *Rosim*, Quito 16-37, is also well stocked.

Tour operators All operators and some hotels offer day trips to Cotopaxi (US$30 per person, includes park entrance fee and lunch) and Quilotoa (US$25 per person, includes lunch and a visit to a market town if on Thu or Sat); prices for 3 or more people. Climbing trips to Cotopaxi run US$120 per person for 2 days (includes equipment, park entrance fee, meals, refuge fees), minimum 2 people. Trekking trips to Cotopaxi, Ilinizas, etc US$30 per person, per day. *Expediciones Amazónicas*, Quito 16-67 y Padre Salcedo, T800375, expedicionesamazonicas@hotmail.com Climbing, trekking and jungle tours (Cuyabeno US$30 per person, per day, shaman tour US$25 per person, per day). Cristhian Varela, knowledgeable. *Metropolitan Touring*, Guayaquil y Quito, T802985, Thomas Cook representative and makes airline reservations. *Montaña Expediciones*, Quito73-99 y Guayaquil, T800227. Climbing and trekking. Fernando Tovar is an ASEGUIM mountain guide. *Neiges*, Guayaquil 5-19 y Quito, T/F811199, neigestours@hotmail.com -Day trips and climbing. Fredy Parreño. *Ruta de los*

Volcanes, Quito opposite main park, T812452. Day trips, tour to Cotopaxi follows a secondary road through interesting country, instead of the Panamericana.

Bus The new bus terminal is operating. Buses to Quito, Ambato, Guayaquil, Quevedo and all regional destinations such a Saquisili, Zumbahua, Chugchilán and Sigchos leave from here. Long distance interprovincial buses which pass through Latacunga, such as Quito-Cuenca, Quito-Riobamba, etc do not go into the terminal. During the day (0600-1700) they go along a bypass road called Av Eloy Alfaro, to the west of the Panamericana. To try to get on one of these buses during daytime you have to ask for the Puente de San Felipe, 4 blocks from the terminal. The bus terminal has some shops, a bakery, cafeteria, restaurant and a municipal tourist information office on the second floor. The tourist office is staffed by local high school students, friendly, Spanish only, open daily 0900-1800. **Transport**

Banks *Filanbanco* for cash advance on Visa, Quito y Guayaquil. Does not change TCs. **Directory**
Communications **Post Office** and **Andinatel:** both at Belisario Quevedo y Maldonado. **Internet:** prices around US$1.50/hr. *A J Cyber Café*, General Maldonado 5-26 y Quito, 2nd flr. *Accomp*, Padre Salcedo y Bellisario Quevedo. *Internet*, Padre Salcedo y Quito, in pedestrian mall. **Hospital** at southern end of Amazonas y Hnos Páez, good service. **Laundry** *Lavandería*, General Maldonado 5-26, $1 per kg, Mon-Fri 0800-1330 and 1500-1800, Sat 0800-1200. **Parking** *Parqueadero Central J S*, Quito y Echeverría, ample.

The Quilotoa Circuit

This is a part of Ecuador that is opening up to tourism and is worth a visit. You could easily spend a few days or more hiking, horse riding, visiting indigenous markets or just relaxing. The scenery is lovely and varied, ranging from the Río Toachi Canyon, patchwork fields, or high páramo to the cloud forest of the Reserva Ecológica Los Ilinizas (see page 192).

A popular and recommended round trip is from Latacunga to Pujilí, Zumbahua, Quilotoa crater, Chugchilán, Sigchos, Isinliví, Toacazo, Saquisilí and back to Latacunga, which can be done in two to three days by bus. Some enjoy riding on the roof for the views and thrills, but hang on tight and wrap up well. The whole loop is around 200 km in total and can be covered in a car or by taxi in seven or eight hours of non-stop driving, but it is a long, hard trip. A better idea is to break it up into two to three days or more. There is accommodation in Saquisilí, Sigchos, Chugchilán, Laguna Quilotoa, Isinliví and Zumbahua. The area is criss-crossed by many small, primitive roads that make for great back-country hiking, biking, trekking and four-wheel driving. **NB** All bus times quoted are approximate, as buses are often late owing to the rough roads or too many requests for photo stops.

Festivals in all the villages are quite lively and include *Año Nuevo* (New Year), *Domingo de Ramos* (Palm Sunday), *Carnaval* (Mardi Gras), *Semana Santa* (Easter Week), *Corpus Cristi, Mama Negra*, and *Finados* (Day of the Dead). Life in these small villages can be very quiet, so people really come alive during their festivals, which are genuine and in no way designed to entertain tourists.

Biking around Quilotoa

This is a great route for biking and only a few sections of the loop are cobbled or rough. The best access is from Lasso or Latacunga. Between **Toacazo** and **Sigchos** on the newer northern route there's quite a lot of cobble. Taking the

Central Highlands

older southern route via Isinliví avoids most of it, but there's a rough 4 km stretch coming down from **Güingopana** (the stunning views almost compensate). The route north from near **Guangaje** to **Guantualo** and **Isinliví** is good, hard-packed earth. From there to Sigchos is good gravel, then to Chugchilán and up to Quilotoa on gravel. It makes four days of good riding in beautiful surroundings.

From Saquisilí there are a series of little lanes which take you up to Yanaurco Alto and then either over Güingopana to Isinliví or south to Cruz Blanco near Guangaje. There's no accommodation here, but with a sleeping bag you can sleep overnight in the local school.

From Zumbahua an interesting route goes south. Take the main road towards Quevedo, turn south at **Apagua** on the pass and then climb to the pass above **Angamarca**. There is one dip on the road at a tiny village, then it is a major descent to Angamarca. You will find a small and very basic *pensión* on the plaza, or ask at the church. Below Angamarca, 3 km downhill, is the village of **Shuyo**, with a small shop with rooms used by bus drivers and if you arrive early there is usually space.

From here the road continues to **El Corazón** (*Hotel Cotopaxi*). From here you can freewheel down to **Moraspungo** (several *pensiónes*) and Quevedo, or continue through the mountains to **Facundo Vela** and up to Radio Loma and into **Salinas** (of cheese fame, see page 227). This latter route has a long tough uphill section from Facundo Vela, and sleeping bags are needed to sleep in village schools or the church.

Latacunga to Zumbahua

A fine paved road leads west to **Pujilí** (15 km, bus US$0.30), which has a beautiful church (but it's closed most of the time). There is some local ceramic work, a good market on Sunday, and a smaller one on Wednesday. Beware of local illicit liquor and pickpockets. The town boasts excellent Corpus Christi celebrations with masked dancers (*danzantes*) and *castillos*, 5-20 m high poles

Quilotoa Circuit

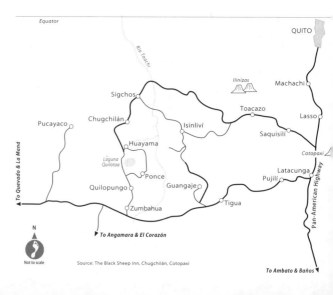

Source: The Black Sheep Inn, Chugchilán, Cotopaxi

which people climb to get prizes suspended from the top (including sacks of potatoes and live sheep!).

The road goes on over the Western Cordillera to Zumbahua, La Maná and Quevedo. Quevedo can also be reached by turning off this road through El Corazón. Transportes Cotopaxi (Calle 5 de Junio 53-44) runs several buses daily to El Corazón via Angamarca (a spectacular ride).

This small indigenous village lies 500 m north of the main Latacunga-Quevedo road, 65 km from Pujilí. It has an excellent hospital, a school and a large church with woodcarvings by local artesans. It is quite sleepy for most of the week, but comes alive on weekends, festivals and market day, which is Saturday. The market starts at 0600, and is only for local produce and animals, but it is interesting nevertheless (best before 1000). Friday nights involve dancing and drinking. Take a windbreaker, as it can be windy and dusty. Many interesting crafts are produced by the Indians in the neighbouring valley of Tigua, such as skin paintings, hand-carved wooden masks and baskets.

Zumbahua
Phone code: 03

Sleeping and eating F per person *Hostal Cóndor Matzi*, on the main plaza, T03-814610. Clean, comfortable, hot showers, kitchen facilities, furnished with beautifully-carved furniture by local students of the Italian missionaries, good beds. Owned by a youth co-operative, can arrange local trips and day-hikes. Recommended as the best in town. Next door in a cement building is **F-G** per person *Richard's*, clean with hot showers. **G** per person *Pensión Quilotoa*, grey, 2-storey building at the bottom of the plaza (look out for the small sign). Clean, with hot shower. **G** per person *Pensión Zumbahua*, green 2-storey building at the top of the plaza. Many rooms. **G** *Residencial Oro Verde*, first place on the left as you enter town. Small store and restaurant, sells purified water, friendly. There is also an unnamed *pensión*, a white 2-storey house behind the church and up the hill a bit (look for someone to open it up for you).

There is no decent restaurant in town, but if you ask Paco at *Hostal Cóndor Matzi* (with a little advance warning) his wife can prepare a tasty traditional meal in their clean kitchen. You can find a cheap meal in the market. Just below the plaza is a shop selling dairy products and cold drinks.

Transport There are many buses daily, and into the evening, on the Latacunga-Quevedo road and transport to and from Latacunga is easy at almost any time. Buses leave every 2 hrs from 0600 from Av 5 de Junio, west of the Panamericana. US$1.25, 2 hrs. Four buses daily with *Trans Vivero* also leave from here, starting at 1100 and then every 30 mins. These buses continue up to **Laguna Quilotoa**, if there are passengers who wish to go. This takes another hour, US$0.75. *Vivero* buses also go to **Guangaje** once a day and to Ponce a few times a week. On Thu and Sat buses leave from La Maná and Pucayaco for **Sigchos**, via Zumbahua, Quilotoa and Chugchilán – they pass **Zumbahua** at around 1000-1200. A pick-up truck can be hired from Zumbahua to go to Quilotoa for US$10-15; also to **Chugchilán** for around US$30-35. On Sat mornings there are many trucks leaving the Zumbahua market for Chugchilán which pass Quilotoa. Return buses from **Quevedo** are every 2 hrs until 1900. The first 30-40 km of road from Pujilí is paved and compacted gravel thereafter. It's a bit bumpy but not too dusty.

Quilotoa

Zumbahua is the point to turn off for a visit to Quilotoa, a volcanic crater filled by a beautiful emerald lake, to which there is a steep path from the rim. From the rim of the crater several snowcapped volcanoes can be seen in the distance.

Phone code: 03
Colour map 4, grid A5
Altitude: 3,850

The crater is reached by a road which runs north from Zumbahua. It's about 12 km and takes three to five hours to walk, or 45 minutes by car. Go down from the village and cross the bridge over the river. After a few kilometres along the dirt road cross another stream and pass through a small community. The road runs along the edge of a canyon, turn right at the fork in the road and then over another bridge – there are no road signs. The road climbs gradually to Quilopungo, with a small school and playground. Continue past the Ponce turn-off on the right and then head up to a colourfully-painted tomb-stone-shaped sign for Quilotoa, where there is a road to the right heading towards a small group of houses (see Sleeping below). The crater is just beyond.

It's a 300-m drop down to the water. The hike down takes about 30 minutes (one hour or more to climb back up). The trail starts to the left of the parking area down a steep, canyon-like cut. You can hire a mule to ride up from the bottom of the crater for US$2-3, but arrange it before heading down. Bring drinking water as there's none at the top of the crater and the water in the lake is salty and sulphurous.

You can walk right round the crater rim in six to seven hours, but parts of the path were destroyed in the 1996 eartquake, others are very slippery and danger-ous. Enquire locally beforehand and take a stick to fend off dogs on the road. Also be prepared for sudden changes in the weather. During the wet season, the best views are in the early morning so those with a tent may wish to camp.

Everyone at the crater tries to sell the famous naïve Tigua pictures and carved wooden masks, and prices are often much cheaper than elsewhere. The best art-ists in the area are the Toaquiza family, at Chimbacucho, by the road at Km 53 on the way to Zumbahua. The father of the family, Julio, began the paintings at the request of the late Olga Fisch, who founded the exclusive handicrafts store in Quito (see page 130). Julio's sons and daughters are now regarded as the most accomplished of the Tigua painters, with exhibitions in the USA and Europe. Try to spread out your business as people here are very poor.

Sleeping G per person *Cabañas Quilotoa*, the first house on the right, owned by Humberto Latacunga (no relation to Jorge below). Accommodation for up to 30, very friendly, warm fireplace, beds and wool blankets, electric shower, cooks traditional food, vegetarian or *cuy* on request, Humberto will lead treks and provide mules, he is a good painter and has a small store. Recommended. Close by is **G** per person *Hostal Quilotoa*, owned by José Guamangate. Friendly, with giant fireplace, offers bicycle rental, food, paintings and excursions. **G** per person *Refugio Quilotoa*, 2-storey build-ing, second on the left. Owned by Jorge Latacunga, take a sleeping bag as you sleep on the floor, he will cook food and take you on a day trek round the lake if you wish, he also paints masks. There is stiff competition for your business in all 3 of these basic places. They all offer mule rental for the day or longer excursions. There are many tal-ented painters, including Humberto and José.

Transport A daily bus, *Trans Vivero*, takes teachers to schools in Zumbahua and Quilapungo, leaving at 0600 and arriving at 0815 in **Quilapungo** (0750 in Zumbahua), from where it is about an hour's walk to the crater. Alternatively, hitch a truck on Sat morning from Zumbahua market bound for Chugchilán and you'll be dropped close to the volcano. Hitching a return trip should not be left till late in the afternoon. Buses bound for **Chugchilán** or **Sigchos** will drop you 5 mins from the lake. *Trans Vivero* has services to Ponce a few times a week. From the **Ponce** turnoff it is about a 40-min walk north. There is a daily milk truck which returns from Latacunga, via Zumbahua/Quilotoa, to **Moreta**, which is a *hacienda* with a bullring, 4 km before Chugchilán. It passes through Zumbahua around midday. (See also under Zumbahua.)

Hiking from Quilotoa to Chugchilán

You can walk around part of the crater rim (enquire locally as to trail conditions), then down to Huayama, and across the canyon (Río Sihui) to Chugchilán (11 km), in about five hours including breaks (longer with a full pack). It's a beautiful but tiring walk which is not recommended on very cloudy days. A mule and guide can be hired at the lake from around US$15. Water is available from small streams, but take a purifier.

Before starting the hike, look out to the left across the crater rim for the lowest and biggest sandy spot, about a quarter of the way round. It'll take about 45 minutes to an hour to reach this spot. When hiking along the rim, make sure you stick to the high trail with views of the lake so as not to miss the sandy spot, which is the third one along. Don't leave the crater rim until you reach it.

Once you reach the third sandy spot you can see the village of Huayama and Chugchilán beyond, across the canyon. Follow a row of eucalyptus trees down and head towards Huayama. There are many trails leading down to the village where you can buy soft drinks (ask around). From here to Chugchilán takes about two hours. Leaving Huayama, take the third right after walking along by the cemetery. This trail leads all the way to Chugchilán. You cross a couple of foot bridges going down into the canyon on a narrow switchback trail. Cross a cement bridge over the Río Sihui. The rest is a climb up to Chugchilán.

Chugchilán It is 22 km (six hours' walk) by road from the Quilotoa crater to Chugchilán, a very poor village in a beautiful setiing. There is a Sunday market.

Sleeping **D** per person *The Black Sheep Inn*, a few mins below the village, run by Andy Hammerman and Michelle Kirby. Accommodation comprises 1 bunk room for up to 6 people and 5 private rooms (each for 3-5 people, at a slightly higher rate), prices include dinner and breakfast or lunch and drinking water, excellent gourmet vegetarian food, they also offer hot showers, maps and hiking advice, 4WD excursions, horse riding (US$10 for 4 hrs) and book exchange, 5% discount for ISIC card holders and South American Explorers (SAE) members, accept travellers' cheques, the whole project is run on an ecologically-sound basis and they use organic farming methods as well as now sponsoring a permaculture course for local *campesinos*, they also have 2 dogs, 2 cats, 2 ducks, 3 llamas and 3 black sheep (of course). Highly recommended and a great base for hiking to Quilotoa, Toachi canyon and nearby Inca ruins. Book 3 days in advance (2 nights minimum stay), write to: Apdo 05-01-240, Correos Central Latacunga, Provincia Cotopaxi, or contact via SAE. **G** per person *Hostal Casa Mama Hilda*, in the village on the road to Sigchos. Four rooms with 10 beds, shared bath with hot shower, laundry facilities, breakfast US$1, lunch and dinner US$2, vegetarian available on request, lovely warm family atmosphere, will arrange horse riding and excursions to the local cheese factory (a beautiful 12 km walk there and back). Recommended. **G** per person *Hospedaje La Dolorosa*, run by Tarjelia, basic, 2 bunk beds with mattresses, sheets and blankets, cheap meals on request.

Transport Four Iliniza buses depart daily from **Latacunga** from 1100-1230 from C Melchor de Benavides, US$1.75, 4 hrs. On Thu a bus leaves from **Saquisilí** market at 1100. On Sat 2 Ilinizas buses leave Latacunga at 1030 and 1500. On Fri and Sat a 14 de Octubre bus leaves from 5 de Junio west of the Panamericana in Latacunga at 1030, via Zumbahua and Quilotoa, 3-4 hrs, US$1.75. Buses return to Latacunga at 0300, via Sigchos. On Sat another bus leaves at 0300 for Latacunga, via Zumbahua. A bus leaves for **Quito**, via Zumbahua, on Sun at 1030. Also on Sun to Sigchos at 1200 and to Latacunga, via Zumbahua, at 0600.

Central Highlands

Sigchos Continuing from Chugchilán the road runs through Sigchos, with its Sunday market. The road east to Toacazo has been improved and from there to Saquisilí it is paved. Sigchos is the main starting point for hiking in the Río Toachi Canyon (this can also be done from Chugchilán). There are a few campsites and you may be able to sleep on the school floor in Asache. There is a basic hotel and restaurant in San Francisco de las Pampas, from where a 0900 bus leaves daily to Latacunga.

Sleeping and eating E *Residencia Sigchos*. Basic but clean, large rooms, shared bath, hot water. *Hostal Tungurahua*. Shared bath, hot water. Cheap accommodation at the *casa campesina*, take sleeping bag. There are a few restaurants in Sigchos, but ask in advance for food to be prepared.

Transport There are 4 buses daily to and from Latacunga (see Chugchilán above), US$1.25, 3 hrs. On Wed there is a bus to Pucayaco, via Zumbahua, Quilotoa and Chugchilán, at 0400, 9 hrs (returns Thu at 0400), also to La Maná, via Zumbahua, Quilotoa and Chugchilán, at 0500, 9 hrs (returns Thu at 0500 and Sat at 0400).

Isinliví Southeast from Sigchos, off the main Quilotoa circuit, is Isinliví, with its colourful Christmas fiestas. There are some spectacular hikes or bike rides in the area and several *pucarás* (hill fortresses). Also here is an excellent carpentry workshop to visit and some birdwatching. The Monday market at nearby **Guantualó** is also an attraction; there is plenty of transport. You can hike from here to the *Black Sheep Inn*, or vice versa, in three hours. A longer hike is to Yanuarco volcano, which will take a full day. Alternatively, catch a morning bus to Güingopana and hike the ridge route from the pass.

Sleeping F per person *Llullu Llama* (pronounced zhu-zhu-zhama). A renovated old house in the village, behind the plaza, 9 bedrooms and a loft dormitory, composting baths, hot showers, breakfast and dinner served, box lunch available early, hot lunch only by previous arrangement. Leave messages in Spanish only at T03-814563.

Transport From M Benavides in **Latacunga**, daily except Thu, at 1100 via Sigchos, 3½ hrs. Direct with Vivero at 1300, 2½ hrs. On Thu these leave from the Saquisilí market around 1100. To Latacunga at 0300 daily except Wed (at 0600 and 0700) and Sun (0600 to Sigchos, connect there for Latacunga and 1200 direct). On Mon there is extra service from Guantaló around 1400.

Saquisilí
Phone code: 03 Some 16 km south of Lasso, and 6 km west of the Panamericana, is this small but very important market town. Its Thursday market (0700-1400) is famous throughout Ecuador for the way in which its seven plazas and most of its streets become jam-packed with people, the great majority of them local Indians with red ponchos and narrow-brimmed felt hats.

Dan Buck and Anne Meadows describe the market thus: "Trucks brimming with oranges and yellow and red bananas; reed mats, fans and baskets. Beef, pork and mutton parts are piled on tables. Indian women squat down beside bundles of onions, radishes and herbs and little pyramids of tomatoes, mandarin oranges, potatoes, okra and avocados. *Cabuya* and *maguey* ropes are laid out like dead snakes, and a food kiosk every few metres offers everything from full *almuerzos* to *tortillas de papa*."

The best time to visit the market is between 0900 and 1200. Be sure to bargain, as there is a lot of competition for your business. The animal market is a little way out of the village and it's best to be there before 0700. Saquisilí has colourful Corpus Christi processions.

Sleeping and eating **D** *Hostería Rancho Muller*, 5 de Junio y González Suárez, at the south end of town, F721103. Cabins with bath and TV in a country setting, restaurant overpriced, German owner organizes tours and rents vehicles. Recommended. **G** *San Carlos*, Bolívar opposite the parque central, T721057. With bath, electric shower, parking. New in 1999, good value, but watch your valuables. **H** *Pensión Chavela*, Bolívar by main park, T721114. Shared bath, water problems. Very basic, friendly. **H** *Salón Pichincha*, Bolívar y Pichincha. Shared bath, warm water, cheap restaurant-bar below, secure motorcycle parking. Basic but friendly.

Café La Fragata, at the main park. Coffee, snacks and set meals. Same owner as Rancho Muller. Mid-range. *El Trébol*, 24 de Mayo near craft market. Set meals. Cheap. *La Abuela*, 24 de Mayo 5-60. Set meals and snacks. Seriously cheap.

Transport The Saquisilí and Cotopaxi bus companies have frequent service between **Latacunga** and Saquisilí, US$0.20, 20 mins, from corner Bolívar and Pichincha. Many buses daily to/from **Quito** bus terminal, from 0530 onwards, US$1, 2½ hrs, leave from Abdón Calderón in Saquisilí. Alternatively you can catch an Ambato bus from Quito, ask the driver to let you off at the junction for Saquisilí and get a passing pick-up truck (US$0.35) from there. The *Hotel Quito* and the *Hotel Hilton Colón* in Quito both organize efficient but expensive taxis for a 2-hr visit to Saquisilí market on Thu. Bus tours cost about US$26 per person, or taxis can be found for US$45, with 2 hrs' wait at the market. Latacunga agencies include Saquisilí in their Quilotoa tours on Thu. Buses and trucks to many outlying villages leave from 1000 onwards.

Eleven kilometres south of Latacunga is Salcedo, with good Thursday and Sunday markets. The town's Mama Negra festival is on 1 November.

Salcedo
Phone code: 03

Sleeping **A** *Hostería Rumipamba de las Rosas*, in Rumipamba, 1 km north of town, T726128, F727103, hrrosas@uio.satnet.net Nice rooms and suites, swimming pool, good expensive restaurant. In pleasant country setting with gardens, a lake with boats, and sport fields. Highly recommended. **G** *Residencial Central*, Bolívar y Sucre, 1 block from main park. Small rooms, with bath, **H** without bath.

Eating *Casa del Marquez*, García Moreno y Quito, at north end of town. International food, set lunch and à la carte, bar. Very good, mid-range prices, recommended. Open 0800-2400. *Ritz*, Bolívar y Sucre. Chicken. *Marisquería Tiburón*, Sucre opposite main park. Seafood. Mid-range, open 0800-2100. *Rocío*, García Moreno y Vicente León, 1 block north of park. Simple, seriously cheap set meals.

Ambato

The capital of the Province of Tungurahua, Ambato is the main commercial hub of the central highlands, an important centre for the leather industry and a major market for nearby fruit growing valleys. It was almost completely destroyed in the great 1949 earthquake and has, therefore, lost the colonial charm found in other Andean cities. The city comes alive during festivals, especially Carnival, and market days. The Monday market is so busy in fact that Lunes de Ambato (an Ambato Monday) *has become synonymous with an unbearably hectic day anywhere in Ecuador.*

Population: 160,302
Altitude: 2,800 m
Phone code: 03
Colour map 4, grid B5

Getting there The main bus station is on Av Colombia y Paraguay, 2 km north from the centre, near the railway station. Town buses go there from Parque Cevallos in the city centre.

Ins & outs

Central Highlands

Getting around Ambato is a pleasant town to wander around. Many hotels are conveniently placed within a block or two of the centre, while others are in the quiet residential neighbourhood of Miraflores. Motorists driving through Ambato to other cities should avoid going into the centre as traffic is very congested.

Tourist offices The *Ministerio de Turismo* is next to the *Hotel Ambato*, Guayaquil y Rocafuerte, T821800. Open 0800-1200, 1400-1800, Mon-Fri, helpful.

Sights

Because of its many orchards, flower and tree lined avenues, parks and gardens, its nickname is 'the city of fruits and flowers'. Since it is the birthplace of the writers Juan Montalvo, Juan León Mera and the artist Juan Benigno Vela, it is also known as the 'city of the three Juanes'. On a clear day Tungurahua and Chimborazo can be seen from the city.

The modern cathedral faces the pleasant **Parque Montalvo**, where there is a statue of the writer Juan Montalvo (1832-89) who is buried in a memorial in a neighbouring street. His house (Bolívar y Montalvo) is open to the public. ■ *Free, T821024.*

In the **Colegio Nacional Bolívar** is the **Museo de Ciencias Naturales Héctor Vásquez** with stuffed birds and other animals, botany samples, a small ethnographic collection and items of local historical interest. Recommended. ■ *Mon-Fri 0800-1200 and 1400-1730, closed for school holidays. US$1, Sucre entre Lalama y Martínez, T827395.* The **Quinta de Mera** is an old mansion in beautiful gardens in Atocha suburb. ■ *0900-1200, 1400-1800, bus from Espejo y 12 de Noviembre.*

Out along the Río Ambato, a pleasant walk from the centre, is the prosperous suburb of Miraflores, which has several hotels and restaurants. Buses leave from the centre to Avenida Miraflores. It is an important centre for the manufacture of leather goods and has some excellent tourist shops, look for colourful and good-quality cloth shoulder bags. Leather clothes can be specially made quite cheaply.

The main market, one of the largest in Ecuador, is held on Monday, and smaller markets on Wednesday and Friday. They are interesting, but have few items for the tourist. Most of the action takes place in the streets, although there are also two market buildings.

A couple of interesting excursions are to **Picaihua** (frequent buses) to see the local work from cabuya fibre, and to Pinllo to see the leather work. At Píllaro, 10 km to the northeast of the city, there is a bull run and fight in early August.

Essentials

Sleeping
■ *on map*
Price codes:
see inside front cover.
There are unfortunately
two street numbering
systems, both in
common use and both
used in this listing

B *Ambato*, Guayaquil 0108 y Rocafuerte, T412005, F412003, hambato@hotmail.com Includes breakfast, good restaurant, casino, squash court. Clean. Recommended. **B** *De las Flores*, Av El Rey y Mulmul, near bus terminal, T/F851424. Includes breakfast and dinner, cafeteria, restaurant. Modern, nice. **B** *Florida*, Av Miraflores 1131, T843040, F843074. Includes breakfast, bath, TV, restaurant, sauna. Clean, pleasant, good set meal. **C** *Hostería Loren*, C Los Taxos, Ficoa, southwest of the centre, T/F846165. Spacious rooms, includes breakfast, restaurant, parking. In residential area, modern, comfortable, new in 2000. **C** *Miraflores*, Av Miraflores 2-27, T843224, F844395. Includes breakfast, heating, fridge, cable TV, good restaurant, sauna, parking. Clean, refurbished. **C** *Villa Hilda*, Av Miraflores 09-116 y Las Lilas, T840700, F845571. Includes breakfast, 2 and 3 bedroom furnished apartments also available, good restaurant, parking, laundry. A bit faded but nice, Italian spoken, limited menu but generous portions (it is acceptable to order one set meal for 2 people to share),

Central Highlands

nice big garden. **D** *Diana Carolina*, Av Miraflores 05-175, T/F821539. Suites, includes breakfast, restaurant, pool, spa. Modern, good views.

E *Cevallos*, Montalvo y Cevallos, T824877. With bath, TV. Good. **E** *Gran*, Lalama 05-11 y Rocafuerte, T/F824235. With bath, hot water, TV, restaurant. Friendly. **E** *Hostal Señorial*, Cevallos y Quito, T825124, F829536. With bath, hot water, cable TV. **F** *Hostal Amazonas*, Av Amazonas y Viteri, via a Baños, T852474, with bath, hot water, parking. **F** *Pirámide Inn*, Cevallos y Mariano Egüez, T842092, F854358. With bath, TV, clean, comfortable, owner speaks fluent English and is very helpful. Recommended. **F** *Tungurahua*, Cevallos 06-55 y Ayllón, T823585. With bath, hot water, TV, overpriced.

G *América*, Vela 737 y JL Mera. Basic, shared bath, hot shower, friendly. **G** *Bellavista*, Oriente y Napo Pastaza, by Bellavista stadium, T851542. With bath, TV. Recommended. **G** *Ejecutivo*, 12 de Noviembre 12-30 y Espejo, T840370, F825866. Bath, small rooms, hot water, TV. **G** *Guayaquil*, JL Mera 7-86 y 12 de Noviembre, T820591. Shared bath. Basic, good. **G** *Imperial Inn*, 12 de Noviembre 24-92 y Av El Rey, near the bus terminal, T844837. With bath, fridge, TV, restaurant. **G** *Madrid*, Juan Cajas y Cumandá, near bus station, T828679. With bath, hot water, TV, cheaper with shared bath, restaurant, disco. **G** *Portugal*, Juan Cajas 01-36 y 12 de Noviembre, near bus station, T822476, F840163. With bath, hot water, TV, good value. **G** *San Francisco*, Egüez 8-37 y Bolívar, T840148. With bath, electric shower, cheaper with shared bath,

Central Highlands

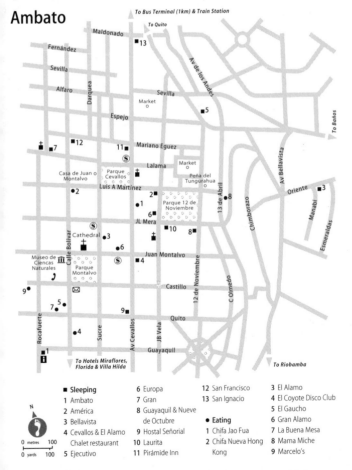

Ambato

■ **Sleeping**	6 Europa	12 San Francisco	3 El Alamo
1 Ambato	7 Gran	13 San Ignacio	4 El Coyote Disco Club
2 América	8 Guayaquil & Nueve		5 El Gaucho
3 Bellavista	de Octubre	● **Eating**	6 Gran Alamo
4 Cevallos & El Alamo	9 Hostal Señorial	1 Chifa Jao Fua	7 La Buena Mesa
Chalet restaurant	10 Laurita	2 Chifa Nueva Hong	8 Mama Miche
5 Ejecutivo	11 Pirámide Inn	Kong	9 Marcelo's

0 metres 100
0 yards 100

central. **G** *San Ignacio*, Maldonado y 12 de Noviembre, T824370. With bath, TV, cafeteria. Recommended. **H** *Europa*, Vela 717 y JL Mera. T823459. Shared bath, hot shower, basic. **H** *Hostal La Liria*, Atahualpa y Caspicara, at the south end of town, T842314. With bath, hot water, carpeted. Recommended. **H** *Laurita*, JL Mera 303 y Vela, T821372. Shared bath, basic. **H** *Nueve de Octubre*, JL Mera 326 y 12 de Noviembre, T820018. Shared bath, hot water, basic.

There are other cheap *residenciales* and restaurants around Parque 12 de Noviembre, but this area is not safe at night.

Accommodation in private homes Rosa Elena López, Av de las Américas y Venezuela, T411785. Two rooms in family home with garden. **E** per person per day, includes meals, laundry service. May arrange pickup at Quito airport.

Eating
● *on map, page 209*
Price categories:
see inside front cover

El Alamo Chalet, Cevallos 1719 y Montalvo, T824704. Ecuadorean and international food. Set meals and *à la carte*, Swiss-owned, good meals. Expensive. Open 0800-2300, Sun until 2200. *Gran Alamo*, Montalvo 520 y Sucre, T820806. International food, meat, chicken, seafood. Expensive. Open 1200-2230, Sun until 1600. *La Buena Mesa*, Quito 924 y Bolívar, T824332. French. Expensive. Recommended. *El Alamo*, Sucre 0617 y JL Mera, T821710. Self-service, 4 main dishes daily, also set meals. Mid-range prices. Open 0800-2000, closed Sun. *Farid*, Bolívar 705 y JL Mera, T824664. Meat served in middle eastern sauces. Mid-range prices. *El Gaucho*, Bolívar y Quito, T828969. Grill. Mid-range prices. *Miramar*, 12 de Noviembre y Juan Cajas, Redondel de Cumandá, near the bus terminal. Seafood. Good. Mid-range prices. *El Coyote Disco Club*, Bolívar y Guayaquil. Mexican-American food, disco at weekends. Mid-range prices. *Cominos*, Guayaquil 9-34 y Bolívar. Good pizza. Mid-range prices. *Carlinho's*, Mariano Egüez y Bolívar. Pizza and good set meals. *La Fornace*, Cevallos 1728 y Montalvo, wood oven pizza. Mid-range prices. There are also several other pizzerías on Cevallos.

Chifa Nueva Hong Kong, Bolívar 768 y Martínez. Good. Cheap. *Chifa Jao Fua*, Cevallos 756. Popular. Cheap.

Mama Miche, 13 de Abril y JL Mera, Centro Comercial Ambato. 24-hr cafeteria. Seriously cheap.

Cafés *Café Marcelo´s*, Rocafuerte y Castillo, Centro Comercial Paseo La Catedral, T828208. Good cafeteria, cheap, 0900-2100. *Pasterlería Quito*, JL Mera y Cevallos, good for breakfast.

Bars, nightclubs
& entertainment

El Coyote, Bolívar y Guayaquil. *Cow-Boys*, Paccha y Los Incas. *Imperio Club*, Paccha y Saraguro, international music. There is a *peña* on Fri and Sat, *Peña del Tungurahua*, in block 2 of the Centro Comercial.

Festivals

Ambato has a famous festival in **Feb or Mar**, the *Fiesta de frutas y flores*, during carnival when there are 4 days of bullfights, parades and festivities. It is impossible to get a hotel room unless you book ahead. The town has taken the bold step of prohibiting water-throwing at carnival (see Festivals, page 456).

Shopping

Supermercado, Centro Comercial Ambato, Parque 12 de Noviembre, or *Supermaxi*, Centro Comercial Caracol, Av de los Capulíes y Mirabeles, in Ficoa, for buying provisions. Good leather hiking boots from *Calzado Piedrahita*, Bolívar 15-08 y Lalama. You can find leather jackets, bags and belts on Vela between Lalama and Montalvo. There are many stores for leather shoes along Bolívar.

Transport

Car hire *Localiza*, Juan Cajas y 12 de Noviembre, near the bus terminal, T849128, localiza@accessinter.net

Bus To **Quito**, 2¾ hrs, US$1.90. To **Guayaquil**, 6½ hrs, US$3.95. To **Cuenca**, US$4.60, 7 hrs. To **Guayaquil**, 6½ hrs, US$6. To **Baños**, 45 mins on a good paved road, US$0.60. To **Riobamba**, US$0.80, 1 hr. To **Guaranda**, US$1.50, 1 hr. To **Latacunga**, 45 mins, US$0.70. To **Santo Domingo de los Colorados**, 4 hrs, US$2.65. To **Tena**, US$4, 6 hrs. To **Puyo**, US$2.60, 3 hrs. To **Macas**, US$3.30, 6½ hrs. To **Esmeraldas**, US$4.80, 8 hrs. To **Loja**, US$6.90, 12 hrs. To **Machala**, US$5.30, 7 hrs.

Airline offices *TAME*, Sucre 09-62 y Guayaquil, T826601. **Banks** *Banco de Guayaquil*, Sucre y JL **Directory** Mera. Visa. *Banco del Pacífico*, Cevallos y Lalama, and Cevallos y Unidad Nacional. TCs and Mastercard. *Produbanco*, Montalvo y Sucre. TCs and various currencies. *Banco del Pichincha*, Lalama y Cevallos, on Parque Cevallos and Av El Rey y Av de las Américas, near the bus terminal. TCs. *Cambiato*, Bolívar 694 y JL Mera. Visa and Amex TCs, some European and Latin American currencies, open Mon-Fri 0900-1300 and 1430-1800, Sat 0900-1230. **Communications** Post Office: Castillo y Bolívar, at Parque Montalvo, 0730-1930. **Andinatel:** Castillo 03-31 y Rocafuerte, open 0800-2130. **Internet:** rates about US$1 per hr. *Café Internet*, Castillo 06-48 y Cevallos, daily 0800-2000. *Ciudadandina*, Castillo 05-28 y Cevallos, daily 0800-2000. *Café de la Casa*, Bolívar y Montalvo, in Casa de la Cultura, Mon-Sat 0800-2000. *El Portal*, Vela 08-23 y Montalvo, good service. **Tour operators** *Metropolitan Touring*, Bolívar 19-22 y Castillo, T824084, F829213 and in Centro Comercial Caracol, for airline tickets. *Coltur*, Cevallos 15-57; 471 y Castillo and Páez 370 y Robles, T548219, F502449. *Ecuadorean Tours*, Cevallos 428. Amex agent, but does not change Tcs.

To the east of Ambato, an important road leads to Salasaca, Pelileo and Baños, **Salasca** and then on along the Pastaza valley to Shell and Puyo, from where there is **& Pelileo** access to other cities in the Oriente (see page 378).

Salasca is a small, modernized village, 14 km from Ambato. The Salasaca Indians wear distinctive black ponchos with white trousers and broad white hats. This is said to reflect perpetual mourning for the death of their Inca emperor, Atahualpa. Most of them are farmers, but they are best known for weaving *tapices*, wall hangings with remarkable bird and animal shapes in the centre. A co-operative has fixed the prices on the *tapices* it sells in its store near the church. Throughout the village the prices are the same, somewhat cheaper than in Quito, and the selection is much better. If you have the time you can order one to be specially made. This takes four to six weeks, but is well worth the wait. You can watch the Indians weaving in the main workshop opposite the church. Fine backstrap weaving can also be seen at Alonso Pilla's; ask around.

Pelileo, 5 km beyond Salasaca, is a lively little market town which has been almost completely rebuilt on a new site since the 1949 earthquake. In all, Pelileo has been destroyed by four earthquakes during its 400-year history. The town springs to life on Saturday, the main market day. This is the blue jean manufacturing capital of Ecuador, with lots of clothing for sale everywhere. There are good views of Tungurahua from the plaza. The town's *Fiesta* is held on 22 July. There are regular buses from Ambato and Baños making the 25-minute journey. There is **G** *Hostal Pelileo*, Eloy Alfaro 641, T871390, shared bath, hot water. There are several simple restaurants near the bus terminal.

Eight kilometres northeast from Pelileo on a paved side-road is Patate, centre **Patate** of the warm, fruit-growing Patate valley. As there are excellent views of Tungurahua from town and its surroundings, it has become a tourist detination since the reactivation of this volcano (see below). It has a well-kept main park and a modern church. The fiesta of Nuestro Señor del Terremoto is held on the weeekend of **February 4**, featuring a parade with beautiful floats made with fruit and flowers, reportedly the most elaborate in Ecuador.

Central Highlands

Arepas, sweets made of squash (unrelated to the Colombian or Venezuelan variety), are the local delicacy; sold around the park

Sleeping and eating **A** *Hacienda Los Manteles*, in the Leito Valley, on the road to El Triunfo, T02-870123, T/F02-505230 (Quito). This converted farm is in a nice setting with great views of Tungurahua and Chimborazo, it has a restaurant and offers hiking and horse riding. **B** *Hostería Viña del Río*, 3 km from town along the old road from Patate to Baños, T/F870139. Cabins for 4-8, restaurant, pool, sauna, games room, horse riding. Busy at weekends, US$3 per day for the use of the facilities. **D** *El Vulcano Lodge*, on the old Patate-Baños road, 15 km from Patate, 4 km before El Pingue, T820068, includes breakfast, good views, horse riding, camping US$7 per tent. **F** *Jardín del Valle*, M Soria y A Calderón, 1 block from the main park, T870209, nicely furnished, good breakfast available, good value, recommended. **H** *Hospedaje Altamira*, Av Ambato y J Montalvo, on the road from Pelileo, shared bath, hot shower, basic. *Los Arupos*, a restaurant at the park, set meals.

From Pelileo, the road gradually descends to Las Juntas, the meeting point of the Patate and Chambo rivers to form the Río Pastaza. One kilometre further east, the road from Riobamba comes in; this intersection is marked by a large sculpture of a macaw and a toucan and the spot is locally known as *los pájaros* (the birds). **NB** Due to landslides and volcanic activity the road from *los pájaros* to Riobamba road was closed in 2000. The road from Ambato then continues along the lower slopes of the volcano Tungurahua to Baños (25 km from Pelileo). The road gives good views of the Pastaza gorge and the volcano.

Baños

Phone code: 03
Colour map 4, grid B6
Population: 16,000
Altitude: 1,800m

The town of Baños, with its beautiful setting and pleasant sub-tropical climate, is a major holiday resort. It is bursting at the seams with hotels, residenciales, *restaurants and tour agencies. The sidewalks of the main street, Calle Ambato, are lined with outdoor cafés and teem with visitors on a Saturday night. Ecuadoreans flock here on weekends and holidays for a dip in the hot springs, to visit the basilica, and to enjoy the* melcochas (toffees), *while escaping the Andean chill. Foreign visitors are also frequent; using Baños as a base for trekking, organizing a visit to the jungle (Baños is the gateway to the central* Oriente), *making local day-trips on horseback or by mountain bike, or just plain hanging out. The town's landmarks include the* Parque de la Basílica, Parque Central *and the* Manto de la Vírgen *waterfall.*

Ins and outs

Getting there
See also Transport, page 220

The bus station is on the Ambato-Puyo road (Av Amazonas) a short way from the centre, on the second floor is the information office. Its patio is the scene of vigorous volleyball games most afternoons. The road from Ambato enters the city from the west, crosses the Riachuelo Bascún and continues to the east along the southern bank of the Río Pastaza towards Puyo.

Getting around
The police make frequent passport checks. Always carry your passport

Bustling with visitors Baños is an easy place to get around with most hotels centrally located. A unique feature of Baños is its sidewalk ramps, which make the centre of town wheelchair accessible. Following the evacuation, there are only a few city buses running to Agoyán, from Alfaro y Martínez. Service to El Salado, the zoo and Lligua had not resumed by late 2000. It is generally safe and tranquil but robberies have been reported along some of the walking trails near town, usually on busy weekends and holidays.

The Municipal tourist office is on the second floor of the bus terminal; open 0800-1300, 1400-1700 (1600 Sat and Sun). There are several private 'tourist information offices' run by travel agencies near the bus station. They offer high-pressure tour sales, maps and pamphlets. Local artist, J Urquizo, produces an accurate pictorial map of Baños, 12 de Noviembre y Ambato, also sold in many shops. **Tourist offices**

Volcanic activity

Baños is nestled between the Río Pastaza and the Tungurahua volcano, only 8 km from its crater. After over 80 years of inactivity, Tungurahua began venting steam and ash in 1999, and the area was evacuated because of the threat of a major eruption between October and December of that year. Such an eruption had not taken place by October 2000, so former residents and tourists returned and the town recovered its previous resort atmosphere despite warnings from scientists that the danger had not entirely passed. The Ambato-Baños-Puyo road was reopened to traffic, but the Baños-Riobamba road remained blocked by landslides. At the close of this edition Tungurahua was relatively quiet, and the thermal baths, most hotels, restaurants and tourist agencies in Baños were operating normally. The volcano is well monitored but it's behaviour can be difficult to predict, and we must therefore advise all travellers to enquire locally before visiting Baños. The Geophysics Institute of the *Escuela Politécnica Nacional* posts daily reports on the web at www.epn.edu.ec/˜igeo and the *El Comercio* newspaper has a small daily summary on its front page. You should also be aware of the areas of highest risk, unless volcanic activity has completely ceased. These include the Bascún Valley (where several hotels and the El Salado baths are located), the valley of the Río Ulba east of Baños and of course Tungurahua itself (above 3,200 m, see Climbing Tungurahua below).

At the same time the area acquired an important new attraction: volcano-watching, which could be enjoyed from Baños, Patate, Pelileo and several other nearby locations. With a little luck, the visitor during 2000 could experience the unforgettable sight of kilometres-high mushroom-clouds being heaved into the sky by day, and red-hot boulders tumbling down the flanks of the volcano by night.

The Río Pastaza rushes past Baños to the Agoyán falls 10 km further down the valley, nearly dry now because of the construction of a hydroelectric dam. The whole area between Pelileo and Baños has a relaxing sub-tropical climate. The rainy season is usually from May to October, especially July and August.

Sights

The **Manto de la Virgen** waterfall at the southeast end of town is a symbol of Baños. The **Basílica** attracts many pilgrims. The paintings of miracles performed by Nuestra Señora del Agua Santa are worth seeing and there is a museum with stuffed birds and Nuestra Señora's clothing. ■ *0700-1600, US$0.40.*

Six sets of thermal baths are in the town. The brown colour of the water is due to its high mineral content. All the baths can be very crowded at weekends and holidays. ■ *US$1 for each bath.* The **Baños de la Virgen** are by the waterfall opposite the *Hotel Sangay*. The water in the hot pools is changed three times a week, and the cold pool is chlorinated. It's best to visit very early in the morning (0430-1700). One small hot pool is open in the evenings only (1800-2200) and its water is changed daily. The **Piscinas Modernas**, with a water slide, are next door and are open weekends and holidays only (0800-1700).

Central Highlands

The **El Salado** baths (several hot pools with water changed daily, plus icy-cold river water) are 1½ km from the centre, off the Ambato road (0430-1700). If walking from town, take a trail that starts at the west end of Martínez and crosses the Bascún river; the baths are at the top of the road on the west side of the river. Note that this is a high risk area during volcanic activity.

The **Santa Clara** baths, at the south end of Calle Rafael Vieira (formerly Santa Clara), are tepid, popular with children and have a gym and sauna, open weekends and holidays (0800-1800). **Eduardo's** baths are next to Santa Clara, with a 25-m cold pool (the best for swimming laps) and a small warm pool (0800-1800). The **Santa Ana** baths, with hot and cold pools, just east of town on the road to Puyo, are open weekends and holidays (0800-1700).

Essentials

Sleeping
■ *on map*
Price codes:
see inside front cover.
Baños can get very
crowded & noisy on
public holidays,
especially Carnival
& Holy Week, when
hotels are fully
booked & prices rise

Baños is amply supplied with accommodation in all categories.

LL *Hostería Luna Runtún*, Caserío Runtún Km 6, T740882/3, F740376, www.lunaruntun.com or wwwlunatravel.com Very comfortable rooms and suites with balconies, restaurant, gardens, price is for half board. Beautiful setting on a hill overlooking Baños, wonderful views. Excellent service, English, French and German spoken. Hiking, horse riding and biking tours, laundry, sports and nanny facilities, videos, internet service, luxurious. Very highly recommended.

B *Monte Selva*, Halflants y Montalvo, T740566, F740244. Private cabins, includes breakfast, bar, restaurant, warm pool, spa. Excellent service. **C** *Cabañas Bascún*, Vía El Salado at the west end of town, near El Salado baths, T740334, T/F740740. **A** for a cabin for 5, pools (cold), sauna, health spa (US$1.50 to non-residents), tennis, good restaurant. Quite comfortable, goodservice. **C** *Palace*, Montalvo 20-03, T740470, F740291, mastalir@tu.pro.ec Newer airy rooms at the front, restaurant, spa (US$1.50 for non-residents), nice garden, small museum. Old-fashioned, good for groups.

D *Isla de Baños*, Halflants 1-31 y Montalvo, T/F740609, islaba@interactive.net.ec Ten clean rooms with bath, **F** without terrace, garden with parrots and monkeys, cafeteria. Owned by Christian Albers, English and German spoken. Recommended. **D** *Hostal Plantas y Blanco*, 12 de Noviembre y Martínez, T741043, F740044. **F** without bath, laundry, excellent breakfast on roof terrace, good restaurant (*El Artesano*), try the fresh fruit pancakes, steam bath 0730-1100, US$2, jeep, motorbike and mountain bike hire, fax and internet service, luggage store, front door keys provided. Very clean, friendly. Warmly recommended. **D** *Sangay*, Plazoleta Isidro Ayora 101,opposite La Virgen baths, T740917, F740490, www.sangayspa.web.com Rooms with views of the waterfall, some cheaper rooms in basement, also more luxurious chalets, **B**, good restaurant, includes breakfast, spa (US$1.50 for day use), tennis and squash courts. Information and some equipment for expeditions to the jungle and volcanoes may be provided. **D** *Villa Gertrudis*, Montalvo 29-75, T740441, F740442. With lovely garden, pool (US$1 for day use), includes breakfast. Reserve in advance. New management in 2000. Recommended. **D-E** *Hostal Cultural*, Pasaje Velasco Ibarra y Montalvo, T/F740083, hostalcultural@yupimail.com Some rooms with chimney, sitting room, restaurant. Nice views of the waterfall. **D-E** *Petit Auberge*, 16 de Diciembre y Montalvo, T740936. Includes breakfast, rooms with fireplace, patio. Quiet and homely.

E *Casa Nahuazo*, Vía a El Salado, just below El Salado baths, T740315. Rooms with bath includes breakfast. Quiet country house. New management in 2000. **E** *Flor de Oriente*, Ambato y Maldonado, at Parque Central, T740418, F740717. Includes breakfast, electric showers, 3 rooms have balconies. Clean, very good, can be noisy on weekends, *Su Café* downstairs. Recommended. **E** *Hospedaje Santa Cruz*, 16 de Diciembre y Martínez, T740648. With bath, hot water. Modern, nice, rooms to the left are noisy. Recommended. **E-F** *Posada El Marqués*, Pasaje Velasco

Ibarra y Montalvo, T740053. Spacious, bright rooms, with bath, hot water, good beds, laundry, garden, good restaurant. View of waterfall, massage service, friendly and helpful. Highly recommended.

F *El Carruaje*, Martínez y 16 de Diciembre, T740913. With bath, hot water, parking. Comfortable. **F** *Charvic*, Oriente y Maldonado, T740298. **G** without bath, restaurant. **F** *El Edén*, 12 de Noviembre y Montalvo, T740616, hostaleleden@andinanet.net With bath, balconies, patio, restaurant parking. Clean. **F** *La Floresta*, Halflants y Montalvo, T740457, F740717. With bath, hot water, nice garden. Friendly, nice. **F** *Grace*, Rocafuerte 522 y Maldonado, at Parque Central, T740907. Modern, with bath, hot water, TV. **F** *Inti Raymi*, Maldonado y Espejo, 1 block from terminal. T740332. With bath, hot water, garden, kitchen facilities. Nice. **F** *Las Rocas*, Espejo opposite bus terminal, T740940, with bath. **F** *Santa Clara*, 12 de Noviembre y Montalvo, T740349. Rooms and cabins, **G** without bath, hot water, use of kitchen, washing facilities, nice garden, good value. Recommended.

G *Achupallas*, 16 de Diciembre, at Parque de la Basílica, T740389. Clean, hot showers, laundry, parking; and **G** *Alborada*, 16 de Diciembre, at Parque de la Basílica, T740614. With shower and luggage store. Modern. **G** *Los Andes*, Oriente 1118 y

Central Highlands

Baños

To Puyo, Agoyan & Luna Runtún

To Ambato

To El Salado

To Statue of the Virgin

To Runtún

To Bellavista Cross

Santa Clara & o Eduardo's Baths

0 metres 100
0 yards 100

■ Sleeping
1 Achupallas & Alborada *B3*
2 Café Cultural & El Marqués *C4*
3 El Castillo *C4*
4 Flor de Oriente *B2*
5 Hospedaje Santa Cruz *C3*
6 Hostal Magdalena *B3*
7 Hostal Plantas y Blanco *C3*
8 Inti Raymi *B2*
9 Isla de Baños & La Floresta *C3*
10 Los Andes & Inca Flame Restaurant *B3*
11 Los Nevados *B4*
12 Lucy *B3*
13 Mariane Hostal & Restaurant *C2*
14 Monte Selva *C2*
15 Palace *C4*
16 Pensión Patty *B3*
17 Petit Auberge & Le Petit Restaurant *C3*
18 Princesa María *B1*
19 Residencial Baños & Donde Marcelo Restaurant *B3*
20 Residencial El Rey *B2*
21 Residencial Rosita *C3*
22 Residencial Teresita *B3*
23 Residencial Timara *C2*
24 Sangay *C4*
25 Santa Clara *C3*
26 Villa Gertrudis *C3*

● Eating
1 Cubanacán *C2*
2 Café Blah Blah & Luzerna *B2*
3 Café Hood *B2*
4 Casa Hood *C3*
5 Closerie des Lilas *B3*
6 Deep Forest Café *C2*
7 Düsseldorf *B3*
8 El Jardín *C3*
9 Higuerón *C3*
10 Paolo's Pizzería *C3*
11 Regine's Café Alemán *B3*
12 Rico Pan *B2*
13 Rincón de Suecia *C3*
14 Sunflower *B3*

● Bars
15 Bamboos *B3*
16 Hard Rock Café *B3*
17 La Bubuja *B4*
18 Peña Ananitay *B3*

Alfaro, T740838. With bath, 24-hr hot water, Mexican restaurant. Clean, English spoken, friendly. **G** *Carolina*, 16 de Diciembre y Martínez, T740592. With bath, TV. **G** *Casa Blanca*, Maldonado y Oriente, near the bus terminal, T/F740092. Modern, with bath, hot water, cable TV, cafeteria. **G** *El Castillo*, Martínez y Rafael Vieira, near the waterfall, T740285. With bath, hot water, good beds, parking, restaurant. Quiet. Recommended. **G** *El Oro*, Ambato y JL Mera, T740736, hostal el oro1@hotmail.com. With bath, hot water, use of kitchen, laundry facilities, includes breakfast. Good value, friendly. Recommended. **G** *Hostal Dinastía*, Oriente y Alfaro. With hot water, good cheap breakfast. Nice rooms, very clean, quiet. Recommended. **G** *Hostal Magdalena*, Oriente y Alfaro, T740364. With bath, warm water, parking. Closes at 2200. Recommended. **G** *Hostal Mariane*, Rocafuerte y Halflants, T740911, patalarcou@hotmail. com With bath, good beds, sitting room with cable TV, cafeteria. Clean, French-run, nice and friendly. **G** *Hostal El Pedrón*, Alfaro y Martínez, T740701. With bath, gardens. Very quiet. **G** *Hostal San Martín*, 2 km from Baños, opposite the zoo. With bath, hot water, meals on request. Peaceful, quiet place overlooking the Pastaza. **G** *Lucy*, Rocafuerte y 16 de Diciembre, T740466. With bath, hot water, **H** without bath, cold water. Friendly, comfortable beds, parking for motorcycles. **G** *Monik's*, Ambato y Pastaza, T740428. With bath, hot water, laundry service. **G** *Montoya*, Oriente y Maldonado, T740640. With bath, hot water, cable TV. Modern, clean. **G** *Los Nevados*, Ambato 1 block east of the Basílica, T740673. With bath, hot water, laundry. Friendly, tours available. **G** *Plaza Agoyán*, Rocafuerte, at Parque de la Basílica, T740177. With bath, hot water, restaurant, garage. **G** *Princesa María*, Rocafuerte y Mera, T741035, princesamaria@andinanet.net With bath, hot water, use of kitchen, laundry service, internet. Good, new in 2000. **G** *Puerta de Alcalá*, Av Amazonas, ½ block east of the bus terminal, T740173. With bath, hot water, restaurant. Convenient for late arrivals, ask for room away from the road. **G** *Residencial Baños*, Ambato y Alfaro, T740284. **H** without bath, washing facilities, luggage store. Good, ask for a top room. **G** *Residencial El Rey*, Oriente y Reyes, T740322. With bath, hot water. Recommended. **G** *Residencial Kattyfer*, 16 de Diciembre y Martínez, T740856. Nice rooms, with bath, hot water, TV, laundry facilities. Clean, very friendly and helpful with local information. Recommended. **G** *Residencial Rosita*, 16 de Diciembre y Martínez, T740396. Big rooms with bath, hot water, sitting room, kitchen for every 2 rooms. Highly recommended.

H *Pensión Patty*, Alfaro 556 y Oriente. T740202. Shared bath. Clean, basement rooms poor, otherwise good facilities, use of kitchen, laundry, comfortable and quiet, family-run, popular. Recommended. **H** *Residencial Dumary*, Halflants 656, T740314. Small rooms, hot water, only 1 shower. Very clean, friendly, private Spanish lessons from English/German speaking daughter. Recommended. **H** *Residencial Teresita*, 12 de Noviembre at Parque de la Basílica. Shared bath, hot water. Very basic, prices vary, shuts early. **H** *Residencial Timara*, Maldonado 381, T740599. Shared bath, hot water, use of kitchen, laundry facilities, nice garden. Friendly. Recommended. **H** *Residencial Torres*, Ambato 2 blocks east of the Basílica, T740403. Shared bath, hot water, clean. On Parque Central are: **H** *Los Pinos*, Rocafuerte y Maldonado, T740252. Clean, electric showers, cheaper without bath. **H** *Olguita*, Rocafuerte y Halflants, T741065. Basic, with bath, electric shower. **H** *La Delicia #1*, Ambato y Halflants; *#2* Maldonado y Ambato, T740417; both with shared bath.

Long term Furnished bachelor apartment (US$150 per month), rooms (US$3 per day, US$10 per day full board), Kathy Vargas at Planeta. Net, on Maldonado 642 y Ambato. *Judy's House*, 12 de Noviembre y Ambato, T740063, rooms for rent in beautifully furnished house, fully equipped kitchen, US$50 per person, per week.

Many establishments serve international food intended for foreign visitors, at mid-range prices. Those serving local fare set meals are usually in the cheap or seriously cheap ranges.

Ecuadorean Calle Ambato has many restaurants serving cheap set meals and local fare. The *picanterías* on the outside of the market serve local delicacies such as *cuy* and *fritada*. *Ambateñito*, Ambato y Eloy Alfaro. Good set meals and barbecued chicken. *La Puerta de Alcalá*, Av Amazonas (main highway), half a block downhill from the bus terminal. Good value set meals.

French *Mariane*, Martínez y Rocafuerte by the Parque Central, T740711. Excellent authentic Provençal cuisine, large portions, pleasant atmosphere, good value and attentive service, open daily 1800-2300. Highly recommended. *Le Petit Restaurant*, 16 de Diciembre y Montalvo, T740936. Vegetarian dishes, meats, fondue. Parisian owner, excellent food, great atmosphere. Open 0800-1500 and 1800-2200, closed Mon. *Closerie des Lilas*, Alfaro y Oriente, T741430. Good food at reasonable prices. Open 1100-2300.

German *Regines Café Alemán*, Rocafuerte y 16 de Diciembre. Good breakfasts, European cooking and cakes, meeting place, very popular. *Sunflower*, Eloy Alfaro y Ambato. Good European food. Good value. Open 1300-2200, closed Mon. Recommended.

International On Calle Ambato are several popular restaurants, some with pavement seating. Between Halflants and Eloy Alfaro are: *La Abuela*, Small, good pizzas, good breakfasts. *La Calderada*, varied menu. *La Casa Vieja de Düsseldorf*, varied menu. Good value. *Luzerna*, set meals and à la carte. *Mama Inés*, Popular.*Pepos*, varied menu. Other locations: *Donde Marcelo*, Ambato near 16 de Diciembre. Good breakfasts, friendly gringo bar upstairs. *Rincón de Suecia*, 12 de Noviembre y Martínez. Varied menu, good, Swedish and English spoken. *Higuerón*, 12 de Noviembre 270 y Martínez. Open daily 0900-2230 except Wed, good European, local and vegetarian food, nice garden, friendly. *El Jardín*, 16 de Diciembre y Rocafuerte. some vegetarian food, juices and bar. Good atmosphere and nice garden.

Italian *La Bella Italia*, 16 de Diciembre entre Montalvo y Martínez. Pasta. OK. *Buono Pizza*, Ambato y Alfaro, T740430. Pizza and Pasta. *Scaligeri*, Alfaro y Ambato. Good home-made pasta. *Paolo's Pizzería*, 16 de Diciembre y Martínez, good pizzas, very friendly. *Pizzería Napolitano*, 12 de Noviembre y Martínez. Pizza and pasta, pleasant atmosphere, pool table. *Il Pappagallo*, Martínez y 16 de Diciembre. Pasta. *Caesar´s*, Martínez y Halflants. Pizza. Wood oven.

Latin American *Cubanacán*, Rocafuerte y Maldonado, at the Parque Central, T740418. Cuban food and drinks. Good atmosphere. Open 1800-2400. *Inca Flame*, Oriente y Alfaro. Mexican food, home made desserts. Good, friendly. Open 1200-2200, closed Mon-Tue.

Vegetarian *Café Hood*, Maldonado y Ambato, at Parque Central, T740537. Some meat dishes. Excellent food, all water and milk boiled, English spoken, always busy, closed Tue. *Casa Hood*, Martínez between Halflants and Alfaro. Varied menu including Indonesian and Thai dishes, some meat dishes, juices, good desserts. Travel books and maps sold, book exchange, repertory cinema. *Deep Forest Café*, Rocafuerte y Halflants, at Parque Central. Middle Eastern and Greek specialties. Good falafel and desserts, good breakfasts, strictly vegetarian. Open 0730-2100. *El Paisano*, Rafael Vieira y Martínez. Variety of herbal teas and meals.

Cafeterias *Café Blah Blah*, good coffee, snacks, small, cosy, popular. Open 0900-2100. *Rico Pan*, Ambato y Maldonado across from Parque Central. Cheap breakfasts, hot bread, good fruit salads and pizzas, also meals. Open Mon-Sat 0700-2100, Sun 0700-1300. *Pancho's*, Ambato y Pasaje Ermita de la Virgen, west of the market. Snacks, coffee. Friendly. Open 0800-2300.

Eating
● *on map, page 215*
*Price categories:
see inside front cover.
There is no shortage
of places to eat.
Many restaurants
close by 2130*

Central Highlands

Local specialities Street vendors sell *canelazo*, a sweet drink of *aguardiente*, naran-jilla, water and cinnamon, and *canario*, aguardiente with egg, milk and sugar. Look out for jawsticking toffee (known as *melcocha*) and the less sticky *alfeñique* made in ropes in shop doorways; another local speciality is *caña de azucar* (sugar cane), sold in slices or as *jugo de caña* (cane juice).

Bars & nightclubs *Córdova Tours* (see below) has a *chiva* (open sided bus) cruising town, playing music, it will take you to different night spots. Eloy Alfaro, between Ambato and Espejo, has many bars including: *Hard Rock Café*, a favourite travellers' hangout, fantastic *piña colada* and juices. *Peña Ananitay*, 16 de Diciembre y Espejo. Good live music and dancing. *La Burbuja*, Ciudadela El Rosario, off Calle Ambato, east of the Basílica. Disco. *Bamboos Bar*, Alfaro and Oriente, popular for *salsa*, live on weekends *Coco Bongo*, Montalvo y 16 de Diciembre. Bar, snacks and pool hall.

Entertainment **Cinema** Films are shown at *Casa Hood* (see Eating above).

Festivals **Oct** *Nuestra Señora del Agua Santa*, with several daily processions, bands, fireworks, sporting events and general partying throughout the month. Week long celebrations ending **16 Dec**, the town's anniversary, with parades, fairs, sports and cultural events and much partying. On the evening of **15 Dec** are the *verbenas* when each *barrio* hires a band and there are many street parties.

Shopping There are craft stalls at Pasaje Ermita de la Virgen, off Calle Ambato, by the market. For painted balsa-wood birds see *El Chaguamango* shop by the Basílica, open 0800-1600 and *Recuerdos*, at the south end of Maldonado, where you can see the crafts-people at work. Shops with a large selection of crafts include: *Tucán*, Maldonado y Ambato; *Monilu T-shirts*, Rocafuerte 275 y Alfaro, good quality handicrafts and T-shirts, reasonable prices; *Las Orquídeas*, Halflants y Montalvo, at Hotel La Floresta, large selection; *Taller Arte*, Ambato y Halflants. T-shirts can be brought from *Latino Shop*, Montalvo y Rafael Vieira. Nice tagua (vegetable ivory made of palm nuts) crafts can be found at 3 shops on Maldonado between Oriente and Espejo, where you can see how the tagua is carved. Ask for the weaver José Masaquiza Caizabanda, Rocafuerte 2-56, who sells Salasacan weaving, gives demonstrations and explains the designs, materials, etc to visitors. *Galería de Arte Contemparáneo Huillac Cuna*, Rafael Vieira y Montalvo, has modern art exhibits and sells paintings including some from well known artists and coffee-table books. Crafts and musical instruments from the Oriente at *Pusanga Women's Cooperative*, Eloy Alfaro y Martínez. Leather shops on Rocafuerte between Halflants and 16 de Diciembre. *Tucán Silver*, Ambato corner Halflants, for jewellery.

There is a fruit and vegetable market all day Sun and Wed morning, in Plaza 5 de Junio on Calle Ambato y JL Mera. A smaller daily market is held at the Mercado Central on Ambato y Alfaro.

Book exchange Artesanía El Tucán, Casa Hood restaurant and Rico Pán Café.

Camping equipment *Varoxi*, Maldonado 651 y Oriente, quality pack manufacturer, repairs luggage. Recommended.

Sports **Climbing** See warning under Climbing Tungurahua, below. For companies offering climbs on nearby peaks, see Tour operators below.

Cycling The road east toward the jungle is very beautiful and popular for mountain biking, see East of Baños (below). Christian at *Hotel Isla de Baños* runs cycling tours with good equipment. US$100 per day, for up to 4 people, includes jeep transport and food. Bike rentals from Adrián Carrillo at *Hotel Charvic*, mountain bikes and motorcycles (reliable machines with helmets). Many other places rent bikes but the quality is variable; check brakes and tyres, find out who has to pay for repairs, and insist on a puncture repair kit and pump. Bicycles cost from US$4 per day; moped US$5 per hr; motorcycles US$10 per hr.

Hiking There are innumerable possibilities for walking and nature observation, near Baños and east towards Oriente (see below). Local agencies offer some treks in the area.

Horse riding Christian at *Hotel Isla de Baños* has excellent horses for rent; 6 hrs with a guide and jeep transport costs US$22 per person, English, Spanish, German spoken, not recommended for novices. *Caballos José*, Maldonado y Martínez, T740746, US$5 per hr, flexible hours; and Angel Aldaz, Montalvo y JL Mera, US$4 per hr (on the road to the statue of the Virgin). There are several others, but check their horses as not all are well cared for.

River rafting Note that the Chambo, Patate and Pastaza rivers are all polluted. Always pay close attention to the quality of equipment (rafts, helmets, life vests, etc) and experience of guides, fatal accidents have taken place here (not with the agency listed). See also the Rafting section, on page 70. *Río Loco*, Maldonado y Martínez, T/F740929, rioloco@ecuadorexplorer.com Héctor Romo, half day, US$25, US$45 for full day (rapids and calm water in jungle), US$120 per person 2 days with camping.

There are many tour agencies in town, some with several offices, as well as independent guides who seek out tourists on the street, or in hotels and restaurants. Quality varies considerably; to obtain a qualified guide and avoid unscrupulous operators, it is best to seek advice from other travellers who have recently returned from a tour. We have received some critical reports of tours out of Baños, but there are also highly respected and qualified operators here. In all cases, insist on a written contract and if possible, try to pay only half the fare up-front. Check any mountaineering or other equipment very carefully before heading out. Most agencies and guides offer trips to the jungle (US$25-$50 per per person per day in 2000) and 2-day climbing trips to Cotopaxi (about US$110 per person) and Chimborazo (about US$120 per person). There are also volcano watching, trekking and horse tours, in addition to the day-trips and sports mentioned above. Baños is a good meeting place to form a group to visit the Oriente. It is more interesting than Misahuallí, if you have to wait a few days, but the tour can be more expensive.

The following agencies and guides have received positive recommendations but the list is not exclusive and there are certainly others. *Rain forestur*, Ambato y Maldonado, T/F740743, rainfor@interactive.net.ec www.ecuador-paginaamarilla. com/rainforestur.htm Run by Santiago Herrera, guides are knowledgeable and environmentally conscious. *Vasco Tours*, Alfaro y Martínez, T741017, vascotours@ andinanet.net Run by Juan Medina, speaks English well, 6-28 day trips available, 6-8 people needed, excellent and plentiful food, up to 4 guides per tour. *Aventurandes*, Alfaro y Oriente (Pensión Patty), T740202. Experienced mountain guides Carlos Alvarez and Fausto Mayorga, also jungle tours. *Caniats*, Residencial Santa Clara, T740349. Run by Carlos Saant Mashu, knowledgeable and honest. *Tsantsa Expeditions-Yawa Jee*, Oriente y Eloy Alfaro, T740957. Good jungle guides, Spanish-speaking only, and they can arrange fly-in trips, eg Sebastián Moya, a Shuar Indian, who will lead tours anywhere. *Córdova Tours*, Maldonado y Espejo, T740923. They run the following tours on board their *chiva Mocambo*, an open sided bus (reserve ahead): waterfall tour, along the Puyo road to Río Verde, 0900-1400, US$5; Baños and environs,1600-1800, US$2.50; night tour with music, 2000-2100, US$1.70 (they will drop you off at the night spot of your choice). *Deep Forest Adventure*, Rocafuerte y Halflants, next to Andinatel, T740403, cellular T09-937137, Eloy Torres, speaks German, English and French, jungle and trekking tours.*Geotours*, Ambato next to Banco del Pichincha, T741344. Geovanny Romo. Small, experienced agency offering jungle tours and horseback tours. *Explorsierra*, Maldonado y Espejo, T740628/302, explorsierra1@hotmail.com Guido Sánchez, Climbing, trekking, jungle and volcano watching tours. *Expediciones Amazónicas*, Oriente 11-68 y Halflants, T740506,

Tour operators
Since the reactivation, of the volcano, access to Tungurahua is restricted. Always obtain safety information before accepting a tour to the volcano

expedicionesamazonicas@hotmail.com Run by Jorge and Dosto Varela, the latter is a recommended mountain guide, also offer trekking and jungle trips. *Willie Navarrete*, at *Café Higuerón* (T09-932411), is a highly recommended guide for climbing, he is an ASEGUIM member. *Huilla Cuna*, there are 3 agencies of the same name: at Rocafuerte y Ambato, T741086, Byron Castillo, helpful and knowledgeable, jungle and mountain tours; at Ambato y Halflants, T741292, huilacuna@yahoo.es, Marcelo Mazo organizes jungle trips; and at Rafael Vieira y Montalvo, T740187, Luis Guevara runs jungle and mountain trips.

Transport
See also Ins & outs,
page 212

Car hire 4WD vehicles with driver can be rented from Córdova Tours, see Tour operators above.

Bus To/from **Quito**, via Ambato, US$3, 3½ hrs, best service with Transportes Baños half hourly, recommended. Going to Quito sit on the right for views of Cotopaxi, and buy tickets early for weekends and holidays. To **Ambato**, 45 mins, US$0.60. To **Riobamba**, landslides caused by Tungurahua's volcanic activity have closed the direct Baños-Riobamba road until further notice, buses go via Ambato, 2 hrs, US$1.50. To **Latacunga**, 2-2½ hrs, US$1.50. To **Puyo**, 2 hrs, US$1.50. Pack your luggage in plastic as it all goes on top of the bus. Puyo-bound buses stop at the corner of Av Amazonas (highway) and Maldonado, opposite the terminal. To **Tena**, 5½ hrs, US$2.50. To **Misahuallí**, change at Tena, or at the Río Napo crossing (see page 375). To **Macas**, 7 hrs, US$3.50, some direct buses or change at Puyo (sit on the right).

Directory

Banks *Banco del Pacífico*, Montalvo y Alfaro. TCs and Mastercard ATM, open Mon-Fri 0845-1630, Sat 0900-1330. *Distracturs*, Ambato y Halflants. Charges 4% comission on TCs. *Don Pedro*, Ambato y Halflants, hardware store opposite Banco del Pichincha. Charges 4% comission on TCs.

Communications Post Office: Halflants y Ambato across from Parque Central. **Andinatel:** Halflants y Rocafuerte by Parque Central, international calls. **Internet:** There are many cyber cafés in town, but these are changing rapidly. Prices range between US$1.60 and US$2 per hr. Some recommended ones are: **Baños.Net**, Alfaro between Ambato and Oriente. **C@fé.Com**, 12 de Noviembre 500 y Oriente. **Planeta.Net**, Maldonado y Ambato, cheaper than average.

Language classes Rates for Spanish lessons in 2000 ranged from US$3 to US$5 per hr. *Baños Spanish Center/Sí Centro de Español e Inglés*, Antonio Páez y Oriente, T740632, elizbasc@uio.satnet.net www.ecuadorexplorer.com/sicentro/home Elizabeth Barrionuevo, English and German speaking, flexible, salsa lessons. Recommended. *Spanish School 16 de Diciembre*, Montalvo 5-26 y Rafael Vieira, T740232. José M Eras, English speaking retired teacher. *International Spanish School*, 16 de Diciembre y Espejo, T/F740612. Martha Vaca F. *Instituto de Español Alternativo IDEA*, Montalvo y Alfaro, T/F740799, idea2@idea.k12.ec Christine Müller. *Raíces Spanish School*, Av 16 de Diciembre y Pablo A Suáres, T/F740090, racefor@hotmail.com.

Laundry Municipal washhouse next to the Virgen baths, US$1 a bundle, or do it yourself for free. *La Herradura*, Martínez y Alfaro, US$0.60 per kg. Several hotels have laundry service, eg *Monik's* and *El Marqués*, see Sleeping for addresses.

Around Baños

There are many interesting **walks** in the Baños area. The **San Martín shrine** is a 45 minute easy walk from town and overlooks a deep rocky canyon with the Río Pastaza thundering below. Beyond the shrine, crossing the San Martín bridge to the north side of the Pastaza, is the **zoo**, with a large variety of regional animals, in well designed enclosures. Recommended. ■ *0800-1800, US$1.* Fifty metres beyond the zoo is a path to the **Inés María waterfall**, a thundering, but sadly polluted, cascade. The road continues on the north side of the Pastaza to the village of **Lligua** which straddles the river of the same name. A trail leads uphill from Lligua two to three hours to **Las Antenas**, a popular place for viewing Tungurahua.

You can also cross the Pastaza by the **Puente San Francisco** suspension bridge, behind the kiosks across the main road from the bus station. From here a series of trails fans out into the surrounding hills, offering excellent views of Tungurahua from the ridgetops in clear weather. A total of six bridges span the Pastaza near Baños, so you can make a round trip.

On the hillside behind Baños, it is a 45-minute hike to the statue of the Virgin, with good views of the valley below. Take the trail at the south end of calle JL Mera, before the street ends, take the last street to the right, at the end of which are stairs leading to the trail. A steep path continues along the ridge, past the statue. Another trail begins at the south end of JL Mera and leads to the *Hotel Luna Runtún*, continuing on to the village of Runtún (five to six hour round-trip).

Along the same hillside, starting at the south end of calle Maldonado, the path to the left leads to the **Bella Vista cross**. It's a steep climb, 45 minutes to one hour, and there's a cafeteria along the way. You can also continue from the cross to the Hotel Luna Runtún.

Caution is advised near the San Francisco bridge as well as on the paths to Bellavista & Runtún. Visitors have occasionally been robbed in these locations

Central Highlands

East of Baños

The road from Baños to Puyo (58 km) is very scenic, with many waterfalls tumbling down to the Pastaza, the first half to Río Negro is unpaved and can get muddy when it rains, the remaining half is paved and in good condition. The area has excellent opportunities for walking and nature observation.

Seventeen kilometres from Baños is the town of **Río Verde** at the junction of the Verde and Pastaza rivers, with several snack bars and simple restaurants.

The Río Verde has crystalline green water and forms several waterfalls along its course, the most spectacular of which is **El Pailón del Diablo** (the devil's cauldron). Cross the Río Verde on the road and take the path to the right after the church, then follow the trail down towards the suspension bridge over the Pastaza, for about 20 minutes. Just before the bridge take a side trail to the right (signposted) which leads you to a viewing platform above the falls; there is a kiosk selling drinks and snacks.

The **San Miguel falls**, smaller but also nice, are some five minutes' walk along a different trail. In town cross the bridge and take the first path to the right.

Take any of the buses bound for Puyo from the corner of Maldonado y Amazonas (main highway), across from the bus terminal. US$0.50, 30 minutes. Córdova Tours offer a tour to Río Verde, stopping at several sites along the way, on a *chiva* (see Tour operators above). For a thrill (not without its hazards), ride on the roof. A worthwhile trip is to cycle to Río Verde and take a bus back to Baños. Leave your bike at one of the snack bars while you go to the falls (tip expected). It is also possible to cycle all the way to Puyo (four to five hours), and the entire route from Baños is very scenic. Unfortunately holdups of bikers have (rarely) taken place here, so enquire about public safety before heading out.

There are excellent hiking opportunities up the Rio Verde. The trail on the west side of the river begins at the town park. This trail makes a good day trip. There is basic lodging three hours up the trail; ask about Angel's cabins at the store just east of the town square.

Sleeping **F** per person *Indillama*, by the San Miguel Falls, T09-785263. Nice cabins, hot water, restaurant, includes breakfast. Beautiful surroundings, German-run. **E** per person *Pequeño Paraíso*, 1½ km east of Río Verde, west of Machay, T09-819756, nina_franco@ hotmail.com Nicely furnished, comfortable cabins, hot water, includes breakfast and dinner. Lovely surroundings, tasty vegetartian meals with homemade bread, small pool, climbing wall, Swiss-run. Camping US$3 per person with use of hot shower. Further east, 9 km past Rio Negro and before Mera, is La Penal, the access point for **Cumandá**, where you will find **F** per person *El Monasterio de Cumandá*, across a foot-bridge over the Pastaza from *La Penal*, then walk 30 mins. Cabins with bath and kitchenette in a lush area, camping permitted, very quiet and relaxing, good walking opportunities. Information and reservations (required) from *Hostal Mariane* in Baños, T740911.

At 2¼ km east of Río Verde is **Machay**, where several waterfalls can be seen, another lovely area for walking. Ten kilometres beyond is the larger village of **Río Negro**, from where there is access to the southeastern region of Parque Nacional Sangay. See page 384 for the section closer to Puyo.

Climbing Tungurahua

Warning Due to the reactivation of the volcano, Tungurahua was officially closed to climbers starting in October 1999. There is nobody to stop you from entering the area, but the dangers are very real and those who ignore this warning do so at considerable risk to their lives. Unless volcanic activity has completely ceased, do not be talked into climbing to the *refugio*, crater or summit. To obtain impartial information, try the municipal tourist office at the Baños bus station; never rely exclusively on an agency who is trying to sell you a climbing tour. At the same time, remember that Tungurahua was a reasonably safe and popular climb for many decades. If the volcano calms down, then in all likelihood it will be reasonably safe once again. Also note that details of the climb as given below may well change once the mountain is re-opened to visitors.

Baños is the access point to climb **Tungurahua** (5,016 m) – part of Sangay National Park. Entry to the park is US$10, but this is generally waived if you will not be staying overnight. A guide is highly recommended for this climb; see Tour operators above. Depending on the season, you may need rubber boots to get to the refuge. You always require a rope, ice axe and crampons for a safe ascent to the summit. The best season is December to March, though in December it can be cloudy in the mornings; check conditions locally.

Getting there

Follow the path at the west end of Martínez across the Bascún river to the El Salado road. Turn right (downhill) and then take the first left (signs for Casa San Juan). Keep an eye out for the beginning of a trail to your left, this will lead you to the village of **Pondoa**. Continue above the town to the park entrance. If you are driving to Pondoa, take the main Ambato road to the turnoff for Riobamba (bird sculptures). Follow the Riobamba road for about 1 km, then take the dirt road to the left which leads to Pondoa. Park at the shop in Pondoa.

The walk from the shop to the beginning of the trail takes 30 mins. A truck leaves at 0900 daily from *Pensión Patty* (you can arrange for pickup at your hotel) to the Park office beyond Pondoa; 1 hr, US$2.50 one way. Trucks return from Pondoa around 1200-1400. A pickup truck from Coop Agoyán on Parque Central, Calle Maldonado, costs US$10 for up to 5 passengers, to the park entrance. The shop in Pondoa and Baños tour operators can arrange for pack animals; guide and mule for 1 pack US$5, for 2 packs, US$7. To hire horses, see page 218.

Route to the summit
The views when the sun rises at 0600 are awesome

From the park entrance to the refuges the trail is clearly signposted. It's a hard but interesting walk through lush vegetation. It is steep in parts and muddy underfoot. From the refuge to the summit takes four to five hours, a tough but rewarding climb. Most parties set out around 0300. At first the path is easy to follow, as far as the antenna and hut, then it becomes a bit vague on fine scree up to the snowline, but still possible to follow. The last hour is on snow. The use of ropes is recommended as it is steep. Crampons and an ice-axe are essential. It takes 1½-2 hours to descend to the refuge, then a further 1½ hours to the park office.

Sleeping

It takes 3-4 hrs from the park entrance up to the shelters at 3,800 m, US$3 per person. There is a stone refuge with capacity for about 40 and electricity, and the older *refugio* Santos Ocaña, preferred by some because the wooden structure is a little warmer, with capacity for about 20 and no electricity. Take a sleeping bag and mat (a hammock can be slung), there is no heating and it can be cold. There are cooking facilities at both shelters, but no eating utensils, take food and a torch. Do not leave baggage unattended in the refuge.

Tungurahua can also be reached from Palitahua at the Río Puela, on the Baños-Riobamba road, at about 2,000 m. A guide is needed through the forest, then you camp at 3,800 m where the forest ends. The snowline is at 4,600 m, so the last 400 m is through snow, requiring crampons and an ice-axe. There are thermal pools at Palitahua, ask where they are. Don't leave anything of value here.

Ambato to Guaranda

To the west of Ambato (see above, page 207), a paved road climbs through tilled fields, past the *páramos* of Carihuairazo and Chimborazo, to the great Arenal, a high desert at the base of Chimborazo where *vicuñas* may be seen. Fifty kilometres from Ambato (44 km from Guaranda) is the access to

Mechahuasca, one of the areas where *vicuñas* were re-introduced to the **Reserva de Producción de Fauna Chimborazo**. The turnoff left is marked by a large orange sign. Thirteen kilometres further is the intersection with the *arenal* road, to the south it leads to the Chimborazo *refugios* (page 236) and the Guaranda-Riobamba road. From the *arenal* the road drops to Guaranda in the Chimbo valley; some parts are badly pot-holed and in need of repair.

Guaranda

Phone code: 03
Colour map 4, grid B5
Population: 15,730
Altitude: 2,650m

This quaint, quiet town, capital of Bolívar Province, proudly calls itself 'the Rome of Ecuador' because it is built on seven hills. The town maintains its colonial flavour, and there are many fine, though fading, old houses along the cobbled streets with narrow sidewalks. There are nice views of the mountains all around, with Chimborazo towering above. The climate can be very pleasant with warm days and cool evenings; however, the area is also subject to rain and fog. Although not on the tourist trail, there are many sights worth visiting in the province, for which Guaranda is the ideal base.

Guaranda is connected by a paved road to Ambato and southwest to Babahoyo (see page 315) and by a narrow but spectacular dirt road to Riobamba. This latter route is known as the Gallo Rumi, so named because of a rock that is not only said to resemble a rooster, but also sound like one in a high wind! Until the beginning of the twentieth century Guaranda was the main crossroads between Quito and Guayaquil, but with the construction of the railroad and later the opening of newer, faster roads, it has since stagnated.

Sights   For tourist information, the *Oficina Municipal de Información Turística*, García Moreno entre 7 de Mayo y Convención de 1884 has useful information and maps about the city and province. It can also arrange guided tours, horse riding and camping in the area. Spanish only. ■ *Mon-Fri 0800-1200 and 1400-1800*.

Locals traditionally take an evening stroll in the palm-fringed main plaza, **Parque Libertador Simón Bolívar**, with a modern statue of Bolívar. Those with an eye for detail will notice that the blade is missing from his sword; every year during carnival the city places a new blade, which is promptly removed by the university students. Around the park are the municipal buildings with an attractive courtyard, paintings in the Salón de la Ciudad and good views from the tower (open Mon-Fri 0800-1200 and 1400-1800), several colonial homes, and a large stone **Cathedral**, with a nice marble altar, wooden ceiling and stained glass windows.

Towering over the city, atop one of the hills, is an impressive statue of '**El Indio Guaranga**', a local Indian leader after whom the city may have been named. The site offers fine views of the city, the surrounding hills and the summit of Chimborazo. A cultural centre at the base of the sculpture includes a regional ethnographic and history museum (open Wed-Sun 0800-1200 and 1400-1700, US$0.20), art gallery and auditorium. To get there, take a taxi (US$0.80), take a 'Guanujo' bus to the stadium and walk 10 minutes from there, or walk 45 minutes from the centre, follow García Moreno to the west end and continue up via the cemetery. Beyond the Indio Guaranga, 2 km towards the Río Salinas is **El Troje**, where you can camp by the river (make arrangements at the tourist office, see above) Walking two hours upriver along the narrow canyon you reach the 8 m high waterfall of **El Infiernillo**.

The **Escuela de Educación de la Cultura Andina** (Universidad de Bolívar), 7 de Mayo y Olmedo, has an anthropology museum with pre-Inca and Inca collections. ■ *Mon-Fri 0800-1200 and 1400-1800, free*.

Market days are Friday and Saturday (larger), when many indigenous people in typical dress from the nearby communities can be seen trading at the market complex at the east end of Calle Azuay, by Plaza 15 de Mayo (9 de Abril y Maldonado), and at Plaza Roja (Avenida General Enríquez). These markets are colourful and interesting. There is also a small daily market at **Mercado 10 de Noviembre** (Sucre y Espejo), busiest on Wednesday.

D *La Colina*, Av Guayaquil 117 on a hill north of the entrance from Ambato, T/F980666. With bath and TV, rooms bright and attractive, terraces give good views of town and surrounding mountains, expensive but mediocre restaurant, pool, nice gardens. Attentive service, restful, friendly. Recommended. **F** *Bolívar*, Sucre 704 y Rocafuerte, T980547. With bath, TV, intermittent hot showers, **G** with shared bath, quiet inner court, restaurant. **F** *Cochabamba*, García Moreno y 7 de Mayo, T981958, F982125, vviteriv@gu.pro.ec With bath, TV, **G** with shared bath, very good expensive restaurant. Somewhat faded, good service. **F** *Ejecutivo*, García Moreno 603 y 9 de Abril near the Plaza Roja, T/F 982044. Shared bath, hot water. New in 1999, simple. **G** *Acapulco*, 10 de Agosto y 9 de Abril. With bath, **H** without bath, restaurant. Basic, small rooms. **G** *Matiaví*, Av Eliza Mariño 314, next to the bus station, T980295. Cold water, not clean. **G** *Santa Fé*, 10 de Agosto y 9 de Abril, T981526. With bath, **H** witout bath, electric shower, TV, restaurant. Basic, friendly, very thin walls, noisy at times. **H** *Pensión Rosa Elvira*, Sucre 606. Shared bath, basic. **H** *Pensión San José*, Sucre 607. Shared bath, very basic. **H** *Pensión Tequendama*, Rocafuerte 309 across from Parque 9 de Octubre. With bath, cheaper with shared bath, safe parking open to non-guests. Very basic, clean. **H** *Residencial La Posada*, General Enríquez y 10 de Agosto, by Plaza Roja, T980867. Shared bath, cold water, not very clean, basic, motorbike parking.

Sleeping
■ *on map*
Price codes:
see inside front cover

Central Highlands

Guaranda

■ Sleeping

1 Acapulco	5 La Colina	9 Residencial La Posada
2 Bolívar	6 Matiaví	10 Sante Fé
3 Cochabamba	7 Pensión Rosa Elvira	
4 Ejecutivo	8 Pensión San José	

● Eating

1 Juad's
2 Rincón del
   Buen Menú
3 Rumipamba

Eating

on map, page 225
Price categories:
see inside front cover.
Most restaurants are
closed on Sun

Cochabamba, at *Hotel Cochabamba*. International food. Best in town, closed Sat evening and Sun. Expensive. Recommended. *La Colina*, at *Hotel La Colina*, international food. Best for Sun lunch when they expect local families, otherwise mediocre. Expensive. *Pizza Buon Giorno*, Av Circunvalación 2 blocks from Plaza Roja on the way to the bus terminal. Pizza and salads. Mid-range prices.

Amazonas, 9 de Abril y García Moreno. Set meals and à la carte. Good, family-run. Cheap. closed Sun. Recommended. *Bolívar*, Sucre 706, at Hotel Bolívar. Good value cheap set meals. Has a nice display of Andean musical instruments, closed Sun. Recommended. *Marisquería El Conchal*, Plaza Roja. Good *ceviche de pescado, camarones* and *mixtos*. Cheap. Not open in the evening, open Sun. Family-run. *Rincón del Buen Menú*, Gen Enríquez at top end of Plaza Roja. Set meals. *Rumipamba*, Gen Enríquez 308, Plaza Roja. Fresh fruit juices, grilled chicken, set meals and à la carte. Cheap.

Seriously cheap   These places offer set meals: *Acapulco*. At hotel; *Central*, Azuay y Marayma Ofir Carvajal, 2 blocks from Plaza Roja; and *Santa Fé*. At hotel. Several more in this category at Plaza Roja near kiosks.

Cafeterías *Juad's Pastelería*, Convención de 1884 y Azuay. Cappuccino, hot chocolate, sandwiches, fruit salad, pastries. Very good, popular, best selection early in the day, closed 1300-1500, closed Sun. Recommended. *Bar-Café Tacuma*, García Moreno across from Parque Bolívar. Coffee and drinks. Open Tue-Sat from 1500. *Heladería El Pingüino*, Sucre accross from Parque Bolívar. Factory ice cream. A popular meeting place in the evenings. *Salinerito*, Plaza Roja. Salinas cheese shop also serves coffee and sandwiches. Closed Sun.

Bars &
nightclubs
Discos are open on Thu,
Fri and Sat nights

Balcones de la Pila Disco Bar, Pichincha y García Moreno. Varied music, drinks, snacks. *No Bar*, Sucre entre Manuela Cañizares y Azuay. Salsa, rock, drinks. *Patatús*, García Moreno entre Sucre y Pichincha. Varied music, drinks, snacks.

Festivals   Carnival in Guaranda is among the best known in the country. People of all walks of life share the festivities; parades, masks, dances, guitars and poetry fill the streets. *Taita Carnaval* (Father Carnival), a landowner who sponsors the party, opens the celebrations when he makes his grand entrance into town. As in other parts of the country water throwing (and at times flour, ink, etc) is common. In the surrounding countryside the celebrations last for 8 days.

Shopping   There are many well stocked shops in town. *Artesanías de PHD*, General Enríquez, Plaza Roja. Crafts from co-operative in nearby Salinas, woollens, decorations. Open Mon-Fri 0900-1300 and 1430-1900, Sat 0900-1700. *Salinerito*, General Enríquez, Plaza Roja, sells good quality cheese from Salinas.

Transport   **Buses** The terminal is at Eliza Mariño Carvajal, on the way out of town towards Riobamba and Babahoyo. If you are staying in town ask to be dropped off closer to the centre. Many daily buses to: **Ambato**, US$1.40, 2 hrs (beautiful views); **Riobamba**,(some along the Gallo Rumi road and others via the arenal) US$1.40, 2 hrs; **Babahoyo**, US$1.65, 3 hrs; **Guayaquil**, US$2.30, 4½ hrs; **Quito**, 3 companies run almost 30 daily services, US$2.30, 4-5 hrs.

Directory   **Banks** *Filanbanco*, on Av Kennedy for Visa cards, 0900-1300 only. **Communications** Post Office: Azuay y Pichincha. **Andinatel**, Rocafuerte 508 y Sucre, 0800-2200 daily; and at the bus terminal. **Laundry** *La Primavera*, Ciudadela 1 de Mayo, T982538. Call for pickup from your hotel, ask for Patricio Zurita. **Tour operators** *Cashcaventura*, Convención de 1884 1112 y García Moreno (no sign), T/F980725, devargas@gye.satnet.net Diego Vargas Guided tours to many destinations in the region including Chimborazo, Salinas, nature reserves, US$20-25 per day depending on accommodation. *Delgado Travel*, García Moreno y 9 de Abril, T/F981719 Airline tickets. Mon-Fri 0900-1700, Sat 0900-1200.

North of Guaranda, 1½ hours by car along poor roads, is **Salinas de** **Excursions from**
Guaranda (*population*: 5,000), in a picturesque setting with interesting geo- **Guaranda**
logical formations. This is the best example of a thoroughly succesful community development project in all of Ecuador. Once a very poor village which
lived from salt mining, it now runs very succesful co-operative projects including a dairy (Salinerito brand cheeses, among the best in the country), a wool
spinning and dyeing mill, and a sweets industry. It is a good area for walking,
horse riding and fishing. ■ *Entry fee to Salinas US$1, guided tour of the com-*
munity projects US$4.

Sleeping **E** *Hotel Refugio Salinas*, T981266. With bath, hot water, **F** with shared
bath, **G** per person in dormitory, meals available. A full board plan including 3 meals,
entry fee and guided tour is **E** per person with bath, **F** per person with shared bath or
in dorm.

Transport Transportes Cándido Rada, daily to Salinas from Verbo Divino School at
the top of Plaza Roja, at about 0600. From Parque Montúfar, Gen Salazar y Sucre,
below the market, at 0700 and 0900. Returning at 0830, 1300, and 1500. A taxi costs
US$10 (US$15 with wait included). Also enquire at the co-operative office or *Salinerito*
cheese shop (Plaza Roja) about their vehicles going to Salinas.

The success achieved in Salinas is starting to spread. In the 1980s a group of
people from Salinas migrated west and founded the town of **La Palma**, which
has established a similar co-operative system and further west, the village of
Chazo Juan also has a dairy co-operative and an experimental farm. Just east
of La Palma is the **Bosque Peña Blanca**, a native cloud forest reserve with a 300
m high waterfall, La Chorrera. A dirt road links this area east to Salinas and
west to **Echeandía** 1½ hours by truck from Chazo Juan, three hours by bus
from Guaranda. In Chazo Juan is **E** *Cabaña Chazo Juan*, T03-970307. Bunk
beds for 16, cooking facilities, bath, an hour's walk from reserve. Echeandía
has several basic **G-H** hotels and restaurants, *Amparito* is the best.

About two thirds of the province of Bolívar is in the foothills of the western *cor-*
dillera, a region known as the *sub-trópico*. This transition zone between the
slopes of Chimborazo and the coastal plain is quite scenic; remnants of cloud
forest still cover some of the higher elevations while the lower reaches produce
sugar cane and citrus. This area sees very little tourism but has great potential;
recommended for off-the-beaten track travellers. Several roads go from the
highlands to the coast, all very scenic.
   The bus ride to Babahoyo (see page 315) is beautiful. **Chimbo** where fireworks and guitars are made is 24 km south of Guaranda. Nearby there is an
interesting church museum in **Huayco** (Santuario de Nuestra Señora de la
Natividad), constructed around a 'Vatican Square', with interesting
pre-Spanish artefacts. The main road continues through **San Miguel**, nearby
is the colonial town of **Santiago** with paintings in the church by a local artist
and the **Bosque Protector Cashca Totoras**. It continues to **San Pablo**, nearby
are the forests of **Bosque de Arrayanes** and **San José de las Palmas**. Further
on is **Bilován**, with the **caves of Las Guardias** to the west, and then
Balsapamba, with waterfall and river beaches, before the road reaches the
coastal plain at Babahoyo. The views along the way are magnificent. An older
route known as *el torneado* runs from Chimbo to Balsapamba, it is very steep,
narrow, there are innumerable hairpin bends and it is extremly scenic. At
Santa Lucía, before reaching Balsapamba, is the interesting, Swiss-run Museo
de las Culturas del Ecuador.

Central Highlands

Ambato to Riobamba After Ambato, the Pananamericana passes apple orchards and onion fields. Between Ambato and Riobamba is **Mocha**, where guinea-pigs (*cuy*) are raised for the table. You can sample roast *cuy* and other typical Ecuadorean dishes at stalls and restaurants by the roadside (*Mariadiocelina* is recommended). The valley's patchwork of fields gives an impression of greater fertility and prosperity than the Riobamba zone that follows. On the houses a small crucifix crowns the roof, where figurines of domestic animals are also found. At the pass there are fine views in the dry season of Chimborazo and its smaller sister mountain, Carihuairazo. For excursions in this area see page 237.

Riobamba

Riobamba is the capital of Chimborazo Province. It is built in the wide Tapi Valley and has broad streets and many ageing but impressive buildings. Because of its central location Riobamba and the surrounding province are known as Corazón de la Patria, *the heartland of Ecuador. It also boasts the nickname* La Sultana de Los Andes (the Sultan of the Andes) *in honour of lofty Mount Chimborazo.*

Riobamba has many good churches and public buildings, and magnificent views of five of the great volcanic peaks: Chimborazo, Altar, Tungurahua, Carihuairazo and, on occasion, Sangay. The city is the commercial centre for the Province of Chimborazo and an important centre of highland culture, both because of the many indigenous communities which live in the province and because of the city's self-styled European aristocracy.

Ins & outs **Getting there** Buses from Quito, Guayaquil, Ambato arrive at the well-run Terminal Terrestre on Epiclachima y Avenida Daniel León Borja. Buses from Baños and the Oriente arrive at the Terminal Oriental, at Espejo y Córdovez. A taxi between terminals is US$0.50. Both terminals are some distance from the centre, a taxi is recommended. The railway station remains a central landmark, although there are hardly any more train services.

Getting around Riobamba is more spread out than most of the towns in the central Sierra so you may want to take a taxi to get from sight to sight.

Tourist offices *Ministerio de Turismo*, Av Daniel L Borja y Brasil, next to the Municipal Library, T/F941213. Open Mon-Fri 0830-1700, very helpful and knowledgeable, English and some French spoken.

Sights

Riobamba has several attractive plazas and parks. The main plaza is **Parque Maldonado**, with a statue to the local scientist Pedro Vicente Maldonado and some interesting wrought-iron fountains. Around it are the **Santa Bárbara Cathedral,** with a beautiful colonial stone façade and an incongrously modern interior, the **Municipality** and several colonial buildings with arcades. Worth visiting is the house on the corner of Primera Constituyente and Espejo, restored in 1996. **Parque Sucre** with a Neptune fountain is located two blocks to the southeast. Standing opposite, along Primera Constituyente, is the imposing building of Colegio Maldonado.

Four blocks northeast of the railway station is the **Parque 21 de Abril**, named after the city's independence date. The Batalla de Tapi was fought in the Riobamba valley, on 21 April 1822. The Argentine General, Juan de Lavalle and 97 patriots defeated 400 Spanish troops. The park, better known as **La**

Loma de Quito, affords an unobstructed view of Riobamba and the peaks. It also has a colourful tile tableau of the history of Ecuador and is especially fine at sunset. **San Antonio de Padua** church, at the east corner of Parque 21 de Abril, tells bible stories in the windows.

West of the centre, along Avenida Daniel León Borja, is **Parque Guayaquil**, the largest in the urban area, with a small lake, a band-shell, a good playground and the **Vaca-Zebra** (zebra-cow), an unusual sculpture by the well known artist Gonzalo Endara Crow. A stylized Simón Bolívar, donated by Venezuela, adorns the traffic circle at Avenida Daniel L Borja and Zambrano.

Markets

Riobamba is an important market centre where indigenous people from many communities congregate. Saturday is the main market day when the city fills with colourfully dressed Indians from many different parts of the province of Chimborazo, each wearing their distinctive costume; trading overflows the markets and buying and selling go on all over town. Wednesday is a smaller market day. The 'tourist' market is in the small **Plaza de la Concepción or Plaza Roja**, on Orozco, south of the Convento de la Concepción (see below). It is a good place to buy local handicrafts and authentic Indian clothing (Saturday and Wednesday only, 0800-1500).

The main produce markets are **San Alfonso** (Argentinos y 5 de Junio) which on Saturday spills over into the nearby streets and also sells clothing, ceramics, baskets and hats, and **La Condamine** (Carabobo y Colombia) open daily, largest market on Fridays. Other markets in the colonial centre are **San Francisco** and **La Merced** (renovated in 2000) near the churches of the same name. The **Mercado de Animales** is at Av Circunvalación y Vía a Chambo, where trading of farm animals takes place early in the morning, busiest on Saturday.

Museums

The **Convento de la Concepción** has been carefully restored by the Banco Central and now functions as a religious art museum. It is a veritable treasure chest of 18th-century religious art. The priceless gold monstrance, Custodia de Riobamba Antigua, is the museum's greatest treasure, one of the richest of its kind in South America. The museum is well worth a visit. The guides are friendly and knowledgeable (tip expected). ■ *Tue-Fri 0900-1200 and 1500-1800, Sat 0900-1800, Sun and holidays 0900-1200, US$1, Orozco y España, entrance at Argentinos y J Larrea, T965212.*

The Brigada Blindada Galápagos runs the **Museo de Armas**, a collection of arms, uniforms and religious artifacts used through different periods of Ecuadorean history. It is housed in a historical *hacienda* house where a peace treaty between liberal and conservative forces was signed. You can also visit the former *hacienda* and ride on horses. ■ *Mon-Fri 0800-1200 and 1400-1600, Ave Héroes de Tapi, T969931.*

The Ateneo de Chimborazo, **Museo Particular Familiar Córdoba-Román**, is a private museum which includes a photo collection, paintings, sculptures, furniture and documents. ■ *Mon-Fri, 1000-1300 and 1500-1700, Velasco 24-25 y Veloz.*

Essentials

Sleeping
■ *on map*
Price codes: see inside front cover

Riobamba suffers from chronic water shortages so make sure your hotel has a water tank. **A-B** *Hostería Abraspungu*, Km 3½ on the road to Guano, T940820, F940819, info@abraspungu.com.ec Beautiful house in country setting, with bath, TV, excellent restaurant, bar, pool, horse riding. **A-B** *Hostería La Andaluza*, 16 km N of Riobamba along the Panamericana, T904223, F904234, handaluz@ch.pro.ec Nice rooms in old *hacienda* house, heaters, good restaurant. With views of Tungurahua and Altar, good

Central Highlands

walking, friendly. **B** *Hostería El Troje*, 4½ km on the road to Chambo, T/F960826, info@eltroje.com Nice rooms, carpeted, some with chimney, good restaurant. Good views, tourist centre, camping (US$5 per person). **C** *El Cisne*, Av Daniel L Borja y Duchicela, T964573, F941982. With bath, TV, restaurant, sauna and Turkish bath, includes breakfast. Modern. **C** *Zeus*, Av Daniel L Borja 41-29, T962292, F963100. With bath, TV, includes breakfast, 24-hr cafeteria, good restaurant. Modern, comfortable, nice, internet next door.

D *Chimborazo Internacional*, Los Cipreces y Argentinos, T963475, F963473. Spacious rooms with fridge and cold drinks, fully carpeted, central heating, pool, sauna, Turkish bath, jacuzzi, noisy discotheque, restaurant overpriced. Attentive service. **E** *Canadá*, Av de la Prensa 23-31 y Av Daniel L Borja, opposite the bus terminal, T/F946677. Laundry service, restaurant, tours. Modern, clean, English spoken. **E** *El Galpón*, Argentinos y Zambrano, T960981. Carpeted rooms, TV, pool, restaurant, bar, disco. Pleasant location on a hill overlooking the city, but a bit run-down. **E** *Humboldt*, Ave D L Borja 3548 y Uruguay, T961788. Clean, with bath, TV, restaurant, parking. **E** *Montecarlo*, Av 10 de Agosto 25-41 entre García Moreno y EspañaT/F960557. Hot water, good restaurant, **F** without window. Clean, comfortable, English spoken, friendly. Recommended. **E** *Riobamba Inn*, Carabobo 23-20 y Primera Constituyente, T961696. Parking, good restaurant. Basic but clean, group discounts. **E** *Segovia*, Primera Constituyente 22-28 y Espejo, near Parque Maldonado, T961259. With bath, **F** with shared bath, cafeteria, laundry service. Clean, good value. **E** *Tren Dorado*, Carabobo 22-35 y 10 de Agosto, T964890. With bath, reliable hot water, parking.

Riobamba

■ **Sleeping**
1 El Cisne *C1*
2 El Galpón *C2*
3 Hostal Ñuca Huasi *C4*
4 Hostal Segovia *C5*
5 Humboldt *C3*
6 Imperial *C4*

7 Los Nevados *D2*
8 Los Shyris *C4*
9 Manabí *D5*
10 Metropolitano *C3*
11 Montecarlo &
   Cafetería Montecarlo *C5*
12 Residencial Colonial *C4*

13 Residencial Rocío *D3*
14 Riobamba Inn *C4*
15 Tren Dorado &
   Café Ashoka *C4*
16 Whymper *C3*
17 Zeus *D2*

Modern, clean, nice. **E** *Whymper*, Av Miguel Angel León 23-10 y Primera Constituyente, T964575, F968137. Private bath, hot water, spacious rooms, safe parking, includes breakfast.

F *El Altar*, Panamericana Norte Km 1, T964872. With bath, TV, restaurant, garage. **F** *Los Alamos*, Av Lizarzaburo on the way north out of town, T967386. With bath, hot water, TV. **F** *Camino Real*, Av de la Prensa y Calle D, opposite the bus terminal, T/F962365, restaurant. **F** *Imperial*, Rocafuerte 22-15 y 10 de Agosto, T960429. Hot water 24 hrs, some rooms with bath, others shared, expensive laundry facilities, stores luggage, good beds. Clean, friendly and comfortable, good views from the roof, loud music from bar on Fri and Sat nights. **F** *Manabí*, Colón 19-58 y Olmedo, T967967/305. With bath, hot water, TV, cheaper with shared bath, restaurant, parking. Clean. **F** *Los Shyris*, 10 de Agosto y Rocafuerte 2160, near the train station, T960323, F967934. With bath, hot water 1700-1100, good rooms and service, rooms at the back are quieter, cheaper without bath. Clean, nicely furnished, friendly, good value.

G *Majestic*, Av Daniel L Borja 43-60 y La 44, near the bus terminal, T968708. With bath, electric shower, parking, cafeteria. **G** *Metropolitano*, Av Daniel L Borja y Lavalle, near train station, T961714. Large rooms with bath, hot water, good beds, noisy, not secure, water problems, basic. **G** *Los Nevados*, Luis Costales 24-37 Av Daniel L Borja, across from Parque Guayaquil, T964696. With bath, constant hot water, laundry. Clean, very good, garage extra. **G** *Ñuca Huasi*, 10 de Agosto 2824 y Dávalos, T966669. With bath, **H** with shared bath, hot water, laundry facilities, poor beds. Noisy, dark and gloomy and not too clean, friendly. **G** *Residencial Rocío*, Brazil 2168 y Av Daniel L Borja, T961848. Bath, hot water, towels and soap supplied, cheaper with shared bath, parking. Clean, friendly, quiet. **G-H** *Fiver*, Epiclachima, opposite the bus terminal, T948538. Shared bath, electric shower, some with TV.

H *Guayaquil*, Montalvo y Unidad Nacional, by the train station, T964512. Shared bath, cold water, very basic. **H** *Monterrey*, Rey Cacha 44-29 y Epiclachima, across from the bus terminal, T962421. Some with bath, hot water only in shared baths. **H** *Residencial Colonial*, Carabobo 21-62 y 10 de Agosto, across from the train station, T966543. Shared bath, hot water. Very basic, run-down colonial house.

Chinese *Chifa Joy Sing*, Guayaquil 29-27 y Carabobo, behind the station, T961285. Cheap, good. Open 1000-2300. *Chifa China*, Av Daniel L Borja 43-49 y la 44. Good, cheap. *Chifa Internacional*, Veloz y Dávalos. Good. *Chifa Pekin*, Av Daniel L Borja y Brasil, T940712. OK, mid-range price. *Chifa Pak Hao*, García Moreno 21-17 y Guayaquil, T964270. Plain setting, cheap.

Ecuadorean *Los Alamos*, Juan de Lavalle 22-41. Good á la carte and set meals. *Bonny*, Diego de Almagro y Villarroel, regional dishes, seafood. Good

To Baños
Baños Oriente
Alvarado
Av México
Buenos Aires
Larrea
Mariana de Jesús
Mercado San Alfonso
Convento de la Concepción
ncepción
La Basílica
Mercado Concepción
Catedral Santa Bárbara
Parque La Libetad
Parque Maldonado
3
Municipality
San Francisco
Espejo
Colón
Parque Sucre
Larrea
Mercado San Francisco
Benalcázar
Velasco
4
9
La Merced
5 de Junio
Tarqui
Chile
5   **6**

● **Eating**
1 Chifa Joy Sing *D4*
2 El Delirio *C4*
3 Los Alamos *C3*
4 Punto Azul *D5*

Eating
● *on map*
Price categories:
see inside front cover.
Most restaurants
close by 2200.
For early departures,
there are several small
cafés at the back of
the bus terminal,
serving breakfast
and other meals

Central Highlands

service, popular. Mid-range prices. Open lunch only. *Don Bolo*, Veloz y Carabobo. Good value set meals. Seriously cheap. *Don Pato*, Carabobo y 10 de Agosto, set meals. Seriously cheap. *Montecarlo*, Primera Constituyente y Pichincha, open 1800-0100, popular. *El Portón Dorado*, Diego Ibarra 22-50 y Av Daniel L Borja. Set meals, à la carte, seafood, open lunch only.

Grill *Che Carlitos*, Colón 22-44, between 10 de Agosto and Primera Constituyente. *Parrilladas Argentinas* and *empanadas*, expensive but authentic, *peña* at weekend. *El Fogón del Chef*, Tarqui y Veloz, across from Andinatel. Chicken and grill. *Parrillada de Fausto*, Uruguay 20-38 y Av Daniel L Borja. T767876. Good meat.

International *Cabaña Montecarlo*, García Moreno 21-40, T968609. Set meals and à la carte. Good food and service, large portions. Mid-range prices. Open 1200-2115, Sun 1200-1530. Recommended. *Café Concierto El Delirio*, Primera Constituyente 2816 y Rocafuerte, T967502. Expensive à la carte and set meals, excellent steaks. Nicely located in Bolivar's house in Riobamba, with patio garden, Andean music starting 2000, popular with tour groups. Open 1200-2130. Recommended. *Cafetería Real Montecarlo*, 10 de Agosto 25-45 y García Moreno, T962844. Excellent food and service large selection, good breakfasts with fresh fruit juices. Mid-range prices. Open 0730-1100 and 1600-2300. Recommended. *Candilejas*, 10 de Agosto 27-33 y Pichincha. A la carte, set meals and pizzas. *Luigi's*, Av Daniel L Borja y Brasil, next to La Ibérica Supermarket, T962397. Spanish, Italian and other international dishes. Exclusive, good. Mid-range prices. Open 1000-2300, Sun 1000-1500. *Tambo de Oro*, Zambrano y Junín, near *Hotel El Galpón*, T962668. Smart, expensive, excellent cuisine, good wine list, one of the best places in town. Open 1200-1500.

Italian *Charlie's Pizzería*, García Moreno entre Guayaquil y 10 de Agosto. Great pizza, vegetarian lasagne, cafeteria. Open Mon-Sat 0930-2100, Sun 1600-2100. *La Pizzería de Paolo*, Av Daniel L Borja corner Epiclachima, near the bus station, T949781. Good pizza and pasta, nice ambience. *Mónaco Pizzería*, Diego Ibarra y Av Daniel L Borja, pizza and pasta, open evenings only. *San Valentín Club Pizzería*, Torres y Borja. Good pizzas, excellent chilli and lasagne, good coffee, bar, cable TV, open daily 0800-1700. Popular with local youth. Recommended.

Seafood *Cevichería Esmeraldas*, J Montalvo y Veloz, good, popular. *Cevichería Las Redes*, Primera Constituyente y Carabobo. Set meals and seafood. *La Fuente*, Primera Consituyente s/n y García Moreno, lower ground floor of building housing the *Ministerio de Obras Públicas*. Very good *sopa marinera*, *ceviches* and fish, reasonably priced, open 0900-1300 and 1500-1900. Recommended. *Punto Azul*, Colón y Olmedo. Excellent seafood, open 0800-1500, closed Sun.

Vegetarian *Ashoka*, Carabobo y 10 de Agosto. Varied vegetarian food.

Cafeterias *Chris's Café*, 10 de Agosto near Parque Sucre. Snacks. *Caffe Johnny*, Espejo 22-45 y Primera Constituyente. Breakfast from 0700, good, closed Sun. *Gran Pan*, García Moreno 22-46, near Primera Constituyente. Bakery and *cafetería*, fresh bread, tasty cakes, good coffee and breakfast, opens at 0800. *Panadería Pan Van*, Primera Constituyente y Larrea, near Parque Maldonado. Great variety of quality bread, sweets and dairy products. *Panadería La Vienesa*, J Larrea 21-26 y Guayaquil, excellent bread, pastries, also sell good local cheese. There are also many snackbars along 10 de Agosto. *Pynn's*, Espejo 21-20 y 10 de Agosto, T943259. Coffee, fruit salad, tacos, set lunches. Cheap. Open 0930-2000.

Bars & nightclubs *Gens-Chop Bar*, Av Daniel L Borja 42-17 y Duchicela. Good music, music and sport videos, open daily, popular. Recommended. *PITS Bar*, Av Daniel L Borja y Zambrano. Popular. *VIP*, Pichincha y 10 de Agosto. Peña, bar, folk music on Fri and Sat. The *Casa de la Cultura*, 10 de Agosto y Rocafuerte. Has a *peña* on Fri and Sat evenings. *La Bruja*, Lizarzaburu s/n, Km 1 on the road to Quito. Disco with varied music. Open Thu to Sat. *Unicornio*, St Armand y Av Lizarzaburo, Vía Ambato Km 2, Piano Bar, Salsoteca, open

Thu-Sat. *Vieja Guardia*, Av Flor 40-43 y Av Zambrano. Good bar and disco. *Milenium*, Ciudadela Los Tulipanes, off Av de la Prensa, 3 blocks south of the bus terminal. Disco, pub, international music, popular. *Grin Livs*, Av de La Prensa y Argentinos, disco. *X-Mix*, Ciudadela Las Retamas, near the bus terminal. Disco, varied music, popular, Open Fri-Sat 2000-0200.

Festivals *Fiesta del Niño Rey de Reyes* starts in Dec and culminates on **6 Jan**, with street parades, music and dancing throughout that period. Riobamba's independence day is **21 Apr**, celebrated for several days with lively parades, concerts, bullfights and drinking. Hotel prices rise and rooms may be difficult to find during this period. Festivals to celebrate the *Foundation of Riobamba* take place on **11 Nov**.

Shopping **Crafts** Nice tagua carvings and other crafts are on sale at *Alta Montaña* Av Daniel L Borja y Diego Ibarra, where you can see how the tagua is carved. *El Buho*, Primera Constituyente 36-31 y Brasil, large selection of regional crafts; workshop on the second floor where you can see the artisans at work, open 1000-1900. Also at several shops on 10 de Agosto near the train station. *Almacén Cacha*, Orozco next to the Plaza Roja, a cooperative of native people from the Cacha area, sells woven bags, wool sweaters and other crafts (closed Sun-Mon). **Supermarkets** *La Ibérica*, Av Daniel L Borja 37-62. *Su Comisariato*, Primera Constituyente 25-24 y España. *Camari*, Espejo y Olmedo, opposite La Merced market.

Sports **Ball games** A local ball game, the *mamona*, in which a solid leather ball is hit with the palm of the hand, is played in the afternoons at the Plaza Roja and in San Alfonso on Sun. A game played with marbles can be seen at Parque Barriga on Av Miguel A León. **Climbing and trekking** Riobamba is a good starting point for Chimborazo, Carihuairazo, Altar and Sangay. See Tour operators and Excursions below. **Cockfights** At Gallera San Francisco, Alvarado y Olmedo, Sat at 1500 and during the city's fiestas. **Mountain biking** *Pro Bici*, at Primera Constituyente 23-51 y Larrea, T960189/961877, F961923. Run by guide and mechanic, Galo J Brito, bike trips and rental, guided tours with support vehicle, full equipment (use Cannondale ATBs), US$25-30 per person per day, excluding meals and overnight stays. *Julio Verne* (see Tour operators below), rental US$6/day, tours including transport, guide, meals, US$25/day. **Swimming** There is a spa *CENAEST*, 5 de Junio y Villarroel, several pools kept at different temperatures, gym, cafeteria. Open 0600-1000 and 1600-2200 daily, US$4.

Tour operators Most companies offer climbing trips (from US$180 per person for 2 days) and trekking (from US$50 per person per day). *Alta Montaña*, Av Daniel L Borja 35-17 y Diego Ibarra, T/F942215, aventurag@laserinter.net Trekking, climbing, cycling, running, birdwatching, volcano watching, photography and horse riding tours in mountains and jungle, logistical support for expeditions, transport, equipment rental, English spoken. Recommended. *Andes Trek*, Colón 22-25 y 10 de Agosto, T940964, F940963. Climbing, trekking and mountain biking tours, transport, equipment rental, good rates, English and German spoken. *Coltur*, Av Daniel L Borja y Vargas Torres, T/F940950. Airline tickets. *Expediciones Andinas*, Via a Guano, Km 3, T964915. Climbing expeditions. *Julio Verne*, 5 de Junio 21-46 y 10 de Agosto, T/F963436, julver@interactive.net.ec, www.julioverne-travel.com Climbing, trekking, cycling, jungle and Galapagos trips, volcano watching tours, river rafting, transport to mountains, equipment rental and sale, Ecuadorean-Dutch run, CLTUR certified, uses official guides. Recommended. *Sangay Expediciones* Argentinos 1140 y Darquea, T962681. Recommended for climbing. *Metropolitan Touring*, Av Daniel L Borja 37-64, T969600, F969601. Airline tickets.

Many hotels offer tours, but note that not all are run by qualified guides

Central Highlands

Railway to the Sierra

A spectacular 464 km railway line (1.067 m gauge), which ran from Durán up to Riobamba, was opened in 1908. It passed through 87 km of delta lands and then, in another 80 km, climbed to 3,238 m. The highest point (3,619 m) was reached at Urbina, between Riobamba and Ambato. It then rose and fell before reaching the Quito plateau at 2,857 m. This was one of the great railway journeys of the world and a fantastic piece of railway engineering, with a maximum gradient of 5.5%. Rail lines also ran from Riobamba south to Cuenca, and from Quito north to Ibarra, then down to the coast at San Lorenzo. There were even more ambitious plans, never achieved, to push the railhead deep into the Oriente jungle, from Ambato as far as Leticia (then Ecuador, today Colombia).

Sadly, time and neglect have taken their toll and today only a few short rail segments remain in service as tourist rides: running a few kilometres outside Ibarra, from Quito to Parque Nacional Cotopaxi, and from Riobamba to Alausí and over the Devil's Nose to Sibambe. There has often been talk of reviving the Ecuadorean railway, but as time passes, the tracks rust and the ties rot, that seems like an ever more remote possibility.

Transport

Bus From the main bus terminal: To **Quito**, US$2.95, 3½ hrs, about every 30 mins. To **Guaranda**, US$1.40, 2 hrs; the road is paved to San Juan, from where there are 2 routes, both very scenic: that via Gallo Rumi is unpaved, while the one via the arenal is partly paved (some Flota Bolívar buses take this route), sit on the right for the beautiful views on either route. To **Ambato**, US$0.85, 1 hr, sit on the right. To **Babahoyo** via Guaranda, US$3, 5 hrs. To **Alausí**, US$1.15, 2 hrs. To **Huigra**, US$2.15, 3 hrs. To **Cuenca**, 6 a day via Alausí, 5½ hrs, US$4. This road is paved but landslides are a constant hazard and the road is often under repair. For a day trip to **Ingapirca** (see page 246), take the 0530 bus to Cuenca and get off at El Tambo at about 1000. The bus back to Riobamba passes through El Tambo at about 1600; the last one about 1930. Bus to **Santo Domingo**, hourly, US$3.30, 5 hrs. To **Huaquillas** at 2100 with Patria, avoiding Guayaquil, daily except Tue and Sat, US$5.45, 9 hrs. To **Guayaquil**, about 35 a day, first one leaves at 0600, US$4, 4½ hrs; the trip is really spectacular for the first 2 hrs.

From the Terminal Oriental: To **Baños**, landslides caused by Tungurahua's volcanic activity have closed the direct Baños-Riobamba road until further notice, buses go via Ambato, 2 hrs, US$1.50. To **Puyo**, also via Ambato, US$2.50, 4½ hrs direct.

See also box above **Train** Train service is very limited, but the most spectacular bit – the Devil's Nose and Alausí Loop – can still be experienced. The train leaves Riobamba on Wed, Fri and Sun at 0700, arrives in Alausí around 1000-1030, reaches Sibambe about 1130-1200, and returns to Alausí by 1330-1400. From Riobamba to Sibambe and back to Alausí costs

US$15 for foreigners; round trip from Alausí US$13. Tickets for the 0700 train go on sale on the eve between 1800 and 1900, or the same morning at 0600, seats are not numbered, best arrive early. Riding on the roof is fun, but hang on tight and remember that it's very chilly early in the morning. It's also a good idea to sit as far back on the roof as possible to avoid getting covered in oil from the exhaust. On the days when the train is not running, you can still experience the devil´s nose and the scenery, by walking along the tracks from from Alausí. A pleasant day trip.

The train service is subject to frequent disruptions and timetables are always changing, best enquire locally about current schedules. The railway administration office is on Espejo, next to the Post Office, where information is available during office hours, T960115, or at the station itself T961909.

Metropolitan Touring, (See Tour operators above) operates a private *autoferro* on the Riobamba-Sibambe route. They require a minimum of 20 passengers and will run any day and time convenient to the group.

Banks *Banco del Pacífico*, Av Miguel A León y Veloz, changes only Amex TCs, US$200 maximum; **Directory** Mastercard through ATM only, open 0845-1700. *Banco de Guayaquil*, Primera Constituyente 2626 y García Moreno, cash advances on Visa, 0900-1600. *Vigo Rianxeira*, 10 de Agosto 25-37 y España, T968608, changes all US$ TCs, major American and European currencies in cash only, good rates and friendly service, Mon-Fri 0830-1330 and 1500-1800, Sat 0900-1700. *Casa de Cambios MM Jaramillo Arteaga*, 10 de Agosto y Pichincha, T940669. TCs, major European and American currencies, fair rates, open Mon-Fri 0830-1700, Sat 0900-1300.

Communications Post Office: 10 de Agosto y Espejo, has fax service. **Telephone:** *Andinatel* at Tarqui entre Primera Constituyente y Veloz, 0800-2200. Also at the bus terminal. **Internet:** rates about US$1 per hr. *Andino Café*, Av Daniel L Borja 35-15 y Diego Ibarra, good service, 0900-2100, Sun 1400-2100. *C@fé Ashoka*, Carabobo y 10 de Agosto, 2nd floor, near the train station, also has book exchange, 0800-2130. *Cybernet Café*, Rocafuerte 21-25 y Guayaquil, pleasant atmosphere, 0900-2100, closed Sun. *Internet Café*, Rocafuerte 22-30 y 10 de Agosto, 2nd floor, 1000-1300 and 1430-2200, often crowded. *Le Monde.net*, Pichincha 21-11 y Guayaquil, 2nd floor, 0800-2100.

Laundry *Café Ashoka*, Carabobo y 10 de Agosto, US$0.60/kg.

Useful addresses Immigration: *Jefatura Provincial de Migración*, is at España 20-50, y Guayaquil, T964697. Open Mon-Fri 0800-1200 and 1500-1800. **Ministerio del Ambiente:** For information about Parque Nacional Sangay, Av 9 de Octubre y Quinta Macají, at the western edge of town, north of the roundabout at the end of Av Isabel de Godin, T963779. Park people are only in the office in the early morning, be there before 0800. From town take a city bus San Gerardo-El Batán.

Excursions

Guano is a sisal-working, leather and carpet-weaving town of 10,000 inhabitants 8 km to the north. There are lovely views of El Altar from the plaza. Chimborazo and Tungurahua can also be seen from a nearby hilltop, try to spot the primitive stone carvings as you walk up. Rugs have been produced here since colonial times when, under the *encomiendas* system, local Indian slaves were trained in this art. You can have rugs made to your own design. There are a number of shops selling rugs, leather goods, and other crafts. You can see how the rugs are made on Calle Asunción, the road that comes in from Riobamba. The town holds a Sunday market and is very quiet other days. **G** *Residencial La Chilenita*, Tomás Ramírez y Juan Montalvo, across from the market, hot water, some rooms with private bath. *Oasis*, at the main park. Set meals and snacks, seriously cheap. Buses for Guano leave from the Mercado Dávalos, García Moreno y New York, every 20 minutes 0600-2200, US$0.10, last bus returns to Riobamba at 1800. Taxi US$2.

After Guano you can take the bus on to Santa Teresita from where it is a 20 minute walk downhill to **Balneario Los Helenes**, with three pools; one tepid, two icy. Camping is possible nearby. There are superb views of El Altar and Tungurahua as you walk through the surrounding pasture land.

In **Cacha**, a small Indian town southwest of Riobamba, the descendants of the indigenous ruling family still live. There have been many articles and books written about the 'Daquilemas'. Textiles and excellent honey are produced here and sold in the Sunday market.

Climbing and trekking around Riobamba

Riobamba is a good starting point for many climbing and trekking expeditions. Chimborazo, Carihuairazo, El Altar, Sangay, Tungurahua, and the Inca Trail to Ingapirca can all be accessed from here. Tour agencies in Riobamba offer transport and trips to all the attractions, see Tour operators above. See also the sections on Climbing (on page 65) and Trekking (on page 68).

Chimborazo At 6,310 m, this is a difficult climb owing to the altitude. No one without mountaineering experience should attempt the climb, and rope, ice-axe and crampons must be used. Acclimatization is esential and the best season is December and June-September. There are two routes up the mountain: the **southwest face** and **northwest face**.

Guides Sr Héctor Vásquez at Colegio Nacional Bolívar, Ambato, has helped many expeditions with travel arrangements and information; he is a top-grade mountaineer. There is a provincial association of mountain guides, Asociación de Andiniso de Chimborazo, which registers approved guides. Some guides who have been recommended are: *Enrique Veloz Coronado* , technical adviser of the Asociación de Andinismo de Chimborazo, Chile 33-21 y Francia, T960916, he is best reached after 1500 and is very helpful, his sons are also guides and work with him. *Marcelo Puruncajas* of *Andes Trek* (see Tour operators above), member of ASEGUIM, highly recommended, speaks English, when not leading tours uses good guides (including his son who speaks German), also offers trekking, four-wheel drive transport and mountain biking. *Silvio Pesántez* of Sangay Expediciones, he is a member of ASEGUIM, an experienced climber and adventure-tour leader, speaks French, recommended. *Marco Cruz* of *Expediciones Andinas* (see Tour companies above), T962845 (house), he is a certified guide of the German Alpine Club and considered among the best and most expensive guides, recommended. *Rodrigo Donoso* of *Alta Montaña* (see Tour companies above), for climbing and a variety of trekking and horse riding trips, speaks English well.

Trekking including guide, transport, equipment, shelter and food will cost US$40-50 per person per day, minimum two persons. Climbing with guides who belong to the Asociación de Andinismo costs about US$140 per person per day.

Youngsters of the communities of Pulinguí San Pablo and La Chorrera, 15 km north of San Juan, along the arenal road, are being trained as *guías nativos*, native guides who lead visitors to the attractions at the base of Chimborazo for US$5 per person per day.

The southwest face From the Whymper refuge to the summit the climb is eight to nine hours and the descent about four hours. The path from the hut to the glacier is marked but difficult to follow at midnight, so it's best to check it out the day before. The route on the glacier is easy to follow as it is marked with flags, though it can be tricky in cloud or mist. There are several crevasses on the route, so you need to rope up. There are three routes depending on your experience and ability. It is recommended to go with a guide and start at 2400 or 0100. There are avalanche problems on the entire mountain.

Getting there   The refuge is 56 km from Riobamba and takes about 1½ hrs. Access is through the scenic *arenal* road, which joins San Juan, on the Riobamba-Guaranda road, with the Ambato-Guaranda road, to the north. Vicuñas can be seen along this route. There are no direct buses so arrange transport with a travel agency, or for a similar price take a taxi from Riobamba; US$35 for 5-6 hrs, US$40 return next day or later, US$20 one way. There are usually several taxis and other vehicles at the car park in the early afternoon. A recommended driver is Segundo López, Taxi 89, found at the taxi stand in Mercado Santa Rosa, Av Guayaquil y Rocafuerte, Riobamba; also Juan Fuenmayor, Veloz 25-31 y España, or arrange through Riobamba hotels. You can also take a Guaranda bound bus which takes the *arenal* route (ask, as not all go this way), alight at the turnoff for the refuge and hitch from there (better chance at the weekend) or walk the remaining steep 5 km and 440 m up.

Entrance fee   Chimborazo lies within the **Reserva de Producción de Fauna Chimborazo**. A US$10 entrance fee is charged at the turnoff for the refuges, from the *arenal* road.

Sleeping   The road ends at 4,800 m, at a large white building, the Hermanos Carrel refuge. It has a guard, bunk beds with mattresses for 8, includes 1 private room for 2, dining area, cooking facilities, running water, toilet, electricity, bring food and warm gear, it gets very cold at night. In about 45 mins you can walk up to the Edward Whymper refuge, a pink building at 5,000 m, which is at the foot of the Thielman glacier. The same facilities are available here, with capacity for 40, in 5 separate rooms. Both refuges are managed by *Alta Montaña* and a US$0.50 fee is charged for a day visit. Overnight stays are US$10 but card carrying members of a club or Youth Hostel Association pay less. Take padlock for the small lockers under the bunks; the guards also have a locked room for valuables, and you can leave your gear with them. If there are only a few people, you will be given the key to your room.

In Totorillas, 7 km south of the turnoff for the refugios is *Base Camp*, in a lovely valley at the foot of Chimborazo, you must make advance arrangements through *Expediciones Andinas* in Riobamba. The views are stunning. In the hamlet of Puiguí San Pablo, 1 km away, is **G** per person *Casa Cóndor*, the local community centre with a couple of rooms and bunk beds, hot shower, use of kitchen (extra) or simple meals on request.

NB Be careful with your belongings in the shelters, parked cars and throughout this area. Some thefts were reported in the past, but the situation appears to have improved with the presence of tourist police.

Getting there   Take the Guaranda bus from Ambato along the new paved road or a truck along the spectacular old road (50 km) to the valley of Pogyos. At Pogyos (4,000 m) there is a house with a metal roof where you can hire mules for US$4 each to carry your luggage. Beware of pilfering from your bags on the ascent. Walk about 3 hrs to the Fabián Zurita refuge (4,900 m) which is uninhabitable. From the refuge to the summit is about an 8-hr climb and 3-4 hrs, descent. It's advisable to start at 2330-2400 at the latest. Take tents and water (obtainable at Pogyos, containers in Ambato). (We are grateful to Enrique Veloz Coronado, page 236, for much of this information.) **The northwest face (Pogyos route)**

From Riobamba to the northwest face, a trip can be made by jeep via San Juan and a road to Arenal, which is west of Pogyos. This road also permits a round-trip Riobamba-Chimborazo-Ambato.

A good area to access Chimborazo for trekking is along the high *páramo* between its eastern slopes and Igualata. There are many walking opportunities here and it is a good area for acclimatization. You can make an excursion (Tuesday, Thursday and Friday) to see the *hieleros* who bring ice blocks down **The eastern slopes**

Central Highlands

from the glacier to sell in the Riobamba market (Riobamba agencies offer this tour). Horses can be hired in **Urbina** and at the village of **12 de Octubre** to the north, ask for Daniel Villacís.

Getting there Urbina is 2 km west of the Panamericana, about half-way between Ambato and Riobamba. The turnoff from the main highway is signed.

Sleeping F per person *Posada de la Estación*, T/F942215 (Riobamba), aventurag@ laserinter.net With shared bath, hot water, good food, dinning room with fireplace. A pleasant inn located in the converted railway station of Urbina. Clean, cold at night, tours, slide shows when the owner is in. Recommended.

El Altar

El Altar is part of Sangay National Park (see below), the most popular trek is to its crater. **NB** In October 2000 an exceptionally large avalanche dammed the outflow of El Altar's crater lake. When this dike burst, the resulting flow of water and debris roared through the Collanes plain leaving much destruction in its wake. Enquire as to current conditions before trekking in this area.

The track (muddy in the wet season) leads on up a steep hill past the *Hacienda Releche* (see below). It is a well-used track and there are small signs at the only two turnings on the route. The track leads up a hill to a ridge where it joins a clearer track. This goes south first and then turns east up the valley of the Río Collanes. It is about six hours to the Collanes plain and another two hours to the crater which is surrounded by magnificent snow-capped peaks. It is possible to camp in the crater, but better still, about 20 minutes before you turn into the broad U-shaped valley leading up to the crater there is a good-sized cave, the floor of which is lined with dry reeds; there is a fire ring at the entrance.

Guides and horses to El Altar can be hired; the approximate cost per day is US$50 for a guide, US$5 per mule, US$5 per porter. Consult the National Park Office in Riobamba about conditions, they are in radio contact with the Guardería at Releche.

Getting there Don't confuse the mountain with the village of the same name. There is an El Altar signpost on the Riobamba-Baños road but this is not the normal route to the mountain. The most used access route is from Penipe, which can be reached by bus from Baños (but note that in late 2000 this road was closed) or Riobamba. From there go to Candelaria by truck, or by bus which passes between 1200 and 1400. Walk out of the village, cross the bridge and go up about 2 km to the park station, a green building with a National Park sign, where you pay your entrance fee of US$10. In Penipe ask for Ernesto Haro, who will take you to the station in his jeep (US$8 one way) and pick you up from there at a pre-arranged time.

Technical climbs For experienced ice climbers the **Ruta Obispo** offers grade 4 and 5 mixed ice and rock. Cima El Obispo is the highest and most southerly of Altar's nine summits, at 5,315 m. Take the turn-off at Cruz de Chania (on the Riobamba-Baños road) to Puelazo. Walk or hire mules (in Puelazo or Inguisay) to the Cañon del Tiaco Chico and beyond to Machay del Negro Paccha (cave). You can camp at the Italian base camp beyond. Another technical route is to **Cima El Canónigo** (5,260 m), the northernmost of the summits. It is mixed ice and rock climbing, grade four and five. Altar's seven other summits are, from north to south: Fraile Grande (5,180 m); Fraile Central (5,070 m); Fraile Oriental (5,060 m); Fraile Beato (5,050 m); Tabernáculo (5,100 m); Monja Chica (5,080 m); and Monja Grande (5,160 m).

F per person *Hostal Capac Urcu* At Hacienda Releche, T03-949761 or 03-960848 (Riobamba). With bath, hot water, use of kitchen (extra) or good meals on request, horses for rent. Pleasant and relaxing. Recommended. You may be able to stay in the park station overnight, although it is not a *refugio*; US$0.50, beds, warm water, shower, cooking facilities and friendly keeper. It is not always open, so it's a good idea to ask in Riobamba beforehand at the the Ministerio del Ambiente office (see Useful addresses above).

Sangay

It is 5,230 m high and lies within **Parque Nacional Sangay**. Access to the mountain takes seven days and is only for those who can endure long, hard days of walking and severe weather. Protection against falling stones is vital. Mecánica Acosta, Plaza Arenas, Quito (near the Basílica), will make shields, arm loops welded to an oil drum top, for US$2-3. December/January is a good time to climb Sangay. Agencies in Quito and Riobamba offer tours or you can organize an expedition independently. A guide is essential. Porters can be hired in the access town of Alao, reached by taxi from Riobamba. Remember you have to provide and organize food for guides and porters. Make sure the fee covers the return journey as well. South American Explorers has further information on organizing a trip, see page 22, also contact the Ministerio del Ambiente in Riobamba (see Useful addresses above). A US$10 charge must be paid in Alao office in Riobamba.

Sangay is one of the most active volcanoes in the world. It can be dangerous even on a quiet day

For the lowland access to Parque Nacional Sangay see page 239.

South of Riobamba

In 1534 the original Riobamba was founded on this site, but in 1797 a disastrous earthquake caused a large section of the hill on the north side of the town to collapse in a great landslide, which can still be seen. It killed several thousand of the original inhabitants of Riobamba and the town was moved almost 20 km northeast to its present site. The new Riobamba has prospered, but Cajabamba has stagnated and is now a small, rather poor town. A colourful, Colta Indian market on Sunday is small but uncommercialized and interesting. The town is easily reached by bus from Riobamba, 25 minutes, US$0.15. There are few restaurants out of town on the Panamericana towards Cuenca.

Cajabamba

A fairly good dirt road leaves the Panamericana 8 km north of Cajabamba, to the west. Known as the Gallo Rumi road, it is one of the oldest of the coast-Sierra routes and links Riobamba with Guaranda and Babahoyo. Five kilometres south of Cajabamba, a paved highway branches southwest to Pallatanga, Bucay, Milagro and Guayaquil.

The road and railway skirt the shores of **Laguna de Colta**, just after the fertile Cajabamba valley. The lake and surroundings are very beautiful and just a short bus trip from Riobamba. At the edge of the village along the main road on the shore of Laguna de Colta is a small chapel, **La Balbanera**, dating from 1534, making it the oldest church in Ecuador, although it has been restored several times because of earthquakes.

Twenty eight kilometres south of Cajabamba is Guamote. It has an interesting and colourful market on Thursday with lots of animals and few tourists, and some good half day walks in the area. There is **F** Hostal *Turista*, at the railway station and **F** *Ramada Inn*, Vela y Riobamba, T916242. There are some places to eat near the station. Many buses from Riobamba, especially on Thursday. Trucks run daily on the unfinished road to Macas (see page 381), which cuts through Parque Nacional Sangay and gives great views of the volcanoes.

Guamote
Altitude: 3,056 m

South of Guamote is **Tixán**, which has a beautifully restored church and many old houses. It is the home of many workers in the nearby sulphur mines. The San Juan Bautista celebrations around June 24 are very colourful.

Osogoche
This is a wild, cold and beautiful area of three large lakes with spectacular mountains towering overhead

Between Guamote and Tixán is the well-signed turnoff to Osogoche, 32 km further on. There are good hiking trails leading north and south. The hike to/from the paved road takes at least five hours across windswept *páramos* with views of Sangay on clear days. The Indians here still live in *chozas* (grass huts) and dress in traditional bright colours. Arrange pack animals and guides with the local community leader, but take all food (none is available) and camping equipment. The best season is November to early March. A small road connects this area with Achupallas (see Inca trail to Ingapirca, page 247).

Alausí

*Population: 5,500
Colour map 4, grid C5*

Eighty four kilometres south of Riobamba, Alausí is the station where many passengers join the train for the amazing descent to Sibambe, via the famous Alausí loop and *Nariz del Diablo* (Devil's Nose). There is also a road which goes from here to the northern Pacific lowlands through Huigra (several basic lodgings and restaurants). The town sits at the foot of Cerro Gampala, on a terrace overlooking the deep Chanchán gorge. The atmosphere is laid-back and friendly. Don't expect too much in the way of exciting diversions, though the Sunday market, in the plaza by the church, just up the hill from the station, brings *campesinos* from the outlying villages and is colourful and interesting. The town celebrates its *fiesta, San Pedro de Alausí,* in late June. The area enjoys a temperate climate and was once a popular holiday destination for Guayaquileños wishing to escape their hottest season.

Sleeping
G *Americano*, García Moreno 159, T930159. Modern, private bath, hot water, friendly, small, recommended as the best in town. **G** *Gampala*, 5 de Junio 122, T930138. With bath, restaurant, good. **G** *Residencial Alausí*, Orozco y 5 de Junio, T930361. Near the coliseo, with bath, **H** without, clean, comfortable, restaurant, one of the best in town. **G** *Residencial Tequendama*. Includes breakfast, clean, friendly, shared bath, hot water, erratic electric shower, and eccentric owners, quieter rooms upstairs. Recommended. Opposite *Residencial Tequendama* is **G** *Europa*. Check that the hot water is free, safe parking in courtyard. **G** *Panamericano*, near the bus stop on the main street, T930156. Has several nice rooms with bath, also with shared bath, quieter at the rear of the hotel, constant hot water, clean, food cheap and good value. **H** *Residencial Guayaquil*, C Eloy Alfaro 149, beside the rail tracks and behind the station. Very noisy, basic, not too clean, friendly.

Eating
Alausí is not the culinary centre of Ecuador, but a few places serve decent meals, prices are cheap: *San Juan*, near the station, on the main street. Owner speaks English, helpful staff, good breakfast and other food. *Gampala*, at the hotel, set meals and à la carte, vegetarian on request, open 0700-0000. *Danielito*, opposite *Tequendama*. Popular for breakfast, will cook vegetarian meals, friendly. *El Flamingo*, behind the *Tequendama*. Good set meals, popular for lunch.

Transport
Buses To/from **Riobamba**, 1½ hrs, US$1, 84 km, all paved. To **Quito**, buses from Cuenca pass through from 0600 onwards, about 20 a day, 5½ hrs, US$3.10; often have to change in Riobamba. To **Cuenca**, 5 hrs, US$3.20. To **Cañar**, US$3. To **Ambato** hourly, 3 hrs, US$1.35. To **Huigra**, 1 hr, US$2. *Coop Patria* has a small office where you can buy bus tickets to Guayaquil, Cuenca, or Riobamba. Other cooperatives have no office, but their buses pass through town, some at the highway and others outside the *Hotel Panamericano*.

Trains The train to Sibambe runs Wed, Fri and Sun. It leaves Riobamba about 0700, arrives Alausí around 1100, gets to Sibambe almost an hour later, stops there for about 15 mins and returns to Alausí about 1330 for a lunch stop, returning to Riobamba at about 1700. Riobamba-Sibambe-Alausí or Alausí-Sibambe-Riobamba costs US$15. Alausí-Sibambe-Alausí US$13. Tickets go on sale at 1030. Further information at the station, T930126. US$13

Chunchi At 2,300 m, 37 km south of Alausí along the Panamericana, is a friendly village with a Sunday market. From here you can hike or cycle down the Huigra road to Chanchán, a scenic area. **G** *Residencial Patricia*, just off the main plaza. Shared bath, basic, clean, beware of overcharging. **H** *Residencial Carmita*, near the station. Clean, basic, hot water. **H** *Residencial Villa Esther*, Av Chimborazo 733, one block from the closed station, T936125. Basic, friendly, helpful, small restaurant. There are many restaurants along the highway, which are better than those in Alausí. Buses leave from the plaza, several daily, to Riobamba.

Southern Highlands

6

Southern Highlands

The Southern Highlands, comprising the provinces of Cañar, Azuay and Loja, may lack the dramatic volcanic peaks of the central and northern highlands, but compensate with their own unique attractions. Within their bounds are Ecuador's prime Inca site, one of its most spectacular national parks, and Cuenca, the focal point of the region, which boasts some of the country's finest colonial architecture. The Cuenca basin, in the northern part of the region, is a major artesanía *centre, producing ceramics, baskets, gold and silver jewellery, textiles and the famous Panama hat, made principally in Cuenca itself, Gualaceo and Girón.*

In addition to the cultural attractions mentioned above, its pleasant climate and magnificent mountain scenery make the Southern Highlands ideal walking country, while undisturbed páramo *and cloud forest are home to many birds and other wildlife.*

Ingapirca

Ecuador's most important Inca ruin lies between Alausí and Cuenca 8½ km east of Cañar, at 3,160 m. Access is from Cañar or El Tambo. ■ *Daily 0900-1800. Entry to the site is US$5, including entry to the site museum and a guided tour in Spanish. They sell a guide book, US$0.80, and will look after your belongings. An audio-visual guide in English is available, and there are guides at the site, as well as some photogenic llamas.*

Though famed as a classic Inca site, Ingapirca, which translates as 'Wall of the Inca', had already been occupied by the native Cañari people for 500 years. It is also known as 'Jatun Cañar', place of the Cañaris. The Inca Huayna Capac took over the site from the conquered Cañaris when his empire expanded North into Ecuador in the third quarter of the 15th century. Ingapirca was strategically placed on the Royal Highway that ran from Cusco to Quito and soldiers were stationed there to keep the troublesome Cañaris under control.

The site, first described by the Frenchman Charles-Marie de la Condamine in 1748, shows typical imperial Cusco-style architecture, such as tightly fitting stonework and trapezoidal doorways, which can be seen on the 'Castillo' and 'Governor's House'. The central structure is an *usnu* platform probably used as a solar observatory.

There is some debate as to Ingapirca's precise function. Though commonly known as a fortress complex, this is contradicted by some archaeologists. From what remains of the site, it probably consisted of storehouses, baths and dwellings for soldiers and other staff, suggesting it could have been a Royal Tambo, or Inn. It could also have been used as a sun temple, judging by the beautiful ellipse, modelled on the Qoricancha in Cusco. Furthermore, John Hemming has noted that the length is exactly three times the diameter of the semicircular ends, which may have been connected with worship of the sun in its morning, midday and afternoon positions. Perhaps then Ingapirca was actually all three: a fortress, a tambo and a sun temple.

A 10 minute walk away from the site is the **Cara del Inca** (face of the Inca), an immense natural formation in the rock looking over the landscape. Nearby is a throne cut into the rock, the **Sillón de Inga** (Inca's Chair) and the **Ingachugana**, a large rock with carved channels. This may have been used for offerings and divination with water, *chicha* or the blood of various sacrificial animals.

One kilometre down the hill off the road to Ingapirca, or 30 minutes' walk along the disused rail line from El Tambo, are the Inca ruins called **Baños del Inca**. This massive rock outcrop has been carved to form baths, showers, water channels and seats overlooking a small plaza or amphitheatre. It's been cleaned up recently and is worth visiting.

On Friday there is an interesting Indian market in the village at Ingapirca. There is a good co-operative craft shop next to the church.

Sleeping & eating
Water supply is poor after midday

B *Posada Ingapirca*, 500 m from the site, T07-290670, or T838508 in Cuenca. Eight luxurious rooms with bath, heating, includes American breakfast, good restaurant and well stocked bar, lunch around US$10, good wine list. In a converted farm, good service, superb views. Warmly recommended. **G** *Inti Huasi*, at the entrance to the the village, T290767. Clean, nice rooms, quiet, hot water, restaurant. **G** *Posada del Sol*, next to Inti Huasi. Clean, restaurant, OK. **G** *Pensión Huasipungo*, in the village.

El Tambo This is situated on the Panamericana 8 km northwest of Ingapirca and is one of the access towns for the ruins. **G** *Pensión Ingapirca* on the main street, at the north end of town, by the turnoff for Ingapirca. hot water, not too clean but friendly, very noisy, can leave luggage for a small fee. **H** *Pensión Estefanía*, on main street, T233126. Shared bath, hot water, friendly.' *Restaurant El Turista*, good and cheap food but unfriendly. Also good is *Restaurant Ingapirca* and *Restaurant Jesús del Gran Poder*, at the truck stop on the hill 400 m north of town, sees more movement than those in the centre. There are several others. Judge the quality by their popularity with truck drivers. There is a small Saturday food market.

Transport A direct bus from the Terminal Terrestre in Cuenca leaves at 0900 daily and 1300 Mon-Fri, returning at 1300 and 1600, 2 hrs, US$1.20, with Transportes Cañar. There are also organized excursions and taxi tours from Cuenca (US$40 from bus terminal). Alternatively take any Guayaquil, Riobamba or Quito bus and get off at El Tambo, 2 hrs, US$1.10. There is a daily 0600 bus from Cañar direct to Ingapirca and a 4 wheel drive can be hired in Cañar for US$2 per person, enquire at Residencial Mónica (slower, rougher road than from El Tambo). From the plaza on the Panamericana in El Tambo, there are regular buses to the ruins with Transportes Ingapirca, about one per hour. A taxi El Tambo-Ingapirca is US$5; camionetas are US$1, but beware of over-charging, especially at the plaza. Taxis can also be caught at the railway station. The last colectivos leave Ingapirca at 1800 for El Tambo. It is a beautiful 2½-hr (16 km) walk from Ingapirca to Cañar. The start of the road is clearly signposted, along the main street; take water.

Inca trail to Ingapirca

The three day hike to Ingapirca on an Inca trail starts at **Achupallas**, 25 km from Alausí. The IGM map (Juncal sheet, 1:50,000) is very useful; also a compass. The name Ingapirca does not appear on the Cañar 1:50,000 sheet and you may have to ask directions near the end. There are persistent beggars, especially children, the length of the hike. If you want to give them something, take pencils or something useful. See Responsible tourism, page 42. Good camping equipment is essential. Take all food and drink with you as there is nothing along the way. A shop in Achupallas sells basic foodstuffs and on Saturday you can buy provisions at the market.

Getting there A truck leaves Alausí almost every day, between 0900-1200 from outside *Residencial Tequendama*, US$0.40 to Achupallas. Transport is more frequent on Sat for the market. The trip takes a couple of hours and is spectacular in its own right. Or take any bus along the Panamericana to **La Moya**, south of Alausí, at the turnoff for Achupallas. Here is **F** *Residencial*, with bath, hot water, new in 2000. Pick-up trucks go from here to Achupallas.

The route
Numbers below correspond to the numbers on the route map, page 248

1 Head for the arch with a cross at the top of the village. Follow the trail to the left of the arch and you'll soon pass the cemetery on the right.
2 The track then deteriorates into a stony footpath and crosses the first footbridge. Continue on the trail which follows alongside the river.
3 About 45 minutes out of the village cross the river again on another footbridge and follow the left bank of the Río Cadrul. Head for a pass ahead between **Cerro Mapahuiña** to the left (4,365 m) and **Cerro Callana Pucará** to the right.
4 At the pass there is an awkward climb over what looks like a huge rockfall. This involves squeezing through a very tight gap, too narrow for you and your backpack at the same time.
5 Soon after you need to cross the river to meet the trail on the other side. In the dry season it can be jumped.
6 About 200 m further on the trail starts to leave the river and climb diagonally up the mountain. There is enough flat ground near the river to pitch a tent for the night, if you're not up to the steep climb.

7 The trail climbs to 4,000 m before following the contours of the west side of the valley.

8 Several kilometres later the trail reaches **Laguna Las Tres Cruces**. From the previous camping spot it is about four to six hours. There are places to camp here.

9 Follow the trail beyond the lake and across the pass. Beyond the pass the trail is not very clear. It crosses some worn rocks and then climbs steeply to the top of the left hand ridge. The views from here are stupendous and make the previous day's hard walking suddenly seem worthwhile.

10 Walk along the top of the ridge to the peak of **Quilloloma**. The trail becomes clear again and then descends sharply to the lush, marshy valley floor below. You can see the vestiges of the old Inca road running in a straight line across the valley floor to the remains of the foundations of an Inca bridge.

11 Follow the Inca road to the river which you have to cross. The best place is a little upstream from the bridge, where it may be narrow enough to jump.

12 There is a clear trail on the left hand side of the **Quebrada Espíndola** which leads past the southern shores of **Laguna Culebrillas** and to a ruined house.

13 It is a comfortable day's hike from Laguna Las Tres Cruces to the ruined house. This is a good place to camp but don't leave your rubbish to accumulate with the rest, especially as part of the house is still, surprisingly, inhabited. The name of the ruined house is **Paredones de Culebrillas** (or simply Paredones).

14 From the ruined house to the ruins of Ingapirca is a steady five to six hours, leaving you enough time to explore the ruins and then find a room for the night. Head southwest on the Inca road, which is at its full width of about 6-7 m. After a short while the trail turns south and continues across the marshy ground, through a landscape strewn with giant boulders.

15 After two to three hours the trail fades out again. Walk in a southerly direction, keeping to the right and as high as possible above the river valley. Eventually you should see signs of cultivation and habitation.

16 Pick up the trail (not the Inca road) and follow it past fields and houses to a road which winds its way up to the ruins of Ingapirca.

The Inca trail to Ingapirca

Achupallas

To Alausí

Cerro Callana Pucará

Cerro Mapahuiña

Río Cadrul

Laguna Las Tres Cruces

Laguna Sansahuín

Quilloloma

Quebrada Espíndola

Laguna Culebrillas

Paredones de Culebrillas

Ingapirca Ruins

Ingapirca Village

Río Cañar

N

0 km 3
0 miles 3

Source: Bradt, *Climbing and hiking in Ecuador*

Galápagos Wildlife

Brown Pelican
(Pelicanus occidentalis)

Right: Land Iguana (Conolphus pallidus *or* subcristatus). *Though less gregarious since the outlawing of feeding by visitors, the land iguana remains a friendly little chap and can be seen at close quarters.*

Above: Marine Iguana (Amblyrynchus cristatus). *This endemic species could be as much as nine million years old, even older than the islands existing today.* ***Right and top left***: Giant Tortoise (Geochelone elephantopus). *The oldest inhabitant of the island is thought to be 170 years old.*

Reptiles

The reptiles found on the Galápagos are represented by five families: **iguanas**, **lava lizards**, **geckos**, **snakes** and, of course, the **giant tortoises**. Of the 27 species of reptiles on the islands, 17 are endemic.

The Galápagos and the Seychelles are the only two island groups in the world which are inhabited by giant tortoises. The name Galápagos derives from the subspecies Saddleback tortoise (*galápago* means saddle). Fourteen subspecies of tortoise have been discovered on the islands, though now only 11 survive, including Lonesome George, a subspecies all by himself.

Giant Tortoises
Geochelone
elephantopus

No one knows the maximum age of these huge reptiles, though the oldest inhabitant of the Darwin Research Station may be as old as 170 (old enough to have met Darwin himself). Perhaps this longevity is due to their living a peaceful life, free from the stresses of modern living. Basically, all they do is eat, sleep and mate.

This latter activity takes place during the wet season from January to March. Later, between February and May, the females head down to the coast to search for a suitable nesting area. The female digs a nest about 30cm deep, lays between three and 16 eggs - depending on the species - then covers them with a protective layer of urine and excrement. Three to eight months later, the eggs hatch, usually between mid-January and March.

In the past, the tortoise population on the islands was estimated at 250,000, but during the 17th and 18th centuries thousands were taken aboard whaling ships. Their ability to survive long periods without food and water made them the ideal source of fresh meat on long voyages. Black rats, feral dogs and pigs, introduced to the islands by pirates, also affected the population by feeding on their eggs and young, until, in 1980, only 15,000 remained.

The Darwin Research Station is now rearing young in captivity for re-introduction into the wild, giving visitors the opportunity to see them close up. To see them in the wild, you can go to the tortoise reserve on Santa Cruz, visit the Los Galápagos site on San Cristóbal or make the long climb up to Volcán Alcedo on Isabela, the island with the largest tortoise population.

Of the eight species of marine turtles in the world only one is found on the islands - the Pacific green turtle. Mating turtles are a common sight around December and January, especially in the Caleta Tortuga Negra, at the northern tip of Santa Cruz. Egg laying usually takes place between January and June, when the female comes ashore to dig a hole and lay 80-120 eggs under cover of darkness. The white sand beach on Floreana is a popular egg-laying spot. After about two months the hatchlings make the hazardous trip across the beach towards the sea, also after dark, in order to avoid the predatory crabs, herons, frigates and lava gulls on the lookout for a midnight feast.

Marine Turtles
Chelonia mydas

This prehistoric-looking endemic species is the only sea-going lizard in the world. The marine iguana is, in fact, from another era. It could be as much as nine million years old, making it even older than the islands existing today. They are found along the coasts of most islands and gather in huge herds on the lava rocks. They vary greatly in size, from 60 centimetres for the smallest variety (Genovesa island) up to one metre for the largest (Isabela island). Their black skin acts as camouflage and allows the iguana to absorb more heat during its exposure to the fierce equatorial sun, although those on

Marine Iguanas
Amblyrynchus
cristatus

***Below**: Land Iguana (Conolphus pallidus or subscristatus). **Right**: Red-footed booby (Sula sula). The only Galápagos booby to nest in trees, thanks to the fact that its feet are adapted to gripping branches.*

***Above**: Galápagos penguin (Spheniscus mendiculus). Although distinctly ungraceful on land, underwater these penguins are speedy and agile and can be seen breaking the surface, like dolphins.*
***Right**: Blue-footed booby (Sula nebouxii). These boobies are best known for their comical and complicated courtship 'dance'.*

Española have red and green colouration. The marine iguana's flat tail is ideal for swimming. But though they can dive to depths of 20 m, and can stay underwater for up to one hour at a time, they prefer to feed on the seaweed on exposed rocks at low tide. Overzealous photographers should note that they frequently spray a salt excess through their nostrils to warn off any unwanted intruders.

There are officially two species of land iguana found on the islands: *conolphus subcristatus* is yellow-orange coloured and inhabits Santa Cruz, Plaza, Isabela and Fernandina islands, while the other, *conolphus pallidus*, is whitish to chocolate brown and found only on Santa Fé. The latter is the biggest land iguana, with the male weighing six to seven kilograms and over a metre in length. Their numbers have been greatly reduced over the years as the young often fall prey to rats and feral animals; the chances of survival for a young land iguana in the wild is less than 10 per cent. Though less gregarious since the outlawing of feeding by visitors, the land iguana remains a friendly little chap and can be seen at close quarters. It now feeds mainly on the fruits and yellow flowers of the prickly pear cactus.

Land Iguana *Conolphus pallidus* or *subcristatus*

Birds

Sea birds were probably the first animals to colonize the archipelago. Half of the resident population of birds is endemic to the Galápagos, but only five of the 19 species of sea birds found on the Galápagos are unique to the islands. These are: the Galápagos penguin, the flightless cormorant, the lava gull, the swallowtail gull and the waved albatross. The endemism rate of land birds is much higher, owing to the fact that they are less often migratory. There are 29 species of land birds in the Galápagos, 22 of which are endemic.

This is the most northerly of the world's penguin species and breeds on Fernandina and Isabela islands, where the Humboldt Current cools the sea. The penguin population is small (under 1,000 in 2000) and fluctuates in response to the El Niño cycle. They may appear distinctly ungraceful on land, hopping clumsily from rock to rock, but underwater they are fast and agile swimmers and can be seen breaking the surface, like dolphins. The best time to see them in the water is between five and seven o'clock in the morning.

Galápagos penguin *Spheniscus mendiculus*

This is one of the rarest birds in the world, with an estimated population of 800 pairs. It is found only on Fernandino island and the west coast of Isabela, where the nutrient-rich Cromwell Current brings a plentiful supply of fish from the central Pacific. Though it has lost the ability to fly, partly due to the lack of predators, the cormorant still insists on spreading its wings to dry in the wind, proving that old habits die hard.

Flightless Cormorant *Nannopetrum harrisi*

The largest bird in the Galápagos, with a wing span of 2½ m, is a cousin of the petrels and the puffins. It is not only endemic to the archipelago but also to the island of Española, for this is the only place in the world where it breeds. Outside the April to December breeding season, the albatross spends its time gliding majestically across the Pacific Ocean, sometimes as far as Japan. It returns after six months to begin the spectacular courtship display, a cross between an exotic dance and fencing duel, which is repeated over and over again. Not surprisingly perhaps, given the effort put into this ritual, albatrosses stay faithful to their mate for life.

Waved Albatross *Dimeda irrorata*

Both the Great Frigatebird, *Fregata minor*, and Magnificent Frigatebird, *Fregata magnificens*, are found on the Galápagos. These 'vultures of the sea' have a wingspan as big as that of the albatross and spend much of their time aloft, gliding in circles with

Frigatebird

their distinctive long forked tail and angled wings. Having lost the waterproofing of its black plumage, the frigate never lands on the sea, instead it pursues other birds – in particular boobies - and harasses them for food, or catches small fish on the surface of the water with its hooked beak. During the courtship display, the male of both species inflates a huge red sac under its throat, like a heart-shaped scarlet balloon, and flutters its spread wings. This seduces and attracts the female to the nest, which the male has already prepared for the purpose of mating. This amazing ritual can be seen in March and April on San Cristóbal and Genovesa, or throughout the year on North Seymour.

Unlike the Great Frigatebird, the Magnificent Frigatebird is an 'inshore feeder' and feeds near the islands. It is very similar in appearance, but the male has a purple sheen on its plumage and the female has a black triangle on the white patch on her throat.

Boobies These are very common in the islands. Three species are found in the Galápagos: the blue-footed, red-footed and masked booby. The name is thought to derive from their extreme tameness, which led to many being killed for sport in earlier times.

The most common booby is the **Blue-footed booby**, *Sula nebouxii*. This is the only booby to lay more than one egg at a time (three is not unusual) though if food is insufficient the stronger firstborn will kick its siblings out of the nest. Unlike its red-footed relative, the blue-footed booby fishes inshore, dropping on its prey like an arrow from the sky. They are best known for their comical and complicated courtship 'dance'.

The **Red-footed booby**, *Sula sula*, is the only Galápagos booby to nest in trees, thanks to the fact that its feet are adapted to gripping branches. It is light brown in colour, although there is also a less common white variety. The largest colony of red-footed boobies is found on Genovesa island.

The **Masked booby**, *Sula dactylactra*, is the heaviest of the three boobies and has a white plumage with a distinctive black mask on the eyes. Like its blue-footed cousin, the white or masked booby nests directly on the ground and surrounds its nest with waste. It chooses to fish between the other two boobies, thus illustrating the idea of the 'ecological niche'.

Mammals

The number of native mammals in the archipelago is limited to two species of bats, a few species of rats and, of course, sea lions and seals. This is explained by the fact that the islands were never connected to the mainland. Since the arrival of man, however, goats, dogs, donkeys, horses and the black rat have been added to the list and now threaten the fragile ecological balance of the islands.

Sea Lion
Zalophus
californianus

As the scientific name suggests, the Galápagos sea lion is related to the Californian species, though smaller. They are common throughout the archipelago, gathering in large colonies on beaches or on the rocks. The male, which is distinguished from the female by its huge size and domed forehead, is very territorial, especially at the beginning of the May to January mating season. He patrols a territory of 40 to 100 sq m with a group of up to 30 females, chasing off intruders and also keeping an eye on the young, which may wander too far from the safety of the beach. Those which are too tired or old to hold a territory gather in 'bachelor clubs'.

Left: *Sea Lion* (Zalophus californianus). *The male sea lion is very territorial, especially during mating season.* **Below**: *Waved Albatross* (Dimeda irrorata). *The spectacular courtship of the albatross is a cross between an exotic dance and a fiery duel.*

Galápagos Wildlife

Above: *Great Frigatebird* (Fregata minor). *During courtship displays, the male inflates a huge red sac under its throat and flutters its spread wings.* **Left**: *Sally lightfoot crab.*

The friendly and inquisitive females provide one of the main tourist attractions, especially when cavorting with swimmers. One of the sea lion's favourite games is surfing the big waves and another popular sport is 'water polo', using a marine iguana instead of a ball.

Sea lion colonies are found on South Plaza, Santa Fé, Rábida, James Bay (Santiago island), Española, San Cristóbal and Isabela.

Fur Seal
Arctocephalus
galapaoensis

Fur seals and sea lions both belong to the Otaridae or eared seal family. The fur seal's dense, luxuriant pelt attracted great interest and the poor creature was hunted almost to extinction at the beginning of the 20th century by whalers and other skin hunters. Fortunately, these *lobos de dos pelos* (double-fur sea wolves), as they are known locally, survived and can be seen most easily in Puerto Egas on Santiago island, usually hiding from the sun under rocks or lava cracks. The fur sea lion is distinguished from the sea lion by its smaller size, its pointed nose, big round sad moist eyes, larger front flippers and more prominent ears.

Marine Life

The Galápagos are washed by three currents: the cold Humboldt and Cromwell currents, and the warm El Niño. This provides the islands with a rich, diverse and unique underwater fauna. The number of species of fish has been estimated at 306, 17 % of which are endemic, though recent research suggests this number could exceed 400. Among the huge number of fish found in the islands' waters, there are 18 species of morays, five species of rays (stingrays, golden ray, marbled ray, spotted eagle ray and manta rays) and about 12 species of sharks. But not to worry, there have been no reported shark attacks on humans! The most common sharks are the white-tip reef shark, the black-tip reef shark, two species of hammerheads, the Galápagos shark, the grey reef shark, the tiger shark, the hornshark and the whale shark.

Among the marine mammals, at least 16 species of whales and seven species of dolphins have been identified. The most common dolphins are the bottle-nosed dolphin, *Tursiops truncatus,* and the common dolphin. Whales include the sperm whale, humpback whale, pilot whale, the orca and the false killer whale, Sei whale, Minke whale, Bryde's whale, Cuvier's beaked whale and the blue whale. These whales can be seen throughout the islands, but most easily to the west of Isabela and Fernandina. The waters are also rich in seastars, sea urchins, sea cucumbers and crustaceans, including the ubiquitous and distinctive Sally lightfoot crab.

South to Cuenca

South of Riobamba, as the Panamericana approaches the southern highlands, it runs through bleak mountainous country. The countryside is poor, dry, chilly and windswept, and the Indians withdrawn and wrapped-up. In the province of Cañar, natives are dressed in black. At Zhud a paved road runs to Cochancay and La Troncal in the coastal lowlands, from where there are paved roads to Guayaquil and Machala. Towards Cuenca the road loses height and the land is more intensively farmed. There is a good paved road which bypasses Biblián and Azogues on the way to Cuenca.

Sixty seven kilometres north of Cuenca and 36 km north of Azogues, Cañar is very much the indigenous capital of the province. It's a lovely, friendly colonial town set in a good area for walking. The town is famous for double-faced weaving, although it is now difficult to find. The jail, Centro de Rehabilitación Social, is one place to find the backstrap weavings that the prisoners sell through the bars to supplement their income and pay for food.

Cañar
Population: 20,000

The market on Sunday is very colourful and it is still relatively easy to find the Cañar hats for sale in several of the small stores in town. The rock work at the base of the church is supposed to be Inca or Cañari, but it has been faced and worked with cement and is difficult to see.

You'll also find the **Ñucanchi Huasi** (Our House), the Cañar Indian centre. It provides a home for students living in town during the week and is a place for conferences and meetings as well as being a discount store for bulk provisions and other services.

Sleeping and eating H *Residencial Mónica*, main plaza, T235486. Some rooms with bath, hot water, laundry facilities. Often full, clean, friendly, owner's daughter offers tour service to Ingapirca, 2 hrs, US$5 (for small group). H *Residencial Cañar*, opposite the park, T235682. Shared bath, hot water. Small, friendly. *Los Maderos Restaurant*, near the centre, is friendly. *Chifa Florida*, on the plaza, serves good and cheap food, not only Chinese.

It's a better idea to stay here, rather than El Tambo, if possible

Transport Buses leave every 30 mins to the Terminal Terrestre in Cuenca, US$1, 1½ hrs; also to Quito and El Tambo (7 km).

Between Cañar and Azogues is Biblián, with a sanctuary to La Virgen del Rocío, built into the rocks above the village. It's a pleasant walk up with impressive views of the river valley and surrounding countryside. One hour west of Azogues is **Cojitambo**; the surrounding area is good for rock climbing. You can stay nearby at Sageo, F *Hostería El Camping*, 3 km from Azoguez, 2½ km from Biblián, T240445, has a pool, spa and restaurant. It gets busy at weekends but is quiet through the week.

Biblián

There is a new route south from Biblián to Cuenca which bypasses Azogues. The road, which is not open to buses, cuts across the valley near Biblián and rejoins the old road to the south of El Descanso (see page 263).

The administrative capital of the province, Azogues is a large, busy city, 31 km north of Cuenca (45 minutes by bus, US$0.60) and a centre of the panama hat industry. Hats are rarely for sale, even at the Saturday morning market, but the *sombrerías* are very happy to show visitors their trade; eg *La Sin Ribal*, Calle Luis Cordero y 3 de Noviembre, or *Cahuzhun*, near the plaza, highly recommended. The market is colourful and beautifully situated on a hill is the city's

Azogues
Population: 21,060

Southern Highlands

huge church and convent **San Francisco de la Virgen de las Nubes**. There's an interesting section below the big church where chickens and other small animals are sold. Just off the main plaza beside the church is a small *artesanía* shop run by the nuns which sells some local knitting, embroidery and other handicrafts. Some of the older buildings around the plaza still have the lovely traditional colonial painted ceilings over the pavements.

Sleeping and eating **F** *El Paraíso*, sector La Playa in the north of town, T242729. With bath, clean. **F** *Rivera*, Av 24 de Mayo y 10 de Agosto, T248113. with bath, hot water, TV, restaurant. Clean and modern. **F** *Cordillera*, overlooking the former bus terminal. With restaurant. **G** *Chicago*, 3 de Noviembre y 24 de Mayo, T241040. With bath, hot water, cable TV. Popular. **H** *Charles*, Solano y Rivera, near plaza, T241364. Shared bath. Clean, simple. *Peleusí*, Emilio Abad y Sucre, T242611. Cafeteria, nice atmosphere, open 0900-1900, closed Sun. *El Padrino*, C Bolívar 609 y 10 de Agosto, T240534. Popular restaurant. *Ochenta y siete*, 3 de Noviembre y 24 de Mayo, next to Hotel Chicago, good restaurant.

Cuenca

Phone code: 07
Colour map 6, grid A4
Population: 400,000
Altitude: 2,530 m

Cuenca is capital of the province of Azuay and the third largest city in Ecuador. The city has preserved much of its colonial air, with many of its old buildings constructed of the marble quarried nearby and recently renovated. The colonial centre is fairly compact and flat, making it easy to get around on foot. Most Ecuadoreans consider this their finest city and few would disagree. Its cobblestone streets, flowering plazas and whitewashed buildings with old wooden doors and ironwork balconies make it a pleasure to explore. In 1999 Cuenca was designated a World Heritage Trust site by UNESCO.

As well as being the economic centre of the Southern Sierra, Cuenca is also an intellectual centre with a long tradition as the birthplace of notable artists, writers, poets and philosophers, earning it the title 'Athens of Ecuador'. It remains a rather formal city, loyal to its conservative traditions. Everything closes for lunch between 1300 and 1500 and many places are closed on Sunday evenings. The climate is spring-like, but the nights are chilly.

Ins and outs

Getting there
See also Transport, page 260
The Terminal Terrestre, well-organized and policed, is on Av España, a 20 min walk northwest of the city centre. The airport is 5 mins' walk from the Terminal Terrestre, both can be reached by city bus. The terminal for local or within-the-province buses is at the Feria Libre on Av las Américas (destinations such as Gima, San Fernando, Deleg, etc). Many city buses also pass here.

Getting around The city is bounded by the Río Machángara to the north. The Río Tomebamba separates the colonial heart from the stadium, universities and newer residential areas to the south. Parque Nacional Cajas can be seen to the west of the city. Av las Américas is a ring road to the north and west of the city. To the south a new multi-lane bypass highway was nearing completion in 2000.

Tourist offices *Ministerio de Turismo*, Presidente Córdova y Benigno Malo, T839337. English spoken. Maps of Cuenca and regional information. A map of the city is also available from the major hotels. ■ *Mon-Fri, 0830-1700*. *Cámara de Turismo*, at the Terminal Terrestre, T846742. Local and regional information, city maps, English spoken. ■ *Daily*

Southern Highlands

0800-2200. *Asociación Hotelera de Cuenca*, Pres Córdova y Padre Aguirre, T836925. Information about accommodation and sights. ■ *Mon-Fri 0830-1300, 1430-1800*.

Cuenca is safer than either Quito or Guayaquil, but routine precautions are nonetheless advised. The city centre is deserted and unsafe after 2200. The area around El Puente del Vado (Av 12 de Abril y Av Loja) is unsafe day and night. Market areas, especially Mercado 9 de Octubre, call for caution at all hours. **Security**

History

Cuenca was originally a Cañari settlement, dating from 500 AD to around 1480, called Guapondeleg, which roughly translates as 'an area as large as heaven'. The suffix 'deleg' is still found in several local place names, a survival of the now extinct Cañari language.

Owing to its geographical location, this was among the first parts of what is now Ecuador to come under the domination of the Inca empire, which had expanded north. The Incas settled the area around Cuenca and called it Tomebamba, which roughly translates as 'River Valley of Knives'. The name survives as one of the region's rivers. Seventy kilometres north of Cuenca, in an area known as *Hatun Cañar*, the Incas built the ceremonial centre of Ingapirca, which remains the most important Inca archaeological site in the country (see page 246). Ingapirca and Tomebamba were the hub of the northern part of the Inca empire.

The city as it is today was founded by the Spanish in 1557 on the site of Tomebamba and named Santa Ana de los Cuatro Ríos de Cuenca. Cuenca then became an important and populous regional centre in the crown colony governed from Quito. The *conquistadores* and the settlers who followed them were interested in the working of precious metals, for which the region's indigenous peoples had earned a well deserved reputation. Following independence from Spain, Cuenca was capital of one of three provinces that made up the new republic, the others being Quito and Guayaquil.

Sights

On the main plaza, **Parque Abdón Calderón**, are both the Old Cathedral (closed for restoration in 2000), also known as **El Sagrario**, begun in 1557 when modern Cuenca was founded, and the immense 'New' **Catedral de la Inmaculada**. The latter was started in 1885 and contains a famous crowned image of the Virgin. It was the work of the German architect Padre Johannes Baptista Stiehle, who also designed many other buildings in the Cuenca area. It was planned to be the largest cathedral in South America but the architect made some miscalculations with the foundations and the final domes on the front towers could not be built for fear that the whole thing would come down. Modern stained glass, a beautiful altar and an exceptional play of light and shade inside the cathedral make it worth a visit. The Sunday evening worship is recommended.

El Sagrario was built on the foundations of an Inca structure and some of the Inca blocks are still visible facing the plaza. The French Geodesic Mission of 1736-1744 came to Ecuador to measure the Equator, and probably also to see what the Spanish were up to. They used El Sagrario as one of the fixed points for their measurements. The interior of the church was recently renovated.

Other churches which deserve a visit are **San Blas**, **San Francisco**, **El Cenáculo**, and **Santo Domingo**. Many churches are open at irregular hours only and for services, because of increasing problems with theft. The

Southern Highlands

17th-century church of **El Carmen de la Asunción** is close to the southwest corner of La Inmaculada and has a flower market in the tiny **Plazoleta El Carmen** in front. The church is open early in the morning and mid-afternoon, but the attached cloister of El Carmen Alto is closed as the nuns inside live in total isolation.

South of the city on Avenida Fray Vicente Solano, beyond the football stadium, is **El Turi church and mirador**, a 40 minute walk from the base or two hours from the colonial city (not safe after dark), or take taxi. It's well worth a visit for the great views and a tiled panorama explains what you see. There is an orphanage attached to the church. There are good walks along attractive country lanes further south.

There is a daily market in **Plaza Cívica** where pottery, clothes, guinea pigs and local produce, especially baskets, are sold. Thursday is the busiest.

The suburb of **San Joaquín**, out west near the tennis club, is famous for its basketwork. There are many houses where you can see the different types of baskets being made. Some of the styles, especially the ones with a waist, are made only in the Cuenca and Azogues areas.

Museums   The excellent **Museo del Banco Central 'Pumapungo'**, on the southeastern edge of the colonial city, is at the actual site of the Tomebamba excavations. The **Museo Arqueológico** contains all the Cañari and Inca remains and artefacts found at this site. Although the Ingapirca ruins are more spectacular, it is believed that Tomebamba was the principal Inca administrative centre in Ecuador. Other halls in the premises house the **Museo Etnográfico**, with information of the different cultures which make up Ecuador, the **Museo de Arte Religioso**, the **Museo Numismático,** and temporary exhibits. There are also book and music libraries and free cultural videos and music events. ■ *Mon-Fri 0900-1800, and Sat 0900-1300, US$1, C Larga y Huayna Capac, T831255. The entrance is on the far left of the building.*

About 300 m from the Pumapungo site there are excavations at the **Todos Los Santos** site, which reveal traces of Inca and Cañari civilizations and show how the Spanish reused the stonework. ■ *Mon-Fri, 0800-1600, C Larga 287.*

The **Instituto Azuayo de Folklore** has an exhibition of popular Latin American arts and crafts.Through CIDAP (Centro Interamericano de Desarollo de Artes Populares), it supports research and promotes sales of artesans' works. There is also a library and a recommended crafts shop. ■ *Mon-Fri 0930-1300, 1430-1800, Sat 100-1300, free. Escalinata 303 y C Larga, extension of C Hermano Miguel.*

Museo de las Culturas Aborígenes A good private collection of precolumbian archaeology, in the house of Dr J Cordero López. There are guided tours in English, Spanish and French. It's well worth a visit. ■ *Mon-Fri 0830-1230, 1430-1830, Sat 0830-1230, but phone in advance, US$2. Av 10 de Agosto 4-70, between F Moscoso y J M Sánchez (taxi from centre US$1.50). T811706.*

Museo del Monasterio de las Conceptas A well displayed collection of religious and folk art, and an extensive collection of lithographs by Guayasamín housed in a cloistered convent founded in 1599. ■ *Mon-Fri 0900-1730, Sat 1000-1300, US$2. Hermano Miguel 6-33 between Pdte Córdova and Juan Jaramillo, T830625.*

The **Museo Municipal de Arte Moderno** has a permanent contemporary art collection and an art library. A biennial international painting competition is held here as well as other cultural activities worth attending. ■ *Mon-Fri 0830-1830, Sat 0900-1500, Sun 0900-1300, free. Sucre 1527 y Talbot, on the Plaza San Sebastián, T831027.*

The **Casa de los Canónigos**, Calle Luis Cordero 888, opposite Parque Calderón, houses the **Galería del Portal**, T833492, with original Latin American works of art for exhibition and sale. There's a small museum, art gallery and bookshop in the **Casa de la Cultura**, Luis Cordero y Sucre (second floor). Look out for the wall of niches in the courtyard; each niche contains a statue of a saint. A lovely, restored colonial house is the **Casa Azul** on Gran Colombia 10-29 y Padre Aguirre, housing a travel agency, restaurant and a little museum.

The **Museo Remigio Crespo Toral**, housed in a beautifully restored colonial mansion, has various regional history collections, including a selection of gold objects from the Cañar and Chordeleg cultures. There is a good café in the basement. ■ *Mon-Fri 0830-1300 and 1500-1830, Sat-Sun 1000-1500, free. C Larga 7-07 y Borreo.*

The **Museo de Artes de Fuego** on Calle las Herrerías, or the blacksmith's road, has a display of wrought iron work and pottery. It is housed in a beautifully restored old building. Outside is a sculpture of a volcano and on special occasions the god Vulkan, wrapped in flames, comes out of the volcano. There is also a shop. ■ *Mon-Fri except for lunchtime and Sat morning. Las Herrerías y 10 de Agosto, across the river from the Museo del Banco Central.*

Essentials

L *Oro Verde*, Av Ordóñez Lazo, on the road to Cajas, T831200, F832849, ecovc@gye.satnet.net Luxury hotel set in lovely gardens on the edge of a lake in the outskirts of town, 77 rooms and 2 suites, one of which has wheelchair access, heated outdoor pool, 2 restaurants, bar, deli, golf, tennis and horse riding all available. **AL** *El Dorado*, Gran Colombia 787 y Luis Cordero, T831390, F847390, eldorado@cue.satnet.net Includes buffet breakfast and airport transfers, good restaurant, gym, spa, good views. **A** *Crespo*, C Larga 793, T842571, F839473, hcrespo@az.pro.ec, www.ecuadorexplorer.com/crespo/ Includes full breakfast, restaurant overlooking the river. Friendly and comfortable, some lovely rooms, others dark or with no windows, a lovely building. **B** *El Conquistador*, Gran Colombia 665, T831788, F831291, hconquis@etapa.com.ec Includes buffet breakfast, free local calls, airport transfer, safety deposit, restaurant, disco (avoid back rooms Fri and Sat). Very clean, good, friendly, good food and wine. **B** *El Conquistador Annex*, Sucre 6-78, T841703. Same services as main hotel. **B** *Inca Real*, General Torres 8-40 y Sucre, T823636, F840699. Includes local calls, all rooms on courtyards, cafeteria with mid-range prices. Central, friendly. **B** *Pinar del Lago*, Av Ordoñez Lazo, next door to the *Oro Verde*, T837339, pinarlag@impsat.net.ec Carpeted rooms with cable TV, laundry service, cafeteria. Good views of river or lake, good.

C *Las Casas de Guapondelig*, Guapondelig y Jaime Roldós, T/F861917, quiet residential area in the northeast of the city, modern individual houses, pool. **C** *Cuenca*, Borrero 1069 y Gran Colombia, T833711, F833819. Includes breakfast, cable TV, restaurant. Clean, attractive. **C** *Nuestra Residencia*, Los Pinos 1-100 y Ordóñez Lazo, T831702, F835576. Six rooms and 1 suite with bath, cable TV, includes full breakfast, living room and bar, arranges bilingual tours, friendly, good atmosphere. **C** *Prado Inn*, Presidente Rocafuerte 3-45 y Av Huayna Cápac, T807164. Warm and comfortable rooms with private bath, TV, clean, friendly, includes breakfast, located in the colonial area. **C** *Posada del Sol*, Bolívar 5-03 y Mariano Cueva, T838695, F838995, pdelsol@impsat.net.ec Refurbished colonial building, includes breakfast, rooms with balcony, laundry, internet. Owner Juan Diego also runs horse and bike treks into Cajas National Park. Recommended. **C** *Presidente*, Gran Colombia 659, T831066, F831979. Includes breakfast. Good value, comfortable, convenient, good restaurant.

D *Atahualpa*, Sucre 3-50 y Tomás Ordóñez, T831841, F842345. Carpeted rooms, TV, includes breakfast, laundry, restaurant, parking. Recommended. **D** *Atenas*, Luis

Sleeping
■ *on map, page 254*
Price codes: see inside front cover

Southern Highlands

Cordero 1189 y Sangurima, T/F827016, hatenas@etapa.com.ec With bath, reliable hot water, small cafeteria, internet café nearby, parking. **D** *Catedral*, Padre Aguirre 8-17 y Sucre, T823204. Includes full breakfast. Clean, cheerful, spacious, modern, but not very warm, English-speaking manager, laundry service, good food, coffee shop opens 0700. **D** *Colonial*, Gran Colombia 10-13 y Padre Aguirre, T/F841644. Includes breakfast. In refurbished colonial house with beautiful patio, cafeteria, clean. **D** *Hostal Macondo*, Tarqui 11-64 y Lamar, T840697, macondo@cedei.org Restored colonial house, **E** with shared bath, hot water, laundry service, friendly, kitchen facilities, includes continental breakfast, but can upgrade to an excellent full breakfast, Quichua and Spanish classes, "a real treat". Highly recommended. **D** *Italia*, Av España y Av Huayna Capac, T840060, F864475. Buffet breakfast included, very clean. **D** *Príncipe*, J Jaramillo 7-82 y Luis Cordero, T821235, F834369. With bath and TV, includes full

Cuenca centre

Southern Highlands

breakfast, pleasant courtyard. **D** *El Quijote*, Hermano Miguel 9-58 y Gran Colombia, T843197, F834573. Breakfast available.

E *Alli-Tiana*, Presidente Córdova y Padre Aguirre, T821955, F821788. Clean, includes breakfast. **E** *Las Américas*, Mariano Cueva 13-59, T831160/835753. Includes breakfast, TV, ask for room with windows, parking, restaurant. Clean, friendly. **E** *Cabañas Cabogana*, in San Miguel de Putushi, 8 km northwest of town, on a side road off El Cajas road, T894044, F894925. Eight cabins with capacity of up to 8, kitchenette, restaurant, gardens, sports fields, fishing. In country setting at the shores of a small river. **E** *Cabañas Yanuncay*, C Cantón Gualaceo 21-49, between Av Loja y Las Américas (Yanuncay), T883716. A 10 min drive from the centre, or take bus 12 or 17 (Av Loja) and get off at the stone bridge. Rustic cabins with bath for 2-4 people, or room with bath, includes breakfast and dinner, fireplace in the house, solarium, library, sauna, organic gardens, good home-cooked meals, run by Beto and Teresa Chico, Spanish and English spoken, helpful, friendly, transport to airport/bus terminal. Recommended. **E** *El Cafecito*, Honorato Vásquez 7-36 y Luis Cordero, T832337. Colonial house, discount for longer stay, with bath (**G** with shared bath), excellent and cheap food in restaurant with charming patio, also vegetarian dishes, often full, good atmosphere. Recommended. **E** *Chordeleg*, Gran Colombia 11-15 y Grl Torres, T822536. Includes breakfast. Charming, clean. **E** *Gran Hotel*, Grl Torres 9-70 y Bolívar, T831934, F833819. With bath, hot water, colour TV, phone, includes breakfast, laundry service, good restaurant, beautiful patio. Clean, popular meeting place. **E** *Hostal La Orquídea*, Borrero 9-31 y Bolívar. Nicely refurbished colonial house, small patios, bright. **E** *Hostal Santo y Seña*, Pasaje 3 de Noviembre 4-71, T841981. With and without bath, garden. Pleasant, quiet. **E** *Hostería El Molino*, Km 7.5 on road Azogues-Cuenca, T800150. Pleasant position between the road and the river, Spanish-run, typical Ecuadorean dishes, pool, rustic style, advisable to book. Recommended. **E** *El Monasterio*, Padre Aguirre 7-24 y Sucre, second floor, T843609. With bath, cheaper with shared bath, kitchen facilities, laundry service.

F *Hostal Caribe Inn*, Gran Colombia 10-51 y Padre Aguirre, T/F835175. Pleasant, comfortable, TV, phone, cheap breakfast available, restaurant. **F** *Hostal Paredes*, Luis Cordero 11-29 y Lamar, T835674, F834910. Beautifully-refurbished colonial mansion, with bath, laundry, luggage stored, garage. Highly

Southern Highlands

recommended. **F** *Milán*, Pres Córdova 989 y Padre Aguirre, T/F831104. With bath, cheaper without, rooms with balconies, clean, often full, best to reserve, mixed reports on security. **F** *Pichincha*, Gral Torres 8-82 y Bolívar, T823868. Includes breakfast, **G** with shared bath, laundry facilities, luggage stored. Spacious, helpful, clean, friendly. **F** *Siberia*, Luis Cordero y C Larga, T840672. Carpeted rooms with bath, some with TV.

G *Hostal Cumandá*, Huayna Cápac 3-76, T836702. One room with bath, others without. **G** *Masdevalias*, Jaramillo 6-35 y Hermano Miguel, T820512. Some with bath, better rooms are on second floor with shared bath, Restaurant *Café Hostal*. **G** *Norte*, Mariano Cueva 11-63 y Sangurima, T827881. Renovated, large rooms, hot showers, cheaper with shared bath. Clean, comfortable, safe although not a good area after dark, motorcycle parking, good restaurant downstairs, friendly. Recommended. **G** *Residencial Astoria*, El Chorro 222 y Gil Ramírez Dávalos, T809252. **H** without bath, hot water. **G** *Residencial Niza*, Mcal Lamar 4-51, T823284/838005. Cheaper with shared bath, clean, helpful. **G** *Residencial París*, Grl Torres 10-48, T842656. Private bath, intermittent hot water, includes breakfast (except Sun), laundry. Clean, friendly. Recommended. **H** *Cantabri*, Pres Córdova 9-21, T823379. Shared bath, electric shower. **H** *Residencial Colombia*, Mariano Cueva 11-61, T827851. Large rooms, shared bath, TV lounge. Clean, basic, noisy, friendly, helpful.

Near the bus terminal E *Hurtado de Mendoza*, Sangurima y Huayna Cápac, T831909. Includes breakfast, with bath, TV, good, restaurant, parking. **F** *Residencial España*, Sangurima 1-17, T831351, F831291. With bath and TV, **G** without bath, includes breakfast, hot water, good restaurant. Clean, friendly, front upstairs rooms are best. **F** *Residencial Tito*, Sangurima 149, T/F843577. Shared bath, safe, clean, hot water, restaurant very good value. **F** *Samay*, Tomás Ordóñez 11-86 y Sangurima, T831119. With bath, TV, **G** without, clean, can be noisy, parking. **G** *Los Alamos No 1*, Madrid 1-42 y Av España, T835771. Cheaper without bath, TV, clean, will store luggage, opposite a noisy reception hall. **G** *Los Helechos*, El Chorro y Gil Ramírez Dávalos, behind the bus terminal, T863401. With bath, TV, cheaper without either. **G** *Los Libertadores*, Av España 1-27, T831487. With bath, TV.

Furnished apartments *El Jardín*, Av Pumapungo y Viracochabamba, T804103, or write to Casilla 298. Equipped apartments with 1-3 bedrooms with cooking facilities, cleaning service, restaurant, parking. US$160-270 per month, daily rate **B-D**. **C** *Apartamentos Otorongo*, Av 12 de Abril y Guayas, T811184. A 10-15 min walk from centre, fully-furnished flats for 4 with kitchenette, TV, phone, cleaning service included, very friendly owners, discount for longer stay.

Eating
● *on map*
Price categories:
see inside front cover
22% tax & service is
added in more
upmarket restaurants

Av Remigio Crespo, between the stadium and the coliseum, has a variety of *pizzerías*, *heladerías*, burger and sandwich bars, steak houses, bars and discos. The area is very popular with young people, and lively at weekends. There are cheap comedores on the second floor of Mercado Modelo, on 10 de Agoste y 18 de Noviembre.

Ecuadorean *Los Capulíes*, Córdova y Borrero, T832339. Bar-restaurant, excellent, friendly, lovely setting, Andean live music Thu-Sat 2030, reservations recommended at the weekend. *Molinos del Batán*, 12 de Abril y Puente El Vado, T811531. Good setting by river, good food, expensive. *El Tequila*, Gran Colombia 20-59, T831847. Good local food, good value and service. *Balcón Quiteño*, Sangurima 6-49 y Borrero, T822581 and Av Ordoñez Lazo 311 y los Pinos, T825251. Popular with the locals after a night's hard partying. *Las Tres Caravelas*, part of hotel *El Conquistador*. Good value, Ecuadorean and international fare. Andean live music at weekends. *A las Riberas del Guayas*, Bolívar 4-40 y Mariano Cueva. Coastal food. *Las Campanas*, Borrero 7-69 y Sucre, good Ecuadorean food, open until 0200.

International *El Jardín*, Presidente Córdova 7-23. Lovely, good food, closed Sun-Mon, very expensive. *Villa Rosa*, Gran Colombia 12-22 y Tarqui. Very elegant, excellent food. *La Rotond*, 12 de Abril y José Peralta, T888111. Excellent French and international cooking, elegant, good view of the river and residential area. *Casa Grande*, San Joaquín-La Cruz Verde, T839992. Grill, good food and value. In picturesque San Joaquín district where flowers and vegetables are grown and baskets made. *Los Sauces*, Bolívar 6-17. Original dishes, reasonable prices. *La Barraca*, Antonio Borrero 9-68 y Gran Colombia, opposite the Post Office, T829967. Breakfast, dinner, quiet music, coffee, excellent, open daily 0800-2300. *El Túnel*, Gral Torres 8-60, T823109. Reasonably priced, quick service, romantic atmosphere, good, cheap lunch menu. *Salad Bar*, Sucre y M Cueva. Popular for lunch.

Italian *Caos*, J Jaramillo y Hermano Miguel. Good food, pleasant atmosphere, cheap. Open Mon-Sat 1800-2400. *La Napolitana*, Federico Proaño 4-20 Nice atmosphere, good food. *NY Pizza*, Gran Colombia 10-43 y Padre Aguirre. Very good especially the *calzones*. *El Pavón Real*, Gran Colombia, 8-33 y Cordero, T816678. Excellent pizzas, pleasant courtyard, friendly. *Los Pibes*, Gran Colombia 776 y Cordero, opposite *Hotel El Dorado*. Good pizzas and lasagne, moderately priced. *Tuna*, Gran Colombia 8-80. Pizzas and trout, popular.

Latin American *El Che Pibe*, Av Remigio Crespo 2-59. *Parrillada Argentina*, good grill, excellent service, also chicken, pizza, pasta, salads etc, open till late, expensive. *El Pedregal Azteca*, Gran Colombia 10-29 y Padre Aguirre. Good Mexican food. *Rancho Chileno*, Av España, next to airport. Good steak and seafood, slow service, pricey. *La Tasca*, Pasaje 3 de Noviembre bajos del Puente Roto. Cuban food.

Oriental *Chifa Pack How*, Presidente Córdova y Cordero. Not cheap. Recommended. *Chifa Asia*, Cueva 11 s/n, entre 34 y 68. Mid-range prices, large portions. Recommended. *Sol Oriental*, Gran Colombia y Vega. Cheap, large portions.

Seafood *La Casa del Marisco*, Av Paucarbamba y Luis Moreno, T843522. *El Gran Manantial*, Presidente Córdova 7-36 y Cordero, T844285. *El Mar*, Gran Colombia 20-33, T843522.

Snackbars and cafés *Raymipampa*, Benigno Malo 8-59, T834159, on Plaza Calderón, also at Sucre 9-13 y Benigno Malo and Remigio Crespo 1-20 y Av del Estadio. Open daily, very popular, especially at lunchtime, local dishes, good ceviche, crêpes, good ice-cream, clean, reasonably priced, excellent value. *Wunderbar*, Hermano Miguel y C Larga, behind the Instituto Azuayo de Folklore. German-run, good atmosphere, good food and coffee, also vegetarian, book exchange, German magazines. *Café Chordeleg*, Gran Colombia 7-87. Open 24 hrs, excellent breakfast for US$3.50-5. *Pity's*, 2 branches, Av Remigio Crespo Toral y Alfonso Borrero, and Ordóñez Lazo y Circunvalación. For sandwiches, hamburgers, recommended. *Café Italia*, Pres Córdova 8-35, entre Luis Cordero y Benigno Malo. Excellent cheap snacks. *Cinema Café*, Luis Cordero y Sucre, above the Casa de la Cultura cinema, snacks, salads, popular. *Jarro Café*, Borrero 5-47 y Honorato Vásquez, cafeteria and some meals, nicely arranged around a courtyard, crafts sold on second floor, live music in evening. *Campoamor*, Hermano Miguel y Presidente Córdova esquina, cafetería.*Helados Honey*, Mcal Lamar 4-21. Clean, recommended milkshakes. *Café Capuchino*, Bolívar y Aguirre. Open 0930, good hamburgers, real coffee and liqueur coffees. *Monte Bianco*, Bolívar 2-80 y Ordóñez, near San Blas church, good cakes, ice cream, open Sun. *Café Austria*, Benigno Malo 5-99. Good cakes, pies, sandwiches, coffee, fruit, ice cream, yoghurt, closed Mon. *Heladería Holanda*, Benigno Malo 9-51. Open 0930, yoghurt for breakfast, good ice cream, fruit salads, great toilets, internet service (see below). *MiPan*, Pres Córdova 824 between Cordero y Malo (also Bolívar y Aguirre). Opens 0730, excellent bread, cakes, tarts, doughnuts, tea, coffee and chocolate.

Vegetarian *El Paraíso*, Tomás Ordóñez 10-45 y Gran Colombi. Open Mon-Sat 0800-1600, good breakfast, excellent food, cheap set lunch. *Govinda*, Juan Jaramillo y Borrero. Limited menu.

Weekends, holidays and by arrangement *Hacienda Sustag*, Km 17 via Joaquín-Soldados, T830834, F832340. Located in the countryside, a farm with beautiful landscapes, camping and picnic area, delicious Ecuadorean food, reasonable. *Dos Chorreras*, via Cajas north road. Excellent for fresh trout.

| Bars & nightclubs | **Bars** *Chaos*, Honorato Vásquez y Hermano Miguel, popular. *Friends*, Pres Córdova y Hermano Miguel, esquina. Café-bar. Opens 1800. *Picadilly Pub*, Borrero 7-46 y Pres Córdova. Upmarket, clean, relaxing. *Saxon*, Av Gran Colombia y Unidad Nacional (Zona Rosa), bar/disco. *Tapas y Canciones*, Remigio Crespo y Galápagos, small quaint *peña*. *UBU Bar*, Honorato Vásquez y Luis Cordero. Popular bar and café. *La Vitrola*, Av Ordóñez Lazo, 500 m from *Hotel Oro Verde*, T837197. Bar, restaurant and *peña* with Latin music, excellent atmosphere.

Discos *Aazúcar*, Pasaje 3 de Noviembre y 12 de Abril, under the Puente Roto bridge. Latin and international music. *Zoom*, Calle Larga y Mariano Cueva. International music, popular with local youth. *Ego*, Unidad Nacional y 3 de Noviembre. Latin music. *IV y 20*, 12 de Abril y Galápagos, international and Latin music, small, informal atmosphere, popular with tourists and locals, unsafe area so take a taxi. *La Mesa Salsoteca*, Gran Colombia 3-36 entre Vargas Machuca y Tomás Ordóñez. No sign, latin music, very popular among locals and travellers. *Papa Galo*, Remigio Crespo y Galápagos, in the Zona Rosa, varied music, popular with local youth. *Pop Art*, Remigio Crespo y Solano, modern music. *Qué Será*, Huayna Capac y Jaime Roldós. Latin music. Also discos in the hotels *Conquistador* and *Alli-Tiana* (older crowd). *Fernández*, near *Capulíes* restaurant. Good disco music, for couples.

| Entertainment | **Cinemas** There are 4 cinemas, the one opposite the Casa de la Cultura shows interesting films at 1430 and 2100. Films also at the Casa de la Cultura itself, evenings. The one at Luis Cordero y Sucre shows double bills at weekends, US$1.75. *Teatro Cuenca*, P Aguirre 10-50, also shows films.

| Festivals | On **Christmas Eve** there is an outstanding parade, *Pase del Niño Viajero*, probably the largest and finest Christmas parade in all Ecuador. Children and adults from all the *barrios* and surrounding villages decorate donkeys, horses, cars and trucks with symbols of abundance. Young children dressed in colourful Indian costumes or as Biblical figures ride through the streets accompanied by musicians. The parade starts at about 1000 at San Sebastián, proceeds along C Simón Bolívar, past Plaza Calderón and ends at San Blas. In the days leading up to and after Christmas there are smaller *Pase del Niño* parades.

On **New Year's Eve**, as elsewhere in Ecuador, the festivities include the parading and burning at midnight of effigies called *Años Viejos* (some political, some fictional) which symbolize the old year.

On **10-13 April** is the *Foundation of Cuenca*. On **Good Friday** there is a fine procession through the town and up to the Mirador Turi. Cuenca hosts an internationally famous *art competition* every 2 years, which begins in **April or May**. Exhibitions occupy museums and galleries around the city for about 4 months. The whole event is coordinated by the Museo de Arte Moderno.

Septenario, the religious festival of *Corpus Christi* in **June**, and lasts a week. On Plaza Calderón a decorated tower with fireworks attached, known as 'castillo', is burnt every night after a mass, 'vacas locas' or mad cows (people carrying a reed structure in the shape of a cow, with lit fireworks) run across the park, and hundreds of hot air paper balloons are released. A spectacular sight which is not to be missed. There are also dozens of dessert sellers and games in the streets.

On **3 November** is *Independence of Cuenca*, with street theatre, art exhibitions and night-time dances all over the city. One such venue is the **Puente Roto**, east of the Escalinata.

Handicrafts The Cuenca region is noted for its *artesanía*. Good souvenirs are carvings, leather, basketwork, ceramics, painted wood, onyx, woven stuffs (cheapest in Ecuador), embroidered shirts and jewellery. There are many craftware shops along Gran Colombia and on Benigno Malo.

Arte Artesanías y Antigüedades at Borrero y Córdova has some lovely textiles, jewellery and antiques. *El Tucán*, Borrero 7-35. Recommended. *Bazaar Susanita*, Benigno Malo 1092. For good woollen sweaters at reasonable prices. *Torres* between Sucre y Córdova, or *Tarqui* between Córdova and the river, for *polleras*, traditional Indian women's skirts. *Galería Claudio Maldonado*, Bolívar 7-75, has unique precolumbian designs in silver and precious stones. *Centro Cultural Jorge Moscoso*, Pres Córdova 6-14 y Hermano Miguel, T822114. Weaving exhibitions, ethnographic museum, antiques and handicrafts. *Galería Pulla*, Jaramillo 6-90. Works by this famous painter, also has sculpture and jewellery. *El Barranco*, Hermano Miguel 3-23 y Av 3 de Noviembre. Artesans' co-operative selling a wide variety of crafts. Also *Yapacunchi*, Luis Cordero y Bolívar. Good quality handicrafts are for sale in the *El Dorado hotel*. *Artesa*, L Cordero 10-31 y Gran Colombia. Several other branches around the city, sells modern Ecuadorean ceramics at good prices. *Galápagos*, Borrero 6-75, excellent selection of crafts. There are several good leather shops in the arcade off Bolívar between Benigno Malo and Luis Cordero, the quality and price are comparable with Cotacachi, near Otavalo in Northern Ecuador.

Panama hats High quality hats are made by *Homero Ortega P e Hijos*, Av Gil Ramírez Dávalos 3-86, T823429, F834045. He will show you his factory opposite the bus station, open 0900-1200, 1500-1800 for visits, they export all over the world. Several other hat shops are on Gran Colombia and Benigno Malo. *Exportadora Cuenca*, Mcal Lamar 3-80. Run by Jaime Ortega Ramírez and his wife, Tania. Highly recommended. Will make to order and won't apply bleach if requested.

Check the quality of Panama hats very carefully as some tend to unravel and shops are unwilling to replace or refund

   Bookshops *Book Exchange*, Gran Colombia 8-41 y Mariano Cueva, 2nd Floor, T831618. Spanish and English titles for rent or exchange. Owner is helpful with general travel information, English spoken.

   Jewellery prices are reported as high, so shop around. *Joyería Turismo*, owned by Leonardo Crespo, at Gran Colombia 9-31. Recommended. He will let wholesale buyers tour his factory. *Unicornio*, L Cordero entre Gran Colombia y Lamar. Good jewellery, ceramics and candelabra.

   Markets Sat is the busiest market day. There's an interesting market behind the new cathedral, and a *Centro Comercial* has opened in the industrial park, with interesting shops. There is a well stocked supermarket behind *Residencial España*. *Supermaxi* is at Gran Colombia y Av de las Américas and on Av José Peralta, near the stadium. Camping Gas is available at several locations; camping equipment can be found at *Bermeo Hnos*, Borrero 8-35 y Sucre, T831522, and *Créditos y Negocios*, Benigno Malo y Pdte Córdova, T829583.

   Photography *Foto Ortiz*, Gran Colombia y Aguirre. Wide range of film, good same day developing. Not recommended for slides. *Asefot*, Gran Colombia 7-18, T/F839342. Recommended for colour prints. *Ecuacolor*, Gran Colombia 7-44 y Cordero. Good service.

Fishing The lakes at Parque Nacional Cajas offer good trout fishing opportunities. **Horse riding** Beatrice and Xavier Malo of *Montaruna Tours* (see Tour operators below) offer horse riding trips (up to 10 days) from their hacienda 30 mins from Cuenca. **Mountain biking** *Eco Rutas*, by the river near the *Hotel Crespo*, T831295, F832920. Rents bikes and helmets, trail information available. A good bike shop is *Tecno Cyclo*, Remigio Tamariz 3-15, T839659. Cheap bike parts at Av Pdte Córdova y Benigno Malo. **Trekking** There are excellent walking opportunities at Parque Nacional Cajas and other areas around Cuenca, see below.

Tour operators *Metropolitan Touring*, Sucre 6-62 y Hermano Miguel, T831463 and Remigio Crespo y

Tours to Ingapirca run US$35-45 per person, excursions to Cajas, Chordeleg, etc, US$35 per person, cheaper for groups of 5 or more

A Cordero, T816937. Tours and tickets *Viajes Enmotur*, Gran Colombia 10-45. Excursions by bus to Ingapirca for US$45. *Ecotrek*, C Larga 7-108 y Luis Cordero, T842531, F835387. Contact Juan Gabriel Carrasco, they run excellent trips to Kapawi Ecological Reserve with experienced guides who offer great adventure travel, monthly departures, specialize in Shaman trips. *Río Arriba Eco-Turismo*, Hno Miguel 7-14 y Córdova, T840031. Recommended. *Apullacta*, Gran Colombia y G Torres. Rent tents (no other equipment rental in Cuenca). *Montaruna Tours*, Gran Colombia 10-29 y Padre Aguirre, T/F846395, montarun@az.pro.ec Horse riding trips, one or several days, US$50 per person per day (includes transport, food, lodging). Jungle tours, trekking, regional tours (Ingapirca, Cajas, Chordeleg) and 4-day excursions to the gold mining area around Zaruma, Also arrange Galápagos tours. Swiss-Ecuadorean run, English and German spoken, friendly and helpful. Recommended. *Costamar Travel*, Sucre 7-60, next to the Old Cathedral, T842984, tours (city, Cajas, Girón waterfalls, Ingapirca), airline tickets, English spoken, friendly.

Recommended guides *José Rivera Baquero*, Pedro Carbo 1-48 y Guapondelig. Extensive knowledge of Cuenca and its surroundings. *Eduardo Quito*, T823018, F834202. Own 4-wheel drive and offers special tours as a professionally qualified guide, transports up to 10 people, speaks good English. Highly recommended. *Luis Astudillo*, C Azuay 1-48 entre Guayas y Tungurahua, T815234. Tours to Ingapirca for US$30, good. The Ministerio de Turismo (see Tourist offices above) has a list of trained guides, *guías carnetizados*.

Transport **Local Bus**: city buses US$0.15. **Taxi**: US$1 for a short journey; US$1.40 to the airport

See also Ins & outs, page 250

or bus station; US$5 per hour; US$22 per day. **Car hire**: *Inter*, Av España, opposite the airport, T801892. *Localiza*, at the airport, T863902.

Long distance **Air**: to **Quito**, 3 flights a day with TAME. To **Guayaquil**, 3 flights a day with TAME and Austo Aereo. To Macas with Austro Aereo, on Mon, Wed and Fri. Reconfirm tickets and beware extra charges at check-in arising from staff claiming incorrectly that your flight has not been confirmed. No ticket reservations can be made at the airport. Arrive at least an hour before departure. Try getting a 'prechequeo' or advanced boarding pass.

Bus: to **Riobamba**, 5½-6 hrs, US$5, scenic, sit on the left. To **Ambato**, US$7, 7½ hrs. To/from **Quito**, 10-11 hrs, US$7, with Panamericana Internacional, Huayna Cápac y España, T840060; luxury coach service with Sucre Express, US$10. To **Loja**, 5-6 hrs with San Luis, US$4, lovely scenery, sit on the left, passport checks are likely. To **Machala**, 4-5 hrs, hourly, US$2.50, sit on the left, wonderful scenery. To **Guayaquil**, via Zhud, 5-6 hrs, US$4; the road is paved – shop around for the most comfortable bus. To **Guayaquil**, via

Cajas and Molleturo, 3-4 hrs, US$4, hourly with San Luis. This road is prone to land-slides, so check if it is open. To **Sucúa**, 10 hrs, US$6 and **Macas**, 11 hrs, US$6.50, with Turismo Oriental (4 daily, better buses) and Coop Sucúa (3 nightly, and one at 1000). The day bus is recommended for spectacular scenery (the left side is best overall although the right side is good for the last part with great views of the approach to the tropical lowlands). To **Huaquillas**, 6 hrs, US$3, buses at 0540, 1300, 1600, 2000, 2230. The bus sometimes stops for 2 hrs in Machala, to avoid the wait get off at the large roundabout (well known to drivers) for the local bus to Huaquillas; the evening bus arrives in Huaquillas at 0300, but passengers can sleep on the bus till daylight. Be pre-pared for frequent police checks on the way. To **Azogues**, US$0.60, 1 hr, buses leave every 30 mins. To **Saraguro**, US$3, 4 hrs. Buses to **Gualaquiza**, US$6, 10 hrs. To **Alausí**, US$4, 4 hrs; all Quito-bound buses pass through, about 20 a day, from 0600 onwards.

Airline offices *TAME*, Benigno Malo 508 y C Larga, T843222. *Austro Aereo*, Hermano Miguel **Directory** 5-42 y Honorato Vázquez, T832677, F848659. *Ecuatoriana*, Bolívar 8-20, T832220, F832280. *American Airlines*, Hermano Miguel 8-67, T831699, F832024. *Iberia*, in the *Hotel El Dorado*.
  Banks *Filanbanco*, several branches, for Visa. *Banco del Pacífico*, Benigno Malo 9-75. Mastercard ATM, best rates for TCs. *Banco del Austro*, Sucre y Borrero, T842492. Citicorp TCs, Visa ATM. *Banco de Guayaquil*, Sucre entre Hermano Miguel y Borrero. For Visa and all TCs. *Banco del Pichincha*, Bolívar 9-74 y B Malo T831544. For TCs. MasterCard office at Bolívar y T Ordóñez, T883577, F817290. *Cambidex*, Luis Cordero 9-77, T835755. Helpful, good rates. *M M Jaramillo Arteaga*, Sucre y Borrero, changes US$ TCs and other currencies, cash only. *Vaz Cambios*, Gran Colombia 7-98 y Cordero, T833434. Open on Sat morning, efficient. No Peruvian currency is available.
  Communications Post Office: on corner of C Gran Colombia and Borrero, helpful. **Pacifictel**: on Benigno Malo between Córdova and Sucre. **Internet**: rates US$0.70-1.00 per hour, net2phone about US$0.35 per minute. *@lo-ETAPA*, Benigno Malo 7-27 y Sucre, also good rates for international phone and fax. *Cuenc@net*, C Larga 6-02 y Hermano Miguel. *Cybercom*, Pres Córdova y Borrero, good rates. *Explore Net*, Padre Aguirre 10-96 y Lamar, T844473, Canadian owner. *Internet Place*, Padre Aguirre y Gran Colombia, good rates. *Internet Service*, Sucre 7-22 y Borrero. *Lasermaster*, Bolívar 4-56, T838677. *Zon@net*, Hermano Miguel 4-46 y C Larga.
  Embassies and consulates Colombian *Consulate*, Cordero 9-55. **British Honorary Consul**, Sr Teodoro Jerves, Pasaje San Alfonso (same block as Iglesia San Alfonso), T831996. *Alliance Française*, Tadeo Torres 1-92. Open Mon-Fri, 0830-1230, 1430-1830.
  Medical facilities *Clínica Santa Inés*, Av D Córdova Toral 2-113, T817888, Dr Jaime Moreno Aguilar speaks English. *Clínica Los Andes*, Mariano Cueva 14-68 y Pío Bravo, T842942/832488, excellent care, clean, 24-hr service. *Hospital Monte Sinai*, Miguel Cordero 6-111 y Av Solano, near the stadium, T885595. *Clínica Santa Ana*, Av Manuel J Calle 1-104, T814068. *Farmacia Botica Internacional*, Gran Colombia 7-20 y Borrero. Experienced staff, wide selection.
  Language courses *Fundación Centro de Estudios Interamericanos*, Gran Colombia 11-02 y Gral Torres, Edif Assoc de Empleados, T839003, F833593, interpro@cedei.org, www.cedei.org Spanish and Quichua, free email service for students, accommodation at short notice, *Hostal Macondo* attached.

Hourly rates for classes US$4.50-8.00

Recommended. *Centro Abraham Lincoln*, Borrero y Honorato Vásquez, T830373. Small Spanish language section. *Nexus*, José Peralta 1-19 y 12 de Abril, T884016, F888221. Also teaches English and German, short-term basis family stays, well-run. Recommended. *Sí Centro de Español e Inglés*, Hermano Miguel 6-86 y Pres Córdova, T846932, jbariio@uio.satnet.net, www. ecuadorexplorer.com/sicentro/home Good, competitive prices, helpful, tourist information available. recommended. *Contacto* Galápagos 5-75 y Esmeraldas, T882703. Spanish, Quichua and English lessons. *Estudio Internacional Sampere*, Hermano Miguel 3-43 y Calle Larga, T/F841986, samperec@samperecen.com.ec At the high end of the price range.

Laundry *La Química*, Borrero 734 y Córdova. Same day service, dry cleaning, expensive. *Lavahora*, Honorato Vásquez 7-72 (next to El Cafecito), T823042. US$1 per load, same day service, helpful and efficient. Recommended. *Fast Klin*, Hermano Miguel y Pres Córdova. Open Mon-Fri 0800-1900, Sat 0800-1300.

Useful addresses Immigration: Policía Nacional de Migración, Luis Cordero 662 y J Jaramillo, T831020.

Excursions from Cuenca

Baños

The hottest commercial baths in Ecuador, so hot that there are steam baths at three of the complexes

There are sulphur baths at Baños, with its domed, blue church in a delightful landscape, 5 km southwest of Cuenca. Water temperatures at the source are measured at 76°C. There are four complexes: Rodas, Marchan, Familiar and Durán. The last are by far the largest and best maintained and although associated with the *Hostería Durán* they are open to the public. There are numerous hot pools and tubs and steam baths open from dawn till 2100 or 2200. They are very crowded at weekends. The country lanes above the village offer some pleasant walks. At the baths is **B** *Hostería Durán*, Km 8 Vía Baños, T892485, F892488. It has a restaurant, its own well maintained and very clean pools, US$1.60 for non-residents, also tennis courts, steam bath US$3; camping is allowed. There are also four *residencias*, all **G**.

Transport Buses marked Baños go to and from Cuenca every 5-10 mins, 0600-2330, US$0.20. Buses turn around at the airport, pass the front of the Terminal Terrestre, cross the city on Vega Muñoz and Cueva, then down Todos los Santos to the river, along 12 de Abril and onto Av Loja to the end where it joins Av de Las Américas. Taxis cost US$2.40. To walk takes 1½ hrs.

East of Cuenca

Gualaceo

Gualaceo is a thriving, modern town set in beautiful landscape, with a charming plaza and fine new church with splendid modern glass. Its Sunday market doesn't cater to tourists. Woollen goods are sold on the main street near the bus station, while embroidered goods are sold from a private home above the general store on the main plaza. Inexpensive good shoes are made locally.

From Gualaceo take a taxi to **Bulzhun** (10 minutes) where backstrap weavers make *macanas* (Ikat dyed shawls). From there walk back down to Bulcay, another weaving community, and catch a bus back to Cuenca. Buses leave from the Terminal Terrestre in Cuenca to Gualaceo, US$0.35, 25 minutes.

Sleeping and eating C *Parador Turístico*, T255110. Outside town, chalets, rooms, modern, nice, swimming pool, good restaurant, also has a little handicrafts museum which is free during the week. On the same street but further down the hill is **E** *Molina*, T255048. With bath, cable TV. Clean. **F** *Residencial Carlos Andrés*, 3 blocks north of the main plaza, T255379. Clean, quiet. **F** *Residencial Gualaceo*, Gran Colombia, T255006. Clean, friendly, camping possible. *Don Q*, The best place to eat in town, clean, fast service, good menu. *Borin Cuba*, Av Jaime Roldós, set meals.

The paved road from El Descanso (between Azogues and Cuenca) to Gualaceo and Paute has been rebuilt, but is only open to small vehicles. Buses to Paute turn off to the east between Azogues and El Descanso, and to Gualaceo turn off south of El Descanso through El Jadán or San Bartolo.

North of Gualaceo, on the Río Palma, is Paute, home to the largest hydroelec- **Paute**
tric plant in Ecuador. Improved access roads have converted much of the original farmland into weekend home developments and the farming has been pushed onto the higher slopes, contributing to deforestation. The rainwater runoff now carries much more mud and soil which is quickly silting up the Paute dam, which has to be continually dredged to function. All this contributes to major dry season electricity cuts nationwide.

Sleeping B *Hostería Huertos de Uzhpud*, Casilla 01-01-1268, Uzhupud, Paute, T250339, T Cuenca 806521, taxi from Cuenca US$8, bargain hard. Set in the beautiful Paute valley. Rooms at the back have best views, swimming pool, sauna, horses, gardens with lots of orchids, quiet, relaxing. Highly recommended. On the edge of town is **D** per person *San Luis*, cabins. **G** *Residencial Cuticay*, T250133. The cheapest, OK.

A paved road runs south from Gualaceo to Chordeleg, a village famous for its **Chordeleg**
crafts in wood, silver and gold filigree (though very little is available nowadays), pottery and panama hats. The village has been described as very touristy (watch out for fake jewellery). *Joyería Dorita* and *Joyería Puerto del Sol*, on Juan B Cobos y Eloy Alfaro, have been recommended. There are some good shops selling beautiful ceramics. Food can be had at the *Restaurante El Turista*. There is plenty of local transport, US$0.15 from Gualaceo market, every 30 minutes. Direct bus from Cuenca, one hour, US$0.40.

The church is interesting with some lovely modern stained glass. Chordeleg has a small Museo de Comunidad with fascinating local textiles, ceramics and straw work, some of which are on sale at reasonable prices. It's a good uphill walk from Gualaceo to Chordeleg, and a pleasant hour downhill in the other direction. With your own vehicle, you can drive back to Cuenca through San Juan and San Bartolomé, which is a lovely colonial town famous for guitar makers. Two small mines after this village welcome visitors.

South of Gualaceo, 83 km from Cuenca, is Sígsig. There's a market on Sunday, **Sígsig**
one *residencial*, **G**, and *Restaurante Turista*, which is OK. Buses from Cuenca, *Another good place to*
1½ hours, US$0.65. There's an hourly bus from Chordeleg. *buy panama hats*

A road has been built between Sígsig and Gualaquiza, along a beautiful and unspoilt route (see page 387). It is open to four-wheel drive and buses during the dry season. From Sígsig take a bus south to Chiqüinda at 0900 (2½ hours); buy tickets the night before. Stay overnight with Sr Fausto, the teacher.

From Chiqüinda the road goes to Aguacate (four to five hours walking), a village **Aguacate**
of 70 people. After about three hours the road divides by a small school on the left. Take the left fork. There are shops and electricity at night only. The village hosts good *fiestas* at Christmas and New Year, and carnival. Sr Jorge Guillermo Vásquez has a *hospedaje*, **G**, very basic but friendly, coffee and popcorn for breakfast, horses can be hired for trekking to caves. Buses to Cuenca leave at 2200. They are often full, try going to Loja instead (at 2200, nine hours).

From Aguacate the road continues southeast to Río Negro, a friendly village. If you wish to stop here, you can then catch a bus or truck at 1300 and 1600 to continue to Gualaquiza (one to two hours, US$0.45).

Southern Highlands

Parque Nacional Cajas

This national park, located 29 km west of Cuenca, is an easily accessible páramo and high elevation forest park speckled with over 250 lakes separated by rocky ridges. It is well managed because it is the source of Cuenca's drinking water and hundreds of Cuencanos go there on the weekends. It is small (29,000 ha), but most tourists do not travel far from the road so it is possible to find solitude. The park is a favourite for birders; 125 species have been identified here, including the Condor and many hummingbirds. The Violet-tailed Metaltail is a hummingbird endemic to this area; others which can be seen include: shining sunbeam, veridean metal-tail, sparkling violet-ear and the sword-billed. The lakes also harbour Andean gulls, speckled teal and yellow-billed pintails.

Treks in the park

There are some trails marked near the visitors' centre but they tend to peter out quickly. For an overnight trek you can follow the routes described below or head out on your own. On the opposite side of the lake from the *refugio* is **Cerro San Luis** (4,200 m) which may be climbed in a day, with excellent views. From the visitors' centre go anticlockwise around the lake; after crossing the outflow look for a sign 'Al San Luis', follow the yellow and black stakes to the summit and beware of a side trail to dangerous ledges.

A strong hiker with a good sense of direction can cross the park in two days. Since the elevation throughout the park is less than 4,500 m there is no permanent snow, but it is cold at night and it can rain and hail. There have been several deaths from exposure so it is important to be prepared with proper clothing. August and September are the driest months but hiking is possible all year round. The best time is August to January, when you can expect clear days, strong winds, night-time temperatures of -8°C and occasional mist. From February to July temperatures are higher but there is much more fog, rain and snow. It is best to arrive in the early morning since it can get very cloudy, wet and cool after about 1300.

Parque Nacional Cajas

Continue past **Laguna Toreadora** on a paved road to the village of **Migüir**. In town ask for the trail that heads up to **Laguna Sunincocha**. Along this path vegetation changes from second growth cloud forest to *páramo*. The trail fades but stay on the south side of Laguna Sunincocha and follow drainage south past **Laguna Valeriana Yacu** to the pass. From here you can see **Laguna Inga Casa** and the Río Soldados drainage. It is about four to five hours to this pass from Migüir and there are good camping spots next to the lakes in the Río Soldados drainage. The walk out to **Soldados** along the Río Soldados the next day takes four to five hours. Since there are only four buses a week to Cuenca via Soldados you should not rely too heavily on transport out.

Migüir to Soldados Trek

It is also possible to follow the Ingañan trail, an old Inca pathway that used to connect Cuenca with the coast. It is in ill-repair or lost in places but there are some interesting ruins above **Laguna Mamamag**. You can access the Ingañan from the park headquarters or from **Migüir**. Beginning in Migüir follow an established path to **Laguna Luspa**. At Laguna Lupsa take a path on the north side of the lake which connects to a stream that flows into Laguna Luspa. From here head east on a trail eventually ascending to a divide where you will be able to see **Laguna Osohuayco**. Continue down to Laguna Osohuaycu. The route passes to the north of Laguna Osohuaycu and then descends to **Laguna Mamamag** where you should stay on the south side of the lake. At the downstream end of the lake cross over the small ridge and descend steeply through cloud forest on an established trail. At the bottom of the hill follow the wide Inca road over pastures to **Laguna Llaviuco**. There is a gate where you should be able to get a ride with fishermen back to Cuenca or walk to the main road in about an hour. This trip takes two to three days.

Ingañan Trail

Essentials

Travel through the park is largely cross-country along way-trails or through the *páramo* grasses, so good topographic maps are necessary. One of the most knowledgeable Cajas guides is Juan Diego Domínguez at the *Posada de Sol* in Cuenca (see page 253). The following IGM 1:50,000 maps cover the whole park: Chaucha, Cuenca, San Felipe de Mollerturo and Chiquintad. Access to some drainages on the eastern edge of the park may be restricted. For more information contact ETAPA in Cuenca (Empresa de Telefonos, Agua Potable y Alcantarillado, T890418/831900). The Ministerio del Ambiente office in Cuenca, Bolívar 5-33, T823074, has limited information.

The main entrance station to the park is about 40 mins from Cuenca on the road to Migüir where you need to pay a fee of US$10. The bus marked Sayausi-Migüir leaves daily at 0600 from the San Sebastián plaza, on the corner of Simón Bolívar y Col Talbot, and takes about 1½ hrs to reach Laguna Toreadora. It returns to Cuenca at 1400, US$1.35. It may also be possible to catch a bus from the terminal terrestre in Cuenca if the road to the coast via Molleturo is open (see page 266). Taxis can be hired in Cuenca for about US$12. Another route into the park is on the bus to Angas, on the south side of the park. Buses leave from Av Loja by the river every day at 0600 and return in the afternoon. Near Laguna Toreadora is a visitors' centre and a *refugio* (see below).

G per person *Refugio*. Cold, with 4 bunks and cooking facilities. There are also 2 primitive shelters by the shore of the lake, a 20- and 40-min walk from the refuge. Take food, fuel, candles, sleeping bags, warm clothes and strong sun cream. Camping costs US$2.

Sleeping

There are organized tours to the lakes from Cuenca, some offering fishing, which cost about US$35 per person. Alternatively, hire a private truck, which costs US$16 with a driver. Jorge Moscoso (see Shopping, page 259), is knowledgeable and helpful about

Tours

Southern Highlands

Cajas. A group of ramblers welcomes visitors for Sunday walks in Aug and Sep, look for posters in Cuenca.

Molleturo &   The road from Cuenca to Guayaquil via Cajas and Molleturo is paved for much
Naranjal   of its length, but it's prone to landslides during the rainy season (February to May) and is often in an appalling state. The road passes through Parque Nacional Cajas and continues over the mountains to the towns of Migüir, Molleturo and on to Naranjal on the coast, between Guayaquil and Machala. The scenery is spectacular and there are still a few places where there is undisturbed forest. There is nowhere to stay after the *refugio* at Laguna Toreadora (see above) until you reach the lowlands between Naranjal and La Troncal. Some buses may be running on this road (for example San Luis and Semeria to Guayaquil, see Transport, page 260), but check on the current situation.

Cuenca to Machala

From Cuenca the Panamericana runs south to La Y, about 20 km away. Here the road divides: one branch continues as the Panamericana to Loja and the other runs through sugar cane fields to Pasaje and Machala on the coast.

One hour from Cuenca is **Girón** whose beauty is spoiled only by a modern concrete church. After the battle on 27 February 1829 between the troops of Gran Colombia, led by Sucre, and those of Peru under Lamar, at nearby Portete de Tarqui, a treaty was signed in Girón. The building, **Casa de los Tratados**, is shown to visitors, as is the site of the Peruvians' capitulation (entry fee US$0.40). Ask directions to **El Chorro** waterfall, a 6 km walk, with cloudforest above.

From Girón trucks take passengers up a winding road to the hamlets of **San Fernando** (rooms at *La Posada*) and **Chumblín**. Friendly inhabitants will act as guides to three lakes high in the *páramo* where excellent trout-fishing is to be had. There is also rock-climbing on San Pablo, overlooking Lago Busa. Take camping gear. Return to the main road through Asunción. There's a beautiful downhill stretch for cyclists.

The route goes through the Yungilla valley and **Santa Isabel**. There's accommodation at **C** *La Molienda*, by Cataviña, just before Santa Isabel; **D** *Sol y Agua*, below the village, a weekend place for *Cuencanos*; **G** *Hostería al Durán*, basic, no water. There are many other small weekend farms. The road then descends through desert to the stark, rocky canyon of the Río Jubones.

The next town is **Casacay** (**E** *Hostería San Luis*, attractive, with pool), after which the road passes through lush banana plantations. Before Casacay, at a military checkpoint, a road climbs south to **Chilla**, see below.

In the lowlands is **Pasaje** (*population*: 27,000) with accommodation at **D** *San Martín*, clean, air conditioning, safe; and many basic *pensiones*, **F**. Most buses travel north to La Troncal or south down the coast to Machala and then to Huaquillas for the Peruvian border (see page 303).

South of Cuenca

The road from Cuenca south to Loja is fully paved; although often in disrepair it is one of the most beautiful and breathtaking in Ecuador.

The road climbs south from La Y to the village of **Cumbe**, which has a small, colourful Wednesday market. The road then rises to the Tinajillas pass, at 3,527 m. Further south at La Ramada a branch road forks left to the lovely, sleepy colonial town of **Nabón**, with its weekend market. There is lovely hiking in the nearby valleys and several unexcavated ruins. A small *pensión* offers accommodation. With a rental car or bikes it is possible to do a loop rejoining the Panamericana at Oña, though this trip is best done in the dry season (June to September).

The road descends sharply into the warm upper Jubones valley past cane fields and rises again after Río León (Km 95, 1,900 m) to the small town of **Oña**, (*population*: 3,244) at Km 105, 2,300 m. There is one hotel on the plaza and several places to eat. The best place to eat is out of town on the old road south, run by the Alvarez sisters, who offer traditional cooking but not much choice. Another recommended restaurant is *San Luis*. From Oña the road weaves and climbs through highland *páramo* pastures (3,040 m) and then descends towards Saraguro (Km 144).

Saraguro
Population: 19,883

This is a very cold town, famed for its weaving and distinctive indigenous population. Here the Indians, the most southerly Andean group in Ecuador, dress all in black. They wear very broad flat-brimmed hard felt hats. The men are notable for their black shorts, sometimes covered by a whitish kind of divided apron, and a particular kind of saddle bag, the *alforja*, and the women for their pleated black skirts, necklaces of coloured beads and silver *topos*, ornate pins fastening their shawls. Many of them drive cattle across the mountains east to the tropical pastures above the Amazonian jungle. The town has a picturesque Sunday market and interesting mass. In the surroundings of Saraguro are several high elevation forest remnants, in which 145 species of birds have been identified. Birdwatching is good even along the main road both north and south of town. Buses to Cuenca with Coop Viajeros, four daily, US$2.65, 4½ hrs. To Loja, US$1.80, 1½ hrs.

Sleeping and eating G *Residencial Armijos*, C Antonio Castro. Cold shower, clean, friendly, quiet, good. **G** *Residencial Saraguro*, C Loja 03-2 y Antonio Castro. Shared bath, friendly, nice courtyard, hot water, laundry facilities. Recommended. *Salón Cristal*, Azuay y Castro, lunch only, simple but good food, clean, on the plaza, OK. *Reina del Cisne*, at the park, set meals. Cheap food is available in the market.

West from Saraguro

From Saraguro a spectacular road (passable June to September) runs through **Celén**, **Selva Alegre**, **Manu**, **Guanazán** and **Chilla** down to the coast. A bus goes to Manu throughout the year and to Guanazán in the dry season. Chilla is famous for its Church of the Virgin and pilgrims flock here in September from all over the country. The only place to stay is the *Casa de Huéspedes* (Pilgrims' Guest House) which is empty the rest of the year. This area has remnants of native forest between 2,800 and 3,000 m and good birdwatching possibilities.

South from Chilla mountain trails run over the mysterious **Cerro de Arcos** to **Zaruma** and **Piñas**, see page 301.

Saraguro to Yacuambi Trek

The trail from Saraguro to the jungle town of **Yacuambi** (called 28 de Mayo on some maps), is a classic old trading route down the eastern slope of the Andes to the jungle. It is perhaps one of the most delightful two to three day walks in Ecuador. It is prone to landslides in the rainy season, so enquire about conditions before starting.

A wide track heads up from the agricultural lands surrounding Saraguro to an expansive swampy bench which is dotted with lakes and a few granite knolls. The track is well-constructed with several sections of stone paving (probably precolumbian) and an interesting stone bridge. The views from this

Southern Highlands

low elevation section of the Andes (3,400 m) into the Amazon Basin on a clear day are awe-inspiring. The path is obvious and still travelled by Saraguros and Oriente settlers. The difficulty of walking is moderate but be prepared for cold, rain and mud during the wet season. The best time to go is during the dry season from August to December. The appropriate maps are IGM 1:50,000 Saraguro and San José de Yacuambi.

Some food can be purchased in the shops in Saraguro but it is best to buy most supplies in a major city. There are also a few basic restaurants. The Saraguro market is open daily and has a good selection of fresh produce. The friendly owner of *Residencial Armijos*, Rogelio Armijos, knows how to get to the beginning of this hike and will take you up in his truck for US$10.

You can also catch any bus heading north on the Panamericana just beyond the town of **Urdaneta** (known locally as Paquishapa) to the turn-off to the village of **Turucachi**. There is a fork in this road about 100 m from the Panamericana; go left towards an area called **Quingueado**. It is possible to drive about 20 minutes to a landslide blocking the road or walk this stretch in about 1½ hours. From the landslide hike up the abandoned roadbed which soon becomes a track. There are several trails but it is best to drop down to a well-worn trail to the right of the roadbed. Head for a couple of houses next to an eroded area which is known as Quingueado.

From Quingueado the trail is an obvious white streak that heads down to **Río Quingueado** then up to a notch. The stone paving is present in this section and is often elevated because of erosion of the surrounding soil. Where the paving is missing years of mule and foot traffic have worn away a path that in places is entrenched 10 m deep into the hillsides. The trail eventually crosses the **Río San Antonio** and then comes to an interesting stone bridge across the boulder strewn **Río Negro**. It is worth stopping here to admire the craftsmanship of the bridge and perhaps take a dip in one of the cool stream pools.

From the Río Negro the trail climbs steeply and within 30 minutes comes to a Y; turn right and up. The trail to the left takes you to the village of **Tutupali** which also could make an interesting hike. Soon you are on a broad flat ridge and pass a glacial erratic (boulder) perched on a hill called **Cerro La Voladora**. Ambling along the granite knolls are views of the **Tres Lagunas** and other lakes on the plateau.

There are good camping spots at the edge of the Andean Slope about six to eight hours from the landslide on the road. There is a small lake on the southeast side of **Cerro Condorcillo** which is a good source of water. Sunsets reflect off the lakes on the plateau and sunrises come up over the Amazon Basin. Although this is one of the lowest points along the crest of the Ecuadorean Andes the views are outstanding. The descent down to the cloud forest is magnificent. From the top on a clear day you can just glimpse where the trail heads

Saraguro to Yacuambi

through a notch in a ridge just above Yacuambi. The notch seems a short stroll but it is really a good six to eight hours of knee pounding descents. The trail has some long sections of paving and seems to blend into the landscape of boulders and shrubby cloud forest vegetation as if in a Japanese garden.

About an hour from Cerro Condorcillo the trail crosses the **Río Corral Huaycu** and enters dense cloud forest. The descent is steep in places and deeply entrenched. Stay on the main path which generally sticks to the ridge crest. In the distance to the right there is a large waterfall above the **Río Garcelán valley**. As you descend it gets hot and humid but there are plenty of streams to refill water bottles. There is one ambiguous intersection about four to five hours from Cerro Condorcillo where you need to turn left. If you head straight you will climb for about five minutes then funnel into a steep deeply eroded trench – this is the wrong way.

Always take the most travelled path and do not be tempted to drop down to the pastures along the **Río Garcelán** since you will only have to climb back up again to get to Yacuambi. In the community of **Tambo Loma** there is electricity. Just beyond you pass through the notch with views of the wide Río Yacuambi (which means clear water in Quichua). From the notch you descend switch-backs to a suspension bridge over the Río Yacuambi. This is also a great spot to go for a swim.

The gravel road from **Zamora** ends at the bridge and from here it is about a 30 minute hike to the town of Yacuambi. There is one very basic hostel near the village plaza which also serves a good and cheap meal. Unión Cariamanga has a nightly bus Yacuambí-Saraguro, at 2000.

The Ministerio del Ambiente is considering the mountains near Yacuambi for a new national park. It is worth stopping by the offices of Fundación Ecológica Yacuambi to find out about their conservation efforts. Trucks leave in the mornings for the 2½ hour drive to Zamora. Once in Zamora there are hotels and numerous buses to Loja which is two hours away (see page 387).

Loja

This friendly, pleasant city, encircled by hills, lies near the Oriente. Loja has been a traditional gateway between the highlands and southern Amazonia. Tropical forest products such as cinchona (the natural base for quinine), first entered the European pharmacopoeia through Loja.

Phone code: 07
Colour map 6, grid B2
Population: 117,365
Altitude: 2,063 m

Ins and outs

The city can be reached by air from Quito or Guayaquil to Catamayo (known locally as La Toma), which is 35 km away by paved road (see page 278). On arrival at La Toma airport, shared taxis will be waiting to take you to Loja; 45 mins, US$3. They fill up quickly so choose a driver, give him your luggage claim ticket and he will collect your checked luggage. There's a bus to Loja (US$0.80), or stay in Catamayo (see page 278). The bus terminal at Av Gran Colombia e Isidro Ayora is to the north of the centre. At the terminal is left luggage, an information desk, shops and Pacifictel office; pay the US$0.15 terminal tax at the information booth by main entrance. There are buses every 2 mins to/from the centre making the 10-min journey. A taxi from the centre is US$0.60.

Getting there
See also Transport, page 273

Loja is a fairly spread out city but the centre is compact with most of the hotels clustered to the west of the cathedral. The Universidad Técnica is a short taxi ride away.

Getting around

Southern Highlands

Tourist offices *Ministerio de Turismo*, Valdiviezo 08-22 y 10 de Agosto, T572964, F570485. Open Mon-Fri, 0800-1300, 1500-1800. *Loja tradición, cultura y turismo*, is a useful guidebook. *La Hora* and *Crónica* give news of events.

Loja was founded on its present site in 1548, having been moved from La Toma, and was rebuilt twice after earthquakes, the last of which occurred in the 1880s. Its first site, in the hotter, lower valley of Catamayo, had too high an incidence of malaria (documentation of this can be found in the Banco Central Museum, see below). The town has the distinction of being the first in the country to have electricity. A small hydro-electric plant was built close by at the end of the last century.

There is an expression in Loja which says that God crumpled the province like a piece of paper and if it were flattened out, it would cover the whole of Ecuador. In other words, this is quite a mountainous area. Much of the accessible land is deforested and it has a tendency to be rather dry. As in the province of Manabí, on the Pacific coast, Loja has a reputation for bad farming practices and high emigration into the newer areas which were opened to

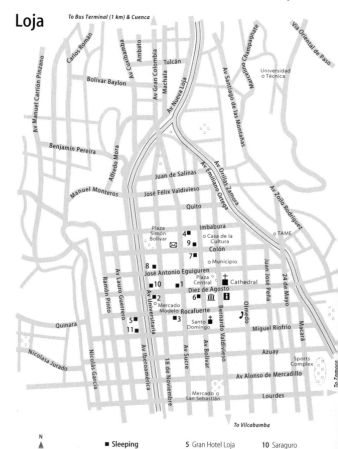

Loja

N
0 metres 200
0 yards 200

■ **Sleeping**
1 Acapulco & Londres
2 Bombuscaro
3 Caribe
4 Chandelier

5 Gran Hotel Loja
6 Las Orquídeas
7 Libertador
8 Metropolitano
9 Ramsés

10 Saraguro Internacional
11 Vilcabamba

colonization by the now defunct IERAC (Instituto Ecuatoriana de Reforma Agraria y Colonización). For this reason the official name of Lago Agrio, capital of the province of Sucumbios, is Nueva Loja.

Sights

At Puente Bolívar, by the northern entrance to town, is a fortress-like monument and a lookout over the city, known as **La Entrada de la Ciudad**. It is a symbol of Loja's role as a gateway between the Pacific and the Amazon basin. Erected in 2000, it will be developed into a cultural centre, a good place to take pictures. ■ *0800-1600.*

The **Cathedral** and **Santo Domingo** church, Bolívar y Rocafuerte, have painted interiors. **El Valle** church, on the south edge of the city, is colonial, with a lovely interior. The **Museo de la Historia y Cultura Lojanas del Banco Central** on the main plaza, 0800-1600, has exhibits of local art, archaeology, folklore and history, and the **Casa de la Cultura**, B Valdiviezo y Colón, sponsors cultural events. **Mercado Centro Comercial Loja**, 10 de Agosto y 18 de Noviembre, rebuilt in 1991, is worth a visit. It is clean and efficient. ■ *Mon-Sat 0800-1800, Sun 0800-1500.* There is a market on Saturday, Sunday and Monday, attended by many Saraguro Indians. There are souvenir and craft shops on 10 de Agosto between Iberoamérica and 18 de Noviembre.

Loja is famed for its musicians and has one of the few musical academies in the country. Musical evenings and concerts are often held around the town. The city also boasts two universities, with a well-known law school. The Universidad Técnica, on the hill to the northeast of the centre, is the Open University for Ecuador, having correspondence students and testing centres scattered across the country. The Universidad Nacional has good murals on some of its buildings. There are also crude but original paintings on the patio walls of many of the old houses.

In the north of the city, a couple of blocks east of the Terminal is the **Parque Recreacional Jipiro**, a good place to walk and relax. A well maintained, clean park, with a small lake, sports fields, pools, an observatory and replicas of different cities. It is popular with Lojanos on weekends, when there are puppet shows, theatre and other activities. Take the city bus marked 'Jipiro', a five-minute ride from the centre.

Excursions

Parque Educacional Ambiental y Recreacional de Argelia is superb, with trails through the forest to the *páramo*. It is 500 m before the police checkpoint on the road south to Vilcabamba. Take a city bus marked 'Argelia'. ■ *0830-1700 except Tue and Wed.* Across the road and 100 m south, the **Jardín Botánico Reynaldo Espinosa** is well laid out and has several cinchona trees. ■ *Mon-Fri 0800-1700, US$0.20.*

Essentials

Sleeping
■ *on map*
Price codes: see inside front cover

C *Bombuscaro*, 10 de Agosto y Av Universitaria, T577021, F570136, mbombus@loja.telconet.net Nice rooms and suites, good service, includes full breakfast. Recommended. **C** *Hostal del Bus*, Av 8 de Diciembre y JJ Flores, opposite the terminal, T575100, F572297, hdelgado@impsat.net.ec Carpeted rooms and suites, with cable TV, restaurant. **C** *Libertador*, Colón 14-30 y Bolívar, T570344, F572119. Bath, TV, suites available, noisy, good restaurant *La Castellana*, parking. **D** *Ramsés*, Colón 14-31 y Bolívar, T571402, F581832. Bath, phone, TV, good restaurant.

Southern Highlands

E *Acapulco*, Sucre 749 y 10 de Agosto, T570651. Clean, hot water, private bath, safe for leaving luggage, first floor rooms are quieter in the mornings. Recommended. **E** *Alborada*, Sucre 1279 y Lourdes. With shower, clean. **E** *Apart Hotel Iberoamérica*, Av Universitaria y J Valdiviezo, with cable TV, laundry service. **E** *Grand Hotel Loja*, Iberoamérica (also known as Av Manuel Agustín Aguirre) y Rocafuerte, T575200, F575202. Bath, TV, phone, cafeteria. **E** *Hostal Aguilera Internacional*, Sucre 01-08 y Emiliano Ortega, T/F572894. Nice rooms with bath, TV, restaurant, sauna, gym parking, includes breakfast. **E** *Podocarpus*, J Eguiguren 16-50 y Bolívar, T584912. Carpeted rooms with bath, cable TV, includes breakfast. **E** *Vilcabamba*, Iberoamérica y Pasaje la FEUE, T573393, F573645. Includes full breakfast. On the river, clean. Discounts for travellers with Footprint Handbook.

F *Hostal Las Orquídeas*, Bolívar 8-59 y 10 de Agosto, T575465. With bath, hot water. Clean, friendly. **F** *Hostal La Riviera*, Universitaria y 10 de Agosto, T572863. Carpeted rooms, TV, phone, good. **F** *Metropolitano*, 18 de Noviembre 6-41 y Colón, T570007. With bath and TV, hot water, clean. **F** *Saraguro Internacional*, Universitaria 724 y 10 de Agosto, T570552. Hot water, TV, parking, restaurant closed Sun. **G** *Caribe*, Rocafuerte 1552 y 18 de Noviembre, T572902. Shared bath, hot water. Recommended. **G** *Chandelier*, Imbabura 14-82 y Sucre, T563061. With bath, TV, friendly. **G** *Londres*, Sucre 741 y 10 de Agosto. Nice big rooms, hot water, clean, friendly. Recommended. There are basic *residenciales* in the **G** and **H** ranges on Rocafuerte, also some along Sucre with mostly short stay customers.

Eating
Meal prices are cheap, often under US$3

José Antonio, Sucre y Eguiguren Excellent *ceviche* and seafood, enthusiastic chef. Highly recommended. *México*, Eguiguren 1585 y Sucre. Good set meals or à la carte, generous portions, popular. Seriously cheap. Recommended. *Chalet Francia*, B Valdiviezo y Eguiguren. Very good food, imaginative cooking, small portions. *La Tullpa*, 18 de Noviembre y Colón. Good *churrasco*. *Parrillada Uruguaya*, Iberoamérica y J de Salinas. Opens 1700, good grilled meat, owner helpful. *La Casona*, 18 de Noviembre 8-56 near Imbabura (the better of 2 branches). Good. *El Paraíso*, Sucre 0435 y Quito. Good vegetarian. *Salud y Vida*, Azuay near Olmedo. Vegetarian. In El Valle area the *Colonial* and *La Lolita* are recommended, try their *cuy*. *Chifa El Arbol de Oro*, Bolívar y Lourdes, opposite Mercado San Sebastián. Good Chinese food. Seriously cheap. *A lo Mero Mero*, Sucre y Colón 6-22. Excellent Mexican food and sandwiches. *La Capiata*, Av Cuxibamba y Tena. Very good seafood. *Don Quijote*, Rocafuerte y Macará. Good pizza. *Unicornio*, Bolívar y 10 de Agosto, on the main plaza. Piano bar. *Plaza Inn*, Bolívar 07-57, at main park. Cheap fast food. Open 0900-2300.

Bakeries Loja has many excellent bakeries, local buns made with raw sugar are called *bollos*. *Pastelería Persa*, Bolívar y Rocafuerte. Good snacks, pastries and yoghurt. *Topoli*, Riofrío y Bolívar. Best coffee and yoghurt in town, good for breakfast (not open for lunch). *El Jugo Natural*, J Eguiguren 14-18 y Bolívar. Very good fresh juices and breakfast. Closed Sun. *Yogur & Helados*, 24 de Mayo y V Vivar, east of the centre. Good ice cream and yoghurt. *Sinaí*, at main park, opposite the Catedral, popular ice cream place.

Local specialities One of the famous dishes from the Loja area is *repe*, a green banana soup made from a special type of banana which only grows in the south. *Cecina* is thinly cut meat, usually pork, often cooked over open flames.

Bars & nightclubs

Siembra, Prolongación 24 de Mayo, Ciudadela Zamora, pizzeria and bar. Popular with foreigners. *Music Bar*, JJ Peña y Azuay. Bar, good music and atmosphere. *El Viejo Minero*, Sucre 10-76 y Azuay. Bar and café. *Fiesta*, 10 de Agosto 10-59 y JJ Peña. Disco with 2 halls, one plays Latin music and the other Techno.

Festivals

The *Fiesta de la Virgen del Cisne* (of the swan) is held **16-20 Aug**, and the image of the Virgin remains in Loja until 1 Nov. The statue of the Virgen del Cisne spends a month each year travelling around the province and hundreds of the faithful walk in procession with it. The most important of these peregrinations is the 3-day 70 km walk from El Cisne to Loja cathedral, which begins on **17 August**. Loja, Catamayo and El Cisne are crowded with religious pilgrims and Ecuadorean tourists during the last **2 weeks of August** and the **first week of September**. It is very difficult to find a room and all prices rise during this period.

Shopping

The Mercado (see Sights above) is well stocked. Health food shop on 10 de Agosto behind the Catedral. Great choice of products. *Procuero*, Av 8 de Diciembre 13-47, for leather crafts. *Cer-Art Ceramics* sells precolumbian designs on mostly high-gloss ceramics, which are produced at the Universidad Técnica with a workshop and retail shop. Above the Universidad Técnica (see Sights above) is the 'Ceramics Plaza', where you can buy directly from the crafts studio. The main shop sells high quality items but if you ask you will be shown the rooms where slightly imperfect ceramics are sold. A little higher on the same road is the Productos Lacteos, where you can buy excellent cheeses and fresh butter, all produced by the university and contributing to its finances. *Loaizacolor*, 10 de Agosto 13-20 for film and developing.

Tour operators

Biotours, JA Eguiguren y Olmedo, T578398, F574696, biotours@loja.telconet.net City, regional and jungle tours, airline tickets, Icaro agents. Friendly service. *Franky Tours*, 10 de Agosto 11-67 y Olmedo, T571031, F562554, fhidalgo@loja.telconet.net Local and regional tours, airline tickets. *Jatunpamba/Aratinga Aventuras*, Lourdes14-80 y Sucre, T/F582434, jatavent@cue.satnet.net Specializes in birdwatching tours, overnight trips to cloud forest. Pablo Andrade is a knowlegeable guide.

Transport

See also Ins & outs, page 269

Local Bus: city buses US$0.15. **Car hire**: *Arricar*, Colón 14-30, T571443, F588014. **Taxirutas** are shared taxis which run on a set route, their stops are clearly marked, US$0.20.

Long distance Air: there are TAME flights to Quito direct or via Guayaquil. Flights are often cancelled due to strong winds and the airport is sometimes closed by 1000. The TAME office is at 24 de Mayo y E Ortega, 0830-1600. Reserve your seat in Cuenca if you want to leave from Loja the next day. Icaro has 3 direct flights per week to Quito, in 19 passenger craft, US$53 one way. Tickets from *Biotours*, see Tour operators above. Flights to Piura (Peru) with ICARO are expected to operate by late 2000.

Bus All leave from the Terminal Terestre at the north of town, some companies also have ticket offices in the centre. To **Cuenca**, 4½ hrs, 7 a day, US$4 with Trans Viajeros (18 de Noviembre y Quito). To **Machala**, 10 a day, 7 hrs, US$3.80. There are 2 routes from Loja to Machala, one goes through Piñas and is rather bumpy with hairpin bends but has the better views, the other is paved and generally quicker. To **Quito**, with Cooperativa Loja (10 de Agosto y Guerrero), and Trans Santa, 4 a day, US$8, 13-14 hrs. To **Guayaquil**, 5 a day, 8 hrs, US$5.20. Panamericana Internacional have a luxury coach service to Quito (US$10) and Guayaquil (US$5.20). Their office is at *Grand Hotel Loja* (see above). To **Huaquillas** at 2030 and 2230, US$3.80, 6-8 hrs; get off at Machala crossroads, *La Avanzada*, and take a local bus from there. To **Macará**, 4 daily, 5-6 hrs, US$4, fully paved. To **Saraguro**, 6 daily, 1½ hrs, US$1. To **Vilcabamba**, a spectacular 1½ hr bus ride; Sur Oriente leave hourly from the bus terminal, US$0.60, Taxiruta (shared taxis) along Av Universitaria, US$1.60, 1 hr; Vilcabaturis vans, from the bus terminal, every 30 mins, US$1, 1 hr. To **Zamora**, 6 daily, 1½ hrs, US$1.25, a beautiful ride on a paved road (landslides are possible with heavy rains). To **Zumba** via Vilcabamba, with Sur Oriente and Unión Cariamanga, 8 daily (1st at 0530, 2nd at 0800), 7 hrs, US$4. To **Piura (Peru)**, luxury coach service with Loja Internacional, at 0700, 1000 and 2300 daily (Piura-Loja at 0600, 1000, 1300), 9 hrs including border formalities, US$7.50.

Southern Highlands

Directory **Banks** *Filanbanco* on the main plaza. Changes Amex TCs, best rates. *Banco de Loja*, Rocafuerte y Bolívar. Good rates for TCs. *Banco Mutualista Pichincha*, on plaza, cash advance on Mastercard. **Communications** **Post Office:** Colón y Sucre. No good for sending parcels. **Pacifictel:** on Rocafuerte y Olmedo. **Internet:** many internet cafés in town, price about US$1.20 per hour. Several around C Colón y Sucre. *Worldnet*, Colón 1469, good service. **Embassies and consulates** *Peru* Sucre y Azuay, T573600. **Useful addresses** **Immigration:** Bolivia y Argentina, T573600.

Parque Nacional Podocarpus

One of the most diverse protected areas in the world Spanning elevations between 950 and 3,700 m, this national park is particularly rich in birdlife, including many rarities and some newly discovered species; there could be up to 800 species in the park. It also includes one of the last major habitats for the spectacled bear. Podocarpus is divided into two areas, an upper premontane section with spectacular walking country, lush tropical cloud forest and excellent birdwatching, and a lower subtropical section, with remote areas of virgin forest and unmatched quantities of flora and fauna.

The park has easy access at several points. Both areas are quite wet, making waterproof hiking boots essential. The upper section is also very cold, so warm clothing and waterproofs are indispensable. ■ *Fee is US$5 in either area.*

Upper premontane section A map of the area and further information may be available at the Ministerio del Ambiente in Loja, Sucre entre Quito e Imbabura, T571534. There is an information centre and camping is possible but it can be very wet. Additional information from conservation groups in Loja: Arco Iris, Segundo Cueva Celi y Clodoveo Carrión, Ciudadela Zamora T572926; Biocorp, J A Eguigurten y Olmedo, T/F576696. Fundación Ecológica Podocarpus, JA Eguiguren y 18 de Noviembre, T572926. Programa Podocarpus, Clodoveo Carrión y Pasaje M de J Lozano, Ciudadela Zamora, T585924.

Access to the upper section of the park is at Cajanuma, about 15 km south of Loja on the Vilcabamba road. Take a Vilcabamba bus, get off in about 20 mins, US$0.60 – then it's an 8 km hike uphill to the guard station. It's possible to sleep here and there are cooking facilities. Direct transport is by taxi, US$8 round trip or with a tour from Loja. You can arrange a pick up later from the guard station. The southwestern section of the park can also be accessed through trails from Vilcabamba and Yangana.

Lower subtropical section There are two possible entrances to the lower subtropical section of the park. **Bombuscara** can be reached from Zamora (see page 387). Take a taxi US$2 to the entrance, then walk 1 km to the refuge, camping is also possible. There are trails to explore beyond.

The other entrance is at **Romerillos**, 2 hrs south by bus. From the bus terminal at Zamora 0630 and 1415, returning to Zamora at 0815 and 1600, there are also some trucks on this route. A 3-5 day hike is possible into this part of the park, contact the Ministerio del Ambiente in Zamora, by the entrance to town from Loja and from Fundación Maquipucuna which also has an office in Zamora and headquarters in Quito: Baquerizo Moreno E9-153 y Tamayo, Quito, T507200, F507201, arodas@uio.satnet.net, www.maqui.org Most food can be obtained in Zamora (but it is expensive), though all camping gear must be brought from larger cities.

Vilcabamba

Phone code: 07
Colour map 6, grid C3
Population: 3,894
Altitude: 1,520 m

Once an isolated village, Vilcabamba has become increasingly popular with foreign visitors, a 'must' along the gringo trail from Ecuador to Peru or vice versa. There are many places to stay and several good restaurants. The whole area is beautiful and tranquil, with an agreeable climate (17°C minimum, 26°C

● ●

Valley of the immortals

The tiny, isolated village of Vilcabamba gained a certain fame in the 1960s when doctors announced that it was home to one of the oldest living populations in the world. It was said that people here often lived to well over 100 years old, some as old as 135. Fame, though, turned to infamy when it was revealed that researchers had been given parish records which corresponded to the the subjects' parents. However, given that first children are often born to parents in their teenage years, this still means that there are some very old people living in these parts.

There is also a high incidence of healthy, active elders. It's not unusual to find people in their seventies and eighties toiling in the fields and covering several miles a day to get there. Such longevity and vitality is not only down to the area's famously healthy climate. Other factors are also at play: physical exercise, strong family ties, a balanced diet low in animal fats and a lack of stress.

● ●

maximum), wonderful for a few days' relaxation. The local economy has benefited from the influx of tourists, but there have been negative effects (see below).

There are many good walks in the Río Yambala valley; maps are available at *Cabañas Río Yambala*. Also good is the Mandango mountain trail, though it's exposed and slippery in parts. Directions are obtainable at *Madre Tierra* (see Sleeping below). There is a Tourist Office on the main plaza next to Pacifictel, which is friendly and helpful, with good information and maps. To the south of town is Parque Recreacional Yamburare, for easy walking.

Vilcabamba has become famous among travellers for its locally-produced hallucinogenic cactus juice called San Pedrillo. In addition to being illegal, it is more dangerous than it may seem because of flashbacks which can occur months or years after use. The resulting medical condition has been named the 'Vilcabamba Syndrome' and can affect sufferers for the rest of their lives. Tourist demand for San Pedrillo and other drugs is changing Vilcambaba for the worse. This has affected local youth and angered much of the population. There are plans for a tough crackdown (see also Drugs, page 46). The principles of responsible tourism and common sense alike advise against involvement with the drug scene in Vilcabamba.

Responsible tourism & common sense

Essentials

NB There are reports of people being pressured to stay in a particular establishment. There is a wide selection, so make your own choice and insist on being taken there.

Sleeping
■ *on map, page 276*
Price codes: see inside front cover

AL-D *Hostal Madre Tierra*, 2 km before the village (coming from Loja, the farm is reached by a dirt track on the right-hand side of the road, just before the bridge), T580269, hmtierra@ecua.net.ec A variety of cabins from new, well decorated, with balcony to refurbished simple, includes breakfast, dinner and free drinking water, discounts for long stays. Excellent home made food, vegetarian to order, non-residents welcome for meals but must reserve a day in advance. Small swimming pool, videos every night, massage (extra charge), steam bath, horse rental (US$10 for 4 hrs), English and French spoken, very popular, run by Jaime Mendoza. Recommended. **D** *Hostería Vilcabamba*, near the northern entrance to town, T580271, F580273. Excellent, comfortable, pool (may be used by non-residents for US$1), jacuzzi, bar, good restaurant serves international food, massage, fitness instruction. **D** *Hostería Las Ruinas de Quinara*, T/F580314, ruinasqui@hotmail.com, www. lasruinasdequinara.com Includes breakfast and dinner, large rooms with double beds

Southern Highlands

and cable TV, hot showers, Turkish steam bath, massage, great vegetarian restaurant, pool room, videos, table tennis, email facilities, swimming pool, helpful staff, will arrange horse riding, rents bikes, hammocks. Recommended.

E *Hostería Paraíso*, 5 mins from town on the main road, cabins with bath, restaurant, pool, sauna, jacuzzi, good value. **E** *Parador Turístico*, at the south end of town, T673122. Good rooms, with restaurant and bar. Recommended. **E** *Hostal La Posada Real*, C Agua del Hierro s/n, T580904. With bath, hot water, very clean, comfortable, excellent views, laundry facilities, relaxing atmosphere. Recommended. **E** *The Hidden Garden*, on Sucre, T/F580281, hiddengarden@latinmail.com Quiet, clean, use of kitchen, lovely gardens, pool. Recommended. **E** *Hostal las Margaritas*, Sucre y Clodoveo esquina. Nice rooms with bath, hot water, includes breakfast, nice garden, pool, homely atmosphere.

F *Pole House and Rumi Huilco Ecolodge*, 10-min walk from town by the Río Chamba (information at Primavera craft shop at the main park), ofalcoecolodge@ yahoo.com The pole house is a cabin built on stilts for 4 people, with fully furnished kitchen, drinking water supplied, there are 4 other equipped, adobe cabins. In relaxed country setting with herb garden, home-grown coffee and homemade granola and jams for sale. Owner Orlando Falco speaks English and runs excellent nature tours in and around Parque Nacional Podocarpus for US$15 per person per day, includes packed lunch.

Vilcabamba

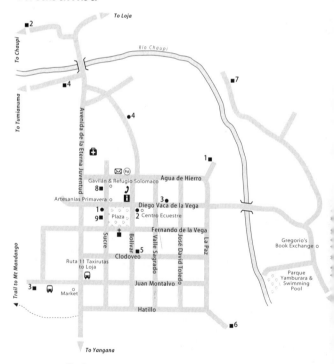

■ **Sleeping**
1 Hostal La Posada Real
2 Hostal Madre Tierra
3 Hostal Mandango
4 Hostería Vilcabamba
5 Libia Toledo's

6 Parador Turístico
7 Pole House & Rumi Huileo Ecolodge
8 The Hidden Garden
9 Valle Sagrado

● **Eating**
1 Huilcopamba
2 La Terraza
3 Le Rendez Vouz
4 Valle de Eterna Juventud

N
Not to scale

G *Hostal Mandango*, behind bus the terminal. Family-run, with bath, hot water, good value. **G** *Valle Sagrado*, on the main plaza. With and without bath, hot water, restaurant, laundry service and facilities. New management and refurbished in 2000. **G** *Sra Libia Toledo*, on Bolívar, corner of Clodoveo, 1 block from the plaza. Shared bath, hot water, family-run, friendly.

At the upper end of the Vilcabamba Valley, a beautiful 4 km walk from the village, are the highly recommended **D-E** *Cabañas Río Yambala*, office in town next to Centro Ecuestre, rio_yambala@yahoo.com Owned by Charlie and Sarah, different types of cabins for 3 to 6, or room, beautiful views in all directions, price includes breakfast and dinner, kitchen facilities if required, shopping done for you, vegetarian restaurant open all day, hot showers, laundry service, clean, helpful and very friendly, do not leave belongings on balcony or porch, horses for rent with or without guide, trekking arranged in the Podocarpus National Park with tents, sleeping bags, food etc provided.

Eating
● *on map*

There are some restaurants on the plaza, including an unnamed, good vegetarian place. *Café Pizzería Manolo's*, 5 mins from the plaza on the road to Quinara. Excellent pizzas and pasta, cheap. Recommended. *Valle de Eterna Juventud*, at the north end of Bolívar. Vegetarian. *La Terraza*, D Vaca de Vega, opposite Pacifictel. International food, one speciality is chicken *fajitas*, garden. *Huilcopamba*, D Vaca de Vega y Sucre. Very good Ecuadorean food. Recommended. *Le Rendez-vous*, C Valle Sagrado. Crêpes speciality. French-run, friendly. Recommended. *Manolo´s*, 5 mins from park on the road to Quinara. Pizza. El Rincón del Abuelo, Av Eterna Juventud y Clodoveo. Seafood. *Camino Real Bar*, Bolívar y J Montalvo.

Shopping

There are a number of well stocked small shops in town. *Artesanías Primavera*, at the main park, has a small selection of crafts and T-shirts.

Tour operators

Caballos Gavilán, New Zealander Gavin Moore offers 3-day horse treks to the cloud forest for US$80 per person, includes food (vegetarian specialities), sleeping bags (if necessary), and basic lodging. Also good for beginners. Repeatedly recommended. Contact him through the tourist office or F573186, or Casilla 1000, Loja. *Centro Ecuestre*, D Vaca de Vega y Bolívar, opposite La Terraza restaurant, T/F673183, centroecuestre@hotmail.com A group of guides who provide horse riding excursions: day trips to Parque Recreacional Yamburare or Parque Recreacional los Huilcos, 1-3 day trips to Podocarpus and trips to archeological ruins. Rates run about US$25 per day. They are part of *Fundación Avetur*, a local nature conservation group. Roger Toledo is one of the recommended guides in the group. *Refugio Solomaco*, Sucre y D Vaca de Vega y Bolívar, T/F673183, solomaco@hotmail.com Trips to Parque Nacional Podocarpus with lodging in a private refuge at the edge of the park, also include transport, guide and French food. One day US$20, 2 days US$50, 3 days US$70 per person, discounts for groups. French-run, friendly. *Las Palmas Nature Reserve*, at the edge of Parque Nacional Podocarpus has a campsite. For further information, contact Charlie or Sarah, at Cabañas Río Yambala, see Sleeping above.

Transport

There are regular buses, vans and taxis to and from Loja, see Loja Transport above. Tickets for bus service Loja-Piura are available from *El Rincón del Abuelo*, see Eating above. Loja-Zumba buses pass Vilcabamba about an hour after departure, see Loja Transport.

Directory

Communications Pacifictel: Bolívar near the park. **Internet**: there are a couple of places by the main park, rates US$1-US$1.25.

Southern Highlands

South from Vilcabamba

A dirt road south continues to **Yangana**, **Valladolid**, **Palanda** and **Zumba**. There are eight daily buses along this route, which is affected by landslides in wet weather, see details in Loja Transport above.

There are some native forests in this area and some interesting trails for walking, including one from **Amaluza** and **Jimbura**, see Loja to Peru below, across the *cordillera* to Zumba. There are several areas between Yangana and Palanda where the locals will tell you that the old Inca trails are walkable. The trails are very beautiful but their archaeological authenticity may be in doubt. Treks into the ancient settlements of Vergel, Porvenir and Loyola in Oriente can be arranged with the locals.

Sleeping and eating Zumba: All in the centre of the village within a block or two of each other. **F** *Oasis*, next to Banco de Fomento. With bath. Modern, new in 2000. **G** *La Choza*. Shared bath, cold water, good restaurant. **G** *Chinchipe*. Shared bath, cold water. **H** *Rosita*. Shared bath, cold water. Basic. *Residencial Miraflores*. New in 2000. For eating, try *Las Cañitas*. Set meals, cheap. *Rincón Zumbeño*. Set meals.

Crossing to Peru A poor road continues south from Zumba 1½ hours to a border crossing (officially opened in 2000) at La Balsa. There are four daily *rancheras* (open-sided trucks with benches) without any fixed schedule, which depart when they fill (two in the morning, one at midday, one in the afternoon), US$1; pickups are also available, US$3 per person. The immigration post is at La Balsa. An oil-drum raft crosses the river to the Peruvian border post, US$0.15, from where there is minibus service to Namballe 15 minutes away (one hotel, **G** per person). A minibus leaves Namballe when full for San Ignacio, three hours south. There are also minibuses and pickups running directly from the border to San Ignacio, 3½ hours, US$3-4. From San Ignacio there is transport to Jaén, 3½ hours further south, along a good unpaved road, US$3. It is reported to be a very relaxed crossing, so much so, that you might have to wake the border officials by knocking on their door. This crossing opens a faster, more direct route between Vilcabamba and Chachapoyas, which can now be done in two days. For more details, see the *Peru Handbook* and the *South American Handbook*.

Loja to the Peruvian border

An established alternative to the Huaquillas border crossing is the more scenic route via Macará. In 2000 other small border posts were being opened. Leaving Loja on the main paved highway going west, the airport at **La Toma** (1,200 m) is reached after 35 km.

Catamayo If flying to or from La Toma, it's best to stay at Catamayo, nearby. There are several weekend resorts around Catamayo where you can go and relax by the pool in a warmer climate. To the northwest of town is one of the largest *ingenios*, sugar processing plants, in Ecuador. High up in the mountains, to the northwest of Catamayo, is the small village and very popular pilgrimage site of **El Cisne**, dominated by its incongruous French-style Gothic church. There is a small museum housing religious art pieces and all the sequinned and jewelled clothes which have been donated to dress the statue of the Virgin del Cisne for every conceivable occasion. There are taxis to the airport, US$1, or it's a 20-minute walk.

Sleeping and eating In Catamayo: E *Hostería Bella Vista*, T962450. Set in tropical gardens with pool. **G** *Hotel San Marcos*, on the plaza. **G** *Hotel El Turista*, Av Isidro Ayora. Shared bath, basic, friendly, poor beds. Opposite is *Restaurant China*. Good, cheap.

At La Toma, where you can catch the Loja-Macará-Piura bus, the Panamericana divides into two branches: one running west and the other south to Cariamang. The former, which is faster, runs via Velacruz and Catacocha, with four passport checks.

West from La Toma, Catacocha is a spectacularly placed town built on a rock. **Catacocha** The views from Shiriculapio, behind the hospital, are marvellous. Ask to walk through the hospital grounds. There are pre-Inca ruins around the town, which was once inhabited by the Palta Indians, a group which now only exists in history books. There are four hotels in town: *Turismo*, behind the church; *Pensión Guayaquil*, between the plaza and the statue; *Mirasol* and *Buena Esperanza* are both down the hill from the statue, south of the town.

From Catacocha, the road runs south to the border at Macará. A turn-off leads **South to Macará** west at the military checkpoint at **El Empalme** to **Alamor**, **Celica** and on to the petrified forest at **Puyango** (see page 302). Between Alamor and Celica is the Guachanamá Ridge with many rare southwestern endemic birds, around 2,000 to 2,800 m.

South from Celica a road heads southwest to **Zapotillo** (*population*: 5,000, *altitude*: 325 m), a charming riverside town on the Peruvian border, southwest of Macará. It is said to be one of the best preserved towns in the south. **G** *Hotel Los Angeles* (the better of the two) and **H** *Pensión Mishel*.

Southwest of Zapotillo is **Lalamor**, where a border post is expected to open. On the Peruvian side there is transport to Lancones and on to Sullana, three hours away.

South from Catamayo

An alternative route to Macará is via **Cariamanga**. The road is paved to Cariamanga. Note that many of the roads shown on maps of this area are very inaccurate and are only passable with a four-wheel drive, and then only in the dry season.

The road runs south to Gonzanamá, a pleasant, sleepy little town famed for the **Gonzanamá** weaving of beautiful *alforjas* (multi-purpose saddlebags). Ask around and buy **& villages** direct from the weavers as there are no handicraft shops. Gonzanamá also pro- **to Macará** duces a good soft cheese. Travellers should note that the town has a somewhat unusual reputation in the south for the high incidence of deafness. So don't be paranoid if everyone seems to be ignoring you! **G** *Residencial Jiménez*, with bath, cold water.

From Gonzanamá there is an old and poorly maintained road to **Malacatos**, passing through the isolated village of **Purunuma**. There is almost no traffic but the views are great. It may be possible to get a ride in the morning up to the village, then it's a long hike down to the river and back up to Malacatos, which has a Saturday market.

Cariamanga, about 27 km southwest from Gonzanamá, has several hotels and banks.

Beyond Cariamanga the two southern roads are unpaved. One heads south-east to **Lucero**, **Amaluza** and **Jimbura**, in the most southerly and least visited parts of the country. There are two small hotels in Amaluza, from where a daily bus runs to Quito, taking about 24 hours. At Jimbura, a border post is expected to open, with connections to Ayabaca in Perú.

The other road twists its way westwards to **Colaisaca** then follows a steep, rough descent, with a loss of about 2,000 m in altitude, to **Utuana** (not recommended for cyclists in the other direction). From there the road heads northwest to **Sozoranga**, 75 km from Gonzanamá. The town has one hotel (**G**, shared cold shower). The road then continues south for 36 km to Macará on the border. North of Sozoranga, a road goes to **Nueva Fátima**, along this route are remnants of a wide variety of native forests between 1,300 and 2,600 m, rich in bird life. A total of 190 species of birds are known from this area, including many southwestern endemics.

Macará

Colour map 6, grid C2
Population: 14,296
Altitude: 600 m

This dusty town on the border is in a rice-growing area. There are road connections to Sullana north of Piura on the Peruvian coast. It is a quiet, pleasant town and a much more relaxed place to cross to Peru than Huaquillas.

Sleeping **E** *Parador Turístico*, on the Pamamericana, not far from the centre. The best in town. Pool, restaurant may not be open. **F** *Espiga de Oro*, opposite the market. With bath, fan, TV, clean. Recommended. **G** *Amazonas*, Rengel 418. Clean, basic, friendly. **G** *Pensión Guayaquil*. With shower, not recommended, fleas, large cell-like rooms. **G** *Residencial Paraíso*, Veintimilla 553. Shared bath, clean, laundry facilities, noisy, unfriendly.

Eating *Colonial Macará*, Rengel y Bolívar. Helpful, but food not too good. *Dragón Dorado*, Calderón. Seafood, popular. *Heladería Cream*, Veintimilla y Sucre. Great ice cream. *Soda Bar Manolo* for breakfast.

Macará

■ Sleeping	3 Parador Turístico	● Eating
1 Amazonas	4 Pensión Guayaquil	1 Colonial Macará
2 Espiga de Oro	5 Residencial Paraíso	2 Dragón Dorado

Southern Highlands

Coop Loja and Cariamanga have frequent buses, daily from Macará to Loja; 5-6 hrs, **Transport**
US$5. Loja Internacional buses which have direct service Loja-Piura, 3 daily, can also
be boarded in Macará. See Loja transport, page 273, for more details.

The international bridge over the Río Macará is 2½ km from town. There is a taxi **Macará-La Tina**
and pick-up service (US$0.50 shared). On the Peruvian side, minivans run La **border**
Tina-Sullana, US$3, three hours. They arrive at a market area on Av Buenos
Aires which is not safe so take a taxi or mototaxi to your hotel or bus station.

Ecuadorean immigration Open 24 hours. Formalities last about 30 minutes. It is reported as a much easier crossing than at Huaquillas. When entering
Ecuador, ask for 90 days if you need it.

Peruvian immigration Open 24 hours.

Exchange During the day there are money changers dealing in Soles at the the
international bridge and in Macará, where there is also a *Banco de Loja* which
changes Soles, open 0900-1700.

The border, on the Peruvian side, is known as **La Tina**. The first 16 km of road, **Into Peru**
to Suyo (one hotel), is not yet paved. From there the road is paved via La
Lomas (two hotels) and on to Sullana (136 km from the border). Minivans run
La Tina-Sullana, US$3, three hours. They arrive at a market area on Av Buenos
Aires which is not very safe so take a taxi or mototaxi to your hotel or bus sta-
tion. **Sullana** is a modern city with an immigration office, banks and *casas de
cambio*, post and phone offices and a range of hotels. Buses can be taken to
Piura, 38 km, which has good connections for Chiclayo, Trujillo and Lima.
There are also direct Sullana-Lima buses. For more details see the *Peru Hand-
book* or *South American Handbook*.

Southern Highlands

Guayaquil and Southern Pacific

7

Guayaquil and Southern Pacific

The coastal plains are the agro-industrial heartland of Ecuador. Rice, sugar, coffee, African palm, mango, cacao and especially bananas are produced in these hot and humid lowlands and processed or exported through Guayaquil. The largest and most dynamic commercial centre in the country, Guayaquil is also Ecuador's main port and the city's influence extends throughout the coast and beyond. This 'working Ecuador' is most frequently seen by business visitors rather than tourists, but Guayaquil is undergoing a cultural revival and has some attractions to offer. Trips to Galápagos can also be organized from here.

The coastline south to the Peruvian border gives the impression of being one giant banana plantation, while increasing numbers of shrimp farmers battle it out with conservation groups over the future of the mangroves that still line parts of the Gulf of Guayaquil.

The climate from May to December is dry with often overcast days but pleasantly cool nights, whereas the hot rainy season from January to April can be oppressively humid.

Guayaquil

Phone code: 04
Colour map 4, grid C3
Population: 3,300,000
Altitude: sea level

Ecuador's largest city and the country's chief sea port and industrial and commercial centre lies on the west bank of the chocolate-brown Río Guayas, some 56 km from its outflow into the Gulf of Guayaquil. Founded in 1535 by Sebastián de Benalcázar near the native settlement of Guayaquile, then again in 1537 by Francisco Orellana, the city couldn't be more different from its highland counterpart and political rival, Quito. It is hot, sticky, fast-paced, bold and brash and with few concessions to tourism. It may lack the capital's colonial charm, but Guayaquileños are certainly more lively, colourful and open than Quiteños.

The Puerto Marítimo, opened in 1964, handles three-quarters of the country's imports and almost half of its exports. It is a constant bone of contention between the *costeños* and the *serranos* that Guayaquil is not given better recognition of its economic importance in the form of more central government aid. Since the late 1990s there have been organized movements for autonomy of Ecuador's coastal provinces, spearheaded by Guayaquil.

Ins and outs

Getting there
See also Transport, page 295

Simón Bolívar International Airport is to the north about 10 mins by taxi from the city centre (recommended, see Taxis below). It costs US$0.15 by bus (take No 2 from the Malecón, No 3 from the Centro Cívico, or No 69 from Plaza Victoria), but this is neither safe nor practical with luggage. If you are going straight on to another city, take a cab directly to the bus station, which is close by. If you are arriving in Guayaquil during the daytime and need a taxi from the airport, walk half a block from the terminal out to Av de las Américas, where taxis and camionetas wait for passengers. The fare will be about half of what you will be charged for the same trip by one of the drivers who belong to the airport taxi cooperative, but it is not safe to leave the terminal area at night. See below for taxi fares.

The Terminal Terrestre is just north of the airport, just off the road to the Guayas bridge. The company offices are on the second floor and buses leave from the top floor. It can sometimes be confusing trying to find out where your bus leaves from. There is no left luggage depot and do not leave anything unattended. The terminal is busy at weekends. There are some expensive restaurants, use of toilet (US$0.10). Lots of local buses go from the bus station to the city centre, but this is not safe with luggage; take a taxi.

Getting around

A new street numbering system is (in principle) scheduled to be implemented by 2001. According to this scheme, the city would be divided into 4 quadrants separated by a north-south axis and an east-west axis. All north-south streets will be called avenidas and the east-west streets will be calles. Each will have an alpha-numeric designation such as Avenida 12 S-E. The airport and bus terminal will be in the northeastern quadrant, the commercial heartland in the southeastern quadrant.

Not surprisingly for a city of this size, you will need to get around by public transport. A number of hotels, however, are centrally located near the riverfront. City buses are often confusing and overcrowded at rush hour (watch out for pickpockets) and cost US$0.15. There are also minibuses (*furgonetas*), US$0.15, which post up their routes in the windscreen. Buses are not allowed in the centre; almost all go along the Malecón. Bus No 15 will take you from the centre to Urdesa, 13 to Policentro, 14 to Albanborja, 74 to La Garzota and Sauces. Outside rush hour, buses are a good, cheap alternative to taxis, but you need to know where you're going. **Taxis** have no meters, so prices are very negotiable and overcharging is notorious. From the airport or bus terminal to the centre is US$2-US$3. From the centre to Urdesa, Policentro or Alborada is US$2. From the airport to the bus terminal and short trips costs US$1. *Taxi rutas* run a set route, charging US$0.25. They are yellow with contrasting bonnets, or stripes over the roof, eg ones with red bonnets run from the Bahía, Centro, Urdesa to Mapasingue and back.

Tourist information

Ministerio de Turismo, P Ycaza 203 y Pichincha, 5th and 6th floors, T568764. Friendly, Spanish only, open 0900-1730, Mon-Fri. They sell a map of Ecuador. Maps also from *INOCAR*, in the planetarium building at the naval base near the port. They have a comprehensive stock of maps. A website about tourism in Guayaquil is www.turismoguayas.com

Safety

People continue to migrate from the countryside to Guayaquil in search of jobs. The population is growing and there are many slums, shanty towns and *invasiones* (squatter settlements); poverty and crime are serious problems. Armed robbery and carjacking are on the increase and visitors should take great care throughout the city. Do not walk anywhere with valuables and always take taxis at night. The Malecón in early morning and from dusk onwards is bad for snatch thieves. You also need to take care downtown in daylight. Be especially careful around hotel or bank entrances and

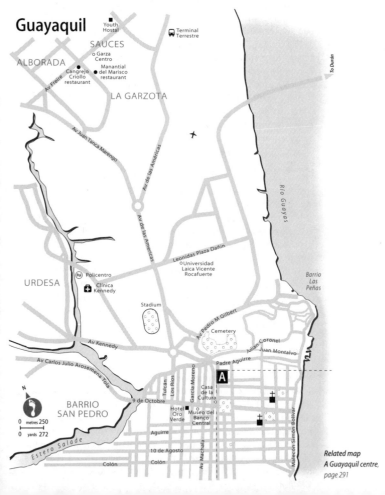

Guayaquil & Southern Pacific

Related map
A Guayaquil centre,
page 291

The Liberators of America

Guayaquil's most famous monument, La Rotonda, commemorates the meeting of the liberators of South America - Simón Bolívar of Venezuela and José San Martín of Argentina - in the city on July 26, 1822. One month later San Martín, who had played a vital role in the independence of Argentina, Chile and Peru, suddenly abandoned his participation in the South American revolutionary campaign.

What happened? The most irreverent commentators suggest that San Martín contracted so violent a case of dysentery as could only be acquired in tropical Guayaquil. Far more plausible however, is that the meeting of the two great heroes of independence was in fact the height of political intrigue, a monumental arm-wrestle on the shores of the Guayas.

Guayaquil was an independent city state and its strategic port was coveted by both of its large emerging neighbours: Colombia to the north and Peru to the south. On June 21, 1822, Bolívar wrote, "We cannot give up Guayaquil, it would make more sense to give up Quito." So both libertadores raced to Guayaquil to woo the city to their respective sides, with

diplomacy and troops. Bolívar got there first, on July 11, while San Martín arrived from Lima two weeks later. Seeing that Colombian forces had already taken up positions at the mouth of the Río Guayas, San Martín ordered his ships to sail back to Peru, and proceeded to meet Bolívar with only a handful of aides.

At their meeting San Martín offered to serve as Bolívar's subordinate in order to conclude the campaign against royalist forces in Peru, but Bolívar (perhaps rightfully suspicious) refused the collaboration. On August 29, San Martín wrote Bolívar that he was unconvinced by the latter's polite excuses and that if, as it seemed, Bolívar wanted all the glory for himself, then he could have it.

Guayaquil became part of Bolívar's Gran Colombia and later the main port of an independent Ecuador. During the many years of border conflict with Peru it was always on the front lines. That conflict was finally settled in 1998, yet political intrigue is alive and well on the shores of the Guayas, in the shadow of La Rotonda and the liberators of America.

at the bus terminal, as attackers usually work in pairs. In late 2000 the newly elected mayor, Jaime Nebot, announced an energetic public safety campaign with the promise of improved security, but visitors are cautioned not to let down their guard.

Another side effect of the population explosion is that the city's services have been stretched beyond the limit. The authorities struggle to control the chaotic transport system, as well as itinerant street vendors and the many informal markets which choke the main downtown traffic arteries and sidewalks. Just to add to the confusion, the authorities have changed the names of several major avenidas and streets; eg Circunvalación Sur in Urdesa is now Avenue Jorge Pérez Concha. Locals still use the old names. It is often quicker to walk short distances in the centre, rather than take a bus or taxi, but on no account walk around after dark.

Sights

A wide, tree-lined waterfront avenue, the Malecón, runs alongside the Río Guayas from the exclusive **Club de la Unión**, by the Moorish clock tower, past the imposing **Palacio Municipal** and **Government Palace** and the old Yacht Club to Las Peñas. This has been the focus of efforts to revive the the city centre, in a project known as 'Malecón 2000'. The riverfront walk has been extensively refurbished; it is attractive and definitely worth a visit. There are restaurants and cafés along its length and a large shopping mall by the south end. Half way along the Malecón, Boulevard 9 de Octubre, the city's main street, starts in front of **La**

Rotonda, a statue to mark the famous yet mysterious meeting between Simón Bolívar and José San Martín in 1822 (see box above). There are 11 piers (*muelles*) running along the Malecón. From the most northerly public pier, near Las Peñas, ferries sail across the river to Durán.

Don't bother looking for ancient monuments in Guayaquil. Most of its history is confined to the history books. There are several noteworthy churches but, because of sackings or fire, almost none of its wooden buildings remain. A notable exception is the old district of **Las Peñas**, a last picturesque, if ramshackle and small, vestige of colonial Guayaquil, with its wooden houses and narrow cobbled street (Numa Pompilio Llona). The entrance is guarded by two cannon pointing riverward, a reminder of the days when pirates sailed up the Guayas to attack the city. Now occupied mostly by artists, there is a large open-air exhibition of paintings and sculpture held here every year in July. It makes a pleasant walk, but this is a poor area and mugging is getting more common at night. You are strongly advised not to walk up the adjacent streets of the Cerro Santa Ana that overlook Las Peñas.

The main plaza halfway up 9 Octubre is the **Plaza Centenario** with a towering monument to the liberation of the city erected in 1920. The pleasant, shady **Parque Bolívar** in front of the **Cathedral** is filled with tame iguanas which scuttle out of the trees for scraps.

There are several noteworthy churches. **Santo Domingo**, the city's first church founded by the Dominicans in 1548, stands just by Las Peñas. It was sacked and burned by pirates in 1624. Its present form was built in 1938, replacing the wooden structure with concrete in classical style. Pirates also sacked the original church of **San Agustín**; the present building dates from 1931.

The original wooden structure of the **Cathedral**, built in 1695, survived both sackings and fire, but the years took their toll and a new building was completed in 1822. In 1924 construction on the present building was started, in the classical Gothic style, and it was inaugurated in the 1950s. Other notable churches are **San Francisco**, with its restored colonial interior, off 9 de Octubre and P Carbo, and the beautiful **La Merced**.

At the north end of the centre, below Cerro El Carmen, the huge, spreading **Cemetery**, with its dazzling, high-rise tombs and the ostentatious mausoleums of the rich, is worth a visit. A flower market over the road sells the best selection of blooms in the city. It's best to go on a Sunday when there are plenty of people about.

There are numerous sports clubs for golf, tennis, swimming, sailing and the horse race track of **El Buijo** is set in lovely surroundings some 5 km outside the city. There are two football stadiums and the enclosed Coliseo Cerrado for boxing, basketball and other sports.

The **Centro Cívico**, heading south, finally finished after 25 years in the making, provides an excellent theatre/concert facility and is home to the Guayaquil Symphony Orchestra which gives free concerts throughout the year. The new **Teatro Centro de Arte** on the road out to the coast is another first class theatre complex, with a wide variety of presentations. The city is also well provided with museums, art galleries and cinemas, details of which are in *El Universo*. Colourful markets are held at the south end of the Malecón or along 6 de Marzo between 10 de Agosto and Ballén. The Mercado Sur, next to Club de la Unión, prefabricated by Eiffel (1905-07), sells fruit, vegetables and illegal wild animals but is not safe to visit. See below under Shopping for the Bahía market.

Barrio Centenario to the south of the centre is the original residential sector, now a peaceful, tree-shaded haven. Newer residential areas are **Urdesa**, northwest of the centre, in between two branches of the Estero Salado (about

15 minutes from downtown, traffic permitting). Near the international airport and bus terminal, which are conveniently close to each other, are the districts of **La Garzota**, **Sauces** and **Alborada**. Cleaner, less congested and safer than the centre, but with all services, entertainment and shops, these areas are 10-15 minutes by taxi from downtown, and five minutes from the airport and Terminal Terrestre.

The **Botanical Gardens** are in the Ciudadela Las Orquídeas to the northwest. There are over 3,000 plants, including 150 species of Ecuadorean and foreign orchids. The views are good and it is the ideal place for a pleasant stroll. Recommended. ■ *0800-1600 daily, US$2, guides available. Av Francisco de Orellana, Las Orquídeas (bus line 63), T417004.*

Guayaquil is also a city of **shopping malls**, where consumerism flourishes in air conditioned comfort. Here you will find many banks, restaurants, bars, discos, cinemas, cyber cafés and of course shops. For a complete list see Shopping, below. Those who yearn for even more of a chill can visit the ice-skating rink called **Zona Fría**, at Km 2.5 on the autopista La Puntilla-Samborondón.

Museums   The **Museo Municipal** is housed in the Biblioteca Municipal (near the *Hotel Continental*), where there are paintings, gold and archaeological collections, shrunken Shuar heads, a section on the history of Guayaquil and also a good newspaper library. ■ *Tue-Sat 0900-1700, free. Sucre y Pedro Carbo.*

The Central Bank's **anthropological museum** has excellent displays of ceramics, gold objects and paintings. There are English speaking guides. ■ *Tue-Fri 1000-1800, Sat-Sun 1000-1400, US$1, Anteparra 900 y 9 de Octubre.* The **Pinacoteca Manuel Rendoy Seminario** is on the first floor of the same building. **Museo del Banco del Pacífico** is a beautiful small museum mainly of archaeological exhibits. ■ *Mon-Fri 0900-1700, free. Ycaza 200 y Pichincha, 3rd floor, T328333.*

There is an impressive collection of prehistoric gold items (not always on display) at the museum of the **Casa de la Cultura**, together with an archaeological museum. ■ *Tue-Fri 1000-1700 and Sat 0900-1500, US$0.20. 9 de Octubre 1200 y Moncayo.* **Religious Art Museum Nahim Isaias Barquet** with a pinacoteca (art gallery) on the ground and first floors. ■ *Tue-Fri 0900-1700, Sat 1000-1300, free. Pichincha y Ballén, T510818.*

Essentials

Sleeping   Hotel prices, which are higher than in Quito, are set by the Tourist Board, which stipu-
■ *on map opposite*   lates their being posted inside hotels. It is common practice to have dual rates in the
& on page 287   more upmarket establishments; one for nationals and a much higher one for foreign-
Price codes: ers. Always check the rate first; also whether 22% service and taxes are included in the
see inside front cover   given price (as they are in the following list). Rooms in the better hotels can be in
demand and booking is advised.

Most hotels are downtown, so take a taxi from the airport or bus station. The cheap hotels are pretty basic, many cater to short stay customers, and singles seem hard to find. **NB** All of the downtown area is unsafe and caution is especially important at night. As an alternative, you can stay in the districts of La Garzota, Sauces and Alborada, near the airport and bus terminal.

LL *Hampton Inn Boulevard*, 9 de Octubre 432 y B Moreno, T566700, F560076, acy@ecua.net.ec Refurbished in 2000, very central, cable TV, casino, shows. Recommended. **LL** *Hilton Colón*, Av Francisco Orellana in Kennedy Norte, T689000, F689149, meeting@hiltonguayaquil.com Luxury hotel with 294 rooms, the largest in

Guayaquil, with full facilities. Five restaurants and bars, 2 pools, outside the city so access and parking are not a problem. **LL** *Oro Verde*, 9 de Octubre y García Moreno, T327999, F329350, ecovg@gye.satnet.net A total of 192 rooms and 61 suites, 4 restaurants (*El Patio* is open 24 hrs), bar, deli, disco, pool, fitness centre, business centre, limo service, airport transfer, gift boutique in lobby. Top class and recommended. **LL** *Unipark*, Clemente Ballén 406 y Chile, T327100, F328352, uni_gye@ oroverdehotels.com Good restaurant and breakfast, 138 rooms, 5-star facilities, good restaurant, café and bar, meeting and banquet facilities, gym, jacuzzi and sauna, golf and tennis facilities and shops nearby.

Guayaquil centre

■ **Sleeping**	8 Palace	15 Vélez
1 Alexander & Nuevo Sander	9 Ramada	
2 Berlín	10 Residencial Pauker	● **Eating**
3 Best Western Doral	11 Ritz	1 Casa Vasca
4 Centenario	12 Rizzo	2 Gran Chifa & Chifa
5 Continental	13 Sol de Oriente	Himalaya
6 Gran Guayaquil	14 Unipark, Plaza	3 La Fontana
7 Hampton Inn Boulevard,	& Unicentro Shopping	4 Melba
TAME & Galasam	Mall	5 Salud Solar

Related map
Guayaquil, page 287

Guayaquil & Southern Pacific

L *Gran Hotel Guayaquil*, Boyacá 1600 y 10 de Agosto, T329690, F327251, www.grandhotelguayaquil.com Good restaurants (La Pepa de Oro is open 24 hrs), swimming pool, sauna, etc, non-residents can use pool, US$2 per day. **L** *Ramada*, Malecón y Orellana, T565555. Pleasantly situated overlooking the river, with pool, mostly used by business travellers. **L** *Presidente*, Chile 303 y Luque, T531300, F531354. Luxury, suites more expensive.

A *Continental*, Chile y 10 de Agosto, T329270, F325454, informe@hotelcontinental. net, www.hotelcontinental.net A KLM Golden Tulip hotel. 5-star, cable TV, 24-hr restaurant *La Canoa*, good coffee shop. Centrally located. Recommended. **A** *Palace*, Chile 214 y Luque, T321080, F322887. Excellent, good value for business travellers, modern, TV, traffic noise on Av Chile side, restaurant, travel agency. Highly recommended. **A** *Tangara Guest House*, Ciudadela Bolivariana, Manuela Sáenz y O'Leary Block F, House 1, T284445, F284039. Clean, safe and friendly, all rooms with private bath, located in a residential area between the airport and town.

B *Sol de Oriente*, Aguirre 603 y Escobedo, T325500, F329352. With a/c, minibar, restaurant, gym. Excellent value. Recommended. **B** *Del Rey*, Aguirre y Marín, T452909. Behind tennis club, includes breakfast, quiet, friendly, a/c, restaurant and bar, laundry. Recommended. **B** *Best Western Doral*, Chile 402 y Aguirre, T328002, hdoral@ gye.satnet.net, www.hdoral.com Good rooms and value, a/c central. Recommended.

C *Alexander*, Luque 1107 y Pedro Moncayo, T532000, F514161. With bath, a/c, comfortable, good value, some rooms without windows, noisy. **C** *Plaza*, Chile 414 y Clemente Ballén, T324006, F324195, jplamas@impsat.net.ec A/c, cafeteria, laundry service, some cheaper rooms available, international newspapers. Recommended. **C** *Rizzo*, Clemente Ballén 319 y Chile, T325210, F326209. TV, bath, a/c, secure, on Parque Bolívar, some rooms without windows, room service, *Café Jambelí* downstairs.

D *Capri*, Luque y Machala, T326341. With bath, a/c, cable TV, fridge, cafeteria, very clean and safe, busy at weekends. **D** *Hostal de Alborada*, Alborada 9a etapa, Mz 935, villa 8, T237251. In the same area as the Youth Hostel (see below), with bath, a/c, TV, fridge, meals on request, friendly. **D** *Paseo Real*, Luque 1011 y 6 de Mayo, T530084. With bath, a/c, TV, **E** for inner rooms, cheaper with fan. **D** *Ritz*, 9 de Octubre y Boyacá, T324134, F322151. With bath, a/c, hot water. **E** *Acuario*, Luque 1204 y Quito, T533715. A/c, bath, fridge, TV, cheaper with fan. **E** *Centenario*, Vélez 726 y Santa Elena, T524467. With bath, TV, fan. **E** *D'Patrick*, Av Barcelona in Bellavista, Mz 73, Villa 13, T332374. Outside the centre on good bus routes and near the Catholic University, with private bath, hot water, TV, owner Patricio León also arranges longer stays in basic apartments around the town for around US$20-25 for a 2-bedroom, minimum stay 1 month. **E** *Nuevo Sander*, Luque 1101 y Pedro Moncayo, T320030. With bath, a/c, cheaper with fan, central but near a dangerous area. **E** *Vélez*, Vélez 1021 y Quito, T530356. With bath, TV, a/c, cheaper without a/c and TV, clean, good value. Recommended.

F *Luque*, Luque 1214 y Quito, T523900. With bath, TV, fan. **G** *Berlín*, Rumichaca 1503, T524648. With bath, fan, clean, front rooms noisy. **G** per person *Libertador*, Santa Elena 803 y VM Rendón, T304637. Fan, with bath. **G** *Hostal Miami*, P Montúfar 534 y Alcedo, T519667. Fan, with bath. **G** *Imperial*, Urdaneta 705, T560512. Basic. **G** *Residencial Pauker*, Baquerizo Moreno 902 y Junín, T565385. Shared bath, run down, old-time haunt for travellers, secure.

Youth hostel E per person *Ecuahogar*, Sauces I, Av Isidro Ayora, opposite Banco Ecuatoriana de La Vivienda, near airport and bus terminal, T248357, F248341, youthost@telconet.net Member of IYHA and Ecuadorean Hostelling Association, non-members welcome, includes breakfast, bunk rooms and rooms with bath, cooking and laundry facilities, tourist information, secure, will pick you up from the bus station and airport, or take buses 2 or 66, discount for longer stay, English and German spoken, set meals in restaurant US$2, very friendly and helpful. Recommended.

The main areas for restaurants are in the centre with many in the larger hotels, around Urdesa, or the newer residential and commercial centres of La Alborada and La Garzota, which have many good eating places. In the smarter places 22% service and tax is added to the bill.

Eating
● *on maps,
page 287 & 291*

French *Decibelius*, Estrada y Cedros, Urdesa. Menu changes frequently, good steaks, crêpes and coffee.

International the *Hotel Continental*, *Gran Hotel Guayaquil* and *Oro Verde* all have good restaurants with international menus. *Posada de las Garzas*, Urdesa Norte, Circunvalación Norte 536. Also French-style dishes. *El Parque*, top floor of Unicentro. For excellent popular buffet lunches at the weekends. *Juan Salvador Gaviota*, Kennedy Norte, Av Fco de Orellana. Good seafood. *La Balandra*, C 5a 504 entre Monjas y Dátiles, Urdesa. For good fish, upmarket ambience, also has a crab house at Circunvalación 506 y Ficus, Urdesa.

Italian *La Trattoria da Enrico*, Bálsamos 504. Expensive but fun surroundings, good antipasto. **Pizzas**: *Trattoria de Pasquale*, Estrada y Guayacanes, Urdesa. Good atmosphere, reasonably priced. *Riviera Urdesa*, Estrada y Ficus, Urdesa. Bright surroundings, good service, also in Mall del Sol. *Pizzería Del Ñato*, Estrada 1219. Good value, sold by the metre.

Oriental A wide variety in the city, most do takeaway and are good value. *Chifa Himalaya*, Sucre 309 y P Carbo. Slow service but good for the price. *Gran Chifa*, P Carbo 1016. Wide variety, good value. *Cantonés*, Av G Pareja y C 43, La Garzota. Huge rather glaring emporium with authentic dishes and all-you-can-eat menu for US$9, karaoke. *Pagoda*, Circunvalación Sur 916 y Ilanes, in Urdesa. Great crab wantan. **Japanese**: *Tsuji*, Estrada 815. Wonderful, authentic dishes, Teppan Yaki, expensive. *UniBar* in *Unipark Hotel* complex. Sushi.

Mexican *Viva Mexico*, Datiles y Estrada, in Urdesa. The best authentic dishes. *Noches Tapatías*, Primera y Dátiles, Urdesa. Fun, good live music at weekends. *Mi Cielito Lindo*, Circunvalación 623 y Ficus. Good.

Seafood *Manny's*, Av Miraflores y Segunda. Not cheap but try the excellent *arroz con cangrejo*. *Casa del Cangrejo*, Av Plaza Dañin, Kennedy. For crab dishes of every kind; several others along the same street. *Red Crab*, Estrada y Laureles, Urdesa. Interesting décor, wide variety. *El Cangrejo Criollo*, Av Principal, Villa 9, La Garzota. Excellent, varied seafood menu. Recommended.

Crab Houses are almost an institution and great fun

Spanish *Casa Basca*, Chile 406 y C Ballén. Wonderful hole-in-the-wall place, specializes in seafood and paellas, expensive, cash only, house wine good value, great atmosphere, gets very crowded. The same owner runs *Tasca Vaska*, Chimborazo between Clemente Ballén y Aguirre. *Caracol Azul*, 9 de Octubre 1918 y Los Ríos. Expensive and very good.

Steak houses *Donde el Ché*, F Boloña S21A. Holds a competition to see who can eat the biggest steak, winner doesn't pay, music, tango and shows. *Parillada Del Ñato*, Estrada 1219. Huge variety and portions, excellent value. *La Selvita*, Av Olmos y Las Brisas, Las Lomas de Urdesa. Good atmosphere and fine panoramic views, also at Calle D y Rosa Borja, Centenario. *Columbus Urdesa*, Las Lomas 206 off Estrada. Good. *Parillada del Tano Liciardi*, Urbanor Av Principal y Av Las Aguas. Excellent quality, open Tue-Sun until 2330.

Typical *Artur's Café*, Numa Pompilio Llona 127, Las Peñas. Wonderful atmosphere and view over the river, live music, popular. *La Canoa* in *Hotel Continental* (see above) and in *Mall del Sol*. Open 24 hrs, for traditional dishes rarely found these days, with different specials during the week. *Salón Melba*, Córdova 720 y Junín. Old fashioned eating house/coffee shop. *Café Jambelí*, in *Rizzo Hotel* for coastal dishes and seafood. *Pique Y Pase*, Lascano 16-17 y Carchi. Popular with students, lively. *Lo Nuestro Urdesa*, VE Estrada 9-03 e Higueras. Traditional décor, great seafood platters. *El Manantial*, VE Estrada y Las Monjas. Good.

Vegetarian *Maranatá I*, Chile y Cuenca, and *II*, Quisquis y Rumichaca. *Super Nutrión I*, Chimborazo y 10 de Agosto, and *II* Chimborazo y Letamendi. *Girasol*, Chile y Colón. *Renacer*, G Avilés y Sucre. *Hare Krishna*, 1 de Mayo y 6 de Marzo. *Salud Solar*, Pedro Moncayo y Luque. *Ollantay*, Tungurahua 508 y 9 de Octubre. *Paraíso*, Av Juan Tanca Marengo, Km 1.5.

Fast food The new shopping malls of *Riocentro Los Ceibos*, *Mall del Sol* and *Riocentro Entrerios* all have chains of **Kentucky Fried Chicken**, **Pollo Tropical**, **Burger King**, **Pizza Hut**, **Taco Bell**, **Miami Subs** and **Dunkin' Donuts**, plus other local chains serving typical Cajun, Chinese, sushi, sandwiches, yoghurt and pastries.

Snacks There are many places selling all sorts of snacks. Try *pan de yuca*, or *empanadas*, but beware of eating at street stalls. Excellent sandwiches at **Submarine**, 9 Octubre y Chile. *Uni Deli* downstairs in the Unicentro, Aguirre y Chimborazo. Good bakery, salami and cheese. *La Chivería*, Circunvalación y Ficus for good yoghurt and *pan de yuca*. *La Selecta*, Estrada y Laureles. Good sandwiches. **Coffee**: great coffee served hot, cold, frozen in milkshakes or ices in the foodhalls of *Riocentro Los Ceibos*, *Riocentro Samborondon* and *El Bopan*, Estrada y Las Monjas, Urdesa. The latter also serves breakfast from 0700. **Ice cream**: *Top Cream*, *Pingüino*, *Baskin Robins*. Many outlets throughout the city.

Bars & nightclubs The **Kennedy Mall** is Guayaquil's main centre for upmarket nightlife, with an ample selection of bars and discos. Prices vary from mid-range to expensive.

Bars In Urdesa are: *Fuente Alemana Peña Bar*, Estrada y Jiguas; *International Pool*, Estrada y Las Monjas, with pool tables.

Discos Most discos charge a cover of around US$5-9 and drinks are expensive. There are discos, bars and casinos in most of the major hotels such as *Oro Verde*, *Unipark*, *Boulevard*. Also *El Garaje*, on Av de las Américas, older crowd, expensive; *TV Bar*, Av Rolando Pareja in La Garzota, good drinks and music, young crowd, moderate prices; *Achumachai*, in Albán Borja, bar and disco, older crowd, expensive; *Jardín de la Salsa*, Av de las Américas, largest in the city, lively, popular, free Salsa classes. There are several others.

Entertainment See *El Universo* or *El Telégrafo* for **cinemas** and other entertainment. Cinemas cost around US$2. **Swimming** Pool at Malecón Simón Bolívar 116.

Festivals The foundation of Guayaquil (actually its relocation from a previous site) is cele-brated on Jul 24-25, and the city's independence on Oct 9-12. Both holidays are lively and there are many public events; cultural happenings are prolonged throughout Oct. Other civic and religious holidays are the same as the rest of the country (see Festivals, page 456).

Shopping
Throughout the city are very cheap, 'dump' stores selling below-market-price clothing. You can find great bargains, but you can also be badly cheated

There are lots of shopping malls. *Centro Comercial Malecón 2000* is the city's newest, at the south end of the Malecón. *Mall del Sol* is near the airport on Av Constitución y Juan Tanca Marengo and is the largest mall in the country. Other malls are: *Riocentro Los Ceibos*, on the coast road beyond Los Ceibos; *Unicentro*, Aguirre y Chile; *Policentro* and *Plaza Quil*, both on Av San Jorge, N Kennedy; *Albán Borja*, Av Arosemena Km 2.7; *Garzocentro 2000*, La Garzota, Av R Pareja; *La Rotonda*, entrance to La Garzota; *Plaza Mayor*, La Alborada, Av R Pareja and, nearby, *Albocentro*; *Riocentro*, Av Samborondón, across the river; and *Puntilla Mall* at La Puntilla. There are several others.

The *Bahía*, a huge bazaar area on either side of Olmedo from Villamil to Chile, is still the most popular place for electrical appliances, clothing and shoes. It was tradition-ally where contraband was sold from boats which put into the bay and is one of the city's oldest market places. It has been cleaned up a bit in recent years but you must still watch your valuables and be prepared to bargain.

Camping equipment Camping gas is available from *Casa Maspons*, Ballén 517 y Boyacá, *Marathon*, 9 de Octubre y Escobedo, or in *Policentro*. *Kao Policentro* has fishing, camping and sports gear at good prices.

Books *Librería Científica*, Luque 223 y Chile and Plaza Triángulo on the Estrada in Urdesa. English books, field guides to flora and fauna and travel in general. *El Librero*, in the Ríocentro, has English books. *Nuevos Horizontes*, 6 de Marzo 924 for book exchange. *Selecciones*, at Av 9 de Octubre 830 and in *Albán Borja* Mall, has a choice of expensive novels and lots of magazines in English.

Handicrafts For the greatest variety try the *Mercado Artesanal* between Loja y Montalvo and Córdova y Chimborazo, almost a whole block of permanent stalls, with good prices. *Artesanías del Ecuador*, 9 Octubre 104 y Malecón are good and reliable as is *Ocepa*, in Urdesa, Estrada 420-A. Prices compare favourably with the towns where the goods are made. There's a good variety of *artesanías* in the *Albán Borja Mall* at *El Telar*, which is expensive but of superb quality, especially ceramics, jewellery and embroidery; and *Ramayana* for reasonable priced ceramics. Also several craft shops in *Centro Comercial Malecón 2000*. *Ceramica Vega Urdesa*, VE Estrada 1200 y Laureles, Urdesa, for brightly-painted Cuenca ceramics. *La Casa de Mimbre*, Eloy Alfaro 1018 y Brasil. A rough area but a fascinating collection of wicker baskets, furniture, hammocks and other bits and pieces at good prices. *Centro de Artesanías Montecristi*, Juan Tanca Marengo Km 0.5. For straw and wicker goods and furniture. *Manos* in Urdesa (Cedros 305 y Primera). Closes until 1530 for lunch. Otavalo Indians sell their crafts along Chile between 9 Octubre y Vélez. Good quality, authentic Panama hats from *Sombrero Barberán*, 1 de Mayo 112, at the north end of Parque Centenario, and in the handicraft market.

Photos Film deteriorates more quickly in the hot climate, always check the expiry date. Photos can be developed reliably at *Rapi-Color*, Boyacá 1418 y Luque, or *Photo Market*, VE Estrada 726 y Guayacanes, Urdesa, prints and slides. There are Kodak stands in most supermarkets which offer a reasonable service. Camera repairs at *Cinefoto*, Luque 314 y Chimborazo, English spoken. Cheap film and instant ID photos from *Discount New York* in *Albán Borja*.

Tour operators *Wanderjahr*, P Icaza 431, Edificio Gran Pasaje, T562111. Also has branches in PlazaQuil, T288400; the *Hotel Oro Verde*; Paseo La Alborada shopping mall, T273054 and Mall del Sol. *Ecuadorean Tours*, 9 Octubre 1900 y Esmeraldas, T287111. Also agent for Amex, and has branches at Chile y 10 de Agosto and in Urdesa, Estrada 117, T388080. *Metropolitan Touring – Galápagos Cruises*, Antepara 915 y 9 de Octubre, T330300. Also has an office at the *Hilton Colón*. *Ecoventura*, Av Francisco de Orellana 222, Mz 12, Solar 22, Kennedy Norte, T283182, 283148. See also under Quito Tour operators and under the Galápagos. *Machiavello Tours*, Antepara 802-A y 9 Octubre, T286079. *Barreiro Insua Viajes*, Malecón 1405 y Aguirre, T519199. *Galasam Cía Ltda*, Edificio Gran Pasaje, 9 Octubre 424, 11th Flr, oficina 1108, T306289. See Galápagos section (page 421) for their Economic Galápagos Tours programmes. *Canodros*, Urb Santa Leonor Mz 5, local 10, T285711, F287651, www.canodros.com Runs luxury Galápagos cruises and also operates the Kapawi Ecological Reserve, www. kapawi.com, in the southern Oriente (see page 384). *Whale Tours*, Vélez 911 y 6 de Marzo, El Forum, 5th Flr, T524608. Recommended for whale watching tours. Whale watching trips can also be arranged out of Puerto López (see page 324). Most agencies arrange city tours, 2½ hrs, US$8-10 per person with English-speaking guide, eg *Royal Tours Service*, T326688. *Viajes Horizontes*, P Solano 1502 y Mascote, T281260. Arranges *chiva* rides and other tours.

Transport
See also Ins & outs, page 286

Car hire There are several car hire firms in booths outside the national terminal of the airport. *Budget* T288510 (airport), 328571 (by *Oro Verde*); *Ecuacars* T283247 (airport); *Avis* T287906 (airport). Also at the airport are *Hertz*, *Localiza* and *Expo Rent a Car*. For rental prices and procedures see Car hire, page 54.

Guayaquil & Southern Pacific

Air Airport facilities: there's an information desk with erratic hours. *Wander Cambio* is open 7 days a week, 0900-1400; also several bank ATMs. There's a modern cafeteria (open 24 hrs) and a post office. Note that to get to the baggage reclaim area you must leave the airport and re-enter further down the building. Show your boarding pass to enter and baggage ticket to leave.

Air services: TAME operates a *puente aereo* (frequent shuttle service) to **Quito**, no reservations, first come first served at the airport.There are also flights to **Cuenca**, **Loja** and **Machala**. Flights to the **Galápagos** leave from here (see page 389). There are daily commuter flights in small 5-17 seater planes from the Terminal de Avionetas on the city side of the international airport: Cedta to Machala, or AECA to Bahía de Caráquez, Manta, Portoviejo and Pedernales (reported unreliable). When passing through Guayaquil by air, do not put valuables into backpacks checked into the hold as things sometimes go missing.

Road There is a 3¼-km bridge (Puente de la Unidad Nacional) in 2 sections across the rivers Daule and Babahoyo to Durán. A paved road runs from there to connect with the Andean Highway at Cajabamba, near Riobamba (see page 228). Also from Durán main roads go to Babahoyo, Quevedo and Santo Domingo (the most frequently used route to Quito), to Cuenca, and to the southern lowlands by Machala.

Bus Several companies to/from **Quito**, 8 hrs, around US$6, up to US$13 for Rey Tours non-stop, a/c service (office in *Gran Hotel*). To **Cuenca**, 5 hrs, US$5. To **Riobamba**, 5 hrs, US$3. To **Santo Domingo de los Colorados**, 5 hrs, US$4. To **Manta**, 3 hrs, US$4. To **Esmeraldas**, 8 hrs, US$5. To **Portoviejo**, 3½ hrs, US$4, and to **Bahía de Caráquez**, 6 hrs, US$4.50. To **Ambato**, 6½ hrs, US$3. Regular and frequent buses to **Playas**, 2 hrs, US$1.50. To **Salinas**, 2½ hrs, US$2. To **Machala** 3½ hrs, US$3. For the **Peruvian border**, to **Huaquillas**, direct, US$3, 4 hrs; via Machala, 6 hrs.

Shipping agent Luis Arteaga, Aguirre 324 y Chile, T533592/670, F533445. Recommended, fast, US$120 for arranging car entry.

Directory **Airline offices** *TAME*, 9 de Octubre 424, Edificio Gran Pasaje, T560728. *Ecuatorianan*, 9 de Octubre 111 y Malecón, T322025, F282020. *Cedta*, T301165. *AECA*, Av de la Américas/Sonapal, T286267. *AeroPerú*, Icaza 451, T563600. *American Airlines*, Gral Córdova y Av 9 de Octubre, Edificio San Francisco, 20th Flr, T564111. *Continental*, Av 9 de Octubre 100 y Malecón, T567241, F567249. *AeroPeru*, Chile 329 y Aguirre, 8th floor, T513691. *Iberia*, Av 9 de Octubre 101 y Malecón, T320664. *KLM*, at the airport, T282713.

Banks *Lloyds Bank*, Pichincha 108-110, with Mercado Central and Urdesa agencies. High commission on TCs. *Citibank*, 9 de Octubre. Citicorp cheques only and before 1330. *Banco del Pacífico*, Icaza 200, p 4. TCs and ATM for MasterCard. *Filanbanco*, 9 de Octubre entre Pichincha y P Carbo. Visa ATM. *American Express*, 9 de Octubre 1900 y Esmeraldas. For purchase of TCs, queues are much longer in the afternoon. *Banco de Guayaquil*, Pichincha y P Ycaza, Visa ATM. Mastercard head office at P Carbo y 9 de Octubre, Edif San Francisco 300, 7th Flr, T561730/511500, F566033, for cash advances. There are fewer *Casas de Cambio* following dollarization: *Cambiosa*, 9 de Octubre y Pichincha; *Wander Cambios* at the airport (see Transport above). Try *Hotel Oro Verde* and similar places for TCs, but service may be only for guests.

Communications *Pacifictel*, the telephone company, and the central post office are in the same block at Pedro Carbo y Aguirre. There are branch post offices in Urdesa, Estrada y Las Lomas by Mi Comisariato supermarket; first floor of Policentro; at the airport and bus terminal. The major hotels also sell stamps. Many courier services for reliable delivery of papers and packages, eg: *DHL*, T287044, is recommended for international service; *Servientrega*, offices throughout the city, for deliveries within Ecuador. **Internet**: There are many cyber cafés in the centre and suburbs alike, the greatest number are concentrated in shopping malls (see above). Also at the Youth hostel (see Sleeping above). Prices around US$0.50 per hour for internet access, U$0.50 per minute for Net2Phone.

Embassies and consulates *Argentina*, Aguirre 104 y Malecón, T323574. *Austria*, 9 de Octubre 1312 y Quito, #1, T282303. *Belgium*, Lizardo García 301 y Vélez, T364429. *Bolivia*, Urdesa Cedros 400 y la 5ta, T889955. *Brazil*, Av San Jorge 312 y Calle 3 Este, Nueva Kennedy, T293046. *Canada*, Edif Torre de la Merced, 21st floor, Córdova 808 y VM Rendón, T563580. *Colombia*, Edif San Francisco, 22nd floor, 9 de Octubre y Córdova, T568753. *Finland*, Luís Urdaneta # 206 y Córdova, T564268. *France*, José Mascote # 909 y Hurtado, T294334. *Germany*, Av Carlos Julio Arosemena Km 2, Ed Berlín, T200500. *Netherlands*, Edif ABN-AMRO Bank, P Ycaza 454 y Baquerizo Moreno, T563857. *Norway*, Av 9 de Octubre 105 y Malecón, T329661. *Peru*, 9 de octubre 411 y Chile, 6th floor, T322738. *Spain*, Urdesa calle Circunvalación, solar #118 y calle Unica, T881691. *Sweden*, Km 6.5 vía a Daule, T254111. *Switzerland*, Av 9 de Octubre 2105, T453607. *UK*, Gen Córdova 623 y Padre Solano, T560400. *USA*, 9 de Octubre 1571 y García Moreno, T323570. *Venezuela*, Chile 329 y Aguirre, T326566.

Medical facilities Doctors: *Dr Angel Serrano Sáenz*, Boyacá 821 y Junín, T301373. English speaking. *Clínica Santa Marianita*, Boyacá 1915 entre Colón y Av Olmedo, T322500. Doctors speak English and Spanish, special rates for Footprint Handbook users. *Dr James Peterson*, C Acacias 608 y Av Las Monjas, T888718, cellular T09-770670. Homeopath and chiropractor, speaks English. **Hospitals:** the main hospital used by the foreign community is the *Clínica Kennedy*, Av San Jorge y la 9na, T289666. Also has a branch in Ciudadela La Alborada XII Mz-1227. It contains the consulting rooms of almost every kind of specialist doctor and diagnostic laboratory (Dr Roberto Morla speaks German, T293470). Very competent emergency department. Also reliable are: *Clínica Alcívar*, Coronel 2301 y Azuay, T580030; *Clínica Guayaquil*, Padre Aguirre 401 y General Córdova, T563-555 (Dr. Roberto Gilbert speaks English).

Laundry *Sistematic*, F Segura y Av Quito, or C 6a y Las Lomas, Urdesa. *Martinizing*, Sucre 517 y Boyacá, and in CC La Gazota, for dry cleaning, many other outlets, but don't rely on their 1 hr service. *Dryclean USA*, VE Estrada 1016, Urdesa.

Places of worship *Anglican-Episcopalian Church*, Calle D entre Bogotá y A Fuentes, T443050. Centro Cristiano de Guayaquil, Pastor John Jerry Smith, Av Juan Tanca Marengo, Km 3, T271423. *Baptist Church*, Ximena 421, T302137. *Watch Tower Bible and Tract Society*, Capitán Zaera 319 y Bolívia, T448764. Many other sects are represented.

Useful addresses Immigration: Av Río Daule, near the bus terminal, T297004. For visa extensions.

Excursions from Guayaquil

This nature reserve is set in tropical dry forest with an impressive variety of birds (over 190 species listed so far), such as the Guayaquil green macaw, crane hawk, snail kite and so on, and with sightings of howler monkeys, ocelot, puma, jaguar and peccaries, among others. The reserve is run by Fundación Pro-Bosque, Edif Promocentro, local 16, Eloy Alfaro y Cuenca, T416975, evonhorst@gu.pro.ec ■ *Reservations required during weekdays and for groups larger than eight on the weekends, and for birders wishing to arrive before or stay after normal opening hours (0800-1530). Guides can be hired, US$5, camping $7 per person. The entrance is beyond the Club Rocafuerte. Taxi from Guayaquil US$10-20. The yellow and green 'Chongonera' buses leave every 30 mins from Parque Victoria and pass the park entrance on the way to Puerto Hondo.*

Cerro Blanco Forest Reserve

On the other side of the road from Cerro Blanco is **Puerto Hondo**. Canoe trips through the mangroves can be made from here. They can be arranged on the spot at weekends from the Fundación Pro-Bosque kiosk for US$7 per person with guides, or during the week with their Guayaquil office (see above).

Heading east then south from Guayaquil, 22 km beyond the main crossroads at Km 26 on the road to Naranjal, lies this ecological reserve. Many waterbirds, animals and dolphins can be seen. Canoe trips into the mangroves with guides must be arranged through the Ministerio del Ambiente office in Guayaquil, Dept Forestal, Avenida Quito 402 y P Solano, 10th floor, T397730; or Bióloga Mirella Pozo, cellular T09-761078. Reservations take three to four days to

Manglares Churute Ecological Reserve

Cocoa

In the late 18th century the Guayas basin, with its fertile soils, hot climate, abundant rainfall and easy river transport, became the most important area in the world for the production and export of cacao, a plant native to the Americas. At the time of independence cacao was the new Republic's only major export. The unhealthy coastal climate, especially notorious for yellow fever, and political instability hindered expansion of plantations until the 1870s. Meanwhile the demand for cacao was small until new processing techniques in Europe and the US in the mid-19th century made chocolate cheaper and more widely available. As it ceased to be an expensive luxury in Europe and the USA and world consumption multiplied eightfold between 1894 and 1924, cocoa plantations expanded rapidly around the Río Guayas estuary. Grown on large plantations, cocoa made fortunes for a new coastal élite, who backed the Radical Liberal Party which seized power in 1895.

By 1900 over 60% of government income came from taxes on cocoa exports. Great development schemes were begun, building roads, ports and railway lines, the most important of which, between Guayaquil and Quito, was completed in 1908.

Although Ecuador maintained its lead in cocoa production until the outbreak of the First World War, the planters were unprepared for a series of setbacks at the end of the war. Competition from African plantations in the British colonies hit the world cocoa price while witch broom disease swept through the plantations. Large areas of land were abandoned, most of the grand building projects were left incomplete and the Guayaquil élite was driven from power by a group of young army officers in the 1925 Revolution.

Today, cacao continues to be produced and exported on a more modest scale. The Ecuadorian variety is prized for its aroma and a small amount is a necessary ingredient in the world's finest chocolates.

arrange a group visit. Trips can also be arranged through *Chasquitur* agency, Urdaneta 1418 y Avenida del Ejército, T281085. ■ *US$10 per person is charged on site just to walk a self-guided nature trail over the hills. A boat trip costs an extra US$50 per boat to cover the cost of fuel. Buses leave the terminal near the airport every 30 mins, going to Naranjal or Machala. Ask to be let off at the Churute information centre. Packages including transport from Guayaquil are available for US$90 per person, minimum 2 persons.*

South to Peru

The road from Durán or Milagro heads south to Naranjal and on to Machala, a main crossroads and useful stopover before heading on to Huaquillas at the Peruvian frontier. Another road leads from Milagro through El Triunfo and La Troncal, then climbs to the Andean highway near Cañar, a useful route to Cuenca. From Machala, roads also run through Pasaje and Girón to Cuenca (188 km), and via Arenillas to Loja (216 km).

Machala

Phone code: 07
Colour map 6, grid B2
Population: 500,000

The capital of the province of El Oro, this booming agricultural town is the centre of a major banana producing and exporting region with an annual international banana fair in September. It is also an important shrimp producing area. The city is not particularly attractive, being somewhat dirty and oppressively hot, but it is prosperous and a good stopping point on the way to Peru.

Hotels are fairly central and the city centre is compact. There are not many sights to speak of in Machala but excursions can be made to **Puerto Bolívar** or the beaches at **Jambelí** (see below). The **Ministerio de Turismo** is located at 9 de Mayo y Pichincha, T932106.

AL *Oro Verde*, Circunvalación Norte, Urb Unioro, T933140, F933150, ecovm@gye.satnet.net Luxury hotel in US southwest style, 70 rooms, beautiful gardens, nice pool (US$6.50 for non-residents), 2 restaurants and deli, tennis courts, casino and cocktail lounge. Best in town. **C** *Oro*, Olmedo y Juan Montalvo, T930032, F937569. Refurbished, with bath, a/c, TV, good, friendly, helpful, expensive restaurant but good, cheaper café downstairs. Recommended. **C** *Rizzo*, Guayas y Bolívar, T921906, F921502. A/c, TV, suites available, recently refurbished, pool (US$2.50 for non-residents), casino, cafeteria, restaurant, noisy late disco.

D *Marsella*, Av Las Palmeras y 9 de Octubre, T932460. A/c, private bath, TV. **D** *Montecarlo*, Guayas y Olmedo, T933104, F931901. A/c, TV, hot water, clean, modern, restaurant. **D** *Ejecutivo*, Sucre y 9 de Mayo, T933992, F933987. With bath, a/c, TV, hot water, modern, in the market area. **D** *Perla del Pacífico*, Sucre 603 y Páez, T930915. TV, a/c, hot water. **D** *San Francisco*, Tarqui entre Sucre y Olmedo, T930915. With a/c, TV, parking, cheaper with fan.

E *Araujo*, 9 de Mayo y Boyacá, T/F935257. With bath, hot water, a/c, TV, parking, cheaper with fan, clean, some rooms are small, disco next door, parking, good value. **E** *Inés*, Montalvo 1509 y Pasaje, T922301, F932301. A/c, TV, parking, good restaurant. **F** *Hostal La Bahía*, Olmedo y Junín, T920581. With bath, fan, cheaper with shared bath, by market, good value, basic. **F** *Residencial Internacional*, Guayas y Sucre, T930244. Water shortages, basic but friendly. **F** *Mosquera*, Olmedo entre Guayas y Ayacucho, T931752, F930390. Cheaper with fan, TV, hot water, restaurant. Recommended. **F** *Hostal Patty*, Boyacá 619 y Ayacucho, T931759. With bath, fan, basic, cheaper with shared bath, some short stay customers. **G** *Julio César*, 9 de Mayo 1319 y Boyacá, T937978. With bath, fan, TV. **G** *Residencial Pichincha*, Sucre 516. Shared bath, very basic. **G** *Residencial Pesantes*, 9 de Mayo y Pasaje, T920154. With bath, fan, basic. **G** *Residencial San Antonio*, 9 de Mayo y Pasaje. With bath, basic.

Sleeping
■ *on map, page 300*
Price codes:
see inside front cover

Cafetería San Francisco, Sucre block 6. Good, filling breakfast. *200 Millas*, 9 de Octubre entre Santa Rosa y Vela. Seafood specialties. *Parrillada Sabor Latina*, Sucre y Guayas. Good steaks and grills. *Don Angelo*, 9 de Mayo just off the main plaza. Open 24 hrs, elaborate set meals and à la carte, good for breakfast. *Copa Cabana*, on the main plaza. Good clean snack bar. *Chifa Central*, Tarqui y 9 de Octubre. Good Chinese. *Chifa Gran Oriental*, 9 de Octubre entre Guayas y Ayacucho. Good food and service. *Mesón Hispano*, Av Las Palmeras y Sucre. Very good grill, attentive service. *Palacio Real*, 9 de Octubre y Ayacucho. Good set meal. *Las Redes*, 9 de Mayo 18-23 y Bolívar. A la carte seafood and choice of cheap set meals. *Aquí es Correita*, Av Arízaga y 9 de Mayo. Popular for seafood, closed Sun. There are 2 branches of *La Fogata*, Av Las Palmeras near the telephone office, for good chicken.

   Ice cream *Zanzibar*, Rocafuerte y Tarqui; *Pingüino*, Juan Montalvo y Rocafuerte; *Tocayo*, Juan Montalvo y Bolívar.

Eating
● *on map, page 300*
The best food is found in the better hotels

There are several cinemas, incuding *El Tauro* and *Unioro*, Ubanización Unioro; both with a/c, cushioned seats and good sound, admission US$1. A development just outside Machala on the Pasaje road has 2 large outdoor swimming pools.

Entertainment

Machala has its fair share of **discos**. Some of the better ones include: *La Contradition*, Av las Palmeras y Callejón 12, good atmosphere; *La Ego*, Tarqui y Rocafuerte, popular with local youth; *Twister Club*, Av Paquisha Km ½, good music and atmosphere, older crowd.

Nightlife

Guayaquil & Southern Pacific

Shopping **Supermarkets** *Unico*, Bolívar y 9 de Mayo. *Frigocentro*, Olmedo y Ayacucho. *Mi Comisiarato* at Unioro Shopping Centre, Circunvalación Norte. *UNO service station*, 9 de Octubre y Tarqui, 24-hr gasoline.

Transport **Air** Daily flights from Guayaquil (connect here for Quito) with *TAME*, Juan Montalvo y Bolívar, T930139. The terminal de Avionetas for flights to Guayaquil is less than 1 km from the centre of town.

For the route Machala-Cuenca, see page 266 **Bus** Most of the bus company offices are also quite central, but there is no *terminal terrestre*. Do not take night buses into or out of Machala as they are not safe. Holdups are especially frequent on the route Guayaquil-Machala.

To **Quito**, with *Occidental* (Buenavista entre Sucre y Olmedo), 12 hrs, US$6, 8 daily between 0815 and 2145; and with *Panamericana* (Colón y Bolívar), 7 daily 0745 to 2230, luxury service, 9 hrs, US$10 with a/c, US$8 without a/c. To **Guayaquil**, 4 hrs, US$3.80, hourly with *Ecuatoriano Pullman* (Colón y 9 de Octubre), *CIFA* (9 de Octubre y Tarqui) and *Rutas Orenses* (9 de Octubre y Tarqui). To **Esmeraldas**, 11 hrs, US$6, with *Occidental* (Buenavista y Sucre) at 2200. To **Loja**, 7 hrs, US$3, several daily with *Transportes Loja* (Tarqui y Bolívar). To **Cuenca**, hourly with *Trans Azuay* (Sucre y Junín), 3½ hrs, US$3.80. To **Huaquillas**, with *CIFA* (Bolívar y Guayas) and *Ecuatoriano Pullman* (Colón y 9 de Octubre), direct, 1 hr, US$1, every 30 mins; via Arenillas and Santa Rosa, 2 hrs, every 10 mins. There are passport checks on this route. **Taxis**: to Guayaquil, *Orotaxis* run a scheduled taxi service between the *Hotel Rizzo*, Machala and *Hotel Rizzo*, Guayaquil, every 30 mins or so, 0600-2000 US$3.50 per person, T934332.

Directory **Banks** *Banco del Austro*, Rocafuerte y Guayas, for Visa. *Banco de Guayaquil* , Rocafuerte y Guayas, for Visa. *Banco del Pacífico*, Rocafuerte y Junín. TCs and MC. *Banco Machala*, Rocafuerte y 9 de Mayo, Visa ATM and cash advance, friendly and efficient. *Filanbanco*, 9 de Octubre y Guayas. For Visa ATM and cash advances. **Communications** Post Office: Bolívar y Montalvo. *Pacifictel*, Av las Palmeras near the stadium. *Internet:* prices around US$1.50 per hour; *Ciber Yogurt*, 9 de Mayo y Pichincha; *Aquinet*, 9 de Octubre y Santa Rosa; *Oro Net*, 9 de Octubre y Buenavista. **Embassies and consulates** *Peruvian Consulate*, at the northwest corner of Colón y Bolívar, 1st Flr, T930680. **Tour operators** *Orotour*, Bolívar 924 y Guayas, T931557. *Glendatur*, Bolívar 513 y Guayas, T937670. Helpful. *La Moneda Tours*, Rocafuerte 518 entre Junín y Tarqui, T562230. Offices in Quito and Guayaquil, specializes in coastal and archaeological tours.

Machala

■ Sleeping
1 Ejecutivo
2 Montecarlo
3 Mosquera
4 Oro
5 Perla del Pacífico
6 Residencial Internacional
7 Rizzo

● Eating
1 Chifa Central
2 La Fogata

🚍 Buses
To Airport (500m)
1 CIFA
2 CIFA (to Huaquillas)
3 Ecuatoriano Pullman
4 Panamericana
5 Rutas Orenses
6 Trans Azuay

0 metres 100
0 yards 100

Excursions from Machala

Puerto Bolívar Built on the Canal de Santa Rosa among mangroves, this is a major export outlet for over two million tonnes of bananas annually. There is a pleasant waterfront and from the old pier a motorized canoe service crosses to the beaches of **Jambelí** on the far side of the mangrove islands which shelter Puerto Bolívar from the Pacific. Canoes can also be hired to **Isla del Amor**, where lots of birdlife can be seen in the mangroves, US$8 per canoe. Or you can just rent a canoe for an hour and explore the narrow channels (take insect repellent). Canoes depart for Jambelí at 0900, 1200, 1500 and 1700 returning at 1300 and 1700, US$1 per person. The beaches of Jambelí are safe and long with straw beach umbrellas for shade (the sun is fierce). Accommodation is moderately priced, and there is good, cheap food in the cafés along the beach.

Longer trips can be made to **Playas Bravita**, 30 minutes away (no shade or facilities), or to **Costa Rica**, which is two hours. Take your passport as a military post has to be crossed. Canoe hire to Costa Rica for the day is about US$70 for 15 people. It's cheaper to arrange a trip from Huaquillas.

Sleeping and eating In Puerto Bolívar: G *Pacífico*, Gral Páez 244. Basic. Or eating, try the following: *Waikiki*, good food, pleasant atmosphere; *Pepe's*, good; *El Portezuela*, Rocafuerte y Córdova. Also *Sarita*. There are lots of seafood kiosks between the old and new piers. Food here is better and cheaper than in Machala.

At Jambelí the following are **F-G**, clean and simple: *María Sol*, T937461. With good restaurant. Also *Niño Turista* and *Acuario Beach*.

Santa Rosa Thirty kilometres south on the main road to the Peruvian border lies Santa Rosa, an agricultural market town. Just by the air strip at Santa Rosa is a turnoff for **Puerto Jelí**, a tiny fishing village 4 km at the road's end, right in the mangroves on a branch of the main *estero*. Good eating at *Riberas del Pacífico*, *El Chino*, *El Pez Dorado* and others. Canoe trips can be arranged through the mangroves with Segundo Oyola (ask for him opposite the dock) to the beach of Las Casitas, for fishing or clam collecting. Price varies according to group size and bargaining is recommended. There is an annual shrimp festival in Santa Rosa, August 24-30, with a contest for the best *ceviche*.

Sleeping and eating E *América*, El Oro y Colón, T943130. With a/c, TV, private bath. **F** *Santa Rosa*, 1 block from plaza. Good with a/c, private bath. Cheap *residencias* on Av Colón. Several *chifas* serve good food.

Zaruma One hundred kilometres southeast from Machala is the gold-mining town of Zaruma. It is reached either by paved road via Piñas (military check point at *Altitude: 1,170 m* Saracay), or via Pasaje and Paccha on a scenic, dirt road.

Founded in 1549 on the orders of Felipe II to try to control the gold extraction, Zaruma is a lovely town perched on a hilltop, with steep, twisting streets and painted wooden buildings. The beautiful main plaza has, unfortunately, been marred by the tasteless cement monstrosity put up by the municipality and facing one of Ecuador's loveliest wooden churches. A preservation order now protects the centre of town from similar acts of architectural vandalism.

Beside the plaza is a lovely little museum showing the history of gold mining in the area. Gold mining is still a major employer here among the noticeably white-skinned, blue-eyed inhabitants of direct Spanish stock. Near Busa is a large *Chancadora*, a primitive rock-crushing operation. Many of the local mines bring their gold-bearing rocks here to be crushed then passed through sluices to wash off the mud. It is possible to visit some of the small roadside mining operations and watch the whole process.

Guayaquil & Southern Pacific

Agricultural production in this area is almost zero, as no one has time, though some coffee is harvested. One small store in Zaruma roasts its own for sale and sends weekly shipments to Quito. On top of the small hill beyond the market is a public swimming pool, from where there are amazing views over the hot, dry valleys.

Sleeping **E** *Rosales de Machay*, up the Busa valley between Zaruma and Piñas. Access is difficult without a car or taxi, it's a long, hot walk upstream then down the other side, pool, restaurant, tennis, popular at weekends, clean, comfortable cabins. Outside town is **F** *Roland*. **G** *Municipal*. Dilapidated, but with good views. **G** *Colombia*, on the main plaza. Very basic. **G** *Pedregal*, on the Malvas road, with 2-3 rooms.

Transport Transportes Paccha departs from Machala near the market, or Trans TAC, Sucre y Colón departs every hour from 0500 to 1700 via Piñas, last bus back at 1800, US$1.70, 3 hrs to Zaruma, US$0.80, 3½ hrs to Piñas.

Piñas Beyond the *Hotel Rosales de Machay* (see above) is the lovely, wooden colonial town of Piñas. Two orchid specialists will show their collections if you ask around. One is a local school teacher and has a museum-like collection of memorabilia in his house. There are three *residencias*, one in town and the others on the hill on the way out of town to Zaruma. There are buses to **Paccha** up in the hills to the north (**F** *Residencial Reina del Cisne*, clean, pleasant), and to **Ayapamba** and many other old gold mining villages. Northwest of Piñas, along the road to Saracay, is **Buenaventura**, to the north of which lies an important area for bird conservation. Here are a few remaining forest tracts in which many rare birds have been found, this area has over 310 bird species. The Jocotoco Foundation protects a 300 ha forest in this region, further information through www.jocotoco.org

Portovelo South of Zaruma, Portovelo was once the headquarters of the Vanderbilt mining company, down in the valley. The huge gold mine took many hundreds of tonnes of gold out of the country but allegedly never paid any taxes. When quizzed by the government, the company pointed to the fact that they had built a new road and not charged them for it. The fact that most of these roads rather conveniently went to new areas ready to be exploited for gold deposits seems to have been ignored.

Portovelo was deemed too hot and unhealthy so the miners' families were moved to the top of the neighbouring hill and the beautiful wooden town of Zaruma was built. There are numerous tiny chapels scattered across the surrounding hills and, in the times when the mines were functioning, it was fashionable to take a trip in the horse and carriage to these outlying chapels for the Sunday services. Many of the roads built by Vanderbilt end at these chapels. There are a couple of small *residencias* in Portovelo. There are lots of buses from Machala, and a local bus runs up and down to Zaruma.

There are hot thermal springs at **Aguas Calientes**, 6 km from Portovelo, but no facilities. A nice walk is 5 km on the Loja road to Río Pindo or Río Luís.

Puyango
This petrified forest is supposedly the most extensive outside Arizona

Over 120 species of birds can be seen at the petrified forest of Puyango, which is due south of Machala. There is no accommodation in the village but ask around for floor space or try at the on-site information centre. If not, basic accommodation is available in Alamor. Campsites are also provided. For further information, contact the Dirección Provincial de Turismo, Machala T932106. Buses for Alamor leave Machala at 0900 and 1330, three hours, US$2.50, ask to be dropped off at Puyango. To return to Machala, you can catch the Loja-Machala bus which passes Puyango around 1500. There are several military checkpoints between Puyango and Machala.

Huaquillas

The most commonly used route overland to Peru is via Machala. Many buses from there (see above) go to Huaquillas, the Ecuadorean border town, which is something of a shopping arcade for Peruvians, though all shops close about 1800. It has grown into a small city with a reasonable selection of hotels and other services. The climate is very hot.

Phone code: 07
Colour map 6, grid B1

A number of the cheaper hotels in Huaquillas are primarily for short stay customers.
D *Lima*, Portovelo y Machala, T907794. Bath, a/c, TV, phone, **E** with fan, mosquito net.
E *Vanessa*, 1 de Mayo 323 y Av Hualtaco, T/F907263. Bath, a/c, TV, phone. **E** *Alameda*,
Tnte Córdovez y José Mendoza. Bath, fan, TV, mosquito net, basic. **E** *Guayaquil*, Remigio
Gómez 125. With bath, **F** without, fan, clean, mosquito net, limited water supply, noisy.
E *Internacional*, Machala y 9 de Octubre, T907963. Bath, fan, small rooms, basic,
cheaper with shared bath. **E** *Rivera*, Portovelo y Machala, T907899. Private bath, a/c.
E *Rodey*, Tnte Córdovez y 10 de Agosto, T907736. Bath, fan, TV, fridge, clean, basic.

F *Gabeli*, Tnte Córdovez 311 y Portovelo, T907149. Bath, fan, mosquito net, cheaper
without bath, parking. **F** *Mini*, Tnte Córdovez y Rocafuerte. Bath, fan, mosquito net,
restaurant, poor water supply. **F** *Residencial Fabiolita*, Tnte Córdovez y Santa Rosa.
Shared bath, mosquito net, basic. **F** *Residencial San Martín*, Av la República opposite
the church, T907083. Shared bath, fan, basic, noisy, mosquito nets. **F** *Rivieras*, Tnte
Córdovez y El Oro. Bath, fan, mosquito net, OK, disco downstairs at weekends.
G *Quito*, Portovelo y Remigio Gómez. Shared bath, mosquito net, basic.

Sleeping
■ *on map*
Price codes:
see inside front cover

Guayaquil & Southern Pacific

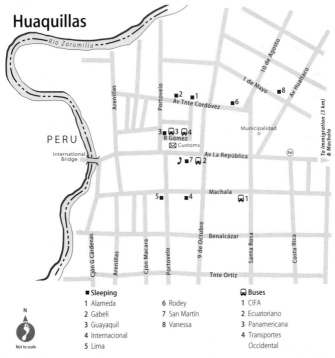

Huaquillas

Río Zarumilla

PERU

International
Bridge

Portovelo

Arenillas

■2 ■1
Av Tnte Córdovez

10 de Agosto

1 de Mayo   ■8

Av Hualtaco

■6

Municipalidad

3■ 🚌3 🚌4
R Gómez
✉ Customs

To Immigration (3 km)
& Machala

🎵■7 🚌2
Av La República

Pol

5■   ■4

Machala
🚌1

Cjón G Cárdenas

Arenillas

Cjón Macara

Portovelo

9 de Octubre

Benalcázar

Santa Rosa

Costa Rica

Tnte Ortiz

N
Not to scale

■ **Sleeping**
1 Alameda
2 Gabeli
3 Guayaquil
4 Internacional
5 Lima

6 Rodey
7 San Martín
8 Vanessa

🚌 **Buses**
1 CIFA
2 Ecuatoriano
3 Panamericana
4 Transportes
   Occidental

Eating *Chic*, behind *Hotel Guayaquil*. Set meal US$1. *Chifa China Norte*, Santa Rosa y Tnte Córdovez. Chinese. *Flamingo*, Tnte Córdovez y 10 de Agosto. *Mini*, opposite Transportes Loja. Good set lunch US$2. *Chesito*, Av la República y Costa Rica. Across from the police station, large portions, good. There are several other cheap and simple places to eat.

Transport **Bus** There are 3 checkpoints (Transit Police, Customs and military) along the road north from Huaquillas, so keep your passport to hand. To **Machala**, with *CIFA* (Santa Rosa y Machala) and *Ecuatoriano Pullman* (Av la República y 9 de Octubre), direct, 1 hr, US$1, every hour between 0400 and 2000; via Arenillas and Santa Rosa, 2 hrs every 10 mins. To **Quito**, with *Occidental* (Remigio Gómez 129 y Portovelo), 3 daily, 12 hrs, US$7; with *Panamericana* (on Remigio Gómez), luxury service, 11½ hrs, 3 daily via Santo Domingo, US$10 with a/c, US$7 without a/c; 2 daily via **Riobamba** and **Ambato**, 12 hrs, US$7. To **Guayaquil**, frequent service with *CIFA* and *Ecuatoriano Pullman*, about 5 hrs, US$3. If in a hurry to reach Quito or Guayaquil, Cuenca or Loja, it might be better to change buses in Machala.

To **Cuenca**, several daily, 6 hrs, US$4. To **Loja**, with *Transportes Loja* (Tnte Córdovez y Arenillas) daily at 1130 and 1830, 7 hrs, US$4. To **Tulcán** for the Colombian border, with *Panamericana*, at 1630, 16 hrs, US$12. The main roads to Guayaquil, Quito and Cuenca are all paved.

Directory **Banks** Check on the rate of exchange with travellers leaving Peru. Fair rates are available for soles and dollars cash on both sides of the border, but you will always be offered a low rate when you first enquire. Ask around before changing, do your own arithmetic and don't be rushed into any transaction. Especially avoid those changers who chase after you. Be sure to count your change carefully. The money changers (recognized by their black briefcases) are very clever, particularly with calculators, and often dishonest. There is now supposed to be an *Asociación de Cambistas*, whose members wear ID tags, but be cautious nonetheless. It is difficult to change TCs but try the banks along the main street. **Communications** **Post Office:** Av la República. **Pacifictel:** Av la República, opposite post office.

Frontier with Peru

Leaving Ecuador The border runs along the Río Zarumilla and is crossed by the international bridge at the western end of Avenida La República. It is a shortish walk from the bus terminals which are just off the main street.

At the border **Ecuadorean immigration** Passports are stamped 3 km north of town along the road to Machala. There is no urban transport; inter-city buses charge US$0.15 from Huaquillas, taxis US$1. The border is open 24 hours. Allow up to one to two hours to complete formalities, although it can sometimes be much quicker. To cross to Peru, walk along the main street in Huaquillas and across the international bridge. At the bridge, the police may check passports.

Crossing by private vehicle Both Ecuadorean and Peruvian customs are located on either side of the international bridge. If there is a problem entering with a car, contact Tulio Campoverde Armijos, Agente Afianzado de Aduanas, Gómez 123 y Portovelo.

Peruvian immigration The main Peruvian immigration and customs complex (open 24 hours) where passports are stamped is outside Zarumilla, about 3 km past the international bridge.

Exchange Coming from Peru, you can sell soles to the money changers outside Peruvian immigration or in Huaquillas, but beware of sharp practices by both.

There are three forms of transport between the frontier and Tumbes in Peru. **Into Peru**
Some colectivos leave from near the bridge. They charge higher prices, especially for foreigners, so beware of rip-offs. Other, cheaper ones leave two blocks down along the main street by a small plaza opposite the church; US$1 per person, or US$6 per car. Colectivos should stop and wait at the immigration complex on the Peruvian side, but they are not always willing to do so. Buses and minivans leave from an esplanade three blocks east from the colectivo stop and go to the market in Tumbes, US$0.75 (they don't wait at immigration). There are also mototaxis from the bridge to the Zarumilla immigration complex, US$0.90 for up to two people. Taxi to Tumbes, including the wait at immigration, US$6.

Coming from Peru into Ecuador: take a bus to Tumbes and a colectivo from there to the border. A ticket out of Ecuador is not usually asked for at this border.

Both the *Peruvian Handbook* and the *South American Handbook* give details on the services and excursions at **Tumbes**. There are national parks and beaches to visit, a fair range of hotels and places to eat and good transport links south down the coast as far as Lima.

The Huaquillas-Tumbes crossing can be harrowing, made worse by the **Alternative** crowds and heat. You must always watch your gear carefully. In addition to **crossings** cheating by money changers and cab drivers (see above), this border is known **to Peru** for its minor shakedowns of travellers. These are annoying but fortunately seldom serious. It is not uncommon to be asked for a small bribe by one of the many officials you will encounter here. Those seeking a more relaxed crossing to or from Peru should consider Macará (see page 280) or enquire about new crossing possibilities which are opening up following the signing of the peace treaty between Ecuador and Peru (eg Zumba, see page 278).

Guayaquil & Southern Pacific

Northern Pacific Lowlands

8

Northern Pacific Lowlands

The coastal region covers a third of Ecuador's total area. Though popular with Quiteños and Guayaquileños, who come here in their droves for weekends and holidays, the Northern Pacific lowlands receive relatively few foreign visitors, which is surprising given the natural beauty, diversity and rich cultural heritage of the coast. You can surf, watch whales at play, visit ancient archaeological sites, or just relax and enjoy the best food that this country has to offer. The jewel in the coastal crown, Parque Nacional Machalilla, protects an important area of primary tropical dry forest, precolumbian ruins, coral reef and a wide variety of wildlife. Further north, in the province of Esmeraldas, there are not only well-known party beaches, but also opportunities to visit the remaining mangroves and experience two unique lifestyles: Afro-Ecuadorean on the coast and native Cayapa further inland.

Even if your time is limited, the coast is easily accessible from Quito, making it the ideal short break from the Andean chill. The water is warm for bathing and the beaches, many of them deserted, are generally attractive, thanks to a number of successful clean-up programmes.

Western Lowlands

Quito to Santo Domingo

From **Alóag**, about one hour's drive south of Quito on the Panamericana, an important paved road goes west to the lowlands. After the pass, it follows the valley of the ríos Naranjal/Pilatón/Blanco, and continues past Tandapi (the official name M Cornejo Astorga is never used), 45 km from Alóag. There are two hotels, **G** (with shared bath), and many roadside restaurants.

Then comes Alluriquín, with accommodation in **F** *Florida* at Km 104, T750232 (with bath, a bit run-down, swimming pool, restaurant, horse riding, busy at weekends).

The drive is scenic, sit on the right for the best views going down, but on the left side look for El Poder Brutal, a devil's face, complete with horns and fangs, carved in the rock face, 2½ km west of Tandapi. This road is very busy. It gets a lot of heavy truck traffic and it can be dangerous owing to careless drivers passing on the many curves, especially when foggy and at night. This is also the route used by rafting agencies in Quito for trips on the Toachi and Blanco rivers (see Rafting, on page 70). Alternative routes from Quito are via Calacalí, and La Independencia, and a much smaller road through Chiriboga, see page 150.

The main road to Santo Domingo passes near some forest remnants with many birds, flowers and butterflies. Seventeen kilometres east of Santo Domingo, to the south of the road, is **Tinalandia**, a great introduction to the world of tropical birds, where more than 360 species have been seen. There are many colourful birds and they are easier to see here than at most other places. There is a pleasant lodge here, **AL** *Tinalandia*, poorly signposted, look for a large rock painted white, T09-494727, in Quito T449028, F442638, tinaland@ramt.com, www.tinalandia.net Chalets with bath, includes excellent meals. There is an unused golf course overlooking the Toachi valley and many trails in the woods behind. Take repellent, there are biting insects in the evening. Lunch (with the right to use the facilities) costs US$10 for non-residents.

Santo Domingo de los Colorados

Phone code: 02
Colour map 2, grid C3
Population: 183,219
Altitude: 500 m

The main route to the coast goes through Santo Domingo de los Colorados, an important commercial centre and a hub for transport between the coast and highlands, 129 km from Quito.

The city became Ecuador's main transport hub in the mid 1960s when the road from Quito through Alóag was completed. Since that time it has experienced very rapid growth and many immigrants from Colombia have settled here. The name de los Colorados is a reference to the native Tsáchila men. The Tsáchila nation are known locally as the Indios Colorados because of their custom of coating their hair with red vegetable dye, although they do not approve of this name. There are less than 2,000 Tsáchilas left, living in eight communities off the roads leading from Santo Domingo to Quevedo, Chone and Quinindé. Their lands make up a reserve of some 8,000 ha.

Today the Tsáchila only wear their native dress on special occasions and they can no longer be seen in traditional garb in the city, except for the Monumento al Colorado statue, at the west end of the city centre where the roads to Quevedo, Chone and Esmeraldas meet.

Santo Domingo is an important commercial centre for the surrounding palm oil and banana producing areas. The city itself is noisy, streets are prone to flooding after heavy rains and it has little to offer the tourist, except for

Climate changes

The local climate, landscape and vegetation vary remarkably both along the coast and from the shore inland towards the highlands. If it were possible to travel north from Machala to the Colombian border in a single day, you would see the sun rise over endless banana plants, eat lunch shivering in a cold, grey drizzle amid parched cactus scrub, and arrive at sundown in tropical heat under the tall, dense canopy of one of the world's wettest rainforests.

The reason for this dramatic difference in climate and vegetation between the north and south coasts is the effects of the opposing and seasonal ocean currents offshore. The cold Humboldt comes north as far as the level of Portoviejo in mid Manabí, which accounts for the semi-arid conditions in the southern coast, particularly in the Santa Elena peninsula. Nevertheless, lush forest grows on hills above about 600 m and in the sheltered Gulf of Guayaquil and humid Guayas delta. Though the overall picture for the coast is of decreasing average temperatures and rainfall from north to south, there is striking local variability.

NB The devastating 1997/98 El Niño wreaked havoc along Ecuador's coastline but the damage has now been completely repaired throughout most of the coast.

access to nature reserves nearby. Sunday is market day and therefore many shops in town are only open from Tuesday to Sunday. The main plaza is Parque Joaquín Zaracay.

There are several options for fishing and bird/butterfly watching excursions in the Santo Domingo area (see out of town Sleeping below). With an all-terrain vehicle, the old road to Quito, via Chiriboga and San Juan, offers access to a forested area on the east bank of the Río Toachi. The turnoff is just east of La Unión del Toachi, between Alluriquín and Tandapi. Tours can be arranged through tour operators, see below. For details on the nature reserves in this area, see Excursions southwest of Quito, page 150. **NB** Santo Domingo is not safe at night. Caution is recommended at all times in the market areas, including the pedestrian walkway along 3 de Julio and in peripheral neighbourhoods.

NB There are many hotels along Av 29 de Mayo, which is a noisy street, so ask for a room away from the road. Several of the cheaper establishments also cater to short stay customers.

Sleeping
■ *on map, page 312*
Price codes:
see inside front cover

In town E *Diana Real*, 29 de Mayo y Loja, T751380, F754091. Modern spacious rooms, with bath, hot water, fan, TV, they are also the local DHL Courier and Western Union representatives. **E** *La Siesta*, Av Quito 606 y Yambo, T751013. With bath, hot water, **F** with shared bath, restaurant, parking, ageing but nice. **F** *Aracelly*, Vía a Quevedo y Galápagos, T750334, F754144. Large rooms, with bath, restaurant, parking. **F** *Caleta*, Ibarra 141, T750277. Good restaurant, private bath, **G** without TV, friendly, good. **F** *Génova*, 29 de Mayo e Ibarra, T759694. Clean, comfortable, **G** without TV, parking, good value. Recommended. **F** *Gran Unicornio*, Ambato y Quito, T768500. With bath, cold water, cable TV, security box, cafeteria, parking. New in 2000.

G *Amambay*, 29 de Mayo y Ambato, T750696. Quite good, water on demand. **F** *El Colorado*, 29 de Mayo y Esmeraldas, T750226. With bath, a bit noisy, restaurant, parking. **G** *Ejecutivo*, 29 de Mayo entre Ambato y Cuenca, T752893. With bath, TV, cafeteria, cheaper without TV, OK. **G** *Jennifer*, 29 de Mayo y Latacunga, T750577. With bath, some with hot water, rooms away from the street are quieter, parking, restaurant, good value. **G** *Las Brisas #2*, Cocaniguas y Río Pilatón, T753283. With bath, clean, modern, parking extra. Under the same management is **G** *Las Brisas #1*, Av Quito y Cocaniguas, T750560. With bath, basic, **F** with shared bath. **G** *Residencial España*, on Av Abraham Calazacón, opposite the bus terminal. Entrance on the side street, with

Northern Pacific Lowlands

bath, clean, basic. **G** *Residencial El Viajero*, 29 de Mayo y Latacunga. With bath, cold water, basic, **H** with shared bath. **G** *San Fernando*, 2 blocks from the bus terminal, T753402. With bath, clean, modern, comfortable, cheaper with shared bath, parking. **G** *Sheraton*, on Av Abraham Calazacón, opposite the bus terminal, T751988. Modern, clean, with bath, hot water, parking, good value. Recommended. **G** *Unicornio*, 29 de Mayo y Ambato, T760147. With bath, cold water, cable TV, restaurant, parking, nice.

H *Residencial Groenlandia*, 29 de Mayo y Ambato, T752877. Shared bath, cold water, basic. **H** *Residencial Madrid*, 3 de Julio 438 y Riobamba. Shared bath, basic. **H** *Aldita* and **H** *Pichincha* (T751052). Both on Tulcán y Quito, both basic. **H** *Hostal Turistas 1* 3 de Julio y Latacunga, T751759. Very basic.

Out of town Along the road to Quito are: **B** *Zaracay*, Av Quito 1639, Km 1½, T750316, F754535. Good rooms and service, full breakfast included, restaurant, slot machines, noisy disco, gardens and a swimming pool. The best hotel in the area, it's advisable to book, especially at weekends. **D** *Tropical Inn*, Av Quito next to the fairground, opposite *Zaracay*, T761771, F761775. Modern, with bath, TV, fridge. **E** *Hostería Los Colorados*, Km 12, just west of the toll booth and police control, T/F753449. Nice cabins with fridge, TV, pool, artificial lake with fish, restaurants, good cafetería. **F** *Hotel del Toachi*, Km 1, just west of *Zaracay*, T/F754688. Spacious rooms, with bath, good showers, TV, swimming pool, parking.

Along other roads out of Santo Domingo: **AL** *Hostería Valle Hermoso*, Km 25 on the road to Esmeraldas, south of La Concordia, T/F759095, office in Santo Domingo:

Santo Domingo de los Colorados

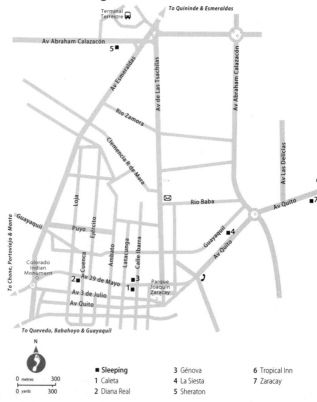

■ Sleeping	3 Génova	6 Tropical Inn
1 Caleta	4 La Siesta	7 Zaracay
2 Diana Real	5 Sheraton	

Cocaniguas 289, T/F759095. Inludes all meals, with bath, hot showers, fan, TV, restaurant, pool, sauna, horse riding, fishing, set in 120 forested hectares on the shores of the Río Blanco, with lakes and waterfalls. **D** *Hostería Rancho Mi Cuchito*, Vía a Chone Km 2, T750636, F755303. With bath, hot water, TV, pool, restaurant. **F** *Complejo Campestre Santa Rosa*, Vía Quevedo Km 16, T754145, F754144. Office in Santo Domingo at *Hotel Aracelly*, on the shores of the Río Baba, rooms with bath, restaurant, swimming, watersports, fishing, salsoteca.

Parrilladas Argentinas, on Quevedo road Km 5. For good barbecues. *Mocambo*, **Eating** Tulcán y Machala. Good. *La Fuente*, Ibarra y 3 de Julio. Good. There are several chicken places in the Cinco Esquinas area where Avs Quito and 29 de Mayo meet, including *Rico Pollo*, Quito y Río Pove. *Tacos Mexicanos*, Quito. A super deli. Highly recommended. *D'Mario*, 1 block southwest of the roundabout for Quito. Good steaks and international food. Several other grills nearby. There are also several *marisquerías* (seafood restaurants) along Av 29 de Mayo. There are several restaurants on Av Abraham Calazacón across from the bus terminal, including *Sheraton*, which is popular.

Ice cream *Heladería* at Edificio San Francisco, Av Quito entre Río Blanco y Río Toachi. Good, made on the premises, also sell fresh cheese. Opposite is *Pingüino*.

Aruba's Disco, Av de los Tsáchilas y 29 de Mayo. *Cervecería-Salsoteca The Jungle*, Av **Entertainment** Quito across from *Hotel La Siesta*. Discos in the peripheral neighbourhoods are not considered safe.

Turismo Zaracay, 29 de Mayo y Cocaniguas, T750546, F750873. Runs tours to the **Tour operators** Tsáchila commune for US$12 per person, minimum 5 persons. Fishing trips US$24 per person, 8 hrs, bird/butterfly watching tours. *Cayapatours*, 29 de Mayo y Tulcán, T/F762933. Tickets and tours.

Road If passing through Santo Domingo, it is not necessary to drive through the **Transport** congested centre of the city, as there is a bypass road around it.

Bus The bus terminal is on Av Abraham Calazacón, at the north end of town, along the city's bypass road. Long-distance buses don't enter the city. A taxi downtown from the terminal costs US$0.60 and public bus is US$0.15.

As it is a very important transportation centre, you can get buses going everywhere in the country. To **Quito** via Alóag US$2, 3 hrs, via San Miguel de los Bancos US$3,50, 5 hrs. To **Guayaquil** US$3.25, 4 hrs. To **Machala**, US$4.55, 6 hrs. To **Huaquillas** US$5.20, 7½ hrs. To **Esmeraldas** US$1.95, 3 hrs. To **Ambato** US$2.60, 4 hrs. To **Loja** US$9.70, 12 hrs. To **Manta** US$4.40, 6 hrs. To **Bahía de Caráquez** US$3.60, 4 hrs. To **Pedernales** US$2.60, 3 hrs.

Banks *Banco Internacional*, Av Quito y Río Blanco. TCs. *Filanbanco*, Av Quito y Av de los **Directory** Tsáchilas, by Parque Zaracay. For Visa and TCs, 0900-1400. Western Union money transfers at *Hotel Diana Real*. **Communications** **Post Office:** Av de los Tsáchilas y Río Baba, 0800-1830. Fax service 0800-1630. *Andinatel*, Edificio San Francisco, Av Quito between Río Blanco y Río Toachi, 2nd Flr, and at the bus terminal, 0800-2200 daily.

Santo Domingo to the Coast

A busy paved highway connects Santo Domingo de los Colorados with Esmeraldas, 185 km to the northwest (see page 343). After 5 km on the new road to Quito you cross the Río Salazar (*Cabanas Don Gaucho*, BBQ, camping, swimming in river, T02-330315, www.ecuador-sommer.com). **La Concordia** (**C** *Hotel Atos*, T02-725445, very good and several cheaper ones), is 40 km from Santo Domingo, just before which is the private **La Perla Forest Reserve**, 40 km from Santo Domingo (you can hike in for free), **La Independencia** (which is the junction with the road from San Miguel de Los Bancos and Quito) and **Quinindé** (**Rosa Zárate**). There are a few hotels in Quinindé: **G** *Sanz*, on the main street, T736522. With bath, TV, clean, parking, very noisy. *Residencial Paraíso*. Clean, quite good, with water 24 hours a day. **G** *Turista*, eight blocks south of town, on the main road, T736784. Quieter than central hotels, with parking. Three blocks south of town on the main road is *Restaurant Jean*, T736831, which serves excellent steaks and seafood, huge portions, good salads, reasonable prices, probably the best restaurant for miles. The road deteriorates north of Quinindé.

Near Quinindé is the **Bilsa Reserve and Biological Station**, owned by the Jatun Sacha Foundation. It protects 3,000 ha of very unusual lowland and foothill forest at 300-750 m above sea level. The forest here contains many bird species virtually impossible to see elsewhere, including the Long-Wattled Umbrellabird and Banded Ground-Cuckoo. From town take a truck to La Y de la Laguna; from there hike three hours to the reserve. Accessibility depends on weather conditions and is easiest July to August; at other times a much longer hike may be required. Accommodation in the **C** range. Contact Jatun Sacha Foundation for visits or volunteer opportunities; see page 80.

Another paved road from Santo Domingo to the coast runs west to **El Carmen**, with a cattle market on the outskirts. There are several basic hotels on the noisy main street, and some quieter ones near the Pacifictel office behind the central plaza. From El Carmen a paved road goes to **Pedernales** on the coast (see page 338). Continuing southwest of El Carmen is Chone where the road divides, either to Bahía de Caráquez (207 km from Santo Domingo, 340 km from Quito, see page 332), or to Portoviejo and Manta (257 km from Santo Domingo, 390 km from Quito).

South from Santo Domingo another highway goes southwest to Quevedo, 1½ hours by bus. At Km 47 is the **Rio Palenque** scientific station, set in one of the last remaining islands of western lowland forest, at an altitude of 200 m. It is a very rich birding area, with 370 species. It has however begun to lose some species because of its isolation from other forests. Here is **B** *Río Palenque*, a lodge with capacity for 20, cooking facilities, US$5 for a day visit. T04-208680 or in Quito T232468 for information and reservations.

Quevedo
Phone code: 05
Population: 120,000

Set in fertile banana lands and often flooded in the rainy season, Quevedo is known as the Chinatown of Ecuador, with a fair-sized Chinese colony. It is a dusty, noisy, crowded and unsafe town which has grown exceptionally rapidly over the last 25 years.

Sleeping and eating B *Olímpico*, Bolívar y 19a. Near the stadium. A/c, huge pool *All hotels are noisy* (open to the public), best restaurant in town. **G** *Quevedo*, Av 7 de Octubre y C 12. Modern rooms with fridge, TV, good restaurant. **G** *Ejecutivo Internacional*, 7 de Octubre y C Cuarta. Modern, large rooms, a/c, private bath, good value, the least noisy. **G** *Rancho Vinicio*, out of town on the road to La Maná. Quiet cabins, with pool.

For eating try, **on 7 de Octubre**: *Rincón Caleño*, No 1103. Colombian. *Chifas* at Nos 806, 809 and 707. *Tungurahua*, No 711. Good breakfast US$1. *Hong Kong*, C Ambato. Recommended.

Transport Bus: Quevedo is an important route centre. To **Quito**, 7 hrs, US$4. To **Portoviejo**, from 7 de Octubre and C 8, 5 hrs, US$1.80. To **Guayaquil**, 3 hrs, US$1.65. Portoviejo, Tosagua and several coastal towns can be reached via Velasco Ibarra, Pichincha, Rocafuerte and Calceta.

Quevedo to Latacunga

The old highway which runs from Quevedo up to Latacunga in the highlands carries very little traffic. It is extremely twisty in parts but it is one of the most beautiful of the routes connecting the highlands with Portoviejo, Manta and the coast. Between **La Maná** and Zumbahua (see page 203) are the pretty little towns of **Pilaló** (two restaurants and petrol pumps) and **El Tingo** (two restaurants and lodging at *Carmita's*). The road is paved from Quevedo to just before Pilaló. This is a great downhill bike route done in reverse from the highlands to the coast.

Sleeping Situated 2½ km before La Maná on the road from Quevedo is: **G** *Rancho Hostería Inmisahu*, T688003/281. Cabins, pool, restaurant. Friendly. *La Herradura*, east of town on the road to Zumbahua.

Quevedo is connected with Guayaquil by two paved highways: one runs through Balzar and Daule; the other passes through the city of Babahoyo, from where another scenic road goes to Guaranda in the highlands (see page 227).

Babahoyo
Phone code: 05
Population: 50,250

Sleeping and eating E *Hotel Cachari*, Bolívar 120 y Gen Barona, T734443, F731317. With bath, a/c, **F** with fan, cable TV, sauna. Acceptable, restaurant nearby. **F** *Hotel Emperador*, Gen Barona, T730535. Bath, a/c, cheaper with fan, TV, restaurant. Eating places include *Chifa Sin Log*, 10 de Agosto y Sucre. Chinese food. *Monich*, Eloy Alfaro y 10 de Agosto. Local and international food.

The coast from Guayaquil to Puerto López

West of Guayaquil is the beach resort of Playas and, further west, the Santa Elena Peninsula. North of Santa Elena, the coastal road passes through the popular surfing resorts of Manglaralto, Montañita and Olón before continuing to the unique Alandaluz Ecological Tourist Centre and on to Puerto López, the perfect base from which to explore the beautiful Machalilla National Park.

There is a good road network on the coast which was rebuilt following El Niño damage in 1997. The beach resorts of Salinas and Playas, are very popular with vacationing Guayaquileños. Several new major projects are in the pipeline, mostly in the shape of high-rise club-style complexes, with casinos, swimming pools, discos, restaurants and the like. Salinas and Playas can be reached along

Northern Pacific Lowlands

a paved toll highway from Guayaquil. The road divides after 63 km at El Progreso (Gómez Rendón).

Playas

One branch of the highway from Guayaquil leads to General Villamil, normally known as Playas, the nearest seaside resort to Guayaquil. Look out for the bottle-shaped ceibo (*kapok*) trees between Guayaquil and Playas as the landscape becomes drier, turning into tropical thorn scrub.

Fishing is important in Playas and a few single-sailed balsa rafts can still be seen among the motor launches returning laden with fish. These rafts are unique, highly ingenious and very simple. The same rafts without sails are used to spread nets close offshore, then two gangs of men take two to three hours to haul them in. The beach shelves gently, and is 200-400 m wide, lined with singular, square canvas tents hired out for the day.

As the closest resort to Guayaquil, Playas is popular with local city dwellers and prone to severe crowding, especially during the high season (*temporada*), December to April, when there are frequent promotional beach parties. The authorities are trying to keep the packed beaches cleaner at the western end as well as by the beach cafés and generally they are less dirty and safer than before. There are showers, toilets and changing rooms along the beach, with fresh water, for a fee.

The Malecón has been improved with new grass and trees. Out of season, when it is cloudier, or midweek the beaches are almost empty especially for anyone who walks north up the beach to Punta Pelado (5 km), although the new Club Casa Blanca, 20 minutes up the beach, will intrude on the isolation. Other hotels are opening up, as well as new restaurants. Playas is also a popular surfing resort with six good surf points.

Sleeping
■ *on map*
Price codes:
see inside front cover

Most hotels are 5 mins' walk from the Transportes Villamil bus station. Some are connected to Guayaquil's mains water supply, but many have wells which take water from the sea which is slightly brackish. Downmarket places have buckets for washing, if you're lucky.

C *Hostería Bellavista*, Km 2 Data Highway, T760600. Rooms or suites in bungalows on the beach, booking necessary, Swiss-run, friendly, clean, camping at the south end

Playas

■ Sleeping		
1 El Galeón	2 Hostería La Gaviota	4 Miraglia
	3 La Terraza	5 Playas
		6 Rey David
		7 Turismo

Golfo de Guayaquil

Not to scale

of beach. **C** *El Tucán*, Km 1.5 Vía Data. Pool, restaurant, parking. **D** *Hostería La Gaviota*, 500 m out on the Data road, T760133. Colour TV, a/c, friendly, good clean restaurant. **D** *Hostería Los Patios*, Km 1½ Data Highway, T760327. Well-equipped suites, restaurant. **D-E** *Playas*, on the Malecón, T760121. Accepts credit cards, plain rooms with fans, clean, safe, restaurant, parking. Recommended.

   E *El Delfín*, Km 1.5, T760125. Old-fashioned, big rooms, on the beach, hacienda type building, nice but sporadic water supply, electric showers, restaurant sometimes closed at night. **E** *El Galeón*, T760270. Beside the church, friendly, clean, mosquito nets or netting over the windows, water all day, cheap restaurant with seafood (closes 1800 Sun), good breakfast, cheaper for long stay. **E** *Hostería Costa Verde*, T760645. Lebanese management, excellent meals, cheaper rates for longer stays. **E** *La Terraza*, Paquisa y Guayaquil, centre of town, T760430. Dingy but clean rooms, substantial and good value meals. **E** *Parasoles*, Principal y Alfonso Jurado, T760532. Clean, helpful. **E** *Rey David*, T760024. Characterless concrete building, clean rooms, sea view. **F** *Miraglia*, T760154. Popular with surfers, run-down but clean, sea view, showers, fresh drinking water, parking for motorcycles, cheaper rates for longer stays. **F** *Turismo*, next door to *El Galeón*. Noisy.

Eating

Excellent seafood and typical dishes are available from over 50 beach cafés (all numbered and named)

Recommended beach cafés are *Cecilia's* at No 7 or *Barzola* at No 9. Good food at *Cabaña Típica* next to *Rey David*. Closed on Mon. *Mario's*, central plaza opposite Banco de Guayaquil. Big hamburgers, good yoghurt. *Los Ajos*, at the end of the street leading from the plaza. Good soups, varied menu but variable quality. Giant oysters and 'mule foot' black conches are opened and served from stalls in a side road down from *La Costa Verde*. Worth a look if nothing else.

Bars & nightclubs

Motivos, at the south end of the Malecón. *Mr Frog*, diagonally opposite *Miraglia*. *Peña de Arturo*, opposite Transportes Villamil bus terminus.

Transport

Bus To **Guayaquil**, frequent, 2 hrs, US$1. Taxi costs US$25.

Directory

Banks *Banco de Guayaquil*. **Communications** Pacifictel: on Av Jaime Roldós Aguilera, service good, open Sun. Post Office: reliable. Mail for collection at the Post Office may be listed under first or last name.

Excursions from Playas

An interesting walk, or short drive, is to the village of **El Morro**, with a disproportionately large wooden church with an impressive façade (under 'permanent' repair) and the nearby mysterious rock formation of the Virgen de la Roca, where there are a small shrine and marble stations of the cross. There is a regular camioneta service from the crossroads of Avenida Guayaquil y Avenida Paquisha.

   Some 3 km further down the road is **Puerto del Morro**, up a scenic mangrove estuary, where there are several working wooden trawlers and other traditional boats. It is possible to rent a canoe for three hours to visit the mangroves and probably see dolphins (about US$25). There's no accommodation, but a few basic eating places.

   Northwest up the coast is **Engabao**, a small settlement where you can find deserted beaches and wooden fishing boats along the coast. There's no food or lodging here, but there are some surfing points. A camioneta goes here from the crossroads, a 30-minute bumpy ride down sandy tracks.

Santa Elena Peninsula

West of El Progreso (Gomez Rendón), a good quality road runs to **Santa Elena** where the road forks west for Salinas or north for the northern coastal towns. In Santa Elena is *Hostal El Cisne* on the plaza, and restaurant *Echeverría*. Near Santa Elena is the **Museo de los Amantes de Sumpa**, which has a very interesting display on the Las Vegas culture (nothing to do with gambling), which lived in this area between 8,800 and 4,600 BC. A burial site with 200 skeletons was found in this spot, including a couple embracing each other, which is displayed *in-situ*, hence the name of the site. These are the oldest remains which have been discovered in Ecuador to date. Beyond Zapotal, by the old race course (now stables), is the turnoff for **Chanduy**, a tiny, picturesque port with accommodation at the restaurant on the east side of the bay. Twelve kilometres along is the **Real Alto Museum**, which offers a well laid-out explanation of the peoples, archaeology and customs of the area. ■ *Daily 1000-1700, US$0.70. T772699.*

Baños San Vicente Seven kilometres before Santa Elena, a well signed turnoff leads 8 km to Baños San Vicente, Ministerio de Turismo-run hot thermal baths, which consist of a swimming pool and a big mudhole which claim to cure assorted ailments. It's best to go early or late to avoid the crowds. ■ *0600-1800, US$0.30, massages extra.* There's accommodation next to the baths at **F** *Hotel Florida*. Basic but clean.

La Libertad To the west of Santa Elena the road passes a petroleum refinery and enters the busy port and regional market centre of La Libertad. It's not the most appealing of towns, and you'll be eager to jump on the first bus out. Thankfully, these are frequent, so there's no need to spend the night here. Car racing takes place at the Autódromo half way between La Libertad and Santa Elena. **Warning** Muggings are frequent.

Sleeping and eating B *Samarina*, Av 9 de Octubre. Ministerio de Turismo-run, some bungalows, swimming pool, restaurant, coffee shop, bar, with views of the oil refinery and tankers. **G** *Hostal Viña del Mar*, in the town centre, T785979. Clean, fan, bath. **G** *Turis Palm*, Av 9 de Octubre, opposite CLP bus terminal. Fan, with bath, **G** without, bit run-down. Next door and similar is **G** *Reina del Pacífico*. **G** *Costa Brava*, Av 12 de Octubre, Barrio 12 de Octubre, near the bus terminal for Montañita and points north T785860. with bath, good. **G** *Seven Seas*, on Malecón, T786858. Very basic. For eating, try *Mar y Tierra*, at the north end of the main street.

Transport Buses to **Guayaquil**, with Coop Libertad Peninsular (opposite *Hotel Turis Palm*) and CICA across the street; US$2, 2½ hrs, every 15 mins (the 2 companies alternate departures). Get off at Progreso for **Playas**, 1 hr, US$1.15. Buses leave every hour, until 1715 to **Manglaralto** (US$1.25), **Puerto López**, **Jipijapa** (US$3.65) and **Manta** (US$4.35) from the terminal on Dagobert Montenegro y C 10, 1 km from town. To **Quito** with Trans Esmeraldas (opposite Coop Libertad Peninsular), 2 nightly, 9½ hrs, US$8.50.

Salinas
Population: 19,298

A few kilometres further on, surrounded by miles of salt flats, is Salinas, Ecuador's answer to Miami Beach. There is safe swimming in the bay and high-rise blocks of holiday flats and hotels line the sea front. The town is dominated by the Chocolatera hill on the southern point of the bay overlooking the well-equipped and very exclusive Salinas Yacht Club.

There are increasing complaints that during *temporada* (December to April/May) it is overcrowded, with traffic jams, rubbish-strewn beaches and food and water shortages. At this time the highway from Guayaquil becomes one-way, depending on the time of day, and is said to resemble a Grand Prix racetrack, especially on Sunday. Obviously not a good time to hitch a lift. During the off season it is quieter, but still not for 'getting away from it all'. Tours, hire of sailing boats, water skis, fishing trips arranged through *Pesca Tours*, on the Malecón, T772391, or *Salitour*, T772800/772789. Buses to Guayaquil, US$2.50, 2½ hours.

Sleeping AL *Calypsso*, Malecón, junto a la Capitanía de Puerto, T773605, F773583, calypsso@gye.satnet.net A/c, pool, gym, crafts shop. **A-B** *El Carruaje*, Malecón 517, T/F774282. A/c, TV, hot water, good restaurant, includes breakfast. **B** *Hostal Francisco 1*, Gral Enríquez Gallo y Rumiñahui, T774106. A/c, hot water, pool, restaurant. Chalet style. **C** *Suites Salinas*, Gral Henríquez Gallo y 27, T/F772759, hotelsalinas@porta.net A/c, hot water, fridge, cable TV, good restaurant, pool, parking, internet. Modern. Under same management, next to one another and with similar services are: **D** *Salinas*, T/F772993. **D** *Salinas Costa Azul*, T774268. **D** *Yulee*, Diagonal Iglesia Central, near the beach, T772028. With bath, **E** without, hot water, cable TV, clean, excellent food, friendly. **E** *Florida*, Malecón y C 2, Chipipe, T772780. With bath, cheaper rooms available. **F** *Albita*, Av 3,y C23, Barrio Barzán, T773211. With bath, good. **F** *Residencial Rachel*, C 17 y Av Quinta, T772526. With bath, TV, fans. A couple more in the **F** range along Av Gral Enríquez Gallo y C 22-25.

Eating *Mar y Tierra*, Malecón y Av 7, excellent seafood, especially lobster. Also nearby is *Flipper*, cheap, simple, clean and friendly. Good freshly cooked seafood in the market, 2 blocks in from the Malecón, *La Lojanita* is recommended. *Oystercatcher*, Malecón y 32. Safe oysters, friendly, bird and whale watchers should ask here for local expert, Ben Haase. Recommended. *La Bella Italia*, Malecón y C 19, near Hotel El Carruaje. Pizzeria. *Ipanema*, near the beach. Good food, expensive. *La Taberna de Chistorra*, near the market. Good food, nice atmosphere, Spanish-Dutch owned. *Perla del Pacífico*, Malecón y Rumiñahui. Chinese food. OK, cheap. *Selva del Mar*, Gral enríquz Gallo y C 23. Good *pescado con menestra*, cheap.

Directory Banks: *Banco del Pacífico* changes TCs and gives good rates on Mastercard. Also *Filanbanco* opposite the market. **Communications**: Pacifictel at Radio Internacional, good service. **Internet:** *Café Planet*, Av 10 y C 25. US$2 per hour.*Salinas.Net*, C 19 y Av 2, US$1.20 per hour.

On the southern shore of the Santa Elena peninsula, 8 km south of La Libertad, is **Punta Carnero**, a magnificent 15 km beach with wild surf and heavy undertow, which is virtually empty during the week. In July, August and September there is great whale watching. Places to stay include **A** *Punta Carnero*, T775450. All rooms with sea view, restaurant, swimming pool. **A-C** *Hostería del Mar*, T775370. With or without air conditioning, restaurant, swimming pool, family suites to let on a weekly basis.

Between Punta Carnero and Mar Bravo are the Ecuasal Ponds (commercial salt pans), which offer the spectacle of thousands, at times tens of thousands, of shorebirds and water birds. Sometimes there are even Chilean Flamingos here, visiting from their breeding grounds in the Peruvian Andes. Birds can be seen from the road, but if you wish to get a closer look, you must get permission from the Ecuasal office in Guayaquil, 10 de Agosto y Malecón, T325666, F320051.

A few kilometres to the east of Punta Carnero, along the coast, lies **Anconcito**, a fishing port at the foot of steep cliffs. Pelicans and frigate birds gather round the colourful boats when the catch is brought in. There's nowhere in town to stay. Further on is **Ancón**, centre of the declining local oilfield.

Northern Pacific Lowlands

North to Puerto López

The coastal road north from Santa Elena to Puerto López is known as the 'Ruta del Sol', it parallels the coastline, gives access to some beautiful beaches and crosses the Chongón-Colonche coastal range. Note that not all beaches are suitable for bathing; the surf and undertow can be strong in some places. Between June and September whales may be seen in this area.

The northern fork of the road at Santa Elena leads past **Ballenita** which has a pleasant beach. At Lomas de Ballenita is **B** *Hostería Farallón Dillon*, T/F786643/785611, Cellular T09-770224, ddillon@gu.pro.ec, which is run by Douglas Dillon who has lots of information on the area. It has air conditioning, hot water, restaurant and also a nautical museum. **C** *Ballenita Inn*, at the fork, T785008, has cottages to rent. There is good food at *La Cabaña*, at the fork, where the filling station has good baths.

Before **Punta Blanca** are several seafood stands on a wild beach. Look for the *semilleros* all along the coast trudging through wave breaks to collect larvae which is then sold via middle men to the shrimp farms. There is basic accommodation in Punta Blanca at *La Cabaña*. Further north is **B** *Hostería Las Olas*, Km 18 Vía Santa Elena, before San Pablo, T610513, F381288. Cabins with hot water, fridge, TV, porch with hammocks, restaurant, pool.

The road hugs the coast, passing **Monteverde**, and then **Palmar**, with popular beaches and beach cafés, but no accommodation.

Continuing north is **Ayangue**, in a horseshoe bay, just off the main highway. It gets very crowded and dirty at peak weekends and holidays. You can stay at **B** *Cumbres de Ayangue*, on the south point of the bay, T916040, which has cabins, a restaurant and impressive views. **G** *Hostal Un Millón De Amigos*, is in town, T916014, with fan and bath. It is very nice and friendly. **G** *Los 5 Hermanos*, T916029, is very basic; clean but overpriced.

Valdivia San Pedro and Valdivia are two unattractive villages which merge together. Just south of San Pedro is **D** *Valdivia Ecolodge*, at Km 40, T916128, valdiviaecolodge@hotmail.com, www.valdiviaecolodge.com It has eight cabins with capacity for four people, with bath, hot water, breakfast included, restaurant, pool. There are many fish stalls; *Cevichería Playa Linda* is reported as reliable. This is the site of the 5,000 year-old Valdivia culture (see History, page 322). Many houses offer 'genuine' artefacts and one resident at north end of the village will show you the skeletons and burial urns dug up in his back garden.

It is illegal to export precolumbian artefacts from Ecuador. The replicas are made in exactly the same manner as their predecessors and copied from genuine designs, so they may not be the real thing, but at least you're not breaking the law and at the same time you can provide some income for the locals. Ask for Juan Orrala, who makes excellent copies, and lives up the hill from the museum. Most of the genuine artefacts discovered at the site are in museums in Quito and Guayaquil. Some pieces remain in the small, local **Ecomuseo Valdivia**, which also has artifacts from other costal cultures and *in-situ* remains. There is also a handicraft section where artisans may be seen at work and lots of local information. ■ *Wed-Sun, US$0.40*. At the museum there is also a restaurant and five rooms with bath to let, **H** per person.

There is an **aquarium** at the entrance to town with three tanks and several huts with exhibits about marine life. ■ *US$1*. By the aquarium are also a restaurant, a cabin to rent at the beach and space for camping. You can rent a boat here for excursions to **Islote El Pelado**, a small island off shore (whales may be seen in season). Eight kiloemtres northeast of Valdivia is **Loma Alta**, a reserve which protects a tract of forest in the Cordillera Chongón-Colonche.

This is the main centre of the region north of Santa Elena, 180 km north of Guayaquil. A tagua nursery has been started and you can ask to see examples of these 'vegetable ivory' nuts being turned into intricate works of art. It is a pleasant place, with a good, quiet, clean beach and good surf. There's little shelter, so take plenty of sun screen.

Manglaralto
Phone code: 04
Population: 18,510

    Pro-pueblo is an organization working with local communities, to foster family-run orchards and cottage craft industry, using *tagua* nuts, *paja toquilla* (used to make Panama hats), and other local products, T901195. *Programa de Manejo de Recursos Costeros PMRC* is an organization promoting ecotourism in the local communities. It encourages tourists to go on trips with locals and stay with families in the villages. A network of community lodgings, *Red de Hospederías Comunitarias*, is being developed (**H**) per person and many interesting routes into the interior have been set up. Their office is opposite the church, T901343, F901118, and they have a tourist information centre in Montañita.

Sleeping and eating **G** *Marakaya*, south of the main plaza, an orange/beige building, 1 block from the beach, T901294. With bath, hot water, clean, safe, fan, mosquito net. **G** *Alegre Calamar*, at the north end of town. Shared bath, mosquito nets, restaurant, refurbished in 2000. *Chacón*, in a modern 3 storey building, was due to open in late 2000. To stay with a family contact the *Red de Hospederías Comunitarias*, see above. Eating places include *La Calderada*, on the beach. Very good seafood, try their *calderada*. *Comedor Familiar* has meals weekends only. Also *Comedor Florencia*. Moderately cheap and friendly. *Cebiches Vico*, near the Plaza, only open in high season and holidays.

Transport **Bus**: to La Libertad, US$1. **Santa Elena**, US$0.80, 1¼ hrs, change here for Guayaquil. To **Jipijapa**, via Salango, US$2, 3½ hrs. To **Puerto López**, 1 hr, US$1.

Situated three kilometres north of Manglaralto, Montañita has a good beach but watch out for stingrays close to the water's edge. If stung, the small hospital in Manglaralto will treat you quickly. Baja Montañita is to the north of the main village, here you'll find the best surfing in Ecuador. Various competitions are held during the year and at weekends the town is full of Guayaquileños. Major development is taking place at the surfing end of the beach. *Oficina de Reservaciones e Información Turística*, opposite the park, run by PMRC (see Manglaralto above), has tourist information and makes reservations for lodging in private homes with the *Red de Hospederías Comunitarias*. There is a surfing school, on the highway, away from the ocean.

Montañita
A good place to hang out, with a relaxed atmosphere

Sleeping **D** *Paradise South*, in residential area between town and Baja Montañita, T901185/244898, paradise_south@hotmail.com With bath, **E** with shared bath, sports fields, laundry, restaurant. Quiet. **E** *Hotel Montañita*, on the beach just north of the village, T901296, F901299, hmontani@telconet.net With bath, hot water, cheaper with cold water, pool, restaurant, internet service, laundry. They run a nature reserve near La Entrada further north. **F** *La Casa Blanca*, T09-892281, lacasablan@hotmail.com With bath, **G** with shared bath, **H** per person in dorm. Large. **F** *El Centro del Mundo II*, 4-storey timber and thatch building on the beach. with bath, **G** with shared bath, **H** per person in the dormitory on the 4th floor. **G** *Rickie*, 1 block from the highway. With bath, mosquito nets, good restaurant. **G** *Villa Rosa*, next to the church. With bath, mosquito nets. **G** *El Puente*, by the bridge on the main road. Very basic.

Northern Pacific Lowlands

In Baja Montañita **C** *Baja Montañita*, T901218, F901227. A/c, cabins and rooms, pool, jacuzzi, 2 restaurants, bars, hosts good beach parties during the high season. **D** *La Casa del Sol*, T/F901302, casasol@ecua.net.ec, www.casasol.com With bath, cable TV, restaurant. US-run, good. **F** *Tres Palmas*, T09-755717. With bath, restaurant serving Tex-Mex and grill. Very nice, good. **G** *Vito's Cabañas*, T241975. A bit run-down, clean and friendly, good cheap food, camping facilities. Mixed reports but generally recommended.

Eating It's cheaper to eat in the village south of the surf beach. *La Cabaña*, at the beach, good and cheap. *La Chiflaa*, good breakfast and meals, grill. *Tiburón*, good pizza. *Lon, Lon, Lon*, Good meals. Recommended. *Las Olas*, Baja Montañita, next to Casa del Sol. *Pelícano*, in Baja Montañita, good pizzas, disco, open till 2200, later in season. *Disco Tiburón*, in town, near the plaza. There are many other restaurants, food and prices quite uniform.

Directory Communications: Internet: in the village, near the church. **Laundry**: *Lavandería Espumita*, near the church, charges by piece.

Olón A few kilometres further north, Olón has a spectacular long beach. There is a sanctuary built atop a cliff by the sea. Nearby is *El Cangrejal de Olón*, a mangrove remnant, home of the blue crab, a species in danger of extinction.

Sleeping and eating **F** *Hostería Olón Beach*, T901191. Clean, basic, with public phone. **G** *Hostería N & J*, on the beach. With bath, OK. **G** *Río Olón*, opposite the church, with bath, basic. **G** *Hospedaje Rosa Mistía*, in family home, part of *Red de Hospederías Comunitarias*, see Manglaralto above. Fanny Tomalá also rents rooms in the village. *Flor de Olón*, in the village, simple but good food. *RSalsa Parrilla*, on the main road. *Verónica*, just off the beach. Scruffy, good seafood, public phone. *Punto de Quiebra* and *Dolphin*, are only open in season.

Transport Bus: Transportes Manglaralto from **Montañita to La Libertad**, 1 hr, US$1. CLP have daily direct buses to **Guayaquil**, at 0500, 1300, 1630 (return 0600, 1300, 1430), US$2.60.

A beautiful beach continues 10 km north to **La Entrada**, at the foot of the Cordillera Chongón Colonche; there are good walking possibilities in this area.

Ayampe The Río Ayampe is the provincial boundary between Guayas and Manabí, just *Phone code: 04* north of it is the village of the same name.

Sleeping and eating **A-AL** *Hotel Atamari*, south of Ayampe, T780430, In Quito: T228470 F234075, atamari@hoy.net Beautiful, cabins with rooms and suites, in spectacular surroundings on cliffs above the sea, restaurant with wonderful food, pool. Buses between Puerto López and Manglaralto go through, it is a 15 min walk from the highway. **D** *Cabañas de la Iguana*, south of the village, 100 m from the beach, T09-775300. Cabins with room for 4, with bath, mosquito nets, meals with advance notice. Clean, quiet, Swiss-French run. **A-B** *Hotel Almare*, south of the village, T09-956015/771306. Rooms with fan, hot water, patio, restaurant. New in 2000.

Puerto Rico Five kilometres north of Ayampe, is Puerto Rico. Just south of town is the **& Piqueros** Alandaluz Ecological Centre, an organization involved in promoting ecologi- *Phone code: 04* cally sound practices in nearby communities, including recycling of rubbish, water and organic agriculture. It is also a very good *hostería* (see below) and gives working demonstrations of its innovative practices.

Seven kilometres north of Puerto Rico is **Piqueros**, where there is a small private museum displaying ceramics, stone artifacts and funerary urns found at the site by archaeologist Presley Norton. These correspond to the Manteña, Valdivia, Machalilla and other pre-historic coastal cultures. A prize piece is the 2 cm high 'Venus de Valdivia' statue, the smallest of its kind.

Sleeping and eating **B-C** *Hostería Alandaluz*, T780184, In Quito T/F543042, alandalu@interactive.net.ec, www.alandaluz.com Bamboo cabins with palm-leaf thatched roofs and private bath and compost toilets. It is a very peaceful place, with a clean beach and stunning organic vegetable and flower gardens in the middle of a desert. Many new cabins were put up after damage from El Niño in 1997. Camping with your own tent is **H** and renting a hotel tent **F-G**. There are student and youth hostel discounts. The hotel offers good homemade organic food, vegetarian or seafood, breakfast costs US$3.70, other meals US$5, and there's a bar. Expensive tours in the area are also offered. Reservations are necessary as it is so popular, friendly and highly recommended.

C *Hostería La Barquita*, by Las Tunas, north of Ayampe and south of Alandaluz, T780051. Includes breakfast, with bath, **E** in room with bunk beds and shared bath, by the beach, expensive restaurant, well set up for partying, bar at the heart of common area. French-run, French, English and German spoken. **D** *Piqueros Patas Azules*, North of Puerto Rico, in Piqueros, near Río Chico, T780279. Cabins overlooking the beach, with bath, fan. Eco-conscious. Price includes entry to the local museum and visit to cave along the beach. **F** per person *Cabaña*, in Puerto Rico, cabin for 6, further information at *The Whale Café* in Puerto López. By the main road at Río Chico is **F** per person *Albergue Río Chico*, T05-604181. Accommodation in dormitories with restaurant. Don Julio Mero, off the main road in Puerto Rico offers meals and rents basic cabins with kitchen and bath for longer stays.

Transport **Bus**: *Trans Manglaralto* buses from **Santa Elena**, US$2, or from **Jipijapa** if coming from Manta and the north. The last bus from the south passes at 1930, from the north at 1730; hitching is difficult. It's 20 mins from Puerto López.

Puerto López

This pleasant little fishing town is beautifully set in a horseshoe bay, with a broad sweep of beach enclosed by headlands to the north and south. The beach is fairly clean at the northern end, away from the fleet of boats moored offshore.

Phone code: 05
Colour map 4, grid B1
Population: 10,212
Altitude: sea level

The town is becoming increasingly visited by foreign tourists who come here between June and September to enjoy a spot of whale-watching. It's also a cheap 'alternative' to the Galápagos, with good snorkelling as well as the other attractions of Parque Nacional Machallila and Isla de la Plata (see below). In town is an information centre about Parque Nacional Machallila, Calle Eloy Alfaro y García Moreno, open Tuesday to Saturday. Though Puerto López boasts several decent restaurants, accommodation is not yet plentiful enough to cope with the increase in visitors during the high season. Note that whales can also be seen further north.

C *Manta Raya Lodge*, 3 km from town, T09-707954. With bath, restaurant, pool. **D-E** *Hotel Pacífico*, just off the Malecón Central, T604133. With bath, hot showers, includes breakfast, clean rooms, friendly, secure, a/c, cheaper with fan, no mosquito nets, restaurants, **F** per person in *cabañas* with shared bath. **D** *La Terraza*, on the hill to the north behind the clinic, T604235. Six apartments for 4 people with great views over the bay, gardens, hot water, spacious and clean, good breakfast, evening meals available on request, run by German Peter Bernhard, very friendly, free car service to/from

Sleeping
Price codes:
see inside front cover

town if called in advance. Highly recommended. **D-E** *Mandala*, beyond the fish market at the north end of the beach, T/F604181. Swiss-Italian-run with pizza restaurant serving Italian dishes, 2-storey cabins, hot water, smaller cabins are cheaper. **E** *Villa Colombia*, behind the market, T604105/604189. Rooms with bath and hot water, cheaper in dormitory for 32 with shared bath and kitchen facilities. Friendly, nice hammocks in the garden. **E** *Los Islotes*, Malecón y Gen Córdova, T604108. Includes breakfast. Private and shared bath. Clean, nice, popular, often booked in high season.

G *Hostal Tuzco*, 500 m inland, uphill behind the market, T604132/604120. With bath, family rooms available, kitchen facilities. **G** *Cueva del Oso*, in the town centre. Above handicrafts shop, well signposted, private rooms or dormitories, clean and friendly, hot water, full kitchen facilities. Recommended. **G** *Hostal Turismar*, on Malecón Sur, 1 street back from park office, T604174. Rooms with bath, cold water and sea view, cheaper without view, discount for longer stays. **G** *Yubarta Guest House*, on Malecón Norte before the fish market. With kitchen and cold water, owned by guide who offers bi-lingual snorkelling and kayaking trips. **G** *Hostal Balandra*, on the Malecón. With shared bath. **G** *Monte Líbano*, at south end of the Malecón.

Eating *Carmita* on the Malecón. Good for fish, also rents rooms for longer stays, **G**. Next door is *Mayflower*. Good for seafood but not cheap. *Spondylus*, on Malecón next to *Exploratur*. Good set lunch but slow service. *Viña del Mar*, on the Malecón. Good food, also rents rooms, friendly but no running water, dirty baths downstairs, serves breakfast from 0700. *Soda Bar Danny*, good cheap lunches for US$1-1.50. *Flipper*, next to the bus stop. Cheap, best meal at best price, friendly. Recommended. *The Whale Café (La Ballena)*, Malecón Sur y Julio Izurieta. Good pizza, good cakes and pies, nice breakfasts. US-run, owners Diana and Kevin are very helpful and provide travel information. *Bellitalia*, on intermediate street between the Malecón and the main road. Very good Italian food, try their spinach soup. Italian run. Recommended. *La Luna*, in back of the market near *Hostal Tuzco*, nice cafetería.The *panadería* behind the church serves excellent banana bread.

Shopping The *Yaguarundi* handicrafts shop is run by local women and sells tagua (vegetable ivory), cactus fibre baskets and pottery. They can also arrange visits to homes to see handicrafts being made and to sample the local cuisine. For details, T04-780184. They also have an outlet at Alandaluz (see above).

Tour operators
The whale-watching season runs from Jun to Sep/Oct

All charge the same rates: US$30 per person for whale-watching, Isla de la Plata and snorkelling. This doesn't include the National Park fee (see below), but does include a soft drink and light snack. All authorized boats have toilets or porta-potty facilities and life-jackets. Trips start at 0730-0800 and return around 1700. *Machalilla Tours*, on the main road, T604206. They also offer horse riding tours around the park for US$20 per day for 2 with a guide. *Manta Raya*, on Malecón Norte, T604233. They have the largest boat, the 16-person sports fisherman *Manta Raya*, which is comfortable and spacious. They also have diving equipment and charge US$100.00 per person, all inclusive.

Exploratur, on Malecón Central next to the *Spondylus* restaurant, T604123. French-run outfit based in Quito, with US manager Kevin Gulash. They have two 8-12 person boats and their own compressor to fill dive tanks. PADI divemaster accompanies qualified divers to various sites, but advance notice is required, US$95 per person for all-inclusive diving day tour. *Bosque Marino*, near the bus stop. Experienced guides, some of whom speak English. They also offer hikes through the forest and birdwatching tours to Agua Blanca (see below) and Las Goteras for US$20 per day for groups of 2-3. *Ecuador Amazing*, Gen Córdova, T542888 in Quito, info@ ecuadoramazing.com, www.ecuadoramazing.com Tours to Isla de la Plata and whale watching. *Sercapez*, Gen Córdova, T604173. Tours to Isla de la Plata, whale watching, San Sebastian, Los Frailes and to the museums at Agua Blanca and Salango. All inclusive trips with camping, local guide and food run US$25 per person, per day. They also work with Guacamayo Bahiatours and organize trips further north (See Bahía de Caráquez below). They also offer transfers to Manta and Portoviejo US$30, and to Bahía de Caráquez US$50 per person. Very friendly and good service. In addition to the above, there are also many fly-by-night operators, so shop around and try to get a personal recommendation from other visitors before you choose a tour.

Bus To/from **Quito**, 1 nightly direct service with Carlos Aray, US$7, 10 hrs. To **Manta**, **Transport** via **Jipijapa**, frequent departures with CITM and CITJ, 1½ hrs, US$1.50. To **Guayaquil**, via Jipijapa, 3 hrs, US$2.25, with *Reina del Camino, Coactur* and *Rutas Portoviejenses*. To **La Libertad**, 2 hrs. To **Manglaralto**, 1 hr, US$1.35. To **Portoviejo**, 1 hr.

The nearby village of Salango is worth visiting for its excellent Presley Norton **Salango** archaeological museum. Artefacts from the excavations in the local fish meal factory's yard are housed in the beautiful museum on the plaza. ■ *US$1*. For eating, *El Delfín Mágico* offers excellent eating but chronically slow service, so it's best to order your meal before visiting the museum; try the *spondilus* (spiny oyster) in fresh coriander and peanut sauce with garlic coated *patacones*. Owner Alfredo also sells attractive t-shirts with precolumbian designs. Also offering excellent seafood is *El Pelícano*, behind the church; reasonable prices, caters for vegetarians.

Bus To and from Puerto López buses normally leave every 20 mins (US$0.40, 10 **Transport** mins), see above under Puerto López.

Parque Nacional Machalilla

The park extends over 55,000 ha, including Isla de la Plata, Isla Salango offshore, and the magnificent beach of Los Frailes. It is concerned with preserving marine ecosystems as well as the dry tropical forest and archaeological sites on shore. The park is recommended for birdwatching, especially in the cloud forest of Cerro San Sebastián, and there are also several species of mammals and reptiles. The continental portion of the park is divided into three sections which are separated by private land, including the town of Machalilla.

Entrance fee for Isla de la Plata and mainland section is US$20 July-September and US$15 October-June. For mainland portion only: US$15 July-September and US$10 October-June. Children under 11 pay half price. It is payable at the park office next to the market in Puerto López (open 0700-1800), or directly to the park rangers (insist on a receipt), ask for five or six days. The park fee is payable not only for land-based trips but also for ocean trips.

To get to this stunning beach, one of the nicest on the entire coast, take a bus **Los Frailes** towards Jipijapa and get off at the turnoff just south of the town of **Machalilla**, then walk for 30 minutes. ■ *Show your national park ticket on arrival. There is no transport back to Puerto López after 1630.*

Sleeping and eating On the main road through Machalilla is **D** *Hotel Internacional Machalilla*, T345905. A conspicuous cement building, clean with fans, overpriced, talk to the manager about cheaper rates for longer stays. Next door is *Comedor La Gaviota. Bar Restaurant Cabaña Tropical* is at the south end of town.

Northern Pacific Lowlands

Agua Blanca   About 5 km north of Puerto López, at Buena Vista, on the road to Machalilla, there is a dirt road to the east marked to Agua Blanca. Here, 5 km from the main road, in the national park, amid hot, arid scrub, is a small village and a fine, small archaeological museum containing some fascinating ceramics from the Manteño civilization found at the site. ■ *0800-1800, US$1.15.* It is cheaper to find a guide for Agua Blanca in the village itself for a visit to the pre-Inca ruins. A two to three hour tour for two people costs US$1.50 each. It's a 45 minute walk to the ruins, or hire horses for US$7.50 per person per day.

Public transport to Agua Blanca leaves Saturday only from *Carmita's* in Puerto López at 0630 and 1200, returning at 0700 and 1300. Camping is possible and there's one very basic room for rent above the museum for US$1.50 per person, with minimal facilities.

San Sebastián   A recommended trip is to San Sebastián, 9 km from Agua Blanca up in tropical moist forest (800 m above sea level), for sightings of orchids and possibly howler monkeys. This is the best nature hike in the park, going through successively more humid forests until reaching true cloud forest at Cerro San Sebastián. Although part of the national park, this area is administered by the *Comuna* of Agua Blanca, which charges its own fees in addition to the park entrance (see above). ■ *A tour to the forest costs US$15 per day for the guide (fixed rate), US$1.50 per person to stay overnight at the guide's house, US$5 for meals, and US$15 per horse. Transportation to Agua Blanca is an extra US$5 per person. It's five hours on foot or by horse. Camping is possible at San Sebastián, US$1.50.*

Isla de la Plata
Trips here have become popular because it's a cheap alternative to the Galápagos, with some of the same bird life

On this island, about 24 km offshore, there are nesting colonies of waved albatross, frigates and three different booby species. Whales can be seen from June to September. It is also a precolumbian site with substantial pottery finds, and there is good diving and snorkelling.

The island can be visited in a day trip. There are two walks, of three and five hours (take water). For details of tours and agencies see above under Tour operators in Puerto López. We recommend only using those agencies listed. Take dry clothes, water, precautions against sun and seasickness and snorkelling equipment.

North of Machalilla

Puerto Cayo   North from Machalilla is Puerto Cayo where the road turns inland for Jipijapa. The beach is not particularly clean here, but improves as you walk away from town. Whale watching tours available from here.

Sleeping and eating C *Hostal Jipijapa Los Frailes*, T616014. A/c, E without a/c, clean, TV, fridge, restaurant, tours. E *Puerto Cayo*, at the south end of the beach, T04-385188, catours@ecuatourism.com, www.ecuatourism.com Rooms with terrace and hammocks, good, expensive restaurant, try their *pescado al ajillo*. Friendly service. G *Residencial Zavala*, on the Malecón. With bath, clean, ask for sea view, meals available. G *Barandhua*, at the north end of the beach. With bath, basic. Expedición Cayo Mar, at the north end of the beach. C Large cabins with kitchen, for up to 6. Ask at *Picantería Avelina* for houses to rent. *La Cabaña* just back from the beach for good seafood. *D'Comer*, next to *Zavala*. Good cheap seafood.

Jipijapa
Population: 32,225

The paved road climbs over humid hills to descend to the dry scrub around Jipijapa, an unattractive town but an important centre for the region's trade in cotton, cocoa, coffee and kapok. Try **D** *Hostal Jipijapa*, T600522, two blocks south of the cemetery, clean, overpriced. **G** per person *Pensión Mejía*, two

A whale of a time

Whale watching has taken off as a major tourist attraction in the tropical Pacific waters off the coast of Ecuador. One of the prime sites to see these massive mammals is around Isla de La Plata.

Between June and September, each year, the acrobatic humpback whale makes the long 8,000 km-long trip from the Antarctic to visit the Ecuadorean coast in search of a partner. The whales spend the northern summer in Antarctica feeding and by the time they leave the icy polar seas on their migration north, their blubber is 15-20 cm thick. Unfortunately for the slow-moving humpbacks, this made them extremely vulnerable to whalers' harpoon guns. Less valuable than sperm whale oil, demand for humpback oil rose suddenly in the 20th century after it became one of the main ingredients in margarine.

By the time whaling nations began to introduce controls in the 1960s, the humpback population had been reduced to less than one-tenth of its original number. The humpback population appears to be recovering, though very slowly, thanks to a ban on commercial hunting since 1966 in all but a few places.

Ironically, the same behaviour that once allowed them to be harpooned so easily makes the humpbacks particularly appealing to whale watchers today. The difference now is that each sighting is greeted with the shooting of film and not lethal harpoons.

Humpbacks got their name from the humped dorsal fins and the way they arch when diving. Their scientific name, Megaptera novaeangliae, which translates roughly as 'large-winged New Englanders', comes from the fact that they were first identified off the coast of New England. Also, when a 30-tonne humpback leaps out of the water with its huge white flippers flapping, it does appear large-winged.

Aside from the acrobatic antics, the whale-watcher may even be treated to a song or two from the multi-talented humpbacks, who are also renowned for their vocal performances. Chirrups, snores, purrs and haunting moans are all emitted by solitary males eager to use their chat-up techniques on a prospective mating partner. And who can blame them after travelling all that way?

blocks from the plaza, no fan, unfriendly, bug-ridden. Buses to Manglaralto, 2 hours, US$2. To Puerto López, 1½ hours, US$1.10. To Manta, one hour. Buses leave from the plaza.

At **La Pila**, due north of Jipijapa, the road turns east for Portoviejo. The village's main industry is fake precolumbian pottery, with a thriving by-line in erotic ceramics.

Montecristi
Population: 37,660

A few kilometres further west from La Pila is this quiet, dusty town, set on the lower slopes of an imposing hill, high enough to be watered by low cloud which gives the region its only source of drinking water. The town is one of the main centres of Panama hat production and is renowned for the high quality of its output (see Arts and Crafts, on page 453). Varied straw and basketware is also produced here (much cheaper than in Quito), and wooden barrels which are strapped to donkeys for carrying water. Ask for José Chávez Franco, Rocafuerte 203, T/F606343, where you can see Panama hats being made. He also sells wholesale and retail. Montecristi is also famous as the birthplace of the statesman Eloy Alfaro.

Manta

Phone code: 05
Colour map 4, grid A1
Population: 156,981
Altitude: sea level

Ecuador's second port after Guayaquil is an important commercial centre, with a large fishing fleet and port. It is a busy, lively town that sweeps round a bay filled with all sorts of boats. The western section comprises steep, narrow streets and the Malecón that fills in the evenings with impromptu parties and cars cruising with blaring music. The constant breeze makes it pleasant to walk along the front or stop for a drink at one of the many small bars. Playa Murciélago at the west end of the Malecón is very wide but not protected. You can walk further west towards the point for spotless beaches and isolation. The town's fine wooden church was burnt down when a Boeing 707 cargo plane flew into it in 1996. Miraculously, the statue of the Virgin survived.

Manta has been the centre of national controversy since 1999, when the Ecuadorean government authorized the use the local airbase for US drug surveillance flights. Fears were expressed about possible retaliation by Colombian insurgents or drug runners. At the same time, Manta's local economy stands to benefit from the influx of money and personnel.

A bridge joins the main town with **Tarqui** on the east side of the Río Manta, where most of the hotels are located along the sea front. The Tarqui beach is more popular, especially at weekends and holidays, but dirtier. Part of it is even used as a makeshift carpark at low tide. The seafront, and the streets leading off behind it, has a decaying, dilapidated look and does not inspire a feeling of security. The Malecón in Manta around Playa Murciélago has been renovated however, and is a lively place especially at weekends. There is good music and seafood, free beach aerobics and lots of action. Hundreds of Ecuadoreans flock here at weekends. There were better police patrols along the beach in 2000, but do not leave **anything** unattended anywhere (in Tarqui or Manta). The **Banco Central** museum, Avenida 8 y Calle 7, behind the bus station, has a small but excellent collection of ceramics of the Huancavilca-Manteño culture (800-1550 AD). ■ *0900-1630, US$1*. Manta has a big new shopping mall called Paseo Shopping, on the main road out of town, Avenida 4 de Noviembre. You can easily get a bus there from the beach end of town. The *Ministerio de Turismo*, Pasaje José María Egas, Avenida 3 y Calle 11, T622944, is helpful; Spanish only.

Sleeping
■ *on map*
Price codes:
see inside front cover

Water shortages are very common. All streets have numbers. Those above 100 are in Tarqui (those above C110 are not safe). Most offices, shops and the bus station are in Manta. There is a wider selection of hotels in Tarqui.

In Manta AL *Oro Verde*, Malecon y Cirunvalación, on the beach front, T629200. With all the luxuries, the best in Manta. **A** *Cabañas Balandra*, Av 8 y C20, Barrio Córdova, T620316, F620545. Cabins with a/c, TV, bath, 3- and 2-bed rooms in each, breakfast included, secure. **B** *Manta Imperial*, on the Malecón by Playa Murciélago, T621955, F623016. Includes taxes, a/c, pool, parking, disco and dancing, plenty of insect life. **C** *Lun-Fun*, near the bridge. 3 blocks from the bus terminal, a/c, with bath, TV, restaurant, expensive.

In Tarqui B *Las Gaviotas*, Malecón 1109 y C 106, T620140, F611840. The best in Tarqui by some length, a/c, poor restaurant, tennis court. **C** *Las Rocas*, C 101 y Av 105, T610856. A/c, TV, cheaper with fan, pool, private parking, poor restaurant. **C** *El Inca*, C 105 y Malecón, T610986. With bath, TV, phone, fan or a/c, good and reasonably priced restaurant, friendly, OK. **E** *Pacífico*, Av 106 y C 102, T622475. With bath, a/c, discount for longer stay. **E** *Panorama Inn*, C 103 y Av 105, T611552. A/c, bath, TV, pool, restaurant, parking, helpful. Recommended. **F** *Boulevard*, Av 105 y C 103, T625333. With bath, TV, garage. **F** *Hostal Miami*, C 108 y Malecón, T611743. Fan, basic, clean, friendly. **F** *Residencial Viña del Mar*, Av 106 y C 104, T610854. With bath and fan.

G *Residencial Monte Carlo*, C 105 y Av 105. With bath, no fan, friendly, dirty and basic.
G *Playita Mía*, Malecón y C 103. Restaurant, shared bath, very basic.

Club Ejecutivo, Av 2 y C 12, top of the Banco de Pichincha building. First class food and **Eating**
service, great view. *Restaurant Riviera*, C 20 y Av 12, first class Italian food. ● *on map*
Restaurante Mexicano, Malecón y C 15. Very good Mexican food. *Guen Roku*,
Malecón y C 16. Good Ecuadorian and international dishes. *Paraná*, C 17 y Malecón,

Manta

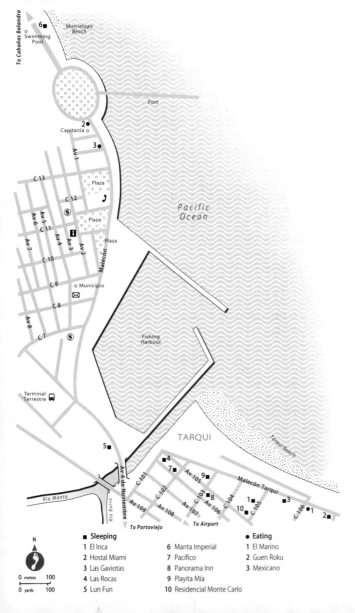

Northern Pacific Lowlands

■ Sleeping		**● Eating**	
1 El Inca	6 Manta Imperial	1 El Marino	
2 Hostal Miami	7 Pacífico	2 Guen Roku	
3 Las Gaviotas	8 Panorama Inn	3 Mexicano	
4 Las Rocas	9 Playita Mía		
5 Lun Fun	10 Residencial Monte Carlo		

N
0 metres 100
0 yards 100

near the port. Local seafood and grill, cheap. Highly recommended. *Shamu*, C 11 No 1-12, downtown. Good set meals and à la carte. *Mima*, C 104 y Malecón, Tarqui. Good fish and seafood, US$3-4. There are many good, cheap *comedores* on Tarqui beach which are open at weekends. *El Marino*, specializes in *sopa marinera*.

Transport **Local** **Car hire**: *Avis*, C Flavio Reyes y C 21, T628512.

Long distance **Air**: Eloy Alfaro airport is southeast of Tarqui. TAME fly to **Quito** daily.
Bus: the Terminal Terrestre behind the new central bank building to the west of the main fishing harbour. To **Quito**, 9 hrs, US$6.60, hourly 0400-2300. To **Guayaquil**, 4 hrs, US$4, hourly. To **Esmeraldas**, at 0630, 0800 and 2000, 8 hrs, US$6.80. To **Santo Domingo**, 4½ hrs, US$5.65. To **Portoviejo**, 45 mins, US$0.70, every 10 mins. To **Jipijapa**, 1 hr, US$1, every 20 mins. To **Bahía de Caráquez**, 3 hrs, US$2.20, hourly.

Directory **Banks** *Banco de Pichincha* and *Banco del Pacífico* change TCs. *Filanbanco* accepts Visa. *Casa de Cambio Zanchi*, Av 2 No 11-28, T613857. *Cambicruz*, Av 2 No 11-22, T622235. **Communications** Post Office: above Banco de Pichincha. **Telephone**: *Pacifictel*, Malecón near C 11. **Tour operators** *Ecuadorean Tours*, at Av 2 y C 13. *Metropolitan Touring* at Av 3 No 11-49. **Useful addresses** Immigration: Av 4 de Noviembre y J-1 (at the police station).

Portoviejo

Phone code: 05
Colour map 4, grid B2
Population: 167,956

Forty kilometres inland from Manta and 65 km northeast from Jipijapa, Portoviejo is the capital of Manabí province and a major commercial centre. It was once a port on the Río Rocafuerte, but as a result of severe deforestation the river has silted and almost completely dried up. In the rainy season, however, it floods badly, often breaking its banks. **Warning** Public safety deteriorated markedly in Portoviejo in 2000, take routine precautions here at all hours.

Sights The cathedral, overlooking Parque Eloy Alfaro, has recently been restored. You can see sloths taking it easy in the plaza's trees and you may be tempted to do the same in this, Ecuador's hottest city. Portoviejo is one of the main places where kapok mattresses and pillows are made from the fluffy fibre of the seed capsule of the *ceibo*. In Calle Alajuela you can buy *montubio* hammocks, bags, hats etc made by the coastal farmers, or *montubios*, as they are known. Ten minutes from town, on the road that later branches to Bahía, is the village of **Sosote**; its main street is lined with workshops where figurines are carved out of *tagua* nuts (vegetable ivory) into innumerable shapes. The *Ministerio de Turismo* is at Pedro Gual y J Montalvo, T630877.

Sleeping
■ on map
Price codes:
see inside front cover

B *Ejecutivo*, 18 de Octubre y 10 de Agosto, T632105, F630876. Very good, expensive, extra charge for the guard, but unfriendly, does not accept Visa despite the sign outside. **B** *Hostería California*, Ciudadela California, T634415. A/c, very good. **B** *Máximo*, C Cumaná y 5 de Junio, T636521. With a/c, cheaper with fan. **C** *Cabrera Internacional*, García Moreno y Pedro Gual, T633201. A/c, clean, noisy. **C** *Conquistador*, 18 de Octubre y 10 de Agosto, T651472. Friendly. **C** *New York*, Fco de P Moreira y Olmedo, T632044. A/c and fridge, **D** with fan, clean, nice, restaurant downstairs. **D** *El Gato*, Pedro Gual y 9 de Octubre, T636908. **F** *Pacheco*, 9 de Octubre 1512 y Morales, T631788. With or without bath, fan. **F** *París*, Plaza Central, T652727. One of the oldest hotels in town, classic. **G** *San Marco*, Olmedo y 9 de Octubre, T630651.

Eating
● on map

La Carreta, C Olmedo y Alajuela. Good food and service. Cervicangrejada Delicias, Pacheco y Diez de Agosto. Good seafood. *La Crema*, Central Park. Clean and cheap, serves lunch and dinner. *El Tomate*, on the road to Crucita and Bahía. Excellent traditional Manabí food. One of the best places to get typical food in the province. *La Fruta Prohibida*, C Chile. Fast food, Portoviejo's gringo hang out. El Galpón, C Quito, very good food and prices, local music at night, very popular. *Zavalito*, Primera Transversal entre Duarte y Alajuela. Lunch only, popular. *Los Geranios*, Chile 508 near Quito. Good set lunch. There are several good *chifas* (chinese restaurants) in town. *El Palatino*, off the main plaza. Good coffee and cheap local specialities.

Viejoteca, for the oldies, good live music. *Discoteques Sótano*, *Pachanguero* and **Bars & discos** *Taguara*, all in the area of Av Manabí.

Air Flights to Quito. **Bus** The bus station is on the edge of town, 1 km from the cen- **Transport** tre. A taxi to/from town costs US$0.90. To **Quito**, 8 hrs. Routes are either east via Quevedo (147 km), or, at Calderón, branch northeast for Calceta, Chone and on to Santo Domingo de los Colorados. Also buses to **Guayaquil**.

Communications Internet: Prices around US$1.75 per hour. Café Royal, C Chile y 10 de Agosto. **Directory** Habla por Menos, C Cordova y Morales. **Tour operators** *Ventura Travel*, Alejo Lascano y Pedro Gual, T634122. International flight changes and confirmations. Very friendly and good service.

A rapidly growing beach resort, 45 minutes by road from Portoviejo, Crucita is **Crucita** popular with bathers on Sunday. It can be crowded and dangerous during car- *Population: 8,300* nival, but is relaxed and friendly at other times. Hang gliding and parasailing are practised from the dry cliffs south of town, some rate this spot as the second best location in the world. The beach and ocean are lovely but it's advisable not to go barefoot near town, as there are many pigs roaming loose and *nigua* (a type of burrowing flea which likes to nest under toenails – *Sarcopsylla penetrans*) are common. Much cleaner beaches are to be found on either side of town. There is an abundance of sea birds in the area, including brown peli- cans, frigates, blue-footed boobies, gulls and sandpipers among others.

Northern Pacific Lowlands

Portoviejo

■ **Sleeping**	4 El Gato	● **Eating**
1 Cabrera Internacional	5 New York	1 El Palatino
2 Conquistador	6 Pacheco	2 La Crema
3 Ejecutivo	7 París	3 Los Geranios

Sleeping and eating From south to north along the beach: **F** *Hipocampo*, the oldest in town. Private bath, basic, friendly, good value. *Barandúa*, on the ocean front. restaurant, pool, disco. Good service. **D** *Hostería Zucasa*, T634908 (Portoviejo). Fully equipped cabins for up to 6, the best accommodation in town. **D** *Hostería Las Cabañitas*, T931037. Cabins for 4-5 people, basic, friendly. There are many simple restaurants and kiosks serving mainly fish and seafood along the seafront. *Alas Delta 1 & 2* Good seafood, try their *conchas asadas*. Both have terrace eating with good ocean views. To the south along the beach are *El Gordo Parapente* and *Las Gaviotas*.

Transport Buses and open sided trucks with slatted seats, called *chivas* or *rancheros*, leave from the beach and plaza for **Portoviejo**, US$0.45, 45 minutes.

Directory Communications: Pacifictel: for long-distance phone calls (no international service), 2 blocks back from the beach on the main road.

Two kilometres north along a paved road running parallel to the beach is the fishing village of **Las Gilces**, which has been less influenced by tourism. Accommodation is available in the *Hotel Centro Turístico Las Amazonas*.

San Clemente & San Jacinto About 60 km north of Portoviejo (60 km northeast of Manta, 30 km south of Bahía de Caráquez) are San Clemente and, 3 km south, San Jacinto, in an area known for its salt production. Both get crowded during the holiday season but are not as nice as they once were owing to the large rocks placed along the beach for protection. The ocean is magnificent but be wary of the strong undertow. Also, do not go barefoot because of the risk of *nigua*, especially in the towns.

Sleeping and eating San Clemente: **C** *Hostería San Clemente*, T420076. Modern clean cabins for 6-10 persons, pool, restaurant, book ahead in season, closed in low season. **E** *Las Acacias*, 150 m from the beach, 800 m north of San Clemente, T541706 (Quito). Nice 3-storey wooden building with huge verandahs, prices go up in high season, with bath, good seafood, clean. Recommended. **E** *Hostal El Edén*, 1 block from beach along the main street. Some rooms have bath, some have sea views, clean, basic. **G** *Cabañas Espumas del Mar*, on the beach. Good restaurant, family-run. Two good, cheap restaurants on the beach are *Tiburón*, and *El Paraíso del Sabor*.
San Jacinto: **E** *Hostal San Jacinto*, on the beach. With bath. **E** *Cabañas del Pacífico*, T09-589801. Private bath, fan, fridge. **F** *Cabañas Los Almendros*, private bath, basic, cramped. **G** *Residencial Virgen de Lajas*, opposite *San Jacinto*. Very basic. **H** *Amarilus*, at the south end of town. Very basic.
Between San Clemente and San Jacinto: **E** *Cabañas Tío Gerard*, T459613, F442954 (Quito). With bath and kitchenette, small rooms, clean, fan. Also *Hostal Chedal*.

Transport Bus: most Guayaquil-Portoviejo-Bahía de Caráquez buses pass San Clemente. To **Jipijapa**, 1 hr, US$1.50. To **Bahía de Caráquez**, 30 mins.

Bahía de Caráquez

Population: 15,308
Altitude: sea level
Phone code: 05
Colour map 4, grid A2

Set on the southern shore at the seaward end of the Chone estuary, Bahía is a friendly, relaxed resort town and a pleasant place in which to spend a few days or more. The river front is attractively laid out with parks on the Malecón Alberto Santos, which becomes Circunvalación Dr Virgilio Ratti and goes right around the point. The beach follows the road around the point and is quite clean. Bahía is small and very manageable. Not surprisingly a number of hotels are clustered around the ferry which links the town with San Vicente, others are along the peninsula, closer to the beach. The *Ministerio de Turismo*,

Malecón y Arenas, T691124, is open Monday to Friday 0830-1630.

The town was badly damaged by *El Niño*, followed by a serious earthquake in 1998, but has since been restored. During reconstruction, local residents with the support of foreign NGOs aimed their efforts towards more sustainable development. As a result Bahía was declared an 'eco-city', where recycling projects, organic gardens and ecoclubs are common (information about the eco-city from Fundación Stuarim, T693490 or the Planet Drum Foundation, planetdrum@igc.org, www.planetdrum.org). The town is also a centre of the less than ecologically friendly shrimp farming industry, which has boosted the local economy but also destroyed much of the estuary's precious mangroves. With awareness of the damage done, there is now a drive for alternative methods. Bahía boasts the first and only certified organic shrimp farm in the world, and a paper recycling scheme, involving communities who previously lived from the mangrove forests. The **archaeological museum** of the Central Bank is in the Casa de la Cultura. It has a collection of precolumbian pottery. ■ *1500-1700, free.*

Bahía de Caráquez

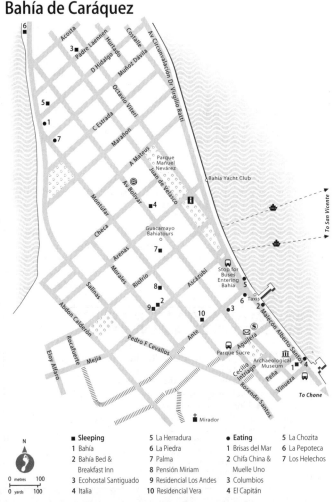

N
0 metres 100
0 yards 100

■ Sleeping	5 La Herradura	● Eating	5 La Chozita
1 Bahía	6 La Piedra	1 Brisas del Mar	6 La Pepoteca
2 Bahía Bed &	7 Palma	2 Chifa China &	7 Los Helechos
Breakfast Inn	8 Pensión Miriam	Muelle Uno	
3 Ecohostal Santiguado	9 Residencial Los Andes	3 Columbios	
4 Italia	10 Residencial Vera	4 El Capitán	

Sleeping
■ on map, page 333
Only hotels with their own supply do not suffer water shortages

A *La Piedra*, Circunvalación near Bolívar, T690780, F690154. Pool, good restaurant but expensive, laundry, modern, good service, access to beach, lovely views. **A** *La Herradura*, Bolívar e Hidalgo, T690446, F690265. A/c, cheaper with fan, friendly, comfortable, restaurant, very pretty. **A** *Casa Grande*, T692097, F692088. Located in an exclusive residential area on the Pacific Ocean, deluxe guest rooms and suites, private bath, outdoor swimming pool and terrace. **D** *Italia*, Bolívar y Checa, T691137, F691092. Private bath, fan, hot water, TV, restaurant. **E** *Ecohostal Santiguado*, Padre Laennen y Juan de Velasco, 2 blocks from the beach in 3 directions. Bed and breakfast, modern rooms, nice terrace bar/café. Clean, friendly, helpful. **F** *Bahía*, on the Malecón near Banco Central. Rooms at the back are better, fan, TV, clean, occasional water shortages. **F** *Bahía Bed & Breakfast Inn*, Ascázubi 322 y Morales, T690146. With bath, fan, some rooms with hot water, restaurant, includes breakfast. Clean, quite good value. **G** *Hostal Querencia*, Malecón 1800 by the main road out of town, T690009. Some rooms with bath, clean, friendly. Recommended. **G** *Palma*, Bolívar 914 y Riofrío, T690467. With bath, clean, basic. **G** *Pensión Miriam*, Montúfar, entre Ascázubi y Riofrío. Shared bath, basic but clean, friendly, rooms at front have windows, has its own water supply. **G** *Residencial Vera*, Montúfar y Ante, T691581. With bath, **H** without. Recommended. **H** *Residencial Los Andes*, Ascázubi 318, T690587. With bath, cheaper without, fan, very basic.

Eating
● on map, page 333

Columbios, Av Bolívar y Ante. Good à la carte and set meals, try the *corvina al pimentón* or the dishes *al ajillo*. Good service and value. *Brisas del Mar*, Hidalgo y Circunvalación. Good fish, cheap. *Los Helechos*, Montúfar y Muñoz Dávila, by Circunvalación. Good and clean. *La Chozita*, on the Malecón near the San Vicente ferry station. Barbecue-style food, good. *Donatella's*, 1 block from Reina del Camino bus terminal. Good, cheap pizza. *Chifa China*, Malecón y Ante, near the wharf. Cheap, good. Nearby is *Muelle Uno*. *La Pepoteca*, Malecón y Ante opposite the wharf. Good food and service. *El Capitán*, Malecón opposite the Hotel Bahia. Cheap chicken and seafood dishes.

Bars & nightclubs

Palma Morena, Morales y Ascázubi. Bar, good music and atmosphere. *Eclipse*, Malecón y Arenas. Disco, open weekends. *Insomnio*, Malecón Nuevo (ask for directions). Disco, open on long weekends.

Tour operators

Both companies listed here offer tours to the estuary islands, wetlands (see Chone below), to see environmental projects in the area including the Río Muchacho farm and the organic shrimp farm, to the Chirije archaeological site, Punta Bellaca dry forest, beaches, whale watching and to Machalilla. See excursions below. *Guacamayo Bahia Tours*, Av Bolívar y Arenas, T/F691412, ecopapel@ecuadorexplorer.com,

Northern Pacific Lowlands

www.qni.com/~mj/riomuchacho Runs tours, rents bikes, sells crafts and is involved in environmental work including Río Muchacho. Part of the tour fees go to community environmental programmes. *Bahía Dolphin Tours*, Av Bolívar 1004 y Riofrío, T692097/086, F692088, archtour@srv1.telconet.net, www.qni.com/~mj/bahia/bahia.html Runs tours, helps with the Puerto Portovelo eco-tourism project and manages the Chirije site.

Air The airport is at San Vicente across the estuary (no regular flights in 2000).   **Transport**

Bus Note that two classes of service operate to Quito and Guayaquil, *ejecutivo* buses are more comfortable, have a/c, videos, and they only stop to pick up passengers at terminals, thus they are safer if not nearly as colourful as the regular service. The Coactur and Reina del Camino offices are on the Malecón 1600 block. All buses coming into Bahía stop by the monument at the Malecón end of Ascázubi before returning to the bus office. Departing buses do not go to the centre.

To **Quito**, ejecutivo, 1 daily, 6 hrs, US$6; regular, 3 daily, 8 hrs, US$4.50. To **Santo Domingo de los Colorados**, 4-4½ hrs, US$3. To **Esmeraldas**, at 1515, 8 hrs, US$6. To **Portoviejo**, 2 hrs, US$1, hourly. To **Puerto López** go to Portoviejo or Jipijapa and change buses. To **Guayaquil**, ejecutivo, 3 daily, 5 hrs, US$4.50; regular service, hourly, US$3. To **Manta**, 3 hrs, US$2, hourly. Open-sided *rancheros* leave from the park on Aguilera to Chone (US$1) and other nearby destinations.

Road From Bahía de Caráquez to the highlands there are 3 main roads. The first one is via Chone and **El Carmen** to Santo Domingo. The road is paved but damaged in places. It climbs quickly over the coastal range, with views of the estuary, the remaining mangroves and the shrimp ponds that destroyed them. In the following wetlands, with more shrimp ponds, are also cattle *fincas* and bamboo houses on stilts. The second road is via San Clemente and Rocafuerte to Pichincha, Velasco Ibarra and on to Quevedo. Alternatively you can go via Calceta, then on an unpaved dry season road directly to Pichincha. This road is very scenic but rarely passable. There are 2 rivers without bridges, which are not deep. A 4-wheel drive vehicle is recommended. The third route is via Pedernales (see page 338), which is quicker.

Banks *Filanbanco*, Aguilera and Bolívar. Cash advance on Visa. *Banco de Guayaquil*, Av Bolívar   **Directory**
and Riofrío. Changes TCs. **Communications Internet:** Rates about US$2.50 per hour. *Genesis Net*, Malecón opposite the Repsol gas station near ferry from San Vicente, also net2phone. *Systemcom*, Calle Riofrio y Av Bolívar.

Excursions from Bahía de Caráquez

The estuary of the Río Chone has several islands with mangrove forest and the area is very rich in birdlife and dolphins may also be seen. **Isla Fragatas**, is 15 minutes by boat from Bahía. It has a stunning number of bird species, including a higher concentration of frigate birds than on the Galápagos. This is an excellent trip for photographers because you can get really close, even under the mangrove trees where they nest. The male frigate birds can be seen displaying their inflated red sacks as part of the mating ritual; best from August to January. ■ *The 3-hr trip costs US$14 per person for 4 (less for larger groups).* Further up the estuary is **Isla Corazón**, where a boardwalk has been built through an area of protected mangrove forest. At the end of the island are some bird colonies which can only be accessed by boat. An information centre for the area with interesting videos is in the village of **Puerto Portovelo**, reached by bus from San Vicente. This community is involved in mangrove reforestation and runs an ecotourism project. ■ *Entrance fee US$5 (does not* *include boat trip to bird colonies). Native guides from the local estuarine commu-nities are available. Tours visiting both islands from the agencies in Bahía (see above), US$35 per person for group of 3, cheaper for larger groups.*

The **Chirije** archaeological site is a 45-minute ride south of Bahía. This site was a seaport of the Bahía Culture (500 BC-500 AD), which traded as far north as Mexico and south to Chile. There is a museum on site. It is surrounded by dry tropical forest and good beaches. There are cabins with ocean views (**D-E**) and a restaurant. There are walking, horse riding and birdwatching possibilities in the area. Tours from Bahía take you in an open-sided *chiva* along the beach. On the way to Chirije is the scenic **Punta Bellaca**, near it is the **Cerro Viejo** or **Cerro de las Orquídeas** hill, with dry tropical forest, worth exploring.

Ten kilometres north of Canoa (see below) is the **Río Muchacho** organic farm which promotes agro-ecology and reforestation in the area and runs an environmental primary school. Three-day horse riding trips to the farm are offered. Accommodation is rustic but comfortable, and the food is mainly veg-etarian. It's an eye opener to rural coastal (*montuvio*) culture and highly rec-ommended, reservations are necessary. Volunteer programmes can be set up for those wishing to stay longer.

Saiananda is a private park owned by biologist Alfredo Harmsen, 5 km from Bahía along the bay. The water front setting is striking, as is the unusual combination of native and domestic animals and birds, many of which inter-act freely with each other and humans. There are sloths, chuchuchos, deer, ostriches, rabbits, macaws, a donkey, a cow, peacocks and geese. There is also a Japanese bonsai garden, cactus collection, spiritual centre, accommodation and restaurant. The food is first class vegetarian. ■ *T398331, reached by taxi or any bus heading out of town.*

Chone
Population: 41,437

Chone is 1½ hours east from Bahía. At the Santo Domingo exit is a strange sculpture of four people suspending a car on wires across a gorge. It represents the difficulty faced in the first ever trip to Quito by car. One of the figures is the famous explorer, Carlos Alberto Aray, who formed one of the first bus compa-nies in Manabí, which still exists. There is a bus terminal just out of town. You can catch a bus there from the centre. The Pacifictel office is opposite the post office at Bolívar y Atahualpa.

Twenty minutes west of Chone, in the Parroquia San Antonio, is the **Ciénega de la Segua**, a huge marshland, home to 158 species of birds, includ-ing 250,000 waterbirds. Tours to this wetland are available from agencies in Bahía and local guides can be hired in the neighbouring towns of La Segua and La Sabana. More information from www.ramsar.org/w.n.ecuador_segua.htm

North of Chone, by an attractive stream, is **La Cueva Dibujada**, a cave with ancient drawings. It was recently discovered and investigations were under-way in 2000 to determine its age. Agencies in Bahía can take you there; be pre-pared to walk or ride a horse uphill for 1½ hours.

Sleeping and eating **D** *Atahualpa de Oro*, Av Atahualpa y Páez, T696627. With bath, TV, restaurant, garage, clean, very good. **E** *Chone*, Pichincha y Páez, T695014. TV, garage, restaurant. **E** *Hostal Los Chonanas*, T695236. Shared bath, poor service. There are others, **G** , which are very basic. Restaurants include *Maikito*, Av Atahualpa. Cheap, typical food, clean. *Rico Pollo*, Bolívar y Colón. Friendly, fast food, clean, cheap.

North to Esmeraldas

San Vicente, on the north side of the Río Chone, can be reached by taking the ferry from Bahía de Caráquez, or the road west from Chone. Its attractive water front and wide sandy beach were lost to El Niño in 1998. However it is still the access point for the impressive stretch of beach between San Vicente and Canoa. It has an airport; however no commercial flights were operating in 2000. There is a small market in town and a newer one on the road to San Isidro. The Santa Rosa church, 100 m to the left of the wharf, is worth checking out for the excellent mosaic and glass work by José María Peli Romeratigui (better known as Peli). There are examples of his work in town. The views of Bahía from town, especially from the hill are excellent.

San Vicente
Phone code: 05

Sleeping and eating On the road to Canoa, across the road from the beach: **C** *Cabañas Alcatraz*, T674179. Cabins for 5, nice, a/c, pool. **C** *Monte Mar*, Malecón s/n, T674197. Excellent food, pool, views, various rooms for rent. **C** *El Velero*. Cabañas and suites, pool, restaurant, good. *El Cangrejo*, close to the bridge on the way out of town to Canoa. Restaurant and bar. *Restaurant La Piedra*, beyond Alcatraz just over the bridge on the way to Canoa, T674451, also rents apartments.
    In town: E *Vacaciones*, near the old market, T674116/8. Bath, a/c, pool, tennis court, restaurant, TV in rooms, disco for residents only. **G** *San Vicente*, Av Primera y C 1, opposite the old market, T674182. With bath, **H** without, basic, clean, mosquito nets. Next door is *Chifa Chunking 2. Pelícano*, on the main road out of town, restaurant.

Transport Bus Coactur, opposite the *panga* dock, to **Portoviejo**, **Manta** and **Guayaquil**. Reina del Camino (near *Hotel Vacaciones*), to **Portoviejo**, 4 daily, US$1.55. To **Chone**, 7 daily, US$1, 45 mins. To **Guayaquil**, 4 daily, US$40, 6 hrs. To **Quito**, at 0630 and 2215, US$5, 7½ hrs. To **Esmeraldas**, US$5. To **Santo Domingo**, US$3. To **Quinindé**, US$4.50. Several companies to **Pedernales**, US$4, 3 hrs, and **Cojimíes**.
    Road A road runs along the bay southeast to Chone. Another goes north to Pedernales and on to Muisne and Esmeraldas.
    Boat *Pangas* cross to Bahía continually until 2200, 10 mins, US$0.20. There's a car ferry every 20 mins or so, which is free for foot passengers. Note that the very steep ramps are difficult for low clearance cars.

The beautiful 17-km beach between San Vicente and Canoa is a good walk or bike ride. You will see many people harvesting shrimp larvae, especially at full and new moon. Just north along the beach are several natural caves at the cliff base. You can walk there at low tide but allow time to return. Canoa is a quiet fishing town, with a 800 m wide, clean and relatively isolated beach. Surfing is excellent, especially during the wet season December to April. In the dry season there is good wind for windsurfing. It is also among the best places in Ecuador for hang gliding and parasailing. Horses can be hired for riding along the beach. Canoa was at the epicentre of a serious earthquake in 1998, it therefore has a new church and school and many bamboo houses built during the relief campaign.

Canoa
The widest beach in Ecuador, great for surfing

Sleeping and eating C-D *Hostería Canoa*, 600 m south of town. Cabins and rooms, pool, sauna, whirlpool, good restaurant and bar. **E** *Sol y Luna*, 3 km south of town. Large rooms with and without bath, restaurant. **F** *Bambú*, on the beach, T09-753696. Shared bath, restaurant with good food, very popular, English and Dutch spoken. Recommended. **F** *Posada de Daniel*, at the back of the village, T691201. An attractive renovated homestead, with or without bath, friendly. **F** *Hostal Shel Mar*, 1 block from the beach. With bath, clean. **F** *Pacific Fun Cabins*, 1 km south of town. Cabins with

Northern Pacific Lowlands

bath, no restaurant but next door is the *Sun Down Inn*, meals available, but not always open. **G** *Tronco Bar*, with bath, cheaper without, restaurant. *Comedor Jixsy* has rooms. *Costa Azul* has good food. *El Torbellino*. Good for typical dishes, cheap, large servings. *Arena Bar* 1 block from the beach. Breakfast, fruit salads, great pizza, snacks, beer, T-shirts for sale, hammocks. Owner Santiago gives surfing lessons, also organizes horse riding tours to **Guaché Forest**, a nice day trip through farmland, bamboo and humid forest. Trips to **Lobster beach**, an isolated beach where you can stay in a cabin and the **Río Muchacho** organic farm (see Excursions from Bahía above) can also be arranged here.

North of Canoa along the shore is **Cabo Pasado**, where howler monkeys might be seen in the forest; it was a stopping point for whalers who used to resupply with water at a spring. From Canoa the road goes inland, through the more humid pasture-lands, north to the small market centre of **Jama**, 2½ hours from San Vicente. There's accommodation at **F-G** *Cabañas Barbudo*, with bath and restaurant, and **H** *Jamaica*, very basic.

Pedernales
Phone code: 05

From Jama the road runs parallel to the beach past coconut groves and shrimp hatcheries, inland across some low hills and across the Equator to Pedernales, a market town and crossroads with good undeveloped beaches to the north; those in town are dirty and unattractive. A mosaic mural on the church overlooking the plaza is one of the best pieces of work by Peli (see San Vicente above), and lovely examples of his stained glass can be seen inside the church. About 50 more examples of his work can be seen throughout the country.

Sleeping and eating **F** *América*, García Moreno, on the road to the beach, T681174. TV, fans, balcony, very comfortable, expensive restaurant. **G** *Playas*, Juan Pereira y Manabí, near the airport, T681125. With bath, TV, fans, nets, clean, comfortable. **G** *Pedernales*, on Av Eloy Alfaro. 2 blocks from the plaza, T681092. With bath, fan, nets, rooms at front have windows. Basic but clean, good value. **G** *César Augusto*, with bath. **H** *Tequendama*, near the beach, with bath. Along the beach to the north is **F** *Cocosolo*, see Cojimies below. *El Rocío*, on Eloy Alfaro. Good cheap food. *La Fontana*, just off main plaza. Good vegetarian food. *Habana Club*, next to *Hotel Playas*. Good seafood, cheap. *San Isidro*, on main street, cheap. There are several good soda bars on Eloy Alfaro.

Transport **Bus**: to **Santo Domingo**, via El Carmen, 6 daily, 2½ hrs, US$3, and on to **Quito**, 6 hrs, US$5.70. To **Chamanga**, 1½ hrs, continuing to **El Salto**, where you can make a connection for **Muisne**, or continue to **Esmeraldas**.

Road A poor unpaved road goes north along the shore to Cojimies. The main coastal road goes south to San Vicente and north to Chamanga, El Salto and Esmeraldas. Another important road goes inland to El Carmen and on to Santo Domingo de los Colorados; this is the most direct route to Quito.

Directory **Banks** Several in town including *Filanbanco* and *Banco del Pacífico*.

Cojimíes

This is a real one-horse town, with unpaved streets. It is continually being eroded by the sea and has been moved about three times in as many decades. Places to stay include **G** *Costa Azul*, with shared bath, very basic. Slightly better looking is **G** *Mi Descanso*, with bath. Ask here for *cabañas* to rent, **F**. *Restaurant Flavio Alfaro*, by the beach where boats leave for Muisne, is friendly amd cheap.

Fourteen kilometres south of Cojimíes on the beach is **F** *Cocosolo*, set among palm trees, French, English and Italian spoken, clean, restaurant, cabins with bath and rooms without bath, camping, horses for hire. Reservations through *Guacamayo Bahia Tours* in Bahía, T05-691412 or *Safari Tours* in Quito, T02-552505. Between Cojimíes and Muisne is Mompeche, with a lovely new French-run hostel. Access is by canoe from Muisne or walk from Las Manchas (see below).

Transport **Bus**: to Pedernales by a rough, unpaved road, 1½ hrs, US$1.90, the last one departs at 1500, minibuses depart more frequently. Pickups also ply back and forth along the beach at low tide, they leave from the beach where the boats land. It's an exhilarating 30-min ride, US$1, the last one leaves at around 1500.

Boat: canoes go to Chamanga and Muisne, 2 hrs, US$8 per person, based on demand. This trip is not for the faint-hearted, those prone to sea-sickness or weak swimmers. The entry into Cojimíes and Muisne is treacherous and many boats have been thrown into the shallows by the swell. Since the Pedernales-Chamanga-Daule-El Salto road opened, it is possible to avoid the boat crossing, however this road does not go through Cojimies, to get to the road you must take a canoe from Cojimies to Daule where you can catch transport north.

Muisne

The town, on an island across a narrow stretch of water, is a bit run-down but lively and friendly. Fifteen minutes' walk from town (or a tricycle ride for US$0.20), is a long expanse of beach, which makes for a pleasant walk at low tide but practically disappears at high tide. The beach end of town is a great place in which to kick back and relax for a few days. The atmosphere is friendly and peaceful and there is some very good food on offer.

Phone code: 06
Colour map 2, grid B1
Altitude: sea level

The main streets in town are Calle Manabí and Calle Isidro Ayora, which run about 500 m between the stretch of water separating it from the mainland, known as Río Muisne, and the beach. Between them and one block from the Río Muisne is the Parque Central; the church is opposite it. Pacifictel is on Ayora, half a block from the park towards the Río Muisne, and the post office is around the corner in a perpendicular street. Buses stop on the mainland. **Warning**: Walking in isolated areas after dark is not safe

The region produces bananas and shrimp. Between 1987 and 2000, over 97% of the 20,000 ha of mangrove forest in the area was destroyed and replaced by shrimp ponds, despite 1994 legislation which prohibits cutting mangroves. There are reforestation efforts underway by the *Fundación de Defensa Ecológica* which works with local communities; this is a slow and difficult process. Marcelo Cotera and Nisvaldo Ortíz arrange boat trips to see the mangrove forests which are being replanted (donations welcome, contact them through the tourist office). On the Río Sucio, inland from Muisne and Cojimíes, is an isolated group of Cayapa Indians, some of whom visit the town on Sunday. There are no banks, instead you can change travellers' cheques at a slightly lower rate at Marco Velasco's store, near the dock.

D *Hostal Mapara*, at the beach. Ample and well furnished rooms, restaurant. Modern wooden construction. Best in town. Recommended. **F** *Oasis*, C Manabí, about 150 m from the beach. With fan, nets. Clean, friendly. Recommended. **F** *Cabañas San Cristóbal*, on the beach to the right coming from town, no sign. Some basic wooden cabins and newer cement rooms, fetch water from well nearby, friendly, cheaper for long stay. **F** *Calade*, 150 m away at the south end of the beach, T480279. With bath, cheaper without, hot water. Clean, comfortable but overpriced, negotiable for longer stays, excellent meals including vegetarian, internet US$6 per hour. **G** *Galápagos*, 200 m from the beach. With bath, fan, mosquito nets, restaurant. Modern, clean.

Sleeping

Northern Pacific Lowlands

Recommended. **G** *Playa Paraíso*. Turn left as you face the sea, then 200 m. Clean, basic, mosquito nets. In town are: **G** *Don José*, with bath. Good. **H** *Residencial Isla*, and **H** *Sarita*, both very basic. Insist on a mosquito net.

Eating *El Tiburón*. Good, cheap. Recommended. *Las Palmeiras*. Excellent seafood, try
Try encocada de *camarones a la plancha*. Near the beach is *Restaurante Suizo-Italiano*. Good pizza
cangrejo, crab and pasta, breakfast on request, good atmosphere. Book exchange. Swiss owner Dan-
in coconut iel is friendly and very knowledgeable about the area. *Doña María*, on the beach.
Good and friendly. *La Riviera*, good. *Mai Tai*, C Manabí by the beach. Italian food,
breakfast, café and disco. Internet US$7 per hour. *Habana Club*. Good rum and reg-
gae. There are several other excellent kiosks on the beach.

Transport **Boat** Canoes ply the narrow stretch of water between the island and mainland (El
Relleno); US$0.10. There are boats going Chamanga-Cojimies. Boats from Muisne to
Cojimíes go when there is demand, US$8 per person, 2 hrs; buy your ticket at the
dock, take waterproofs and be prepared to wait until the boat is full. It is also possible
to reach Cojimies going by bus towards Chamanga and getting off at Daule, north of
Chamanga, from where you walk and take a canoe to Cojimies.

Bus To **Esmeraldas** US$1.50, 3 hrs. There is a direct bus to **Quito** once a night. For
Pedernales, take a bus to **El Salto**, US$0.25, 30 mins, on the Esmeraldas road, from
where there are buses going south to **Chamanga**, US$0.75, 1½ hrs, where you
change for Pedernales, 1½ hrs. At 0600 there is a direct bus Muisne-Chamanga.

Tonchigüe is a quiet little fishing village, two hours north from Muisne and
1½ hours southwest of Esmeraldas. There's accommodation in expensive
cabañas and two small hotels, **G** *Hostal Tonchigüe*, with bath, OK, and **G** *Luz
del Mar*, with bath, basic. There are buses to Atacames (US$0.50) and to
Esmeraldas (US$1).

Playa Two kilometres south of Tonchigüe a road goes west and follows the shore to
Escondida **Punta Galera,** from where it continues south to **Quingüe**, **Estero del Plátano**
and **San Francisco**. Between June and September, whales are sometimes seen
from the shore at Estero del Plátano. Boat excursions to see the whales go from
Súa and Atacames (see below). At Km 10 between Tonchigüe and Punta
Galera is **Playa Escondida**, a charming beach hideaway, set in 100 ha stretching back to secondary tropical dry forest. It is run by Canadian Judith Barett on
an ecologically sound basis. Accommodation is in rustic cabins overlooking a
lovely little bay in **D** range and camping **G** per person, breakfast runs US$2-3,
meals US$4 and up. The food is excellent, swimming is safe, and you can walk
along the beach at low tide. The place is completely isolated and wonderfully
relaxing. For reservations, T09-733368/06-733106, judithbarett@hotmail.
com, www.intergate.ca/playaescondida Volunteers are welcome for a reforestation project in the area.

To get there take a *ranchera* or bus from Esmeraldas for Punta Galera. River
Tavesao departs at 0530, 0830 and 1200 and La Costeñita at 0730 and 1600,
two hours. From Quito take a bus to Esmeraldas or Tonchigüe and transfer
there. A taxi from Atacames is US$12 and a pickup from Tonchigüe US$5.

Same Northeast of Tonchigüe is Playa de Same, with a beautiful, long, clean, grey
Phone code: 06 sandy beach lined with palms. It's safe for swimming and there's good
birdwatching in the lagoon behind the beach. There is no cheap accommodation here, but mostly high-rise apartment blocks for rich Quiteños.

Northern Pacific Lowlands

Sleeping and eating Booking is advisable at holiday times and weekends. In the low season good deals can be negotiated. **L** *Club Casablanca*, T252077, F253452 (Quito), casablan@uio.satnet.net, www.ccasablanca.com Restaurant, tennis courts, swimming pool, luxurious. **B** *Seaflower*, on the beach, T733369. Nice rooms, good expensive restaurant. German-Chilean-run. **B** *El Rampiral*, at south end of the beach, T/F264134 (Quito), rampiral@uio.satnet.net Cabins by the sea. **C** *El Acantilado*, on the hill by the sea, south of Same, T453606 (Quito). Fourteen rooms for 2-3 people, 30 cabins up to 5 people, excellent food, pool, whale watching tours in season. **C** *Cabañas Isla del Sol*, at south end of beach, T733470. Cabins with fan, kitchenette, pool, cafeteria serves breakfast. **D** *La Terraza*, on the beach, T544507/09-476949. Eleven cabins for 3-4, with bath, fan, hammocks, Spanish and Italian owners, good restaurant. *Unicornio Azul* and *Moscú* are both reasonable eating places.

Transport Buses every 30 mins to and from **Atacames**; La Costeñita, 15 mins, 18 km, US$0.35. Make sure it drops you at Same and not at *Club Casablanca*. To **Muisne**, US$0.60.

This is another beach resort, a 15 minute bus ride southwest of Atacames. It is a quiet and friendly little place, set in a beautiful bay with pelicans and frigate birds wheeling overhead when the fishing boats land their catches. Hotel prices are lower out of season. Between June and September there are whale watching excursions from here. The sighting area is to the south of Punta Galera (see above), 40-60 minutes by boat. ■ *Boats depart at 0800, US$20, per person.*

Súa
Phone code: 06

Sleeping and eating **F** *Hostal Los Jardines*, 150 m from the beach, T731181. With bath, fan, parking. Very nice, new in 2000. **F** *Chagra Ramos*, on the beach, T731006. With bath, fan, good restaurant, disco. Clean, good value. **F** *El Peñón de Súa*, T731013. With bath, restaurant, parking. **F** *Las Acacias*, on the beach. Cabins with bath, fan. Nice. **F** *Clint*, on the beach. With bath. Basic. **F-G** *Buganvillas*, on the beach, T731008. With bath. Very nice, room 10 has the best views. **F** *Mar y Mar*. Cabins, **D** for group to 6. **F** *Malibu*, on the beach, T731012. With bath, **G** without, basic. **G** *Cabañas El Triángulo*, on the street going to the beach, With bath, fan, parking. **G** *Cabañas San Fernando*, near the road, T726441. Cabins, parking. Basic. **G** *Gabi*, on the beach past Buganvillas. With bath, basic. **G** *Mar y Sol*, on the Malecón, T731293. With bath. **G** *El Shamán*, on the Malecón. With bath, basic. **G** *Súa*, on the beach, T731004. 6 rooms, fan, café-restaurant. Clean, comfortable. *Restaurant Bahía*, big portions. *Café-Bar*, on the beach past Hotel Buganvillas, Reggae.

Atacames

Twenty-five kilometres south of Esmeraldas, Atacames is one of the main resorts on the Ecuadorean coast. It's a real 24-hour party town during the high season (April-October), at weekends and national holiday times, and the beach is none too clean at these times. Those who enjoy peace and isolation and who like to sleep at night should avoid the place; nearby Súa is a more tranquil alternative (see above).

Phone code: 06
Colour map 2, grid A2
Altitude: sea level

The main park and services such as the post office, Pacifictel and the bus stops are to the south of the Río Atacames. Most hotels are in a peninsula between the river and the ocean. There are whale watching tours from here in season (see Caída del Sol, Sleeping below). **NB** The sale of black coral jewellery has led to the destruction of much of the offshore reef. Consider the environmental implications before buying.

Security Many assaults on campers and beach strollers have been reported in recent years. People walking along the beach from Atacames to Súa

Northern Pacific Lowlands

regularly get assaulted at knife point where there is a small tunnel. Gangs seem to work daily. Note also that the sea can be very dangerous, there is a powerful undertow and many people have been drowned.

Sleeping
■ *on map*
Price codes:
see inside front cover

Prices quoted are for the high season. Discounts are available in the low season. Hotels are, generally, expensive for Ecuador. Most accommodation has salt water in the baths. Fresh water is not always available and not very good. It's best to bring a mosquito net as few hotels supply them.

AL *Juan Sebastián*, towards the east end of the beach, T731049, hotelj.s@uio.satnet.net A/c, TV, restaurant, pool, parking. Luxurious. **B** *Le Marimba*, at the west end of the beach, T731321. Cabins, pool. **B** *Lé Castell*, T731542, F731442. Cabins with bath, TV, phone, includes breakfast, pool, garage, restaurant. Comfortable. **B** *Villas Arco Iris*, at the east end of the beach, T731069, F731437, arcoiris@waccom.net.ec, www.VillasArcoiris.com With bath, fridge. Clean, charming, English, German and French spoken. Recommended. **C-D** *Tahiti*. With bath, TV, pool, fan, nets, friendly, breakfast, good restaurant, cabins are cheaper. **D** *Cabañas Caída del Sol*, Malecón del Río, 150 m from the beach, T/F731479. With bath, fan, fridge, parking. Clean, spacious, quiet, good value, Swiss-run. Organizes whale watching tours, US$25 per person. **D** *Playa Hermosa*, at the west end of the beach, T731238, F731518. A/c, TV, pool. **D** *Rincón Sage*, 120 m from beach, T731246. With bath, restaurant. Quiet, clean, comfortable. **D** *Hostal María*, at the west end of the beach. With bath, pool. **D** *Grand Hotel Paraíso*, T731425. With bath, pool.

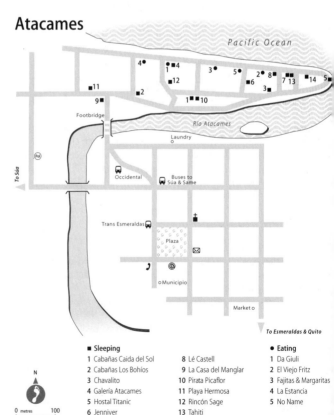

Atacames

Pacific Ocean

Río Atacames

Footbridge

Laundry

To Súa

Occidental

Buses to Súa & Same

Trans Esmeraldas

Plaza

Municipio

Market

To Esmeraldas & Quito

N

0 metres 100
0 yards 100

■ **Sleeping**
1 Cabañas Caída del Sol
2 Cabañas Los Bohíos
3 Chavalito
4 Galería Atacames
5 Hostal Titanic
6 Jenniver
7 Juan Sebastián
8 Lé Castell
9 La Casa del Manglar
10 Pirata Picaflor
11 Playa Hermosa
12 Rincón Sage
13 Tahiti
14 Villa Arcos Iris

● **Eating**
1 Da Giuli
2 El Viejo Fritz
3 Fajitas & Margaritas
4 La Estancia
5 No Name

E *Cabañas Los Bohíos*, 1 block from the beach by the pedestrian bridge, T731089. Bungalows with fresh water showers, clean, comfortable, quite good value. **E** *Cabañas de Rogers*, at the west end of the beach, T751011. Quiet, constant water supply, restaurant, bar. Beware of dogs. Recommended. **E** *Rodelú*, T731033. With bath, fridge, fan, clean, OK. **E** *Titanic*, at east end of the beach, T730093. With bath, restaurant, parking. German and English spoken. **F** *Cabañas Rincón del Mar*, on the beach, T731064. With bath, fresh water. Clean, friendly, secure, cosy, English, French and German spoken. Highly recommended. **F** *La Casa del Manglar*, 150 m from the beach beside the footbridge, T731464. With bath, cheaper without, fan, sweet water, laundry. Clean, friendly. Recommended. **F** *Galería Atacames*, on the beach, T731149. With bath, fresh water. Clean, book exchange, safe deposit. **F** *Hostal Chavalito*, along the river, T731113. With bath. Quiet. **F** *Hotel de mi Nati*, at west end of the beach, T731271. With bath, large rooms for up to 8 available. Quiet. **F** *Pirata Picaflor*, Malecón del Río, 1 block from the beach, T09-928084. With bath. Italian-run. **G** *Jennifer*, ½ block from the beach on a perpendicular street. With bath, cheaper with shared bath, **F** in cabins with cooking facilities and fridge.

Apartments by the ocean with a/c, TV, balconies, with capacity for 8. For rent from *El Viejo Fritz Restaurant*, T09-451777, **F** per person.

Eating
● *on map*
Many restaurants on the beach rent rooms

The beach is packed with bars and restaurants, too numerous to list. Most offer seafood at similar prices. The best and cheapest *ceviche* is found at the stands at the west end of the beach and at the market, but avoid *concha*. *Marco's*. Good steak and fish. Recommended. *El Tiburón*, on the beach. Good seafood, cheap. *Paco Foco*. Great seafood, very popular. Along the Malecón are: *La Estancia*. Very good food, expensive. Recommended. *Da Giuli*. Spanish and Italian food. Good. *El Viejo Fritz*. German and International food, seafood, meat, good breakfasts, bar. *No Name*, good pizza. *Fajitas & Margaritas*, Mexican food. *Cocada*, a sweet made from coconut, peanut and brown sugar, is sold in the main plaza.

Bars & nightclubs

Scala, on the Malecón, disco, admission US$1. Recommended. *Sambaye Club*, Malecón, by Hotel Tahiti, bar.

Transport

Bus To/from **Esmeraldas**, every 15 mins, US$0.70, 40 mins. To/from **Muisne**, hourly. To **Guayaquil**, US$5.60, 8 hrs. To **Quito**, 3 daily, US$5.20, 6½ hrs. Trans Esmeraldas station is by the main park.

Directory

Banks *Pacífico*, by the main park, for TCs and Mastercard. **Communications** Internet: by the main park, US$3.60 per hour. **Laundry** A couple of blocks east of the pedestrian bridge, on the south side of the river, US$1 per kg.

Northern Pacific Lowlands

Esmeraldas

The city itself has little to recommend it. It is hot, sticky, not too friendly and suffers from water shortages. The beaches to the north, though, are quieter and cleaner than those around Atacames and good for swimming. A new and mostly paved road has been completed from Esmeraldas north to Borbón and San Lorenzo.

There are gold mines in the area, tobacco and cacao grown inland, cattle ranching along the coast, timber exports (which are decimating the rainforest), and an oil pipeline from the Oriente to the oil refinery at the ocean terminal at nearby Balao. The development of shrimp farms has destroyed much of the surrounding mangrove forest. Despite the wealth in natural resources, Esmeraldas is among the poorest provinces in the country.

Phone code: 06
Colour map 2, grid A2
Population: 117,722
Altitude: sea level

The area is however rich in culture. La Tolita, one of the earliest cultures in Ecuador, developed in this region, and the most important archaeological site is in **La Tolita** island to the north. This culture's ceramic legacy can be seen at the **Museo del Banco Central**, Espejo entre Olmedo y Colón. Esmeraldas is also the heartland of Ecuador's Afro-Ecuadorean community. Its *marimba* music and dance is worth experincing, as is the local cuisine which makes extensive use of coconut and plantain. The *Ministerio de Turismo*, Bolívar 221 entre Mejía y Salinas, is open Monday to Friday 0830-1700.

NB Mosquitoes and malaria are a serious problem throughout the province of Esmeraldas, especially in the rainy season. Take plenty of insect repellent because the Detán sold locally does not work well. Most *residenciales* provide mosquito nets (*toldos* or *mosquiteros*). It's best to visit in the June-December dry season.

Sleeping
■ *on map*
Price codes:
see inside front cover
Generally, hotels on
the outskirts are better
than those in the centre

C *Apart Hotel Casino*, Libertad 407 y Ramón Tello, T728700, F728704. Excellent, good restaurant, casino. **F** *Galeón*, Piedrahita 330 y Olmedo, T723820. With bath, a/c, **G** with fan. **F** *Hostal El Cisne*, 10 de Agosto y Olmedo, T723411. With bath, TV. Very good. **G** *Diana*, Cañizares y Sucre, T727923. With bath, Secure. **G** *Asia*, 9 de Octubre 116, near the bus station, T711852. With bath, cheaper without. Basic but clean. **G** *Turismo*, Bolívar 843. With bath, TV and fan. Basic, clean and friendly. **G** *Zulema 2*, Malecón y Rocafuerte, T726757. Modern, with bath, TV, parking. **G** *Zulema 1*, Olmedo y Piedrahita, T723827. With bath, TV, parking. Not as nice as No 2. **H** *Miraflores*, on plaza. Shared bath, fan. Basic, clean, good. **H** *Valparaíso I*, Libertad y Pichincha. Very basic but good value, cheap restaurant.

Eating
● *on map*

Chifa Restaurante Asiático, Cañizares y Bolívar. Chinese, excellent. *La Marimba Internacional*, Libertad y Lavallén. Recommended. *Las Redes*, main plaza. Good fish, cheap, friendly. *Budapest*, Cañizares 214 y Bolívar. Hungarian-run, clean, pleasant. *Balcón del Pacífico*, Bolívar y 10 de Agosto. Nice atmosphere, good view overlooking the city, cheap drinks. *Los Alamos*, 9 de Octubre, near the plaza. Good, popular. There are numerous typical restaurants and bars by the beach selling *ceviche*, fried fish and *patacones*.

Entertainment

El Portón peña and discotheque, Colón y Piedrahita. *El Guadal de Ña Mencha*, 6 de Diciembre y Quito, peña upstairs, marimba school at weekends. *Bar Asia* on Bolívar by Parque Central. Good.

Shopping

There is a Cayapa basket market across from the Post Office, behind the vegetables. Also 3 doors down, Tolita artefacts and basketry. The market near the bus station is good for buying mosquito nets. *Más por Menos* supermarket has a good selection of imported goods.

Transport

Air General Rivadeneira Airport is on the road to La Tola. A taxi to the city centre (30 km) is about US$5. Buses to the Terminal Terrestre from the road outside the airport pass about every 30 mins. Daily flights except Sat to **Quito** with TAME, 30 mins, US$24 one way. Check in early as planes may leave 30 mins before scheduled time. Buses to La Tola, Borbón or San Lorenzo pass near the airport so it is not necessary to go into town if northbound.

Bus To **Quito**, US$4.40, 5-6 hrs, via Santo Domingo, frequent service on a good paved road, with Trans-Esmeraldas (10 de Agosto y Bolívar, recommendedAv), Occidental (9 de Octubre y Olmedo) and Aerotaxi (near the main park); also with Panamericana (Colón y Piedrahita) twice daily, slow but luxurious, US$8,Alternatively, it's 7 hrs via San Miguel de los Bancos and La Independencia. To **Santo Domingo**,

US$2, 4 hrs. To **Ambato**, 5 times a day with Coop Sudamericana, 8 hrs, US$6. To **Guayaquil**, hourly, US$5.30, 7 hrs. To **Bahía de Caráquez**, via Santo Domingo de los Colorados, US$6.50. To **Portoviejo**, US$2.75. To **Manta**, US$6.50. To **Quevedo**, 6 hrs. There are buses to **La Tola** 7 daily with La Costeñita, US$1.50, 3½ hrs. Also to **Borbón**, US$3, 4 hrs. To **San Lorenzo**, 6 daily, US$5, 6 hrs. To **Muisne**, hourly, US$1.50, 3½ hrs. To **Súa**, **Same** and **Atacames**, every 15 mins from 0630 to 2030.

Boat You can take a bus to La Tola from where there are launches to points north. For the occasional boat sailing north, enquire at the Capitanía de Puerto in Las Palmas, see below.

Banks *Filanbanco*, for TCs and Visa, upstairs at both until 1400. *Banco del Austro*, Bolívar y Cañizares, for Visa. **Communications** Post Office: Av Colón y 10 de Agosto. *Andinatel*, Malecón Maldonado y J Montalvo. **Internet:** *T@ipe.net*, Olmedo y 10 de Agosto, US$2.40 per hour. Another internet place at 9 de Octubre y Colón. **Useful addresses** Immigration: At Police Headquarters in La Propicia neighbourhood, at the entrance to town, T724624. **Directory**

This resort is just north of Esmeraldas and has several hotels and restaurants. There is a broad sandy beach but it is reported unsafe because of theft; it is also filthy and used as a speedway. Even the water is muddy. Outsiders, especially **Las Palmas**

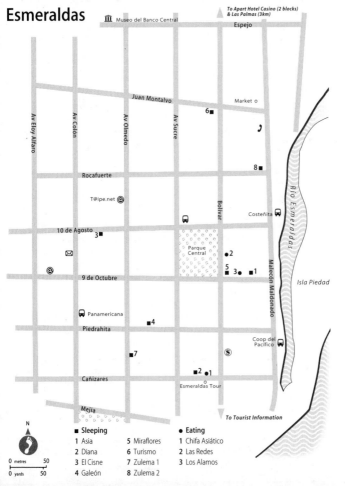

Esmeraldas

Sleeping ■
1 Asia
2 Diana
3 El Cisne
4 Galeón
5 Miraflores
6 Turismo
7 Zulema 1
8 Zulema 2

Eating ●
1 Chifa Asiático
2 Las Redes
3 Los Alamos

Northern Pacific Lowlands

single women, are advised to avoid the shanty-town on the Malecón and to take care everywhere. To get to Las Palmas take bus No 1 which leaves regularly from the main plaza in Esmeraldas, US$0.15. A taxi costs US$0.60.

Sleeping C *Costa Verde Suites*, Luis Tello 809 e Hilda Padilla, 1 block from the shore, T728714. Carpeted suites with kitchen, cable TV, parking, restaurant with local and international food. Friendly. Many good hotels in Las Palmas are along Av Kennedy: **D** *Cayapas*, T711022. A/c, showers and hot water in all rooms, overpriced, good restaurant. **D-E** *Del Mar*, on the sea front, T723708. Modern, a/c and mosquito-proofed rooms, restaurant. **F** *Ambato*, Kennedy y Guerra, T721144. With bath, TV, fan, restaurant. Camping at *El Edén* south of town near the beach.

North of Esmeraldas

There are good beaches for swimming north of Esmeraldas. The polluted water of the Río Esmeraldas reaches no further than **Camarones**, 20 km north of the city. Here is *Hostería La Fragata*, T701038/09-849889, which has cabins with bath, restaurant serving regional specialities, parasailing, fishing and land tours. **Río Verde**, which was the setting for Moritz Thompson's books on Peace Corps life, *Living Poor* and *Farm on the River of Emeralds*, is a good place to spend a few relaxing days. It's two hours north of Esmeraldas. The water temperature is pleasant all year round.

Sleeping F *Hostería Pura Vida*, on a stretch of deserted beach. To get there, take a bus from Esmeraldas to Palestina and get off just before Palestina. Five rooms in the *hostería* with or without bath and 7 rooms in *cabañas* all with bath, balcony and hammocks, all rooms have nets and are very clean. Excellent restaurant and bar with a wide range of fruit juices. Owned by Thomas Meier and Narcisa Obando who will arrange fishing trips or tours of the nearby mangroves. English, French, German and Italian spoken. Recommended as beautiful and peaceful.

Beyond Río Verde is **Rocafuerte**, recommended as having the best seafood in the province.

At the outflow of the Río Cayapas, 122 km north of Esmeraldas is **La Tola**. Here the shoreline changes from sandy beaches to the south, to mangrove swamp to the north. The wildlife is varied and spectacular, especially the birds. East of town is **El Majagual** forest with the tallest mangrove trees in the world. In this area, Action for Mangrove Reforestation (ACTMANG), a Japanese NGO, is working with the community of **Olmedo**, just south of La Tola, on environmental protection projects. The Women's Union of Olmedo runs an ecotourism project, they have accommodation (**H** per person with shared bath), cheap meals and tours in the area. You can go without reservations (boat ride or 20 minutes' walk from La Tola) or call Sra Carmen Mina in San Lorenzo (T06-780239), if advised they will pick you up at La Tola.

To the northeast of La Tola and on an island on the northern shore of the Río Cayapas is **La Tolita**, a small, poor village, where the culture of the same name thrived between 300 BC and 700 AD. Many remains have been found here, several burial mounds remain to be explored and looters continue to take out artifacts to sell. A small site museum was set up, but it too has been looted.

Sleeping and eating In La Tola: Try to avoid staying overnight. Women especially are harassed. **H** *El Jhonny* and **H** *Arist*, both basic with shared bath. For meals *Bero*, opposite Arist. **In Olmedo**: see above.

Transport There are 7 daily buses between La Tola and Esmeraldas (see Esmeraldas transport). Boats between La Tola and San Lorenzo connect with buses to/from Esmeraldas; see San Lorenzo transport below. There are hourly launches between La Tola and Limones, 1 hr, US$1.

Officially called Valdez, but generally known as Limones, the town is the focus of **Limones** traffic downriver from much of northern Esmeraldas Province, where bananas from the Río Santiago are sent to Esmeraldas for export. The Cayapa Indians live up the Río Cayapas and can sometimes be seen in Limones, especially during the crowded weekend market, but they are more frequently seen at Borbón.

Nancy Alexander, of Chicago, writes that about 75% of the population of Limones, Borbón and San Lorenzo has come from Colombia in the last 50 years. The people are mostly black and many are illegal immigrants. Smuggling between Limones and Tumaco in Colombia is big business (hammocks, manufactured goods, drugs) and there are occasional drug searches along the north coastal road.

Limones has two good shops selling the very attractive Cayapa basketry, including items from Colombia. Limones is 'the mosquito and rat capital of Ecuador', a title disputed by Borbón which has the highest rate of malaria in the country.

Sleeping Accommodation is very basic, San Lorenzo has much better choices. **G** *Mauricio Real*, by the dock, T789219. With bath, **H** without. **H** *Puerto Libre* and **H** *Limones*, both shared bath, very basic.

Transport There are hourly launches between La Tola and Limones, 1 hr, US$1, and frequent launches to San Lorenzo, 1 hr US$2. Launches to Borbón see below. A hired launch provides a fascinating trip through mangrove islands, passing hundreds of hunting pelicans; 6 people US$1.75 per person, 1½ hrs. Information on boat journeys from the Capitanía del Puerto in Las Palmas (see above). From Limones you can also get a canoe or boat to Borbón.

On the Río Cayapas past the mangrove swamps, Borbón is a dirty, unattrac- **Borbón** tive, busy, dangerous place and best avoided. It is a centre of the timber industry. Ask for Papá Roncón, the King of Marimba, who, for a beer or two, will put on a one-man show. Across from his house are the offices of *Subir*, the NGO working in the Cotacachi-Cayapas reserve; they have information on entering the reserve and guide services. *Ministerio del Ambiente* in Quito can also provide information (see page 145). Buses to/from Esmeraldas, several companies, US$2, four hours. To San Lorenzo, two hours, US$1.60.

Sleeping and eating **G** *Tolita Pampa de Oro*, T Quito 566075. Bath, cheaper without, clean, mosquito nets, helpful. **G** *Residencial Capri*. **H** *Panama City*. Mosquito nets, noisy. There is one restaurant *Comedor*, where the *chiva* buses stop. Excellent fish.

Upstream are Cayapa Indian villages. From Borbón hire a motor launch or go **Upriver from** as a passenger on launches running daily around 1100-1200 to the mouth of **Borbón** the Río Onzole; US$5 per person, 3½ hours. **Santa María** is just beyond the confluence of the Cayapas and Onzole rivers.

Sleeping Board and lodging with Sra Pastora at the missionary station, **F**, basic, mosquito nets, meals US$2, unfriendly, her brother offers river trips. Or at the **G** *Residencial*, basic, will prepare food but fix the price beforehand, the owner offers 5 hr jungle trips to visit Cayapa villages (beware deadly red and black river snakes).

Northern Pacific Lowlands

You can camp in front of school for free. At the confluence of the Cayapas and Onzole rivers, there is a fine lodge built by Hungarian Stephan Tarjany: **C** with full board, good value, clean, warm showers. Jungle walk with guide and small canoes at no extra charge. Water skiing available, US$12 per hour. Steve organizes special tours to visit remote areas and a trip to the Ecological Reserve, US$250 for 3 days including transport and food. For advance bookings write to Stephan Tarjany, Casilla 187, Esmeraldas.

Zapallo Grande, further upriver, is a friendly village with many gardens, where the American missionary Dr Meisenheimer has established a hospital, pharmacy, church and school. There is an expensive shop. You will see the Cayapa Indians passing in their canoes and in their open long houses on the shore. **San Miguel** has a church, a shop (but supplies are cheaper in Borbón) and a few houses beautifully situated on a hill at the confluence of two rivers. Borbón to San Miguel, US$8 per person, five hours, none too comfortable but an interesting jungle trip.

Trips from San Miguel into the **Reserva Ecológica Cotacachi-Cayapas** (entry US$5) cost US$22.50 for a group with a guide, US$5 for boat rental, US$5 per meal. One guide in this area is Don Cristóbal. You can sleep in the rangers' hut, **G**, basic (no running water, no electricity, shared dormitory, cooking facilities), or camp alongside, but beware of chiggers in the grass; also **F** *residencial*.

San Lorenzo

Phone code: 06
Colour map 2, grid A4
Altitude: sea level

The hot, humid town of San Lorenzo stands on the Bahía del Pailón, which is characterized by a maze of canals. The town was once notable as the disembarkation point on the thrilling train journey from Ibarra, high up in the sierra (see below). The train has now been replaced by the bus, but San Lorenzo is still worth visiting. There's a very different feel to the place, owing to a large number of Colombian immigrants, and the people are open and friendly. The culture is distinct and there are opportunities for trips into virgin rainforest. This is also a good place to hear marimba music and see the wonderfully sensual dances.

The area around San Lorenzo is rich in timber and other plants, but unrestricted logging is putting the forests under threat. The prehistoric La Tolita culture thrived in the region. The local festival is held August 6-10. When arriving in San Lorenzo, expect to be hassled by children wanting a tip to show you to a hotel or restaurant. During the rainy season, insect repellent is a 'must'.

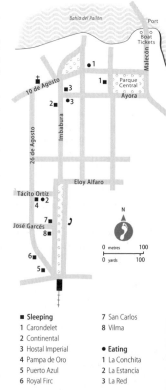

San Lorenzo

■ **Sleeping**
1 Carondelet
2 Continental
3 Hostal Imperial
4 Pampa de Oro
5 Puerto Azul
6 Royal Firc
7 San Carlos
8 Vilma

● **Eating**
1 La Conchita
2 La Estancia
3 La Red

E *Continental*, C Imbabura, T780125, F780127. With bath, hot water, TV, mosquito nets, more expensive with a/c. Clean, family-run, breakfast on request, parking. F *Pampa de Oro*, C 26 de Agosto, T780214. With bath, a/c, cheaper with fan, TV. Clean, friendly. F *Puerto Azul*, C 26 de Agosto, near the train station, T780220. with bath, TV, a/c, **G** with fan. **G** *Carondelet*, on the plaza, T780202. With or without bath, some rooms are small, fans, mosquito nets, friendly. **G** *San Carlos*, C Imbabura, near the train station, T780240, F780284. With bath, cheaper without, fan, nets. Clean, friendly. Recommended. **G** *Hostal Imperial*. With bath, **H** without, fan, nets. Clean, friendly. **G** *Royal Firc*, C 26 de Agosto, with bath, **H** without. Basic. **H** *Vilma*, near the train station. Very basic, ask for rooms 15 or 16, they are newer and bigger.

Sleeping
■ *on map*
Price codes:
see inside front cover

La Red, Imbabura y Ayora, good seafood, not too clean. *La Conchita*, 10 de Agosto. Excellent fish. Recommended. *La Estancia*, next to *Hotel San Carlos*. Good food and service but expensive. Highly recommended. *Casablanca*, near the train station.

Eating
● *on map*

Marimba can be seen during the local fiestas in August. Groups practise Thu-Sat. One on C Eloy Alfaro, another near the train workshops. Ask the kids at the train station (for a price). There are 2 discos near the plaza.

Entertainment

The train station is in the south of town, some buses also arrive at the train station, others opposite the *Hotel San Carlos*. The pier is at the north of town, 1 block from the main park. **Bus** To **Ibarra**, 10 daily, 5-6 hrs, US$3.20 They leave from the train station or near *Hotel San Carlos*. This road is prone to landslides, in 2000 it was in poor condition. To **Esmeraldas** via Borbón and Camarones, 6 daily, 6 hrs, US$5. **Train** The spectacular train journey to Ibarra, up in the highlands, has been replaced by buses (see under **Ibarra**, page 176). **Boat** Two companies offer launch service. To **Limones**, frequent service, 1 hr, US$2. **Limones-La Tola**, hourly, 1 hr, US$1. For direct service to **La Tola**, you must hire the launch, US$24.

Transport

Excursions from San Lorenzo

San Lorenzo is in the Chocó bio-geographic region (see Flora and Fauna, page 445). There are a number of nature reserves including the **Reserva Ecológica Cayapas-Mataje**, which protects some of the islands in the estuary northwest of town; the lowland section of the **Reserva Ecológica Cotacachi-Cayapas**, inland and upriver along the Río Cayapas (see above); **Reserva Playa de Oro**, upriver along the Río Santiago; **Bosque Protector La Chiquita**, at the junction of the Mataje and Ibarra roads; **Bosque Humedal del Yalare**, a wetland on the road to Esmeraldas; and **El Majagual** (see La Tola above). There are also some reserves which protect the last indigenous groups of the Ecuadorean coast, the Awa and the Cayapas or Chachi.

Launches can be hired for excursions, Coopseturi, Calle Imbabura, T/F780161 and Costeñita, on the same street, offer transport and tours in the region, US$4 per hour. Jaime Burgos is a guide who knows the area well, he can be reached at *Restaurant La Estancia* (see above), T780230. To visit the **Reserva Playa de Oro**, enquire with Victor Grueso, who has a store in town and also works for the Instituto Permacultura Madre Selva, on the outskirts of San Lorenzo, near the football field (T780257). Basic accommodation is available on the trip, but bring your own food and water; meals are cooked on request. The truly adventurous can take a trip upriver from Playa de Oro into unspoiled rainforest, where you can see howler and spider monkeys and maybe even jaguars. Contact Mauro Caicedo in San Lorenzo. For information on how to contact Mauro, T529727 (Quito), or contact Jean Brown at *Safari Tours* in Quito (see page 135). It is possible to stay at Madre Selva, **G** per

Northern Pacific Lowlands

person including breakfast; you can find out about permaculture and do various trips in the area.

At the seaward end of the bay is a sandy beach at San Pedro, with fishing huts but no facilities. It can be reached by canoe on Saturday and Sunday at 0700 and 1500, one hour. Contact Arturo or Doris, who will cook meals.

Crossing to Colombia

Leaving Ecuador From San Lorenzo there are boats to **Tumaco** in Colombia every other day at 0700 and 1400. It's 1½ hours to the frontier at **Palmarreal**, US$2, from there take another canoe to **Monte Alto** and then a *ranchero* to **Puerto Palmas**, cross the Río Mira, then take a Land Rover taxi to Tumaco. It takes six to seven hours in total.

At the border Entry stamps in Colombia must be obtained by crossing the border at Ipiales and returning again. When arriving in San Lorenzo from Tumaco, the customs office, run by navy personnel, is in the harbour, but you have to get your passport stamped at the immigration office in Ibarra or Esmeraldas. Problems may arise if you delay more than a day or two before getting an entry stamp, as the immigration police in Ibarra are less easygoing.

NB If taking an unscheduled boat from Colombia, be prepared for anti-narcotics searches (at least). This can be a dangerous trip, try to seek advice before taking a boat. Gringos are not normally welcome as passengers because contraband is being carried.

Warning Enquire locally about public safety before going to the border (see Dangerous areas, page 46).

Northern Pacific Lowlands

Oriente Jungle

Oriente Jungle

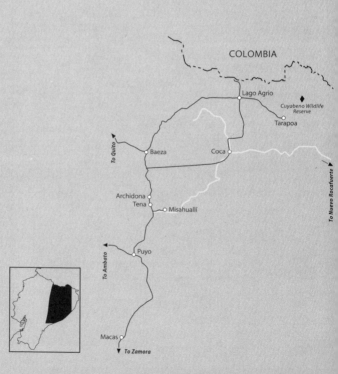

East of the Andes the hills fall away to the vast green carpet of tropical lowlands. Much of this beautiful wilderness remains unspoiled, unexplored and sparsely populated with indigenous settlements along the tributaries of the Amazon. The Ecuadorean jungle has the added advantage of being relatively accessible and the tourist infrastructure is well developed, with emphasis on environmental and cultural awareness and conservation.

A large proportion of the Northern Oriente – the provinces of Sucumbíos, Orellana, Napo and Pastaza – is taken up by the protected areas of Yasuní National Park, the Cuyabeno Wildlife Reserve and most of the Cayambe-Coca Ecological Reserve, but is nevertheless under threat. Colonists have cleared parts of the forest for agriculture, while other areas are the site of petroleum exploration and production. The ever increasing demand for land and resources must be weighed against the region's irreplaceable biodiversity and traditional ways of life.

The southern Oriente, made up of the provinces of Morona-Santiago and Zamora-Chinchipe is less developed, for tourism as well as other activities. Precisely for this reason, it offers unique opportunities and demands extraordinary respect. An increase of tourism in this area is expected now that the long-standing border conflict with Peru has been settled.

Ins and outs

Getting there Ecuador's Eastern tropical lowlands can be reached by four different road routes: from Quito, Ambato, Cuenca or Loja. These roads are narrow and tortuous and subject to landslides in the rainy season, but all have regular, if poor, bus services and all can be attempted in a jeep or in an ordinary car with good ground clearance. Their construction has led to considerable colonization by highlanders in the lowland areas. Several of the towns and villages on the roads can be reached by air services from Quito and places further into the immense Amazonian forests are generally accessible by river canoe or small aircraft from Shell-Mera or Macas. A fifth road route, from Guamote (south of Riobamba) to Macas is nearing completion, but remains controversial due to its impact on Parque Nacional Sangay, (see page 383). Transport details are given under the relevant destination; see also Getting around (page 50).

Public safety
Enquire before visiting remote areas in northern Oriente

There are frequent military checks in the Oriente, so always have your passport handy. You may be required to register at Shell-Mera, Coca and Lago Agrio. The Oriente, especially the northern Oriente, is also at risk of being affected by conflict in neighbouring Colombia. Always enquire about public safety before visiting remote sites, particularly north of the Río Napo, and avoid areas immediately adjacent to the Colombian border. (Also see Dangerous areas, page 46.) At the same time, you should remember that the Ecuadorean Amazon has traditionally been safe and tranquil, and the very few incidents which have taken place mostly involved foreign oil workers rather than tourists. Baeza, Tena, Misahuallí, Puyo and their surroundings, as well as jungle areas to the south, have experienced no difficulties.

Health Anti-malaria tablets are recommended and be sure to take a mosquito net and an effective repellent, especially below 600 m. A yellow fever vaccination is also strongly recommended for travel into the Oriente.

Ecotourism in the Oriente

The Northern Oriente offers an extensive variety of ecotourism services and programmes, which can be divided into three basic types: lodges; guided tours; and indigenous ecotourism. A fourth option is independent travel without a guide, but this is not advisable, for the reasons given below. The Southern Oriente, comprising the province of Morona-Santiago and Zamora-Chinchipe, is less developed and lacks the same level of tourist infrastructure.

Jungle lodges These cabaña complexes are normally located in natural settings away from towns and villages and are in most cases built to blend into the environment through the use of local materials and elements of indigenous design. They are generally owned by urban-based nationals or foreigners, have offices in Quito and often deal with national or international travel agencies. When staying at a jungle lodge, you will need to take a torch, insect repellent, protection against the sun and a rain poncho that will keep you dry when walking and when sitting in a canoe. Rubber boots can be hired.

Experiencing the jungle in this way usually involves the purchase of an all-inclusive package in Quito or abroad, quick and convenient transport to the lodge, a comfortable stay at the lodge and a leisurely programme of activities suited to special interests. Getting to the lodge may involve a long canoe ride, with a longer return journey upstream to the airport, perhaps with a pre-dawn start. Standards of services are generally high and most lodges show a relatively high degree of environmental awareness, have standardized arrangements with neighbouring indigenous communities and rely on

Orellana and the Amazon

The legends of the Incas only served to fuel the greed and ambition of the Spanish invaders, who dreamed of untold riches buried deep in the Amazon jungle. The most famous and enduring of these was the legend of El Dorado which inspired a spate of ill-fated expeditions deep into this mysterious and inhospitable world.

Francisco Pizarro, conqueror of the Incas, sent his younger brother, Gonzalo, to seek out this fantastic empire of gold. An expedition under the command of Gonzalo Pizarro left Quito with 220 Spanish soldiers, 4,000 Indian slaves, 150 horses and 900 dogs, as well as a great many llamas and livestock. They headed across the Andes and down through the cloud forest until they reached the Río Coca. In 1541 Pizarro's expedition was joined by Francisco de Orellana, the founder of Guayaquil, accompanied by 23 more conquistadores.

After following the Coca for some distance, the expedition began to run out of food. Rumours that they would find food once they reached the Río Napo led Orellana to set out with his men to look for this river and bring back provisions. But the jungle natives fled their small farms as soon as they saw the Spanish approach and Orellana and his party found nothing.

Without food and not being able to return up river against the current, Orellana sent three messengers on foot to inform Gonzalo Pizarro of their decision to continue downstream. On February 12, 1542, Orellana reached the confluence of the Napo and the Amazon – so called by him because he claimed to have been attacked by the legendary women warriors of the same name.

On August 26, 1542, 559 days after he had left Guayaquil, Orellana and his men arrived at the mouth of the Amazon, having become the first Europeans to cross the breadth of South America and follow the world's greatest river from the Andes to the Atlantic. Totally lost, they followed the coastline north and managed to reach the port of Cubagua in Venezuela. In the meantime, Gonzalo Pizarro had suffered enormous losses and limped back to Quito with only 80 starving survivors.

Orellana returned to Spain and organized a second expedition which sailed up the Amazon in 1544, only to meet with disaster. Three of his four vessels were shipwrecked and many of the survivors, including Orellana himself, died of fever (most likely yellow fever). The 'discoverer' of the Amazon was buried near the present site of Monte Alegre, Brazil.

well-qualified personnel. Their contribution to local employment and the local economy varies.

Guided tours of varying length are offered by tour operators, river cruise companies and independent guides. These should be licensed by the Ministerio de Turismo. Tour companies and guides are mainly concentrated in Quito, Baños, Puyo, Tena, Misahuallí, Coca and Lago Agrio – and to a lesser extent in Macas and Zamora – where travellers tend to congregate to form or join groups and arrange a jungle tour, usually of between one and seven days. In these towns there is always a sufficient number of guides offering a range of tours to suit most needs, but there may be a shortage of tourists for group travel outside the months of July and August. **Guided tours**

Since the cost of a tour largely depends on group size, the more budget-conscious travellers may find that in the off-season it will take several days to assemble a reasonably sized group. In order to avoid such delays, it may be easier to form a group in Quito or Baños, before heading for the Oriente. Conversely, the lack of tourists in the off-season can give you more bargaining power in negotiating a price.

When shopping around for a guided tour ensure that the guide or agency specifies the details of the programme, the services to be provided and whether park fees and payments to indigenous communities are involved. Serious breaches of contract can be reported to the Ministerio de Turismo and to South American Explorers in Quito, but you should be reasonable about minor details. Most guided tours involve sleeping in simple cabañas or camping shelters (open-sided with raised platforms) which the guides own or rent. On trips to more remote areas, camping in tents or sleeping under plastic sheets is common.

Indigenous ecotourism In recent years a number of indigenous communities and families have started to offer ecotourism programmes on their properties. These are either community-controlled and operated, or organized as joint ventures between the indigenous community or family and a non-indigenous partner. These programmes usually involve guides who are licensed as *guías natívos* with the right to guide within their communities.

Accommodation typically is in simple cabañas of varying, but generally adequate, quality, and safe food. A growing number of independent indigenous guides are working out of Puyo, Tena, Coca and Misahuallí, offering tours to their home communities.

Essential items for a trip of any length are: rubber boots (or, if you prefer, two pairs of suitable light shoes – keep one pair dry); sleeping bag; rain jacket; trousers (not shorts); binoculars; insect repellent; sunscreen lotions; mosquito net; water-purifying tablets; sticking plasters. Wrap everything in several small plastic bags.

Tours without a guide Though attractive from a financial point of view, this is not to be encouraged, for several reasons. From a responsible travel perspective, it does not contribute adequately to the local economy and to intercultural understanding and it may be environmentally damaging. Furthermore, it involves a greater risk of accident or injury.

While unguided trekking is possible in some settled areas, such as around Baeza, and in cleared areas, particularly in the Tena region, travellers should definitely avoid unguided river travel, unguided hiking in remote forested areas and unguided entry into indigenous community lands.

Choosing a rain forest A tropical rain forest is one of the most exciting things to see in Ecuador, but it isn't easy to find a good one. The key is to have realistic expectations and choose accordingly. Think carefully about your interests. If you simply want to relax in nature and see some interesting plants, insects, small birds and mammals, you have many choices, including some that are quite economical and/or easily accessible. If you want to experience something of the cultures of rain forest people, you must go farther. If you want the full experience, with large mammals and birds, you will have to go farther still and spend more, because large things have been hunted out around settled areas.

A visit to a rain forest is not like a visit to the Galápagos. The diversity of life in a good rain forest far exceeds that of the Galapagos, but creatures don't sit around and let themselves be seen. You will need to work to find them but the more nearly virgin the forest, the less you will have to work. In forests where people hunt, the few animals that remain will do their best to avoid you. In a truly untouched forest, on the other hand, even the larger animals and birds do not fear people, and it is possible to have intimate encounters with them instead of mere glimpses. Nevertheless, even in the best forests, your experiences will be unpredictable — none of this 'today is Wednesday, time to see sea lions'. A rain forest trip is a real adventure; the only guarantee is that the surprises will be genuine, and hence all the more unforgettable.

There are things that can increase the odds of really special surprises. One of the most important is the presence of a canopy tower. Even the most colourful rain forest birds are mere specks up in the branches against a glaring sky, unless you are above them looking down. Towers add an important dimension to bird and mammal watching. A good guide is another necessity. Because the life of the rain forest is subtle, you will depend on your guide's eyes and ears to find things. If you are a birder, search for a guide who knows bird calls, since most birds are initially detected by ear. Point out a few birds in your field guide (Rusty-belted Tapaculo or Black-faced Antthrush would be good choices) and ask him to imitate them. If he can't, go elsewhere. Avoid guides (and lodges) that emphasize medicinal plants over everything else. This usually means that there isn't anything else around to show. If you are interested in exploring indigenous cultures, give preference to a guide from the same ethnic group as the village you will visit.

If you want to see real wilderness, with big birds and mammals, don't go to any lodges you can drive to. Expect to travel at least a couple of hours in a motorized canoe. Don't stay near villages even if they are in the middle of nowhere. In remote villages people hunt a lot, and animals will be scarce. Indigenous villages are no different in this regard; most indigenous groups (except for a very few, such as certain Cofán villages that now specialize in ecotourism) are ruthlessly efficient hunters.

If economy is important, the newest and least well established lodges offer the best values. An economic alternative to a lodge is a canoe camping trip on a remote river like the Cononaco. These trips are also a good way to experience real jungle cultures. Just make sure there are whole days spent in the forest; some guides turn these trips into canoe marathons and forget that the forest is the reason for your visit. Another economic alternative to the fancy jungle lodges are the community-based lodges run by local people. An added advantage of these lodges is that your money goes straight to the community, providing an economic incentive for conservation.

Responsible jungle tourism

Some guides or their boatmen will try to hunt meat for your dinner – don't let them, and report such practices to South American Explorers when you get back to Quito. Don't buy anything made with animal or bird parts. Avoid making a pest of yourself in indigenous villages; don't take photographs or videos without permission, and don't insist. Many native people believe that photographs can steal one's soul. In short, try to minimize your impact on the forest and its people. Also remember when choosing a guide that the cheapest is **not** the best. What happens is that guides undercut each other and offer services that are unsafe or harm local communities and the environment. Do not encourage this practice.

Oriente Jungle

Northern Oriente

Quito to Lago Agrio

The most northerly route into the Oriente is from Quito via Baeza to Lago Agrio. The road crosses the Eastern Cordillera at a pass, just north of the volcano **Antisana** (5,705 m), and then descends via the small villages of **Papallacta** (excellent thermal baths, see page 152) and **Cuyuja** to the old mission settlements of **Baeza** and **Borja**. The road is paved and in very good condition until 5 km before Papallacta, and the trip between the pass and Baeza has beautiful views of Antisana (clouds permitting), high waterfalls, *páramo* and a lake contained by an old lava flow.

Antisana gets vast quantities of snow and has huge glaciers. It is very difficult to climb, so experience is essential. There are two accesses: one is from Pintag to *Hacienda Pinantura*, then to *Hacienda El Hato* from where it is four to five hours on foot (one hour by four-wheel drive) to Crespo Norte (morraine); the second access is from *Hacienda El Tambo* above Papallacta Lake to Laguna del Volcán (northwest of Antisana). Permission may be required to go beyond *Hacienda Pinantura*. It can be obtained from *Fundación Antisana*, Avenida Mariana de Jesús y La Isla, T433851, in Quito.

This is a colonist dairy-farming region with little indigenous presence, surrounded by the Cayambe-Coca, Antisana and Sumaco-Galeras Biological Reserves. Its mountainous landscape and high rainfall have created many spectacular waterfalls, pristine rivers and dense vegetation. Because of the climate, *ceja de montaña* (cloud forest), orchids and bromeliads abound. The numerous hiking trails make this ideal territory for trekking, and for fishing enthusiasts, the rivers have trout.

Baeza At the heart of this region is this small town, in the beautiful setting of the Quijos pass. The town is about 1 km from the main junction of the Lago Agrio and Tena roads. You need to get off the Lago Agrio bus at the police checkpoint and walk up the hill, but the Tena bus goes through the town. The town of Baeza is divided in two: **Baeza Colonial** (Old Baeza) and **Andalucía** (New Baeza). The old settlement, however, is dying as people have moved to the new town, 1 km down the road towards Tena, where the post office and Andinatel are located. Regular buses to Tena can be caught outside the *Hostal San Rafael*; two hours. Buses to Quito stop at the bus stop just below the *Hotel Jumandí* in the old town.

Sleeping and eating **G** *Samay*, in the new town. Shared bath, basic, clean, friendly. **G** *Hostal San Rafael*, in the new town. Shared bath, clean, friendly, spacious, cheaper cabins at rear, parking, restaurant. Recommended. **G** *Jumandí*, in the old town. Basic, full of character, very friendly (walls have holes). **G** *Oro Negro*, with restaurant, good, friendly. The better restaurants are in the old town. The best is *Gina*, cheap, friendly. *Guaña*. Breakfasts US$1, friendly, TV. Everything closes by 2030.

Hikes around There are many hiking trails in this region which generally can be done without
Baeza a guide. A recommended source for maps and route descriptions is *The Ecotourist's Guide to the Ecuadorian Amazon*, by Rolf Wesche, which is available in Quito, or in the *Hostal San Rafael*.

Camino de la Antena This is a three to four hour round trip, with a moderate climb and beautiful views along a mountain road which passes through pasture and, at the top, dense cloud forest. The trail is straightforward and easily accessible, with lots of birdlife to be seen. In the rainy season parts can be difficult due to deep mud.

The climb starts in Old Baeza, beside the church. Pass the cemetery and head up the antenna maintenance road. After about 500 m, you cross a wooden bridge and turn left. Then there's a steep uphill climb to the top (accessible with four-wheel drive vehicles), but on a clear day the views of the Quijos Valley are fantastic.

Baeza to Tena

At Baeza the road divides. One branch heads south to Tena, with a branch road going directly via Loreto to Coca (seven hours). The route from Baeza to Tena passes near several important reserves and national parks. Near **Cosanga**, approximately 30 minutes from Baeza, is LL *Cabañas San Isidro*, including three excellent meals. This is a 1,200 ha private reserve with rich bird life, comfortable accommodation with private bath, hot water and warm hospitality. Recommended. There is a small easily accessible Cock-of-the-Rock lek on the reserve, and feeders make the local hummingbirds easy to see. Reservations are necessary: Quito T547403, F228902, birdecua@hoy.net, www.ecuadorexplorer.com/sanisidro

Higher up in the same area is L *SierrAzul*, including three meals. This is an ecotourism development with a slightly different set of birds than San Isidro. Cabins are very nice, private bath, hot water; access is via a 1 km walk starting at the end of the road 12 km beyond San Isidro. Mountain Tapir tracks are sometimes seen. US$22 transport from Quito and back. Contact Quito T264484 ext 501, F449464, sierrazul@access.net.ec, www.sierrazul.com

Between San Isidro and SierrAzul is a biological station which was being developed in 2000, **Yanayacu**, run by Harold Greeney. This is intended as a base for students studying the cloud forest. Contact Harold at yanayacu@hotmail.com

Twenty minutes towards Tena from Cosanga is the **Guacamayos Ridge**, part of the Reserva Ecológica Antisana. There is a good stone path at the antennae (just before the shrine on the right side of the road), which enters one of the wettest and most interesting cloud forests in the area. Many rare birds and plants are found here, including several orchids found nowhere else in the world. On a clear day there is a view of the vast Oriente spread out below.

Much of the Baeza-Tena road southeast of the Guacamayos antennas is flanked by very good forest, making this stretch ideal for birdwatching or 'botanizing'. Another excellent forested road nearby is the Hollín-Loreto road which branches off the Baeza-Tena road near Narupa and goes on to Coca. The upper half of this road is famous for exciting and colourful birds, butterflies and plants. Even such rare birds as Military Macaws can sometimes be seen from there. It is worth going at least as far as the beautiful gorge of the Rio Hollín. A car is necessary, as buses are scarce.

Baeza to Lago Agrio

The other branch of the road from Baeza goes northeast to Lago Agrio, following the Río Quijos past the villages of **Borja**, a few kilometres from Baeza, and **El Chaco** (cabins on the edge of town and excellent food at the restaurant on the road) to the slopes of **Volcán Reventador** (see below for a description of the trail to the summit). At the village there is *Pensión de los Andes*. Basic, clean, and a restaurant. Also *Hotel Amazonas*.

Oriente Jungle

Reventador Trek

Views of the rain forest and the Eastern Slope peaks of Cayambe & Antisana are outstanding from the top

Volcán Reventador (3,560 m) is an active volcano which lies on the edge of the Cayambe-Coca Ecological Reserve poking up from the Oriente rain forests. It consists of a blown-out crater opening to the south. In the centre is an active cone with a small crater and fumeroles venting steam and volcanic gases. Eruptions of lava occurred as recently as the mid-1970s so the upper part of the mountain is covered only with moss and shrubs. There is no indication that another eruption is imminent but conditions may change.

The summit is only 8 km from the road as the toucan flies but longer and arduous by foot. The three to five day route to the summit and back is not technical but is physically challenging. The trail first crosses a chaotic volcanic rain forest covered landscape, which abruptly changes to a blocky lava flow, then there is a final scramble up loose scree slopes. It is important to wear rubber boots for the first section and boots with good ankle support for the rest of the hike. The driest months are usually September through December but it is foggy and rainy all year around. The appropriate map is IGM 1:50,000 Volcán El Reventador.

Getting there Take a bus from Quito towards Lago Agrio and get off at the San Rafael Waterfall (see below). There is a little cement block hut with an INECEL sign at a turn-off to your right which leads to the falls. You can stay at the former INECEL cabins beside the park guards hut, on the way to the falls, or there is a cheaper option of accommodation in the village of Reventador (see above), 13 km beyond the falls turn-off.

Guides The trail can become overgrown (bring a machete) but several local guides know the route well. Guillermo Vasquez, who lives in the Pampas 3 km before the falls, cut the original trail. Also recommended are Luis 'Lucho' Viteri from Baeza and Edgar Ortíz at the *Hotel Amazonas* in the village of Reventador.

The trek The beginning of the trek is tricky since there are pastures to cross before entering the forest. If in doubt ask locals to guide you for the first hour. On the main road walk 20 minutes past the falls turn-off where there is a large INEFAN sign (note that information on hiking time is incorrect on the sign). Head up the trail to the left to a wood ladder over the oil pipeline just before the

Oriente Jungle

Reventador Trek

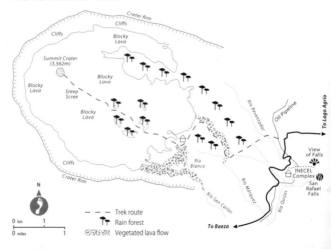

pipeline heads up a very steep incline. On the other side of the pipeline head northwest passing to the right of a wood shack in a flat field.

There is a vague trail in the grass that soon enters forest where it becomes more defined. Soon you reach a small stream choked with cobbles – jump across and look for the trail several metres upstream. A few minutes later the trail forks; stay left, the right fork heads up to pastures. Descend to the clear Río Reventador with great swimming holes.

The trail continues slightly upstream and from here there are no more branches but it still may be hard to follow in places. The trail ascends over two ridges with rotting steps and descends into ravines with small streams finally ascending to the toe of a forest covered lava flow. The surface of the trail changes from mud to awkward boulders and heads northwest up the flow. An hour along the trail it climbs to the left up to a muddy plateau then heads southwest to the Río Blanco (not named on IGM map) and a wooden refuge.

It should take four to five hours from the road to the refuge, which was built in 1994 and is still in good condition but not currently maintained. From the porch there are great views of the summit and across a vegetated plain. There are eight basic bunks without mattresses in two rooms and a cooking area with a fireplace and benches. No one is there to guard your belongings while climbing but the area is rarely visited.

It is possible to climb and return in one long day or set up a high camp at the base of the cone or summit rim. It is 10-13 hours of walking round trip from the refuge depending how comfortable you are at hopping the mossy boulders. Remember once it gets dark finding your way on the lava flows is difficult. The problem with camping at the base of the cone or at the summit is that there is no water source. You need to carry all your water with you from the refuge. You should have a minimum of five litres of water per day.

Cross the small stream known as the Río Blanco (slightly white from volcanic minerals) and head across a swampy area and up a steep vegetated hill. About an hour from the refuge you reach the edge of the blocky lava flow with a clear view of the cone 4 km in the distance. There is an obvious and abrupt change in vegetation to moss and shrubs. This spot should be marked by wood poles and flagging.

Head northwest for the summit cone across the lava blocks. There is a vague trail that can be followed to the base of the cone which is distinguished by crushed moss and may be marked with flagging. Re-mark the route if the flagging is gone. Orientation during a clear day is easy but in fog or at night you could easily spend hours or perhaps days wandering around the lava flows.

Head over several low ridges and climb to the left of two islands of cloud forest. Traverse right into a dry stream bed where it may be possible to find flat ground to camp. It takes two to three hours to reach this point from the toe of the lava flow. The trail gets steeper but the footing is easier. Beware of rockfall, though.

It takes three to four hours to reach the summit from here. Near the crater rim are steaming fumaroles and the soil is warm. The actual summit requires a short jaunt around to the west side of the rim. Total time from the refuge to the summit is six to eight hours. The descent takes four to five hours.

San Rafael Falls

The road to Lago Agrio winds along the north side of the Río Quijos, past these falls. To get to them take a Quito-Baeza-Lago Agrio bus. About two to three hours past Baeza (500 m before the bridge crossing the Río Reventador), look for a

These are an impressive 145 m, believed to be the highest in Ecuador

Oriente Jungle

covered bus stop and an INECEL sign on the right-hand side of the road. From here, walk about five minutes on a gravel road to the guard's hut, just beyond a small bridge, where you must pay the US$3.75 entry fee. Near the guard's hut accommodation in some functional cabins (the former INECEL complex).

The path to the falls begins behind the INECEL complex. It's an easy 1½ hour round trip through cloud forest. After about five minutes, you will come to an intersection; take the right-hand path, then cross the river and it's a further 30 minute walk to falls. At the ridge overlooking the falls is a small cross commemorating the death of a Canadian photographer who got too close to the edge. Camping is possible, but take all equipment and food. An extremely steep, slippery trail leads down to the bottom of the falls and should only be attempted by the most experienced of trekkers, preferably with a guide.

Many birds can be spotted along the trail, including Cock-of-the-Rock, and there are swimming holes and waterfalls near the INECEL complex, making this a worthwhile stopover on the way to or from Coca or Lago Agrio.

From San Rafael the road crosses the watershed between the Coca and Aguarico rivers and runs along the north bank of the river to the developing oil towns of Santa Cecilia and Lago Agrio.

Lago Agrio

Phone code: 06
Colour map 3, grid B3
Population: 20,000

Despite its importance for tourists as the access for Cuyabeno Wildlife Reserve, Lago Agrio is first and foremost an oil town. It is also has close connections with neighbouring Colombia. It retains the feel of a primitive and dangerous frontier town, despite the fact that the infrastructure has improved and most of the streets in the centre have been paved or cobbled, making it a much cleaner place. It is the capital of the province of Sucumbíos.

The road from Quito enters from the west. Virtually everything in the town is along the main road, Avenida Quito. The *Camara de Turismo de Sucumbíos* is located on Av Quito, between Colombia and Gonzanamá, cellular T09-848248. *Comercial Calvopeña* is the best place to buy groceries and supplies.

Lago Agrio is among the places in Ecuador most likely to receive significant impact from developments in neighbouring Colombia (see Dangerous areas, page 46). Enquire about public safety before travelling here and enquire again in Lago Agrio before visiting outlying areas in the province of Sucumbíos.

History The town's official name is Nueva Loja, owing to the fact that the majority of the first colonizers were from the province of Loja. The name Lago Agrio comes from Sour Lake, the US headquarters of Texaco, the first oil company to exploit the huge crude reserves beneath Ecuador's rainforest. They were in effect the new *conquistadores* and turned the Ecuadorean Amazon into a place where oil barrels mean more than human rights. Hundreds of thousands of barrels of oil flow out of Lago Agrio every day along a pipeline that snakes over the Andes and down to the coast for export. Wells and pipelines criss-cross the devastated terrain. The natural habitat around Lago Agrio is destroyed and the rivers poisoned, while its history threatens to be repeated elsewhere in Oriente.

The oil companies also broke up the indigenous communities, displacing people who had lived here for centuries, just to give us petrol in our cars. The Cofan, Siona and Secoya Indians were traditionally at least partially nomadic, but with the arrival of oil drilling, they have been forced to stay in one place and alter their lifestyles accordingly. They now have villages not far from Lago Agrio and come into town at the weekend, though you'll rarely see them in traditional dress. Some of these indigenous groups have recently become more aware of tourism as a way of earning a living.

Oriente Jungle

As if all this weren't bad enough, cattle have been introduced to the region to feed the hamburger industry. However, these are unsuitable animals for grazing on the poor or non-existent soils of the rainforest and now there are desert-like areas where only poor, useless grasses cover the land. For more information, see *Amazon Crude*, by Judith Kimerling.

B *Arazá*, Quito 610 y Narváez, T830223. With a/c, secure, restaurant, includes breakfast. New in 2000, best in town. Recommended. **B** *Gran Hotel de Lago*, km 1½ via Quito, T830015. Cabins with a/c, pool (open to non guests on weekends), restaurant, nice gardens, quiet. Includes breakfast. Recommended. **D** *D'Mario*, Quito 171, T880989. With a/c, cheaper with fan. Restaurant, central, a meeting place. Recommended. **D** *El Cofán*, 12 de Febrero y Av Quito, T830009. TV, fridge, clean, restaurant mediocre and expensive. Overpriced. **D** *Cuyabeno*, 18 de noviembre y Colombia, T830775. With a/c. New in 2000, good.

E *Gran Colombia*, Quito y Pasaje Gonzanamá, T831032. Clean, convenient location. **E** *París*, Añasco y Gonzanamá, T830496. With a/c. Clean and quiet. **F** *Shalom*, Quito y Av del Chofer, away from centre, T831494. With fan. **F** *Casablanca*, Quito 130 y Colombia, T830181. With fan. **F** *La Cabaña*, Av Quito next to Hotel Willigram. Clean. **F** *Lago Imperial*, Colombia y Quito, T830453. With fan. Convenient location, good value. **F** *La Posada*, Quito y Orellana, T830302. With fan. Clean, good value. **F** *Machala 2*, Colombia y Quito, T830037. With bath, TV, fan, clean, safe, friendly, restaurant, sometimes water shortages. **F** *Americano*, Quito y Gonzanamá, T831787. OK. **F** *Sayonara*, Quito y Colombia, T830193. OK.

F *Chimborazo*, Manabí y Quito, T830502. **F** *Guacamayos*, Quito y Colombia, T830601. Adequate. **F** *San Carlos*, 9 de octubre y Colombia, T830122. Clean, safe, a/c, cheaper with fan. Several others in this price range. **G** *Secoya*, Quito 222, T830451. Basic. **G** *Oro Negro*, Quito 164, T830174. Basic. **H** *Willigram*, Quito 400, T830163. Very basic. **H** *Marcella*, on Gonzanamá, T830199. Very basic.

Sleeping
■ *on map*
Price codes:
see inside front cover

Oriente Jungle

Lago Agrio

To Colombia

To Native Life Tour Operator & Terminal Terrestre

10 de Agosto

Sionatour

9 de Octubre

■ 16

Progreso · Vilcabamba · 24 de Mayo · Narváez · Guayaquil · Orellana

TAME

Av Colombia

To Hotel Shalom, Gran Lago & Quito

Magic River Tours

La Ronda
Plaza

18 de Noviembre

■ 4

Eloy Alfaro

12 de Febrero

Añasco

■ 14

■ 11

10

To Airport (5 km)

Caiman Safari

■ 6

■ 3

12 ■

Manabí

Pasaje Gonzanamá

■ 13

■ 1

■ 2

9 ■

17 ■

■ 7

Market

Av Quito

8 ■

15 ■

■ 5

■ 7

Harpia Eagle Tours

Rainforestur

Biotravel

Cuyabeno Tours

Av Río Amazonas

○ Pioneer Tours

N

0 metres 100
0 yards 100

■ **Sleeping**
1 Americano, Casa Blanca & Sayonara
2 Arazá
3 Chimborazo
4 Cuyabeno
5 D'Mario & Gran Colombia
6 El Cofán
7 Guacamayos
8 La Cabaña
9 La Posada
10 Lago Imperial
11 Machala 2
12 Marcella
13 Oro Negro
14 París
15 Putumayo & Willigram
16 San Carlos
17 Secoya

Eating There are restaurants at the better hotels (see above). *Mi Cuchita* beside *El Cofán*. Cheap, good chicken.

Tour operators
Shop around and try to get a recommendation from other travellers who have just returned from an excursion

All of the following offer tours to Cuyabeno: *Biotravel*, Quito y Gonzanamá, T830779; *Caiman Safari*, Quito y Orellana, T830177; *Cuyabeno Tours*, Quito y Gonzanamá, T831737; *Magic River Tours*, 18 de noviembre y Guayaquil, T831003; *Native Life*, Venezuela y 23 de septiembre, cellular T09-210858, also have Quito office; *Pioneer Tours*, Barrio Colinas Petroleras, T831845; *Rain Forestur*, Amazonas y Quito, celluar T09-200157, also have Quito office; *Sionatour*, 12 de febrero y 10 de agosto, T830232.

Transport **Air** The airport is 5 km southeast of the centre. TAME flies to **Quito**, daily except Sun, US$55 one way. It's best to book 1-2 days in advance, and reconfirm often. **Bus** To Quito, US$7.50, 10-11 hrs. To **Baeza**, 7 hrs. To **Coca**, 3 hrs; also many *ranchero* buses which leave when full. To **Tena**, US$8.30, 9 hrs.

Directory **Exchange** TCs are very difficult to negotiate in Lago Agrio and credit cards can only be used in the best hotels; no cash advances.

Cuyabeno Wildlife Reserve

Twenty years ago Lago Agrio was set deep in the jungle and a favourite of entomologists who came here to collect the vast array of insects attracted by the night light of the oil camps. Today, there is no virgin jungle anywhere close. It is, however, the best access for the Cuyabeno Wildlife Reserve, a huge tract of pristine rainforest covering 602,000 ha.

Down the Aguarico from Lago Agrio, Cuyabeno is an extensive jungle river area on the Río Cuyabeno, which drains eventually into the Aguarico 150 km to the east. In the Reserve there are many lagoons and a great variety of wildlife, including river dolphins, tapirs, capybaras, five species of caiman, ocelots, 15 species of monkey and over 500 species of birds. Tourist pressure has been heavy however, and it is becoming increasingly rare to see many animals close to the big lake. There are almost a dozen agencies offering trips and most take up to 12 in a group (which is too many). If your aim is to see animals, then look for a smaller tour which keeps away from the most heavily visited areas and scrupulously adheres to responsible tourism practices. ■ *Entry for foreigners is US$20 Jul-Sep, US$15 Oct-Jun. Transport is mainly by canoe and motorboat, except for one road to Río Cuyabeno, 3 hrs by truck from Lago Agrio.*

Jungle lodges & tour operators *Neotropic Turis*, operates the Grand Cuyabeno Lake lodge; cabins with private or shared baths, US$350 per person for 4 days and 3 nights, and including all meals, bilingual guides but excluding transport to and from Lago Agrio (see above) and the park entry fee. Contact: *Centro de Reservaciones Cultura (CRC)*, Robles y Reina Victoria, Quito, T/F02-558889, info@ecuadortravel.com, www.ecuadortravel.com, or *Neotropic Turis*, T521212/478016, F554902, neotropi@uio.satnet.net, ecuadorexplorer.com/neotropic *Transturi*, of Quito, Isla Pinzón 701 near Río Coca, T245055, do trips into the jungle on a floating hotel, *Flotel Orellana*, US$567 (4 nights, 3 days) per person in double cabin with fan, including all meals, guides, etc. Services and food are good. Flights extra (US$125): bus to Chiritza on the Río Aguarico, then launch to the *Flotel*. Different itineraries for different interests are available on the *Flotel*. Prices are quoted by Metropolitan Touring. They run their own excursions (3/4, 4/5, 5 night/6 day) to the Imuya and Iripari camps. Depending on length, tours involve stops at the Aguarico Base Camp and the Flotel; Imuya (220 km from Lago Agrio) involves a speedboat trip to get there, earplugs provided; it is very unspoilt, with good birdlife. Iripari, on Lake Zancudo, involves a 5 km walk, plus a paddle across the largest lake in Ecuador's Oriente; the camp itself is basic but adequate. Prices do not include the Quito-Lago Agrio air fare: low season, 4-day US$375, 5-day US$450, 6-day US$510; high season (1 January-15 March, 15 June-31 August, 1 November-31 December) 4-day US$470, 5-day US$560, 6-day US$635 (all per person, double occupancy).

Native Life, Foch E4-167 y Amazonas, Quito, T505158, F229077, natlife1@natlife. com.ec Lincoln Reyes runs tours to their Nativo Lodge in Cuyabeno Reserve. Five days/4 nights for US$240. *Jungletur*, Amazonas 854 y Veintimilla, Quito, have 6-day tours of the area. *Pacarina*, in the same Quito office as *Hostería Alandaluz* (see page 322), runs 5 day tours to a Secoya community down the Río Aguarico. There are a great many others; shop around and only use responsible agencies and guides.

Frontier with Colombia

The road to the north connects Lago Agrio with Colombia, but goes through an area which has suffered terrorist and kidnapping problems. There is regular transport to the frontier on the Río San Miguel. Crossing here is possible but neither easy nor recommended.

Leaving Ecuador
Warning: this is a dangerous border area and best avoided

Get an exit stamp from Migración in Lago Agrio before taking a bus north to **La Punta** (US$0.50, 1¼ hours), where you hand in your Tourist Card to the military and cross the bridge over the Río San Miguel to the village of **San Miguel** in Colombia (La Punta-San Miguel, one hour, US$2.65).

At the border

From there you can catch a jeep or bus (five hours) to **Puerto Asís** and on to **La Hormiga** (one hour, hotels and restaurants), then a bus to Mocoa and on to Pasto. There are DAS office and border formalities at Mocoa. A Colombian entry stamp might be obtained at the Consulate in Lago Agrio. In late 2000 the Colombian province of Putumayo was extremely dangerous due to the presence of guerrillas and paramilitaries. Unless the situation has improved dramatically, you are strongly advised not to enter Colombia here.

Into Colombia
Warning: in late 2000 this part of Colombia was extremely dangerous

At Lago Agrio, a temporary ferry crosses the Río Aguarico (bridge washed away), then the road heads south to Coca. The route from Tena via Loreto also involves a ferry crossing a few kilometres before Coca, US$2 per car.

South to Coca

Coca

Officially named Puerto Francisco de Orellana, Coca is a hot, dusty, noisy, sprawling oil town at the junction of the Ríos Coca and Napo. It is the capital of the province of Orellana. As a tourist centre it offers few attractions other than being closer to undisturbed primary rainforest than the main jungle towns further west. Hotel and restaurant provision is adequate and there are plenty of bars and discos. Considering its relative isolation, food and supplies are not that much more expensive than other, more accessible parts of the country. The town's power supply is erratic; there is usually no electricity after midnight.

Phone code: 06
Colour map 3, grid B3
Population: 15,199

The road from Lago Agrio enters from the northeast. There is also a rougher but very scenic road from Baeza or Tena, through Loreto. Most hotels are on or near the riverfront and are very convenient for the dock. It is a small town and easy to walk around. It's about a 20 minute walk to the bus terminal from *Hotel Auca*.

Although further from the Colombian border, and generally more *tranquilo* than Lago Agrio, the same general precautions apply to Coca (see Lago Agrio above). All foreigners going beyond town into the jungle have to register with the police and all guides who accompany foreigners have to be

Oriente Jungle

licensed. If going alone beyond the bridge at Coca into the jungle, you must get permission from the Ministerio de Defensa in Quito (full details from South American Explorers in Quito, page 22).

Sleeping
■ *on map*
Price codes:
see inside front cover

D *La Misión*, by riverfront, T880260, Quito contact T553674, F564675. A/c, very smart, English spoken, pool, restaurant and disco, arranges tours. Recommended. **E** *El Auca*, Napo entre Rocafurte y García Moreno, T880600. Cabins with bath, hot water, TV, comfortable, big garden with hammocks, manager speaks English, friendly, good meeting place to make up a tour party, restaurant and disco. Recommended. **E** *Amazonas*, 12 de Febrero y Espejo, T880444. Away from the centre, quiet, with restaurant. Recommended. **F** *Florida*, on main road from the airport, T880177. With fan, basic, dark rooms, clean. **G** *Oasis*, near the bridge at the end of town, T880206. Hot water and fans. Mixed reports. **G** *Lojanita*, Cuenca y Napo, T880032. With private bath, cheaper without. New rooms, clean, good. Other hotels and *residencias* are populated by oil workers and range from basic to barely inhabitable.

Eating

There are good restaurants at the larger hotels (see above). *Los Cedros*, down by the river, 2 blocks from the Capitanía. Good fish, *patacones*, *yuca*, fairly expensive. *Dragón Dorado*, Bolívar between Quito and Napo. Chinese. The set meal at *Doña Erma* is cheap and filling. *Ocaso*, Eloy Alfaro between Napo and Amazonas, set meals. *Pappa Dan's*, Napo y Chimborazo, by river. Hamburgers, chilli, tacos etc, good. *Mama Carmen*. Good for early breakfast. *Media Noche*, C Napo, in front of *Hotel El Auca*. Chicken dishes. Inexpensive. *Parrilladas Argentinas*, Cuenca y Amazonas. Grill. *El Buho*. Good food, jungle specialities such as capybara, reasonably priced.

Bars

Two friendly bars are *Riverside Bar* (formerly Papa Dan's), Chimborazo y Napo, and *Maito's*, Napo y Eloy Alfaro.

Oriente Jungle

Coca

■ Sleeping
1 Amazonas
2 El Auca & Paushi Tours
3 Florida
4 Lojanita
5 Oasis

● Eating
1 Dragón Dorado
2 Media Noche
3 Ocaso
4 Pappa Dan's
5 Parrilladas Argentinas

🚍 Buses
1 Flota Pelileo
2 Trans Baños
3 Zaracay
4 Putumayo
5 Trans Esmeraldas

Air The airport is in the north of the town, on the same road as the bus terminal. Daily to and from **Quito** with Aerogal Mon-Sat US$55 one way; reserve 48 hrs in advance and always reconfirm, planes are small and flights can be very bumpy, flights in and out of Coca are heavily booked, military and oil workers have priority on standby. Also flights to **Tena** and **Shell-Mera** from Coca. Aerogal office is at the airport. TAME office is at Napo y Rocafuerte, T881078; TAME flights suspended in late 2000, but may be resumed.

Bus To **Quito**, 10 hrs, US$10.50, several daily 1030-2200, Trans Baños and Putumayo, depart from their offices on Napo y Cuenca. To **Lago Agrio**, 3 hrs, US$3.40. To **Tena**, 6 hrs, US$6. To **Misahuallí**, 14 hrs. To **Baeza**, 8 hrs.

Boat For **passenger boats** out of Coca, ask the Capitanía at the dock; there is no more regular passenger service to Misahuallí; Nueva Rocafuerte, US$28; canoes go if there are 8 or more passengers, taking about 14 hrs, if it is not reached before nightfall, the party will camp beside the river. For a price, of course, the willing traveller can hire a canoe with owner and outboard motor to take them anywhere along the Napo.

Banks Banks won't change TCs. **Communications** Andinatel on Eloy Alfaro. 0800-1100 and 1300-1700. **Internet**: prices around US$7 per hour and access is unreliable due to poor telephone lines. Internet access is offered by hotels *Auca* and *La Misión* (see above).

Jungle tours from Coca

Most of the Coca region is taken up by the Yasuní National Park and Huaorani Reserve. This uninterrupted lowland rainforest offers excellent opportunities for a true jungle experience, but wildlife in this area is under threat and visitors should insist that guides and all members of their party take all litter back and ban all hunting and shooting; it really can make a difference.

This area is unsuited to tours of less than three days owing to the remoteness of its main attractions. Most tours, including visits to lodges, require extended periods of canoe travel there and back. Shorter visits of three to four days are worthwhile in the Coca-Yuturi segment of the Río Napo, where the lodges are concentrated. Tours to the Huaorani Reserve and Yasuní Park really need a minimum of four or five days. Trips which do not go beyond the Río Napo itself are not worth taking since you will see nothing. To see animals you should go downstream from Coca to the Río Tiputini, or south to the Río Shiripuno, or to the Cuyabeno Wildlife Reserve (see above under Lago Agrio).

NB If a guide offers a tour to visit the Huaorani, ask to see his/her permission to do so. The only guides permitted to take tourists into Huaorani territory are those who have made agreements with the Huaorani organization ONHAE.

All guides out of Coca charge about US$40-60 per person per day, but you may have to bargain down to this. At popular times it may be difficult to find a choice of worthwhile tours or English-speaking guides. You are strongly advised to check what precisely is being offered, and that the price includes equipment such as rubber boots, tents, mosquito nets, cooking equipment and food, and transport.

Note that all Napo area lodges count travel days as part of their package, which means that often a 'three-day tour' spends only one day actually in the forest. Also, keep in mind that the return trip must start before dawn if it is to connect to that day's Coca-Quito flight; if it starts later it will be necessary to spend the night in Coca. Most lodges have fixed departure days from Coca (eg Mon and Fri) and it is very expensive

Oriente Jungle

to get a special departure on another day. Ask the lodges for up-to-date departure day information before planning your trip.

La Selva is an upmarket lodge 2½ hrs downstream from Coca, professionally run, on a picturesque lake surrounded by excellent forest (especially on the far side of Mandicocha). Bird and animal life is exceptionally diverse. Many species of monkey are seen regularly. A total of 580 bird species can be found here, one of the highest totals in the world for a site at a single elevation, and some of the local guides (eg José) are very good at finding them. There is a biological station on the grounds (the Neotropical Field Biology Institute) as well as a butterfly farm. Cabins have private baths. Meals are excellent. Usually the guides are biologists, and in general the guiding is of very high quality. A new canopy tower was due to be built in 2001. Four-night packages from Quito including all transport, lodging, and food, cost US$684 per person. Quito office: 6 de Diciembre 2816, Quito, T550995, F567297, laselva@uio.satnet.net, www.laselvajunglelodge.com, or book through most tour agencies in Quito.

Sacha is another upmarket lodge close to La Selva, 2½ hrs downstream from Coca. Cabins are very comfortable, with private bath and hot water, and meals are excellent. The bird list is outstanding, and they have a local bird expert, Oscar Tapuy (T06-881486), who can be requested in advance by birders. Guides are generally knowledgeable. Boardwalks through swamp habitats allow access to some species that are difficult to see at other lodges, and nearby river islands provide another distinct habitat. They also have a butterfly farm, an exciting canopy tower and a canopy walkway. Several species of monkey are commonly seen. A 5-day package costs US$720 per person, excluding flight from Quito. Quito office: Julio Zaldumbide 375 y Toledo, Quito, T566090, F236521, sachalod@pi.pro.ec, www.sachalodge.com

Yuturi Forest Lodge is 4 hrs downstream from Coca and less expensive than La Selva or Sacha. Birdwatching is excellent, and there are some species (e.g. Black-necked Red Cotinga) that are difficult to find at the previous two lodges. There is a wide variety of habitats here, and a modest canopy tower. Wildlife is good. The

The Huaorani people

South of Coca is the homeland of the Huaorani, a forest people who traditionally lived a simple, nomadic life in the jungle as hunters and subsistence farmers. They refer to anyone living outside their communities as cohuode, meaning either 'those that cut everything to pieces' or 'people from other places/not living in the territory', and, until recently, lived in complete isolation. There are presently 18 Huaorani communities spread over a large area reaching south into Pastaza province.

Since the 1970s the Huaorani have been greatly affected by the activities of the petroleum industry and have suffered at the hands of an uncontrolled tourist trade. Both have dramatically changed their culture and disturbed their traditional village life. The Huaorani have responded to the tourist invasion by imposing tolls for the use of their rivers and entrance fees to their communities as well as demanding gifts. This latter practice has been encouraged by oil companies who have used it to their advantage when bargaining with Huaorani communities. There has even been some conflict between the indigenous people and tour guides, with violent confrontation in the past. Overall, though, tourism has had a negative effect on the Huaorani people.

Randy Smith, author of Crisis Under the Canopy, who has worked with the indigenous peoples of Ecuador on the development of ecotourism projects, states that tourism has taken a major toll in the deculturation process of the Huaorani as the guides offer gifts or cash for the use of their lands or services. He continues that the tourist dollar offers the Huaorani a chance to join the cash economy. The Huaorani visit the various centres outside their territory for food, staples and clothes and therefore require money to sustain this new way of life that many of them have chosen.

For some time, ONHAE (the Huaorani Indigenous organization) opposed tourism, but revised its position in 1992, allowing a number of ONHAE-approved guides to operate in their territory. Lately a number of communities have shown greater interest in getting involved in ecotourism, as the Huaorani have become more integrated into the money economy and are now aware of the amount of money that outside guides receive for taking tourists through their land. They would like to have more control over the tourism that comes through their area and derive more benefits from it.

guides are usually local people accompanied by translators. Four nights cost US$340, exclusive of airfare. Quito office: Amazonas 1324 y Colón, T/F504037, yuturi@yuturi.com.ec, www.yuturi.com

Cabañas Bataburo, a lodge in Parque Nacional Yasuní is on the Río Tigüino, a 3-6 hr canoe ride from the end of the Via Auca out of Coca. Two cabins have private baths, while the others share baths. There are shared shower facilities. Guides are mostly local people. The birds here have been little studied but macaws and other large species are present. The mammal population also appears to be quite good. Prices are US$295 for 5 days/4 nights; cabin with private bath US$20 additional. Quito office: Kempery Tours, Pinto 539 y Amazonas, T226715, kempery@ecuadorexplorer.com, www.ecuadorexplorer.com/kempery/home

Añangucocha is a facility being built in 2000 by and for the local Añangu community, across the Napo from La Selva, 2½ hrs downstream from Coca. This area of hilly forest is rather different from the low flat forest of some other sites, and the diversity is slightly higher. There are big caimans, good mammals, including Giant Otters, and the birding is excellent. The local guide, Giovanny Rivadeneyra, is one of the most knowledgeable birders in the Oriente. Facilities are basic at present, palm-thatch huts and an outhouse, but the price is very low compared to the big-name lodges (US$27 per day) and most of the money goes directly to the community. More elaborate facilities and a

Oriente Jungle

canopy tower are planned. For more information contact Chris Canaday, Quito T447463, canaday@accessinter.net Bookings through Cecilia, Coca T881486.

Sani Isla is another lodge near La Selva. All proceeds go to the Sani Isla community, who run the lodge with the help of outside experts. It is located on a remote lagoon which seems to contain the nearly extinct Amazonian Manatee (droppings were reported from here) and also has 12-15 ft long Black Caiman. This area is rich in wildlife and birds. Good accommodation were being built in 2000 and an effort has been made to make the lodge accessible to people who have difficulty walking; the lodge can be reached by canoe (total 4 hrs from Coca) without a walk. A canopy tower is planned. US$95 per night. Contact c/o elmontelodge@hotmail.com

Pañacocha is located halfway between Coca and Nuevo Rocafuerte, nearby is the magnificent lagoon of Pañacocha on the Río Panayacu. This has been declared a protected forest region. Canadian Randy Smith (contact through River Dolphin Expeditions in Coca) is working on a management plan for the area in order to ensure that the local Quichua community get the best out of tourism. Several agencies and guides run tours from Coca (see above). Accommodation is available at **G** *Pensión*, in Pañacocha. Friendly, but watch out for chiggers in the mattresses.

Tiputini Biodiversity Station is far from any settlement and has experienced very little hunting, not even by native people. The result is the best site in Ecuador for observing the full range of Amazonian wildlife and birds. Facilities are extremely well designed and merge into the forest; the canopy tower and canopy walkway are exceptional. Food is good. It is a scientific station, not a tourist facility, and potential visitors must form or join an educational group and receive approval in advance; services are oriented towards scientists. Spider monkeys, curassows, large macaws, large raptors and other threatened wildlife are more common and more confiding here than at most other sites, and this is the best place in Ecuador for jaguar (but you still have to be lucky to see one). If you would like to join an educational workshop contact Carol Walton, USA T1-512-2630830, F1-512-2632721, tiputini@aol.com Scientists wishing to do research should contact tbs@mail.usfq.edu.ec

Hacienda Primavera is 2 hrs downstream from Coca in an area with little wildlife. There are clean, basic rooms **G**, or you can camp (US$0.50). Meals available. Excursions from here are not cheap, however; agree all prices carefully in advance.

Tour operators & guides A common misconception is that it is always easy to find a cheap tour in Coca. For people travelling alone in the low season (especially February to May) it is difficult to find a big enough group to get a bargain rate. Most jungle tours out of Coca cost US$30-$50 per person per day. Furthermore, you should beware of cut-rate operators who may compromise on safety, quality or responsible practices. The following operators and guides have been recommended, and there are many others.

Safari offers 4-day all-inclusive trips with the Huaorani; responsible practices, contributions made to the community. Quito office: Calama 380 y JL Mera, T552505, F223381, admin@safari.com.ec, www.safari.com.ec *Emerald Forest Expeditions*, Amazonas 1023 y Pinto, 2nd Flr, Quito, T/F541543, T526403 (ext 13). Guide Luis Alberto García has many years experience, speaks English, and runs tours to the Pañacocha area. Recommended. *Tropic Ecological Adventures*, Av República 307 y Almagro, Edif Taurus, Dpto 1-A, Quito, T225907, F560756, tropic@uio.satnet.net Runs ecologically-sound tours with local and bilingual naturalist guides, and work closely with Cofan, Secoya and Huaorani communities. Highly recommended. *Jumandy Explorers*, Wilson 718 y JL Mera, T220518/551205, Quito. Guide Isaias Cerda is an indigenous Quichua, very knowledgeable, speaks some English, does trips on the Río

Arajuno. *Ejarsytur*, opposite *Hotel Oasis*, T887142, in Quito at Santa Prisca 260 y 10 de Agosto, T583120. Run by the Jarrín family, German and English spoken, US$40 per person per day, recommended. *Etnoturismo Amasanga Supay*, an indigenous Quichua co-operative which offers a variety of trips and which helps local communities. They are opposite the Capitanía at the port, or contact César Andi at *Hotel Oasis*.

Recommended guides are Klever and Braulio Llori, T880487. Also Wymper Torres, T880336, or speak to his sister, Mady in Quito, T659311. He specializes in the Río Shiripuno and Pañacocha areas, speaks Spanish only. Carlos Sevilla runs tours of 5-15 days in the Huaorani Reserve and Parque Nacional Yasuní, small groups of 3-6, speaks Spanish only but recommended. Contact through *Hotel Auca* in Coca, or through his family in Quito, T244205.

Coca to Nuevo Rocafuerte

An irregular canoe service (best to hire your own) passes Coca carrying passengers and cargo downriver to **Limoncocha**, the Capuchin mission at **Pompeya** with a school and museum of Napo culture, **Pañacocha** (see Jungle lodges, above) and on to **Nuevo Rocafuerte**, on the border with Peru. Canoes from Nuevo Rocafuerte return to Coca.

The Laguna de Limoncocha is an excellent spot for birding. The area was once used by Metropolitan Touring, until 1991, but they moved on and left the cabaña complex to the local villagers, who have created a Biological Reserve. The facilities are beautifully situated, overlooking the lagoon.

Nearby is the **Pompeya Capuchin mission**, on the left bank of the river, about two hours downriver from Coca. Upriver from Pompeya is **Monkey Island**. You can rent a canoe to visit the small island with free-roaming monkeys.

The end of the line is Nuevo Rocafuerte, where the missionaries and Sra Jesús let rooms. There are no restaurants. It is possible to hire a boat and guide in Nuevo Rocafuerte, but it would be unwise to add tourism to the pressures to which the Huaorani Indians are already subjected by the oil industry.

There is a boat from Coca to Nuevo Rocafuerte but you must get a military permit to enter the area. The officer has to write exactly the area you wish to visit and you have to leave your passport. The boat takes eight hours (hammocks provided). There is a cargo boat back on Monday, but it doesn't always run and you may have to wait until Friday. To Coca it is a 2½-day ferry ride (US$9) with an overnight stop at Sinchichieta and a meal stop at Pañacocha. It is not yet possible to cross from Nuevo Rocafuerte into Peru, but this border might be opened now that the border dispute between the two countries has been resolved.

Archidona

Roads from both Baeza and Coca go south to Archidona, 65 km from Baeza. Founded in 1560, at the same time as Tena, 10 km to the south, this was an important mission and trading centre. The small painted church is striking and said to be a replica of one in Italy (possibly in Sienna). The plaza, once planted with tall, shady trees, has been 'renovated', leaving a rather boring and shade-free replacement. The gas station to the north of town rarely has petrol. Next door is the only handicrafts store in town, which sells feathered stuff, as well as some interesting local medicines, spears, *shigras*, basket work and endangered animal skins (which it is illegal to take out of the country).

AL *Orchid Paradise*, 2 km north of town, T889232, Quito T526223. Cabins in nice secondary forest with lots of birds. Meals not included, restaurant on site. **E** *Residencial*   **Sleeping & eating**

Oriente Jungle

Regina, Rocafuerte 446, T889144. Modern, clean, cheaper without bath, pleasant and friendly. Recommended. *Hostal Archidona*, hidden down a back street, 5 blocks south of the plaza. There are few decent places to eat, though *Restaurant Los Pinos*, near *Residencial Regina*, is good.

Excursions from Archidona

Orchid Paradise owns a private forest reserve, 45 minutes from Archidona by car. The site has many rare birds like the Reddish-winged Bare-eye, various flatbills, and the Striated Antbird (known in Ecuador only from this site). See contact information under Sleeping and eating above.

The road leaving the plaza to the east goes 10 km to an old bridge over the Río Hollín and on to the access for the **Parque Nacional Sumaco-Napo-Galeras**. To enter the park you must have a guide and permission, entry US$5.

Tours can be arranged by special arrangement to the **Izu Mangallpa Urcu (IMU) Foundation**, 3 km east of town off a side turning down the road to Galeras, set up by the Mamallacta family to protect territory on Galeras mountain. They have started work on a women's healing centre, for which they have received some foreign aid, to work with local women on traditional medicines. They charge US$35 per day for accommodation and day trips, taking groups of eight to 10; US$65 per day for five days' trekking, groups of two minimum. It's tough going but the forest is wonderful. Ask around or book through *Safari Tours* in Quito (see page 133).

Just outside Archidona, to the south, a small turning leads to the river. About 200 m along there is a large rock with many petroglyphs carved on its surface. There are quite a few others within a 30 km radius of Archidona, but most are very difficult to find. These precolumbian petroglyphs are unique to this area. The symbols depict mysterious stories and messages whose meanings are no longer known by the local Quichua people.

Tena

Phone code: 06
Colour map 3, grid C1
Population: 13,790

Seventy-five kilometres south of Baeza, is Tena, the capital of Napo Province. Once one of the important early colonial missionary and trading posts of the Amazon, it is now a commercial centre with a plaza overlooking the confluence of the Ríos Tena and Pano. Along the rivers are several popular sand and pebble beaches. There is a beautiful riverside walk starting down the steps behind town.

The road from the north passes the airstrip and market and heads through the town centre as Avenida 15 de Noviembre on its way to the bus station, nearly 1 km south of the river. Tena is quite spread out. There is a pedestrian bridge which links the two halves of the town. The tourist office is located at Bolívar y García Moreno, near the market at the north end of town.

Tena has a large lowland Quichua Indian population living in the vicinity, some of whom are panning for gold in the rivers. These Indians are unlike the Indian groups further into the Oriente forests, they are Quijos, of Chibcha stock. Despite external pressure from the ever-encroaching modern world, many of these communities have maintained their distinct ethnicity, mythologies and customs. The Tena area, which lacks the pristine jungle found deeper in the Oriente, has instead developed interesting and worthwhile opportunities for ethno-tourism.

Sleeping
■ *on map*
Price codes:
see inside front cover
The water supply
in most cheaper
hotels is poor

C *Establo de Tomás*, via a San Antonio, 20 min out of town, T886318. Cabins on river shore, clean, friendly. Good restaurant. **C** *Puma Rosa*, on Malecón near vehicle bridge, T/F886320. With a/c, TV, private bath, hot water, nice grounds, parking. **C** *Los Yutzos*, at the south end of town overlooking the Río Pano. Clean, comfortable, beautiful grounds, family-run. **D** *Mol*, Sucre 432, T886215. With bath, clean, garage. Recommended. **D** *Hostal Turismo Amazónico*, Amazonas y Abdón Calderón, T886487. With

Oriente Jungle

bath, TV, fan, fridge, parking. **E** *Caribe*, 15 de Noviembre y Eloy Alfaro, T886518. **E** *Hostal Indiana*, Bolívar, between Amazonas and García Moreno, T886334. Private bath, hot water, TV, restaurant for breakfast only. Tour agency for jungle trips. **E** *Hostal Traveler's Lodging*, 15 de Noviembre 422, T886372, F886015. Basic, clean, helpful, cheaper with cold shower, good food, friendly, run by *Amarongachi Tours* (see Tour operators below). **E** *Hostal Villa Belén*, on Baeza road (Av Jumandy), north of town, T886228. Friendly, clean, cold shower, quiet. Recommended. **E** *Media Noche*, 15 de Noviembre 1125, near the bus station, T886490. With bath, cheaper without, good, clean, inexpensive restaurant. **E** *Residencial Alemana*, Díaz de Pineda 210 y Av 15 de Noviembre, T886409. OK, fairly clean, cold water only, **D** for cabin. **E** *Vista Hermosa*, 15 de Noviembre 622, T886521.

Tena

To Hostal Villa Belén (200m), Hotel Auca (1 km), Archidona, Coca & Quito

Oriente Jungle

■ **Sleeping**
1 Camba Huasi & Ríos Ecuador Office
2 Caribe
3 Hostal Indiana
4 Hostal Traveller's Lodging
5 Hostal Turismo Amazónico

6 Jumandy
7 Media Noche
8 Mol
9 Puma Rosa
10 Residencial Alemana
11 Residencial Nápoli

12 Yutzos

● **Eating**
1 Chuquitos
2 Cositas Ricas
3 Pollo Good

F *Jumandy*, Amazonas y Abdón Calderón, T886329. Clean, friendly, balcony, breakfast from 0600, the Cerda family also arrange jungle tours for US$25 per person per day (see Jungle tours below). **F** *Residencial Laurita*, opposite the bus terminal. Shared bath, basic. **F** *Residencial Nápoli*, Díaz de Pineda 147, T886194. Fan, shared bath, parking, friendly. **G** *Hostal Camba Huasi*, near the bus terminal, T887429. Basic but clean. **G** *Hostal Limoncocha*, Ita 533, on the hill, 300 m from the bus terminal, T887583, welschingerm@yahoo.de Five rooms, 1 with bath, others shared, laundry and kitchen facilities, terrace with hammocks, breakfast and drinks available, parking. German-Ecuadorean run, clean, friendly and relaxed. Also organizes tours.

Eating *Cositas Ricas*, 15 de Noviembre, next to *Hostal Traveler's Lodging*. Tasty meals, vege-
● *on map, page 373* tarian available, good fruit juices, run by Patricia Corral of *Amarongachi Tours*. *Chuquitos*, García Moreno by Plaza. Popular. *Pollo Good*, 15 de Noviembre 1 block north of bus terminal. Tasty chicken. *El Toro Asado*, on the left arriving from Archidona. Good *almuerzo*. There are also *chifas* in town.

Tour operators *Amarongachi Tours* (see *Hostal Traveler's Lodging* above for address and phone; see also Jungle tours below). *Ríos Ecuador*, 15 de Noviembre y 9 de Octubre, T887438, Quito T553727, info@riosecuedor.com Gynner Coronel runs highly recommended white-water rafting and kayak trips and a 5-day kayak school. See also Rafting, on page 73. *Voyages Fantastic*, opposite bus station. *Kanoa Tours*, 15 de Noviembre, opposite Cositas Ricas. *Ecoindiana*, inside *Hostal Indiana* (see above). *Limoncocha*, at *Hostal Limoncocha*. Rafting US$35 and jungle trips US$25 per person per day, German spoken.

Transport **Air** Flights to Shell-Mera (see page 380). You can take short flights over the jungle canopy in a superlight plane, 1 person at a time; contact Jorge through *Ríos Ecuador* (see Tour operators above).

Bus To **Quito**, regular service via Baeza, 0200-2345, US$4.50, 5 hrs, book in advance. To **Baeza**, 2 hrs. To **Ambato**, via Baños, 10 daily, US$5, 5 hrs. To **Baños**, 4-5 hrs, US$3.25. To **Riobamba**, via Puyo and Baños, 6 daily from 0200, 5-6 hrs, US$4.50. To **Archidona** every 20 mins, US$0.20, 15 mins. To **Misahuallí**, hourly, US$0.70, 45 mins, buses leave from the local bus station not the long distance terminal. To **Coca**, 6 hrs, US$6, 8 daily 0600-2200. To **Lago Agrio**, with Jumandy at 1830, 9 hrs, US$8.30. To **Puyo**, 3-4 hrs. To **Ahuano** hourly 0700-1800.

Directory **Communications** Andinatel: Olmedo y Juan Motalvo. **Internet**: *Tena Systems*, Bolívar y García Moreno. *Piraña Net*, 9 de Octubre y Tarqui. *Yacu Runa Net*, 15 de Noviembre y Rueda.

Excursions The numerous limestone caves of the Tena area are of special significance to
from Tena the Quichua. Caves are generally feared and respected and are seldom entered by local people. The intrepid tourist who dares to defy local beliefs can visit the famous **Jumandí caves**, 5-6 km north of Archidona. Take a taxi, or bus from Archidona; 30 minutes. It is necessary to go with a guide. Also take good boots, a strong torch and spare batteries. It is very muddy (sometimes full of water) so it can be useful to take spare clothes. The side ducts of the caves are extremely narrow and claustrophobic. There are several colonies of vampire bat (*Desmodus rotundus*) in the caves. A tourist complex has been built with swimming pool, waterslide and restaurant. The pool and the caves are always open but the other facilities usually only at weekends and holidays.

The cave complex is large and several of the entrances are on private land. In an attempt to preserve some of the caves from stalactite thieves and graffiti artists, some of the landowners have denied access to the caves on their land. The caves are subject to flash flooding in the rainy season and care should be taken when entering beyond the first chamber. Before going, make full enquiries about routes and conditions.

Sumaco Volcano can be climbed from Tena. It is an extremely long, difficult
expedition because of the steepness and dense vegetation. But the trek allows
you to enjoy stunning views of the surrounding rainforest. Expect to take five
to six days. Contact Don Francisco in Huamani on the new Tena-Coca road.

Trips are organized to **Amarongachi** by Jesús Uribe at *Amarongachi Tours*, 15
de Noviembre 422, T/F886372. Highly recommended. This co-operative travel
agency works closely with local people, and also runs a hotel and restaurant (see
Sleeping and Eating above). You can stay in the *Shangri-La* cabins south of Río
Jatunyacu, or with an indigenous family; US$30 per person per day.

Comunidad Capirona is one hour by bus, then three hours on foot from
Tena. Visits can be arranged here or to nine other communities in the area,
US$30-40 per person per day. This is part of a highly regarded project which
combines eco/ethno-tourism and community development. There are also
opportunities for volunteers. Contact the *Red Indigena de las Comunidades del
Alto Napo para la Convivencia Intercultural y El Ecoturismo (Ricancie)*, 15 de
Noviembre 722, T/F887072, ricancie@ecuanex.net.ec

The **Cerda family** provide tours of various lengths, camping or staying in
cabañas. Tours focus on local indigenous life and cost US$25 per person per
day. They also offer rafting trips on the Río Jatunyacu (US$40 per person
including meal and equipment) and one day motorized canoe tours from
Misahuallí to Ahuano (US$30 per person). You must call from Quito to let
them know when you're leaving so they can meet you at the terminal in Tena;
T886250/887181. Both Olmedo and Oswaldo (son) are recommended guides
and speak German as well as Spanish. You can also contact them through
Hotel Jumandy in Tena, see above.

Sr Delfín Pauchi, T886434/886088, Casilla 245, Tena, has built *Cabañas
Pimpilala*, 45 minutes by taxi from Tena, where for two to four days you can live
with a Quichua family for US$35 per person per day, including lodging, meals,
transport and guide. Trails for hiking have been made on his 30 ha of undeveloped land, but emphasis is on culture rather than wildlife. Delfín speaks only
Quichua and Spanish. He knows about plants and their medicinal uses, legends
and music. He will meet you at the terminal in Tena if you call ahead. Also contact through *Naturgal* in Quito, Reina Victoria y Foch, T522681.

Also, *Hacienda Jatún Yacu*, a family farm in the rainforest, is excellent. Contact through *Ríos Ecuador* (see above) or *Safari Tours* in Quito (see page 133).

From Tena the main highway runs south towards Puyo (curiously, only the
northbound lane is paved). **Puerto Napo**, a few kilometres south of Tena, has
a bridge across the Río Napo. Pato García, a guide, has a good room to rent, **G**.
On the north bank a road runs east to Misahuallí, about 17 km downstream.
From Puerto Napo you can catch a local bus from Tena to Misahuallí. If you're
travelling north from Puyo, avoid going into Tena by getting off the bus here.

Misahuallí

This small port at the junction of the Napo and Misahuallí rivers was once the *Phone code: 06*
westernmost access for navigation on the Río Napo and very important *Colour map 3, grid C2*
because of the lack of roads. Its decline as a port began with the opening of the *Population: 3,579*
Loreto road to Coca. Fortunately for Misahuallí the tourist trade was already
established, and as commerce declined, tourism replaced it. Now, the town is
almost totally devoted to tourism.

The near Oriente Misahuallí is perhaps the best place in Ecuador from which to visit the 'near Oriente', but your expectations should be realistic. The area has been colonized for many years and there is no extensive virgin forest nearby (except at Jatun Sacha, see below). Access is very easy however, prices are reasonable, and while you will not encounter large animals in the wild, you can still see birds, butterflies and exuberant vegetation – enough to get a taste for the jungle. There is a fine, sandy beach on the Río Misahuallí, but don't camp on it as the river can rise unexpectedly.

Sleeping **AL** *Jardín Alemán*, on the shores of the Río Misahuallí, several kilometres from town, access is along a road north before you reach Misahuallí. Suites and rooms with hot water, fan, terraces. In a pleasant garden setting. Tours, Spanish school. **A** *Misahuallí Jungle Hotel*, across the river from town. Cabins for up to 6, nice setting, pool, friendly, restaurant operates sporadically, packages available. Quito office: Ramírez Dávalos 251 y Páez, T520043, F504872, miltour@accessinter.net, www.miltour.com **D** *El Albergue Español*, on J Arteaga. All rooms with bath, clean and screened with balconies overlooking the Napo. Good expensive restaurant. Recommended. Also operates *Hotel Jaguar* jungle lodge (see below). Quito office: Eloy Alfaro 3147 y CJ Arosemena, T453703, F466911, alb-esp@uio.satnet.net **D** *France Amazonia*, on road from Tena across from high school, Tena F887499, france_amazonia@hotmail.com Small rooms (not for tall people), with private bath. Includes good breakfast. French run, friendly and helpful.

E *El Paisano*, on G Rivadeneyra. Private bath, hot water. Meals only for groups. Pleasant atmosphere. **F** *Marena Inn*, on Juan Arteaga, Tena T/F887584. Private bath, cold water, fan. **F** *La Posada*, Napo opposite the plaza. With bath, restaurant. Renovated rooms. **F** *Shaw*, Santander on Plaza, ecoselva@yahoo.es Simple rooms with private bath, cheaper without. Operate their own tours, English spoken. Very friendly and knowledgeable. Recommended. **F** *Granilandia*, on Santander at entrance to town, Quito T350256, F350873. Private bath, cold water, fan. Operated by the military on a former base. Unusual but friendly. Good views. **G** *Hostal Casa Eduardo*, Napo 3 blocks form park in private house (no sign, ask), Quito T254950. Clean, with fan, shared bath with electric shower, use of kitchen, book exchange. **H** *Sacha*, by beach. Basic but OK. Good location (take insect repellent). **H** *Balcón del Napo*, J Arteaga on Plaza. Basic, clean and friendly.

Eating
There are a handful of general stores well stocked with basic supplies
Doña Gloria, Arteaga y Rivadeneyra by corner of plaza. Open 0730-2030 daily. Very good set meals. Recommended. *Le Peroquet Bleu*, Santander y Napo by corner of plaza. A la carte. Slightly upmarket, not cheap. Also upmarket is the restaurant at *Albergue Español* (see above). *Bar Atarraya*, at the end of Santander. Good atmosphere. *La Posada*, at the Plaza. Varied à la carte menu, nice porch setting, slow service.

Transport **Bus** Local buses run from the plaza to Tena every 45 mins 0745-1800, US$0.50, 1 hr. Make all long distance connections in Tena, or get off at Puerto Napo to catch southbound buses although you may not get a seat.

Boat With the increase in roads, river traffic is diminishing along the upper Napo. All scheduled passenger service from Misahuallí has been discontinued. Motorized canoes wait at the beach and can be hired for touring (but better to go with a guide) or transport to the location of your choice.

Excursions from Misahuallí
Always wear rubber boots when walking in this area
A good walk is along the **Río Latas**, 7 km west of Misahuallí, where there are some small waterfalls. You walk through dense vegetation for about 1½ hours, often muddy, to get to the largest fall where you can bathe. To get there catch the bus towards Tena and ask to get off by the river at the metal bridge, the third one out of Misahuallí. On the west shore of the river a short path leads to a commercial bathing area, popular with locals. On the east shore, the longer and more difficult trail described above leads to the falls.

Oriente Jungle

A strenuous day trip can be made to **Palmeras**. Take the road north and cross the bridge over the Río Misahuallí, a muddy road (rubber boots essential) goes through fields skirting the jungle. There are many birds in this area. Palmeras, a friendly village with no services (take food and water), is reached after about three hours. Continue to a patch of primary forest where there are side trails. If you are lucky, and quiet, you may see monkeys.

There is a *mariposario* (butterfly farm) 15 minutes downstream from Misahuallí on the north shore of the Río Napo. Several colourful species can be observed and photographed close up. Interesting. Make arrangements through *Ecoselva* (see Tour operators below).

Jungle tours from Misahuallí

There are many guides available to take parties into the jungle for trips of one to 10 days, all involving canoeing and varying amounts of hiking. Travellers should ask to see a guide's licence (we have received reports of unlicensed guides cheating tourists). Try to pay part of the cost on completion of the trip. The going rate is between US$25 and US$40 per person per day, depending on the season, size of group and length of trip. This should include food and rubber boots, which are absolutely essential.

Tour operators

Cruceros y Expediciones Dayuma, run tours to their ecological reserve, 15 mins by canoe plus a 4-hr walk from Misahuallí, with accommodation in bungalows with baths, hammocks and restaurant. They can also organize longer trips. Guides include Douglas and Wilfred Clarke, who speak English. Office on J Arteaga on the plaza and in Quito: Av 10 de Agosto 3815 y Mariana de Jesús, edif Villacis Pazos, #301, T564924/664490, dayuma@hoy.net

Ecoselva, Santander on the plaza, ecoselva@yahoo.es Recommended guide Pepe Tapia speaks English and has a biology background. Trips from 1-6 days. Well organized and reliable.

Viajes y Aventuras Amazónicas, on the plaza. Friendly, good food.

Guides

The following guides have all been recommended. *Pepe Tapia González* speaks English and is recommended as honest and knowledgeable (see *Ecoselva* above). *Héctor Fiallos*, contact via *Sacha Hotel* on the beach (see above), Quito T239044 or Tena T740002.

Marcos Estrada is knowledgeable, honest and offers tours of different lengths. Contact *France Amazonia* office on plaza or enquire at the hotel (see above). *Jaime Recalde* is interesting on fauna and flora and offers good meals; contact him at *Balcón del Napo* (see above).

Oriente Jungle

Sócrates Nevárez, runs well-organized 1-10 day tours including trips further down the Río Napo; PO Box 239, Tena. *Carlos Herbert Licuy Licuy*, locally born, is good on history, legends and culture of the area. *Alfredo Andrade*, speaks English; T584965.

Jungle lodges on the upper Napo **B** *Anaconda*, on Anaconda Island in the Río Napo, about 1 hr down river by canoe from Misahuallí. It consists of 10 bungalows of bamboo and thatch, with space for about 48 guests, no electric lights, but flush toilets and cold showers. The meals are good. Canoe and hiking trips arranged, guides only speak Spanish.

Opposite, on the north bank at **Ahuano**, is **A** per person *Casa del Suizo*. Swiss/Ecuadorean-owned, price includes all meals, buffet meals only which cater for vegetarians, every room has a private bath, 24 hr electricity, pool, animal sanctuary, trips arranged. Highly recommended for hospitality and location. For further information contact their office at Julio Zaldumbide 375 y Toledo, Quito, T566090, F236521, sachalod@pi.pro.ec, www.casadelsuizo.com

The south shore of the Napo has road access from Tena, with frequent bus service. Along this road are several hotels, including **C** *Isla Amazonica*, near **Venecia**, Baños T03-740609. Rustic cabins on riverfront, with private bath, hot water. Meals available.

C per person *Hotel Jaguar*, 1½ hrs downstream from Misahuallí, congenial atmosphere, includes meals, vegetarian available. Tours arranged. Operated by *El Albergue Español*, see Misahuallí hotels above. **AL** per person *Yachana Lodge*, is based in the indigenous village of Mondaña, 2 hrs downstream from Misahuallí. All proceeds from the lodge go towards supporting community development projects. The lodge is comfortable, has 10 double rooms and family cabins and solar power. US$10 extra for a private cabin. *Yachana* offers highly recommended packages which include transport from Quito, all meals, lodging and guides; US$425 for 5 days. Quito office: Francisco Andrade Marín 188 y Diego de Almagro, Quito, T237278, F220362, dtm@pi.pro.ec

Jatun Sacha Eight kilometres downriver from Misahuallí, reached by road or river, is the **Jatun Sacha Biological Station** ('big forest' in Quichua), a reserve set aside for environmental education, field research, community extension and ecotourism. The biological station and the adjacent Aliñahui project together conserve 1,300 ha of tropical wet forest. So far, 507 birds, 2,500 plants and 765 butterfly species have been identified at Jatun Sacha. They offer excursions with good views and walking on a well-developed trail system.

Lodging is at **A** per person *Cabañas Aliñahui*. Eight cabins with 2 bedrooms and bath, lush tropical garden, rainforest and nature trails. Includes 3 delicious meals in the dining hall. US$6 for entrance only. Profits contribute to conservation of the area's rainforest. Quito office: *Fundación Jatun Sacha*, Pasaje Eugenio de Santillán N34-248 y Maurian, T432246, F453583, alinahui@jatunsacha.org, www.jatunsacha.org

Puyo

Phone code: 03
Colour map 5, grid A2
Population: 15,563

The capital of the province of Pastaza is the largest centre in the whole Oriente. It feels more like a small lowland city anywhere, rather than a typical jungle town. Visits can nonetheless be made to nearby forest reserves and tours deeper into the jungle can also be arranged from Puyo. It is the junction for road travel into the northern and southern Oriente, and for traffic heading to or from Ambato via Baños. The road from Macas enters from the southeast, the road to Tena leaves to the north. The Sangay and Altar volcanoes can occasionally be seen from town.

The *Ministerio de Turismo* office is in the Centro Shopping Carmelita, fourth floor, Ceslao Marín y 9 de Octubre. ■ *Mon-Fri 0900-1700.* There is a second tourist office, which is friendly and helpful, run by the *Consejo Provincial.* They are moving, so ask around for the address.

The **Museo Etno-Arqueológico**, Atahualpa y 9 de Octubre, third floor, has a small collection of artefacts. ■ *Mon-Fri 1000-1230 and 1400-1700, US$0.50.*

A *Hostería Safari*, outside town at Km 5 on the road to Tena, T885465. Includes breakfast. Ample grounds. Peaceful. **D** *Gran Hotel Amazónico*, Ceslao Marín y Atahualpa, T883094. Private bath, hot water, TV, fan. Restaurant downstairs. Nice. **D** *Hostería Turingia*, Ceslao Marín 294, T885180, F885384, turingia@punto.net.ec Private bath, hot water, garden, small pool, restaurant. Comfortable. Older rooms cheaper. **E** *El Araucano*, Ceslao Marín 576, T883834. Private bath, hot water, TV, restaurant, stores luggage. Includes breakfast, cheaper without. Clean and friendly. **E** *Los Cofanes*, 27 de Febrero 6-29 y Ceslao Marín, T885560, F884791, loscofanes@yahoo.com Private bath, hot water, TV, fan. Modern. **E** *Cristhian's*, Atahualpa between 9 de Octubre and 27 de Febrero, T/F883081. Large modern rooms with private bath, hot water, TV. **E** *Majestic Inn*, Ceslao Marín y Villamil, T885417. Private bath, hot water, clean, TV. **F** *Chasi*, 9 de Octubre y Orellana, T883059. Clean, basic. **G** *California*, 9 de Octubre 1354, T885189. Private bath, cold water. Centrally located and noisy. **G** *Hostal El Colibrí*, C Manabí between Bolívar and Galápagos, T883054. Away from centre, private bath, cold water, parking. Clean, modern, friendly, good value. Recommended. **G** *Rizzo*, 9 de Octubre y Bolívar, T883279. Private bath, cold water. Modern, good value. **G** *El Cafecito*, 27 de Febrero y Ceslao Marín, T885267. Private bath, cold water. Basic.

Mesón Europeo, Mons Alberto Zambrano, near the bus station. Upmarket dining. The restaurants in *Turingia* and *Gran Hotel Amazonico* are reliable. *Casa Verde*, Azuay y Cotopaxi in Barrio Obrero. Good quality. Not cheap. *Rincón Chileno*, in *Hotel El Araucano*. Good grill. *Pizzería Buon Giorno*, in a small shopping arcade at 9 de Octubre y Orellana. Good pizza and salads. Mid-range prices. Pleasant atmosphere. Popular. Recommended. *Rincón de Suecia*, at the end of 9 de Octubre. Pizza. *Chifa China*, 9 de Octubre y 24 de Mayo. Clean. *Mistral*, Atahualpa y 9 de Octubre. Set meals. *Sal y*

Sleeping
■ *on map*
Price codes:
see inside front cover

Eating
● *on maps*
Price categories:
see inside front cover

Oriente Jungle

Puyo

To La Casa Verde Restaurant (1.5 km) & Omaere Reserve

To Tena

C 4 de Enero

Río Puyo Yacu

C Sucre

C Bolívar

Av 20 de Julio

Av Manabí

C Ceslao Marín

C 27 de Febrero

C 9 de Octubre

C 10 de Agosto

C Bolívar

J Vargas

Gral Villamil

C Francisco de Orellana

Centro de Cómputo Amazonas

Organización de Pueblos Indígenas de Pastaza

Museo Etno-Arqueológico

Casa de Cambios Puyo

C Atahualpa

C Jacinto Dávila

Market

C 24 de Mayo

To Bus Terminal, Shell-Mera, Baños & Ambato

To Macas

N

0 metres 200
0 yards 200

■ **Sleeping**
1 Araucano
2 California
3 Chasi
4 Colibrí
5 Cristhian's

6 El Cafecito
7 Gran Hotel Amazónico & Majestic Inn
8 Los Cofanes
9 Rizzo
10 Turingia

● **Eating**
1 Pizzería Buon Giorno
2 Rincón de Suecia
3 Sal y Pimienta

Pimienta, Atahualpa y 27 de Febrero. Grilled meats. Cheap and popular. *Cafetería Panadería Susanita*, Ceslao Marín y Villamil. Bakery, also serves breakfast and lunch.

Bars & nightclubs At Barrio Obrero, along the river on the road north to Tena, are several bars and discos in a pleasant setting. *Disco Caribe 2000*, Sucre y 9 de Octubre downstairs, popular with local troops from the military base at Shell.

Shopping There are many well stocked shops for supplies. *Amazonía Touring*, Atahualpa y 9 de Octubre, has a good selection of local crafts. There is also a craft shop at *OPIP*, 9 de Octubre y Atahualpa.

Tour operators *Amazonía Touring*, Atahualpa y 9 de Octubre, T883219. Operates 1-5 day visits to nearby reserves and Indian communities. US$40 per person per day. The *Organización de Pueblos Indígenas de Pastaza (OPIP)* operates *Papangu Tours*, 9 de Octubre y Orellana, T883875. One to six day jungle trips, US$40-$50 per person per day. *Entsa Tours*, PO Box 16-01-856, T885500. Recommended for tours into the jungle, Mentor Marino is helpful and knowledgeable.

Transport **Air** There are military flights from Shell to Quito and villages deep in the Oriente. These are generally not open to foreigners. Also two commercial flights a week to Quito (see Shell, below).

Bus The new Terminal Terrestre on the outskirts of town, on the Shell-Mera and Baños road in the southwest, a 10-15 min walk from the centre. To **Baños**, US$1.50, 2 hrs. To **Ambato**, US$2, 3 hrs. To **Quito**, US$2.75, 6 hrs via Ambato (9 hrs via Baeza, US$3.50). To **Tena**, US$1.50, 3 hrs on a rough road. To **Macas**, US$4, 6 hrs. To **Riobamba**, US$1.60, 5 hrs.

Directory **Banks** *Casa de Cambios Puyo*, Atahualpa y 9 de Octubre, T/F883064. 3% commission for US$ TCs. Also other currencies, cash only. Helpful and friendly. **Communications** Andinatel, Villamil y Orellana. Long lineups. **Internet:** *Centro de Cómputo Amazonas*, Atahualpa 2000 y 9 de Octubre, 2nd floor, US$5 per hour, no Net2Phone. **Post Office** 27 de Febrero between Atahualpa and Orellana.

Excursions from Puyo **Omaere** is a 15.6 ha ethnobotanical reserve located 2 km north of Puyo on the road to Tena. It offers 1½ hour guided tours with indigenous experts, US$4 per person. There are examples of different traditional dwellings and a botanical garden with plants used by native people. You can swim nearby in the Río Puyo. Contact: Fundación Omaere, T883001, admin@omaere.ecuanex.net.ec, www.ecuanex.apc.org/omaere

There are other small private reserves of varying quality in the Puyo area and visits are arranged by local tour operators (see above). You cannot however expect to see large tracts of undisturbed primary jungle here. Sites include: **Criadero de Vida Silvestre Fátima**, 9 km north on the road to Tena, which attempts to 'rehabilitate' captive jungle animals, entry US$2; **Jadín Botánico La Orquideas**, 3 km south on the road to Macas, with orchids and other tropical plants; **Fundación Ecologica Hola Vida**, 27 km from Puyo near **Porvenir**, which offers rustic accommodation in the forest, and a 30-minute canoe trip.

Puyo to Baños The road from Puyo to Baños is a spectacular journey with superb views of the Pastaza valley and a plethora of waterfalls.

Shell is 13 km west of Puyo, 50 km from Baños (1½ hours). It has an airfield (watch out for aircraft crossing the road!) and an army checkpoint where foreigners must sometimes register; passport required.

Sleeping and eating **F** *Los Copales*, west of Shell on the road to Baños, T795290. Comfortable cabins with private bath and electric shower. Restaurant on site, quiet setting. Friendly. **F** *Germany Hostal*, down a side street (not easy to find), T795134. Private bath, hot water on request, restaurant. Nice quiet setting. Family-run, very friendly. **G** *Hostal Cordillera*, on main street. With bath, cheaper without. Restaurant. Basic, friendly. **G** *Hostal Amazonas*, at east end of main street. Shared bath, cold water. Basic. There are several cheap and simple *comedores* on the main street; *El Portón*, near the west end, is good.

Transport Military flights from Shell are generally not open to foreigners. *Servicio Aereo Regional*, T Quito 592032; (Shell) 795175, flies to Quito Mon and Fri, US$45. Also charters a light aircraft for 7 passengers, US$320 per hour.

Southern Oriente

Stretching south of the Río Pastaza, the southern Oriente is made up of the provinces of Morona-Santiago and part of Zamora-Chinchipe. This is a less developed region and tourism is only just getting started. The area has maintained its natural and cultural integrity in part because of the traditionally determined – at times hostile – attitude of the Shuar and Achuar people who live here. Also because there has been relatively little petroleum development to date, although mining poses a hazard. The signing of a peace treaty in 1998 between Ecuador and Peru over their disputed border is helping to introduce tourism to the region. There is a great deal to explore here, but all visitors to virgin territory should remember that they have an especially important obligation to be responsible tourists (see page 42).

The first leg of the Puyo-Macas bus journey goes as far as Sharupi on the Río Pastaza (three hours). There is a hair-raising suspension bridge suitable only for cars and small busetas. On the opposite shore, another bus carries passengers the rest of the way (2½ hours) to a second suspension bridge over the Río Upano, just before Macas. It stops often at small settlements, mostly inhabited by Shuar. The ride is slow and rough, the road hard packed dirt, full of potholes. The jungle which borders this road is rapidly being removed.

Puyo to Macas (margin)

Oriente Jungle (margin, vertical)

Macas

Capital of Morona-Santiago province, situated high above the broad Río Upano valley, Macas is developing rapidly thanks to nearby oil deposits. It is a clean-looking town, established by missionaries over 400 years ago. The immense snow-capped Sangay volcano can be seen on rare clear mornings from the plaza, creating an amazing backdrop to the tropical jungle surrounding the town. Puffs of smoke may be seen and a red glow at night from the crater of this still very active volcano.

*Phone code: 07
Colour map 5, grid B1
Population: 9,720
Altitude: 1,000 m* (margin)

The modern cathedral, completed in 1992, with beautiful stained-glass windows, houses the much venerated image of La Purísima de Macas. Several blocks to the north of the cathedral, in the park which also affords great views of the Upano Valley, is an excellent orchid collection. Several blocks south of the cathedral there is a public swimming pool, which is open at weekends and holidays. There is good birdwatching down the hill from Macas into the Upano Valley and alongside the tributary streams. The whole area has been developed for beef production. The climate is not too hot and the nights are even cool. The town is small enough to walk around. Hotels are dotted around a bit but most of the restaurants are close to the bus terminal.

Sleeping
■ *on map*
Price codes:
see inside front cover

C *Cabañas Ecológicas Yuquipa*, a 3 km walk from Km 12 on the road to Puyo, T700071. Minimum 3 days stay, package includes accommodation, guides, meals and transport, cheaper for groups of 6 or more, contact *Pan Francesa* bakery at Soasti y Tarqui. **E** *Cabañas del Valle*, Via Sur Km 1.5, T700700300. Quiet and helpful. **E** *Peñón del Oriente*, Domingo Comín 837 y Amazonas, T700124, F700450. Modern, clean, secure, hot water, good views from roof. Recommended. **E** *Esplendid*, Soasti 1518, T700120. With bath, rooms without are cheaper, clean, modern, hot water, parking. **E** *Manzana Real*, Av 29 de mayo at southern entrance to town, T700637. Comfortable rooms with private bath, hot water, pool, meals on request. Recommended. **E** *Esmeralda*, Cuenca 612 y Soasti, T700160. Modern, clean, hot water, cheaper with cold. **E** *La Orquídea*, 9 de Octubre 1305 y Sucre, T700970. With bath, hot water, cheaper with cold. Clean and bright, quiet. **E** *Casa Blanca*, Soasti y Domingo Comín.

F *Amazonas*, Guamote y 29 de Mayo, near the University, T700198. With bath, cheaper without. **F** *Emperatriz*, Amazonas y Tarqui, T700748. With bath, cheaper without. **F** *Liria*, 12 de Febrero y 1 de Mayo. **F** *Cabañas El Abanico*, Km 18 Vía Macas-Guamote, T700394.

G *Residencial Macas*, 24 de Mayo y Sucre, T700254. Above *Restaurante Carmitas* (good, simple cooking), quiet, clean, cheaper without bath. **G** *Casa de La Suerte*, Tarqui 626 y Soasti, T700139. Basic, helpful. **G** *Sangay*, Tarqui 605, T700457. Basic, friendly.

Eating
There is not a lot to choose from & prices are rather high

Chifa Pagoda China, Amazonas y Domingo Comín, next to *Peñon del Oriente*. Good expensive Chinese food. *La Randipampa*, 24 de Mayo, on Parque Central. Bar-restaurant, good Cuban food (also cigars). *Los Helechos*, Soasti, between Cuenca y Sucre. Good, popular with guides. *Café El Jardín*, Amazonas y Domingo Comín. Expensive. *Bohemio*, 10 de Agosto y Loja. Mid-range prices. Cheaper places include *Imperial*, on Domingo Comín and *Super Pollo*, 10 de Agosto y Guamote.

Bars & nightclubs

Discos *Acuario*, Tarqui y Amazonas, good music. *Extasis*, on Tarqui, expensive. *Luna Azul*, Amazonas y Riobamba. Live music on Fri, expensive.

Tour operators

ETSA, 24 de Mayo y 10 de Agosto, T700550. *Ikiaam*, 10 de Agosto, 2nd floor in house opposite the bus terminal, T700457. Tours to the jungle and Sangay National Park. *Tuntiak Tours*, in the bus terminal, T700082. Carlos Arcos is half Shuar and speaks the language, very experienced. *Aventura Tsunki Touring*, Amazonas y Domingo Comín, T/F700464, tsunki@cue.satnet.net Hiking tours with a Shuar guide and English interpreter, also canoe trips and cave exploration. *Winia Sunka*, Amazonas y Pasaje Turístico, opposite *Hotel Peñón del Oriente*, T/F700088, visunka@juvenilemedia.com Runs cabins and tours in the Santa Rosa area north of Macas, as well as tours east of the Cordillera de Cutucú, near the Peruvian border. The owner, Pablo Velín, is a recommended guide. *ROW*, Amazonas y Quito. A US company from Idaho offering whitewater rafting on the Río Upano (See River rafting, page 72).

Transport

Air The small local airport is a couple of blocks to the north but it may be difficult to get flights at times. There are flights to and from **Quito** with TAME on Mon, Wed and Fri (sit on the left for the best views of Sangay).

The paved runway at Macas is the main access for the southern jungle, but DAC (Dirección de Aviación Civil) occasionally tightens up the regulations making it almost impossible for tourists to fly with local airlines, who, they claim, are only licensed to transport missionaries, volunteers, Indians and people needing medical attention. Tour operators have tried to change this policy as it restricts the development of tourism in the area. The only way round this is to charter a plane from a licensed company in Shell or Quito, which is obviously much more expensive. It may sometimes be possible to get a flight from Sucúa's grass strip, a 40-min taxi ride to the south (see below).

Bus The road from Puyo crosses the Río Upano before going across the small town centre to reach the bus terminal in the west. To **Cuenca**, 12 hrs, US$7, 4 a day with Turismo Oriental, also Transportes Sucúa at 1700; the views are spectacular, take a 0530 bus to see it in daylight. To **Sucúa**, 1 hr, every hour but no regular service on Thu. Two bus companies run to **Puyo**, Coop San Francisco 5 a day, US$4.50, 6 hrs; and Coop Macas almost hourly from 0600-1500.

A controversial new road runs from **Macas to Guamote** in the central Andes, cutting through Parque Nacional Sangay (see page 384). It had been almost completed in late 2000. You can travel this route by public transport, walking the missing section. Enquire in advance at the Macas bus terminal.

Banks *Banco del Austro*, 24 de Mayo y 10 de Agosto. Visa. **Communications** Post Office: 9 de Octubre y Domingo Comín, next to the park. **Andinatel:** 24 de Mayo y Sucre, F700110 (use this fax number to contact any establishment in town; be patient). **Directory**

Macas

■ **Sleeping**	5 La Orquídea	● **Eating**
1 Amazonas	6 Peñon del Oriente	1 Café El Jardín
2 Casa de la Suerte	& Chifa Pagoda	
3 Esmeralda	7 Residencial Macas	
4 Esplendid	8 Sangay	

Oriente Jungle

Excursions from Macas

The Salesian **Sevilla-Don Bosco mission** is east of town. The modern archae-ological museum, Don Bosco y Montalba, is a good place to rest and see views of the Río Upano, and there is a recreation area nearby. Three kilometres north is **La Cascada**, beside the Río Copueno, with a picnic area, with swimming, slide, football and volleyball.

Complejo Hombre Jaguar is an archaeological site with many *tolas*. It is north of town near Santa Rosa and Guapula on the way to Sangay National Park (see below). Allow two days to see everything; ask for directions if you're using public transport. Day tours can be arranged with *Sunka* for US$25 per person (see below).

Tours from Macas
See also Tour operators above

It is possible to visit the jungle from Macas and there are agencies specializing in tours to villages. However, it is advisable to contact the appropriate Shuar Federation (there are several, see Sucúa below) before taking a tour and verify what is involved before signing any contract.

Native guides

An intimate encounter with the Shuar culture is possible by taking a trek to a tradi-tional village in the company of a Shuar guide/host. The Shuar have traditionally kept outsiders from entering their territory, but are willing to share their traditions with appropriately prepared guests. A Shuar chief, **Alfredo Uyungara**, and his Eng-lish-speaking son offer trips by light plane (US$200 per flight) or canoe (US$20 per trip) from Macas to the village of **Yaupi**, with visits to caves and lagoons in the sur-rounding forest. Also treks from Macas to the small village of **Wisui** and an enchanted cave, **Jurijri**. Price US$35 per person per day plus transport. Their office in Macas is above Delgado Travel, T07701578, uyungaraalfredo@hotmail.com

Fundacion Tuntui offers a hike of 5-7 hrs to **Makuma** and nearby villages. Con-tact Gustavo Umanya or María Guadalupe de Herida, T898321, cellular T09-707369. US$35 per person per day plus US$10 entrance fee.

Jungle lodges

Kapawi Ecological Reserve is a top-of-the-line jungle lodge located on the Río Pastaza in the heart of Achuar territory. It is accessible only by small aircraft and motor canoe. The lodge was built in partnership with the indigenous organization OINAE and offers flexible programmes adapting to the interests and conditions of the ecotourist. It is also built according to the Achuar concept of architecture, using typi-cal materials, and emphasizes environmentally friendly methods such as solar energy, biodegradable soaps and rubbish recycling. It is in a zone rich in biodiversity, with many opportunities for seeing the forest and its inhabitants. Four nights in a double cabin costs US$700, plus US$150 for transport to and from Quito. The location, quality of service, cabin accommodation and food have all been highly recommended. www.kapawi.com Quito office: Canodoros: Av Portugal 448 e Isabel de Aldaz, T256759, eco-tourism1@ecu.net.ec, www.canodros.com

Parque Nacional Sangay

In clear weather the surrounding hills give excellent views of the active volcano **Sangay**, within Parque Nacional Sangay. The lowland area of the park has interesting walking and can be reached by taking a bus to the village of 9 de Octubre, on Wednesday, Friday and Sunday at 0730 and 1600. It is 1½ hours' walk from there to the park entrance (entry fee US$10); information from Ministerio del Ambiente in Macas, Juan de la Cruz y 29 de Mayo. For informa-tion about climbing Sangay, see page 239.

Sucúa

Twenty-three kilometres from Macas, Sucúa is of particular interest as the centre of a branch of the ex-head-hunting Shuar (Jívaro) Indians. Their crafts can be seen and bought but it is tactless to ask them about head-hunting and shrinking (a practice designed to punish those who bewitched others and to deter anyone wishing to cause sickness or disaster in future). Outside the school, scenes from Shuar mythology are displayed in painted tableaux.

You can contact the **Shuar Federation** at Domingo Comín 17-38 (or C Tarqui 809), T/F740108, for information about visiting traditional villages. This is possible with an Indian guide, but takes time as the application must be considered by a council of seven and then you will be interviewed and told how you should behave. Allow at least 1½ days. There is a small craft shop across the street from the Shuar Federation. There is an interesting bookshop and, 10 minutes' walk from the town centre, a small museum and zoo (very few animals) run by Shuar Indians, in the Centro de Formación.

Nearby is the Río Upano, a 1½ hour walk, with plenty of Morpho butterflies. A cable car crosses the river. Also close by is the Río Namangoza, a 15 minute walk, with rapids and good swimming, but be careful of the current after rain.

Sleeping & eating

F *Hostal Karina*, on the southwest corner of the plaza, above the *farmacia*. Clean and bright. **F** *Hostería Orellana*, at the south end of town, T740193. One room with bath, others without. **F** *Hostal Alborada*, Domingo Comín. T740149. With restaurant. **F** *Hostal Cuenca*, T740129. **G** *Rincón Oriental*. Shared bath, clean, parking. Recommended. **H** *Sangay*. Very basic.

Restaurant La Fuente, Domingo Comín near the plaza. Bar/restaurant, good. *Sangay*, opposite *Rincón Oriental*. *Paolita*, Domingo Comín south of centre. On the same street are *Oasis* and *Sabor del Oriente*. *Jefralisavi*, north of the plaza. Snacks and drinks, open till midnight. *Tropical Bar's*, Victoriano Abarca s/n, snacks and music. *Discoteca Caña Brava*, Av Sucua y Abarca.

Sucúa to Morona

From Sucúa, the road heads south for one hour to Logroño. A short walk out of town are extensive limestone caves; take a torch, rope, etc. They are subject to flash floods during rainstorms. There is a gate; get the key before walking out of the village. A guide is useful. Another one hour south is (Santiago de) **Méndez**, a nice town with a modern church.

Sleeping & eating

G *Hostal Los Ceibos*, C Cuenca just off plaza, T760133. Private bath, hot water. Impeccably clean and friendly. Recommended. **G** *Hostal Los Sauces*, T760165. **G** *Hostal Los Alamos*. **H** *Pensión Vanesa*. Places to eat include *El Reportero*, Domingo Comín y Cuenca; and *16 de Agosto*, Cuenca y Guayaquil.

Oriente Jungle

The family of Achuar

The Achuar is one of the four groups of the linguistic family Jívaro: Achuar, Shuar (or Shiwiar), Aguaruna and Huambisa. This is by far the most important remaining indigenous culture in the Amazon Basin, with a population of around 80,000, and occupying huge tracts of Ecuador and Peru's rainforest. They get their name from the Shuar word achu meaning morete, a kind of palm that grows in flooded areas, and shuar, meaning people.

Though known in the past for their internal wars, the Achuar live today in peace, mostly in small villages. They hunt, fish and forage in the forests and also tend small plots (chacras) where they practise slash-and-burn cultivation. This is a necessary practice given that the rainforest soils are particularly infertile. Each chacra covers an area of roughly 4,000 sq m, generally near a river, and is used for an average of three years before being left in favour of a new plot of land.

The Achuar believe in multiple spirits that give them guidance for a harmonious relationship with the rainforest and its wildlife. Magic and healing powers are used by the shaman (uwishin), who gets his force by means of hallucinogenic plants like natem. They maintain a very intimate relationship with nature and its processes. Primarily based in astronomical calculations and biological cycles, the Achuar have created a model of representation of annual cycles in the rainforest much more precise than any developed by modern biologists or meteorologists. Since they did not have a written language before the arrival of missionaries, the use of myths has been very important in keeping the traditions alive.

Until the end of the 18th century, the region occupied by the Achuar was only occasionally visited by the most determined of missionaries. The region was not affected by the rubber boom, which converted thousands of Indians into slaves during the 19th century. Although from the end of the 19th century to the 1950s this area was visited by some explorers and naturalists, it was, for the most part, considered terra incognita until the late 1960s. Between 1968 and 1970 Catholics and Evangelists established the first contacts with the group in order to convert them to Christianity, a process that drastically altered their way of living. Since 1991 the majority of the Achuar belong to OINAE (Organization of Ecuadorean Achuar Nationalities). Today OINAE is divided into three groups, each one with its own centre.

South of Méndez, passports are checked at a checkpoint at **Patuca**, the first village after the bridge over the Río Upano. Note that photocopies are not accepted; if permission to proceed is denied, don't argue. This road is subject to landlsides in the rainy season.

Near Méndez a road (one bus daily) goes east into the jungle to **Morona**. Along the road is the junction of the Zamora-Coangos rivers. East of the confluence, at the village of Santiago, a canoe can be hired (about US$30) to a point from where you can walk in 2½ hours to the **Cueva de Los Tayos**, a huge cave, 85 m in depth. The trail is obscure, and a guide is necessary. Mario Cruz, in conjunction with Metropolitan Touring in Quito, organizes treks from the capital.

It is nine hours to the village of (San José de) **Morona**, located on the Río Morona near the Peruvian border. There is no accommodation but camping is possible, and there is a house where you can get meals and drinks. No border crossing is permitted.

Limón Two hours, 50 km south of Méndez is Limón, official name General Leónidas Plaza, a mission town founded in 1935, now a busy, friendly place, surrounded by high jungle. Buses, all from Calle Quito, go to Cuenca, Macas and Gualaquiza.

F *Dream House*, C Quito. Friendly. **G** *Residencial Limón*, T770114. Modern, basic, clean and friendly, front rooms noisy. **G** *Residencial Dianita*, T770122. **H** *Residencial Santo Domingo*. Basic. There are several basic *chifas* in town and the *El Viajero* restaurant at bus the terminal.

Sleeping & eating

From Limón, a road to Cuenca (132 km) passes through Gualaceo, via Jadán. From Limón the road rises steeply with many breathtaking turns and the vegetation changes frequently, partly through cloud forest and then, at 4,000 m, through the *páramo*, before dropping very fast down to the valley of Gualaceo. There is a police checkpoint at Plan de Milagro, where foreigners have to register. There is nowhere to stay along the Limón-Gualaceo road.

Limón to Cuenca
This is one of the best roads in Ecuador for birdwatching

South to Zamora

Continuing south from Limón the road passes **Indanza** (very basic *residencial* and *comedor*), before reaching Gualaquiza, a pioneer town off the tourist track. It is surrounded by densely forested mountains, in which many interesting side trips can be made. If you intend to explore the area, bring a tent and sleeping bag.

Gualaquiza

Among the excursions from Gualaquiza are the caves near Nuevo Tarqui and the Salesian mission at Bomboiza, which has a small museum. The Tutusa Gorge is three hours' walk, then two hours by boat; take a guide, such as Sr José Castillo, for example.

It's a six hour walk to **Aguacate**, near which are precolumbian ruins (food and bed at Sr Jorge Guillermo Vázquez). **Yumaza** is a 40 minute walk, for more precolumbian ruins (two sites).

Sleeping and eating F *Amazonas No 2*, Domingo Comín 08-65 y Gonzalo Pesantes. Basic, friendly. **F** *Hostal de Guadalupe*, Gonzalo Pesantes 08-16, T780113. **F** without bath, dirty, smelly and noisy. **F** per person. *Guakiz*, Orellana 08-52, T780138. With bath, friendly, the best in town. The best restaurant is *Oro Verde*, near the *Hotel Guakiz*. Excellent food and service. Also *Cabaña*, and *Los Helechos*, opposite the bus station. Both recommended.

Transport Bus: To **Cuenca**, at 1900, 2000 and 2100, 6 hrs. To **Loja**, at 0300 and 2200. To **Macas**, at 1800, 10 hrs. *Rancheros* leave for Yantzaza in the morning, from where a bus reaches Zamora before dark (see below).

Directory Communications: Andinatel: García Moreno y Ciudad de Cuenca. Open Mon-Sat 0800-1100, 1400-1700, 1900-2100.

From Loja (see page 269) the road to the Oriente crosses a low pass and descends rapidly to Zamora. It was paved and in good condition in 2000, but is subject to frequent landslides and deteriorates rapidly during heavy rains. The road is beautiful as it wanders from *páramo* down to high jungle, crossing mountain ranges of spectacular cloud forest, weaving high above narrow gorges as it runs alongside the Río Zamora.

Zamora

The southernmost city in Oriente and capital of the province of Zamora-Chinchipe, Zamora is an old mission settlement at the confluence of the Ríos Zamora and Bombuscara. It has traditionally been far off the beaten path but is now opening up to tourism, and there are great expectations in this

Colour map 6, grid B4
Population: 8,736

Oriente Jungle

regard following the peace treaty with Peru. Mining is an important part of the province's economy and also a threat to its natural environment.

The **Orquideario Tzanka**, one block from the plaza, features an interesting collection of almost 1,000 plants including rare specimens (not for sale). ■ *Contact Mario González, T605692.* There is also **Orquideario Paphinia**, 5 km from town.

Excursions Zamora's most important attraction is the easy access it provides to the sub-tropical part of **Podocarpus National Park**, via the **Bombuscara** entrance. The entrance trail along the Bombuscara River is very pleasant and full of sub-tropical birds hard to find elsewhere in Ecuador (such as Coppery-chested Jacamar, White-breasted Parakeet, several rare Fruiteaters, and many more). Take the road east out of Zamora and turn right when you reach the Rio Bombuscara. Do not cross the river; take the road that follows the river upstream. The road ends in a car park, where the trail begins. Thirty minutes' walk takes you to the visitors' centre and more trails, including a river trail and a 30 minute loop trail. It is highly recommended for nature lovers, especially those who might have difficulty walking on steep trails. The trail to the visitors' centre is virtually flat, unlike almost all other trails at this elevation in Ecuador. Information is available from the Ministerio del Ambiente office at the entrance to town from Loja.

Sleeping **E** *Orillas del Zamora*, Diego de Vaca near the car bridge. Refurbished in 2000. **E** *Cabañas Tzanka*, enquire at the Orquideario Tzanka (see above). Spacious cabins with bath and kitchen. **F** *Gymyfa*, Diego de Vaca one block from Plaza. With bath, TV. Nice. **F** *Internacional Torres*. Good. **F** *Maguna*, Diego de Vaca, T605113. Fridge, TV, bath, electric shower, parking. Very friendly. **F** *Seyma*, 24 de Mayo y Amazonas, T605583. Clean, friendly, recommended. **G** *Zamora*, Sevilla de Oro y Pío Jaramillo, T605253. Shared bath, clean. **G** *Residencial Venecia*, Sevilla de Oro. Shared bath, basic.

Eating The restaurant in *Hotel Maguna* is good, *Comedor Don Pepe* set meals and à la carte. *Esmeraldas*, in the market area opposite the bus terminal. Good, recommended. *Las Gemelitas*, opposite market. *200 Millas*, in bus terminal. Varied menu. *King Burger*, by park. Snacks.

Transport Bus: leave from the Terminal Terrestre. To **Loja**, frequent service, 2 hrs, US$1.50. To **Cuenca**, 4 daily via Loja, 6-7 hrs. To **Yantzaza** and **La Paz**, 6 a day. To **Gualquiza**, 3 a day, 7 hrs.

Nambija Nambija is a gold mining town outside Zamora. Once a frontier town with its
& Zumbi own limited law and order, it has calmed down since an international company took over the mines. North of Nambija is Zumbi, reached by 0800 bus from Zamora. The last bus back is at 1500. It's a very scenic ride.

The road north from Zamora passes through **Yantzaza** (four hotels, including the new *Inca*, **G**, and several *comedores*) and **El Pangui** (**H** *Hotel Estrella del Oriente*) on its way to Gualaquiza, allowing for connections to Cuenca, Macas and Puyo (see above).

Galápagos Islands

10

Galápagos Islands

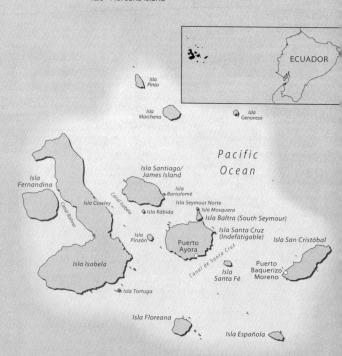

A trip to the Galápagos is a unique and unforgettable experience. As Charles Darwin put it, 'the Natural History of this archipelago is very remarkable: it seems to be a little world within itself'. The islands are world-renowned for their fearless wildlife but no amount of hype can prepare the visitor for such a close encounter with nature. Here, you can snorkel with penguins and sea-lions, watch giant 200 kg tortoises lumbering through cactus forest and enjoy the courtship display of the blue-footed booby and frigatebird, all in startling close-up.

A visit to the islands doesn't come cheap. The return flight from Quito and national park fee add up to almost US$500; plus a bare minimum of US$55 per person per day for sailing on the most basic boat, when you can find space at this price. Luxury vessels cost up to five times as much, or even more in high season. Sleeping on land may provide a slightly more economical alternative but there is at present simply no way to enjoy Galápagos on a shoestring. For those with the money and interest however, the experience is well worth the cost. At the same time, these high prices are one way of keeping the number of visitors within reasonable levels in order to limit impact on the islands and their wildlife.

Galápagos Islands

Facts about the islands

See also the colour wildlife section in the middle of the book & the box on Charles Darwin, page 396

Lying on the Equator, 970 km west of the Ecuadorean coast, the Galápagos consist of six main islands: San Cristóbal, Santa Cruz, Isabela, Floreana, Santiago and Fernandina (the last two are uninhabited). There are also 12 smaller islands – Baltra and the uninhabited islands of Santa Fe, Pinzón, Española, Rábida, Daphne, Seymour, Genovesa, Marchena, Pinta, Darwin and Wolf – as well as over 40 small islets.

The Galápagos have never been connected with the continent. Gradually, over many hundreds of thousands of years, animals and plants from over the sea somehow migrated there and as time went by they adapted themselves to Galápagos conditions and came to differ more and more from their continental ancestors. Thus many of them are unique: a quarter of the species of shore fish, half of the plants and almost all the reptiles are found nowhere else. In many cases different forms have evolved on the different islands. Charles Darwin recognized this speciation within the archipelago when he visited the Galápagos on the *Beagle* in 1835 and his observations played a substantial part in his formulation of the theory of evolution. Since no large land mammals reached the islands (until they were recently introduced by man), reptiles were dominant just as they had been all over the world in the very distant past. Another of the extraordinary features of the islands is the tameness of the animals. The islands were uninhabited when they were discovered in 1535 and the animals still have little instinctive fear of man.

Classification Plant and animal species in the Galápagos are grouped into the following three categories. These are terms which you will hear often during your visit to the islands. **Endemic species** are those which occur only in the Galápagos and nowhere else on the planet. Examples are the Marine and Land Iguana, Galápagos Fur Seal, Flightless Cormorant and the 'Daisy tree' (*Scalesia pedunculata*). **Native species** make their homes in the Galápagos as well as other parts of the world. Examples include all three species of boobies, Frigate birds and the various types of mangroves. Although not unique to the islands, these native species have been an integral part of the Galápagos ecosystems for a very long time. **Introduced species** on the other hand are very recent arrivals, brought by man, and inevitably the cause of much damage. They include cattle, goats, donkeys, pigs, dogs, cats, rats and over 500 species of plants such as elephant grass (for grazing cattle), and fruit trees such as the raspberry and guava. The unchecked expansion of these introduced species has upset the natural balance and seriously threatens the unique endemic species for which Galápagos is so famous.

Geology The islands are the peaks of gigantic undersea volcanoes, composed almost exclusively of basalt. Most of them rise from about 2,000 to 3,500 m above the surrounding seabed, but over 7,000 m above the deepest parts of the adjacent ocean floor to the west of Fernandina. The highest summit is Volcán Wolf on Isabela island, 1,660 m above sea level. Eruptions have taken place in historical times on Fernandina, Isabela, Pinta, Marchena and Santiago. The most active today are Fernandina, Isabela, Pinta and Marchena, and fumarolic activity may be seen intermittently on each of these islands. The islands are also very gradually drifting eastward, due to the movement of the tectonic plate on which they rest. Hence the oldest islands lie to the east, including San Cristóbal and Española which are approximately three to 3½ million years old. The youngest islands, such as Fernandina and Isabela are in the west of the archipelago, and have been in existence for some 700,000 to 800,000 years. (See also Geology, on page 441).

The Galápagos climate can be divided into a hot season (December to May), when the sea temperature rises and there is a possibility of brief heavy showers, and the cool or *garúa* season (June to November), when the ocean is cooler and days generally are more cloudy with some mist or light drizzle. During July and August the southeast trade winds can be very strong. At night, temperatures can fall below 15°C, particularly at sea. The underwater visibility is best from January to March. Ocean temperatures are usually higher to the east and lower at the western end of the archipelago. Despite all these variations, conditions are generally favourable for visiting Galápagos throughout the year.

Climate
See graph below for details of rainfall, air & sea temperatures

The islands' climate and hence their wildlife are also affected by the phenomenon known as El Niño (see page 444). This cyclical increase in ocean temperature alters the food chain upon which depend the Galápagos marine fauna. The result is high levels of mortality especially among sea lions, penguins and other seabirds. This is, however, part of the natural life cycle. When the phenomenon subsides, food supplies are replenished and the different species recover. An El Niño year is also when you can see the islands at their greenest.

The islands were discovered accidentally by Tomás de Berlanga, the Bishop of Panama, in 1535. He was on his way to Peru when his ship was becalmed and swept 800 km off course by the currents. Like most of the early arrivals, Bishop Tomás and his crew arrived thirsty and disappointed at the dryness of the place. He did not even give the islands a name, although he did dub the giant tortoises 'Galápagos' because of the resemblence of their shell to a Spanish riding saddle.

History of human settlement

The islands first appeared on a map in 1574, as 'Islands of Galápagos', which has remained in common use ever since. The individual islands, though, have had several names, both Spanish and English. The latter names come from a visit in 1680 by English buccaneers who, with the blessing of the English king, attacked Spanish ships carrying gold and relieved them of their heavy load. The pirates used the Galápagos as a hide-out, in particular a spot North of James Bay on Santiago island, still known as Buccaneers' Cove. The pirates were the first to visit many of the islands and they named them after English kings and aristocracy or famous captains of the day.

The Spanish also called the islands 'enchanted', or 'bewitched', owing to the fact that for much of the year they are surrounded by mists giving the impression that they appear and disappear as if by magic. Also, the tides and currents were so confusing that they thought the islands were floating and not real islands.

Between 1780 and 1860, the waters of the Galápagos became a favourite place for British and American whaling ships. At the beginning of the whaling era, in 1793, a British naval

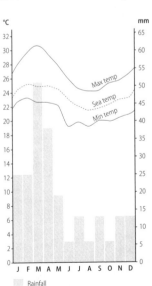

Climate: Galápagos Islands

Galápagos Islands

captain erected a barrel on Floreana island, to facilitate communication between boats and the land. It is still in place today, at Post Office bay.

The first island to be inhabited was Floreana, in 1807, by a lone Irishman named Patrick Watkins. After his departure they were more or less uninhabited, until 1832, when Ecuadorean General José Villamil founded a colony on Floreana, mainly composed of convicts and political prisoners, who traded meat and vegetables with whalers. In February 1832, following the creation of the young republic, Colonel Ignacio Hernández took official possession of the archipelago in the name of Ecuador. Spanish names were given to the islands, in addition to the existing English ones.

The Galápagos Affair One of the more bizarre and notorious periods began in 1929 with the arrival of German doctor, Friedrich Ritter, and his mistress, Dore Strauch. Three years later, the Wittmer family also decided to settle on the island, and Floreana soon became so fashionable that luxury yachts used to call in. One of these visitors was Baroness von Wagner de Bosquet, an Austrian woman who settled on the island with her two lovers and grandiose plans to build a luxury hotel. Soon after landing she had proclaimed herself Empress of Floreana, which was not to the liking of Dr Ritter or the Wittmer family, and tensions rose. There followed several years of mysterious and unsavoury goings-on, during which everyone died or disappeared, except Dore Strauch and the Wittmer family. The longest survivor of this still unexplained drama was Margret Wittmer, who lived at Black Beach on Floreana until her death in 2000, at age 95. Her account of life there, entitled *Floreana, Poste Restante*, was published in 1961 and became a bestseller.

Current settlements Human settlement on the Galápagos is currently limited to about 3% of the islands' land area of 7,882 sq km, but nevertheless, the resident population of the islands has grown very rapidly in recent years; there were an estimated 20,000 to 25,000 inhabitants in 2000. The population is concentrated in eight settlements. Two are on San Cristóbal (Chatham), at Puerto Baquerizo

Moreno and a small village inland called El Progreso. San Cristóbal has a population of around 7,000, and Puerto Baquerizo Moreno is the administrative capital of the province of Galápagos and Ecuador's second naval base. There are three settlements on Santa Cruz (Indefatigable) – Puerto Ayora, the largest town and the main tourist centre, Bellavista and Santa Rosa, two small farming communities inland. Santa Cruz is the most populated island, with around 15,000 inhabitants. On Floreana, the longest inhabited island, there are 70 souls, most of which are at Black Beach and on Isabela (Albemarle), the largest island, there is a thriving community of 3,000 at Puerto Villamil and a village inland at Tomás de Berlanga. Additionally, there is a navy base on Baltra (South Seymour) at the site of an old US Airforce camp. Flights from the mainland arrive either at Baltra, which has a good road to Puerto Ayora, or on San Cristóbal. There is also an airstrip for light aircraft at Puerto Villamil on Isabela. All the other islands are accessible only by sea.

Evolution and conservation

The continuing volcanic formation of the islands in the west of the archipelago has not only created a unique marine environment, but the drift eastwards of the whole island group at the nexus of several major marine currents has created laboratory-type conditions where only certain species have been allowed access. Others have been excluded; most significantly, practically the whole of the terrestrial kingdom of mammals. The resulting ecology has evolved in a unique direction, with many of the ecological niches being filled from some unexpected angles. A highly-evolved sunflower, for instance, has in some areas taken over the niche left vacant by the absence of trees.

Within the islands, evolutionary pressures are so intense that there is a very high level of endemism (species confined to a particular area). For example, not only have the tortoises evolved differently from those in the rest of the world, but each of the five main volcanoes on Isabela has evolved its own sub-species of giant tortoise. This natural experiment has been under threat ever since the arrival of the first whaling ships and even more so since the first permanent human settlement. New species such as horses, cattle, donkeys, goats, pigs, dogs, cats and rats, as well as over 500 species of plants, were introduced and spread very rapidly. The unique endemic species that had gradually evolved to fill the ecological niches in the Galápagos are now at risk of being evicted and destroyed by the more recent introductions. More recently still, quarantine programs have been implemented by the authorities in an attempt to prevent the introduction of even more species. There have also been campaigns to eradicate some introduced species on some islands, but this is inevitably a very slow, expensive and difficult process.

The most devastating of the newly introduced species are human beings, both visitors and settlers. To a large degree, the two groups are connected, one supporting the other economically, but there is also a sizeable proportion, over half of the islands' permanent residents, who make an income independent of tourism from working the land or at sea.

While no great wealth has accumulated to those who farm, fortunes have been made by fishermen in a series of particularly destructive fisheries: black coral, lobster, shark fin and sea cucumber. Sharks were caught by setting gill nets across a bay. These nets took a wide range of marine animals and birds as a by-catch, including pelicans, boobies, seals, turtles and dolphins. As none have any commercial value, they were dumped. Each successive fishery was encouraged by foreign demand involving large amounts of money.

The human effect

In January 2001, as this book went to press, there was a serious oil spill from a small tanker which supplied fuel for tour boats & locals, affecting the surrounding marine reserve & San Cristóbal Island

Charles Darwin and the Galápagos

Without doubt, the most famous visitor to the islands is Charles Darwin. His short stay in the archipelago proved hugely significant for science and for the study of evolution.

In September 1835, Darwin sailed into Galápagos waters on board the HMS Beagle, captained by the aristocratic Robert FitzRoy whose job was to chart lesser known parts of the world. FitzRoy had wanted on board a companion of his own social status and a naturalist, to study the strange new animals and plants they would find en route. He chose Charles Darwin to fill both roles.

Darwin was only 22 years old when he set sail from England in 1831 and it would be five years before he saw home again. They were to sail around the world, but most of the voyage was devoted to surveying the shores of South America, giving Darwin the chance to explore a great deal of the continent. The visit to the Galápagos had been planned as a short stop on the return journey, by which time Darwin had become an experienced observer. It was indeed a stroke of luck that he had been picked for this unique cruise.

During the five weeks that the Beagle spent in the Galápagos Darwin went ashore to collect plants, rocks, insects and birds. The unusual life forms and their adaptations to the harsh surroundings made a deep impression on him and eventually inspired his revolutionary theory on the evolution of species. The Galápagos provided a kind of model of

the world in miniature. Darwin realized that these recently created volcanoes were young in comparison with the age of the Earth, and that life on the islands showed special adaptations. Yet the plants and animals also showed similarities to those from the South American mainland, where he guessed they had originally come from.

Darwin concluded that the life on the islands had probably arrived there by chance drifting, swimming or flying from the mainland and had not been created on the spot. Once the plants and animals had arrived, they evolved into forms better suited to the strange environment in which they found themselves. Darwin also noted that the animals were extremely tame, because of the lack of predatory mammals. The islands' isolation also meant that the giant tortoises did not face competition from agile mammals and could survive.

On his return to England, Darwin in effect spent the rest of his life publishing the findings of his voyage and developing the ideas it inspired. It was however only when another scientist, named Alfred Russell Wallace, arrived at a similar conclusion to his own that he dared to publish a paper on his theory of evolution. Then followed his all-embracing The Origin of the Species by means of Natural Selection, in 1859. It was to cause a major storm of controversy and to earn Darwin recognition as the man who "provided a foundation for the entire structure of modern biology".

It is, however, farmers who are responsible for the largest number of introduced species. Recent introductions (since the formation of the National Park) include elephant grass to provide pastures, the ani to eat parasites living on cattle (although in the Galápagos it prefers baby finches when it can get them) and walnut trees planted on Isabela.

Conflicting interests Each of the colonizing groups on the islands – scientists, the tourist industry, settlers, farmers and fishermen – have all become powerful pressure groups. Each has its own agenda, with different expectations of the islands. The most sophisticated pressure groups are probably those involved in tourism, divided between boat owners and guides. Being mostly Ecuadorean, the boat owners are easily identified and, as they are looking for long-term stability and profit, they can be monitored through a system of licences and permits issued by both the Ministerio del Ambiente and the Navy. Of all the commercial groups, the boat owners are the most likely to support attempts by the Park authorities to conserve the islands. Among the guides, there has been some rivalry between foreigners (such as multilingual and specialist guides) on the one hand, and local or Ecuadorean guides on the other. Needless to say, the *'colonos'*, colonist farmers and especially fishermen, have a completely different set of priorities which have at times led to overt conflict with the National Park.

The number of tourists to the island is controlled by the authorities to protect the environment but critics claim that the ecology is seriously threatened by current levels. Limits were increased from 25,000 in 1981, reaching a record number of 60,000 visitors in 1997, and roughly maintained ever since. There were almost 90 tourist boats operating in Galápagos in 2000, ranging in capacity from 10 to 100 passengers, as well as growing land-based tourism; but no new permits are supposed to be issued in the near future. Even by international standards, tourism in Galápagos is quite well organized and regulated; by Latin American standards or those of mainland Ecuador, it is remarkably so.

At least five different authorities have a say in running Galápagos – the islands and surrounding marine reserve. These include: 1) Instituto Nacional Galápagos (INGALA), under control of the president of Ecuador, which was once responsible for most of the islands' infrastructure and today decides who is entitled to the status of *'colono'* (colonist, or Galápagos resident); 2) the National Park Service, under the authority of the Ministerio del Ambiente, which regulates tourism and manages the 97% of the archipelago which is parkland; 3) the Charles Darwin Research Station, part of an international non-profit organization devoted to supporting scientific research and channelling international funds for conservation; 4) the Ecuadorean Navy, which patrols the waters of the archipelago and attempts to enforce regulations regarding both tourism and fishing; 5) local elected authorities including municipalities and the provincial council, which – in principle – advocate the interests of all the islands' residents. All of the above must work together but since they represent rather different sets of interests, this is not always an easy task. **The authorities**

Those planning to carry out scientific research, commercial or documentary filming and any other special activities which are not part of usual tourism may require permits. It is best to enquire and make all arrangements well in advance. A useful contact is Roslyn Cameron at the Charles Darwin Research Station in Puerto Ayora, T05-526146, cdrs@fcdarwin.org.ec, www.darwinfoundation.org The National Park Service in Puerto Ayora may be reached at T05-526189, F05-526190, infopng@fcdarwin.org.ec

Because tourism is so easily controlled and involves relatively large amounts of money, it is this area which has been debated more than any other. Tourists and their guides form the vast majority of the visitors to the 97% land area that is Park, but it is equally true that, from the point of view of the islands as a whole, it is settlers who are responsible for the largest amount of damage. The remains of abandoned habitations can be seen on Floreana, at Post Office Bay, at Puerto Egas (an abandoned salt works on Santiago Island), near Puerto Villamil and most extensively on Baltra. There is no will to remove them. **The impact of tourism**

The impact of tourism in the Park can best be seen at places like the Plaza islands on the east side of Santa Cruz and a photostudy by the Darwin Station shows many of the changes. Tourists are limited to some 56 landing sites throughout the entire island group. Each has a clearly defined trail from which visitors are not allowed to deviate. The impact that a farmer can have, importing just one species, or one family of settlers, is therefore far greater than that of tourism, which has been largely successfully controlled.

Galápagos Islands

The impact of immigration

Among the other pressing problems that have accumulated over the past two decades, top of the list was uncontrolled immigration. For some Ecuadoreans, the Galápagos Islands are an El Dorado, with strong economic growth, plenty of work opportunities and salaries about 50% higher than on the mainland. Population growth has been astronomic and land prices have soared. Legislation passed in 1998 and finally implemented two years later restricts migration from mainland Ecuador and attempts to better regulate tourism, fishing and agriculture. At the same time, it enshrines the rights of those residents who were established in Galápagos prior to 1996. The current population of the islands is young and, even without further immigration, is likely to grow steadily in coming years. The human threat to Galápagos is therefore far from under control.

But Ecuador is a poor country and it has many pressing social problems. The economy needs the foreign currency generated in the Galápagos Islands, by tourism as well as other activities. Having gained international support for its efforts to conserve the land-based ecology of the Galápagos, Ecuador also needs international support for marine conservation. It therefore faces a difficult task in balancing domestic political opinion, the nation's urgent needs and international credibility when drawing up policies for the benefit of the islands.

Visitor sites

The Galápagos have been declared a World Heritage Site by UNESCO and 97% of the land area and 100% of the surrounding ocean are now part of the Galápagos National Park and Marine Reserve. Within the area of the park there are some 56 landing sites, each with defined trails, so the impact of visitors to this fragile environment is minimized and the park preserved for future generations.

Each of the landing sites has been carefully chosen to show the different flora and fauna, and with the high level of endemism nearly every trail has flora and fauna that can be seen nowhere else in the world. The itineraries of tourist boats are strictly regulated in order to avoid crowding at the visitor sites and some sites are periodically closed by the park authorities in order to allow them to recover from the impact of tourism. Certain sites are only open to smaller boats, and additionally limited to a maximum number of visits per month.

The total lack of fear exhibited by the birds and reptiles that inhabit the islands enables visitors and scientists a unique opportunity to see and study nature. Never miss the opportunity to go snorkelling when visiting. There is plenty of underwater life to see, including rays, turtles, sharks, sea lions, penguins and many spectacular fish and invertebrates. The other islands not mentioned below are closed to tourists.

NB Never touch any of the animals, birds or plants. Do not transfer sand or soil from one island to another. Do not leave litter anywhere – it is highly undesirable in a National Park and is a safety and health hazard for wildlife – and do not take food on to the islands.

Santa Cruz

This island is the principal inhabited island with a population of about 15,000

Most of the inhabitants live in and around **Puerto Ayora**, but there are farming settlements inland at **Bellavista** and **Santa Rosa**. Puerto Ayora is the economic centre of the Galápagos and every cruise visits it for one day anchoring at Academy Bay. The main visit is to **Charles Darwin Research Station** and there is free time to do some shopping, make phone calls and so on.

In 1959, the centenary of the publication of Darwin's *Origin of Species*, the Government of Ecuador and the International Charles Darwin Foundation established, with the support of UNESCO, the Charles Darwin Research Station at Academy Bay, a 20-minute walk from Puerto Ayora. A visit to the station is a good introduction to the islands as it provides a lot of information. Collections of several of the rare sub-species of giant tortoise are maintained on the station as breeding nuclei, though, sadly, no mating partner has yet been found for Lonesome George, the sole remaining member of the Isla Pinta sub-species. There is also a tortoise-rearing area where the young can be seen. The Darwin Foundation staff will help bona fide students of the fauna to plan an itinerary, if they stay some time, and hire a boat. There are several beaches by the Darwin Station, which get crowded at weekends (see Puerto Ayora). ■ *The station offices are open Mon-Fri 0700-1600, visitor areas 0600-1800 daily.*

Some itineraries include a guided visit to the interior of the island. The highlands and settlement area of Santa Cruz are worth seeing for the contrast of the vegetation with the arid coastal zones. There are five main vegetation zones while going inland from Puerto Ayora on the southern side of the island. The highest point is at 864 m. You can hike to the higher parts of the island called **Media Luna**, **Puntudo** and **Cerro Crocker**. The trail starts at Bellavista, 7 km from Puerto Ayora. A round trip from Bellavista is four to eight hours, depending on the distance hiked (10-18 km). A permit and guide are not required, but a guide is advisable. Also take water, sun block and long-sleeved shirt and long trousers to protect against razor grass.

There are a number of sites worth visiting in the interior, including **Los Gemelos**, a pair of twin sinkholes, formed by a collapse of the ground above a fault. The sinkholes straddle the road to Baltra, beyond Santa Rosa. If you're lucky, you can take a *camioneta* all the way, otherwise take a bus to Santa Rosa (see below), then walk. It's a good place to see the Galápagos hawk and barn owl.

There are several **lava tubes** (natural tunnels) on the island. There are some 3 km from Puerto Ayora on the road to Bellavista. They are unsigned, but look on the left for the black-and-white posts. Barn owls can be seen here. Two more lava tubes are 1 km from Bellavista. They are on private land, and therefore can be visited without an official guide. It costs US$1.50 to enter the tunnels (bring a torch or hire one) and it takes about 30 minutes to walk through the tunnels. Tours to the lava tubes can be arranged in Puerto Ayora.

Another worthwhile trip is to the **El Chato Tortoise Reserve**, which is a 7 km hike. The trail starts at Santa Rosa, 22 km from Puerto Ayora. Horses can be hired at Santa Rosa for US$6 each, and a guide is compulsory; US$6.50. A round trip takes one day. The Puerto Ayora-Bellavista bus (see below) stops at the turn off for the track for the reserve. It's a hot walk, so take food and drink. To walk to the Reserve from Santa Rosa, turn left past the school, follow the track at the edge of fields for 40 minutes, turn right at the memorial to the Israeli, 20 minutes later turn left down a track to Chato Trucha.

Next to the reserve is Steve Devine's Butterfly Ranch (Hacienda Mariposa), where you can also see giant tortoises in the wild, but only in the dry season. In the wet season the tortoises are breeding down in the arid zone. Vermillion flycatchers can be seen here also. The ranch is beyond Bellavista on the road to Santa Rosa (the bus passes the turn-off). ■ *US$3, including a cup of hierba luisa tea, or juice.*

Santa Rosa and **Bellavista** From San Francisco school in Puerto Ayora, 3 daily buses **Transport** leave for Santa Rosa and Bellavista. It's a 30-min trip, and buses return immediately. The fare for all destinations is US$0.40. There are also trucks, which are cheaper. On roads to the main sites hitching is easy but expect to pay a small fee.

Galápagos Islands

Other sites on Santa Cruz include **Caleta Tortuga Negra**, on the northern part of the island (restricted to small groups). Here you can drift by dinghy through the mangrove swamps which are home to marine turtles, white-tipped sharks, spotted eagle rays and yellow cow-nosed rays. Nearby is **Las Bachas**, a swimming beach, also on the north shore. **Conway Bay** is a rarely visited landing site on the northwest coast, inhabited by a large colony of sea lions. **Whaler Bay** is the site of one of the oldest whaling camps on Santa Cruz. It was to here and the other similar camps that the giant tortoises were brought before being loaded on board the whalers. **Cerro Dragón** is located on the north shore of Santa Cruz, where land iguanas may be seen as well as the occasional flamingo.

Baltra   Once a US Airforce base, Baltra is now a small military base for Ecuador and also the main airport into the islands. The island is quite arid and that, along with the rubble left by the USAF, gives it the appearance of a junk yard. Also known as South Seymour, this is the island most affected by human habitation. **Mosquera** is a small sandy bank just north of Baltra, home to a large colony of sea lions.

Seymour Norte   Just north of Baltra, Seymour Norte is home to sea lions, marine iguanas, swallow-tailed gulls, magnificent frigatebirds and blue-footed boobies. The tourist trail leads through mangroves in one of the main nesting sites for blue-footed boobies and frigates in this part of the archipelago.

Daphne Major   West of Baltra, Daphne island has a very rich birdlife, in particular the nesting boobies. Because of the possible problems of erosion, only small boats may land here and are limited to one visit each month.

Plaza Sur   One of the closest islands to Puerto Ayora is Plaza Sur. It's an example of a geological uplift and the southern part of the island has formed cliffs with spectacular views. It has a combination of both dry and coastal vegetation zones. Walking along the sea cliffs is a pleasant experience as the swallowtail gull, shearwaters and red billed tropic birds nest here. This is the home of the Men's Club, a rather sad looking colony of bachelor sea lions who are too old to mate and who get together to console each other. There are also lots of blue-footed boobies and a large population of land iguanas.

Santa Fe   This island is located on the southeastern part of Galápagos, between Santa Cruz and San Cristóbal, and was formed by volcanic uplift. The lagoon is home to a large colony of sea lions who are happy to join you for a swim. From the beach the trail goes inland, through a semi-arid landscape of cactus. This little island has its own sub-species of land iguana.

San Cristóbal   San Cristóbal is the easternmost island of Galápagos and one of the oldest. The principal town is **Puerto Baquerizo Moreno** which is the capital of the province of Galápagos.

There are four buses a day inland from Puerto Baquerizo Moreno to **El Progreso** (6 km, 15 minutes, US$0.15), then it's a 2½ hour walk to El Junco lake, the largest body of fresh water in Galápagos. There are also frequent pickup trucks to El Progreso (US$1), or you can hire a pickup in Puerto Baquerizo Moreno for touring: US$15 to El Junco, US$35 continuing to the beaches at Puerto Chino on the other side of the island, past a planned tortoise reserve. Prices are return and include waiting. At El Junco there is a path to walk around the lake in 20 minutes. The views are lovely in clear weather but it is cool and wet in the *garúa* season, so take adequate clothing. In El Progreso is

La Casa del Ceibo, a tree house, for rent, and there are some eating places. Another road from El Progreso continues to **La Soledad**, a school above which is a shrine, a deserted restaurant and a *mirador* overlooking the different types of vegetation stretching to the coast. There are two buses to La Soledad, on Sundays only, when the restaurant is open. From El Progreso a trail also crosses the highlands to **Cerro Brujo** and **Hobbs Bay**, and also to **Stephens Bay**, past some lakes.

It's a three hour hike to **Galapaguera** in the northeast, which allows you to see tortoises in the wild. Isla Lobos is a large sea lion colony and nesting site for sea birds northeast of Puerto Baquerizo Moreno.

NB Always take food and plenty of water when hiking on your own on San Cristóbal. There are many crisscrossing animal trails and it is easy to get lost. Also watch out for the large-spined opuntia cactus and the poisonwood tree (*manzanillo*), which is a relative of poison ivy and can cause severe skin reactions.

Kicker Rock (León Dormido), the basalt remains of a crater, is not strictly speaking a landing site, but the rock is split by a narrow channel and is navigable to the smaller yachts. It is home to a large colony of many seabirds, including masked and blue-footed boobies, nesting in the cliffs rising vertically from the channel. This is also a diving site. **Punta Pitt**, in the far northeast of the island, is a tuff formation which serves as a nesting site for many sea birds, including all three boobies. Up the coast is **Cerro Brujo** beach with sea lions, birds and crabs, though not in any abundance.

Española

This is the southernmost island of the Galápagos and, following a successful programme to remove all the feral species, is now the most pristine of the islands with many migrant, resident and endemic sea birds. **Gardner Bay**, on the northeastern coast, is a beautiful white sand beach with excellent swimming and snorkelling. **Punta Suárez**, on the western tip of the island, has a trail through a rookery. As well as a wide range of sea birds (including blue-footed and masked boobies) there is a great selection of wildlife including sea lions, the largest and most colourful marine iguanas of the Galápagos and the original home of the waved albatrosses.

Floreana

This is the longest inhabited of the islands and the site of the mysterious 'Galápagos Affair' in the 1930s (see page 394). There are opportunities for accommodation or camping with some of the 70 residents here, but you should be as self-sufficient as possible (see page 426).

Devil's Crown, a dramatic snorkelling site to the north of Punta Cormorant, is an almost completely submerged volcano. Erosion has transformed the cone into a series of jagged peaks with the resulting look of a crown. There is usually a wide selection of fish, sharks and turtles easily visible in about 6 m of water.

Punta Cormorant is on the northern part of Floreana. The landing is on a beach of green sand coloured by olivine crystals, volcanic-derived silicates of magnesium and iron. The trail leads to a lake normally inhabited by flamingos and other shore birds and continues to a beach of fine white sand particles known as Flour Beach, an important nesting site for turtles.

Post Office Bay is west of Punta Cormorant. The Post Office barrel was placed and used in the late 18th century by English whaling vessels and later by the American whalers. It is the custom for visitors to place unstamped letters and cards in the barrel, and deliver, free of charge, any addressed to their own destinations. There is a short walk to look at the remains of a Norwegian commercial fish drying and canning operation that was started in 1926 and abandoned after a couple of years. A lava tube that extends to the sea is also visited. **Black Beach** is a small settlement on the western side of the island (see History of human settlement above).

One of the most famous sites in the islands

Galápagos Islands

Isabela This is the largest island in the archipelago. The extensive lava flows from the six volcanoes – Alcedo, Cerro Azul, Darwin, Ecuador, Sierra Negra and Wolf – joined together and formed Isabela. Five of the six volcanoes are active and each have (or had) their own separate sub-species of giant tortoise.

Puerto Villamil on the south coast, the main settlement, was founded in 1897 by Antonio Gil as the centre of a lime producing operation. It is today inhabited by some 3,000 people. Nearby are several lagoons, nesting sites of flamingos and common stilts. A visit to **Punta Moreno**, on the southwest part of Isabela, starts with a dinghy ride along the beautiful rocky shores where penguins and shore birds are usually seen. After a dry landing there is a hike through sharp lava rocks.

Elizabeth Bay, on the west coast, is home to a small colony of penguins living on a series of small rocky islets and visited by dinghy. **Sierra Negra Volcano** is reached from Villamil. The crater, some three miles across, is the biggest volcanic crater in the world. It takes at least a full day to climb up the volcano to see the tortoises. It can be climbed on foot, horseback or by pick-up.

Punta García, across the Isabela Channel from Santiago Island, is the only landing site on the eastern side of Isabela. From here it is possible to hike up to **Alcedo volcano** with its own sub-species of giant tortoise. You can see flightless cormorants here and there are also several active fumaroles.

Urbina Bay, at the base of Alcedo Volcano on the west coast, was the site of a major uplift in 1954, when the land rose up about 5 m. This event was associated with an eruption of Alcedo volcano. The coastline rose as far as 1 km out to the sea and exposed giant coral heads. The uplift was so sudden that lobster and fish were stranded on what is now the shore. **Tagus Cove**, located on the west coast across the narrow channel from Fernandina island, is an anchorage that has been used by visiting ships going back to the 1800s, and the ships' names can still be seen painted on the cliffs. A trail leads inland from Tagus Cove past **Laguna Darwin**, a large salt water lake, and then further uphill to a ridge with lovely views. **Punta Tortuga**, on the north of Tagus Cove on the west coast of Isabela, is a bathing beach surrounded by mangroves. **Punta Albermarle**, on the northern part of Isabela, was used as a radar base by the US during the Second World War.

Fernandina This is the youngest of the islands, about 700,000 years old. **Punta Espinosa** is
The most volcanically on the northeast coast of Fernandina. The trail from the landing site goes up
active of the islands, through a sandy nesting site for huge colonies of marine iguanas. The nests
with eruptions every appear as small hollows in the sand. You can also see flightless cormorants dry-
few years ing their atrophied wings in the sun and go snorkelling in the bay.

Santiago This large island, also known as James, is northwest of Santa Cruz. It has a volcanic landscape full of cliffs and pinnacles, home to several species of marine birds. This island has a large population of goats, one of the four species of animals introduced in the early 1800s.

James Bay is on the western side of the island, where there is a wet landing on the dark sands of **Puerto Egas**. The trail leads to the remains of an unsuccessful salt mining operation. Fur seals are seen nearby. **Espumilla Beach** is another famous visitor site. After landing on a large beach, walk through a mangrove forest that leads to a lake usually inhabited by flamingos, pintail ducks and stilts. There are nesting and feeding sites for flamingos. Sea turtles dig their nests at the edge of the mangroves. **Buccaneer Cove**, on the northwest part of the island, was a haven for pirates during the 1600s and 1700s. **Sullivan Bay** is on the eastern coast of Santiago, opposite Bartolomé Island. The visitor trail leads across an impressive lunar landscape of lava fields formed in eruptions in 1890.

This is probably the most easily recognized – the most visited and most photographed – of the islands in the Galápagos with its distinctive **Pinnacle Rock**. It is a small island located in Sullivan Bay off the eastern shore of Santiago. The trail leads steeply up to the summit, taking between 30 to 40 minutes, from where there are panoramic views. At the second landing site on the island there is a lovely beach from which you can snorkel or swim and see the penguins.

Bartolomé
One of the most popular and impressive sites

This island is just to the south of Santiago. The trail leads to a salt water lagoon, occasionally home to flamingos. There is an area of mangroves near the lagoon where brown pelicans nest. This island is said to have the most diversified volcanic rocks of all the islands. You can snorkel and swim from the beach.

Rábida

This is just off the southeastern tip of Santiago, or James, and its name refers to its shape. It is most noted for the volcanic landscape including sharp outcroppings, cracked lava formations, lava tubes and volcanic rubble. This site is only available to yachts of less than 12 passengers capacity.

Sombrero Chino

Located at the northeast part of the archipelago, this is an outpost for many sea birds. It is not an easy trip for the captain and crew since it takes an 8-10 hour all-night sail from Puerto Ayora. Genovesa and Fernandina are best visited on longer cruises or ships with larger range.

Genovesa

One of the most famous sites is **Prince Phillip's Steps**, an amazing walk through a seabird rookery that is full of life. You will see tropic birds, all three boobies, frigates, petrels, swallow-tailed and lava gulls, and many others. There is also good snorkelling at the foot of the steps, with lots of marine iguanas. The entrance to **Darwin Bay**, on the eastern side of the island, is very narrow and shallow and the anchorage in the lagoon is surrounded by mangroves, home to a large breeding colony of frigates and other seabirds.

Scuba diving

The Galápagos Islands are among the most desirable scuba diving destinations. At first look you might wonder why. During much of the year the water is cold enough to require thick wetsuits with hood and boots. Strong currents make many sites into drift dives, and can sometimes turn threatening if the unpredictable moving water becomes a downward flow at walls or steep reefs. There is no convenient place where you can just start your dive from the shore. Thirty metres (100 ft) of visibility here is considered great, but usually it's 15 m or less. So what is the attraction?

There are animals here in such profusion and variety that you won't find in any other place, and so close up that you won't mind the low visibility. Not just reef fish and schooling fish and pelagic fish, also sea lions, turtles, whale sharks, schools of hammerheads, flocks of several species of rays, diving birds, whales and dolphins; an exuberant diversity including many unique endemic species, and representing every kind of environment, from parrot fish to penguins. You could be with a Galápagos marine iguana, the world's only lizard that dives and feeds in the sea, or perhaps meet a glittering man-size sailfish. Make no mistake, this is no tame theme park, nor like some other well-travelled dive destinations where a predictable fish is given a pet name by the locals. Galápagos is adventure diving where any moment could surprise you.

Marine life

There are basically two options for diving in the Galápagos: live-aboard cruises and hotel-based day trips. Live-aboard operations usually expect the divers to

Dive options

Galápagos Islands

bring their own equipment, and supply only lead and tanks. The day trip dive operators supply everything. At the time of writing, day trip diving is mostly offered by boats operating out of Puerto Ayora on Santa Cruz, and one small operator in Puerto Baquerizo Moreno on San Cristobal (but service is not always available here).

Live-aboard cruises usually are reserved many months in advance. This is the only way to travel all around the archipelago, combining shore visits to the National Park and up to three dives per day and occasional night dives, on an itinerary of a week or more. The live-aboards take passengers to some of the National Park's most outstanding wildlife colonies, using a system of assigned itineraries, naturalist guides, and marked trails to protect these natural treasures. A few of the live-aboard cruises voyage to the isolated northern islands of Wolf and Darwin. Shore visits are forbidden there, but the extraordinary diving makes the long trip worthwhile.

Day trip diving is more economical and spontaneous, often arranged at the dive shop the evening before. The distances between islands limit the range of the day trip boats to the central islands. Nevertheless, day boats can offer reliable service and superb dive locations including Gordon Rocks, world famous for schooling hammerheads. The day trip dive boats do not take passengers ashore at the more frequently visited marked trail sites, but can offer special trips to isolated landings for travellers who want a less structured experience of this teeming ecology. Non-diving day tour boats also go to the National Park trail sites.

A third option is a combination of the first two. Through your agent or by email, make prior arrangements to combine the day trip dive services with one of the non-diving live-aboard cruise yachts. Before or after the live-aboard cruise, visitors based at a hotel can make day trip dives. Another way is a rendezvous of cruise yacht and dive boat at some other island.

For full details of companies which offer day trips, live-aboard diving tours or equipment rental, see under Puerto Ayora (page 420) and Puerto Baquerizo Moreno (page 422).

General advice   Visitors should be aware of some of the special conditions in Galápagos. The National Park includes practically all of the land and the surrounding waters. The National Park prohibits collecting samples or souvenirs, spear-fishing, touching animals, or other environmental disruptions. Guides apply the National Park rules, and they can stop your participation if you do not cooperate. The experienced dive guides can help visitors have the most spectacular opportunities to enjoy the wildlife.

Nonetheless, diving requires self reliance and divers are encouraged to refresh their skills and have equipment serviced before the trip. Though the day trip operators can offer introductory dives and complete certification training, this is not a place where a complete novice should come for a diving vacation. On many dives you could meet any combination of current, surge, cold water, poor visibility, deep bottom and big animals. Like many exotic dive destinations, medical care is limited, as are communications and transportation. The nearest recompression chamber is 650 miles away on the mainland (and not always functioning). To avoid the risk of decompression sickness, divers are advised to stay an extra day on the islands after their last dive, before flying to the mainland, especially Quito at 2,840 m above sea level.

Santa Fe This site offers wall dives, rock reefs, shallow caves, fantastic scenery and usually has clear calm water. You can dive with sea lions, schooling fish, pelagic fish, moray eels, rays, Galápagos sharks. Like everywhere in Galápagos, you can expect the unexpected.

Seymour Norte You can see sea lions, reef fish, hammerhead sharks, giant manta rays, white tip reef sharks, invertebrates. Occasionally whale sharks, humpback whale and porpoises.

Floreana Island The dive sites are offshore islets, each with its own character and scenery. **Devil's Crown** is a fractured ring of spiked lava around coral reefs. **Champion** is a little crater with a nesting colony of boobies, sea lion beaches and underwater rocky shelves of coral and reef fish. **Enderby** is an eroded tuff cone where you often meet large pelagics; rays, turtles, tunas and sharks. **Gardner** has a huge natural arch like a cathedral's flying buttress. These and other islets offer diving with reef fish, schooling fish, sea lions, invertebrates, rays, moray eels, white tip reef sharks, turtles, big fish including amberjack, red snapper, and grouper. Sometimes you can see giant mantas, hammerheads, Galápagos sharks, whales, seahorses, and the bizarre red lipped batfish.

Gordon Rocks This is a wall dive, with a deep bottom. Usually there is strong current, making this a drift dive along the wall. It is not recommended for novices. Gordon Rocks is world famous for diving with schools of hammerhead sharks, but there are also reef fish, amberjacks, snappers, barracudas, white tip reef sharks, turtles, invertebrates, rays, octopi and morays. Big pelagic fish could include wahoo, tuna, and even sailfish. Sometimes there are mantas, porpoise, whales and Galápagos sharks.

Dive sites
These are some of the better known dive sites in the central islands

Ins and outs

There are two airports which receive flights from mainland Ecuador, but no international flights to Galápagos. The most frequently used airport is at Baltra (South Seymour), across a narrow strait from Santa Cruz, the other at Puerto Baquerizo Moreno, on San Cristóbal. The two islands are 96 km apart and on most days there are local flights in light aircraft between them, as well as to Puerto Villamil on Isabela island. There is also an irregular boat service between Puerto Ayora, Puerto Baquerizo Moreno, Puerto Villamil and Floreana island. See Getting around, below.

Airports

At the close of this edition only TAME was operating flights to Galápagos (2 daily to Baltra and 2 a week to San Cristóbal), although it was hoped that Aerogal would soon begin flights to San Cristóbal and make a long stopover in Guayaquil. The return fare in high season (1 Dec-5 Jan and 15 Jun-31 Aug) is US$385 from Quito (US$340 from Guayaquil). The low season fare costs US$330 from Quito, and US$295 from Guayaquil. The same prices apply regardless of whether you fly to San Cristóbal or Baltra; you can arrive at one and return from the other. The ticket is valid for 21 days from the date of departure. Independent travellers must get their boarding pass (*pre-chequeo*) for outward and return flights 2 days before departure. This is especially critical during high season and from San Cristóbal at all times.

All flights originate in Quito

The prices indicated above are subject to change without notice. Discount fares for Ecuadorean nationals and residents of Galápagos are not available to foreigners and these rules are strictly enforced. A 15% discount is available to students with an ISIC card; details from TAME office at Edif Pichincha, 4th Floor, Amazonas y Colón, Quito.

Galápagos Islands

Boat owners make block bookings with the airlines in the hope of filling their boat. Visitors may buy tickets where they like, but in the busy season will have to take the ticket to the tour operator for the reservation. Tickets are the same price everywhere, except for student discounts with TAME as above.

Air Force flights, known as *logísticos*, may only be booked in person at the military airport in Quito. In 2000 however, foreigners were not permitted to use these flights and the rules were strictly enforced. This option is, at best, a long shot.

To and from the airport   Two buses meet flights from the mainland at Baltra: one runs to the port or *muelle* (10 mins, no charge) where the cruise boats wait; the other goes to Canal de Itabaca, the narrow channel which separates Baltra from Santa Cruz. It is 15 mins to the Canal, US$1.50, then you cross on a small ferry for US$0.30, another bus waits on the Santa Cruz side to take you to Puerto Ayora in 45 mins, included in the first fare. If you arrive at Baltra on one of the local inter-island flights (see below) then you have to wait until the next flight from the mainland for bus service, or you might be able to hire a taxi. For the return trip to the airport, CITTEG buses leave from opposite the company's office/café near the pier (see map, page 418) to meet flights at Baltra (enquire locally for current schedules). It's best to buy a ticket the night before, though this is not possible for the Saturday bus. Hotels may make prior arrangements.

The pleasant airport in **Puerto Baquerizo Moreno** is within walking distance of town, but those on prearranged tours will be met by transport. Pickup trucks can be hired if you are on your own and have have lots of gear.

Sea   Several small cargo vessels sail for Galápagos from from the Muelle Sur Naval by Calle 'K' in Guayaquil. Each ship sails about every 2-3 weeks. The journey usually takes 3 days and return fares are approximately US$160 per person, including food, in 3 or 4 bunk berths. It costs extra to stay with the ship while it calls on various ports in Galápagos. Take care of the cranes, etc, and be very alert to theft at all times (reports of very basic facilities, inadequate food and accommodation). It is described as "an experience, but not a way to see the Galápagos". The park entry tax must be paid on arrival.

In 2000 The *Virgen de Monserrat* was authorized to carry passengers; contact their Guayaquil office at Av Dr Elias Muñoz Vicuña e Isla Santa Cruz, T296785, F399475. Other vessels sailing this route include: *Paola*, Colón 103 y Malecón, T524325, F524525; and *Marina 91*, Chile y Urdaneta, T/F397370. Enquire in advance by phone about sailing dates but final arrangements are best made on site. Always take a look at the ship beforehand and make sure you understand what is involved. You may have to obtain special permission from the Capitanía del Puerto to sail aboard some ships.

Entry tax

Every foreign visitor has to pay a National Park Tax of US$100 on arrival, cash only. Be sure to have your passport on hand. Do not lose your park tax receipt; boat captains need to record it. A 50% reduction on the national park fee is available to children under 12, but only those foreigners who are enrolled in an Ecuadorean university are entitled to the reduced fee for students.

Getting around

Emetebe Avionetas offers inter-island flights in 2 light twin-engine aircraft (a 5-seater and a 9-seater). There is no firm schedule but flights usually operate Mon-Sat in the morning between Puerto Baquerizo Moreno (San Cristóbal), Baltra and Puerto Villamil (Isabela), depending on passenger demand. Baggage allowance 30 lbs, strictly enforced. Fares range from US$80 to US$100 one way, including taxes; charter rates from US$400 to US$500 per hour. Emetebe offices in Puerto Baquerizo Moreno, Puerto Ayora and Puerto Villamil are given in the corresponding sections below. In Guayaquil T292492, emetebe@ecua.net.ec

In 2000 the *Estrella del Mar* sailed from Puerto Villamil (Isabela) to Puerto Ayora (Santa Cruz) on Mon and Thu, returning Tue and Fri, 6 hrs, US$30 one way. The *Galamar*, sailed from Puerto Baquerizo Moreno (San Cristóbal) to Puerto Ayora on Mon, Wed and Fri, returning on Tue, Thu and Sat, 5 hrs, US$30 one way; this boat can also be chartered for trips to Floreana, US$400 and Isabela US$500. These schedules are subject to change. There is also an irregular boat service from Puerto Ayora to Floreana; check at the Capitanía de Puerto. You must be flexible in your itinerary and allow plenty of time if you wish to travel between islands in this way.

Island cruises

There are two ways to travel around the islands: a 'tour navegable', where you sleep on the boat, or less expensive tours where you sleep ashore at night and travel during the day. On the former you travel at night, arriving at a new landing site each day, with more time ashore. On the latter you spend less time ashore and the boats are smaller with a tendency to overcrowding in high season. All tours begin with a morning flight from the mainland on the first day and end on the last day with an afternoon flight back to the mainland. Prices are no longer significantly cheaper in the low season (February-May, September-November), but you will have more options available. The islands get very busy in July and August (high season), when it is impossible to make last minute arrangements.

It is not possible to generalize about exactly what you will find on the boat in which you cruise around the Galápagos Islands. The standard of facilities varies from one craft to another and you basically get what you pay for. Once on shore at the visitor sites, no matter what price you have paid, each visitor is shown the same things because of the strict park rules on limited access. Note however that smaller and cheaper boats may not visit as many or as distant sites. On the other hand, larger vessels may not be allowed to take passengers to some of the more fragile landings (Daphne Major, for example).

Each day starts early and schedules are usually full (if they aren't you're not getting your money's worth). If you are sailing overnight, your boat will probably have reached its destination before breakfast. After eating, you disembark for a morning on the island. The usual time for snorkelling is between the morning excursion and lunch. The midday meal is taken on board because no food is allowed on the islands. If the island requires two visits (for example Genovesa/Tower, or Española/Hood), you will return to shore after lunch, otherwise part of the afternoon may be taken up with a sea voyage. After the day's activities, there is time to clean up, have a drink and relax before the briefing for the next day and supper.

Itineraries are controlled by the National Park to distribute tourism evenly throughout the islands. Boats are expected to be on certain islands on certain days. They can cut landings, but have to get special permission to add to a planned itinerary. An itinerary change may be made if time would be better spent elsewhere. A good guide will explain this and you can trust their advice. Altering an itinerary to spend more time in Puerto Ayora or San Cristóbal is unacceptable (except in extreme bad weather). This sometimes occurs because not all passengers are on the same length of tours and boats come into port to change passengers.

Galápagos Islands

Choosing a tour

The less expensive boats are normally smaller and less powerful so you see less and spend more time travelling; also the guiding is likely to be in Spanish only (there are some exceptions to this). The more expensive boats will probably have 110 volts, a/c, video and private baths, all of which can be nice, but not critically important. All boats have to conform to certain minimum safety standards (check that there are enough life-rafts) and have VHF radio, but the rules tend to be quite arbitrary (for example windows and portholes may have domestic, rather than safety glass). A water maker can make quite a difference as the town water from Puerto Ayora or Puerto Baquerizo Moreno should not be drunk. Note that boats with over 18 passengers take quite a time to disembark and re-embark people, while the smaller boats have a more lively motion, which is important if you are prone to seasickness. Note also that there may be severe limitations for vegetarians on the cheaper boats.

The least expensive boats (called economy class) cost about US$60 per day; they tend to travel during the day, with nights spent at anchor. For around US$75 per day (tourist class) you will also be on a small boat but travelling at night, with more time ashore in daylight. US$100 per day ('superior tourist' or first class) is the price of the majority of better boats, most with English guiding. Over US$200 per day is entering the luxury bracket, with English guiding the norm, far more comfortable cabins and a superior level of service and cuisine. No boat may sail without a park-trained guide.

It must be stressed that a boat is only as good as its crew and when the staff change, so will these recommendations. The South American Explorers in Quito (see page 145) has an extensive file of trip reports for members to consult. *Safari Tours* in Quito (see page 133) also keep abreast of developments.

Booking a cruise

You can book a Galápagos cruise in several different ways: 1) from either a travel agency or directly though a Galápagos wholesaler in your home country, 2) from one of the very many agencies found throughout Ecuador, especially in Quito but also Guayaquil, or 3) from agencies in Puerto Ayora but not Puerto Baquerizo Moreno. The tradeoff is always between time and money: booking from home is most efficient and expensive, Puerto Ayora cheapest and most time-consuming, while Quito and Guayaquil are intermediate. Prices for a given category of boat do not vary all that much however, and it is not possible to obtain discounts or make last-minute arrangements in high season. Those who attempt to do so in July, August or over Christmas/New Years often spend several very frustrating weeks in Puerto Ayora without ever seeing the islands. The following section lists recommended agencies and operators based in Quito, Guayaquil, Puerto Ayora and abroad. See also the list of recommended boats below.

UK In Britain, contact David Horwell, who arranges tailor-made tours to Ecuador and the Galápagos Islands. For further details contact **Galapagos Adventure Tours**, 37-39 Great Guildford Street, London SE1 0ES, T/F020-7261 9890, david@galapagos.co.uk, www.galapagos.co.uk Penelope Kellie also comes recommended, pkellie@yachtors.u-net.com, T01962-779317, F779458, www.quasarnauticatumbaco.com She is the UK agent for **Quasar Nautica** (see Quito Tour operators, on page 133). **Galapagos Classic Cruises**, 6 Keyes Road, London NW2 3XA, T020-89330613, F84525248, GalapagosCruises@compuserve.com, www.galapagoscruises.co.uk

specializes in tailor-made cruises and diving holidays to the islands with additional land tours to Ecuador and Peru available on request.

Galápagos Network, 6303 Blue Lagoon Drive, Suite 140, Miami, FL 33126, **USA** T305-2626264, T800-6337972 (toll free), F305-2629609, info@galapagosnetwork. com, www.ecoventura.com *Sol International*, 13780 S. W., 56 St, Suite 107, Miami, FL 33175, T305-3826575, T1800-7655657 (toll free), F305-3829284, solint@ cwixmail.com *International Expeditions*, One Environs Park, Helena, Alabama, 35080, T205-4281700, T1-800-6334734 (toll free), nature@ietravel.com, www.ietravel.com *Wilderness Travel* (801 Allston Way, Berkeley, CA 94710, T1-800-3682704) and *Inca Floats* (Bill Robertson, 1311 63rd Street, Emeryville, CA 94608) have also been recommended.

Quito & Guayaquil Shopping around the many agencies in Quito is a good way of securing a value-for-money cruise, if you have the time. It is worth asking if the vessel has 1-3 spaces to fill on a cruise; you can try to get them at a discount. See Quito Tour operators (page 133) for complete contact information for the agencies listed below. *Safari Tours* have a data base on all boats with current vacancies and will sell trips at fair prices. They are highly recommended. Also recommended are the following operators with Quito offices, all of whom have a well established reputation for quality Galápagos cruises: *Angermeyer's Enchanted Expeditions*, *Quasar Nautica*, *Rolf Wittmer* and *Metropolitan Touring*. The following equally recommended operators have offices in both Quito and Guayaquil: *Ecoventura*, *Galasam and Canodros* (see the corresponding sections for contact information).

Other recommended agencies in Quito are *Galacruises Expeditions*, Jorge Washington 748 b/, Av Amazonas and 9 de Octubre, Quito, T556036/523324, T/F224893, seaman@uio.satnet.net, www.galapagosseaman.com.ec Owners of the *Sea Man* yacht offer diving and nature cruises. *Islas Galápagos Turismo y Vapores*, Av República de El Salvador N36-43 y Suecia, Quito, T446884/3, F439888/446882, www.ambasadorcruises.com, offers cruises aboard *Ambasador I*.

There are of course a great many other agencies throughout Ecuador which sell Galápagos tours; the key is to shop around carefully and not let yourself be rushed into a decision.

Puerto Ayora If you wish to wait until you reach the islands, Puerto Ayora is the only practical place for arranging a cruise; this cannot be done in Puerto Baquerizo Moreno. In Puerto Ayora you may find slightly better prices than the mainland, especially in the last minute, but bear in mind that you could be faced with a long wait. In the high season (July, August, and mid-December to mid-January) there is no space available on a last minute basis, so at these times of the year you must purchase your cruise before arriving in Galápagos.

Galápagos Islands

To arrange last-minute tours, a highly recommended contact is Yenny Montenegro de Divine at the *Moonrise* travel agency. There are also several other agencies, including *Galasam*, in Puerto Ayora who offer this service (see Puerto Ayora, below). Especially on cheaper boats, check carefully about what is and is not included (for example drinking water, snorkelling equipment and so on).

Recommended boats

Almost 90 boats were operating in the islands in 2000; we cannot list them all. We list those for which we have received positive recommendations. Exclusion does not imply poor service. Also remember that captains, crews and guides regularly change on all boats. These factors, as well as the sea, weather and your fellow passengers will all influence the quality of your experience.

Two boats with consistently high recommendations are the sailing brigantine *Andando* and the motor trawler *Samba*, both owned by Jane and Fiddi

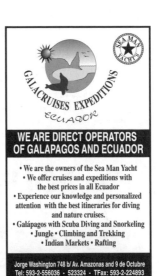

Galápagos Islands

Angermeyer (book through *Angermeyer* tour operator in Quito or *Moonrise* in Puerto Ayora). Georgina and Agustín Cruz' *Beagle III* offers friendly service with good cooking (bookable through *Metropolitan Touring*).

The 22-passenger luxury motor yachts *Eric, Flamingo I* and *Letty* all offer top quality comfort and service, and have excellent cruising range to cover distant parts of the archipelago. They are operated by *Ecoventura* tour operator (see Quito, Guayaquil and Galapagos Network USA above), who also run *Sky Dancer* specifically for live-aboard diving tours. The *Galápagos Explorer II* is a 100-passenger luxury ship with all facilities, operated by *Canodros* tour agency (see Quito and Guayaquil). Also good are the motor yacht *Orca* (book through *Etnotours*, JL Mera y Cordero, Quito, T230552) and *Angelique* (owner Franklin Angermeyer). Highly recommended are *Quasar Nautica's Parranda, Resting Cloud, Lammer Law* and *Alta*.

Rolf Wittmer, son of Margaret Wittmer of the famous 1930s Galápagos Affair, owns and runs *Tiptop III* (no snorkelling equipment). His son has the sailing yacht *Symbol*, a converted ship's lifeboat, which is very basic, but a good way to drift between the islands (*Wittmer Turismo*, see Quito Tour operators). *Seaman*, run by *Galacruises Expeditions*, has good tours but cramped lower cabins (see Quito agencies above)). The sailing catamaran *Pulsar* is recommended, but it is best when the owner Patric is on board; it is run by *Galaptur* (JL Mera 358 y Robles, Quito, T226432, F567622, aaagalap@uio.satnet.net, www.galapagostour.com).

The *Golondrina* and *Fragata* offer a good service; book through *Golondrina Turismo*, JL Mera 639 y Carrión, Quito, T528570, F528570. *Isla Galápagos* is recommended; the guide Peter Freire speaks quite good English. *Elizabeth II* has good crew and food. Also good is the *Angelito* of Hugo Andrade (with a new

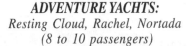
Galápagos Islands

ISLAS GALAPAGOS M/V AMBASADOR I

THE MOST COMFORTABLE VESSEL CRUISING THE GALAPAGOS ISLANDS

Discover the magic of the enchanted archipelago, the flora and fauna of its remote islands, combined with the excellent service on board 3, 4 & 7 night cruises with shore excursions that are lead by naturalist guides.

The Ambasador I accommodates 100 passengers on three different decks. Other facilities include sundeck, swimming pool, bar-saloon, gift shop and library. We also offer land services in continental Ecuador such as sightseeing in Quito, Indian Markets, Highlands & Hotels.

Fax: 593-2-439888 or 593-2 446882 Phone: 593-2-446884/3
E-mail: ambasador@impsat.net.ec or ambasador@galapagos.com.ec
Address: Av. República de El Salvador N36-43 y Suecia
URL Web: www.ambasadorcruises.com
Quito - Ecuador

Angelito in service); *Española* (eight passengers, good food); *Lobo del Mar* (12 passengers); *Daphne* (8 passengers – good cook); *Stella Maris* (book through Yenny Divine); and *San Antonio* (12 passengers, good food, nice crew).

Day tours can be arranged on *North Star*, which is small but fast (contact David Asencio at *Hotel Darwin* in Puero Ayora). Also *Santa Fe II*, owned by Byron Rueda (T526593), and *Esmeraldas*, owned by *Ninfa Tours* (see Quito Tour operators).

General advice

A ship's crew and guides are usually tipped separately. The amount is a very personal matter; you may be guided by suggestions made onboard or in the agency's brochures, but the key factors should always be the quality of service received and – of course – your own resources.

Tipping

Legitimate complaints may be made to any or all of the following: the Jefe de Turismo at the national park office in Puerto Ayora, the Ministerio de Turismo office or the Capitanía de Puerto. Any 'tour navegable' will include the days of arrival and departure as full days. Insist on a written itinerary or contract prior to departure as any effort not to provide this probably indicates problems later. South American Explorers (see page 145) has produced a useful, brief guide to the Galápagos which includes a specimen contract for itinerary and living conditions.

Problems

If a crew member comes on strong with a woman passenger, the matter should first be raised with the guide or captain. If this does not yield results, a formal complaint, in Spanish, giving the crew member's full name, the boat's name and the date of the cruise, should be sent to Sr Capitán del Puerto, Base Militar de Armada Ecuatoriana, Puerto Ayora, Santa Cruz, Galápagos. Failure to report such behaviour will mean it will continue. To avoid pilfering, never leave belongings unattended on a beach when another boat is in the bay.

Daytime clothing should be lightweight, and even on 'luxury cruises', should be casual and comfortable. At night, particularly at sea and at higher altitudes, warm clothing is required. Note that boots and shoes soon wear out on the lava terrain. A remedy for seasickness is recommended; the waters south of Santa Cruz are particularly rough. A good supply of sun block and skin cream to prevent windburn and chapped lips is essential, as are a hat and sunglasses. You should be prepared for dry and wet landings. The latter involves wading ashore.

What to take

Take plenty of film with you. The animals are so tame that you will use far more than you expected. Two 36-exposure rolls a day will barely be enough for the least enthusiastic of photographers. A telephoto lens is not essential, but if you have one, bring it. Also take filters suitable for strong sunlight. An underwater camera is also an excellent idea. Snorkelling equipment is particularly useful as much of the sea-life is only visible under water. Most of the cheaper boats do not provide equipment and those that do may not have good snorkelling gear. If in doubt, bring your own, rent in Puerto Ayora, or buy it in Quito (available at *KAO* in the Ecuatoriana building at Colón y Almagro). It is possible to sell it afterwards either on the islands or back in Quito.

Galápagos: A Natural History Guide, Michael H Jackson (University of Calgary Press, 1985). This is considered the Bible by all guides and staff at the Charles Darwin Research Station. Also good is *The Galápagos Islands*, by Pierre Constant (Odyssey, 2000).

Recommended reading

The *Galápagos Guide* by Alan White and Bruce White Epler, with photographs by Charles Gilbert, is published in several languages. These can be bought in Guayaquil in Librería Científica and Libri Mundi in Quito. South American Explorers in Quito sells a useful brief guide, *Galapagos Package*, US$4.

Galápagos: the Enchanted Isles by David Horwell (London: Dryad Press, 1988). Available through his UK agency (see Booking a cruise above).

The Enchanted Isles. The Galápagos Discovered, John Hickman (Anthony Nelson, 1985).

The Galápagos Affair, John Treherne (Jonathan Cape, 1983) describes the bizarre events on Floreana in the 1930s. More personal is Margret Wittmer's autobiography: *Floreana* (Michael Joseph, London, 1961).

Journal of the Voyage of HMS Beagle, by Charles Darwin, first published in 1845. Penguin Books of the UK have published Darwin's account of the Galápagos in their Penguin 60s Classics series. Another interesting historical work is Herman Melville's *The Encantadas* [1854], published in *Billy Bud, Sailor and Other Stories* (Penguin Books, London, 1971).

Reef Fish Identification, Paul Humann (Libri Mundi, 1993).

A Field Guide to the Fishes of Galápagos, Godfrey Merlen (Libri Mundi, 1988).

Plants of the Galápagos Islands, Eileen Schofield (New York: Universe Books, 1984).

A Guide to the Birds of the Galápagos Islands, Isabel Castro and Antonia Phillips (Christopher Helm, 1996).

The Galápagos Conservation Trust (18 Curzon St, London W1Y 7AD, T0171-6295049, F0171-6294149, galapagosconstrust@compuserve.com), publishes a quarterly Newsletter for its members.

Noticias de Galápagos is a twice-yearly publication about science and conservation in the islands. It is the official publication of the Charles Darwin Foundation. 'Friends of the Galápagos' (US$25 per year membership) receive the journal as a part of their membership.

Websites about Ecuador and Galápagos are listed under Tourist information, page 22.

A recommended map is *The Galápagos Islands*, 1:500,000 map by Kevin Healey and Hilary Bradt (Bradt Publications, 1985). Also recommended is the *Galápagos Pocket Guide* (and map) by Nelson Gómez, available in most Quito bookshops.

Puerto Ayora

Phone code: 05
Colour map 1
Population:
around 10,000

Puerto Ayora is the largest town of the Galápagos archipelago and the main tourist centre, with a wide range of hotels, restaurants and shops. If you choose to arrange a tour from here, instead of from the mainland, it's a pleasant place to spend a few quiet days waiting.

The cost of living in Puerto Ayora, and throughout the Galápagos, is higher than in the mainland, particularly in the peak season (December, July and August). Most food has to be imported although certain meats, fish, vegetables and fruit are locally produced. Bottled drinks are relatively expensive; for example a gallon (4 litre) bottle of mineral water is US$1 and a beer costs between US$1 and US$3.

The *Ministerio de Turismo/CAPTURGAL*, on Avenida Charles Darwin by south end of Pelican Bay, T526174, cptg@pa.ga.pro.ec, is open Monday to Friday 0800-1200, 1500-1600. Information also available at the boat owners' cooperative office nearby.

Excursions from Puerto Ayora

For a detailed description of the various sites around Santa Cruz see Visitor sites, page 398

One of the most beautiful beaches in the Galápagos Islands is at **Tortuga Bay**, an hour's walk (5 km) west from Puerto Ayora on a marked and cobbled path. Start at the west end of Calle Charles Binford; further on there is a gate where you must register, open 0600-1830 daily. The sunsets here are excellent. Take drinking water and do not go alone (occasional incidents have been reported). Also take care of the very strong undertow, the surf is calmer on the next cove to the west. Camping is not permitted.

Las Grietas is a beautiful gorge with a pool at the bottom which is ideal for bathing. It is to the southwest of town, a 20-minute walk from *Hotel Delfín* (see Sleeping below). Follow the signs to the lagoon, then walk round the left side of the lagoon (follow the green and white posts) and head uphill at the far end of the lagoon on a clear path. Strong shoes or boots are advised. It can also be accessed by boat.

There are some areas of interest at and near the grounds of the Darwin Station. A small rocky beach is halfway between the interpretation centre and the entrance and is popular with local families at weekends. Past the interpretation centre on the paved road, and to the right of the Tomas Fischer Science building, a trail leads to a rocky beach where marine iguanas and crabs can be observed. Following a small trail between the gift shop at the entrance and the *Hotel Galápagos*, you can see the stone house built by the Norwegian pioneer Sigurd Graffer in 1933.

Tour operators in Puerto Ayora (see below) run excursions to the highland sites for US$10-20 per person, depending on the number of sites visited and the size of the group. These may include visits to ranches such as Rancho Mariposa (enquire at *Moonrise Travel*).

Bay excursions in glass-bottom boats (*Aqua Video*, best visibility, and *Mainao*, small glass window) visit sites near Puerto Ayora such as Isla Caamaño, Punta Estrada, Las Grietas, Franklin Bay and Playa de los Perros. It involves some walking and you are likely to see sea lions, birds, marine iguanas and marine life including sharks. Snorkelling can be part of the tour. Half-day tours (at 0900 and 1400) run US$25 per person and can be arranged at the pier or through travel agencies.

Essentials

Hotel space at the upper end of the market is limited and reservations are strongly recommended in the high season. There is a wide choice of budget hotels and a room shouldn't be difficult to find, except at the busiest times. Some hotels charge national and foreign rates; ask for national rates in the low season.

Sleeping
■ *on map*
Price codes:
see inside front cover

L *Delfín*, Barrio Punta Estrada, on a small bay to the south of Puerto Ayora and accessible only by boat, T526297, F526283, indefati@ayora.ecua.net.ec A lovely beach, pool, bar, restaurant, good service, comfortable rooms. Book through *Metropolitan Touring* (see Quito Tour operators) for hotel and related day-cruises. L *Galápagos*, Av Charles Darwin, near Darwin Research Station, T526296, T/F526330, hotelgps@pa.ga.pro.ec Fourteen cabins in 5 acres of seaside park, with bath, hot water, fan, great ocean views, laundry service, restaurant with fixed menu, fruit and meat from the hotel farm. Friendly service. Day trips and diving available, works in association with *Scuba Iguana* (see Diving below). Highly recommended. **L-AL** *Red Mangrove Inn*, Av Charles Darwin y las Fragatas, on the way to the Research Station, T/F526564, redmangrove@ecuadorexplorer.com, www.ecuadorexplorer.com/redmangrove or book through the *Cultura Reservation Center* in Quito, T558889, F224271. Six rooms decorated in a unique style with ocean views, hot showers, jacuzzi, deck bar, restaurant, warmly recommended. Also offer tours including sea kayaking, windsurfing, highland farm, cruises in the *Azul*, 5 and 8 day land-based tours, cruises in the *Ecuador Explorer*, diving (with *Nauti Diving*), bicycle rentals and horse riding.

AL *Angermeyer*, Av Charles Darwin y Los Piqueros, T/F526277 (Quito T/F269626). A/c rooms, solar water heating, good restaurant, pool, laundry, tours arranged, bicycle hire, diving trips. Comfortable and attractive. **AL** *Fernandina*, 12 de Noviembre y

Los Piqueros, T526499, F526122. A/c, hot water, restaurant, pool (open to non guests), jacuzzi. **A** *Las Ninfas*, Los Colonos y Berlanga, near the harbour, T526127, F526359. Full range of services, includes breakfast, a/c, hot water, pool, jacuzzi, good restaurant, own boat at reasonable price for day trips.

B-C *Sol y Mar*, Av Charles Darwin, next to Banco del Pacifico, T526281, F527015. Ten rooms with bath, hot water, fan, balconies, those with ocean views are the most

Puerto Ayora

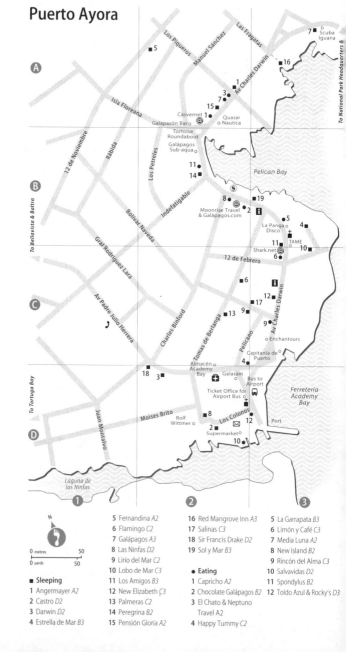

Galápagos Islands

expensive. Long stay discounts. **C** *Castro*, Los Colonos near the harbour, T526508, F526113. With bath, cold water, fan. Popular. Owner Sr Miguel Castro arranges 7-day tours and is an authority on wildlife. **C** *Estrella de Mar*, Av Charles Darwin y 12 de Febrero, T526427. Spacious rooms with bath, hot water, fan, communal sitting area, room with balcony and sea view. Clean, comfortable. Recommended. **D** *Gran Hotel Fiesta*, Moises Brito y Las Ninfas, a 15-min walk inland from the seafront, T/F526440 (Quito T509654), fiestur@pi.pro.ec With bath, hot water, fan, hammocks, restaurant, laundry. Very quiet, reasonable value but a bit remote. **D** *Palmeras*, Av Tomás de Berlanga y Naveda, T526139, F526373. With bath, fan, restaurant, terrace with pool. Good value. Also run day tours. **E** *Salinas*, Naveda y Berlanga, T/F526107. With bath, cold water, fan, restaurant. Clean, good value.

F-G *Los Amigos*, Av Charles Darwin, opposite TAME office, T526265. Cool and airy rooms (upstairs best), most with shared bath, laundry facilities. Friendly, family-run, clean. Recommended. **F** *New Elizabeth*, Av Charles Darwin, near the Capitanía de Puerto, T526178. With bath, cold water, breakfast available, laundry. Reasonable, owner very helpful. **F** *Flamingo*. Berlanga y Naveda, T526556. With bath, fan, laundry, interior patio. Hot, clean, OK. **F** *Lirio del Mar*, Naveda y Berlanga, near the bus stop, T526212. Private bath, cold water, fan, cafeteria, laundry facilities. Clean, not too friendly but otherwise OK. **F** *Lobo de Mar*, 12 de Febrero y Av Charles Darwin, T526188, F526569. With bath, cold water, fan, balconies, laundry facilities. Clean, popular with nationals, noisy on occasions, OK. **F** *Peregrina*, on Av Charles Darwin e Indefatigable, T526323. With bath, most rooms with fan, garden, shady terrace, includes good breakfast. Friendly. Recommended. **F** *Sir Francis Drake*, Padre J Herrera y Binford, T526222. With bath, cold water, fan. OK. **G** *Darwin*, Padre J Herrera y Binford, 526193. With bath, fan, shady patio, restaurant (order meals in advance). Ageing. **G** *Pensión Gloria*, Av Charles Darwin y Los Piqueros. Cold water. Very basic. Friendly. **G** *Santa Cruz*, Padre J Herrera e Indefatigable, T526573. Shared bath, cold water. Small, friendly, family run.

For longer stays there are houses for rent for US$15 per person per day. Enquire at *Moonrise Travel*.

Don't leave valuables unattended in your room in cheaper hotels

The following restaurants are on the main street unless mentioned otherwise, starting at the harbour and moving north towards the Darwin Station. *Salvavidas*, right on the seafront overlooking the activity at the pier. Good set lunch, good breakfast, seafood, hamburgers, or just a beer while you wait. *Toldo Azul*, at the harbour. Popular with tour groups, good reputation for seafood and fish. *Rocky´s*, overlooking the bay. Bar and grill, in 2 separate sections, popular. *Cucuve*. Traditional snacks like *humitas* and *tamales*, hamburgers, juice, coffee. *Sabrosón*, open-air grill. OK food, nice décor. *Happy Tummy*, opposite the Capitanía de Puerto. Varied menu, meals and snacks. Good, open late even Sun. *Rincón del Alma*, north of the harbour. Good food, reasonable prices. *Limón y Café*, corner 12 de Febrero. Good snacks and drinks, lots of music, pool table, open evenings only, popular. *La Garrapata*, north of TAME, next to *La Panga* disco. Considered as the best food in town, try their *parrillada de pescado*. Attractive setting and good music. Popular meeting place for travellers, open morning and evening but not Sun, drinks expensive. *New Island*, by Charles Binford, near *Moonrise Travel*. Breakfast, fruit juices, seafood, ceviches. *Chocolate Galápagos*, opposite *Banco del Pacífico*. Good snacks, burgers, raclette. Popular with locals. *Spondylus*, north of Indefatigable. Regional and international food, good Italian dishes. *Capricho*, by the tortoise roundabout. Good vegetarian food, salads and juices, breakfast. Friendly, also sells souvenirs. Recommended. *Media Luna*, near corner Los Piqueros. Good food, pizza, also sandwiches, excellent brownies. Open evenings only. *El Chato*, corner Los Piqueros. Set meals and à la carte. *Viña del Mar*. Padre J Herrera. Popular with locals. Along Charles Binford, near Padre J Herrera are a series of kiosks selling traditional food at economic prices; *Tía Juanita* cooks well, seafood.

Eating
● *on map*

Galápagos Islands

Bakeries There is one on Charles Binford and the most popular one is almost opposite the telephone office, it opens early and serves hot bread and drinking yoghurt before the early bus leaves for the airport. The restaurant at the bus company office also does a cheap breakfast.

Outside Puerto Ayora There are some expensive restaurants in ranches in the highlands serving lunch, meals run about US$16. Arrangements have to be made in advance, agencies or hotels with a VHF radio can help you make a reservation. *Narwhal*, at Km 14 on the way to Santa Rosa. Set meals, food is OK. *Rancho Mariposa*, also near Santa Rosa. For groups only, reserve through *Moonrise Travel*. *Rancho Altair*, in the Cascajo area, near the lava tunnels. Ask for Tim Gray and Anita Salcedo at *Garrapata* restaurant.

Bars & nightclubs *La Panga*, Av Charles Darwin y Berlanga and *Five Fingers*, Av Charles Darwin opposite the Capitanía de Puerto, are popular bar/discos. *Galapasón* is a popular salsa bar at the tortoise roundabout. *Salsa 10*, on Naveda, good latin music.

Shopping For boat charters and camping trips most basic foodstuffs generally can be purchased on the islands, but cost more than on the mainland. The *Proinsular* supermarket opposite the pier is the best place (try their delicious locally-made yoghurt drink). The *mercado municipal* is on Padre J Herrera, beyond the telephone office, on the way out of town to Santa Rosa. Medicines, sun lotions, mosquito coils, film, and other useful items all cost more than on the mainland and at times might not be available. *Galapaguito* can meet most tourists' needs, the owners are very helpful. There is a wide variety of T-shirt and souvenir shops along the length of Av Charles Darwin. Do not buy items made of black coral as it is an endangered species.

Sports **Cycling** Mountain bikes can be hired from travel agencies in town, US$10 per day; or at the *Red Mangrove Inn*, US$5 per hour. *Galápagos Discovery* runs cycling tours in the highlands, US$25 per day.

Diving There are several diving agencies in Puerto Ayora, they offer courses, equipment rental, dives within Academy Bay (2 dives for US$75-80), dives to other central islands (2 dives, US$110-120), daily tours for 1 week in the central islands (12 dives, US$1,260) and several day live-aboard tours (1 week tour of central islands US$1,960). Two agencies that offer all services and have been repeatedly recommended are: *Galápagos Sub-Aqua*, Av Charles Darwin by Pelican Bay (Quito: Pinto 439 y Amazonas, office 101, T565294, F569956; Guayaquil: Dátiles 506 y Sexta, T304132, F314510), sub_aqua@accessinter.net, www.galapagos_sub_aqua.com.ec Instructor Fernando Zambrano offers full certificate courses up to divemaster level (PADI or NAUI). Open 0800-1200 and 1430-1830. *Scuba Iguana*, at the *Hotel Galápagos*, T526296, T/F526330, mathiase@pa.ga.pro.ec, www.scuba-iguana.com (Quito: *Scala Tours*, Foch 746 y Amazonas, T545856, F258655). Run by Jack Nelson and Mathias Espinosa, who are both experienced and knowledgeable about different sites, Mathias offers full certificate courses up to instructor level. Open 0730-1900. Divers must have their certificates and log books and can expect to be asked to do a test dive in the bay before going to more advanced sites. Making arrangements in advance, you can be met by a divemaster during a regular Galápagos cruise, you dive while your companions do a land visit.

Horse riding For horse riding at highland ranches, enquire with *Moonrise Travel*.

Kayaking and windsurfing Equipment rental and tours available from the *Red Mangrove Inn*, US$10 per hour.

Snorkelling Masks, snorkels and fins can be rented from travel agencies and dive shops, US$4-5 a day, US$60 deposit. Some bay tours include snorkelling. A full day snorkelling tour with *Scuba Iguana* is US$35 including equipment, wet suit and lunch. The closest place to snorkel is by the beaches near the Darwin Station.

Surfing There is surfing at Tortuga Bay (see excursions, above) and at other more distant beaches accessed by boat. Note that there is better surfing near Puerto Baquerizo Moreno on San Cristóbal. *Galápagos Discovery* rents surfboards US$10 per day and organizes surfing tours, US$55 and up. Vladimir Palma is a local surfer who can be found at *Discovery* or *Galapasón* bar.

Moonrise Travel Agency, Av Charles Darwin, opposite *Banco del Pacífico*, T526348, T/F526403, sdivine@pa.ga.pro.ec Last minute cruise bookings, day tours to different islands, bay tours, highland tours, airline reservations. Knowledgeable, helpful and reliable. Highly recommended. Run by Yenny and Steve Divine, Steve is a qualified recommended guide, his services run US$80 per day. *Galasam*, Padre J Herrera y Pelícano, near the port, T/F526126, heparton@ayora.ecua.net.ec Last minute tours, tickets for boat to Isabela. Helpful and friendly. *Sr Victor López*, at Ferretería Academy Bay, Padre J Herrera, opposite the hospital, T526136. Runs economical tours on the *Elizabeth*, very cheap. *Galápagos Discovery*, Padre J Herrera, opposite the hospital, T526245. Bicycle rentals and tours, surf boards, snorkelling gear, motorcycle rentals US$40. Run by Victor Vaca who also arranges last minute tours, they work with the *Free Enterprise* (this boat has received some negative reports). *Neptuno Tours*, Av Charles Darwin, at *El Chato* restaurant, near *Hotel Angermeyer*, T526246, economic highland tours. There are several agencies along Av Charles Darwin on the block opposite the Capitanía de Puerto offering the full range of tours. Among them: *Enchantours*, T526657, also rents snorkelling gear; *Galápagos Cruises 2000*, T526097, in the same premises, they are agents for DHL courier and Western Union.

Tour operators

Bus To **Bellavista** and **Santa Rosa** in the highlands, 3 daily, US$0.40. **Taxi** To **Santa Rosa** US$4. **Boat** Water taxis from the pier to nearby beaches such as **Las Grietas**, US$0.40. Tickets for the *Estrella de Mar* to **Puerto Villamil**, sold at *Galasam* agency or speak to the captain when the boat arrives Mon and Thu around 1300, for travel the next day. Tickets for the *Galamar* to **Puerto Baquerizo Moreno**, from Pablo López, Padre J Herrera y Binford, near *Rico Pan* bakery, T526413 or from *Galápagos Discovery* agency.

Transport
See also Getting there, page 405 and Getting around, page 406 for buses to the airport, flights and boats between islands, etc

Airline offices *TAME*, Av Charles Darwin north of 12 de Febrero, T526165. Open Mon-Sat 0830-1230, Mon-Fri 1400-1730. *Emetebe*, Av Charles Darwin opposite the port, 3rd floor of post office building, T526177.

Directory

Banks *Banco del Pacífico*, Av Charles Darwin by Pelican Bay. Open 0800-1500, US$3 commission per transaction to change TCs, Cirrus ATM and cash advance on Mastercard only. Note that there is nowhere in the islands to get cash advances on Visa or other credit cards and no other ATM networks. Mastercard is the most commonly accepted card on the islands, although the more upmarket businesses may take others. A surcharge is often applied to credit card purchases, and many places do not accept any credit cards at all. Most boats accept TCs.

Communications Post Office:, by the port. It often runs out of stamps (never leave money and letters), ask in the 'red boat' (*Galería Jahanna*) or *Artesanías Bambú*. Many postcards do not reach their destination, so it's probably best to wait until you return home (see Postal services, page 59). **Telecommunications:** *Pacifictel*, the telephone office, is on Padre J Herrera, 4 blocks from Av Charles Darwin. No collect or country-direct calls can be made from here. International calls can also be made from public cellular card phones (both Bell South and Porta), you can also receive calls at these phones. **Internet:** Rates run US$5-6 per hour. *Galapagos.Com*, Av Charles Darwin in back of Moonrise Travel. *Casvernet*, Pelican Bay, near the tortoise roundabout. *Shark.Net*, Av Charles Darwin y 12 de Febrero.

Embassies and consulates *British Consul*, David Balfour, c/o Etica, Barrio Estrada, Puerto Ayora.

Laundry *Lavagal*, by the football stadium, machine wash and dry US$1.50 per kilo, good, reliable, US$1 taxi ride from town.

Medical facilities Hospitals: there is a hospital on Padre J Herrera. Consultations cost US$10, medicines reasonably priced, but they cannot perform operations.

Galápagos Islands

Useful services Immigration: Only the immigration police in Puerto Baquerizo Moreno (San Cristóbal) are authorized to extend tourist visas. **Lost property:** information and retrieval of lost property from Radio Santa Cruz, next to the Catholic Church.

Puerto Baquerizo Moreno

On San Cristóbal island to the east, this is the capital of the province of Galápagos. The island is being developed as a second tourist centre. It is a pleasant place to spend a few days, with interesting excursions in the area.

Sights To the north of town, opposite Playa Mann, is the Galápagos National Park visitors' centre or **Centro de Interpretación**. It has an excellent display of the natural and human history of the islands. Highly recommended. ■ *Mon-Fri 0700-1200 and 1300-1700, Sat 0730-1300 and 1330-1730, Sun 0730-1200 and 1300-1700. Free. T520138.*

In town, the cathedral, on Avenida Northía, two blocks up from the post office, has interesting, mixed-media relief pictures on the walls and altar. ■ *0900-1200 and 1600-1800.* Next door is the small Franciscan museum of natural history. It has stuffed exhibits, old photos, and a tortoise called Pepe. ■ *Mon-Fri 0800-1200, 1500-1730, US$1.*

The provincial chamber of tourism, *CAPTURGAL*, on Malecón Charles Darwin y Española. has a list of services in town. *Asociación de Guías*, Malecón Charles Darwin y Wolf, is helpful with general information and has a book exchange. In the same office is the *Fundación Ecológica Albatros*, a local environmental group.

Excursions For a detailed description of the various sites around San Cristóbal, see Visitor sites, on page 398. A good trail goes from the Centro de Interpretación to the northeast through scrub forest to **Cerro Tijeretas**, a hill overlooking town and the ocean, 30 minutes away (take water). Side trails branch off to some lookouts on cliffs over the sea. Frigate birds (*tijeretas* or *fragatas*) nest in this area and can be observed gliding about, there are sea lions on the beaches below. To go back, if you take the trail which follows the coast, you will end up at **Playa Punta Carola,** a popular surfing beach, too rough for swimming. Closer to town is the small **Playa Mann** (follow Avenida Northía to the north), more suited for swimming and in town is **Playa de Oro**, where some hotels are located. Right in the centre of town, along the sand by the tidal pool, sea lions can be seen, be careful with the male who 'owns' the beach. Further afield to the northeast, and reached by boat (15 minutes) is **Puerto Ochoa**, another beach popular with locals.

To the south of town, 20 minutes' walk past the airport, is **La Lobería,** a

rocky bay with shore birds, sea lions and marine iguanas. You can continue along the cliff to see tortoises and rays, but do not leave the trail.

Sleeping

A *Hostal Northía*, Av Northía y 12 de Febrero, T/F520041. With a/c, hot water, TV, includes breakfast. Clean and friendly, but overpriced. **B** *Orca*, Playa de Oro, T/F520233, pat@etnot.ecx.ec With a/c, fridge, good food. OK, often filled with groups, has its own boat for cruises. **C** *Islas Galápagos*, Esmeraldas y Colón, T520203, F520162. With bath, hot shower, a/c, TV in sitting room. A bit run down. **B** *Hostal Galápagos*, at Playa de Oro, T520157. A/c cabins, hot water, fridge. Often unattended. **D** *Cabañas Don Jorge*, above Playa Mann, T520208, terana@ga.pro.ec Simple cabins in a quiet setting overlooking the ocean, with bath, hot water, fan, meals available. Clean, friendly. **E** *Chatham*, Av Northía y Av de la Armada Nacional, on the road to the airport, T520137. With bath, hot shower, fan, TV, meals on request. Nice courtyard with hammocks, very clean, friendly. **F** *Mar Azul*, Av Northía y Esmeraldas, on the road to the airport, T520139, F520384. With bath, hot shower, fan, nice gardens. Clean, good value. Highly recommended. **F** *Los Cactus*, Juan José Flores y Av Quito, near Pacifictel, T520078. With bath, hot shower. Family-run, friendly. **G** *Residencial San Francisco*, Malecón Charles Darwin y Villamil, T520304. With bath, cold water, fan. Rooms in front overlooking the harbour are nicer.

Puerto Baquerizo Moreno

■ Sleeping
1 Cabañas Don Jorge
2 Chatham
3 El Cactus
4 Flamingo
5 Hostal Galápagos
6 Islas Galápagos
7 Mar Azul
8 Northía
9 Orca

● Eating
1 Albacora
2 Bambú
3 Barracuda
4 Miconia
5 Panadería Fragata
6 Rosita
7 Sabor Latino

● Bars & Nightclubs
8 Blue Bay
9 El Barquero
10 La Terraza
11 Neptuno

Galápagos Islands

Simple, good, clean, friendly. **G** *Residencial Flamingo*, Hernández y Av Quito, T520204. With bath, cold water. Basic, friendly.

Out of town In El Progreso in the highlands is **G** *La Casa del Ceibo*, T520248. A cane treehouse atop a kapoc, equipped for short or long stays.

Eating There are several restaurants by the intersection of Ignacio de Hernández y General Villamil, including: *Rosita*. Set meals and varied à la carte menu. Very good, long known among the yacht crowd and considered as the best in town. *Barracuda*. Grilled meat, fish, and *menestras*. Cheap. *Pizzería Bambú*. Good economical set meals and pricey pizza and à la carte dishes.

Sabor Latino, Hernández y Manuel J Cobos. Good set meals, busy at lunch. *Miconia*, Av de la Armada Nacional, by the navy base. Varied menu, meat, fish, pizza, Italian. Nice breezy location, pleasant bar in the evening. *Albacora*, Av Northía y Española. Good set meals. In simple thached roof structure, cheap, very popular with locals. *Casa Blanca*, Malecón by the whale statue next to the pier. Breakfast, *ceviche*, Mexican snacks, grill on the weekends. Closed Mon. *Genoa*, Malecón Charles Darwin by Post office. A la carte. Open evenings only, music, good atmosphere. *Galapaluz*, Malecón Charles Darwin y Manuel J Cobos. Snacks, coffee, drinks. Small, with character, also gift shop. *Panadería Fragata*, Northía y Rocafuerte. Excellent bread and pastries, refrigerated cheese and yoghurt, good selection.

Out of town In El Progreso in the highlands are *La Casa del Ceibo* and *Quinta de Christi* open at weekends only and serving Ecuadorean dishes and *parrilladas*.

Bars & nightclubs *El Barquero*, Hernández y Manuel J Cobos. Bar and *peña*. Open daily. *Blue Bay* and *Neptuno*, both at Malecón Charles Darwin y Herman Melville, opposite the whale and opposite each other. Discos, young crowd, open Tue-Sat 2030-0300. *La Terraza*, at bottom of Manuel J Cobos, by the waterfront. Disco, large dance floor. There are other bars along Av de la Armada Nacional towards the waterfront.

Shopping There are a few souvenir shops along the Malecón selling T-shirts and a some crafts. Do not buy black coral. Paintings with Galápagos motifs can be bought from the following artists: *Arni Creaciones*, Av Quito y Juan José Flores, near Pacifictel. Humberto Muñoz, very nice work. Recommended. *Fabo Galería de Arte*, Malecón Charles Darwin, opposite the whale statue. Paintings by the owner Fabián, silk screened T-shirts. He also directs the *Mar de Lava* theatre group which has periodic presentations at the Centro de Interpretación. There is small produce market in town.

Sports **Cycling** Mountain bikes can be hired from travel agencies in town, US$0.80 per hour. **Diving** There are several diving sites around San Cristóbal, most popular being Kicker Rock, Roca Ballena and Punta Pitt (at the northeastern side). Gonzalo Quiroga of *Chalo Tours* is a divemaster offering tours to these sites, however he is not always available. **Surfing** There is good surfing in San Cristóbal, the best season is Dec-Mar. **Punta Carola** near town is the closest surfing beach; popular among locals. There is a championship during the local *fiestas*, the second week of Feb.

Tour operators *Chalo Tours*, Malecón Charles Darwin y Villamil, T520953. Bay tours US$35 per person (minimum 5 people) to Kicker Rock, Isla de los Lobos, boat tours to the north end of the island US$65 per person, highland tours to El Junco and Puerto Chino beach, US$20 per person, diving tours US$75-90 per person, bike rentals, snorkelling gear, surf boards, book exchange.

Transport **Bus** See also Getting there, page 405 and Getting around, page 406. To El Progreso in the highlands, see Visitor Sites, page 398. **Boat** Tickets for the *Galamar* to Puerto Ayora are sold by José Montero, at *Hostal Galápagos*, in Playa de Oro.

Airline offices *TAME*, at the airport, entrance around the side of main building, T521089. Reconfirm here and pick up your boarding pass 2 days in advance, there is a shortage of space on all flights. Open Mon-Fri 0900-1230 and 1400-1600, Sat 0900-1230. *Emetebe*, at the airport terminal, T520036. Open Mon-Fri 0700-1300 and 1500-1730, Sat 0700-1300. **Banks** *Banco del Pacífico*, Malecón Charles Darwin y 12 de Febrero, by the waterfront. Same services as in Puerto Ayora. Open Mon-Fri 0800-1530, Sat 1000-1200. **Book exchange** At the *Asociación de guías* and *Chalo Tours*. **Communications** Post Office: Malecón Charles Darwin y 12 de Febrero. **Telephone office:** Pacifictel on Av Quito, 3 blocks from the Malecón, same services as in Puerto Ayora, there are also card operated public cellular phones. **Internet** prices run US$5-US$6 per hour. *Cyber Jean Carlos*, Española y Malecón, Mon-Sat 0800-1230, 1430-2130, Sun 1630-1930. *Iguana Net 1*, Hernández corner Manuel J Cobos, Mon-Fri 0800-1300, 1430-1900, Sat 0900-1300. *Iguana Net 2*, Malecón Charles Darwin y Villamil, Mon-Sat 0800-1230, 1500-2000. **Laundry** *Lavandería Limpio y Seco*, Av Northía y 12 de Febrero. Wash and dry for US$2. Open daily 0900-2100. **Medical facilities** There is a hospital providing only basic medical services. Dr David Basantes, opposite *Hotel Mar Azul* is a helpful general practitioner. *Farmacia San Cristóbal*, Villamil y Hernández, is the best stocked pharmacy in town. **Useful services** Immigration: at Police Station, Malecón Charles Darwin y Española, T/F520129.

Isabela Island

Isabela is not highly developed for tourism but if you have a few days to spare it is worthwhile spending time there. It looks like most people's image of a Pacific island: coconut palms, azure ocean, white sand beaches, rocky inlets, mangroves, laid back lifestyle, funky little seafood restaurants offering lobster all the year round – and very few tourists. Just the place for some to pursue hardcore relaxation while the more energetic tramp round the island.

For a description of the various tourist sites, see under Visitor sites (page 398). All the accommodation listed below is in Puerto Villamil. There is a Pacifictel office four blocks from the plaza. There are no banks.

Horses can be rented for US$5 to US$10, depending on the destination. Book one day in advance: Sr Modesto Tupiza T529217 (he also has a truck for hire) or Sr Tenelema T529102. Antonio Gil is a guide.

It is 2½ hours each way to **Muro de las Lágrimas**, built by convict labour; horses available for part of route. The **Centro de Crianza** is 30 minutes' walk west of town, a breeding centre for seven species of giant tortoise. There are several good **beaches** ; west of town for surfing, east of town for mangroves and rocky inlets for snorkelling, in front of town for swimming. Fishermen can take you to see the white-tipped sharks at **Las Grietas,** US$8 per boat. In the **agricultural zone** you can visit small farms, harvest citrus fruit and so on.

Day trips can be arranged through *Isabela Tours*, on the plaza, T529207, F529201, expensive. Dora at *Ballena Azul* will help arrange trips, for example volcano tours US$20 per person, minimum two people. Tours are also arranged by *La Casa de Marita* and *Hotel San Vicente* (see below).

B *La Casa de Marita*, at east end of village, T529238, F529201, hcmarita@ga.pro.ec Includes breakfast, other meals on request. Various rooms with different prices (none cheap), all with private bath, hot water, fan; some with a/c and fridge. Also runs an expensive travel agency. **C** *Ballena Azul* and *Isabela del Mar*, next door to each other, same owner, T/F529125, isabela@ga.pro.ec, www.hosteriaisabela.com Private bath, solar hot water, fan. Meals available. Swiss-run, recommended. **E** *Tero Real*, C Tero Real y Opuntia, T529195. Private bath, cold water, fan, fridge. **F** *Loja*, on the road to airport and highlands, T529174. Private bath, cold water, fan, patio. Clean, basic, sometimes water shortages, friendly staff, cheap, very good restaurant. **F** *San Vicente*, C Cormorán y Las Escalecias, T529140. Private bath, cold water, fan, fridge. Meals on request. Clean, good value, often full. Also runs tours. There are several other basic places.

Eating   *El Encanto de la Pepa*, east of the plaza. Lots of character, good food, attractive setting, friendly. Best and most expensive in town. *Casa de Marita*, at hotel. Elegant, family-style, one set meal per day, order in advance. *Ballena Azul*, at hotel. Very pleasant, good food, many choices, but order in advance. *Costa Azul*, facing the Capitanía. Clean, modern, good daily specials. *La Ruta*, on the plaza. Simple, small, set meals and à la carte. *La Iguana*, on the beach in the Parque Iguana. Pizza and more, but mostly serves drinks under the palms. Try ordering in advance. Open mostly weekends and holidays. *Caracol*, kiosk next to police station. One set meal per day, good and cheap, but arrive early or they sell out. *Campo Duro*, in the highlands at Merceditas. Parrilladas, weekends only, popular. Comedores: *Jacqueline* and *Perla del Pacifico*, both good and cheap but limited menu.

Transport   **Bus** Two daily to the highlands, 48 km round trip: departs 0700 by the market,
There is a regular service   returns 0845; second trip at 1200, returns around 1400. The bus passes villages of
from Baltra and Puerto   Santo Tomás, Marianitas, La Esperanza and La Cura. From La Cura it is a 20 min walk to
Ayora by light aircraft   where one can take horses up to the Sierra Negra volcano. Trucks can be rented to var-
and boat, respectively.   ious destinations around the village or in the agricultural zone.
See Getting around,
page 406 for details

Floreana Island

Floreana, the island with the richest human history (see Recommended reading, page 415) has 70 inhabitants, 40 in Puerto Velasco Ibarra, the rest in the highlands. There is one school in town and one telephone at the Wittmers. There are about 14 people who were born on the island, they now include a director of the National Park, a boat owner, several naturalist guides and captains.

Unless you visit with one of the few boats which land at black beach for a few hours, it is difficult to get onto and off the inhabited part of the island. This is an ideal place for someone who wants peace and quiet to write or escape the world. Services are limited however; don't go unless you can be self-sufficient and very flexible about travel times. Staying with the Wittmers is delightful, the pace of life is gentle and locally produced food is good, but you will not be entertained. Margret Wittmer died in 2000 at age 95, however you can meet her daughter, granddaughters and great grandsons.

The climate in the highlands is fresh and comfortable, good for birdwatching – of special note is the Floreana finch. Some 200 species of ants have also been described here. Visit the natural water source for the island at Asilo de la Paz. A three hour hike goes to flamingo lagoons and a marine turtle nesting site.

Sleeping   **A** *Pensión Wittmer*, T05-520150 (only evenings when the generator is on). Includes 3
& eating   good meals. Rooms with private bath, hot water and fan (when there is electricity), also 2 family bungalows. Or, with the Wittmers' permission camp near the caves where the island's first inhabitant, Patrick Watkins, lived in the early 1800s.

Transport   **Boat** There is an irregular service from Puerto Ayora (Santa Cruz), and occasionally other islands. No fixed schedule. **Bus** Mixto bus/truck 0600 to highlands Mon-Sat returns 0730 for school, 1500 to highlands returns 1700; Sun up 0700 returns 1000. The bus journey takes 30 mins, walking down takes 2½ hrs, 8 km from Asilo de la Paz.

Background

11

Background

History and politics

Pre-conquest history

The oldest archaeological artefacts which have been uncovered in Ecuador date back to approximately 10,000 BC. They include obsidian spear tips and belong to a pre-ceramic period during which the region's inhabitants are thought to have been nomadic hunters, fishers and gatherers. A subsequent formative period (4,000 to 500 BC) saw the development of pottery, presumably alongside agriculture and fixed settlements. One of these settlements, known as Valdivia, existed along the coast of Ecuador and remains of buildings and earthenware figures have been found dating from between 3,500 and 1,500 BC (see box, page 430).

Earliest history

Between 500 BC and 500 AD, many different cultures evolved in all the geographic regions of what is today Ecuador. Among these were the Bahía, Guangalá, Jambelí and Duale-Tejar of the coast; Narrío, Tuncahuán and Panzaleo in the highlands; and Upano, Cosanga and Yasuní in Oriente. The period from 500 to 1480 AD was an era of integration, during which dominant or amalgamated groups emerged. These included, from north to south in the Sierra, the Imbayas, Shyris, Quitus, Puruhaes and Cañaris; and the Caras, Manteños and Huancavilcas along the coast.

This rich and varied mosaic of ancient cultures is today considered the bedrock of Ecuador's national identity. It was confronted, in the mid-15th century, with the relentless northward expansion of the most powerful pre-Hispanic empire on the continent: the Incas.

The Inca kingdom already existed in southern Peru from the 11th century. It was not until the mid-15th century that they began to expand their empire by conquering the highlands of Ecuador, led by Yupanqui and his son, Túpac Yupanqui. The Cañaris resisted for many years but eventually secured favourable peace terms around 1470, and their northern counterparts fought on for another few decades.

Huayna Capac, Túpac Yupanqui's son, was born in Tomebamba, site of present-day Cuenca, and established himself at Ingapirca before turning his attention to the domination of the Quitu/Caras further north. Quito was finally captured in 1492 (a rather significant year) and became the base from which the Incas extended their territory even further north.

A great road was built between Cusco and Quito, but the empire was eventually divided; ruled after the death of Huayna Capac by his two sons, Huáscar at Cusco and Atahualpa at Quito.

Conquest and colonial rule

Civil war broke out between the two halves of the empire, and in 1532 Atahualpa secured victory over Huáscar and established his capital in Cajamarca, in northern Peru. In the same year, Pizarro's main Peruvian expedition set out from Tumbes, on the Peru-Ecuador border, finally reaching Cajamarca. There, Pizarro captured the Inca leader and put him to death in 1533. This effectively ended Inca resistance and their empire collapsed.

Pizarro claimed the northern kingdom of Quito, and his lieutenants Sebastián de Benalcázar and Diego de Almagro took the city in 1534. Pizarro founded Lima in 1535 as capital of the whole region, and four years later replaced Benalcázar at Quito with Gonzalo, his brother. Gonzalo Pizarro later set out on the exploration of the Oriente. He moved down the Napo River, and sent Francisco de Orellana ahead to prospect. Orellana did not return. He drifted down the river finally to reach the mouth of the Amazon, thus becoming the first white man to cross the continent in

Background

The Valdivia culture

The village of Valdivia gave its name to one of the earliest of Ecuador's cultures, dating back to 3,300 BC, and famed for its ceramics. In the 1950s and 1960s these were the earliest ceramics known in the Americas. The superficial similarities between Valdivia ceramics and those of the Jomon Culture of Japan led many archaeologists to the conclusion that the Valdivia ceramics were first introduced to the Americas by Japanese fishermen.

However, discoveries over the past 35 years show that ceramic manufacture in the Americas has its own long path of development and that the idea of a Japanese contribution to pre-European cultures in South America should be discarded.

A much more compelling notion is that ceramic production in Ecuador had its origins in the non-Ecuadorean eastern Amazon basin. New claims from Brazilian sites place early pottery there at between 6,000-5,000 BC. It is possible that ceramic technology was transmitted from the Amazon basin through commerce or movement of people. The third alternative is that the development of pottery

occurred locally and may have accompanied the development of a more sedentary lifestyle on the Colombian, Venezuelan and Ecuadorean coasts.

The impressive Valdivia figurines are, in general, female representations and are nude and display breasts and a prominent pubic area. Some show pregnancy and in the womb of these are placed one or more seeds or small stones. Others have infants in their hands and some have two heads.

These figurines fill museum cases throughout the country (notably the excellent museums of the Banco Central in Guayaquil, Quito and Cuenca). They are still being produced by artesans in the fishing village of Valdivia today and can be purchased here or at the site museum in Salango, further north near Puerto López. In fact, according to several Ecuadorean archaeologists, many of the figurines housed in the museum collections were made in the 1950s and 1960s because the archaeologists working at that time would pay for any figurines that were found. (Jonathan D Kent, PhD, Associate Professor, Metropolitan State College of Denver).

this way; an event which is still considered significant in the history of Ecuador (see box, page 355).

Quito became a *real audiencia* under the Viceroyalty of Peru. For the next 280 years Ecuador reluctantly accepted the new ways brought by the conqueror. Gonzalo Pizarro had already introduced pigs and cattle; wheat was now added. The Indians were Christianized, and colonial laws, customs and ideas introduced. The marriage of the arts of Spain to those of the Incas led to a remarkable efflorescence of painting, sculpting and building at Quito, one of the very few positive effects of conquest.

The Spanish introduced the *encomienda* into the Audiencia. This feudal system assigned the Indians to a Spanish landowner. They lived on his land and were forced to work for him, in exchange for a tiny piece of land, a few crumbs of food and religious guidance. Of course, the Indians were permanently in debt to their landowner and their children inherited this debt.

So the indigenous people effectively became slaves, with the size of the population greatly reduced by death and disease as a result. Following economic recession at the beginning of the 18th century the Spanish began to take over the remaining areas of land in Indian hands and turn them into huge private estates, called *haciendas*. Those Indians whose land had been confiscated had little choice but to work for the Spanish landlords under the same conditions as had existed during the *encomienda* system. In Quichua, this new form of serfdom was known as *huasipungo*, which means 'at the door of the house', referring to the tiny plot of infertile land on which they lived. This system actually survived until the 1964 land reforms (see below). In the 18th century the production and export of cocoa began and black slave labour was brought in to work cocoa and sugar plantations near the coast.

Independence and after

Ecuadorean independence came about in several stages. In 1809, taking advantage of the chaos produced in Spain by Napoleon's invasion and the forced abdication of the Spanish king, some members of the Quito élite formed a junta and declared independence. This lasted only three months before being put down by royalist troops. Fearing further trouble, the royalists executed the leaders of the junta the following year, provoking an uprising and the establishment of another junta which governed in Quito until it was crushed by a royalist army two years later. The defeat of these early moves for independence discouraged any further opposition to Spanish rule in Quito, though members of the coastal élites led an uprising in 1820. Independence therefore had to wait until royalist forces were defeated by Antonio José de Sucre in the Battle of Pichincha in 1822. For the next eight years Ecuador was a province of Gran Colombia under the leadership of Simón Bolívar. As Gran Colombia collapsed in 1830 Ecuador became an independent state.

After independence Ecuadorean politics were dominated by the small élite, divided between a coastal faction, based in Guayaquil, and a faction from the Sierra, based in Quito. Separated by different landholding systems, distinct economic patterns and interests and widely divergent social attitudes, these two factions struggled for control of Ecuador through the 19th century and beyond. Although there were several presidents from the coast, all governments until 1895 represented the interests of the conservative landowners of the Sierra against the commercial interests of the agro-exporting landowners and traders of Guayaquil and the coast whom they disdainfully called *monos* (monkeys), an epithet which persists to the present day.

After 1830 Ecuador became a chronic example of the political chaos and instability which affected much of Spanish America in the 19th century. Of the 21 individuals and juntas who occupied the presidency for a total of 34 times between 1830 and 1895, only six completed their constitutional terms of office. Four men stand out as the most notorious of the *caudillos* (political strongmen) who dominated politics, either as presidents or from behind the scene: General Juan José Flores (president 1830-34, 1839-45), a Venezuelan who led the struggle for independence from Gran Colombia; José María Urbina (1851-56) who abolished slavery but imposed stern military rule; Gabriel García Moreno (1860-65 and 1869-75) who built roads linking the coast and highlands but was most renowned for his attempts to force Catholicism on the population and for eventually being hacked to death by machete at the entrance of the presidential palace; and Ignacio Veintimilla (1876-83), who was so unpopular that he united all the factions in the country against his dictatorship.

The 20th century

The seizure of power in 1895 by the coastal élite, led by the Radical Liberal *caudillo* Eloy Alfaro (president 1895-1901 and 1906-11), was followed by important changes as the Radical Liberals began to implement a programme which they saw as bringing Ecuador into the modern world. A key part of this was reducing the power of the church. Secular education, civil marriage and divorce were introduced and church lands were confiscated. Ambitious plans were drawn up for construction of a railroad deep into the Oriente and capital punishment was abolished.

The overthrow of the Radical Liberals by a group of military officers (Alfaro, his two brothers and closest allies were killed and their bodies dragged through the streets of

Cursed treasure

When Francisco Pizarro, at the head of only 63 conquistadores, managed to take Atahualpa prisoner at Cajamarca, he probably knew little or nothing about the proportions of the empire – larger than all of Spain – whose sovereign he had just captured. What Pizarro and his men did know was that the Incas had gold and that they, the Spaniards, wanted it.

Legend-cum-history tells us that Atahualpa offered, in exchange for his freedom, to fill a room nearly 7m long by 5m wide with gold and silver to the height of his fully raised arm. Chasquis (messengers) were sent forth at once to the four suyos (cardinal points) of the great empire, and caravans of llamas and porters eventually began to return with the coveted treasure. Cajamarca however is located almost 800 km south of Quito and over 1,000 km northwest of Cuzco, as the condor flies, and delivering the ransom took time.

As the weeks dragged into months something even more powerful than greed began to grip the conquistadores: fear. The natives fanned the flames of the white men's paranoia with rumours of a great army commanded by a general from Quito named Rumiñahui (literally 'stone-face'), who was allegedly marching on Cajamarca with over 200,000 warriors. After eight months they could stand it no longer, and Pizarro and his men put Atahualpa to death on August 29, 1533, well before the ransom could be completed.

Once again word spread throughout the provinces that the Inca was dead. Rumiñahui apparently took the reins of the crumbling empire, razed Quito before the Spanish could capture it, and hid all the treasure that was still en route to Cajamarca, by far the greater part of the promised ransom. The lesser part, that which was delivered to the Spaniards, came to over six tons of 22½ carat gold and almost 12 tons of fine silver.

Where is the hiding place of so fabulous a fortune? Five hundred years of history and generations of treasure hunters, many of whom perished or went mad in their quest, have yet to provide a definitive answer. Most trails seem to lead to the Llanganates, a particularly inaccessible chain of mountains situated roughly between Baños and the Cotopaxi volcano. Rumiñahui, who remains a national hero in Ecuador, was a nobleman of the Puruhá nation which lived near the Llanganates. Further legend has it that he not only hid the treasure but also cursed it. Or was it the greed of the conquerors which cursed the treasures of the New World?

Quito before being publicly burned), led to the restoration to power of the Quito élite. Between 1925 and 1931 the military-backed government of Isidro Ayora carried out some of the reforms suggested by a team of economic advisors from the US, including the establishment of a Central Bank. The onset of the Great Depression, however, led to severe economic problems as demand for Ecuador's exports collapsed and prices fell. In the following years the country experienced its worst period of political instability. Between 1931 and 1948 there were 21 governments, none of which succeeded in completing its term of office. "There were ministers who lasted hours, presidents who lasted for days, and dictators who lasted for weeks." (G Abad, *El proceso de lucha por el poder en el Ecuador*, Mexico 1970.)

Political stability was only restored after 1948 when Ecuador entered another period of economic expansion, this time based on the production of bananas on coastal plantations. Banana exports grew from 18,000 tons in 1945 to 900,000 tons in 1960, by which time they accounted for two-thirds of exports. With cocoa and coffee prices also improving, there was a shift in population from the Sierra to the coast, where Guayaquil grew rapidly.

Between 1948 and 1960 three successive presidents managed to complete their terms of office. However, conflict between Velasco Ibarra and Congress in 1961 brought a return to instability. Velasco was succeeded by his Vice-president, Carlos

Political parties and conflict in modern Ecuador

Although Ecuadorean political parties reflect the regionalism of the country, this alone does not explain the myriad of parties which exist. The country's oldest parties, the Partido Conservador *and the* Partido Liberal Radical, *were formed to represent the élites of the* sierra *and the* costa *respectively. Marxist parties have never enjoyed much support, both the* Socialist party *(founded in 1926) and the* Communist party *(established in 1931) remaining small organisations. Most other parties have tended to be based around personalities, rising and falling with their leaders' fortunes:* Velasco Ibarra *who claimed to dislike political parties, ran for election supported by a variety of parties, but* Velasquismo *died with its founder. By contrast the* Concentración de Fuerzas Populares, *a party which draws its main support from the shantytowns of Guayaquil, managed to survive the death of its charismatic leader, Asaad Bucaram. Asaad's equally charismatic nephew, Abdalá, won the presidency in 1996 at the head of his own* Partido Roldosista Ecuatoriano *(see box, page 434).*

Since the return to constitutional rule in 1979 the most important parties have included two centre-left parties Democracia Popular *(the party of Osvaldo Hurtado, but today more centre than left) and* Izquierda Democrática *(the party of Rodrigo Borja). The main right-wing parties include the* Partido Social Cristiano *(the party of León Febres Cordero) and the traditional Conservatives. New parties include* Pachacutic, *which claims to represent the interests of the country's indigenous population.*

The proliferation of parties has contributed to the problems of governing since 1979. To win the presidency candidates need to form electoral alliances with other parties: these often disintegrate shortly afterwards leaving the president facing a hostile majority in Congress.

More than any coherent ideology however, the vast majority of Ecuador's political parties follow the path of greatest expediency. As a result, the image of the political establishment in general - and Congress in particular - has been badly eroded. In 2000, following months of shameless wrangling over the election of the president of the legislative body, which led to fist fights among its members, there were calls for the dissolution of Congress.

Julio Arosemena, a *costeño* who was attacked by the Quito elite who saw him as favourable to the Cuban Revolution. Arosemena scandalized *quiteños* and the military with his indecorous behaviour. He was incapably drunk at a formal reception for the Chilean President, once received a visiting mission dressed in his bathrobe and enjoyed visiting sleazy bars and shooting at the waiters. Insulting the US ambassador at a banquet provided the military with an excuse to overthrow him.

Between 1963 and 1979 Ecuador experienced two periods of military rule. The first, from 1963 to 1966, took strong measures against what it saw as a threat of Communism. An Agrarian Reform Law introduced in 1964, though inadequate to challenge many of the country's outdated landholding practices, was enough to upset the élite and the *junta* was forced from office. During the brief interlude of civilian rule which followed, new elections in 1968 led to the return of Velasco Ibarra. His overthrow by the armed forces in 1972 coincided with the increase in oil revenues from the Oriente and was followed by seven years of military rule.

Between 1972 and 1976 General Rodríguez Lara led a 'revolutionary and nationalist' government, of which the aim was to use the oil revenues to build up the country's infrastructure and to finance agricultural, industrial and social projects. In fact, the Rodríguez Lara government lacked clear objectives, while disagreements within the armed forces and the opposition of many of the powerful sections of Ecuadorean society eventually led to the president's replacement by a junta which promised to return the country to civilian rule.

Background

An Ecuadorean political dynasty?

Few newly elected presidents have celebrated their victory by launching a career as a pop singer. Shortly after his election in 1996, Abdalá Bucaram, who had campaigned as El Loco (the Madman) released an album called De un Loco con Amor *(From a Madman with Love)* and was performing to packed audiences in Guayaquil. Unusual though Bucaram's political style may have been, he was merely the latest member of Ecuador's most colourful political family to achieve fame.

Bucaram's uncle, Asaad, a man of humble origins who started his adult life as a travelling salesman for a textile company, dominated Guayaquil politics for two decades. Elected to Congress in 1958 Asaad Bucaram soon made a name for himself with his unconventional debating methods, on one occasion brandishing a pistol in the chamber. After seizing control of the Concentración de Fuerzas Populares (CFP) in the early 1960s, he was twice elected mayor of Guayaquil. His fiery oratory and personal popularity among the poor of Guayaquil's shantytowns (where he was known affectionately as 'Don Buca') earned him the hatred and distrust of Ecuador's élite who saw him as a Communist. The Ecuadorean left regarded him as a fascist, pointing to his lack of real interest in redistributing power or wealth and to his practice of employing gangs of thugs to intimidate opponents.

He was arrested and exiled four times between 1963 and 1972 by the armed forces, who seized power in 1972 to prevent his election to the presidency after he had emerged as the leading candidate. On the return to civilian rule in 1978 the military and their civilian supporters insisted that the new constitution should stipulate that only those born of parents who were Ecuadorean citizens at the time of birth were eligible as presidential candidates, thus excluding Bucaram, whose parents were Lebanese immigrants. Bucaram's niece's husband, Jaime Roldós, took his uncle's place as CFP candidate under the slogan 'Roldós to govern, Bucaram to power' but after Roldós's victory, the two men fell out: Roldós forming his own party (People, Change, Democracy) while Bucaram led the CFP in a bitter anti-government campaign which was cut short by his death in 1981.

Return to democracy

Since 1979 Ecuador has enjoyed its longest period of civilian constitutional government since independence. In 1978 a young and charismatic Jaime Roldós was elected president on a platform of using oil revenues to build up the country's infrastructure. By the time of Roldós' death in a plane crash in 1981 his plans had been frustrated by a decline in oil prices and the opposition of Congress. Roldós' successor, his Vice-president Oswaldo Hurtado of the Democracia Popular (DP) party, was threatened by a series of political and economic crises which might have led to military intervention. He managed to hold out however and eventually became one of the very few respected elder statesmen in Ecuadorean politics.

In 1984 elections, León Febres Cordero of the right-wing Partido Social Cristiano (PSC) obtained a narrow victory. His attempt to introduce a neoliberal economic programme failed to control inflation or end recession, but sparked an upsurge in political violence and confrontation including coup attempts and clashes with students and workers. Febres Cordero was subsequently elected to two consecutive terms as mayor of Guayaquil and, although in failing health, he retained a very strong following among *guayaquileños* and the country's political right as well as considerable influence in all circles of power.

When Rodrigo Borja of the centre-left Izquierda Democrática (ID) won the 1988 election, his inheritance from Febres Cordero was difficult: high inflation, high unemployment and a large public spending deficit. The latter half of Borja's presidency was marked by conflict with Congress and labour unrest.

Background

Constitutions and revolutions

Two prominent features of Ecuador's turbulent history are its numerous constitutions and its frequent revolutions. Since the creation of the republic in 1830 Ecuador has had 18 constitutions although few of the changes in these have made much difference to the lives of most of the population. One of the most notable was the so-called 'Black Charter' of 1869 decreed by Gabriel García Moreno, which enhanced the power of the Catholic church giving it complete control over education and denying citizenship to non-Catholics. The 1906 Constitution introduced by the Radical Liberal Eloy Alfaro separated church and state. Women gained the vote in the 1929 Charter but illiterates had to wait until the Constitution of 1979. The latest contitution, passed in 1998, enshrined a number of additional civil rights.

Although there have been many violent and unconstitutional changes of government, it is hard to accept Ecuador's image as a country of revolutions: few of these uprisings have led to anything more than a change of the faces in power. Only the Revolutions of 1895 and 1925 deserve the title: the first brought the coastal Radical Liberal Party to power and led to important social, political and economic changes; the second ended the rule of the Radical Liberals and brought the Conservatives of the sierra back into office.

The most recent governments to be overthrown were those of Abdalá Bucaram in 1997 and Jamil Mahuad in 2000, both – it should be pointed out – almost without violence. When the dust settled however most Ecuadoreans realized that, yet again, very little had changed. Irreverent comments, like "We have a new mascot but on the same old leash" reveal an insight into how little room for maneuvering most Ecuadorean presidents actually have.

1992 to the present day

The elections of 1992 were won by Sixto Durán Ballén of the centre-right Partido de Unidad Republicana in coalition with Alberto Dahik of the Partido Conservador (who became vice-president). The popularity of Durán Ballén's government declined steadily with his attempts to implement an economic modernization programme. The resulting strikes and protests were temporarily interrupted when Ecuadoreans responded to the 1995 border conflict with Peru (see below) with a massive display of national unity, backing their government and armed forces to an extent not seen before. This backing was short-lived however and followed by a major corruption scandal which culminated with Vice-president Dahik fleeing the country in 1996 at the controls of his private aircraft. He became the first of many contemporary national figures to seek asylum and self-imposed exile.

Durán Ballén's government limped to the end of its term in 1996, but disenchantment with the political establishment as a whole was so great that a flamboyant populist named Abdalá Bucaram of the Partido Roldosista Ecuatoriano (PRE) was swept to power in the next elections (see box, page 434). Bucaram's erratic government lasted barely six months and by February 1997 all manner of scandal had implicated his entire government and family. A 48-hour national strike and mass demonstrations were followed by a congressional vote to remove Bucaram from office on the grounds of 'mental incapacity'. There followed a period of political chaos during which Ecuador had three simultaneous presidents: Bucaram, vice-president Rosalía Arteaga, who claimed the office, and Fabián Alarcón, chosen by Congress, of which he was president. The military sided with Alarcón and Bucaram fled to Panama form where he remained closely involved with Ecuadorean politics by remote control, as his PRE party kept an important following especially among poor *costeños*.

After the departure of Bucaram, Alacrón was overwhelmingly elected president by Congress until new general elections were held in 1998. His interim government was marred by further accusations of corruption and continuing economic decline.

Background

A number of his closest collaborators eventually fled the country and Alarcón himself was imprisoned for several months on corruption charges after the end of his presidency, but later released. A constituent assembly was convened during the interim government and drew up the country's 18th constitution. It was in many ways a noble and progressive document but contributed little or nothing to solving the country's problems (see box, page 435).

Jamil Mahuad of the DP, a former mayor of Quito, was narrowly elected president in 1998, amid renewed border tensions with Peru. He immediately diffused this explosive situation and in less than three months had signed a definitive peace treaty, putting an end to decades – even centuries – of conflict (see below). This early success was Mahuad's last, as a series of bank failures (some allegedly fraudulent and perpetrated by bankers who had helped finance the president's election campaign) sent the country into an economic and political tailspin (also see Economy, page 437). In March 1999 Mahuad decreed an austerity package including a freeze on bank accounts, effectively confiscating all assets on deposit in excess of US$200. A popular uprising followed and the president was forced to back down on some of his harshest austerity measures but not the bank freeze. Even the freeze did not prevent additional banks from collapsing however, and the mortally wounded economy embarked on a process of hyperinflation, previously unknown in Ecuador.

By December 1999 the country's social, political and economic situation was completely out of control and Mahuad decreed the adoption of the US dollar as the national currency in a desperate bid for monetary stability. Less than a month later, on 21 January 2000, he was forced out of office by Ecuador's indigenous people led by the Confederación de Nacionalidades Indígenas del Ecuador (CONAIE) and disgruntled members of the armed forces. This was the first overt military *coup* in South America in more than two decades, but it lasted barely three hours before a combination of local intrigue and international pressure handed power to vice-president Gustavo Noboa. Mahuad displayed courage and dignity during his removal from office; shortly thereafter he joined the ranks of other Ecuadorean politicians in exile. The colonels involved in the *coup* were subsequently pardoned but dismissed from the military. Most significantly, all of the foregoing years of social unrest were never accompanied by serious bloodshed.

Noboa, a political outsider and academic, stepped into Mahuad's shoes with remarkable aplomb. With assistance from the US and the International Monetary Fund (IMF), his government managed to flesh out and implement the dollarization scheme, thus achieving economic stabilization and the beginnings of recovery. They continued the previous administration's drive for better tax collection which, although criticized by some as arbitrary and heavy handed, helped (along with high oil revenues) to bolster the national budget and inspire renewed international confidence. The new executive also passed omnibus economic legislation through a constitutional loophole, without congressional debate. The sweeping package included controversial measures for privatizing state enterprises, the same measures which had lead to social strife during so many previous governments. This time however, attempts at national strikes and uprisings by the country's labour movement and CONAIE did not receive any grassroots support.

At the close of this edition Ecuador was convalescing surprisingly well from the political convulsions of recent years, but the country could hardly be given a clean bill of health. Deeply ingrained institutional corruption remained a serious problem and a new concern was the US-sponsored 'Plan Colombia', which threatened to involve Ecuador in the long-standing guerrilla conflict of its northern neighbour. Looking toward the future, much seemed to depend on the government's ability to simultaneously satisfy international political and economic demands (mostly from the US), demands which were all the more difficult to resist in the context of a US dollar economy; and, at the same time, to help Ecuadoreans recover their national self-esteem as well as a tolerable standard of living.

End of border dispute with Peru

After the dissolution of Gran Colombia in 1830 (largely present-day Venezuela, Colombia and Ecuador), repeated attempts to determine the extent of Ecuador's eastern jungle territory failed. While Ecuador claimed that its territory has been reduced from that of the old Real Audiencia de Quito by gradual Colombian and especially Peruvian infiltration, Peru insisted that its Amazonian territory was established in law and in fact before the foundation of Ecuador as an independent state.

The dispute reached an acute phase in 1941 when war broke out between the two countries. The war ended with military defeat for Ecuador and the signing of the Rio de Janeiro Protocol of 1942 which allotted most of the disputed territory to Peru. Since 1960 Ecuador denounced the Protocol as unjust (because it was imposed by force of arms) and as technically flawed (because it refers to certain non-existent geographic features). According to Peru, the Protocol adequately demarcated the entire boundary.

Sporadic border skirmishes continued throughout subsequent decades. In January 1995 these escalated into an undeclared war over control of the headwaters of the Río Cenepa. Argentina, Brazil, Chile and the USA (guarantors of the Rio de Janeiro Protocol) intervened diplomatically and a ceasefire took effect after six weeks of combat, during which both sides made conflicting claims of military success. Negotiations followed and a definitive peace treaty was signed on October 26, 1998, finally ending the seemingly interminable dispute.

Under the terms of the agreement Ecuador gained access to two Peruvian ports on the Amazon, Ecuador's navigation rights on the river were confirmed and, in the area of the most recent conflict, it was given a symbolic square kilometre of Peruvian territory as private property. Although there was initial discontent among hardliners on both sides, relations have improved rapidly between the two former adversaries. Ambitious plans were drawn up for economic cooperation, opening new border crossings and developing a tourism circuit involving both countries. By mid-2000 Peruvian visitors were flocking to Cuenca, while some Ecuadoreans were – for the first time – enjoying the beaches of northern Peru.

Government

There are 22 provinces, including the Galápagos Islands. Provinces are divided into *cantones* which are subdivided into *parroquias* for administration.

Under the 1998 constitution, all citizens over the age of 18 are both entitled and required to vote. The president and vice-president are elected for a four-year term and may be re-elected. The president appoints cabinet ministers and provincial governors. The parliament, or Congress (Congreso Nacional), has 123 members who are elected for a four-year term at the same time as the president. The next elections are due in mid-2002.

Economy

In the 1970s, Ecuador underwent a transformation from an essentially agricultural economy to a predominantly petroleum economy. Substantial oil output began in 1972, from when economic growth has largely followed the fortunes of the international oil market and the country as a whole – economically, politically and socially – has been extremely vulnerable to these fluctuations.

The contribution of agriculture and fishing to gdp has dwindled from over 22% in 1972 to about 17% in the mid-1990s, but about one third of jobs are still in farming and agro-exports generate almost 50% of foreign earnings. Ecuador is the world's

Farming & fishing

largest exporter of bananas. Efforts have been made to expand markets following the introduction of EU import restrictions, to introduce a variety of banana resistant to black sigatoka disease and to reduce costs and increase efficiency; all with limited success. Coffee is the most extensive of Ecuador's cash crops, accounting for over 20% of total agricultural land, but it is very low yielding. Cocoa yields have also fallen and a programme for better maintenance and replacement of old trees is under way. Several non-traditional crops are expanding rapidly, especially roses and other flowers in the Sierra within reach of Quito airport; also mangoes, strawberries, palm hearts, asparagus and other fruits and vegetables, many of which are processed before export.

The fishing industry is a major export earner, partly from the catch offshore of tuna, sardines and white fish, but mostly from shrimp farming along the coast. Shrimp farms offer employment in underdeveloped areas where other jobs are scarce, but their development is controversial and a large portion of Ecuador's mangroves has been destroyed. Most of the forest around Bahía and Muisne is gone and that which remains is threatened. In the Gulf of Guayaquil, the shrimp have suffered from high mortality in recent years, allegedly because of pollution from agrochemicals used intensively by banana growers. In 1999-2000, the shrimp industry as a whole was dealt a further blow by an epidemic disease known as *mancha blanca* (white spot) which caused mortality rates up to 100% on some farms.

Oil production Although Ecuador's share of total world oil production is small (about 1%), foreign exchange earnings from oil exports are crucial, accounting for almost one half of total exports and government revenues alike. In 1999, oil production represented 14.6% of GDP. Ecuador left Opec in 1992 because of production quota disagreements and in 2000 was producing approximately 410,000 barrels per day, of which 250,000 barrels per day were exported. The main producing area is in the northern Oriente, and a 495-km trans-Andean pipeline carries the oil to Esmeraldas on the coast, where it is refined and/or exported. A second smaller pipeline takes oil to Colombia, from where it is exported through that country's pipeline system, but neither has the capacity required for planned development of new wells. A new pipeline for heavy crude was being planned in late 2000. Over the years, millions of hectares of Amazon forest have been opened to exploration (totally disregarding Indian reserves and national parks). The oil industry has had a considerable adverse affect on the Oriente's unique biodiversity as well as on indigenous communities, who have seen their lands polluted and deforested, and their way of life irreparably altered.

Tourism Tourism is a rapidly growing sector of the Ecuadorean economy, and the country's third most important source of foreign revenue. Ecuador received 637,000 visitors in 2000 generating US$400 million. Beach vacationers from Colombia have traditionally been the most numerous tourists in Ecuador but, following the signing of the peace treaty with Peru in 1998 there has been an important influx of Peruvians, contributing to the development of tourism in the south. The Galápagos islands remain a particularly important destination for visitors from Europe and North America, but there is an increasing trend toward eco- and ethno-tourism in both the highlands and Oriente jungle. At the same time, tourism remains highly focused on certain well-known centres in Ecuador, with the economies of places like Galápagos, Otavalo, Baños and Vilcabamba very heavily dependent on foreign visitors.

Mining Mining is not yet an important sector, but the discovery of about 700 tonnes of gold reserves around Nambija (Zamora) in the southeast created intense interest in the late 1980s, and over 12,000 independent miners rushed to prospect there. Over nine tonnes of gold are produced a year by prospectors along the Andean slopes, polluting the waters with cyanide and mercury. Legislation has been designed to encourage investors in large projects with better technology which would – in principle - be less harmful and could be more strictly controlled. Foreign companies are interested in deposits of gold, silver, lead, zinc and copper in the south.

Despite the abundance of oil, over two-thirds of electricity generation comes from hydropower. Hydroelectric projects on the Paute, Pastaza and Coca rivers could raise capacity from 2,300MW to 12,000MW. However, in the mid-1990s drought revealed the dangers of overdependence and power shortages were widespread. Several thermal plants subsequently came into operation and the Government eased restrictions on diesel imports. Privatization, especially in the electric energy sector, has long been resisted by the labour movement. Recent governments have none-the-less managed to break up the nationwide public electric company (INECEL) into a number of smaller regional operators, which are due to be sold off in 2001 or 2002.

Hydropower

After a sharp rise in debt during the 1970s, Ecuador joined other debtor nations in the 1980s in attempting to refinance its external obligations. The cycle was repeated during the 1990s, synchronized to the roller-coaster of international oil prices. During the same period the economy was adversely affected by such local circumstances as the 1995 border war with Peru, the devastating 1997 *El Niño* floods and social and political unrest between 1997 and 2000. Throughout this time, repeated attempts at structural reform were made under the tutelage of the IMF, but these were always blocked by the country's labour movement, most recently allied with native people and elements of the military (see 1992 to the present day, page 435).

Recent trends

By the second half of the 1990s inflation and devaluation were growing apace while productivity declined, but the death knell for Ecuador's economy was sounded by the collapse of *Filanbanco*, the country's largest bank, at the end of 1998. The government bail-out of *Filanbanco* cost somewhere between US$500 million and US$800 million (depending on whom you believe) and, along with the subsequent failure of other banks, left approximately 70% of financial institutions in state hands while the implicated bankers fled the country to avoid prosecution. In March 1999 President Mahuad decreed a freeze on all deposits over US$200, in an attempt to halt the run on both the banks and the Sucre. It failed to do either, but deprived many Ecuadoreans of their life savings, only some of which had been reimbursed by the end of 2000.

In October 1999 the government of Ecuador defaulted on all its debts, national and foreign. By December 1999, the sucre – which had been the nation's currency for the previous 116 years – reached 25,000 to US$1 (75% devaluation in one year) and Mahuad announced the adoption of the US dollar as the national currency in a desperate bid for monetary stability. He was deposed shortly thereafter and the government of his successor, Gustavo Noboa, was left to implement the dollarization scheme. In all, 1999 was a catastrophic year: 8% decrease in GDP (9.8% decrease per capita), 52.2% inflation, 1% decline in exports, 50.1% drop in imports and 20.3% contraction of private sector credit.

Having hit bottom, the economy began a gradual process of stabilization and recovery during 2000. The previous year's commotion attracted international attention and, with the help of the USA and IMF, dollarization was made to take hold. The country renegotiated its international obligations with bond holders and the Paris Club, under ostensibly favourable terms, although debt service continued to account for a disproportionate share of government spending. Tax collection was improved, albeit by controversial means, and a balanced budget proposed for 2001. Things were looking a bit better but 100% real annual inflation (mostly at the beginning of 2000 as prices adjusted to the new US dollar economy), hit hard at the already battered population.

Background

Long-postponed structural adjustments were once again placed on the agenda, due in part to leverage being applied to the Ecuadorean government from abroad; the increased leverage made possible by dollarization. At the close of this edition the government and IMF appeared to be have gained the upper hand over Ecuador's labour and indigenous movements and plans for privatization seemed ready to move forward, but only time will tell.

Society

Poverty & migration

Accurate up-to-date figures on these areas are scarce, because the last census was carried out in 1990, but Ecuador is undoubtedly one of the poorer countries in South America. As in other Andean countries with large indigenous populations, wealth is distributed along ethnic lines, with indigenous people and blacks suffering the greatest poverty. At the same time there is a tiny – mostly white – élite, who are spectrally wealthy. Recent estimates are that more than 70% of the population live in poverty. Many of those who are fortunate enough to be formally employed (the minority) must survive on a monthly take-home pay of barely US$100. As well as poverty, some Ecuadorean women also suffer domestic violence from drunken husbands, but in this macho culture such abuse often goes unreported and may even be tolerated, although attitudes have gradually begun to change.

In an attempt to escape rural poverty, many have migrated from the coast and the highlands to the towns and cities, particularly Guayaquil and Quito, where they are usually even worse off. In the countryside those with even a tiny plot of land or a fishing net can usually manage to eat, whereas in the city one must either earn or steal money in order to survive. This can be seen by the increase in crime as well as the many people trying to scrape together an honest living as *ambulantes*: by selling various goods or offering services on the streets of the major cities, particularly Quito. Rather worryingly, a high percentage are young children.

The most recent economic crises forced many Ecuadoreans to seek even more distant opportunities, in North America and Europe, especially Spain. So many Ecuadoreans wanted to leave that passports became scarce and, once they managed to get one, people queued for days outside the Spanish embassy in Quito in hopes of obtaining a visa. Families were often split up as one spouse migrated in search of work, while the other remained behind with the children, and tearful farewells were an everyday sight at Quito and Guayaquil airports. Illegal emigrants faced much greater hardship; they typically paid US$5,000 to US$10,000 to a *coyote* who offered to guide them overland through Central America, or in small vessels by sea, to the US. Some were defrauded of their savings without ever reaching the 'promised land' while others perished *en route*. Once in Spain, Italy, Germany, the US or Canada, many of the illegal migrants were mistreated and underpaid, but there was sufficient demand for cheap labour in these countries that Ecuadoreans continued to emigrate. Some, especially those who eventually legalized their status, did well economically and began to send funds back to their relatives in Ecuador. This income is increasingly important for the country as a whole, though it has yet to reach the proportions of Cuba or Mexico.

Health

The gulf between rich and poor in Ecuador is exacerbated by the two-tier healthcare system. This division works on two levels – rural and urban and state and private. Two thirds of doctors and hospitals are concentrated in Quito and Guayaquil, and private hospitals thrive at the expense of a badly under-funded and crumbling state health service.

Despite this, things have improved in recent decades. Infant mortality has been halved to 45 per 1,000 and life expectancy has increased to an average of 65½ years. The main causes of death are no longer those associated with a typical developing country but those of the developed world: cancer, heart and lung disease. A large number of people are also killed in traffic accidents. Although abortion is illegal, it is commonly carried out in unsanitary conditions and roughly 12% of admissions to gynaecological departments are related to the termination of pregnancies.

Population pressure is strong on Ecuador's most elemental resources – land and water, and an important threat to the country's outstanding biodiversity. Migration and a slowly declining birth rate have eased this pressure only slightly in recent years and the country's future depends, more than anything else, on achieving a sustainable balance between its population and renewable resources. Family planning programs exist but are not widely accepted, and such efforts must contend with the great power and influence of the Roman Catholic Church.

Children are entitled to nine years of compulsory education by law, but in practice this is not always the case. In rural areas most complete elementary school, but not all go on to secondary education. This is mainly because the rural population is greatly dispersed and the cost of travelling such large distances is prohibitive. Other factors are that many families cannot afford the costs of uniforms and materials and schools lack teaching resources.

Education

Illiteracy is no longer the problem it was a generation or two ago, and bilingual (Spanish and Quichua) education is available in some highland Indian communities. Overall standards for public education are extremely variable however, with a handful of highly regarded state schools in Quito and provincial capitals, while more remote classrooms and teachers can be severely deficient. Funds are always scarce and education, especially much needed investment in teacher training, has not been a priority for recent governments.

Land and environment

Ecuador, named for its position on the equator, is the smallest country of South America (256,370 sq km) after Uruguay and the Guianas. It is bounded by Colombia in the north, by Peru to the east and south, and by the Pacific Ocean to the west. Its population of approximately 13 million (a rough estimate since the last census was carried out in 1990) is also small, but is larger than Bolivia and Paraguay as well as Uruguay and the Guianas. It has the highest population density of any of the South American republics, at about 50 inhabitants per square kilometre.

The border had been a source of conflict with its neighbours, and Ecuador lost a significant part of its former territory towards the Amazon to Peru in 1941-42 (see above).

The Galápagos Islands were annexed by Ecuador in 1832. They lie in the Pacific, 970 km west of the mainland, on the equator, and consist of six principal islands and numerous smaller islands and rocks totalling about 8,000 sq km and scattered over 60,000 sq km of ocean. They are the most significant island group in the eastern Pacific Ocean.

Geology

Geologically, Ecuador is the creation of the Andean mountain-building process, caused in turn by the South American Plate moving west, meeting the Nasca plate which is moving east and sinking beneath the continent. This process began in the late Cretaceous Period around 80 million years ago and has continued to the present day. Before this, and until as late as perhaps 25 million years ago, the Amazon basin tilted west and the river drained into the Pacific through what is now southern Ecuador.

The Andes between Peru and Colombia are at their narrowest (apart from their extremities in Venezuela and southern Chile), ranging from 100-200 km in width. Nevertheless, they are comparatively high with one point, Chimborazo, over 6,000 m and several others not much lower. Unlike Peru to the south, most of the peaks in Ecuador are volcanoes, and Cotopaxi is one of the highest active volcanoes in the world, at 5,897 m. The 55 volcanic craters which dot the landscape of the northern highlands suggest a fractured and unstable area beneath the surface. A dramatic example of volcanic activity was an eruption of Cotopaxi in 1877 which was followed by a *nuée ardente* (literally, a burning cloud) which flowed down the side of the volcano engulfing many settlements. Snow and ice at the summit melted to create another volcanic phenomenon called a *lahar*, or mud flow, which reached Esmeraldas (150 km away) in 18 hours! The most recently volcanic episodes began in 1999, with the eruptions of Guagua Pichincha and Tungurahua.

The eastern third of the country is part of the Amazon basin filled with sedimentary deposits from the east, since the formation of the Andes, from the mountains to the west. The coastlands rise up to 1,000 m and are mainly remnants of Tertiary basalts, similar to the base rocks of the Amazon basin on the other side of the Andes.

The Galápagos are not structurally connected to the mainland and, so far as is known, were never part of the South American Plate. They lie near the boundary between the Nasca Plate and the Cocos Plate to the north. A line of weakness, evidenced by a ridge of undersea lava flows, stretches southwest from the coast of Panama. This meets another undersea ridge running along the equator from Ecuador but separated from the continental shelf by a deep trench. At this conjuncture appear the Galápagos. Volcanic activity here has been particularly intense and the islands are the peaks of structures that rise over 7,000 m from the deepest parts of the adjacent ocean floor. The oldest islands are San Cristóbal and Española in the east of the archipelago: three to 3.5 million years old. The youngest ones, Fernandina and Isabela, lie to the west, and are between 700,000 and 800,000 years old. In geological terms, therefore, these islands have only recently appeared from the ocean and volcanic activity continues on at least five of them.

The Andes The Andes form the backbone of the country. In Colombia to the north, three distinct ranges come together near Pasto, with three volcanoes overlooking the border near Tulcán. Although it is essentially one range through Ecuador, there is a trough of between 1,800 m and 3,000 m above sea level running south for over 400 km with volcanoes, many active on either side. The snowline is at about 5,000 m, and with 10 peaks over that height, this makes for a dramatic landscape.

Overlooking Quito to the west is Pichincha which was climbed by Charles-Marie de La Condamine in 1742, and in 1802 by Alexander Von Humboldt. Humboldt climbed many other Ecuadorean volcanoes, including Chimborazo, where he reached over 6,000 m (though not the top), the first recorded climb to this height. He christened the road through the central Andes the 'Avenue of the Volcanoes'.

Further south, near Riobamba, is Volcán Sangay, 5,230 m, which today is the most continuously active of Ecuador's volcanoes. There are fewer volcanoes towards the Peruvian border and the scenery is less dramatic. The mountains rarely exceed 4,000 m and the passes are as low as 2,200 m. Although active volcanoes are concentrated in the northern half of the country, there are many places where there are sulphur baths or hot springs and the whole Andean area is seismically active with severe earthquakes from time to time.

The central trough is crossed by several transversal ranges of extruded volcanic material, creating separate basins. South of Quito, the basins are lower, the climate hotter and drier with semi-desert stretches. The lack of surface water is aggravated by large quantities of volcanic dust which is easily eroded by wind and water and can produce dry 'badland' topography. Landslides in this unstable and precipitous terrain are common. A serious example was in the Paute valley near Cuenca in 1993 when a hillside which had been intensively cultivated gave way in unusually heavy rains. An earth dam was formed which later collapsed, causing further damage downstream.

The coast

West of the Andes, there are 100-200 km of lowlands with some hilly ground up to 1,000 m. The greater part is drained by the Daule, Vinces and Babahoyo rivers that run north to south to form the Guayas, the largest river on the Pacific coast of South America, which meets the sea at Guayaquil. There are several shorter rivers in the north including the Esmeraldas, whose headwaters include the Río Machángara which unfortunately is the open sewer of Quito. Another system reaches the ocean at La Tola. All of these rivers have created fertile lowlands which are used for banana, cacao and rice production, and there are good cattle lands in the Guayas basin. This is one of the best agricultural areas of South America.

Mangrove swamps thrived on coastal mudflats in tropical rainforest zones and were typical of parts of Esmeraldas, Manabí and Guayas provinces. These are now having to compete with shrimp fisheries, an important export product. Attempts are being made to restrict the destruction of mangroves in the Guayas estuary. South of Guayaquil, the mangroves disappear, and by the border with Peru, it is semi-arid.

Amazonia

The eastern foothills of the Andes are mainly older granite (Mezozoic) rocks, more typical of Brazil than the Pacific coast countries. As with most of the western Amazon basin, it has a heavy rainfall coming in from the east and much is covered with tropical forest along a dozen or so significant tributaries of the Amazon. Partly as a result of the territory being opened up by oil field exploitation, land is being cleared for crops at a high rate. However, certain areas are being developed for ecotourism and it remains to be seen if this will help to arrest the destruction of the environment.

With good water flow and easy gradients, many of the rivers of this region are navigable at least to small craft. The Napo in particular is a significant communications route to Iquitos in Peru and the Brazilian Amazon beyond. Following the end of the border conflict with Peru in 1998, international navigation downstream from ports in the Ecuadorean Oriente has become an interesting prospect for the future.

Climate

Background

In spite of its small size, the range of tropical climates in Ecuador is large. The meeting of the north-flowing Humboldt current with the warm Pacific equatorial water takes place normally off Ecuador, giving the contrast between high rainfall to the north and desert conditions further south in Peru. Changes in the balance between these huge bodies of water, known as the *El Niño* phenomenon, can lead to heavy rains to the south, and this anomaly has affected the region and the world several times during the 1990s (see box, page 444).

Coast

The climate along the Pacific coast is a transition area between the heavy tropical rainfall of Colombia and the deserts of Peru. The rainfall is progressively less south of Guayaquil. This change of climate is due to the offshore Humboldt current which flows north along the South American Pacific coast from Chile to Ecuador. This relatively cold water inhibits rain-producing clouds from 27° south northwards, but just south of the equator, the current is turned west and the climate is dramatically changed.

Andes & Oriente

Inland, the size of the Andean peaks and volcanoes create many different mini-climates, from the permanent snows over 5,000 m to the semi-desert hollows in the central trough. Most of the basins and the adjoining slopes have a moderate

El Niño

What is El Niño and how can it so dramatically alter the world's climate? Aboriginal peoples of Ecuador appear to have been aware of these cyclical changes in weather, attributing them to the position of the earth relative to other heavenly bodies.

Among the early European scientists to visit South America, the German Alexander von Humboldt observed that a powerful ocean current flows from south to north along the coast of Peru; it was later given his name. Under normal conditions, this cold Humboldt current follows South America's Pacific coastline northward as far as the equator, causing very low precipitation (because of low evaporation from its cool waters) and creating deserts in northern Chile, Peru and southern Ecuador. At the equator the Humboldt current turns due west, sweeping past the Galápagos islands into the central Pacific.

Situated north of the equator, a warm countercurrent flows in the opposite direction, eastward towards Panama and then south along the Pacific coast (where it is called the Panama current) until it meets the Humboldt current at the equator. This warm current brings warm moist air and high precipitation to the Pacific coasts of Panama, Colombia and northern Ecuador.

The relative strength of these two currents, warm and cold, varies with the time of year. The warm Panama current can be stronger around Christmas and hence was dubbed the Corriente del Niño, the current of the (Christ) child. Under certain circumstances, which tend to recur in an irregular 5-10 year cycle, this warm current can be exceptionally strong and sweep as far south as Chile, causing very heavy rains and associated calamities in these normally desert areas.

More recently, scientists have looked beyond the explanations offered by these regional Pacific currents. They now regard the El Niño phenomenon, its causes and effects, as truly global; bringing a combination of floods and droughts to the entire planet. They note that under normal conditions the trade winds, which blow westward across the tropical Pacific Ocean, pile up warm sea surface water in the west. Consequently, the sea level by Indonesia is normally about 50 cm higher than it is by Ecuador. This movement of warm water to the west causes an upwelling of deeper cold water in the east (the Humboldt current) resulting in a temperature difference of about 8°C at the same latitude, between the water by the coast of South America and that by Southeast Asia.

When the trade winds diminish in intensity, there is a gradual eastward-moving warming of surface water in the Pacific. Heavy rainfall follows the warmer water east to the Pacific coast of South America (the El Niño phenomenon) and is accompanied by simultaneous drought in Southeast Asia and Australia. The level of the ocean rises along the west coast of South America causing marejadas, exceptionally high tides which can destroy beaches and seaside property. The earth's entire atmospheric circulation is altered and important weather changes result in areas far removed from the equatorial Pacific. The two most recent El Niños took place in 1992-93 and 1997-98, and both were devastating for the Ecuadorean coast as well as many other parts of the world.

Despite some of the simplified explanations presented here, El Niño remains a mystery to even the most sophisticated scientific theories. Why do the trade winds ease off in the first place, apparently initiating the phenomenon? Could it have something to do with the gravitational forces of other planets? Could the ancient inhabitants of El Niño's realm have understood something about these complex relationships which we still do not?

Adapted from the Latin American Travel Advisor, Issue 14, July 1997.

climate, though at altitude daily temperature fluctuations can be considerable. In the north, the basins are higher and temperatures are warm by day and cool at night. It rains mostly between October and May; Quito has an average of 1,300 mm per year. Near the border with Peru, the mountain climate can be very pleasant. Vilcabamba in Loja province is reputed to have a most favourable climate for a long and healthy life. In the Oriente the climate is indistinguishable from the hot, very humid lands of the western Amazon basin. There is heavy rainfall all year round, particularly May to December.

Although lying on the equator, there is considerable variation in the weather of the Galápagos Islands. The islands are affected by the cool water from the southeast Pacific which turns west near the equator. Surface water temperatures can fall to 16°C in July-September, causing low cloud and cool air conditions. Temperatures are highest from January to May and tropical downpours occur frequently at this time. September and October also have a lot of rainfall.

Galápagos
See also graph, page 393

Flora and fauna

No country in the world has as much biological diversity in as little space as Ecuador. The geologically recent uplift of the Andes has caused this diversity by dividing the country into two parts, west and east, and by creating a complex topography that fosters the evolution of new species. It is an exciting thing to experience this diversity firsthand, and Ecuador's extensive road system makes it easy. Here we will make a quick survey of this diversity, from west to east, to give an idea of the enormous range of Ecuador's life forms.

For the Galápagos islands, see the colour wildlife section in the middle of the book

The westernmost part of mainland Ecuador is a broad rolling plain covered in the north by some of the wettest rainforest in the world. (There are some low coastal mountains but they do not reach significant elevations.) The biological centre of this region is the Chocó forest of neighbouring Colombia, so Ecuador's northwest shares many species with that area. Among the so-called Chocó endemics that reach Ecuador are some very fancy birds like the Long-wattled Umbrellabird, Banded Ground-Cuckoo and Scarlet-breasted Dacnis. Many other birds, mammals and plants of this region are found all along the wet Pacific lowlands from northwest Ecuador to Central America. Visitors familiar with Central American wildlife will feel at home here amongst the Mantled Howler Monkeys, Chestnut-mandibled Toucans and Red-capped Manakins. Unfortunately this forest is severely endangered by commercial logging, cattle ranching and farming, and good examples of it are now hard to find.

Northwestern lowlands

The cold Humboldt ocean current creates a completely different environment in the southwestern lowlands. Here the forest is deciduous (driest in July and August), and the southernmost parts of this area are desert-like. The birds and plants of this region are very different from those of the wet northwest; they belong to the Tumbesian bioregion and many are restricted to this small corner of Ecuador and adjacent northwest Peru. Some of the Tumbesian endemic birds are the recently-discovered El Oro Parakeet, Rufous-headed Chachalaca and Elegant Crescent-chest. This is a densely populated region however, and many of the species endemic to it are threatened with extinction.

Southwestern lowlands

Rising suddenly from these flat lowlands are the western Andes, very steep and irregular. Here the constant mists keep the forest wet all the way from north to south. In southern Ecuador it is therefore possible to go from desert to cloud forest in the space of a few hundred metres of elevation. This cloud forest is thick, tall and

Western slopes

Background

dark, and every branch is loaded with bromeliads, orchids and mosses. Orchids reach their maximum diversity in Ecuadorean cloud forests, and many spectacular varieties are found in the west, especially the weird Draculas. Many of the birds in these mountains are restricted to western Ecuador and western Colombia, including spectacular species like the gaudy Plate-billed Mountain-Toucan. At higher elevations there are more similarities with the eastern slope of the Andes. Among the highlights of these forests are the mixed foraging flocks of colourful tanagers, with exotic names like Glistening-green, Beryl-spangled and Flame-faced Tanagers. Mammals are scarce; lower elevations have capuchin, spider and howler monkeys, while high elevations have the elusive Spectacled Bear. Insects too diminish as elevation increases and their role as flower pollinators is taken over by myriads of hummingbirds, including the Violet-tailed Sylph, Velvet-purple Coronet and Gorgeted Sunangel, to name but a few.

Western páramo The cloud forest becomes low and stunted above about 3,300 m, and at higher elevations the forest is replaced by the grassland environment called *páramo*. Here, in contrast to the lower forests, the plant are largely from familiar temperate-zone families like the daisy and blueberry. They take on increasingly bizarre forms as the altitude increases, and the species of the highest elevations look like cushions of moss. Mammals are scarce but include Spectacled Bear, which feeds on the terrestrial bromeliads called Puyas or *achupallas* (which look a lot like pineapple plants); and rabbits, which can be so numerous that they make broad trails in the vegetation. Also preying on the rabbits are a form of Great Horned Owl and the Andean Fox. The birds and insects of these elevations are mostly drab, and many of the families represented here have their origins in North America or temperate southern South America. Forming islands of high forest in the *páramos* are the Polylepis trees, in the rose family; their distinctive flaky reddish bark is the favorite foraging substrate for the Giant Conebill.

Inter-Andean basins Between the western and the eastern Andes lies the Inter-Andean Basin, really a series of basins formed by various river valleys. This region is in the rain shadows of both the western and eastern Andes, so it is relatively dry all year. Much of the original vegetation was destroyed centuries ago, replaced with grasses and more recently with introduced pine and eucalyptus trees. Only on high mountains like Chimborazo or Cotopaxi do relatively undisturbed habitats remain. Here a desolate zone of volcanic ash and bare rock marks the upper end of the *páramo*. There is little vegetation beyond, apart from the valiant colonization attempts of lichens, which grow well even up to 5,000 m.

Eastern páramo To the east of the Inter-Andean Basins are the high eastern *páramos*, very much like the western ones but wetter. Here Mountain Tapirs are the largest animal, but they, like all big chunks of meat in Ecuador, survive only in remote regions. Spectacled Bears are here too, along with White-tailed Deer and its faithful predator the Mountain Lion. A miniature deer, the pudu, also lives here but is rarely seen. Andean Condors, one of the largest flying birds in the world, can be seen soaring majestically overhead. Condors are scavengers and clean up the larger animals after they die.

Eastern slopes The eastern slope of the Andes is clothed in cloud forest like the western slope, but this cloud forest is much less seasonal, and has a higher diversity. Many west slope species of plants and birds have east slope sister species; the Plate-billed Mountain-Toucan, for example, is here replaced by the Black-billed Mountain-Toucan. The lower elevations have some Amazonian species like Woolly Monkey, and there are a few birds that have no western or Amazonian counterparts, like the strange White-capped Tanager. Plant diversity is very high here; orchids are especially diverse, even more so than in the west. The eastern cloud forests are much less damaged by man than the western ones, and there are still large wildernesses that are virtually unknown biologically.

The eastern Amazonian lowland rainforest is the most diverse habitat in Ecuador for birds and mammals, with up to 14 primate species and 550 bird species at a single site. This is as diverse as life gets on this planet. Here is the home of the biggest snake in the world, the semiaquatic Anaconda, and various species of alligator-like caimans. The birds are very impressive, like the multicoloured macaws, the monkey-eating Harpy Eagle, the comical Hoatzin and the elusive Nocturnal Curassow. Mammals include five species of cats, three anteaters, a couple of sloths, two dolphins and an endless variety of bats – bats that troll for fish, bats that suck nectar, bats that catch sleeping birds by smelling them, bats that eat fruit, bats that catch insects, and even vampire bats that really drink blood. The variety of fish is even greater than the variety of birds and bats, and include piranhas, stingrays, giant catfish and electric eels. There are fewer epiphytes here than in cloud forests, but many more species of trees; 1 ha can have over 300 species of trees! Insect life reflects the diversity of plants; for example, there can be over 700 species of butterflies at a single site, including several species of huge shining blue Morphos. If one wants to see spectacular birds and animals and has only one opportunity to visit one mainland region of Ecuador, then this should be it. But you must choose the site carefully if you really want to see these things, see Choosing a rainforest, page 356.

Eastern lowlands

National parks

Reserva Ecológica Antisana, 120,000 ha in Pichincha and Napo provinces. Features varied altitude, Antisana volcano and Andean condors. ■ *US$5*.

Highland parks

Parque Nacional Sangay, 517,725 ha, in Chimborazo, Tungurahua and Morona-Santiago provinces. Covers an area from 800 m up to 5,319 m. Features Altar, Sangay and Tungurahua volcanoes, rain forest, and contains several threatened mammals, eg spectacled bear, tigrillo, mountain tapir. ■ *US$10*.

Parque Nacional Cotopaxi, 33,939 ha, in Cotopaxi, Pichincha and Napo provinces, centred around the Cotopaxi Volcano. ■ *Jul-Sep US$10, Oct-Jun- US$7*.

Reserva Ecológica Cayambe-Coca, 403,103 ha, in Imbabura, Pichincha and Sucumbíos provinces. Features a varied altitude with a diversity of flora and fauna, Cayambe volcano (dormant), lakes and waterfalls. ■ *US$5*.

Reserva de Producción Faunística Chimborazo, 58,560 ha, in Chimborazo, Bolívar and Tungurahua provinces. A centre for the preservation of llama, alpaca and vicuña, also features Chimborazo and Carihuairazo mountains. ■ *US$10*.

Reserva Geobotánica Pululahua, 3,383 ha, located 13 km northwest of Quito near the Mitad del Mundo monument. Features the extinct crater of Pululahua volcano. ■ *US$5*.

Parque Nacional Cajas, 28,800 ha, located 30 km from Cuenca. Features lakes and good trekking. ■ *US$10*.

Area de Recreación El Boliche, 1,077 ha, adjacent to Cotopaxi National Park. ■ *US$5*.

Reserva Ecológica El Angel, 15,715 ha, in Carchi province. Features *frailejones* plants, Chiles volcano, lakes and rivers. ■ *US$10*.

Parque Nacional Llanganates, 219,707 ha in the provinces of Cotopaxi and Tungurahua, Napo and Pastaza. Features Andean lakes and forest; access is difficult. ■ *US$5*.

Reserva Ecológica Cotacachi-Cayapas, 204,420 ha, in Imbabura and Esmeraldas provinces. Runs from the western slopes of the Andes to the coast. Features tropical

Mixed habitats

National parks & reserves

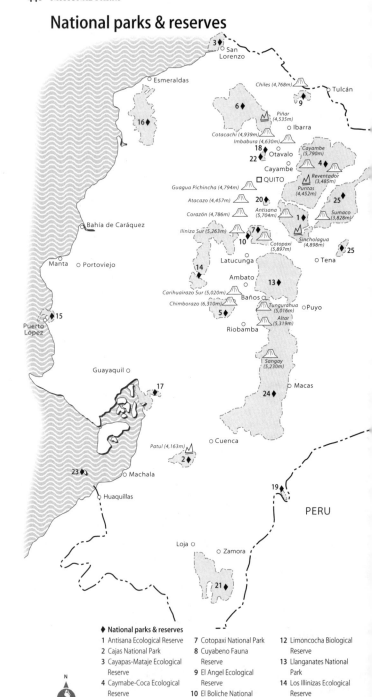

○ San Lorenzo

3 ♦

○ Esmeraldas

Chiles (4,768m)

9 ♦

○ Tulcán

6 ♦

Piñar (4,535m)

○ Ibarra

Cotacachi (4,939m)
Imbabura (4,630m)

18 ♦

○ Otavalo

22 ♦

Cayambe (5,790m)

4 ♦

□ QUITO

Cayambe ○

Reventador (3,485m)

Guagua Pichincha (4,794m)

Atacazo (4,457m)

20 ♦

Puntas (4,452m)

25 ♦

Antisana (5,704m)

Corazón (4,786m)

1 ♦

Sumaco (3,828m)

Iliniza Sur (5,263m)

7 ♦

10 ♦

Sincholagua (4,898m)

○ Bahía de Caráquez

Cotopaxi (5,897m)

25 ♦

Latucunga ○

○ Tena

○ Manta ○ Portoviejo

14 ♦

Ambato ○

13 ♦

Carihuairazo Sur (5,020m)
Chimborazo (6,310m)

Baños ○

Tungurahua (5,016m)

○ Puyo

5 ♦

Altar (5,319m)

Puerto López ○ ♦ 15

Riobamba ○

Sangay (5,230m)

Guayaquil ○

17 ♦

24 ♦

○ Macas

Patul (4,163m)

2 ♦

○ Cuenca

23 ♦

○ Machala

○ Huaquillas

19 ♦

PERU

Loja ○ ○ Zamora

21 ♦

N

0 km   20
0 miles   20

♦ **National parks & reserves**

1 Antisana Ecological Reserve	7 Cotopaxi National Park
2 Cajas National Park	8 Cuyabeno Fauna Reserve
3 Cayapas-Mataje Ecological Reserve	9 El Angel Ecological Reserve
4 Caymabe-Coca Ecological Reserve	10 El Boliche National Recreational Area
5 Chimborazo Fauna Reserve	11 Galápagos National Park
6 Cotacahi-Cayapas Ecological Reserve	

12 Limoncocha Biological Reserve

13 Llanganates National Park

14 Los Illinizas Ecological Reserve

15 Machalilla National Park

16 Mache-Chindul Ecological Reserve

forests, lakes (including Cuicocha) and rivers. ■ *US$5; no fee charged to visit only Cuicocha.*

Parque Nacional Podocarpus, 146,200 ha, in Loja and Zamora provinces. Features cloud forest, rivers and birdlife. ■ *US$5.*

Parque Nacional Sumaco-Napo-Galeras, 205,249 ha, in Napo province. Features Andean and sub-tropical forests, rivers, and much fauna, including river otters, jaguar and spectacled bear. ■ *US$5.*

Parque Nacional Yasuní, 982,006 ha, in Napo province. Amazonian rainforest with lakes, animals and birdlife. ■ *US$10.*

Amazonian parks

Reserva de Producción Faunística Cuyabeno, 655,781 ha, in Sucumbíos province. Rainforest, with lakes and abundant wildlife, although this is coming under increasingly heavy pressure from tourism. ■ *Jul-Sep US$20, Oct-Jun US$15.*

Reserva Biológica Limoncocha, 4,613 ha, in Sucumbíos province. Features Limoncocha lake, with black caiman and good birdlife. ■ *US$5.*

Parque Nacional Machalilla, 55,000 ha, in Manabí province. Features dry coastal forest, beaches, archaeology and Isla de la Plata. ■ *For Isla de la Plata and mainland portion: Jul-Sep US$20, Oct-Jun US$15. For mainland portion only: Jul-Sep US$15, Oct-Jun US$10.*

Coastal parks

Reserva Ecológica Manglares-Churute, 49,383 ha, in Guayas province. Features mangroves and dry tropical forest. ■ *US$10.*

Reserva Ecológica Cayapas-Mataje, 51,300 ha, in Esmeraldas province. Features islands rich in mangroves and bird life. ■ *US$5.*

The Galápagos Islands, 693,700 ha. A description of the archipelago's unique wildlife are given in the colour section in the middle of the book. Entry fees for Galápagos are given on page 406.

Galápagos

The entry fees given above are those officially established by the Ministerio del Ambiente in 2000. They are subject

Entry fees & offices

COLOMBIA

Lago Agrio

12 ◆
oca

8 ◆

26 ◆

N
Not to scale

Galápagos Marine
Biological Reserve

To Ecuador coast (1,000 km)

Pinta
(Abingdon)

Marchena
(Bindloe)

Santiago (San
Salvador/James)

Fernandina
(Narborough)

Santa Cruz
(Indefatigable)

11 ◆

Isabela

San Cristóbal
(Chatham)

Floreana
(Charles, Santa María)

Background

to change without notice and there may also be local variation in both the amounts charged and the dates for high and low season. Whatever fee you are charged, always insist on an official receipt. In the more remote areas there may not be any park infrastructure nor anyone to collect fees.

The offices of the Ministerio del Abiente are located in Quito, in the Ministerio de Agricultura y Ganadería building, 8th floor, Amazonas y Eloy Alfaro, T529845, F564037. They can provide some limited tourist information but it is best to contact the office in the city nearest the park you wish to visit, for example the Cuenca office for Cajas, Loja for Podocarpus and so on. Ecuador's national parks were previously administered by a government agency called INEFAN. Although this no longer exists some people still use the name when referring to the national park authorities.

Culture

People

About half of Ecuador's 13 million people are *mestizo*, descendants of Indians and Spaniards. Those in the Sierra who are an ethnic mixture of white and Indian are sometimes referred to as *cholos*, a name also given to people of white/Indian/black descent who live in the Santa Elena peninsula, west of Guayaquil. Another, more common, name given to people of this three-way mixture in the area around Guayaquil and throughout the northern Pacific lowlands, is *montuvios*.

Indigenous cultures

Mother Earth

Pachamama, or Mother Earth, occupies a very privileged place in Andean culture because she is the generative source of life. The Andean people believe that Man was created from the land, and thus he is fraternally tied to all the living beings that share the earth. According to them, the earth is our mother, and it is on the basis of this understanding that all of human society is organized, always maintaining the cosmic norms and laws.

Women's and men's relationship with nature is what the indigenous highlanders call ecology, harmony and equilibrium. They furthermore believe that private land ownership is a social sin because the land is for everyone. It is meant to be shared and not only used for the benefit of a few.

Vicenta Mamani Bernabé of the

Andean Regional Superior Institute of Theological Studies states: "Land is life because it produces all that we need to live. Water emanates from the land as if from the veins of a human body, there is also the natural wealth of minerals, and pasture grows from it to feed the animals. Therefore, the Pachamama is sacred and since we are her children, we are also sacred. No one can replace the earth, she is not meant to be exploited, or to be converted into merchandise. Our duty is to respect and care for the earth. This is what white people today are just beginning to realize, and it is called ecology. Respect for the Pachamama is respect for ourselves as she is life. Today, she is threatened with death and must be liberated for the sake of her children's liberation."

Andean peoples

Roughly a quarter of all Ecuadoreans today belong to one of 11 different indigenous peoples, though this figure has declined greatly over the centuries through disease, oppression and forced expulsion from their lands. The largest indigenous group are the Andean Quichuas, who number around two million. The common language, Quichua, was introduced by the Incas and is closely related to the Quechua spoken in parts of Peru and Bolivia. Though they speak a common language, indigenous dress differs from region to region. In the north, Otavaleño women are very distinctive with their blue skirts and embroidered blouses, while in the south the Saraguros traditionally wear black, in constant mourning for their dead leader, Atahualpa. The most important part of indigenous dress is the hat, not surprising in a part of the world where the tropical sun can bleach your brains in no time.

Rainforest peoples

The largest groups in the Oriente are the Quichuas in the Pastaza and Napo provinces (around 60,000) and the Shuar and Achuar in the province of Morona Santiago in the south (around 40,000). The Amazonian Quichuas may speak the same language as their highland counterparts, but their way of life is very different. They practise a form of itinerant farming which requires large areas of land, in order to allow the jungle to recover, but their way of life is under threat and many Amazonian Indian communities are fighting for land rights in the face of oil exploration and colonization from the highlands.

The Quichua, Shuar and Siona-Secoya Indians in Pastaza welcome tourists in a controlled way, in order to sell their beautiful products, and some work as guides. But care is required when visiting the Oriente and taking tours to Huaorani villages without prior arrangement. The Huaorani are at great risk from the tourist invasion and do not appreciate being treated as a spectacle. ONHAE, the Huaorani Indigenous organization, has stated that it will only allow guides approved by them to enter their territories (see box, page 369).

There are also small groups of Indians on the coastal plain: in Esmeraldas and Carchi provinces live around 4,000 Cuaiquer, also known as Awas; nearer the coast and a little further south live around 7,000 Cayapas, also known as Chachi; in the lowlands of Pichincha around Santo Domingo are some 2,000 Tsáchilas, also known as Colorados. These coastal Indians are also under threat from colonization.

Background

Native organizations Despite the many pressures they have faced throughout history and still today, the various indigenous groups of the Sierra, the coast and the Amazon rainforest have managed, to some degree, to survive and preserve their cultural identity. The interests of these different groups vary widely. Whereas in the Sierra and on the coast the main issues are obtaining infrastructure for native communities and access to water for irrigation, in the Amazon it is resistance to colonization and the ever-encroaching oil and timber industries. The single biggest threat to the Amazonian rainforest is the oil industry and its irresponsible methods.

Today, Ecuador's native people are among the best organized and politically savvy of any in Latin America. They have grouped themselves into various regional bodies as well as some other entities set up along religious lines (ie Catholic or Protestant). The national body which brings together many, but not all, of these regional organizations is the Confederación de Nacionalidades Indígenas del Ecuador (CONAIE). There is also a loosely allied political party called Pachacutic, which claims to represent the interests of native peoples. In addition to their political activities, these groups work with foreign NGOs and at times with the government, to foster native interests. In 2000 for example, plans were announced for the establishment of a National Indian University in Quito.

CONAIE in particular has played a key role in recent national political events, such as the overthrow of former president Jamil Mahuad. The organization's leadership has at times been criticized for pursuing its own political agenda rather than lobbying for the most immediate needs of its rank and file communities. The matter is controversial. Whatever the case, there can be little doubt that the *Indígenas* of Ecuador have made their voices heard in recent years and will certainly continue to do so in the future.

Those wishing to visit the Oriente independently may contact the Organización de Indígenas de Pastaza (OPIP) in Puyo, T3885461; they can also give you a list of indigenous museums and artesan workshops. Also contact Federación de Centros Shuar-Achuar, Domingo Comín 17-38, Sucúa, Morona-Santiago, T/F7740108 (or in Quito, T2504264). CONFENIAE, the confederation of Amazon Indians, is another good contact at Km 5 outside Puyo, T3885343, or at their office in Quito, Avenida 6 de Diciembre y Pazmino, Edif Parlamento, fourth Floor, oficina 408, T2543973, F2220325.

Afro-Ecuadoreans Ecuador's black population is estimated at almost one million. They live mostly in the coastal province of Esmeraldas and in neighbouring Imbabura, and are descended from slaves who were brought from Africa in the 18th century to work on coastal plantations. Although the slave trade was abolished in 1821, slavery itself continued until 1852. Even then, freedom was not guaranteed until the system of debt tenancy was ended in 1881, and slaves could at last leave the plantations. However, the social status of Ecuador's blacks remains low and most of them still work on banana plantations or in other types of agriculture. Furthermore, they suffer from poor education and the racism endemic in all levels of society.

Racism in Ecuador is not solely aimed at black people, but Indians in general. Its roots run deep and some whites and *mestizos* still view Indians as second-class citizens.

Religion

According to official statistics, 93% of the population belongs to the Roman Catholic faith and the church remains a formidable force in society. In recent decades a variety of Evangelical Protestant groups from the US, Seventh-Day Adventists, Mormons and Jehovah's Witnesses, have increased their influence. Freedom of worship is guaranteed by the Ecuadorean constitution.

Arts and crafts

Ecuador is a shopper's paradise. Everywhere you turn there's some particularly seductive piece of *artesanía* being offered. This word loosely translates as handicrafts, but that doesn't really do them justice. The indigenous peoples make no distinction between fine arts and crafts, so *artesanía* are valued as much for their practical use as their beauty.

Most people don't even know that the Panama hat, Ecuador's most famous export, comes from Ecuador. The confusion over the origin of this natty piece of headwear dates back over 100 years.

Panama hats

    The major trading post for South American goods until the 20th century was at the Isthmus of Panama, the quickest and safest seafaring route to Europe and North America. Sugar, fruit, minerals, cloth and dozens of other products, including the Ecuadorean straw hats, passed through the Isthmus. In the mid-1800s gold seekers from the east coast of the US heading for the California gold rush picked up the straw hats on their way west. Fifty years later, workers on the Panama Canal found these hats ideal for protection against the tropical sun and, like the forty-niners before them, named the hats after their point of purchase, rather than their place of origin. The name stuck.

    The plant from which the hat is made – *Carludovica Palmata* – grows best in the low hills west of Guayaquil, owing to the unique climate. The hats are woven from the very fine fronds of the plant, which are boiled, then dried in the sun before being taken to the weaving centres – Montecristi and Jipijapa in Manabí, and Azogues, Biblián and Sigsíg in Azuay. Montecristi, though, enjoys the reputation of producing the best *superfinos*. These are Panama hats of the highest quality, requiring up to three months work. They are tightly woven, using the thinnest, lightest straw. When turned upside down they should hold water as surely as a glass, and when rolled up, should be able to pass through a wedding ring.

    From the weaver, the hat passes to a middleman, who then sells it on to the factory. The loose ends are trimmed, the hat is bleached and the brim ironed into shape and then softened with a mallet. The hat is then rolled into a cone and wrapped in paper in a balsawood box ready for exporting. The main export centre, and site of most of the factories, is Cuenca, where countless shops also sell the *sombreros de paja toquilla*, as they are known locally, direct to tourists.

During Inca times, textiles held pride of place, and things are no different today. Throughout the highlands beautiful woven textiles are still produced, often using techniques unchanged for centuries. One of the main weaving centres is Otavalo, which is a nucleus of trade for more than 75 scattered Otavaleño communities, and home of the famous handicrafts market which attracts tourists in their thousands.

Weavers of Otavalo

    The history of weaving in Otavalo goes back to the time of conquest when the Spanish instead exploited the country's human resources through the feudal system of *encomiendas* (see History, page 429). A textile workshop (*obraje*) was soon established in Otavalo using forced indigenous labour. *Obrajes* were also set up elsewhere in the region, for example in Peguche and Cotacachi, using technology exported from Europe: the spinning wheel and treadle loom. These are still in use today.

    Though the *encomiendas* were eventually abolished, they were replaced by the equally infamous *huasipungo* system, which rendered the indigenous people virtual serfs on the large *haciendas* that were created. Many of these estates continued to operate weaving workshops, producing cloth in huge quantities for commercial purposes.

Background

The textile industry as it is known today was started in 1917 when weaving techniques and styles from Scotland were introduced to the native workers on the Hacienda Cusín. These proved successful in the national market and soon spread to other families and villages in the surrounding area. The development of the industry received a further boost with the ending of the *huasipungo* system in 1964. The *indígenas* were granted title to their plots of land, allowing them to weave at home.

Today, weaving in Otavalo is almost exclusively for the tourist and export trades by which it is quite naturally influenced. Alongside traditional local motifs, are found many designs from as far afield as Argentina and Guatemala. The Otavaleños are not only renowned for their skilled weaving, but also for their considerable success as traders. They travel extensively, to Colombia, Venezuela, North America and as far afield as Europe, in search of new markets for their products.

Woodcarving During the colonial era, uses of woodcarving were extended to provide the church with carved pieces to adorn the interiors of its many fine edifices. Wealthy families also commissioned work such as benches and chairs, mirrors and huge *barqueños* (chests) to decorate their salons.

In the 16th and 17th centuries woodcarvers from Spain settled north of Quito, where San Antonio de Ibarra has become the largest and most important woodcarving centre in South America.

Initially the *mudéjar*, or Spanish-Moorish styles, were imported to the New World, but as the workshops of San Antonio spread north to Colombia and south to Chile and Argentina, they evolved their own styles. Today, everyone in San Antonio is involved with woodcarving and almost every shop sells carved wooden figures, or will make items to order.

Bags Plant fibre is used not only for weaving but is also sewn into fabric for bags and other articles. *Mochilas* (bags) are used throughout the continent as everyday holdalls.

In Cotopaxi province, *shigras*, which are bags made from sisal, were originally used to store dry foodstuffs around the home. It is said that very finely woven ones were even used to carry water from the wells, the fibres swelling when wet to make the bags impermeable. These bags almost died out with the arrival of plastic containers, until Western demands ensured that the art survived. *Shigras* can be found at the market in Salcedo.

Like the small backstrap looms and drop spindles of the Andes, the bags are portable and can be sewn while women are herding animals in the fields. Today, women's production is often organized by suppliers who provide dyed fibres for sewing and later buy the bags to sell. A large, blunt needle is used to sew the strong fibres and the finished article is likely to last a lot longer than the user.

Bread figures The inhabitants of the town of Calderón, northeast of Quito, know how to make dough. The main street is lined with shops selling the vibrantly-coloured figures made of flour and water which have become hugely popular in recent years.

The origins of this practice are traced back to the small dolls made of bread for the annual celebrations of All Soul's Day. The original edible figures, made in wooden moulds in the village bakery, were decorated with a simple cross over the chest in red, green and black, and were placed in cemeteries as offerings to the hungry souls of the dead. Gradually, different types of figures appeared and people started giving them as gifts for children and friends. Special pieces are still made for All Soul's Day, such as donkeys and men and women in traditional costume.

In the province of Cotopaxi, near Zumbahua and the Quilotoa crater, a regional craft has developed specifically in response to tourist demand. It is the production of 'primitivist' paintings on leather, now carried out by many of the area's residents, depicting typical rural or village scenes and even current events. Following the volcanic eruptions of 1999, these began to figure prominently in the Tigua paintings – named after the town where the work originated. The paintings do vary in price and quality and are now also widely available in Quito, Otavalo and other tourist destinations.

Primitivist paintings

The dress of pre-Hispanic women in the Andean region consisted basically of the *urku*, the *llicila* and the *chumpi*, or belt. The *urku*, the principal vestment, was a large rectangular cloak which covered the woman from her shoulders to her feet in the manner of a tunic. It was fastened at shoulder level with a pair of metal *tupu* and at the waist with a belt.

Andean dress pins

This garb was widely used in rural areas up until about 100 years ago, and survives today in a shortened and modified form. The *llicila* was the outermost shawl, which covered the shoulders and was fastened at the chest with a single pin or a smaller clasp called a *ttipqui*. This garment is still worn today in the rural Andean world, although it is slowly being replaced by other western-style items of clothing.

Tupu and *ttipqui* are the ancient Quechua names for the two types of dress pins, but today all metal pins used by Indian women to fasten their clothing are known as *topos*, which is a Castellanization of the Quechua word *tupu*.

The use of the *tupu* and *ttipqui* is thought to have spread North from the Huari-Tiahuanuco empire throughout the entire Andean region. The first dress pins were simply cactus spines or carved from thin pieces of wood and of a strictly functional nature. However, the development of metallurgy allowed artesans to make the pins from metal, at first hammering gold and silver, and later through the smelting and moulding of copper.

Music and dance

Culturally, ethnically and geographically, Ecuador is very much two countries – the Andean highlands with their centre at Quito and the northern Pacific lowlands behind Guayaquil. In spite of this, the music is relatively homogeneous and it is the Andean music that would be regarded as 'typically Ecuadorean'.

The principal highland rhythms are the Sanjuanito, Cachullapi, Albaza, Yumbo and Danzante, danced by Indian and mestizo alike. These may be played by brass bands, guitar trios or groups of wind instruments, but it is the *rondador*, a small panpipe, that provides the classic Ecuadorean sound, although of late the Peruvian *quena* has been making heavy inroads via pan-Andean groups and has become a threat to the local instrument.

The coastal region has its own song form, the Amorfino, but the most genuinely 'national' song and dance genres, both of European origin, are the Pasillo (shared with Colombia) in waltz time and the Pasacalle, similar to the Spanish Pasodoble. Of Ecuador's three best loved songs, 'El Chulla Quiteño', 'Romántico Quito' and 'Vasija de Barro', the first two are both Pasacalles. Even the Ecuadorean mestizo music has a melancholy quality not found in Peruvian 'Música Criolla', perhaps due to Quito being in the mountains, while Lima is on the coast.

Music of the highland Indian communities is, as elsewhere in the region, related to religious feasts and ceremonies and geared to wind instruments such as the *rondador*, the *pinkullo* and *pifano* flutes and the great long *guarumo* horn with its mournful note. The guitar is also usually present and brass bands with well worn instruments can be found in even the smallest villages. Among the best known musical groups who have recorded are Los Embajadores (whose 'Tormentos' is superb), and the duo Benítez-Valencia for guitar-accompanied vocal harmony, Ñanda-Mañachi and the Conjunto Peguche (both from Otavalo) for highland Indian music and Jatari and Huayanay for pan-Andean music.

There is one totally different cultural area, that of the black inhabitants of the Province of Esmeraldas and the highland valley of the Río Chota in Imbabura. The former is a southern extension of the Colombian Pacific coast negro culture, centred round the marimba, a huge wooden xylophone. The musical genres are also shared with black Colombians, including the Bunde, Bambuco, Caderona, Torbellino and Currulao dances and this music is some of the most African sounding in the whole of South America. The Chota Valley is an inverted oasis of desert in the Andes and here the black people dance the Bomba. It is also home to the unique Bandas Mochas, whose primitive instruments include leaves that are doubled over and blown through.

Festivals

Festivals are an intrinsic part of Ecuadorean life. In pre-Hispanic times they were organized around the solar cycle and agricultural calendar. After the conquest, the church integrated the indigenous festivals with their own feast days and so today's festivals are a mix of Roman Catholicism and indigenous traditions. Every community in every part of the country celebrates their own particular festival in honour of their patron saint and there are many more that are celebrated in common up and down the country, particularly in the Sierra.

Carnival Carnival is held in February or March during the week before Lent and ends on Ash Wednesday. While the Ecuadorean version can't rival that of Brazil for fame or colour, Ecuador has its own carnival speciality: throwing balloons filled with water or, less frequently, bags of flour and any other missile guaranteed to cause a mess. Water pistols are sold on every street corner at this time of year and even the odd bucket gets put to use. It can take visitors aback at first, but if you can keep your composure or – better yet – join in the mayhem, it can all be good fun. For the more sensitive tourist, there is the option of heading to Ambato, one hour south of Quito, where water-throwing is banned and flour is replaced by flowers at the city's *Fiesta de las Frutas y las Flores*.

Holy week The next major event of the festival calendar is Holy Week, or *Semana Santa*, which is held the week before Easter and begins on Palm Sunday (*Domingo de Ramos*). This is celebrated throughout the country, but is especially dramatic in Quito, where there is a spectacularly solemn procession through the streets on Good Friday. A particularly important part of Holy Week is the tradition of eating *fanesca* with family and friends. *Fanesca* is a soup made with salt fish and many different grains, and a good example of the syncretism of Catholic and earlier beliefs. In this case the Catholic component is the lack of meat, which was not consumed during Lent, while the many grains came from native traditions to celebrate the beginning of the harvest at this time of year.

Summer & *Corpus Cristi* is a moveable feast held on Thursday after Trinity Sunday, usually in
autumn mid-June. This is a major event in the central highlands, especially in the provinces of Cotopaxi and Tungurahua, but also in Chimborazo province and in Saraguro and Loja. In Salasaca the festival is celebrated with music, dance and elaborate costumes, while in Pujilí (Cotopaxi) groups of masked *danzantes* make their way through the streets and the valiant climb *palos encebados*, 10m-high greased poles, in order to obtain prizes.

San Juan Bautista takes place on 24 June and is the main festival of the Otavalo valley. For an entire week, the local men dress up in a variety of costumes and dance constantly, moving from house to house. At one point, they head to the chapel of San Juan and start throwing rocks at each other, so keep your distance. This ritual spilling of blood is apparently a sacrifice to *Pachamama*, or Mother Earth.

Another major fiesta in Imbabura province is *San Pedro y San Pablo* (Saints Peter and Paul). This is held on 29 June, but the night before bonfires are lit in the streets and young women who want to have children are supposed to jump over the fires. This festival is particularly important in Cotacachi and Cayambe, and is also celebrated in southern Chimborazo, in Alausi and Achupallas.

Other important festivals include *Virgen del Carmen*, on 16 July, with the biggest celebrations going on in Cuenca and in Chambo, just outside Riobamba. *La Virgen de la Merced*, on 24 September, is a big festival in Latacunga, where a man dressed as *La Mama Negra*, the black mother, dances through the streets.

Day of the Dead

Two of the most important dates in the indigenous people's calendar are 1 and 2 November, All Saints' Day and Day of the Dead (*Todos Santos* and *Día de los Difuntos*, respectively). This tradition has been practised since time immemorial. In the Incaic calendar, November was the eighth month and meant *Ayamarca*, or land of the dead. The celebration is another example of religious adaptation in which the ancient beliefs of ethnic cultures are mixed with the rites of the Catholic Church.

According to ancient belief, the spirit visits its relatives at this time of the year and is fed in order to continue its journey before its reincarnation. The relatives of the dead prepare for the arrival of the spirit days in advance. Among the many items necessary for these meticulous preparations are little bread dolls, each one of which has a particular significance. Horse-shaped breads are prepared that will serve as a means of transport for the soul in order to avoid fatigue.

Inside the home, the relatives construct a tomb supported by boxes over which is laid a black cloth. Here they put the bread, along with various other items important in the ritual. The tomb is also adorned with the dead relative's favourite food and drink. Most households also share a glass of *colada morada*, a syrupy, purple-coloured drink made from various fruits. Once the spirit has arrived and feasted with their living relatives, the entire ceremony is then transported to the graveside in the local cemetery, where it is carried out again, along with the many other mourning families.

This meeting of the living and their dead relatives is re-enacted the following year, though less ostentatiously, and again for the final time in the third year, the year of the farewell. It does not continue after this, which is just as well as the costs can be crippling for the family concerned. Today, most Ecuadoreans commemorate *Día de los Difuntos* in more prosaic fashion; by visiting the cemetery and placing flowers at the graveside of their deceased relatives.

Christmas

Among the local Christmas (*Navidad*) celebrations is the *Pase del Niño* (procession of the child). On Christmas Eve all families which possess a statue of the baby Jesus carry them in procession to the local church, where they are blessed during a special Mass. The most famous *Pase del Niño* is in Cuenca on the morning of 24 December. Other notable celebrations take place in Saraguro, in Loja province, in Pujilí and Tanicuchí in Cotopaxi province and throughout the province of Cañar.

New Year

A typically Ecuadorean aspect of New Year's celebrations are the *años viejos* (literally 'old years'), life-size effigies or puppets which are constructed and displayed throughout the country on December 31. They usually depict politicians or other prominent local, national or international personalities and important events of the year gone by. Children dressed in black are the old year's

Background

widows, and beg for alms: candy or coins. Just before midnight the *años viejo's* will is read, full of satire, and at the stroke of midnight the effigies are doused with gasoline and burned, wiping out the old year and all that it had brought with it. In addition to sawdust, the *años viejos* usually contain a few firecrackers making for an exciting finale; best keep your distance.

Appropriate behaviour Outsiders are usually welcome at all but the most intimate and spiritual of celebrations and, as a *gringo*, you might even be a guest of honour. Ecuadoreans can be very sensitive however and you should make every effort not to offend (for example by not taking a ceremony seriously or by refusing food, drink or an invitation to dance). At the same time, you should keep in mind that most *fiestas* are accompanied by heavy drinking and the resulting disinhibition is not always pleasant. It is best to enjoy the usually solemn beginning of most celebrations as well as the liveliness which follows, but politely depart before things get totally out of control.

Literature

Much Ecuadorean literature has reflected political issues such as the rivalry between Liberals and Conservatives and between Costa and Sierra, and the position of the Indian and the marginalized in society, and many of the country's writers have adopted a strongly political line. Among them were Francisco Eugenio de Santa Cruz y Espejo, who led a rebellion against Spain in 1795, José Joaquín de Olmedo, Federico González Suárez (archbishop of Quito) and Juan Montalvo.

The 19th century José Joaquín de Olmedo (born Guayaquil 1780, died 1847) was a disciple of Espejo and was heavily involved first in the independence movement and then the formative years of the young republic. In 1825 he published *La Victoria de Junín, Canto a Bolívar*, a heroic poem glorifying the Liberator. His second famous poem was the *Canto al General Flores, Al Vencedor de Miñarica* (Juan José Flores was the Venezuelan appointed by Bolívar to govern Ecuador). In addition to poetry, Olmedo wrote political works such as *Discurso sobre las mitas* and *Manifiesto político sobre la Revolución del Seis de Marzo*.

Juan Montalvo (born Ambato 1832, died 1889) was an essayist who was influenced by French Romantics such as Victor Hugo and Lamartine, also by Lord Byron and by Cervantes. One of his main objectives as a writer was to attack what he saw as the failings of Ecuador's rulers, but his position as a liberal, in opposition to conservatism such as García Moreno's, encompassed a passionate opposition to all injustice. 'Ojeada sobre América', for instance (in *El cosmopólita*, 1866-68), is a diatribe against the 'natural law' of man, namely war and killing. Other collections of essays included *Los siete tratados* (1881-82) and *El espectador* (1886), in which he wrote, "If my pen had the gift of tears, I would write a book called *The Indian*, which would make the whole world weep." He never wrote that book. His *Capítulos que se le olvidaron a Cervantes* (1895) was an attempt to imitate the creator of Don Quijote, translating him into an Ecuadorean setting.

Montalvo's contemporary and enemy, Juan León Mera (born Ambato 1832, died 1894), did write a book about the Indian, *Cumandá* (1979). But this dealt not so much with the humiliated Sierra Indians as the unsubjugated Amazonian Indians, 'los errantes y salvajes hijos de las selvas' (the wandering and savage sons of the forests). The book has provoked much debate, which has revolved around the concepts of civilization and barbarism, how colonialism leads to exploitation, but also the value of using nature and the 'savage' solely for ideological ends so that characters are reduced to nothing more than symbols.

The writing on the wall

One of Ecuador's great writers, Jorge Enrique Adoum, once wrote: "Here the only way to get read is by writing on the walls and door of the toilet." The people of Quito have certainly taken that opinion to heart. Graffiti now seems to pervade almost every part of Quito and the city's cultural élite are proud of this phenomenon. The Institute of Culture even published a book with hundreds of examples recorded for posterity.

The sentiments expressed vary from outrage and bitterness to irony and humour and cover everything from existential philosophy to environmental issues. One example warns: 'Forget your dreams, your dreams were sold'. Another offers the rather pertinent advice: 'Help the police - torture yourself'. Disenchantment with the government's economic policies wrought: 'Country with ocean view for sale, inquire at the Presidential Palace'. On a more humorous note is: 'Blessed are the alcoholics, for they shall see God twice'.

Quito's many graffiti poets belong to permanent groups, each with its own 'signature', and most of them are students from wealthy or middle-class families, venting their frustrations at the country's social injustices.

In 1904, Luis A Martínez (1869-1909) published *A la costa*, which attempts to present **The 20th** two very different sides of the country (the coast and the highlands) and the **century** different customs and problems in each. *Plata y bronce* (1927) and *La embrujada* (1923), both by Fernando Chávez, portray the gulf between the white and the Indian communities. In their distinct ways, the two writers moved beyond León Mera's use of an Ecuadorean setting for a Christian Romantic theme (shared, for example, by Chateaubriand in France – *René*) to books which are just Ecuadorean.

For the next 15-20 years, novelists in Ecuador produced a realist literature heavily influenced by French writers like Emile Zola and Maupassant, Russians like Gorki and the North Americans Sinclair Lewis, Dos Passos, John Steinbeck and Ernest Hemingway. This was realism at the expense of beauty. They wrote politically committed stories about marginalized people in crude language and stripped-down prose.

The first indication of this radically different prose was *Los que van*, a collection of stories by Joaquín Gallegos Lara (1911-47), Enrique Gil Gilbert (1912-75) and Demetrio Aguilera Malta (1909-81). These stories created a scandal. They describe incidents in the lives of poor people whose own violence and sexual passions bring about their tragedy. Their dialect is transcribed faithfully, adding to the realism. Interestingly, *Los que van* initiated a movement of protest literature without actually denouncing anyone or anything. The stories deal with social injustice, but in isolated, extreme cases.

Along with two other writers, José de la Cuadra (1903-41) and Alfredo Pareja Diezcanseco (1908), they formed the Grupo de Guayaquil. A sixth member, Adalberto Ortiz (born 1914), joined later. Among the books of these writers are: Gallegos Lara, *Las cruces sobre el agua* (novel, 1946); Gil Gilbert, *Yunga* (stories, 1933), *Nuestro pan* (novel, 1941); Aguilera Malta, the novels *Don Goyo* (1933), *Canal zone* (1935), *La isla virgen* (1942), *La caballeresa del sol* (1964), *Siete lunas y siete serpientes* (1970) and *El secuestro del General* (1973); de la Cuadra, many short stories, *Repisas* (1931), *Horno* (1934), and the novels *Los sangurinos* (1934), *Guasinto* (1938) and *Los monos enloquecidos* (1951). Pareja Diezcanseco's novels are concerned more with urban themes than the stories of his colleagues, for example *El muelle* (1933, set in Guayaquil and New York), *Baldomera* (1938), *Hombres sin tiempo* (1941), *Las tres ratas* (1944). He also wrote a group of books under the general title of *Los años nuevos* (including *La advertencia*, 1956, *El aire y los recuerdos*, 1959, *Los poderes omnímodos*, 1964) which show him breaking away from the Guayaquil Group, taking as his

Background

starting point the political events of 9 July 1925 and the founding of the Socialist Party. With *Las pequeñas estaturas* (1970) and *La manticora* (1974) he became more experimental with narrative forms, while introducing more imaginative material into the same historical lines. Adalberto Ortiz was born in Esmeraldas: his novel *Juyungo* (1943) relates the life of a black/Indian of that region. He also wrote *El espejo y la ventana* (1967), *La envoltura del sueño* (1981) and is a poet.

A slightly later Guayaquileño writer is Pedro Jorge Vera (born 1914), author of poetry in the 1930s and 1940s and novels such as *Los animales puros* (1946), *La semilla estéril* (1962), *Tiempo de muñecos* (1971) and *El pueblo soy yo* (1976), about Velasco Ibarra.

Of the writers of the 1930s and 1940s, outside Guayaquil, Pablo Palacio (1906-47) described himself as an observer. Besides the stories of *Un hombre muerto a puntapies* and *Débora* (1927), his best known book is *Vida del ahorcado* (1932), which is described as one of the rare cries of existential anguish in Ecuadorean literature.

A contemporary group, from Cuenca and Loja, included Angel F Rojas (born 1909), a poet and novelist (*Banca*, 1940, *Un idilio bobo*, 1946, *El éxodo de Yangana*, 1949), G Humberto Mata (born 1904), writer of the indigenist novels *Sal* (1963), *Sumac-Allpa* and *Sanagüín*, and Alfonso Cuesta y Cuesta.

Another group of famous writers, from Quito, were Fernando Chávez (see above), Humberto Salvador (born 1909 – *Camarada*, 1933; *Trabajadores*, 1935; *Noviembre*, 1939) and Jorge Icaza (1906-78). Icaza's novel of 1934, *Huasipungo*, has been described as "the most controversial novel in the history of Latin American narrative". Unlike some indigenist fiction (basically, writing about the Latin American Indian, especially in Peru and Bolivia), there is absolutely no attempt to portray the life of the Sierra Indians as anything other than brutal, inhuman, violent and hopeless. Even the landscape - cold, muddy, drenched in rain - has none of the beauty that is frequently the background to indigenist writing. The book has aroused much anger, either at the Indians' plight, or at Icaza's motives as a novelist. He wrote many other novels, among them *En las calles* (1935), *Cholos* (1938), *Media vida deslumbrados* (1942) and *Huairapamuchas* (1948), but none achieved the fame of *Huasipungo*.

The 1960s ushered in the so-called Boom, with writers such as Gabriel García Márquez, Mario Vargas Llosa, Carlos Fuentes and Julio Cortázar gaining international recognition for the Latin American novel. At the same time, the Ecuadorean poet and novelist, Jorge Enrique Adoum (born 1923), wrote *Entre Marx y una mujer desnuda* (1976). This extraordinary novel is a dense investigation of itself, of novel-writing, of Marxism and politics, sex, love and Ecuador, loosely based around the story of the writer and his friends in a writing group, their loves and theorizing. Adoum has also written *Ciudad sin angel* (1995), and several collections of poetry, which is also intense and inventive (see, for example, *No son todos los que están, 1949-79*).

Other contemporary novelists include Abdón Ubidia (*Ciudad de invierno*; *Palacio de los espejos*; *Sueño de lobos*), Eliecer Cárdenas Espinosa (*Polvo y ceniza*; *Diario de un idolatra*), Raul Pérez Torres, writer of prose and poetry, Javier Vásconez (*El secreto*, *Ciudad lejana*), Miguel Donoso Pareja – who is also a poet (*Henry Black*, *El hombre que mataba a sus hijos*), Alicia Yáñez Cossió (*La casa del sano placer* – described as a satire of traditional sexual norms) and Nelson Estupiñán Bass (*Cuando los guayacanes florecían*). See also *Diez cuentistas ecuatorianos*, Libri Mundi, 1993.

20th century poetry In *Lírica ecuatoriana contemporánea* (two volumes, Quito 1979), Hernán Rodríguez Castelo says that a generation of powerful lyric poets was born between 1890 and 1905. This included modernists like Ernesto Noboa y Caamaño and José María Egas, and many post-modernists. Among this second group were Miguel Angel Zambrano (born 1898, *Diálogo de los seres profundos*, 1956), Gonzalo Escudero (born 1903, *Estatua del aire*, *Materia de ángel*, *Autorretrato*, *Introducción a la muerte*, written in the 1950s and 1960s), Alfredo Gangotena (born 1904, *Poesía*, 1956) and Aurora Estrada y Ayala (born 1902, *Como el incienso*, 1925).

The major figure, perhaps of all Ecuadorean poetry, was Jorge Carrera Andrade (1903-78). Son of a liberal lawyer, Carrera Andrade was involved in socialist politics in the 1920s before going to Europe. In the 1930s and 1940s, Carrera Andrade moved beyond the socialist realist, revolutionary stance of his contemporaries and of his own earlier views, seeking instead to explore universal themes. His first goal was to write beautiful poetry. He published many volumes, including the haiku-like *Microgramas*; see *Registro del mundo: antología poética* (1922-39), *El alba llama a la puerta* (1965-66), *Misterios naturales* and others. See also *Selected Poems*, translated by H R Hayes, Albany, New York, 1972, and *Winds of Exile* by Peter R Beardsell, Oxford, 1977.

From the 1940s onwards, many groups were writing in different parts of the country. A poet who was a major link between Carrera Andrade's generation and the new writers was César Dávila Andrade (1919-67: *Oda al arquitecto*, 1946; *Catedral salvaje*, 1951; *Arco de instantes*, 1959; *En un lugar no identificado*, 1963; *Materia real*, 1970). He was a member of the Madrugada group, as were Enrique Noboa Arízaga (*Orbita de la púpila iluminada*, 1947; *Biografía atlántida*, 1967) and Jorge Crespo Toral. There were two groups called Elan, in Cuenca and Quito. Other Quito groups were Presencia (eg Francisco Granizo Ribadeneira, *Muerte y caza de la madre*, 1978; Gonzalo Pesántez Reinoso, *Palabras*, 1951), Umbral (1952, including Alicia Yáñez Cossió) and Caminos, whose stated concern was for the Ecuadorean people, denouncing social disorder. In Guayaquil in the 1950s the Club 7 de Poesía included David Ledesma, Gastón Hidalgo Ortega, Sergio Román Armendáriz and Alvaro San Félix (both also playwrights) and Ileana Espinel, whose introspective, bitter poems confronted the meaninglessness of the 20th century human condition.

In the heat of the Cuban Revolution, Los Tzántzicos formed in Quito in 1961. They used shock tactics with direct, anti-bourgeois poetry, inciting people to revolution. A chief enemy was the conformist Caminos group. Some of the Quito Tzántzicos were Ulises Estrella, Iván Egüez, Rafael Larrea and Raúl Arias, while in Guayaquil Lenín Bohórquez, Sonia Manzano, Luis Delgadillo and others followed the same line. Many schools and workshops continue to promote poetry in Ecuador, notably the Centro Internacional de Estudios Poéticos del Ecuador (CIEPE), which has published collections like *Poemas de luz y ternura* (Quito 1993).

Bibliographical note Many sources have been used in the preparation of this brief survey. Apart from books quoted in the text above, mention should be made of: Jorge Enrique Adoum, *La gran literatura ecuatoriana del 30* (Quito: El Conejo, 1984); Benjamín Carrión, *El pensamiento vivo de Montalvo* (Buenos Aires: Losada, 1961); Jean Franco, *Spanish American Literature since Independence* (London, New York: Benn, 1973); Karl H Heise, *El Grupo de Guayaquil* (Madrid: Nova Scholar, 1975); Gerald Martin, *Journeys through the Labyrinth* (London, New York: Verso, 1989); Antonio Sacoto, *Catorce novelas claves de la literatura ecuatoriana* (Cuenca: 1990) and *The Indian in the Ecuadorean Novel* (New York: Las Americas, 1967); Darío Villanueva y José María Viña Liste, *Trayectoria de la novela hispanoamericana actual* (Madrid: Austral, 1991); Jason Wilson, *Traveller's Literary Companion: South and Central America* (Brighton: In Print, 1993). Thanks are also due to Anja Louis of Grant and Cutler, London, and Libri Mundi, Quito.

Fine art and sculpture

Colonial Quito was a flourishing centre of artistic production, exporting works to many other regions of Spanish South America. The origins of this trade date back to the year of the Spanish foundation of Quito, 1534, when the Franciscans established a college to train Indians in European arts and crafts. Two Flemish friars, Jodoco Ricke and Pedro Gosseal, are credited with teaching a generation of Indians how to paint the pictures and carve the sculptures and altarpieces that were so urgently needed by the many newly-founded churches and monasteries in the region.

16th & 17th centuries

Background

The college's success, based on the Franciscans' liberal attitude towards the Indians, became a political issue and in 1581 control was transferred to the Augustinians. By that time, however, Quito had an established population of indigenous craftsmen, and the legacy of the first Franciscan college is confirmed in the interior of San Francisco itself, lavishly furnished with 16th and early 17th century altarpieces, paintings and decorative carving. The influence of the ideology of the 16th century Franciscan missionary friars, their taste for images of ascetic penitent saints and badly wounded Christs, their fondness for theological allegory, and their devotion to the Virgin of the Immaculate Conception, can be discerned in religious art until the 19th century and beyond.

As well as the initial Flemish bias of the first Franciscans, stylistic influences on the Quito school came from Spain, particularly from the strong Andalucian sculptural tradition. Quito churches preserve several works imported from Seville in the later 16th and early 17th century which served as models for local craftsmen, and there are records of Quiteñan craftsmen going to Spain to broaden their experience, but few Spanish craftsmen emigrated to Ecuador. The Toledan Diego de Robles (died 1594), who worked in Madrid and Seville before arriving in Quito in 1584, is an exception, important not so much for the quality of his few surviving works but because the workshop he ran together with the painter Luis de Ribera provided the expertise in the techniques of painted and gilded statuary for which Quito was to become so famous.

Colonial painting was as much influenced by Italy as by Spain. An important early figure in this was the Quito-born mestizo Pedro Bedón (1556-1621). Educated in Lima where he probably had contact with the Italian painter Bernardo Bitti, Bedón returned home to combine the duties of Dominican priest with work as a painter. He is best-known for his illuminated manuscripts, where his decorated initials include all manner of grotesque heads, but he also established a religious brotherhood attached to the church of Santo Domingo whose membership included many of the painters trained by the Franciscans, where the influence of his slightly archaic Italian manner was considerable.

Indigenous influence is not immediately apparent in painting or sculpture despite the fact that so much of it was produced by Indians. The features of Christ, the Virgin and saints are European, but in sculpture the proportions of the bodies are often distinctly Andean: broad-chested and short-legged. This is especially true of figures of Christ, such as the anonymous late 17th-century *Ecce homo* in the San Francisco museum. In both painting and sculpture the taste – so characteristic of colonial art in the Andes – for patterns in gold applied over the surface of garments may perhaps be related to the high value accorded to textiles in pre-conquest times.

Important names in the field of 17th-century colonial sculpture include the shadowy Padre Carlos, active between 1620 and 1680, to whom is attributed the bleeding and emaciated San Pedro de Alcántara in the Franciscan chapel of the Cantuña. José Olmos, known as Pampite, also very poorly documented but perhaps a pupil of Padre Carlos, produced gory crucifixions, including one in the church of San Francisco and one now in the Museo del Banco Central where Christ's wounds are more like suppurating sores, contrasting starkly with the pale shiny flesh.

In painting the mestizo, Miguel de Santiago (died 1706) represents a break from the Italian mannerist style of Bedón. In 1656 he produced a monumental series of canvases on the Life of St Augustine for the Augustinian cloister based on engravings by the Flemish Schelte de Bolswert, but with local settings. He later devised a set of eight ingeniously complex allegories on the theme of Christian Doctrine for the Franciscans, which can be seen in the Museo de San Francisco. Santiago's daughter Isabel and nephew Nicolás de Goríbar (active 1685-1736) were also painters, influenced by the chiaroscuro of earlier Spanish artists – particularly Zurbarán and Murillo.

Representations of the Virgin are very common, especially that of the Virgin Immaculate, patron of the Franciscans and of the city of Quito. This curious local version of the Immaculate Conception represents the Virgin standing on a serpent and crescent moon as tradition dictates, but unconventionally supplied with a pair of wings. It was popularized by Miguel de Santiago in the mid-17th century (Museo del Banco Central) perhaps with earlier roots, and is best known from the modern monument on the Panecillo hill, while 18th-century carved versions survive in churches throughout Ecuador.

The prolific Bernardo de Legarda (died 1773) was responsible for many of these including that on the high altar of San Francisco (1734), a lively, dancing figure with swirling robes. The theatricality of 18th-century Quiteñan sculpture is evident in Legarda's tableau in the old Carmelite convent (Carmen Alto) depicting the death of the Virgin, where 16 life-size free-standing figures of saints and angels mourn at the bedside.

In the later 18th century the sculptor Manuel Chili, known to his contemporaries as Caspicara 'the pockmarked', continued the tradition of polychrome images with powerful emotional appeal ranging from the dead Christ (examples in the Museo del Banco Central) to sweet-faced Virgins and chubby infant Christs (Museo de San Francisco). Outside Quito the best-known sculptor was Gaspar Sangurima of Cuenca who was still producing vividly realistic polychrome crucifixions in the early 19th century (example in the Carmen de la Asunción, Cuenca). After the declaration of Independence in 1822 Bolívar appointed him Director of the first School of Fine Arts, so confirming Cuenca's importance as a centre of artistic activity, an importance the city retains to this day.

Painting in the later 18th century is dominated by the much lighter, brighter palette of Manuel Samaniego (died 1824), author of a treatise on painting which includes instructions on the correct human proportions and Christian iconography, as well as details of technical procedures and recipes for paint.

As elsewhere in Latin America, the struggle for Independence created a demand for subjects of local and national significance and portraits of local heroes. Antonio Salas (1795-1860) became the unofficial portrait painter of the Independence movement. His paintings of heroes, military leaders and notable churchmen can be seen in Quito's Museo Jijón y Caamaño. Antonio's son, Rafael Salas (1828-1906), was among those to make the Ecuadorean landscape a subject of nationalist pride, as in his famous birds-eye view of Quito sheltering below its distinctive family of mountain peaks (private collection).

Rafael Salas and other promising young artists of the later 19th century, including Luis Cadena (1830-89) and Juan Manosalvas (1840-1906), studied in Europe, returning to develop a style of portraiture which brings together both the European rediscovery of 17th-century Dutch and Spanish art and Ecuador's own conservative artistic tradition where the tenebrism of Zurbarán and his contemporaries had never been forgotten. They also brought back from their travels a new appreciation of the customs and costumes of their own country. The best-known exponent of this new range of subject matter was Joaquín Pinto (1842-1906). Although he did not travel to Europe and received little formal training, his affectionate, often humorous paintings and sketches present an unrivalled panorama of Ecuadorean landscape and peoples.

Pinto's documentation of the plight of the Indian, particularly the urban Indian, presaged the 20th-century indigenist tendency in painting whose exponents include Camilo Egas (1899-1962), Eduardo Kingman (1913-97) and most famously Oswaldo Guayasamin (1919-99). Their brand of social realism, while influenced by the Mexican muralists, has a peculiarly bitter hopelessness of its own. Guayasamin's home also includes a museum which is well worth a visit and Kingman's work can be seen at the Posada de las Artes Kingman.

Their contemporary, Manuel Rendón (1894-?), seems superficially more modern but his subject matter is traditional and often religious, the curvaceous patchwork designs reminiscent of stained glass windows. Several interesting artists of the subsequent generation have rejected social realism and explored aspects of precolumbian and popular art. Aníbal Villacís (born 1927) and Enrique Tábara (born 1930) use textures and glyphic motifs to evoke ancient pottery and textiles, while Osvaldo Viteri (born 1931) incorporates brightly-clad dolls into his compositions, contrasting the tiny popular figures with large areas of paint and canvas.

The civic authorities in Ecuador, particularly during the middle years of this century, have been energetic in peopling their public spaces with monuments to commemorate local and national heroes and events. Inevitably such sculpture is representational and often conservative in style, but within these constraints there are powerful examples in most major town plazas and public buildings are generously adorned with sculptural friezes, such as in the work of Jaime Andrade (born 1913) on the Central University and Social Security buildings in Quito. Estuardo Maldonado (born 1930) works in an abstract mode using coloured stainless steel to create dramatic works for public and private spaces.

In recent years there have been lots of interesting artistic experiments which can be appreciated in museums and especially the galleries of the Casa de Cultura across the country: the lively expressionism of Ramiro Jácome, the hyperrealism of Julio Montesinos or the complex dramas of Nicolás Svistoonoff, for example, or the spare engravings of María Salazar and Clara Hidalgo. Jorge Chalco makes inventive use of popular motifs while Gonzalo Endara Crow's success has led to numerous imitators of his picturesque formula combining faux-naif landscapes with elements of surrealism. His giant mosaic-tiled hummingbird has become a landmark in the Valle de los Chillos east of Quito.

Cuenca hosts an important Biennial and Ecuador is unusual among the smaller Latin American countries for its lively international art scene.

Footnotes

12

Footnotes

Spanish words and phrases

No amount of dictionaries, phrase books or word lists will provide the same enjoyment as being able to communicate directly with the people of the country you are visiting. Learning Spanish is a useful part of the preparation for a trip to Ecuador and you are encouraged to make an effort to grasp the basics before you go. As you travel you will pick up more of the language and the more you know, the more you will benefit from your stay. The following section is designed to be a simple point of departure.

Whether you have been taught the 'Castillian' pronunciation (all *z*'s, and *c*'s followed by *i* or *e*, are pronounced as the 'th' in 'think') or the 'American' pronunciation (they are pronounced as *s*), you will encounter little difficulty in understanding either; Spanish pronunciation varies geographically much less than English. There are, of course, regional accents and usages; but the basic language is essentially the same everywhere.

General pronunciation
The stress in a Spanish word conforms to one of three rules: 1) if the word ends in a vowel, or in n or s, the accent falls on the penultimate syllable *(ventana, ventanas)*; 2) if the word ends in a consonant other than n or s, the accent falls on the last syllable *(hablar)*; 3) if the word is to be stressed on a syllable contrary to either of the above rules, the acute accent on the relevant vowel indicates where the stress is to be placed *(pantalón, merálona)*. Note that adverbs such as *cuando* (when), take an accent when used interrogatively; *¿cuándo?* (when?).

Vowels
A	not quite as short as in English 'cat'
E	as in English 'pay', but shorter in a syllable ending in a consonant
I	as in English 'seek'
O	as in English 'shop', but more like 'pope' when the vowel ends a syllable
U	as in English 'food', after 'q' and in 'gue', 'gui' u is unpronounced; in 'güe' and 'güi' it is pronounced
y	when a vowel, pronounced like 'I'; when a semiconsonant or consonant, it is pronounced like English 'yes'
ai, ay	as in English 'ride'
el, ey	as in English 'they'
oi, oy	as in English 'toy'

Consonants
Unless listed below consonants can be pronounced in Spanish as they are in English.

b, v	their sound is interchangeable and is a cross between the English **b** and **v**, except at the beginning of a word or after **m** or **n** when it is like English **b**
C	like English **k**, except before **e** or **i** when it is the **s** in English 'sip'
G	before **e** and **i** it is the same as **j**
H	when on its own, never pronounced

J	as the **ch** in the Scottish 'loch'
Ll	as the **g** in English 'beige'; sometimes as the 'lli' in 'million'
Ñ	as the 'ni' in English 'onion'
Rr	trilled much more strongly than in English
X	depending on its location, pronounced as in English 'fox', or 'sip', or like 'gs'
Z	as the **s** in English 'sip'
G	before **e** and **i** it is the same as **j**
H	when on its own, never pronounced

Pronouns

In the Americas, the plural, familiar pronoun *vosotros* (with the verb endings - *áis*, - *éis*), though much used in Spain, is never heard. Two or more people, including small children, are always addressed as *ustedes* (*uds*).

Inappropriate use of the familiar forms (*tú, vos*) can sound imperious, condescending, infantile, or imply a presumption of intimacy that could annoy officials, one's elders, or, if coming from a man, women.

To avoid cultural complications if your Spanish is limited, stick to the polite forms: *usted* (*ud*) in the singular, *ustedes* in the plural, and you will never give offence. Remember also that a person who addresses you as *tú* does not necessarily expect to be *tuteada* (so addressed) in return.

You should, however, violate this rule when dealing with a small child, who might be intimidated by *usted*; he/she is, after all, normally so addressed only in admonitions such as '*¡No, Señor, ud no tomará un helado antes del almuerzo!*' 'No, Sir, you will not have ice cream before lunch!'

General hints

Note that in Ecuador the common response to *¡Gracias!* is as often as not *¡A la orden!* ('Yours to command!') rather than the '*¡De nada!*' ('It's nothing!') taught in school.

Travellers whose names include b's and v's should learn to distinguish between them when spelling aloud as *be larga* and *ve corta* or *uve*. (Children often say *ve de vaca* and *be de burro* to distinguish between the two letters, pronounced interchangeably, either as b or v, in Spanish.)

Expressions of time

Many misunderstandings about engagements stem from terminology rather than tardiness. *Ahora* is often used as a synonym for *hoy*, 'today', not the 'now' in the dictionary; 'now' or 'soon' are *ahorita*; 'right now' is *ahora mismo* or *enseguida*. *Ahora* can also mean 'in a little while' or 'in a bit'.

Greetings, courtesies

excuse me/I beg your pardon	*permiso*
Go away!	*¡Váyase!*
good afternoon/evening/night	*buenas tardes/noches*
good morning	*buenos días*
goodbye	*adiós/chao*
hello	*hola*
How are you?	*¿cómo está?/¿cómo estás?*
I do not understand	*no entiendo*
leave me alone	*déjame en paz/no me moleste*
no	*no*
please	*por favor*
pleased to meet you	*mucho gusto/encantado/encantada*
see you later	*hasta luego*
thank you (very much)	*(muchas) gracias*

What is your name?	*¿Cómo se llama?*
yes	*sí*
I speak ...	*Hablo ...*
I speak Spanish	*Hablo español*
I don't speak Spanish	*No hablo español*
Do you speak English?	*¿Habla usted inglés?*
We speak German	*Hablamos alemán*
They speak French	*Hablan francés*
Please speak slowly	*hable despacio por favor*
I am very sorry	*lo siento mucho/disculpe*
I'm fine	*muy bien gracias*
I'm called_	*me llamo_*
What do you want?	*¿Que quiere?*
I want	*quiero*
I don't want it	*No lo quiero*
long distance phone call	*la llamada a larga distancia*
good	*bueno*
bad	*malo*

Nationalities and languages

American *Americano/a*
Australian *Australiano/a*
Austrian *Austriaco/a*
British *Britanico/á*
Canadian *Canadiense*
Danish *Danés/Danesa*
Dutch *Holandés/Holandesa*
English *Inglés/Inglesa*
French *Francés/Francesa*
German *Alemán/Alemana*
Irish *Irlandés/Irlandesa*

Italian *Italiano/a*
Mexican *Mexicano/a*
New Zea-
land *Neozelandés/Neozelandesa*
Norwegian *Noruego/a*
Portuguese *Portugués/Portuguesa*
Scottish *Escocés/Escocesa*
Spanish *Español/a*
Swedish *Sueco/a*
Swiss *Suizo/a*
Welsh *Gallego/a*

Basic questions

Have you got a room for two people?
  ¿Tiene habitación para dos personas?
How do I get to_? *¿Cómo llegar a_?*
How much does it cost? *¿ Cuánto vale?*
How much is it? *¿Cuánto es?*
When does the bus leave? *¿A qué hora sale el bus?*

-arrive? *-llega-*
When? *¿Cuándo?*
Where is_? *¿Dónde está_?*
Where is the nearest petrol station?
  ¿Dónde está la gasolinera más cerca?
Why? *¿Por qué?*

Basics

bank *el banco*
bathroom/toilet *el baño*
bill *la factura/la cuenta*
cash *el efectivo*
cheap *barato*
church/cathedral *La iglesia/catedral*
exchange house *la casa de cambio*
exchange rate *la tasa de cambio*
expensive *caro*

market *el mercado*
notes/coins *los billetes/las monedas*
police (policeman) *la policia (el policia)*
post office *el correo*
supermarket *el supermercado*
telephone office *el centro de llamadas*
travellers' cheques *los travelers/los cheques de viajero*

Getting around

aeroplane/airplane *el avión*
airport *el aeropuerto*
bus station *la terminal (terrestre)*
bus stop *la parada*
bus *el bus/el autobus*
bus route *el corredor*
first/second class *primera/segunda clase*
on the left/right *a la izquierdo/derecha*
second street on the left
 la segunda calle a la izquierda
straight on *derecho*
ticket office *la taquilla*
ticket *el boleto/tiquete*

to walk *caminar*
Where can I buy tickets?
 ¿Dónde se puede comprar boletos?
Where can I park?
 ¿Dónde se puede parquear?
straight on *derecho*
ticket office *la taquilia*
ticket *el bolero/tiquete*
to walk *caminar*
Where can I buy tickets?
 ¿Dónde se puede comprar boletos?
Where can I park?
 ¿Dónde se puede parquear?

Orientation and motoring

arrival *la llegada*
avenue *la avenida*
block *la cuadra*
border *la frontera*
corner *la esquina*
customs *la aduana*
departure *la salida*
east *el este, el oriente*
empty *vacío*
full *lleno*
immigration *la inmigración*
insurance *el seguro*
the insured *el asegurado/la asegurada*
to insure yourself against *asegurarse
 contra*
luggage *el equipaje*

north *el norte*
oil *el aceite*
passport *el pasaporte*
petrol/gasoline *la gasolina*
puncture *el pinchazo*
south *el sur*
street *la calle*
that way *por allí/por allá*
this way *por aquí/por acá*
tourist card *la tarjeta de turista*
tyre *la llanta*
unleaded *sin plomo*
visa *el visado*
waiting room *la sala de espera*
west *el oeste/el poniente*

Accommodation

air conditioning *el aire acondicionado*
all-inclusive *todo incluído*
blankets *las mantas*
clean/dirty towels *las toallas
 limpias/sucias*
dining room *el comedor*
double bed *la cama matrimonial*
guest house *la casa de huéspedes*
hot/cold water *el agua caliente/frío*
hotel *el hotel*
Is service included? *¿Está incluído el
 servicio?*
Is tax included? *¿Están incluidos los
 impuestos?*

noisy *ruidoso*
pillows *las almohadas*
restaurant el restaurante
room *el cuarto/la habitación*
sheets *las sábanas*
shower *la ducha*
single/double *sencillo/doble*
soap *el jabón*
to make up/clean *limpiar*
toilet *el sanitario*
toilet paper *el papel higiénico*
with private bathroom *con baño privado*
with two beds *con dos camas*

Health

aspirin *la aspirina*
blood *la sangre*
chemist/phar-
macy *la farmacia*
condoms *los*
preservativos
contact lenses *las*
lentes de contacto
contraceptive
(pill) *el*
anticonceptivo (la
píldora
anticonceptiva)
diarrhoea *la diarrea*
doctor *el médico*
fever/sweat *la*
fiebre/el sudor
(for) pain *(para)*
dolor
head *la cabeza*
period/towels *la*
regla/las toallas
stomach *el*
estómago

Time

At one o'clock *a la una*
At half past two/two thirty
 a las dos y media
At a quarter to three *a cuarto para las*
tres or *a las tres menos quince*
It's one o'clock *es la una*
It's seven o'clock *son las siete*
It's twenty past six/six twenty
 son las seis y veinte
It's five to nine *son cinco para las*
nueve/son las nueve menos cinco
In ten minutes *en diez minutos*
five hours *cinco horas*
Does it take long? *¿Tarda mucho?*
We will be back at ... *Regresamos a las ...*
What time is it? *¿Qué hora es?*
Monday *lunes*
Tuesday *martes*
Wednesday *miércoles*
Thursday *jueves*
Friday *viernes*
Saturday *sábado*
Sunday *domingo*
January *enero*
February *febrero*
March *marzo*
April *abril*
May *mayo*
June *junio*
July *julio*
August *agosto*
September *septiembre*
October *octubre*
November *noviembre*
December *diciembre*

Numbers
one *uno/una*
two *dos*
three *tres*
four *cuatro*
five *cinco*
six *seis*
seven *siete*
eight *ocho*
nine *nuevo*
ten *diez*
eleven *once*
twelve *doce*
thirteen *trece*
fourteen *catorce*
fifteen *quince*
sixteen *dieciseis*
seventeen *diecisiete*
eighteen *dieciocho*
nineteen *diecinueve*
twenty *veinte*
twenty one,
two *veintiuno,*
veintidos etc
thirty *treinta*
forty *cuarenta*
fifty *cincuenta*
sixty *sesenta*
seventy *setenta*
eighty *ochenta*
ninety *noventa*
hundred *cien or*
ciento
thousand *mil*

Family

aunt *la tía*	grandmother *la abuela*
brother *el hermano*	husband *el esposo/marido*
cousin *la/el prima/o*	married *casado/a*
daughter *la hija*	mother *la madre*
family *la familia*	single/unmarried *soltero/a*
father *el padre*	sister *la hermana*
fiance/fiancee *el novio/la novia*	son *el hijo*
friend *el amigo/la amiga*	uncle *el tío*
grandfather *el abuelo*	wife *la esposa*

Key verbs

To go *ir*
I go *voy*
you go (familiar singular) *vas*
he, she, it goes, you (unfamiliar singular) go *va*
we go *vamos*
they, you (plural) go *van*
To have (possess) *tener*
I have *tengo*
You have *tienes*
He she, it have, you have *tiene*
We have *tenemos*
They, you have *tienen*
(Also used as 'To be', as in 'I am hungry' *tengo hambre*)
(NB *Haber* also means 'to have', but is used with other verbs, as in 'he has gone' *ha ido*)
I have gone *he ido*
You have said *has dicho*
He, she, it has, you have done *ha hecho*
We have eaten *hemos comido*
They, you have arrived *han llegado*
Hay means 'there is' and is used in questions such as ¿*Hay cuartos?* 'Are there any rooms?'; perhaps more common is *No hay* meaning 'there isn't any'

To be (in a permanent state) *ser*
I am (a teacher) *soy (profesor)*
You are *eres*
He, she, it is, you are *es*
We are *somos*
They, you are *son*
To be (positional or temporary state) *estar*
I am (in London) *estoy (en Londres)*
You are *estás*
He, she, it is, you are (happy) *está (contenta)*
We are *estámos*
They, you are *están*
To do/make *Hacer*
I do *hago*
You do *haces*
He, she, it does, you do *hace*
We do *hacemos*
They, you do *hacen*
The above section was compiled on the basis of glossaries by André de Mendonça and David Gilmour of South American Experience, London, and the Latin American Travel Advisor, *No 9, March 1996*

Useful Ecuadorean words and phrases

how are you? what's up? ¿*qué tal?*
right now (but it usually means you've got a long wait ahead of you) *ahorita*
lodging, basic accommodation *alojamiento*
high Andean plain *altiplano*
mountain pass *apacheta*
suburb or district of city *barrio*
cabin *cabaña*
person from the countryside *campesino*
shared taxi *colectivo*

restaurant specializing in meat dishes *churrasquería*
pastry filled with meat or cheese *empanada*
corner *esquina*
bus company *flota*
soft fizzy drink *gaseosa*
Latin American term for an American, but not derogatory *gringo/a*
ranch *hacienda*
ice cream parlour *heladería*

juice *jugo*
small bus or minibus *micro*
office *oficina*
treeless plains *pampas*
mixed grill *parrillada*
floor *piso*
town or village *pueblo*

soft drink *refresco*
small change (and very difficult to find)
sueltito
shop *tienda*
barrier across road at beginning
of village *tranca*

Food

avocado *el aguacate*
baked *al horno*
bakery *la panadería*
banana chips *los tostones*
banana (sweet) *el guineo*
beans *los frijoles/las habichuelas*
beef *la carne de res*
beef steak or pork fillet *el bistec*
boiled rice *el arroz blanco*
bread *el pan*
breakfast *el desayuno*
butter *la mantequilla*
cassava, yucca *la yuca*
casserole *la cazuela*
chewing gum *el chicle*
chicken *el pollo*
chilli pepper or green pepper *el ají*
clear soup, stock *el caldo*
cod, salt cod *el bacalao*
conch *el lambi*
cooked *cocido*
dining room *el comedor*
egg *el huevo*
fish *el pescado*
fork *el tenedor*
fried *frito*
fritters *las frituras*
garlic *el ajo*
goat *el chivo*
grapefruit *el pomelo*
grill *la parrilla*
grilled/griddled *a la plancha*
guava *la guayaba*
guinea foul *la guinea*
ham *el jamón*
hamburger *la hamburgueso*
hot, spicy *picante*
ice cream *el helado*
jam *la mermelada*
knife *el cuchillo*
lime *el limón*
lobster *la langosta*

lunch *el almuerzo*
margarine, fat *la manteca*
meal, supper, dinner *la comida*
meat *la carne*
minced meat *el picadillo*
mixed salad *la ensalada mixta*
onion *la cebolla*
orange *la naranja*
pepper *el pimiento*
plantain, green banana *el plátano*
pasty, turnover *la empanada/el*
pastelito
pork *el cerdo*
potato *la papa*
prawns *los camarones*
raw *crudo*
restaurant *el restaurante*
roast *el asado*
root or starchy vegetables *las viandas*
salad *la ensalada*
salt *el sal*
sandwich *el bocadillo*
sauce *la salsa*
sausage *la longaniza*
scrambled eggs *los huevos revueltos*
seafood *los mariscos*
small sandwich, filled roll *el bocadito*
soup *la sopa*
spoon *la cuchara*
squash *la calabaza*
squid *los calamares*
supper *la cena*
sweet *dulce*
sweet potato *la batata*
to eat *comer*
toasted *tostado*
turkey *el pavo*
turtle *la tortuga*
vegetables *los legumbres/vegetales*
without meat *sin carne*
yam *el ñame*

Drink

aged rum *el ron añejo*
beer *la cerveza*
boiled *hervido*
bottled *en botella*
camomile tea *la manzanilla*
canned *en lata*
cocktail *el coctel*
coconut milk *la leche de coco*
coffee *el café*
coffee, small, strong *el cafecito*
coffee, white *el café con leche*
cold *frío*
condensed milk *la leche condensada*
cup *la taza*
drink *la bebida*
drunk *borracho*
fruit milk shake *el batido*
fruit punch *el ponche de frutas
(non-alcoholic)*
glass *el vaso*
glass of liqueur *la copa de licor*
hot *caliente*
ice *el hielo*

juice *el jugo*
lemonade *la limonada*
milk *la leche*
mint *la menta*
orange juice *el jugo de china/naranja*
pineapple milkshake *el batido de piña
con leche*
rough rum, firewater *el aguardiente*
rum *el ron*
soft drink *el refresco*
soft fizzy drink *la gaseosa/cola*
sugar *el azúcar*
sugar cane juice *la guarapa*
tea *el té*
to drink *beber/tomar*
water *el agua*
water, carbonated *el agua mineral con
gas*
water, still mineral *el agua mineral nat-
ural/sin gas*
wine, red *el vino tinto*
wine, white *el vino blanco*

Index

Map index

Shorts

Advertisers

Galapagos & Ecuador

^{M/V} Galapagos Legend

Galapagos Island Cruises

starting at $219 per night/pp.

On board our yachts:
^{M/Y} **Coral**
^{M/Y} **Coral II**
The new ^{M/Y} Grand Coral
16 - 32 passengers capacity, Charters and individuals.

Coming soon:

The new
^{M/V} **Galapagos Legend**
for 90 passengers

^{M/Y} Grand Coral

^{M/Y} Coral

^{M/Y} Coral II

Ecuador land excursions:

Otavalo Indian Market	starting at $ 58 pp
Cotopaxi national park & volcano	starting at $ 76 pp
Amazon rainforest expedition	starting at $112 per day/pp
all inclusive packages	starting at $100 per day/pp

Many more special offers, just mention this add!!!

We make Galapagos and Ecuador easy!

KLEIN TOURS

QUITO - ECUADOR Av. Shyris 1000 & Holanda Ph: (593-2) 430345-267000
Fax: (593-2) 442389   E-mail: ecuador@kleintours.com.ec
Web site: www.galapagosecuador.com / www.kleintours.com

GALAPAGOS ISLANDS
an ecological adventure

Breathe the curiosity of modern biology. Discover Darwin's "living laboratory" where the wildlife wander freely. Hike ancient lava flows and contemplate giant tortoises. Slip into a sea kayak Breathe the curiosity of modern biology. Discover Darwin's "living laboratory" where the wildlife wander freely. Hike ancient lava flows and contemplate giant tortoises. Slip into a sea kayak and explore hidden bays snorkel with a penguin on the equator, swim with sea lions o walk along pristine powder sand beaches. Marvel a prehistoric reptiles and the most comical sea birds on the planet. Visit these enchanting Islands in maximum comfor and safety aboard one of ou first class, expedition vessels a fleet of (3) 20-passenge motor yachts; the M/Y Eric Flamingo I or Letty, a 200-foot 48-passenger expedition ship the M/V Corinthian and a 16-passenger custom dive live-aboard, the M/Y Sky Dancer.

galapagosnetwork
ecoventura

800-633-7972
info@galapagosnetwork.com
www.ecoventura.com

expedition cruising

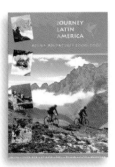

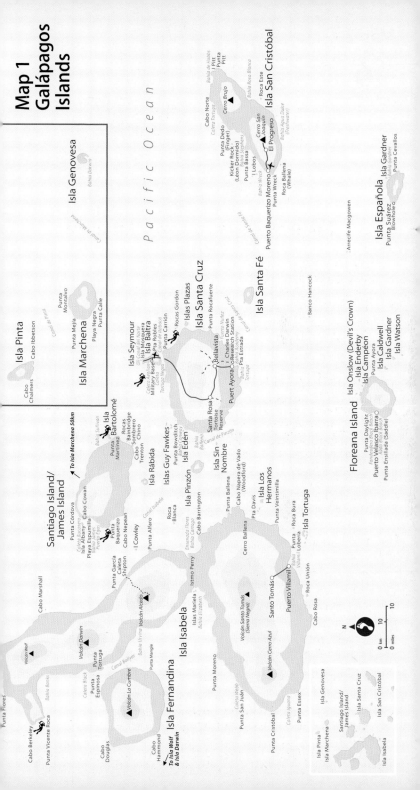

Map 1
Galápagos Islands

Pacific Ocean

Isla Genovesa

Isla Pinta
Cabo Ibbetson

Isla Marchena
Playa Negra
Punta Calle
Punta Montalvo
Punta Mejía

Canal de Pinta
Canal de Mayor (Big Channel)
Bahía Sullivan
Bahía Darwin

To Isla Marchena 50km

Cabo Chalmers

Santiago Island/ James Island
Punta Córdova
Isla Albany
Cabo Cowan
Playa Espumilla
Isla Cousins
Isla Sombrero Chino
Rocas Bainbridge
Punta Martínez
Cabo Trenton
Bahía James (Puerto Egas)
Punta Baquerizo
Punta Espinosa

Isla Bartolomé

Isla Rábida

Isla Seymour
Isla Mosquera
Military Base
Isla Baltra
Pta Robles
Punta Carrión
Rocas Gordon

Caleta

Isla Santa Cruz
Punta Rocafuerte
Canal de Itabaca
Tortuga Negra
Islas Plazas
Bellavista
Charles Darwin Research Station
Puert Ayora
Bahía Pta Estrada
Bahía Tortuga

Isla Santa Fé

Islas Guy Fawkes
Isla Edén

Isla Sin Nombre
Punta Bowditch

Isla Pinzón
Roca Blanca
Cabo Barrington

Santa Rosa
Tortoise Reserve
Bahía Ballena
Canal de Pinzón
Bahía Borrero

Banco Hancock

Cerro Nuñez
Sierra Crucita
Punta Rocafuerte

Cabo Norte
Caleta Tortuga
Bahía de Hoobs
I Pitt
Punta Pitt
Bahía Rosa Blanca

Isla San Cristóbal
Cerro Brujo
Cerro San Joaquín
El Progreso
Punta Dedo (Finger)
Kicker Rock (León Dormido)
Punta Bassa
I Lobos
Bahía Stephens
Bahía Blanca
Bahía Agua Dulce (Freshwater)
Bahía Wreck
Roca Este
Puerto Baquerizo Moreno
Punta Ballena (Whale)
Roca Ballena (Whale)
Punta Carola
Canal de Santa Fé

Arrecife Macgowen

Isla Española
Punta Suárez
Bahía Gardner
Punta Cevallos

Isla Gardner
Punta Gardner

Floreana Island
Isla Onslow (Devil's Crown)
Isla Enderby
Isla Campeón
Punta Daylight
Punta Ayora
Punta Cormorant
Cerro Pajas
Puerto Velasco Ibarra
Radio Block Bacon
Punta Ensillada (Saddle)

Isla Caldwell
Isla Watson

Isla Napean
Cabo Nepean

I Cowley

Isla Los Hermanos
Pta Davis
Roca Bura
Punta Veintimilla
Punta Ballena
Cabo Napera de Vado (Woodford)

Isla Tortuga

Volcán Wolf

Cabo Marshall

Volcán Darwin
Punta Tortuga

Volcán Alcedo
Punta García
Caleta Shipton
Bahía Urbina
Bahía Cartago
Ensenada Flores
Islas Mariela
Bahía Elizabeth
Istmo Perry

Volcán Santo Tomás (Sierra Negra)
Santo Tomás
Volcán Cerro Azul

Volcán La Cumbre
Punta Espinosa
Punta Mangle

Isla Fernandina

Isla Isabela
Punta Moreno
Punta Essex
Punta Cristóbal

Puerto Villamil
Bahía Villamil
Punta Lobería
Cerro Ballena
Roca Unión
Cabo Rosa

Volcán Cerro Azul

Canal Bolívar
Caleta Black
Bahía Banks
Cabo Berkeley
Punta Vicente Roca
Cabo Douglas
Cabo Hammond
To Isla Wolf & Isla Darwin
Caleta Webb
Caleta San Juan
Canal Webb
Punta San Juan
Caleta Iguana

Punta Flores

N
0 km   10
0 miles   10

Isla Pinta
Isla Marchena
Isla Genovesa
Santiago Island/ James Island
Isla Santa Cruz
Isla San Cristóbal
Isla Isabela

Map 2

N

0 km 30
0 miles 30

===== Paved road
——— Unpaved road

A

Pacific Ocean

I Sta

Limones (Valde

La Tola

Borbó

Lagarto

Rioverde

Rocafuerte

Anchayacu

Las Palmas

Atacames
Same
Tonchigüe   Súa

ESMERALDAS

Esmeraldas

Viche

ESMERALDAS

B

Muisne

Ens de Mompiche

Bolívar

I de Cojimíes
Cojimíes

Guayllabamba

Rosa Zárate (Quinindé)

Maldona

Pedernales

Palmar
Tabuga

Mtas de Chindul

PICHINCH

Jama   Map 3

Santo Domingo
de los Colorados

El Carmen

C

San Isidro

Mtas Jama

Eloy Alfaro

MANABÍ

COTAPAX

Chone
San
Antonio

Chone

S
Chugo

Tosagua

Laguna Qu

Zumba

1   **2**   **3**

A

COLOMBIA

CARCHI

Map 2

orenzo

ón

San Juan

va Ecológico
achi-Cayapas

Lita

Maldonado

Trufiño

TULCAN

Reserva Ecológica
El Angel

La Libertad

El Angel   San Gabriel

Mira

Bolívar   Gruta de La Paz

El Juncal

Pimampiro

San Francisco
de Sigsigpamba

Cotacachi
(4,939m)

IMBABURA

Urcuqui

IBARRA

San Antonio de Ibarra

Laguna
Cuicocha Quiroga   Cotacachi

Apuela

Lago de
San Pablo

Otavalo

Caricocha

B

SUCUMBIOS

Maquipucuna
Biological
Reserve

Puéllaro
Crater

Cayambe

Calacalí

Rumicucho

San Antonio
de Pichincha

Mitad del Mundo

Vol Cayambe
(5,790m)

Reventador

Vol Reventador
(3.562m)

lindo

Nono

Pomasqui

Guayllabamba

Calderón

Vol Guagua
Pichincha
(4,794m)

Vol Rucu Pichincha
(4,627m)

QUITO

Alangasí

Sangolquí

Pintag

Papallacta

Sta Rosa de Chicos

El Chaco

Pan de Azucár

Borja

NAPO

Baeza

Machachi

Vol Antisana
(5,758m)

Vol Sumaco
(3,732m)

Vols Iliniza
(5,126m/5,263m)

Lasso

C

Parque
Nacional
Cotopaxi

Cosanga

Vol Cotopaxi
(5,897m)

Cord Galeras

Map 4

Saquisili

Pujili

4

LATACUNGA

5

6

Map 3

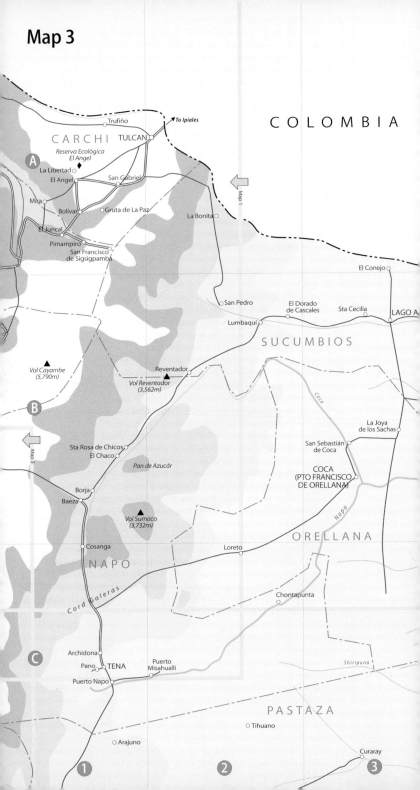

N

| 0 km | 30 |
| 0 miles | 30 |

═════ Paved road
───── Unpaved road

Pta Carmen de Putumayo ○

Putumayo

R Faun Cuyabeno

Güeppi

○ Tarapoa

hushifindi

Cuyabeno
Wildlife ◆
Reserve

○ Cuyabeno

Aguarico

moncocha
ta

Napo

○ Pañacocha

○ Zancudo

Tiputini

○ Tiputini

◆
Parque
Nacional
Yasuní

↓ Map 4

Nuevo Rocafuerte ○

Nashino

P E R U

Cononaco

4   5   6

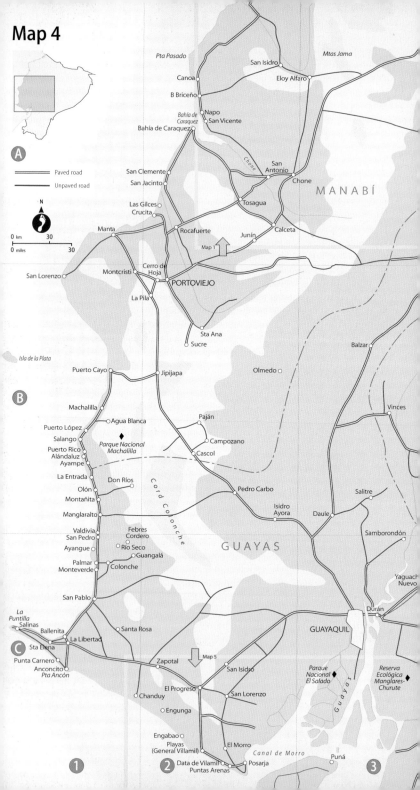

Map 5

NAPO

Archidona
Pano TENA
Puerto Napo
Puerto Misahuallí

Map 2

○ Tihuano

Cord Llanganates

○ Arajuno

(A)

Baños
Shell-Mera

Villano

Vol Tungurahua (5,016m)

PUYO

Canellos

PASTAZA

▲ *El Altar (5,319m)*

○ Pallora

○ Sarayacu

Bobonaza

○ Chuigaza

▲ *Vol Sangay (5,230m)*

MORONA SANTIAGO

Pastaza

(B)

○ Zuñac

Upano

○ Macas

Map 5

○ Taisha

Huasaga ○

○ Sucúa

Méndez ○

Map 3

Morona

○ Yaupi

Morona ○

(C)

Zamora

Santiago

Santiago

PERU

(1)   (2)   (3)

Map 6

San Lorenzo

Engunga

Engabao

Playas
(General
Villamil)

El Morro

Data de Vilamil

Posarja

Puntas
Arenas

Puná

GUAYAS

Naranjal

Cañar

Parque
Nacional ◆
Cajas

↑ Map 4

Canal de Morro

A

Golfo de
Guayaquil

Pacific Ocean

I Puná

Balao

Pta Carnero

AZUAY

Chumblín Girón

San Fernando

Canal Jambeli

I Sta Clara

MACHALA

Guabo

Sta Isabel

Jumbones Casacay

Pasaje

Chilla Guanazán

Oña

Sta Rosa

EL ORO

Selva Alegre

Celén Saraguro

Huaquillas

To Tumbes ▲

Cerro de Arcos

Arenillas

Piñas Zaruma

B

Cord Larga

Chuquiribamba

El Cisne

Puyango

LOJA

Catamayo

LOJA

Alamor

Catacocha

Celica

Paletillas

Catamayo

Purunuma Malacatos

Gonzanamá Vilcabamba

Colaisaca Yangana

Macará Sozoranga Cariamanga

Utuana

Zapotillo

To Sullana & Piura ▶

C

Valledolid

Amaluza

PERU

Palanda

Zum...

1   **2**   **3**

Ingapirca

Biblián

AZOGUES

Paute

Bulcay

Gualaceo
Chordeleg

JENCA

Sigsig

Chigüinda

S de Mayo
(acuambi)

Cumbaratza

ZAMORA
CHINCHIPE

ZAMORA

Je
ar
rpus

Map 4

Sucúa

Méndez

MORONA
SANTIAGO

Yaupi

Morona

Gral El Plaza Gutiérrez (Limón)

Indanza

Zamora

Santiago

Santiago

S Carlos de Limón

Gualaquiza

El Panguí

Los Encuentros

Yantzaza
Nambija

PERU

N

0 km   30
0 miles   30

Paved road

Unpaved road

A

B

C

4   5   6

"Head, shoulders and spine ahead of the rest."
Adventure Travel

"If 'the essence of real travel' is what you have been secretly yearning for all these years, then Footprint are the guides for you."
Under 26

"While Wallpaper shies away from the standard handbook when packing our Vuitton, we are prepared to make an exception for the Footprint series when it comes to South America."
Wallpaper

"Footprint can be depended on for accurate travel information and for imparting a deep sense of respect for the lands and people they cover."
World News

"Intelligently written, amazingly accurate and bang up-to-date. Footprint have combined nearly 80 years' experience with a stunning new format to bring us guidebooks that leave the competition standing."
John Pilkington, writer and broadcaster

Mail order
Available worldwide in bookshops and on-line. Footprint travel guides can also be ordered directly from us in Bath, via our website **www.footprintbooks.com** or from the address at the beginning of this book.

Acknowledgements

The authors were ably assisted by the following contributors, without whom this work would not have been possible. The project brought together a varied group of people with one thing in common: a desire to share their fascination with Ecuador.

Jean Brown, originally from England, has lived for more than two decades in Ecuador and is well known for her encyclopaedic memory, and her connections with absolutely everyone. Jean is a founding member of *South American Explorers* in Quito, a partner in *Safari Tours* and a long-standing contributor to the *South American Handbook* as well as other Footprint titles. She is also an avid supporter of various grassroots environmental protection organizations. Jean helped update the Northern Highlands chapter, the Quilotoa circuit and has provided much useful general assistance.

Lou Jost is an accomplished botanist, ornithologist, and wildlife painter, who hails from Milwaukee in the USA. Lou worked for many years as a naturalist guide in Costa Rica and Ecuador, and he is illustrator of *Common Birds of Amazonian Ecuador* (Ediciones Libri-Mundi, Quito, 1997). He currently lives near Quito and travels throughout the country to discover and study new species of miniature orchids. Lou helped update information about birdwatching, nature lodges and flora and fauna, as well as providing much useful general assistance.

Michael Resch arrived in Ecuador in 1996 from Hallein, Austria. He came the long way, after journeying through most of the world during the previous 17 years, in the course of which he learned a thing or two about travel and guidebooks. Michael currently makes his home near Baños where he teaches German and English, lovingly tends his garden, and watches eruptions of Tungurahua to the sounds of classical music. He helped update the Northern Pacific Lowlands chapter, Ibarra, Baños and Ambato.

Delia María Torres is a native *guayaquileña* who truly loves her city. She works for the historical archives of the Central Bank and, when not travelling to other regions of Ecuador, enjoys introducing visitors to the sights and sounds of her bustling metropolis. Delia María helped update Guayaquil, Salinas and surroundings.

Nicola Mears is a New Zealander who has lived on the coast of Ecuador since 1989. She jointly owns *Guacamayo Bahía Tours* and is also dedicated to many environmental projects including paper recycling and the creation of the first organic shrimp farm in the world. Nicola has combined all of these activities with tourism in what she calls 'tourism for a better planet'.

Jeaneth and Guido Abad come from Baños and Cuenca, respectively. Professional language teachers, they owned and operated the *Sí Centro de Español e Inglés* in Baños until 1999, when the Tungurahua volcano encouraged them to relocate back to Cuenca. There they continue to run the language school and are active in the travel industry. Guido and Jeaneth prepared an excellent update of Loja, Vilcambamba and other parts of the Southern Highlands chapter.

Beatrice Malo first came to Ecuador in 1987 from her native Switzerland, where she was a nurse. With her *azuayo* husband **Xavier**, an accomplished horse breeder and trainer, she owns and operates *Montaruna Tours* in Cuenca. They specialize in horseback riding tours and are well connected with the local travel scene. With the assistance of **María José Andrade**, a professional guide, Beatrice and Xavier helped update Cuenca, Ingapirca and surroundings.

Susana Bermeo was born and raised in Quito, she is knowledgeably proud of her city and its traditions. Susana works in education, and keeps busy in her spare time by raising her six children. She helped update Quito hotels and museums and the lowlands around Santo Domingo.

Grace Naranjo is also an avid *quiteña*, who vigorously defends the capital against the wisecracks of her many Riobamaba-born relatives. Grace works with computers and is known for her ability to do three things at once. She helped update Quito restaurants and directory, the southern Oriente and provided general assistance.

Carolyn (Caz) Bointon left a lawyer's career in London, England, to wander the wilds of South America. She has lived in Cusco, Peru, and contributed to the *South American Handbook* and *Bolivia Handbook*. Caz currently lives in Quito, where she helped update language schools and nightlife.

Kerry Alley is a freelance guide, originally from Maine in the USA. She lives in Quito and guides regularly in the Oriente. Kerry helped update Lago Agrio and Coca.

The authors would particularly like to thank the Ecuadorean government's **Ministerio de Turismo**, their various regional offices, and the many members of their staff (too numerous to list here) who very kindly provided assistance with the preparation of this edition. We would also like thank the following individuals, all of whom provided valuable assistance: **Patricio Ballesteros,** Oficina Municipal de Información Turística, Guaranda; **Franco DeAntoni; Beatriz Gómez; Dr Nelson Gómez**, Centro Internacional de Estudios de los Espacios y Sociedades Andinas; **Pablo Gómez; Jason Halberstat; Minard (Pete) Hall; Joanna May; Patricia Mothes; Dr John Rosenberg; Nina Senti; Pepe and Margarita Tapia; Wellington Valdiviezo.**

This third edition of the *Ecuador Handbook* is built on the insights and hard work of several generations of travel editors. For many decades editor of the *South American Handbook*, the late **John Brooks** helped lay the foundations of the current volume. The present author of the *South American Handbook*, **Ben Box**, was instrumental in the creation of Footprint's single-country Latin American editions including this title. Ben also wrote the literature section. **Alan Murphy** turned Ecuador into an independent handbook. He wrote the first and second editions. Ben and Alan have long been a source of moral support for the authors. Thanks are also due to the following contributors to previous editions. The late **Yossi Brain**, a sorely missed friend who was tragically killed in an avalanche in Bolivia in 1999, wrote the mountaineering section for the second edition. **Steve Nomchong** wrote the rafting and kayaking section for the second edition and updated this material for the current edition. **Mark Thurber** (co-author of Bradt's *Climbing and Hiking in Ecuador* 4th edition) wrote the trekking sections and **Jack Nelson** wrote the Galápagos diving section for the second edition.

We likewise thank the entire Footprint editorial and production team, and in particular the following specialist contributors who either wrote or reviewed the corresponding sections: Peter Pollard, Land and environment; Dr Nigel Dunstone (University of Durham), Flora and fauna; Dr Valerie Fraser (University of Essex), Fine art and sculpture; Nigel Gallop, Music and dance; Mark Eckstein, Responsible travel; Sarah Cameron, Economy. The material in the Arts and crafts section was used courtesy of Lucy Davies and Mo Fini of *Tumi*.

By far our most important vote of thanks, however, goes to you - the readers and travellers who make this book a living, evolving thing and who took the time and trouble to send in their comments and recommendations.

Robert and Daisy Kunstaetter

Daisy was born and raised in Ecuador (Riobamba and Quito) and went to Montreal, Canada, to attend university. There she met Robert, who suggested they travel 'a bit' before continuing with their careers in medicine and occupational therapy. That was in 1986 and they have yet to settle, instead they have lived and travelled in every country in South and Central America and a few others besides.

Over the years and miles, Robert and Daisy became regular correspondents for Footprint, helping to update annual editions of the *South American Handbook* and other Latin American titles. Based back in Ecuador since 1993, where Daisy's pet peeve is being mistaken for a *gringa*, she and Robert have been involved with the *Ecuador Handbook* since the first edition. They are also founders of the *Latin American Travel Advisor*, contributors to various other publications and are currently writing a book about trekking in Ecuador.

Once known for their gracious hospitality, Robert and Daisy lived a less sociable existence while preparing this edition. When not writing, travelling, fleeing erupting volcanoes or butting heads with bureaucracy during this period, they were usually sound asleep.